CHARACTER AND SCRIPTURE

CHARACTER AND SCRIPTURE

*Moral Formation, Community,
and Biblical Interpretation*

Edited by

WILLIAM P. BROWN

WILLIAM B. EERDMANS PUBLISHING COMPANY

GRAND RAPIDS, MICHIGAN / CAMBRIDGE, U.K.

© 2002 Wm. B. Eerdmans Publishing Co.

Wm. B. Eerdmans Publishing Co.
255 Jefferson Ave. S.E., Grand Rapids, Michigan 49503 /
P.O. Box 163, Cambridge CB3 9PU U.K.
www.eerdmans.com

Printed in the United States of America

07 06 05 04 03 02   7 6 5 4 3 2 1

Library of Congress Cataloging-in-Publication Data

Character and Scripture: moral formation, community,
and biblical interpretation / edited by William P. Brown.
     p.   cm.
  Includes bibliographical references.
  ISBN 0-8028-4625-4 (pbk.: alk. paper)
  1. Ethics in the Bible.   I. Brown, William P., 1958-

  BS680.E84 C44   2002
  220.6 — dc21

                  2002026356

Unless otherwise noted, the Scripture quotations in this publication are from the New
Revised Standard Version of the Bible, copyright © 1989 by the Division of Christian
Education of the National Council of Churches of Christ in the U.S.A., and used by
permission.

Contents

Contributors   viii

Preface   xi

Abbreviations   xvii

THE SCOPE AND LIMITS OF CHARACTER ETHICS

Christian Character, Biblical Community, and Human Values   3
  Lisa Sowle Cahill

Formed and Transformed by Scripture:
Character, Community, and Authority in Biblical Interpretation   18
  L. Gregory Jones

Images of Scripture and Contemporary Theological Ethics   34
  William Schweiker

BIBLICAL INTERPRETATION

The Good Neighborhood: Identity and Community
through the Commandments   55
  Patrick D. Miller

The Complexity of Character and the Ethics of Complexity:
The Case of King David   73
  Richard G. Bowman

A Character Ethics Reading of 1 Chronicles 29:1-25   98
  M. Patrick Graham

Narrative Ethics, Character, and the Prose Tale of Job   121
  Carol A. Newsom

"The Way of the Righteous" in the Psalms:
Character Formation and Cultural Crisis   135
  J. Clinton McCann, Jr.

The Pedagogy of Proverbs 10:1–31:9   150
  William P. Brown

Preserving Virtues: Renewing the Tradition of the Sages   183
  Ellen F. Davis

The Ethics of Narrative Wisdom: Qoheleth as Test Case   202
  Eric S. Christianson

The Character of God in Jeremiah   211
  Terence E. Fretheim

Ecumenism as the Shared Practice of a Peculiar Identity   231
  Walter Brueggemann

The Education of Human Wanting: Formation by *Pater Noster*   248
  C. Clifton Black

Character Formation or Character Transformation?
The Challenge of Cruciform Exegesis for Character Ethics in Paul   264
  Alexandra R. Brown

Accepting Affliction: Paul's Preaching on Suffering   290
  L. Ann Jervis

Believing Forms Seeing: Formation for Martyrdom in Philippians   317
   Stephen E. Fowl

The Function of Moral Typology in 2 Peter   331
   J. Daryl Charles

"A Sharp Two-Edged Sword": Pastoral Implications of Apocalyptic   344
   Ellen T. Charry

PRACTICE ——————————————————————

Embodied Remembering: Wisdom, Character, and Worship   363
   Jill Y. Crainshaw

Sightings of Primal Visions: Community and Ecology   389
   Larry L. Rasmussen

Character Ethics and Moral Education for Liberation   410
   Marcia Y. Riggs

Acknowledgments   423

Index of Subjects and Names   424

Index of Scripture References   428

Contributors

C. Clifton Black
Otto A. Piper Professor of Biblical Theology
Princeton Theological Seminary

Richard G. Bowman
Professor of Religion
Augustana College

Alexandra R. Brown
Professor of Religion
Washington and Lee University

William P. Brown
Aubrey Lee Brooks Professor of Biblical Theology
Union Theological Seminary
and Presbyterian School of Christian Education

Walter Brueggemann
William Marcellus McPheeters Professor of Old Testament
Columbia Theological Seminary

Lisa Sowle Cahill
Professor of Christian Ethics
Boston College

J. Daryl Charles
Associate Professor of Religion and Philosophy
Taylor University

Ellen T. Charry
Margaret W. Harmon Associate Professor of Systematic Theology
Princeton Theological Seminary

Eric S. Christianson
Lecturer in Biblical Studies at the Department of Theology
Chester College, Chester, U.K.

Jill Y. Crainshaw
Assistant Professor of Ministerial Studies
Wake Forest University Divinity School

Ellen F. Davis
Associate Professor of Bible and Practical Theology
Duke Divinity School

Stephen E. Fowl
Professor of Theology
Loyola College in Maryland

Terence E. Fretheim
Elba B. Lovell Professor of Old Testament
Luther Seminary

M. Patrick Graham
Margaret A. Pitts Associate Professor of Theological Bibliography and
Director of Pitts Theology Library
Candler School of Theology
Emory University

L. Ann Jervis
Professor of New Testament
Wycliffe College
Toronto School of Theology

L. Gregory Jones
Dean of the Divinity School and Professor of Theology
Duke University

J. Clinton McCann, Jr.
Evangelical Professor of Biblical Interpretation
Eden Theological Seminary

Patrick D. Miller
Charles T. Haley Professor of Old Testament Theology
Princeton Theological Seminary

Carol A. Newsom
Professor of Old Testament
Candler School of Theology
Emory University

Larry L. Rasmussen
Reinhold Niebuhr Professor of Social Ethics
Union Theological Seminary

Marcia Y. Riggs
Associate Professor of Christian Ethics
Columbia Theological Seminary

William Schweiker
Professor of Theological Ethics
University of Chicago Divinity School

Preface

The following collection of essays does not provide another literary or socio-historical analysis of the Bible. The volume, rather, offers ways of reading Scripture that have been all but lost in the guild and, to some extent, in the church. The essays, diverse as they are, share a common thesis: the interpretation of Scripture and the moral formation of reading communities are inextricably bound. Scripture forms community as much as community informs the reading of Scripture. To explore the intersection between "character" and Scripture, thus, is to probe the variegated communities that produced the biblical corpus and sustained it over the centuries, as well as to inquire about the impact Scripture has upon the community's life *coram deo* and *in mundo*, "before God" and "in the world." In a time when ideologically deconstructing the text is the game and the hermeneutics of suspicion remains the norm, this collection dares to explore the *constructive* ways Scripture forms moral character and faith, to discern how the theological and ethical contours of the text can shape, subvert, and reshape the contours of community.[1]

Drawing on various fields of study, from hermeneutics to historical criticism, a "character ethics" approach — more a shared outlook than an established methodology — to the text's interpretive threshold investigates the *formative*, as well as normative, impact that Scripture *qua Scripture* makes upon reading communities, both ancient and (post)modern. At the same time, it recognizes the community's role in formulating the ways Scripture can be appropriated in the life of faith. Largely absent in other perspectives that have gained a measure of

---

1. As will be demonstrated in several of the following essays, a character ethics approach to the biblical text easily appropriates the important critical gains of various hermeneutical perspectives.

currency in biblical studies, such an approach integrates issues of moral formation and identity, on the one hand, and textual normativity and valuation, on the
other. Specific concerns and issues that may be found within the scope of character ethics include virtue, moral education, faith and culture, worldview, moral vision and imagination, wisdom, narrative ethics, ethos and moral space, agency,
conscience, communal remembrance, and reader response. A character ethics approach to biblical exegesis fully acknowledges that the *interpretation* of Scripture
within the context of a community of faith entails the *appropriation* of Scripture,
and that such appropriation is essentially dynamic insofar as character and faith
denote an ongoing process of formation and, yes, transformation.

Advanced by contemporary ethicists such as Alasdair MacIntyre and
Stanley Hauerwas, character ethics has established itself as a discrete discipline.
It explores the morphology of the self and seeks, thereby, to identify the dimensions that give moral coherence and depth to human agency by addressing matters, as traditionally delineated, of perception, intention, and disposition,[2] or,
more broadly, the affective, cognitive, and volitional, along with their deep interrelations.[3] Such distinctions are more heuristic than essential. Moreover, the
environment or habitat, in all its physical, social, and moral contours, is recognized to be a powerful shaping force in the formation of agency and character.

Having its roots in Aristotle, Augustine, and Aquinas, such a mode of inquiry is far from new. It could be said that a distinctly Christian view of character ethics conjoins Aristotle's emphasis on practical wisdom[4] and the cultivation of sound character with Augustine's distinctly moral concern for an
adequate hermeneutics. Augustine recognized that moral judgments, in an
ecclesial context at least, are also hermeneutical judgments, and vice versa. In
his manual on biblical interpretation, *De doctrina christiana* ("On Teaching
Christianity"), the Bishop of Hippo grounds all biblical interpretation in the
"right order of love," specifically the love of God and neighbor, the sum of what
Scripture teaches.[5] The ultimate test of exegetical correctness, which begins
with the literal or plain sense of the text, is whether one's interpretation contributes "to the reign of charity."[6] A Christian character ethics, thus, lodges

---

2. See the discussion in Bruce C. Birch and Larry L. Rasmussen, *Bible and Ethics in the
Christian Life*, rev. ed. (Minneapolis: Augsburg, 1989), pp. 74-81.

3. See the brief discussion in James M. Gustafson, *Ethics from a Theocentric Perspective*,
vol. 1: *Theology and Ethics* (Chicago: University of Chicago Press, 1981), pp. 117-20.

4. "Practical wisdom" *(phronēsis)* was considered by Aristotle as both a moral and an intellectual virtue *(Nicomachean Ethics* 6.3-7; 6.5.20).

5. *De doctrina christiana* 1.36.40.

6. *De doctrina christiana* 3.15.23. Translation from D. W. Robertson, Jr., *Saint Augustine:
On Christian Doctrine*, LLA 80 (New York: Liberal Arts Press, 1958), p. 93.

moral discourse within an ongoing conversation with Scripture in its particularity and plurality, while also engaging with and in behalf of the world. At base, character ethics is an exegetically based ethics. This moral engagement with Scripture marks a serious attempt, on the one hand, to eschew sectarianism and, on the other, to resist the move to accommodate faith-based identity to prevailing cultures. A community of faith that is *in* and *for* the world, enabling the global community to recognize what it was created to be, remains also distinct *from* the world. Avoiding provincialism while forming inviolable identity, having an all-encompassing outlook yet remaining uncompromising in conviction and conduct, is the fine line character ethics attempts to walk.

Although sometimes critiqued for being excessively Thomistic in orientation, character ethics is by no means limited to certain classical forms found in Western Christianity and philosophy that stress the formation of virtue or moral disposition. Broader issues related to moral identity and the formation of community also fall within its purview. Moreover, it is the objective of this volume to demonstrate that the traditions of ancient Israel and the early church — expressed in various literary genres, from law and proverb to narrative and apocalyptic — serve to form, sustain, and reform the theological and moral identity of community. Attempts to limit moral formation to the rhetorical and social dynamics of any one literary genre have proven unnecessarily limiting, as has been done for narrative (as opposed to moral principle).[7] It is a reductive mistake to limit the discursive basis for moral formation to any *single* genre. The textual factors that catalyze and direct the formation of character are as numerous and variegated as Scripture is generically diverse.

The formation of this volume began as a dialogue. Under the sponsorship of the Society of Biblical Literature,[8] a modest consultation designed to bring together biblical interpreters, ethicists, and theologians was launched in 1996. The steering committee for the "Character Ethics and Biblical Interpretation" group was co-chaired by Beverly Stratton and myself and guided by Bruce C. Birch, Lois K. Daly, M. Daniel Carroll R., L. Ann Jervis, and Stephen E. Fowl. In its first session, Catholic ethicist Lisa Sowle Cahill and Protestant biblical scholar Walter Brueggemann shared papers that sparked a spirited discussion among 150 members crammed into a room with a maximum capacity of fifty. Since then, the group has flourished and continues to hold sessions at the na-

---

7. This is recognized even by Stanley Hauerwas, "The Self as Story: A Reconsideration of the Relation of Religion and Morality from the Agent's Perspective," in *Vision and Virtue: Essays in Christian Ethical Reflection* (Notre Dame, Ind.: Fides, 1974), p. 89.

8. The original plan was to have the program unit co-sponsored by the American Academy of Religion, which prematurely rejected the proposal for not having sufficient potential for cross-disciplinary conversation.

tional meeting of the SBL. Featured presenters have included ethicists L. Gregory Jones, Marcia Y. Riggs, William Schweiker, Michael G. Cartwright, Larry L. Rasmussen, and Ellen T. Charry; as well as biblical scholars Patrick D. Miller, Carol A. Newsom, Terence E. Fretheim, Bernard M. Levinson, Stephen E. Fowl, L. Ann Jervis, Luke Timothy Johnson, Alexandra R. Brown, Richard Burridge, and J. Daryl Charles, among others. This volume features many of the presentations given at the annual meetings, but also includes several essays that were developed or enlisted especially for this volume.

The overall shape of this collection is dictated by the range of perspectives and convictions of its contributors, all united by a common concern for theory, canonical breadth, and contextual practice. The essays are arranged along three major, albeit relative, divisions. The first set of essays ("Scope and Limits"), contributed by Christian ethicists committed to serious engagement with Scripture, explores the promises and challenges of character ethics as both a viable model for moral discourse and a hermeneutical tool. Lisa Sowle Cahill's essay opens the volume by programmatically exploring the various ways character ethics is used in moral theory and hermeneutics. The second set of essays ("Biblical Interpretation") includes contributions from scholars who engage particular biblical texts or corpora with an eye toward issues of moral identity and formation. The essays are arranged in canonical order beginning with Patrick Miller's essay on the Decalogue and concluding with Ellen Charry's essay on Revelation. One may note a cluster of essays that deal primarily with the wisdom literature, which is perhaps the most explicit in dealing with issues related to moral formation, virtue, and practical wisdom. However, the range of essays covers a wide variety of literary forms and books, from legal code to narrative, from prophetic pronouncement to intercessory prayer. The last set of essays ("Practice") comprises three essays that devote attention to contemporary contextual issues in moral education (from an African-American perspective), ecology, and worship. Despite the overt arrangement of the volume, each essay integrates to some degree the movement from biblical interpretation and theory to praxis. Moreover, the contributors cover the theological and sociological spectrum, yet are united in concern for conveying something of the formative power of Scripture within various communities for the life of faith.[9] For those who contributed to this volume, the exercise to integrate biblical interpretation and ethics has been meaningful, if not liberating. The hope is that the reader will also find it so.

---

9. The wide range of ideologies and standpoints reflected in this collection counters the charge that "character ethics" is essentially a white, middle-class, male-dominated ethical system. See particularly the essays by Cahill, Newsom, Rasmussen, Crainshaw, and Riggs.

Many works that have informed and continue to sustain this growing discipline can be found among the footnotes given in the following essays. As a point of departure, however, a very select bibliography of recent studies, both foundational and applied, is provided below. Some of the works listed do not explicitly promulgate a character ethics, but they do provide important resources for the field.

Select Bibliography

Albrecht, Gloria H. *The Character of Our Communities: Toward an Ethic of Liberation for the Church.* Nashville: Abingdon, 1995.

Birch, Bruce C., and Larry L. Rasmussen. *Bible and Ethics in the Christian Life.* Rev. ed. Minneapolis: Augsburg, 1989.

Bondi, Richard. "The Elements of Character." *JRE* 12 (1984): 201-18.

Bonhoeffer, Dietrich. *Ethics.* Trans. N. H. Smith. Ed. E. Bethge. New York: Macmillan, 1955, esp. pp. 64-119 ("Ethics as Formation").

Brown, William P. *The Ethos of the Cosmos: The Genesis of Moral Imagination in the Bible.* Grand Rapids: Eerdmans, 1999.

―――. *Character in Crisis: A Fresh Approach to the Wisdom Literature of the Old Testament.* Grand Rapids: Eerdmans, 1996.

Fowl, Stephen E., and L. Gregory Jones. *Reading in Communion: Scripture and Ethics in the Christian Life.* Grand Rapids: Eerdmans, 1991.

Gustafson, James M. *Christian Ethics and the Community.* Philadelphia: Pilgrim, 1971.

Hauerwas, Stanley. *The Peaceable Kingdom: A Primer in Christian Ethics.* Notre Dame, Ind.: University of Notre Dame Press, 1983.

―――. *A Community of Character: Toward a Constructive Christian Social Ethic.* Notre Dame, Ind.: University of Notre Dame Press, 1981.

―――. *Character and the Christian Life: A Study in Theological Ethics.* San Antonio, Tex.: Trinity University Press, 1975.

Hauerwas, Stanley, and Charles Pinches. *Christians among the Virtues: Theological Conversations with Ancient and Modern Ethics.* Notre Dame, Ind.: University of Notre Dame Press, 1997.

Hays, Richard. *The Moral Vision of the New Testament — Community, Cross, New Creation: A Contemporary Introduction to New Testament Ethics.* San Francisco: HarperSanFrancisco, 1996.

―――. "Scripture-Shaped Community: The Problem of Method in New Testament Ethics." *Int* 54 (1990): 42-55.

Janzen, Waldemar. *Old Testament Ethics: A Paradigmatic Approach.* Louisville: Westminster/John Knox, 1994.

Jones, L. Gregory. *Transformed Judgment: Toward a Trinitarian Account of the Moral Life.* Notre Dame, Ind.: University of Notre Dame Press, 1990.

Lapsley, Jacqueline E. *Can These Bones Live? The Problem of the Moral Self in the Book of Ezekiel.* BZAW 301. Berlin and New York: Walter de Gruyter, 2000.

MacIntyre, Alasdair C. *After Virtue: A Study in Moral Theory.* 2nd ed. Notre Dame, Ind.: University of Notre Dame Press, 1984.

Matties, Gordon. *Ezekiel 18 and the Rhetoric of Moral Discourse.* SBLDS 126. Atlanta: Scholars Press, 1990.

Meeks, Wayne A. *The Origins of Christian Morality: The First Two Centuries.* New Haven: Yale University Press, 1993.

————. *The Moral World of the First Christians.* LEC 6. Philadelphia: Westminster, 1986.

Taylor, Charles. *Sources of the Self: The Making of Modern Identity.* Cambridge, Mass.: Harvard University Press, 1989.

Abbreviations

AARS	American Academy of Religion Academy Series
AB	Anchor Bible
ABD	*Anchor Bible Dictionary.* Ed. D. N. Freedman. 6 vols. New York: Doubleday, 1992.
ABRL	Anchor Bible Reference Library
ACNT	Augsburg Commentary on the New Testament
ACW	Ancient Christian Writers
AnBib	Analecta biblica
AOTS	Augsburg Old Testament Series
APOT	*The Apocrypha and Pseudepigrapha of the Old Testament.* Ed. R. H. Charles. 2 vols. Oxford: Clarendon, 1913.
APQ	*American Philosophical Quarterly*
ATR	*Anglican Theological Review*
BAGD	Bauer, W., W. F. Arndt, F. W. Gingrich, and F. W. Danker. *Greek-English Lexicon of the New Testament and Other Early Christian Literature.* 2nd ed. Chicago: University of Chicago Press, 1979.
BBR	*Bulletin for Biblical Research*
BEATJ	Beiträge zur Erforschung des Alten Testaments und des antiken Judentum
BETL	Bibliotheca ephemeridum theologicarum lovaniensium
Bib	*Biblica*
BibS(N)	Biblische Studien (Neukirchen, 1951-)
BKAT	Biblischer Kommentar, Altes Testament. Ed. M. Noth and H. W. Wolff
BLS	Bible and Literature Series
BNTC	Black's New Testament Commentaries
BR	*Bible Review*

BSNA	Biblical Scholarship in North America
BZAW	Beihefte zur Zeitschrift für die alttestamentliche Wissenschaft
CBQ	*Catholic Biblical Quarterly*
CBQMS	Catholic Biblical Quarterly Monograph Series
ConBNT	Coniectanea biblica: New Testament Series
ECC	Early Church Classics
FOTL	Forms of the Old Testament Literature
FRLANT	Forschungen zur Religion und Literatur des Alten und Neuen Testaments
FTS	Freiburger theologische Studien
GQ	*Gentlemen's Quarterly*
HBT	*Horizons in Biblical Theology*
HNTC	Harper's New Testament Commentaries
HTR	*Harvard Theological Review*
IBC	Interpretation: A Bible Commentary for Teaching and Preaching
ICC	International Critical Commentary
Int	*Interpretation: A Journal of Bible and Theology*
ISBL	Indiana Studies in Biblical Literature
JAAR	*Journal of the American Academy of Religion*
JANES	*Journal of the Ancient Near Eastern Society of Columbia University*
JBL	*Journal of Biblical Literature*
JBR	*Journal of Bible and Religion*
JME	*Journal of Moral Education*
JNSL	*Journal of Northwest Semitic Languages*
JQR	*Jewish Quarterly Review*
JR	*Journal of Religion*
JRE	*Journal of Religious Ethics*
JSNT	*Journal for the Study of the New Testament*
JSNTSup	Journal for the Study of the New Testament: Supplement Series
JSOT	*Journal for the Study of the Old Testament*
JSOTSup	Journal for the Study of the Old Testament: Supplement Series
JTS	*Journal of Theological Studies*
LCBI	Literary Currents in Biblical Interpretation
LCL	Loeb Classical Library
LEC	Library of Early Christianity
LLA	The Library of Liberal Arts
LXX	Septuagint
MT	Masoretic text
NCB	New Century Bible
NEB	New English Bible
NIBCNT	New International Biblical Commentary on the New Testament

NJPS	*Tanakh: The Holy Scriptures: The New JPS Translation according to the Traditional Hebrew Text*
NovTSup	Supplements to Novum Testamentum
NRSV	New Revised Standard Version
NT	New Testament
NTAbh	Neutestamentliche Abhandlungen
NTS	*New Testament Studies*
OBT	Overtures to Biblical Theology
Or	*Orientalia*
OT	Old Testament
OTL	Old Testament Library
OtSt	*Oudtestamentische Studiën*
PSB	*Princeton Seminary Bulletin*
PTMS	Pittsburgh Theological Monograph Series
RB	*Revue biblique*
RSR	*Religious Studies Review*
RSV	Revised Standard Version
SBLDS	Society of Biblical Literature Dissertation Series
SBLMS	Society of Biblical Literature Monograph Series
SBLSCS	Society of Biblical Literature Septuagint and Cognate Studies
SBLSS	Society of Biblical Literature Semeia Studies
SJLA	Studies in Judaism in Late Antiquity
SNTSMS	Society for New Testament Studies Monograph Series
SP	Sacra pagina
SPOT	Studies on Personalities of the Old Testament
SSN	Studia Semitica Neerlandica
StPB	Studia post-biblica
TDNT	*Theological Dictionary of the New Testament.* Ed. G. Kittel and G. Friedrich. Trans. G. W. Bromiley. 10 vols. Grand Rapids: Eerdmans, 1964-76.
TDOT	*Theological Dictionary of the Old Testament.* Ed. G. J. Botterweck and H. Ringgren. Trans. J. T. Willis, G. W. Bromiley, and D. E. Green. 8 vols. Grand Rapids: Eerdmans, 1974-.
ThT	*Theology Today*
TNTC	Tyndale New Testament Commentaries
TS	*Theological Studies*
VT	*Vetus Testamentum*
WBC	Word Biblical Commentary
WMANT	Wissenschaftliche Monographien zum Alten und Neuen Testament
WO	*Die Welt des Orients*
WTJ	*Westminster Theological Journal*
WUNT	Wissenschaftliche Untersuchungen zum Neuen Testament

WW   *Word and World*
ZAW   *Zeitschrift für die alttestamentliche Wissenschaft*
ZNW   *Zeitschrift für die neutestamentliche Wissenschaft und die Kunde der
            älteren Kirche*

THE SCOPE AND LIMITS
OF CHARACTER ETHICS

Christian Character, Biblical Community, and Human Values

Lisa Sowle Cahill

From the perspective of a Christian ethicist, the term "character" can have a variety of theological, epistemological, and practical implications. In this essay, I will differentiate two basic ways in which the notion of character is used by ethicists, then indicate some possible uses by biblical interpreters interested in ethics. The two models of character can be loosely associated with Protestant and Roman Catholic authors, though this division is not sharp. In the approach typical of several Protestant theologians, the language of character ethics is a way to highlight the faith-based nature of the Christian life, understood as intrinsically communal. The ways of "faith active in love" characterize a community called to discipleship in Christ, a community in which the moral agent's individual identity is formed, and against which it is tested. The term "character" links the agent to this community and this process. In an approach more typical of Catholic moral theologians, the interest in character ethics emerges against a different ecclesial and theological history. The practice of individual confession created a moral tradition in which the evaluation of individual acts was highly important, even excessively so. "Character" here is a way of stressing the fact that acts do not have an intrinsic moral character outside of the life orientation and intentions of the agent. Acts must be understood in relation to the character of the whole moral life that they express.

Before expanding a bit further on these models, I want to make three basic points about the challenges of relating biblical materials to ethics, all of which impinge on the way a category like "Christian character" is understood. First is the fact of pluralism in the Bible and in the Christian churches. As has been amply argued in recent biblical scholarship, there is significant diversity of moral perspective and instruction in the Bible itself, even if we confine our attention to the New Testament. Even less debatable is the fact of pluralism among the communities of moral identity in our culture and globally that identify themselves as "Christian." Second, however, neither individuals nor communities can arrive at moral judgments or take action without some relatively focused idea of what is morally good and right. Irreducible pluralism cannot result in decisive and consistent moral action. An adequate, if not complete, understanding of Christian character will demand that we acknowledge and reply to the fact of pluralism, deciding whether, in spite of pluralism, there are some stable reference points for the formation of character in Bible and Christian tradition.

Third, Christians and their communities have not lived in isolation from their cultures, either in the first century or today. Contemporary Christian ethicists are perhaps more aware, however, of an ability and a duty to exercise responsibility for justice and the common good, which requires dialogue and cooperation across confessional and cultural lines. First-century Christians and twenty-first-century Christians share the problem of how to negotiate the spaces between Christian character and the characters of other morally committed persons with whom we must address common practical problems. Yet the internal pluralism of modern societies, and the urgent nature of global issues like the economy, the environment, violence, and human rights, make Christians today even more interested than their forebears in understanding the intersections between Christian communities and other communities of moral identity.

Two Models of Character Ethics

Now to the senses in which and purposes for which a notion of character is most often employed in ethics. These uses of character, far from being mutually exclusive, are often intertwined and interdependent. However, it is useful to distinguish them as foci of attention, particularly in a conversation in which participants might be approaching character ethics with different assumptions and agendas.

1. For many ethicists, perhaps especially for those rooted in the Catholic tradition, an ethics of character holds up the basic moral dispositions of the agent as more important than individual acts. Character refers to the long-term formation and moral self-expression of the person. The concern to avoid excessive concentration on the nature of particular kinds of actions and on moral norms specifying act-focused morality has been especially characteristic of recent Roman Catholicism. Catholic moral theology prior to the Second Vatican Council was defined predominantly by a deductive and systematic casuistry of moral rules, which seemed to make the moral status of individuals contingent

on the nature of their acts, taken more or less in isolation, and not as a series, or as part of an integrated direction of life. From this perspective, character ethics is a way of returning to and revivifying the Thomistic category of virtue as a habitual disposition to act in favor of certain goods, an interior disposition that is more essential to moral identity and moral goodness than any external act that expresses character. This use of character is exemplified in Richard Gula's *Reason Informed by Faith:*

> Morality is often associated exclusively with behavior guided by rules. . . . While we are certainly called to do what is right as Christians, we are first of all called to be loving persons in the imitation of Christ. . . . Morality, then, has a great interest in the interiority of the person, or the person's character. . . . Here is where we locate the classical idea of the virtues — those personal qualities disposing us to act in certain ways.[1]

2. Another, complementary, use of character in theological ethics aims to situate individual moral agency within a community of formation. For Protestants in particular, this can be a way of clarifying that Scripture guides morality by forming a community in which the agent's primary loyalties are directed by faith in Christ. Such a use can be illustrated by the work of Stanley Hauerwas, who sees personal moral agency as embodying a community's "narrative" or "story." While dispositional continuity and interior commitment are important, the key function of character here is to highlight or sustain the integrity and distinctiveness of communal identity and practices. For example, the Christian individual and community are both morally committed to nonviolence, because both are formed by Jesus' sacrificial death on the cross, an action the meaning and truth of which will be obscure or even unintelligible to outsiders. But the Christian lives faithfully and truthfully by conforming his or her being and actions to Christ's example. In a book emblematically entitled *A Community of Character,* Hauerwas contends that there is no neutral point in evaluating competing stories, nor any "story of stories" in light of which a multitude of communal narratives could be adjudicated. "Rather objectivity comes from being formed by a truthful narrative and community within history." The only test of the truth of a story is the lives of its adherents, and Christians witness to the Christian narrative by means of their practices.[2]

Hauerwas objects particularly to abstract, universal ethics of the Kantian

---

1. Richard M. Gula, *Reason Informed by Faith: Foundations of Catholic Morality* (New York: Paulist, 1989), p. 7.

2. Stanley M. Hauerwas, *A Community of Character: Toward a Constructive Christian Social Ethic* (Notre Dame, Ind. and London: University of Notre Dame Press, 1981), p. 96.

variety and, following Alasdair MacIntyre, wants to return to the historicity and particularity of moral actions and ethical theories alike. To an extent, he is willing to accept relativism as a consequence (though not of the "vicious" or "vulgar" variety). I would describe Hauerwas's position by saying that he, like Karl Barth or H. Richard Niebuhr, is committed to the objective truth of moral obligations revealed in Christ, but knowledge of that truth is relative to Christian community and not easily communicable to outsiders. To be God's people, "a forgiven people," is to be in a sense separated from the world. The world assumes, to the contrary, that "power and violence rule history," and so it refuses to live by the memory of forgiveness sustained by the community formed by scriptural narratives.[3] "Christians are forbidden to despair in the face of the dividedness of the world. . . . The task of the Christian is not to defeat relativism by argument but to witness to a God who requires confrontation."[4]

Many Catholic authors, working from the notion of virtue in Aquinas, also highlight the historical and practical nature of ethics, but they do so by employing a notion of prudence or practical reason. Prudence, understood as a virtue of the intellect that allows the agent to discern what would instantiate the virtues in any given set of circumstances, is highly context-dependent.[5] However, for these authors, prudence still works against a backdrop of reasonable, shared, and generally intelligible objective goods. More communitarian proponents of character, however, avoid assertions about shared or shareable values in favor of a distinctive moral identity that offers a witness against culture without expecting persuasion or consensus.

While writers in the first category of character ethics often choose the term "virtue" to describe their enterprise, those writing more in the mode of narrative or story ethics use the designation "character" more frequently. The preference of terminology reveals the more basic difference in perspective. Virtue connotes *aspiration to* or *cultivation of* certain goods, values, or ideals, to which the moral agent is positively and habitually disposed. Character carries an overtone of *resistance to* and *steadfastness against* threatening powers or forces against which the strong must stand firm. In the background of these connotations, we may perceive the age-old theological debates about the primacy of a created nature that is able to discern basic goods and to strive after them in the present moral order versus the primacy of sin in human experience and the need for conversion away from the order of the world.

---

3. Hauerwas, *Community of Character*, p. 69.

4. Hauerwas, *Community of Character*, p. 105.

5. Jean Porter, *The Recovery of Virtue: The Relevance of Aquinas for Christian Ethics* (Louisville: Westminster/John Knox, 1990), p. 159.

A Model of Biblical "Community"

When we move to issues of morality and ethics as they appear in the writings of biblical scholars, we find that neither the term "virtue" nor the term "character" has as high a profile as the term "community" itself. "Community" as a more common framing term for the nature of early Christian morality functions in many ways parallel to character but carries a suggestion of *conformance to* or *integration of* the individual with the worldview of his or her social group. For example, in *The Moral World of the First Christians*, Wayne Meeks interprets the moral formation of the early Christian communities in terms of resocialization from one symbolic world to another, with distinctive (though not separate) patterns of belief and behavior. Within these worlds, there was a strong interdependence of community and self.[6] In contrast to Hauerwas, what is stressed here is not the distinctive, commanding, obligatory nature of Christian morality but its dependence on social location and historical and cultural influences from the Jewish and Greco-Roman worlds.

The new emphasis on community or social world as shaping the ethos and ethics of a particular biblical author or the community for which he wrote reflects the strong indebtedness of contemporary biblical interpretation to the social sciences. It can also represent a deconstructionist agenda, either soft or strong, deployed against some traditional theological and ethical interpretations of biblical texts that virtually excised the texts in question from their roots in ancient cultures and tried to convert them into timeless representations of theological and moral doctrine. My point is not to repudiate sociology and social history as approaches to biblical narratives, for I would in fact affirm them. I also affirm, for example, the healthy iconoclasm of a feminist hermeneutic in the face of standard accounts of biblical ethics. My point is simply that we need to be careful about the tacit theological and epistemological premises of a biblical character ethics, and that there are several different directions in which such an ethics might go.

Community, Character, and Biblical Authority

The assimilation of character ethics by biblical interpretation takes the above-mentioned concerns about placing moral dispositions before rules and about stressing communal formation over abstract moral reasoning and transposes

---

6. Wayne A. Meeks, *The Moral World of the First Christians* (Philadelphia: Westminster, 1986), pp. 12-14.

them into a framework explicitly shaped by concerns about biblical authority. The crisis of biblical authority today is deeply informed by postmodern trends in the contemporary intellectual disciplines, as noted by Walter Brueggemann in his positive review of Leo Perdue's *The Collapse of History*:[7]

> The new pluralism, which pays attention to vested interest in knowledge, and relies on "interested" judgments . . . [is] part of a much wider and deeper epistemological crisis in the West, wherein what was taken to be "objectively given" is much more likely now to be seen as the conclusion of an interpretive elite, whose privilege is now eroded.[8]

As reflecting this epistemological crisis, the issue of the authority of the Bible for ethics entails at least four problems. Stated succinctly, these are whether the message of the Bible is unitary or fragmented; whether the biblical message about ethics is unique; whether the Bible can ground moral rules and offer concrete guidance; and whether the moral message of the Bible has sense and significance outside of Christianity. First, as has already been stated, there is textual pluralism within the Bible, and a historical pluralism of the communities that produced it, as well as historical diffuseness and contingency of the processes by which the canon itself was selected and defined. The fact of pluralism leads some to question whether values such as love and cross-bearing are in fact the only or primary ones the canon (even the New Testament canon) provides. In a particularly strong statement, Burton Mack refers to "the Jesus schools, the Christ cults, the Pauline churches, Thomas Christianity, the Johannine enclaves, Jewish-Christian communities, Gnostic-Christian groups, the Pauline school, and others." Mack ultimately concludes that, even though all the above claim Jesus as their founder, they are so diverse that they "are very difficult to comprehend as variants of a common persuasion."[9]

Furthermore, to see the Bible itself as forming more historical communities over time also indicates pluralism in the concrete interpretation of what identified "biblical" values and virtues mean in practice, for communities are by definition particular and diverse. The Bible functions as an authority only by virtue of the privileged place it occupies within a certain community (or communities) of interpretation, not by virtue of invariant, self-evident meanings of scriptural texts. If the Bible must be understood as the "Church's" book — or

---

7. Leo Perdue, *The Collapse of History: Reconstructing Old Testament Theology* (Minneapolis: Fortress, 1994).

8. Walter Brueggemann, "Leo G. Perdue, *The Collapse of History* . . . ," *JR* 76 (1996): 352.

9. Burton Mack, "Many Movements, Many Myths: Redescribing Attractions of Early Christianities: Toward a Conversation with Rodney Stark," *RSR* 25 (1999): 133.

the book of many churches — in order to function as authoritative Scripture, then, so some might argue, the epistemological claims that can be made for its moral content are limited.

An ethics of character can appear to resolve the uncertainty pluralism and cultural relativity created by making this pluralism itself normative. For instance, taking his lead from "postmodern critics" who "have preferred indeterminacy to closure and order, pluralism to unity," Burke O. Long urges biblical critics "to choose socially rooted loss of privilege or indeterminacy, a clash of rival gods as it were, as a condition appropriate to their postmodern future."[10] By granting that biblical meaning varies so radically among communal readings of the Bible, we sidestep the issue of whether there is or should be any consistent, recognizably "Christian" identity and behavior that the Bible should engender if interpreted properly. We absolve ourselves from the responsibility of determining in any general terms what is or is not an appropriate moral interpretation of the Bible, or what, for that matter, would constitute the shape of a faithful community or life. Hermeneutically, this may be attractive, and it has some value morally as a form of resistance to hegemonic readings of texts. But is it enough?

Two further dimensions of the problem of biblical authority are whether the Bible's message is unique to Christianity, and whether it can be heard beyond Christianity's parameters. Uniqueness and nongeneralizability correlate with Hauerwas's insight into the nature of Christian community as a witness to a reality and to values that are violently rejected by groups formed around competing centers of value. Richard B. Hays asserts that "[t]he community, in its corporate life, is called to embody an alternative order that stands as a sign of God's redemptive purposes in the world," an order Hays develops in terms of community, cross, and new creation.[11] Christian community is the bearer of an objective and true revelation to a favored people; that revelation is not known outside Christianity; and it will make no sense to those who are not redeemed in Christ. The Bible is then an authority for ethics by virtue of its ability to form community and character in a manner consistent with this revelation of God.

A fourth problem is whether the Bible can function, as has sometimes been assumed in the past, as a source of timeless rules for action. Historical study of the vast differences in context between the moral instructions found in the Bible and the dilemmas of later cultures has fairly decisively eroded the no-

---

10. Burke O. Long, "Ambitions of Dissent: Biblical Theology in a Postmodern Future," *JR* 76 (1996): 279, 289.

11. Richard B. Hays, "Scripture-Shaped Community: The Problem of Method in New Testament Ethics," *Int* 54 (1990): 46.

tion that the Bible is an ahistorical rule book. But the remaining question today is in what sense the Bible does function as an authority for ethics, or at what level it does so. One possible answer is that the Bible operates more foundationally and pervasively in forming community and character than in providing moral proscriptions and prescriptions about specific kinds of activity. Specific instructions that it does provide are of continuing relevance only in proportion to the similarity between our situation and their original one; otherwise, they should be taken as culturally limited attempts to communicate the gospel — or simply dismissed as not authoritative for us.

In a framework of character ethics in which "character" indicates a process of communal formation of individual identity, the Bible does not necessarily have to produce specific moral rules in order to be authoritative. Rather, it orients Christian persons and communities around general values, principles, or virtues that reflect God's self-disclosure in Christ. Central among these are, for example, repentance, love of neighbor, self-sacrifice, cross bearing, forgiveness, nonviolence (closer to a moral rule), and compassion.

Toward Unity in Diversity

In an article that resulted from a conference at the University of Chicago, Carol Newsom recounts the story of an amusingly frustrating exchange between a theologian at her institution, the Candler School of Theology, and a biblical scholar who had come for a job interview. The theologian inquired as to whether there might be some theological center to the Old Testament, some unifying theme such as creation or covenant, or even some common referent such as "God." All these suggestions were rebuffed by the biblical scholar, who observed that "there may be *some* prominent themes among *certain* large blocks of material . . . but identifying any one or two of those as the unifying theme of the Old Testament betrays its extraordinary variety and distorts its historical particularity." Finally the theologian pleaded, "I'm not trying to do violence to the historical particularity of the Bible or its cultural context. . . . I'm just trying to find something that theology can work with."[12]

Many interpreters point to the pluralistic, internally dynamic structure of the biblical canon itself as a model for theological reflection, and Newsom herself is sympathetic to this approach. She advocates "dialogic truth and the polyphonic text," in which the different voices in the text are brought into intersection at the level of practical engagement and conversation among interpreters.

12. Carol A. Newsom, "Bakhtin, the Bible, and Dialogic Truth," *JR* 76 (1996): 290.

Similarly to Newsom, Werner Jeanrond calls for a new form of interdisciplinary, reading-centered biblical theology that is both critical of ideologies in the text and resistant to any final systematization, especially one that is "ecclesially imposed." "Biblical theology encourages all nondogmatic models and paradigms of describing continuities and discontinuities in the complex development and religious challenge of biblical monotheism. It calls for an ongoing ideology critique of any systematizing attempt."[13]

This leads John Collins to wonder whether any approach to biblical interpretation that emphasizes diversity and historicity is not "inherently unsystematic" and "opposed to conferring any kind of theological normativity on literary and historical interpretation."[14] He cites others who apparently agree — including Leo Perdue, in *The Collapse of History* (see above), and Elizabeth Castelli, editor of *The Postmodern Bible*[15] — before concluding that renewed dialogue between theology and biblical scholarship will of necessity "be marked by the celebration of diversity rather than the search for unity."[16]

On the one hand, I endorse the Bible's internal pluralism as a model for a dialogic theology and ethics. On the other hand, I wonder whether essentially procedural solutions ("let all be heard in dialogue") move very confidently toward the content Newsom's theologian friend felt was needed. From the standpoint of an ethicist, the simple celebration of diversity is quite an anemic response to genocide in Hitler's Germany, in the colonial Americas, or in today's Bosnia, Rwanda, or Kosovo; to exploitation of child labor in other countries by U.S. manufacturers; to the international sex trade; or to the rape and murder of women not only by criminals and political terrorists but even by their own fathers and husbands. Even the celebration of a uniquely Christian set of moral qualities with little hope of social impact would not be adequate from my point of view. Yet the identification of some distinctive, if not unique, qualities of Christian character is at least a place to begin real moral engagement.

My own conviction is that sheer pluralism is not adequate as a Christian moral response to injustice in the world. Christian morality requires some more determinate understanding of what it means to begin to live in the reign of God, to form a community as body of Christ, or to be transformed by the Lord's Spirit. Christian morality can and should be centered in virtues like repentance, reconciliation, love, compassion, solidarity, mercy, and forgiveness. Moreover — and this may be even more controversial — Christian biblical ethics has social

---

13. Werner Jeanrond, "Criteria for New Biblical Theologies," *JR* 76 (1996): 247.

14. John J. Collins, "The Bible and Christian Theology," *JR* 76 (1996): 170.

15. Elizabeth Castelli, ed., *The Postmodern Bible* (New Haven: Yale University Press, 1985).

16. Castelli, *Postmodern Bible*, p. 171.

implications that draw us ineluctably into moral debate and partnership with other moral communities (of some of which we, still Christians, are also a part).

The first Christians' moral identity was neither absolutely unique nor insulated from cultural influence and from the opportunities for conversion and transformation that cultural embeddedness provided. As far as I can tell, a certain permeability and communicability of moral identity characterized early Christianity, as it continues, appropriately so, to characterize Christianity today. For instance, the distinctive New Testament love command (Matt 22:37-39; Mark 12:29-31; Luke 10:27) has Jewish roots (Deut 6:5; Lev 19:18). Finding redemptive meaning in a sacrificial death was not unique to Christians, and they borrowed formulations and symbols from Jewish and Greco-Roman religions to express their experience of the death of Christ.[17] Common meals were a way to enact the unity of other voluntary associations and religious cults.[18] Inclusiveness across class lines and more equal roles for women in the Christian churches reflected tendencies in the Greco-Roman culture.[19]

Yet the interdependence of Christian moral community and character on other moral worldviews (e.g., Jewish and Greek) need not signify that Christian moral identity is reducible to those worldviews, rather than being true and transformative. Why not see cultural parallels as confirmatory evidence of the truth of the Christian worldview rather than as threats to its supposed uniqueness? Christians adapt values, virtues, and practices from other communities and traditions, refocusing them in relation to their experience of Jesus as Christ, and embodying them within a community in which the presence of God actually enables moral relationships of compassion, inclusion, and forgiveness.

Is There a Moral Vision in the New Testament?

Discussing literary methods of biblical interpretation as a link between narrative theology and the Bible, and taking note of the influence of deconstruction

17. John T. Carroll and Joel B. Green, *The Death of Jesus in Early Christianity* (Peabody, Mass.: Hendrickson, 1995); Adela Yarbro Collins, "Finding Meaning in the Death of Jesus," *JR* 78 (1998): 175-96.

18. Robert L. Wilken, *The Christians As the Romans Saw Them* (New Haven and London: Yale University Press, 1984), p. 44.

19. Wilken, *Christians*, p. 39; Ross Shepard Kraemer, *Her Share of the Blessings: Women's Religions among Pagans, Jews, and Christians in the Greco-Roman World* (New York and Oxford: Oxford University Press, 1992); Carolyn Osiek and David L. Balch, *Families in the New Testament World: Households and House Churches* (Louisville: Westminster/John Knox, 1997), pp. 54-64.

and a new historicism, John Donahue notes that biblical interpreters are often reluctant to move from questions of "the world of the text" to questions of theological meaning. Yet he expects or hopes, drawing on Elizabeth Castelli, that the creative interaction of many forms of literary criticism, including feminism, womanism, and ideological analysis, may bring us to "the threshold of new theological constructs."[20]

Although the celebrators of diversity eschew the Candler theologian's interest in something substantial as the working material of theology, I find it essential to Christian character ethics to define at least a few desirable *characteristics*. It is astounding to me that so many biblical interpreters today are so highly reluctant to acknowledge that a profile of such characteristics is clearly projected by the "single, fairly coherent story" (Newsom) of Jesus as the Christ. In an article on the diversity of presentations constituting the "third quest" for the historical Jesus (Hellenistic Cynic Sage, Jewish Cynic Peasant, Jewish "spirit Person," Egalitarian Prophet of Wisdom, Eschatological Prophet of the Present and Coming Kingdom, and Prophet of Imminent Restoration Eschatology), M. Eugene Boring clearly demonstrates that

> there is considerable agreement that, whatever else Jesus was, he was something of a subversive sage, provocatively challenging the common-sense wisdom of people from the perspective of a new vision of the kingdom of God. In addition, there is agreement that Jesus mediated, in word and deed, the merciful, inclusive presence of God imaged as a loving father and the womb-like compassion he directed especially to outsiders.[21]

Of course, questers of the historical Jesus are not making specific theological claims about the relation of Jesus to a transcendent, redeeming God, claims that are presupposed by speaking of Jesus as Christ. To speak of Jesus in that way is to assert the presence of God in the life Jesus lived and the vision he proclaimed, and it is also to express confidence in the continuing presence of God and God's reign in the historical believing community. However, historically informed biblical scholarship leaves little doubt as to the ethical and moral shape that a community formed in Jesus' name should assume, whether or not one also grants its transcendent origin and destiny. Wolfgang Schrage is among those who appropriate such historical research more theologically: while the basis of Christian conduct is "God's sovereignty and Jesus' cross and resurrection," the content of Christian ethics is defined by "the radical rejection of all

20. John R. Donahue, S.J., "The Literary Turn and New Testament Theology: Detour or New Direction?" *JR* 76 (1996): 272-73.

21. M. Eugene Boring, "The 'Third Quest' and the Apostolic Faith," *Int* 50 (1996): 344.

limits on" love of neighbor, which is open "precisely to those whom we would naturally say are not worth loving."[22]

The idea that once critical, academic study of the Bible gives up the kind of dominating and exclusivist interpretations associated with privileged social and ecclesial locations then the necessary and desirable result is "indeterminacy" and even "a clash of rival gods" becomes all the more ludicrous when moral concerns are placed on the table. Although overly confident specific extrapolations of biblical ethics can and have been unjust and oppressive, complete deconstruction of normative meaning is not an acceptable alternative. It is not enough to say Christian character will be formed in a number of quite disparate communities that have in common only that they have read Scripture idiosyncratically. The general virtues Christian character should exhibit are evident enough from the standpoint of even a historically oriented and critical biblical hermeneutic. Furthermore, both the historical fact that the identity of even the earliest Christians was formed interactively with other cultural groups and the ethical demand that Christians interact with others to define and defend a more just society should lead us to seek ways in which to make the moral ideals of Christianity communicable to, plausible to, and resonant with other contemporaneous cultures and worldviews.

Where more indeterminacy and dialogue come legitimately into play is at the level of specific decisions, actions, practices, and policies, as is acknowledged in the prudential aspects of virtue ethics, in the communalism of narrative character ethics, and in dialogic proposals for the discernment and testing of moral truth in practice. Of course, it is not the purpose of character ethics to settle in advance the rightness or wrongness of all specific types of actions, nor even to supply general rules for such determinations. Yet what it can and should do is establish a clear orientation and set of priorities that will guide them by shaping Christian persons and communities in certain distinctive ways.

The Sermon on the Mount

Let me turn briefly to the Sermon on the Mount (Matthew 5–7) as an example.[23] This text, especially the "hard sayings" of 5:38-48, has long been a favor-

---

22. Wolfgang Schrage, *The Ethics of the New Testament*, trans. David E. Green (Philadelphia: Fortress, 1988), pp. 76-77.

23. The following is adapted from a review I wrote of Hans Dieter Betz's *The Sermon on the Mount*, ed. Adela Yarbro Collins, Hermeneia (Minneapolis: Fortress, 1995), for *BR* 12/4 (1996): 14, 16.

ite of ethicists because it seems so clearly to present what is unique about Christian morality, and to do so in a way that sets it off from Jewish and pagan practice. The Beatitudes seem to represent a thorough reversal of worldly standards. Considering Jesus' Jewish background, many see the "antitheses" (5:21-48) as exemplary of Jesus' self-distancing from the religion of his hearers: Jesus seems to substitute an original and more heartfelt reading of morality for the old prescriptions of "the law." Moreover, Jesus' commands to love our enemies, turn the other cheek, and give away possessions have often been taken as warrants for specific and relatively unvarying rules for moral behavior, especially nonviolence.

Yet many scholars now stress the correspondence of Matthew's Gospel to its Jewish context, and even of the ideals of love and forgiveness to Jewish precedent.[24] In his massive commentary on the Sermon on the Mount, Hans Dieter Betz follows the emergent consensus that Jesus' ministry and teaching are strongly indebted to his Jewish background, and that the Sermon on the Mount appears in a Gospel intended for a largely Jewish community.[25] Betz's thesis that a pre-Matthean author wrote the Sermon just as we now have it, and that Matthew simply incorporated it into his Gospel, will no doubt prove controversial. Yet, whatever one's stance on that particular issue, it will be difficult to deny that Betz lays to rest the assumption that the Sermon on the Mount is morally unique. On the contrary, it displays many similarities with the Judaism familiar to Jesus and his first followers. The Sermon on the Plain (Luke 6:20-49) is a catechetical adaptation of similar material for culturally Greek disciples. Since some variant on the Golden Rule can be found in virtually every culture, it is considered self-evident by Luke (6:31), while Matthew backs it up by Jewish teaching (Matt 7:12). Likewise, the principle of nonretaliation was a common ideal in ancient literature, both Jewish and Greek. For early followers of Jesus, the enemy is the fellow Jew who sees them as heretics. Betz also discerns Jewish roots in the belief that to forgo satisfaction or reward now will preserve it in the world to come.

Betz sees the Beatitudes as historically the best-known and most-valued portion of the Sermon. He maintains that a key function of the Beatitudes is to set out conditions under which disciples enjoy a new existence, a salvation that will be completed at the end of the world if the necessary conditions are fulfilled. Eschatology is often considered to be the touchstone for the distinctiveness of Jesus, insofar as he proclaimed the kingdom of God both as a future

24. See Anthony J. Saldarini, *Matthew's Jewish-Christian Community* (Chicago and London: University of Chicago Press, 1994).
25. Betz, *Sermon on the Mount*.

event and as accessible to believers now. Yet Betz provides evidence that the belief that either salvation or condemnation can be experienced in the present life, and that their completion depends upon future judgment, is common both to Judaism and to early Christianity. Finally, Betz believes that the Lord's Prayer (Matt 6:9-13) originated with the historical Jesus but reflects merely his particular insights "into the Jewish religion and life as it was understood and practiced in his environment."[26] One distinctive, if not unique, note arises in the universality of Jesus' view of the relation of God to humanity. God is "our" Father, including all human beings on earth.

There are, perhaps, two fundamental points to be learned here about the relevance of the Sermon on the Mount — as *epitome* of Jesus' remembered teaching — for Christian, biblical character ethics. First, the Scriptures are most influential morally as they form the Christian worldview, communal life, and *character*. Christian dispositions and intentions, evoked by trust in and loyalty to Christ, provide a sense of direction out of which we make specific decisions and judgments, even though other loyalties and commitments can and should contribute to specific moral actions.[27] Second, we can and should maintain that Scripture and authentically biblical communities will form character in a recognizable way. Plurality, dialogue, and practice are still essential in generating self-criticism and constant reformation of our concrete moral standards. If self-promotion, dominance, and exploitation constitute the status quo, Jesus pushes a vision in which compassion, forgiveness, mercy, and solidarity are the transformative edge of an experience of God in which "business as usual" is no longer possible. Jesus takes familiar cultural and religious values and, without introducing any unheard of moral value or norm, rearranges virtues into a new pattern, so that love, mercy, and justice are at the very center of righteous existence under God. In the words of James Gustafson,

> The Gospels bear witness to Jesus' own confidence in the goodness and mercy of God, his indiscriminating care for the just and the unjust. The deeds of Jesus narrated in the Gospels testify to his faith that renewal, healing, and reconciliation are possible for all men [and women]: for those who have fallen into degradation, those who are without respectable status, those who serve the human oppressors, those who are sick, those who are one's enemies.[28]

26. Betz, *Sermon on the Mount*, p. 377.

27. James M. Gustafson, *Christ and the Moral Life* (New York: Harper and Row, 1968), pp. 262-63.

28. Gustafson, *Christ and the Moral Life*, p. 244.

Neither totally unique nor reducible to cultural influences, this pattern defines the experience of God that Jesus Christ mediates. What is profoundly original about Christian ethics and about Christian understandings of moral character is the claim that, in and through Jesus, disciples are really empowered to exist in this way.

Symbol, Story, and Character Formation

On a final note, I want to introduce an aspect of biblical character ethics that is receiving more attention today. The Bible's narratives, parables, and symbols have great potential to transform the affections, perceptions, motivations, and intentions of the moral agent, and to place moral commitment against the horizon of God's reign. This fact is increasingly appreciated due to a more nuanced moral anthropology that goes beyond reason to imagination and the emotions as media of moral discernment. As the Catholic author William Spohn has stated it, "Jesus of Nazareth lived a particular human life that has universal meaning; the analogical imagination recognizes how to be faithful to Jesus in ever new situations."[29] Also, recognition of the imaginative and affective dimensions of morality helps make room for the relevance of religious language and symbols in what is ultimately "public" dialogue about ethics and justice. The parable of Lazarus at the gate or of the Good Samaritan has far more engaging and motivating power than Kant's categorical imperative; the example of Jesus' death on the cross than Kierkegaard's ruminations on the "works of love." At the level of character formation, the Bible as story and narrative can engage and educate the full panoply of our moral capacities — the imagination, affections, and emotions, as well as the intellect. All of these are necessary to bring ethical theory and reasoning to the endpoint of committed action.

29. William C. Spohn, *Go and Do Likewise: Jesus and Ethics* (New York: Continuum, 1999), p. 186.

Formed and Transformed by Scripture: Character, Community, and Authority in Biblical Interpretation

L. Gregory Jones

The seminary students had been anxiously awaiting the time when their homiletics professor would post the list that assigned each student in the class a biblical text. Each student was to write an exegesis of and a sermon on that text. Students were anxious because, while some would undoubtedly be assigned the Prodigal Son or another favorite text, many feared they would get an obscure passage from 1 or 2 Chronicles or, even worse, the story of Balaam's ass. A crowd quickly gathered as soon as the list was posted. A third-year seminary student, nearing graduation, was distressed when he saw his text. "Darn it," he said. "I got a text from Hebrews. I really wanted a New Testament text."

I have often wondered what that student's ministry has been like in the parishes to which he has been appointed. More broadly, though, the lack of familiarity with Scripture that this story illustrates has become an increasing problem among clergy and laity across the traditions. I showed a group of sixty undergraduates, almost all of whom identified themselves (at least nominally so) as Christians, a video of Martin Luther King, Jr.'s "I Have a Dream" speech from 1963. After watching the video, I noted to the students that at a pivotal point in the speech King declared, "Let justice roll down like waters, and righteousness like an ever-flowing stream." Where, I asked the students, did that phrase come from? After an awkward silence, one student suggested that King was such a good orator that he had probably coined the phrase himself. Another student hazarded the guess that King had gotten it from either the Bible

Portions of the first part of this essay appeared as "The Word That Journeys with Us: Bible, Character Formation, and Christian Community," *ThT* 55/1 (1998): 69-76, and are reproduced with permission.

or Shakespeare. But not one student could specify that it was from the Bible, or more specifically from the prophets — much less from Amos. Yet King, just thirty-five years ago, did not think he would need to say, "As the prophet Amos, in the Old Testament of the Christian Bible, said. . . ." He presumed, I think rightly, that no matter how poor Christian performance of the Scriptures might have been in the United States, the vast majority of his listeners would hear those words as Amos's critique of people who worship God without practicing justice.

Yet this familiarity with biblical texts has diminished in recent decades. There are complex reasons that account for this loss, but the key point in this context is that we have lost a sense of the Bible as a (or the) central text in the formation of Christian character and identity. This is not to say that the interpretations of the Bible today are excellent or poor, constructive or destructive. It is to say that, rather than struggling to provide wise readings and performances of the biblical texts, we in the United States have largely marginalized those texts in Christian community and Christian life. As a result, we have lost a clear sense of the ways in which Scripture's words (and the Word) shape both our minds and our bodies.

There is an obvious objection to this claim: Whom do I mean by the "we" in the previous sentence? After all, large numbers of people in the United States gather in small groups on a regular basis for "Bible study." According to Robert Wuthnow, perhaps as many as two-thirds of all small groups in America gather specifically as "Bible study" groups.[1] Surely such groups must constitute a crucial counterexample to my claim. Yet what Wuthnow and his associates discovered is that these groups are far more focused on providing personal support to one another than on learning the Bible. Indeed, he discovered that such groups often produce wooden interpretations of the Bible with little increase in knowledge of the Bible's content (e.g., "The Bible helped me get a job, therefore it must be true.").

A more decisive objection is that the "we" refers to people from middle-class, white (and perhaps Protestant) America. After all, King's own practice was nourished in the black church, and the rich patterns of biblical interpretation in black preaching and black music would seem to provide important counterexamples to my claims. This is an important point, and I want to return below to the black church as a resource for a richer conception of the Bible's role in the formation of community and character. At this point I would simply observe that, while the black church is not in as bad a shape on these matters as

1. See Robert Wuthnow, *Sharing the Journey: Support Groups and America's New Quest for Community* (New York: The Free Press, 1994).

are most Euro-American churches, my impression is that these issues are becoming more and more pressing even within the black church.

The heart of my concern is that American Christians have increasingly lost a familiarity with ruled patterns for reading the Bible, the kind of familiarity that shapes people's lives and, at its best, enlivens a scriptural imagination. Indeed, this loss is at least in part a consequence of an increasing preoccupation with questions of biblical method and biblical authority. As Christians in modernity have increasingly argued about the appropriate method or methods for biblical study, as well as the perceived status of Scripture's authority, we have failed to attend adequately to the task of actually reading the texts themselves. This is a particular problem within predominantly white, mainline Protestant churches in the United States, but it is more and more problematic across traditions and across the theological spectrum. Even evangelicals who have a very high view of Scripture's authority often have a rather low competence in biblical knowledge.

Further, our loss of familiarity with Scripture is also a cause of our preoccupation with biblical method and biblical authority. The less familiar we are with the texts of Scripture in all their diversity and complexity, the easier it is for us to remain at a more generalized level of argument about whether Scripture has authority or not — or, more accurately put, what kind of authority diverse people are willing to ascribe to Scripture.

Perhaps most importantly, our loss of knowledge about Scripture is also morally convenient. As United Methodist Bishop Kenneth Carder has suggested, "It is much easier to argue about evolution and creation than it is to live as though this is God's world. Or, debating whether a 'great fish' really swallowed Jonah is far less costly and risky than acknowledging that God loves our enemies as much as God loves us."[2] Carder's point hit home autobiographically, for as I began to absorb the significance of Jonah's judgment with regard to some of my own attitudes, I simultaneously discovered that I prefer debates about its historicity. Such debates do not put my own character at risk, whereas the force of the story challenges my refusal to be open to God's work of transforming my character.

I have also discovered that Jonah has significant relevance for challenging how we tend to even articulate our disagreements with fellow Christians about biblical method, biblical authority, and biblical texts. We construct these people as enemies to be defeated, not as fellow children of God with whom we ought to engage both in the hope that they will be converted *and* in the openness that we *need* to be converted.

2. Bishop Kenneth L. Carder, "Bible's True Authority Lies in Power to Change," a United Methodist News Service commentary, June 2, 1999.

To be sure, we cannot presume that we can evade questions of method or authority simply by immersing ourselves once again in Scripture. The questions are unavoidable, particularly on this side of modernity's questioning. However, I am suggesting that we can make an important difference in addressing these questions by developing habits of effective and faithful reading of Scripture.

We develop such habits through a lively scriptural imagination. In such an imagination, people know the stories and convictions embedded in Scripture in ways that then provide the freedom for creatively (and faithfully) "imagining the world Scripture imagines."[3] Such scriptural imagination can be found in the great theologians of the tradition, and also in great literature such as John Milton, Flannery O'Connor, and Toni Morrison.[4]

In order to cultivate such a scriptural imagination, we need to rediscover Scripture as the "word that journeys with us" in Christian living. This is a phrase I borrow from the Roman Catholic theologian Hans Urs von Balthasar in order to suggest the sense in which we need to learn to live with the texts of Scripture throughout our lives.[5] In the first part of this essay, I suggest that learning to live with, and immersing ourselves in, Scripture requires our engaging it in three distinct but overlapping contexts: in catechesis, in critical study, and in reflection on patterns of social engagement. I briefly identify how each of these contexts provides us with opportunities for reenlivening Scripture as a word that journeys with us, and point to two figures who are exemplars of the kind of practice I am suggesting: Augustine of Hippo and Martin Luther King, Jr.

In the second section of the essay, I explore how a disciplined and creative scriptural imagination will enable us to address issues of biblical authority more faithfully and effectively. Despite the obvious differences between the premodern Augustine and the modern Martin Luther King, Jr. in time, culture, denominational presumptions, and formal biblical method, I will suggest that they share a great deal in common because of their commitment to Scripture as the word that journeys with us.

---

3. This phrase comes from the title of Luke Timothy Johnson's essay, "Imagining the World Scripture Imagines," in *Theology and Scriptural Imagination*, ed. L. Gregory Jones and James J. Buckley (Oxford and Malden, Mass.: Blackwell, 1998), pp. 3-18.

4. It is indicative of my larger concern about the loss of familiarity with Scripture that college English departments are finding it increasingly difficult to teach English and American literature to students who cannot understand the multifaceted biblical allusions that pervade much of that literature. There are now footnotes in Oxford "classics" that explain the scriptural references.

5. See Hans Urs von Balthasar, *Theo-Drama*, 4 vols., trans. Graham Harrison (San Francisco: Ignatius, 1990), 2:102-4.

Throughout, I will suggest that reclaiming a rich familiarity with Scripture, nurtured through better reading habits than we typically provide, will provide us with greater resources for challenging bad readings of Scripture and discovering afresh Scripture's formative and transformative power to change people's lives and bear faithful witness to God.

Catechesis

Christians need to reclaim the centrality of catechesis if Scripture is to be formative for our character and our communal life. Most basically, we need to learn the stories, to have Moses and Deborah, Amos and Paul, Mary and John become people we know. My colleague Willie J. Jennings, raised in the African-American Christian tradition, indicates that his parents talked so much about biblical characters that when he was young he really thought that people such as Ruth and Naomi were members of his extended family. Those stories are crucial for forming a Christian understanding of, and desire for, God.

Even more, we need to locate the practice of learning and interpreting Scripture within the context of other practices of Christian living, both individually and as communities. This was at the heart of one of the most powerful examples of catechesis, the ancient catechumenate.[6] In the early church, there was a commitment to Scripture as the word that journeys with us, and it formed the heart of shaping Christian life. Wherever they occur, such "dramatic" interpretations immerse people in the actual texts of Scripture and offer more complex, and more imaginative, sets of practices for dealing with difficult texts than we tend to deploy in modernity. In so doing, readers immersed in the text embody their reading, thereby making the words and stories part of the fabric of their very being and identity. (We would do well to recall the monastic metaphors of "consuming" the text.)

St. Augustine was integrally involved with catechumenal practices and provides exemplary catechetical engagements with Scripture. As William Harmless has documented, Augustine's preaching and theological reflection were often shaped by concerns for his congregation's developing relationships with Scripture and other practices of Christian living. Augustine thought that a

---

6. The convictions and practices of the ancient catechumenate are being reclaimed in such contemporary contexts as the Roman Catholic Rite of Christian Initiation of Adults. Even so, the RCIA has not been as influential in reshaping engagement with Scripture as I suggest needs to be done in this essay — in part because it has not really confronted the crises of ecclesial biblical interpretation.

long period for catechesis (typically two years for adults) was necessary in order to "hear what the faith and pattern of Christian life should be."[7] One can hear in Augustine's preaching the rich resonances of someone for whom Scripture has been a word journeying with the community and why these particular words and stories matter. He tells catechumens,

> Your sins will be like the Egyptians following the Israelites, pursuing you only up to the Red Sea. What does up to the Red Sea mean? Up to the font, consecrated by the cross and blood of Christ. For, because that font is red, it reddens [the water]. . . . Baptism is signified by the sign of the cross, that is, by the water in which you are immersed and through which you pass, as it were, in the Red Sea. Your sins are your enemies. They follow you, but only up to the Red Sea. When you have entered, you will escape; they will be destroyed, just as the Egyptians were engulfed by the waters while the Israelites escaped on dry land.[8]

Augustine's imagery is intelligible only to people who have become familiar with the story of the Exodus, with the Gospels, and with the stakes involved in baptism.

Similarly, Martin Luther King, Jr. was nurtured in practices of interpreting Scripture, learned both through his own participation in black preaching and through the rich biblical allusions and performances of spirituals and other music of the black church. His life and the power of his witness do not make sense apart from an extraordinary scriptural imagination learned through catechetical practices of the church. Richard Lischer's study *The Preacher King: Martin Luther King, Jr. and The Word That Moved America* wonderfully displays the tapestry of King's engagements with Scripture. As Lischer puts it, King's formation in the African-Baptist Church

> prepared him to be the public advocate of God's justice for black people in America, which in the African-American tradition meant that he would take a church and preach. From this environment he absorbed key theological strategies for dealing with injustice that he would never relinquish. He learned more from the Negro preacher's methods of sustaining a people and readying it for action than from any of his courses in graduate school; he absorbed more from his own church's identification with the Suffering Servant than from anything he read in Gandhi. What came earliest to him

---

7. Augustine, *De fide et operibus* 6.9, cited in William Harmless, *Augustine and the Catechumenate* (Collegeville, Minn.: Liturgical Press, 1995), p. 156.

8. Augustine, *Sermons*, 213.8, cited in Harmless, *Augustine and the Catechumenate*, p. 282.

remained longest and enabled him to put a distinctively Christian seal on the struggle for civil rights in the United States.[9]

Note, for example, one sentence in which King evokes a complex set of biblical images. In Holt Street Baptist Church in Montgomery, King interpreted the events unfolding with the bus boycott in the following way: "We, the disinherited of this land," he cried, "we who have been oppressed so long, are tired of going through the long night of captivity."[10] Lischer goes on to argue that King's preaching actually sounded like the Bible. Its words and the patterns of its words had significantly shaped the practices of his life as well as his rhetoric.

Critical Study

Even so, both Augustine and King also knew that Scripture must be studied critically as a part of journeying with the text. Of course, what we mean by "critically" is a contestable issue that involves interpretive debates about the methods of "higher criticism" that were unavailable in Augustine's time. My point here is more modest. Anyone who journeys with Scripture for very long will discover issues and perplexities with which they will undoubtedly struggle. Perhaps it is the difficult textual transmissions of Job, or the gaps in the Gospels, or the fact that different Gospels tell the "same" story differently. Or perhaps it is because there are passages that seem to defy understanding in relation to other fields of inquiry, passages that bear striking similarity to other stories in the ancient Near East, or because there are texts that we simply find difficult to understand or to accept.

Such critical study may occur through formal education, but it need not. It might occur through the sorts of practices we associate with the rabbis in ancient Judaism, or through studying the Talmud as contemporary Jews do. Wherever it is practiced and in whatever setting, we need to be schooled in critical engagement with Scripture. Augustine described Scripture — or, more accurately, the church in which Scripture is primarily read — as a "school," and those who come to hear Scripture read as "students of divine letters."[11] Notably, he did not hesitate to acknowledge that there were texts he did not understand and avoided speaking about (e.g., Matt 12:31-32 on the sin against the Holy Spirit), although he did not stop "seeking, asking, knocking" about

9. Richard Lischer, *The Preacher King: Martin Luther King, Jr. and The Word That Moved America* (Oxford: Oxford University Press, 1995), p. 6.

10. Cited in Lischer, *The Preacher King*, p. 198.

11. Augustine, *Sermons*, 32.2 and 33A.4.

them.[12] He also turned to the philosophical tools of Neoplatonism to help him understand issues in Scripture that seemed perplexing.

Similarly, King engaged in critical study of Scripture throughout his formal education at Morehouse College, in seminary, and through his graduate education at Boston University. His engagements with Scripture were informed by the liberal theological tradition that helped to shape his social activism. His acquired language of liberal theology became a means by which his Scriptural imagination was hammered out in his preaching and teaching.

Interestingly, King's formal education in historical criticism did not seem to influence him much; his own interpretations of Scripture were far more shaped by the sophisticated patterns of allegory and typology characteristic of scholarly study of the Bible in premodern periods. In this, King was truly a person of the black church. For even in engaging difficult texts, and those texts *made* difficult by ideologically oppressive white readings of texts (e.g., the "curse of Ham" in nineteenth- and early-twentieth-century America),[13] the black church's critical study of Scripture has been much more similar to premodern than to historical-critical readings.

Both Augustine and King utilized the diverse historical, philological, philosophical, literary, and rhetorical tools available to them in order to develop the richest and most faithful interpretations of Scripture possible. We may disagree with their interpretations, but their scriptural imaginations were shaped by powerful, ongoing, subtle interpretations of Scripture that transformed their own lives as well as those to whom they preached and with whom they read.

Social Engagement

A third context in which Scripture journeys with us is in reflection on our engagements in the world. This context comes to life in communities as diverse as Wesleyan class meetings in the eighteenth century and Latin American base communities in the late twentieth century. Common to such contexts is the struggle to reflect on Scripture in the wake of particular experiences of joy and grief, triumph and suffering, blessing and oppression. Such struggle may pro-

---

12. See Augustine's discussion in *Sermons*, 71.7-8. I am indebted to John Cavadini for directing me to this sermon.

13. For an instructive discussion of this passage in the context of African-American biblical interpretation, see Michael G. Cartwright, "Ideology and the Interpretation of the Bible in the African-American Christian Tradition," *Modern Theology* 9 (April 1993): 141-58.

duce difficulties in understanding or accepting what the text seems to be saying and may pose significant interpretive obstacles for a variety of reasons. Yet such struggle may also produce a deep engagement with the texts and with the God who Christians believe is revealed through them.

Augustine reflected in quite provocative ways on the divisions and vices he saw within his world. He knew that a lack of forgiveness was a local vice, and so he focused on it in reflection. For example, he noted in a sermon that people tended to bring their fierce resentments and their desires for revenge to prayer: "Each day, people come, bend their knees, touch the earth with their foreheads, sometimes moistening their faces with tears, and in all this great humility and distress say: 'Lord, avenge me. Kill my enemy.'" He insisted that they recognize their enemies as children of God and that, when praying for those enemies: "Let your prayer be against the malice of your enemy; may his malice die, but may he live. . . . If his malice should die, then you would have lost an enemy and gained a friend."[14]

King's reflections were tested in the crucible of fire that was the civil rights movement in the United States. King transposed biblical themes of love, suffering, deliverance, and justice into the great social and political debates of the day. His sermons and speeches showed the power, and the interpretive freedom, of one whose scriptural imagination was so fertile that he could "move America" through the power of the Word — even when he did not explicitly appeal to any scriptural or theological language. Lischer nicely summarizes the power of King's witness in the context of social engagements: "The black church not only sought to locate truth *in* the Bible, in order to derive lessons from it, but also extended the Bible into its own worldly experience. King found the ancient methods of interpretation useful in his effort to enroll the Civil Rights Movement in the saga of divine revelation. These techniques he joined to the black church's practice of 'performing' the Scripture in its music, its rhythmic pattern of call and response, and a variety of rhetorical adornments — all of which he exported from the church's Sunday worship to political mass meetings around the country."[15]

I have been suggesting that if we want to understand the role of the Bible in forming Christian character and Christian community we need to see Scripture as the Word that journeys with us through the diverse contexts of our lives. We need more intensive schooling in catechesis, in critical study, and in reflecting on our engagements in the world. While these contexts are distinct, they re-

---

14. Augustine, *Sermons*, 56.13-14 and 211.6, cited in Harmless, *Augustine and the Catechumenate*, pp. 290-91.

15. Lischer, *The Preacher King*, p. 7.

quire rich interrelation for character formation and transformation. These are the sources that fund a fertile scriptural imagination and shape habits of thought and life. We need virtues of wise reading and performance of Scripture, bound up with other practices of Christian thought and life.[16]

There is, of course, much more to be said, and many issues and objections that would need to be addressed in order to develop my proposal more fully. After all, I am well aware that the Devil is adept at quoting Scripture. Nevertheless, I think Augustine and King, along with literary compatriots such as Milton, O'Connor, and Morrison, display the transformative possibilities of scriptural imagination. This does not foreclose counterarguments, nor does it guarantee that our readings will be formative (much less transformative) rather than malformative. But it does suggest a much better and more life-giving set of options than the biblical illiteracy that afflicts so many of our churches and so many of us. It does so because our language is not only ideal but material, and the words and language that shape our imaginations also shape our bodies, our communities, and our life together.

Indeed, developing habits of wise and faithful readings of Scripture — readings that will not preclude ongoing disagreements but indeed sharpen them into fruitful disagreements — will enable us to address issues of biblical method and biblical authority in more life-giving ways. How might this be the case?

Wise and Faithful Readings

I can only sketch here the contours of an answer that would require a much longer and more extended analysis. However, there are several guiding judgments that are crucial to displaying how a focus on wise and faithful readings of Scripture can move us forward in debates and disagreements. I believe that each of these judgments would be shared by Augustine and King, as well as by many other exemplary readers of Scripture despite other methodological and substantive disagreements and divergences.[17]

16. For an insightful and imaginative account of the virtues and practices needed for the wise reading of Scripture, see Stephen Fowl, *Engaging Scripture* (Oxford: Blackwells, 1999).

17. These guiding judgments reflect, at times explicitly and at times implicitly, claims developed by my colleague Richard Hays and I in the forthcoming essay "Ten Theses on the Interpretation of Scripture." This essay is scheduled to appear in a book emerging out of the Center of Theological Inquiry's "The Scripture Project."

The Company of Interpreters

The first is that "habits of wise and faithful readings of Scripture" is a contested notion that can be assessed only in the ongoing interpretations we offer in conversation with others. A primary way in which we adjudicate what constitutes wisdom and faithfulness is whether it bears appropriate witness to the God of Jesus Christ. Or, as Augustine puts it in *De doctrina christiana,* all Scripture, when correctly interpreted, is conducive to the knowledge and love of God and neighbor. He emphasizes that, in this light, "correct" interpretation requires an understanding of the multiple senses of Scripture (see my fourth judgment below). Augustine writes, "Whatever appears in the divine Word that does not literally pertain to virtuous behavior or to the truth of faith you must take to be figurative. Virtuous behavior pertains to the love of God and of one's neighbor; the truth of faith pertains to a knowledge of God and of one's neighbor."[18]

An important component of recognizing the contested character of interpretation is to cultivate an expansive notion of the "us" with whom Scripture journeys throughout life. If we have such an expansive sense of who the "us" is, we will more likely be able to check our tendencies toward malformation and ideological paralysis. That is, we need to read Scripture in a wide company of interpreters who both nurture and challenge us. In this sense, we need to read, hear, and perform Scripture "in communion" with the whole company of disciples of Jesus Christ (while also engaging, and listening to, external critics and other readers).[19] Even more, we also need to read Scripture in conversation with readers outside the church whose challenges and objections offer crucial contexts for us to recognize our capacity for blindness and ideological distortions, even as we also offer challenges and objections to our interlocutors.

Christocentric Focus

The second guiding judgment is that we ought to interpret Scripture not with *my* interests foremost in mind, but with a discerning focus on the God who gives life. Once again, Augustine offers an eloquent testimony. He proposes that we are all joint-inquirers in which Christ is our ultimate Teacher:

18. Augustine, *On Christian Doctrine,* trans. D. W. Robertson (New York: Macmillan, 1958), p. 88 (III.10).

19. See the longer argument in Stephen E. Fowl and L. Gregory Jones, *Reading in Communion* (Grand Rapids: Eerdmans, 1991), esp. pp. 110-34.

Your graces know that all of us have one Teacher, and that under him we are fellow disciples, fellow pupils. And the fact that we bishops speak to you from a higher place does not make us your teachers; but it's the one who dwells in all of us that is the Teacher of us all. He was talking to all of us just now in the gospel, and saying to us what I am also saying to you; he says it, though about us, about both me and you: *If you remain in my word* — not mine, of course, not Augustine's, now speaking, but his, who was speaking just now from the gospel. . . .[20]

Given by God

The third guiding judgment, particularly relevant to biblical authority, is that Christians trust that the texts of the Bible are Christian Scripture given by God for the sake of human redemption and salvation.[21] This is a general claim to which I believe all Christians ought to assent. I would add, based on more substantive (and thereby controversial) material convictions about the content of Scripture, that Christian Scripture is given by God in order to build up the body of Christ and to reconcile men and women to God in the church. The biblical texts cohere because the Triune God who is revealed through those texts speaks through Scripture to the church.

We can trust in Scripture, even amid its complexities and its potential for ideologically destructive readings of Scripture, because God is the guarantor of Scripture's unity and coherence for the sake of the knowledge and love of God and neighbor. When wisely and faithfully interpreted, Scripture does not bind or oppress; it heals and liberates. The story of Scripture is inherently open to the future and to the God who continues to surprise us and to call us to freedom in Christ by the power of the Holy Spirit.

Scripture's Multivalence

A fourth guiding judgment, already implied in the earlier judgments, is that the texts of Scripture have multiple complex senses rather than one single meaning.

20. Augustine, *Sermons*, 134.1, cited in John Cavadini, "Simplifying Augustine," unpublished paper.

21. On the centrality of trust for biblical interpretation, see Richard Hays, "Salvation by Trust? Reading the Bible Faithfully," *The Christian Century* (February 26, 1997): 218-23. On the formal arguments for such a claim in the designation of these texts as Christian Scripture, see Charles Wood, "Hermeneutics and the Authority of Scripture," in *An Invitation to Theological Study* (Valley Forge, Pa.: Trinity Press International, 1994), pp. 55-70.

The church's premodern interpretations presumed Scripture's multivalence, which was exemplified in the medieval "fourfold" approach to interpretation.[22] Though he did not characterize it as such, Martin Luther King, Jr. exemplifies this pattern; he regularly wove together biblical types and allusions in order to illumine God's work in the contemporary plight of African-Americans.

Further, Scripture is and ought to be interpreted "intertextually," where texts are read in complex conversation with one another.[23] This sometimes occurs within Scripture itself, as in the ongoing engagement over who is included in the scope of "neighbor." Is, for example, the Canaanite a neighbor? Note the conquest narrative in Joshua, the judgment on the purported wickedness of the Canaanites (e.g., Deut 9:5), and the villainous Jezebel, on the one hand, as well as the faithful confession of Rahab, the Canaanite harlot (Joshua 2), and the faithful Canaanite woman who challenges Jesus (Matt 15:21-28), on the other. Such intertextuality is also exemplified by Paul in his complex rendering of Israel's story, sometimes in remarkable continuity with the story as it is told elsewhere and at other places in dramatic reinterpretation of what would have seemed to be the plain sense of the scriptural text (see Galatians 4 and his retelling of the story of Hagar and Sarah).[24]

This intertextual reading continues in the work of faithful interpreters. So, for example, Augustine's interpretation of baptism (see above) weaves together the story of the Exodus with the narrative of Christ's crucifixion. Similarly, Christian readers have sought, and should continue to seek, to read particular passages of Scripture in light of the whole.

Historical-critical readings of Scripture play an indispensable role in the interpretation of Scripture, even as we acknowledge the multiple senses of Scripture. We ought to avail ourselves of the best possible sources of interpretation of particular texts, whether they be historical, philological, comparative, literary, or socio-political. But we need to see them in light of the entirety of the canon of Scripture.

22. See the discussion in David Steinmetz, "The Superiority of Pre-Critical Exegesis," in *The Theological Interpretation of Scripture*, ed. Stephen E. Fowl (Oxford: Blackwells, 1997), pp. 26-38. See also Henri de Lubac, *Medieval Exegesis: The Four Senses of Scripture*, 2 vols. (Grand Rapids: Eerdmans, 1998, 2000).

23. For a powerful exposition of this intertextuality within the Jewish tradition, see Michael Fishbane, *Biblical Interpretation in Ancient Israel* (Oxford: Clarendon, 1985).

24. Richard Hays offers a powerful rendering of Paul as interpreter of Scripture in his *Echoes of Scripture in the Letters of Paul* (New Haven: Yale University Press, 1989).

Unity of the Testaments

This leads to a fifth judgment, namely, that interpreting Scripture faithfully requires an engagement with the entire narrative: the New Testament cannot be rightly understood apart from the Old, nor for Christians can the Old be rightly understood apart from the New. We cannot adequately understand the complex interrelations of the two Testaments apart from an intimate familiarity with the texts and the stories, and an ability to see connections that are missed by those with only a superficial awareness of Scripture. As Richard Hays and I have suggested elsewhere,

> The Bible must be read "back to front" — that is, understanding the plot of the whole drama in light of the death and resurrection of Jesus Christ. This suggests a strategy not of messianic prooftexting but of figural reading, showing how the Old Testament opens proleptically towards the New. Yet the Bible must also be read "front to back" — that is, understanding the climax of the drama, God's revelation in Christ, in light of the long history of God's self-revelation to Israel. This suggests an interpretation of the relationship between Israel and the Church that is neither supersessionist nor Marcionite.[25]

Open to Transformation

A sixth guiding judgment is that readers who attempt to remain detached and neutral in their interpretation of the Bible will typically understand it less deeply than those who discipline their lives by studying Scripture as the vehicle of God's Word. Scripture bears witness to the God of Jesus Christ so that we may be transformed by the power of the Holy Spirit into the likeness of Christ. We find it easier, and morally convenient, to evade the actual claims of Scripture through debates about Scripture. Yet the call of Scripture is for us to be open to the transformation of our own lives and to see the necessity of such transformation. Hence, whether in the ancient catechumenate or in the African-American church of King's day, there is a presumption that wise and faithful readings of Scripture are inextricably linked to the disciplined pursuit of holy living in other practices of Christian life. Interpreting Scripture both presupposes and creates communities of worship, critical study, and witness. Such

---

25. Richard B. Hays and L. Gregory Jones, "Ten Theses on the Interpretation of Scripture," forthcoming.

communities must exhibit ongoing vigilance against sinful readings and practices as we seek to be wise and faithful in our readings and practices — always seeking the right knowledge and love of God and of neighbor.

Embodied Virtues

A seventh guiding judgment is that the saints of the church provide guidance in how to interpret and perform Scripture. We need several interpretive virtues for wise and faithful reading of Scripture. Prominent among them are receptivity, humility, truthfulness, courage, charity, and imagination. The writings of saintly figures sometimes offer explicit guidance in the interpretation of Scripture, but in other cases their guidance is to be found implicitly in the pattern of their lives as exemplary performances of Scripture.

Conclusion

I have suggested that these guiding judgments, shaping people who seek to cultivate a scriptural imagination by immersing themselves in the Word that journeys with us, offer a way forward for the church in grappling even with issues of biblical method and biblical authority. I believe that disputes even about some of our time's most controversial matters, including the ordination of women and diverse issues of sexuality, would be more faithfully conducted if we were to engage in readings of Scripture along the lines suggested above.

I offer one example by way of conclusion that will suggest how these guiding judgments might move us forward if we focus on the Bible's role in forming and transforming Christian life in relation to God. Ellen Davis, an artful interpreter of Scripture (and professional biblical exegete), presents a suggestive reading of how Jesus' reinterpretation of the levitical legislation offers a key resource for the contemporary church's deliberations. She suggests that the focal question for the levitical material is this: "What constitutes a holy people? In other words, what is the nature and discipline of a community capable of hosting the presence of God in its midst (cf. Lev 9:6)?"[26] She indicates that the simplest answer is that "it is hospitality toward God, living in such a way that God may feel at home in our midst."[27]

---

26. Ellen F. Davis, "Critical Traditioning: Seeking an Inner Biblical Hermeneutic," *ATR* 82 (2000): 744.

27. Davis, "Critical Traditioning," p. 744.

She then suggests that at the heart of Jesus' reinterpretation is a reconception of holiness by extending hospitality in significantly new ways. This is true of the parable of the Good Samaritan in particular, but this extension of hospitality is found throughout his teachings and actions. Davis's conclusion is significant:

> Henceforth, holiness must be demonstrated, not as internal consolidation within the Jewish community, but rather as the power to reach out to the stranger without losing one's own footing in the tradition. The levitical Holiness Code, as we have seen, welcomes the sojourner who immigrates to the people Israel (Lev 19:34). But Jesus himself becomes an emigrant, at least for a time, when he enters the district of Tyre and Sidon. Even more, there he submits to be instructed on no small point of holiness by a woman whom Matthew pointedly designates a "Canaanite." This story is the most dramatic illustration in all Scripture of what it means to be a critical traditionalist. It means exercising the profound, even godly humility, to be able to learn something previously unimaginable about the fundaments of your life with God — and further, to learn it from "the least of these."[28]

Davis's analysis, grounded in a wise and faithful reading of Scripture as canon, offers a context for discernment in the midst of conflicts in the present. Her analysis could lead to competing judgments about the morality of homosexual practice, or about the ordination of women. But now the debates are set in the context of intertextual readings of Scripture, in which the horizon is shaped by the question of what constitutes a holy people. Might we learn something previously unimaginable from saintly ordained women? Or saintly persons who happen(ed) to be gay or lesbian? How does their life bear witness, or fail to bear witness, to the normative judgments we see rendered in Scripture?

As I indicated at the outset, we cannot avoid questions of both biblical method and biblical authority. But neither do they resolve debates, especially when we recognize the rich complexity of Scripture. We would be better off if, following such examples as Augustine and King in all of the complexity of their interpretations and the fallibility of their own lives, we continually immerse ourselves in Scripture as the Word that journeys with us through catechesis, critical study, and witness. With Christ as our true teacher, we are called to become people of character, a holy people, who perform the Scriptures wisely and faithfully so that God may be at home in our midst.

28. Davis, "Critical Traditioning," pp. 747-48.

Images of Scripture and Contemporary Theological Ethics

William Schweiker

The human world is electrified by the imagination. Images scurry around the planet thanks to the global media system. New religions with new myths are given birth; displaced peoples weave together highly textured identities by imaginatively mixing old practices with novel meanings; theologians "re-imagine" God in light of distinctive legacies of belief, experience, and community. As cultural anthropologist Arjun Appadurai notes, "People throughout the world see their lives through the prisms of the possible lives offered by mass media in all their forms. That is, fantasy is now a social practice; it enters, in a host of ways, into the fabrication of social lives for many people in many societies."[1] The global media system circulates an infinite array of images of possible worlds and lives. This fact poses with new force an enduring moral challenge: given the explosion of the global imaginary, persons and communities must assess the images, symbols, ideas, and narratives that saturate self-consciousness and thus determine how life is to be lived.

Scripture and the Imaginary

Mindful of this challenge, theologians nowadays need to consider the meaning and truth of religious symbols, narratives, and beliefs in the work of culture. Of course, symbols and narratives have always played a role in cultural existence. Peasants in "Palestine" listened to Jesus portray the reign of God as a mustard seed and thus imagined a new world far removed from their poverty

---

1. Arjun Appadurai, *Modernity at Large: Cultural Dimensions of Globalization* (Minneapolis: University of Minnesota Press, 1996), pp. 53-54.

and hurt and the ruthless justice of Rome (Matt 13:31-32). They imagined the triumph of one power structure (God's reign) over another (imperial Rome).[2] Within the *pax Romana*, life was defined by status and role; within the reign of God, it was possible to overcome the difference of Jew and Gentile, male and female, slave and free (Gal 3:28). But the imagination was in many ways limited by the walls of political power and recalcitrant dimensions of existence. Not so today. The media circulate a vast array of images that overturn social and political boundaries by fueling perceptions and possibilities for life. Amid cultural flows, the Bible has become an inexhaustible text of possible lives. It goads the unrelenting work of interpreting the meaning and purpose of life and the world.

One can specify the place of Scripture in the work of culture more boldly. The Bible provides a space in history for the West. Biblical scholar Burton Mack writes:

> A vague collection of the biblical story seems to be in everyone's mind, a story that begins at the creation of the world with Adam and Eve in the garden, that courses through the Bible and then the history of Western civilization to flow into the fulfillment of its promise in America with a culmination in the future consequence for all the people of the world.[3]

Mack's reading of the Bible as underwriting the American dream is a bit exaggerated, especially in a postcolonial age that witnesses liberating and destructive readings of these texts in diverse cultures. One must not overestimate the force of the Bible on Western and other societies. Yet, unless blinded by ideology, it seems clear that for societies shaped by Judaism and Christianity biblical texts are basic to a worldview. Remove these texts from cultural memory, and the shape of present Western societies would be decisively changed. (That removal might be the real social experiment currently under way in the West.)

In this essay, I want to explore ideas about Scripture in current theological ethics against the background of the global explosion of the imaginary. My argument moves between two poles of reflection: (1) a textual pole concerned with how Scripture is pictured, and (2) a normative pole of inquiry with respect to the moral life before God. In the next section, we can isolate widely shared

---

2. See N. T. Wright, "Paul's Gospel and Caesar's Empire," *Reflections: Center of Theological Inquiry* 2 (Spring 1999): 42-65.

3. Burton Mack, *Who Wrote the New Testament? The Making of the Christian Myth* (New York: HarperCollins, 1995), p. 3. In this essay, I use "Bible" and "Scripture" as synonymous terms; in other contexts a distinction would need to be drawn.

moral concerns vis-à-vis the place of imagination in the moral life. Following that, I will bring together the poles of reflection by exploring two dominant strands of contemporary ethics, what I call narrative and encounter ethics. These ethics risk reducing Scripture to one form, to "narrative" or "encounter," consistent with a normative outlook. Their insight is to insist that an "image" of Scripture must display the most basic feature of the moral life.

As David Tracy notes, the strategy of seeking one "form" to assert the continuity of reason and reality is the essential trait of "modern" thought. Relatedly, James M. Gustafson has rejected one dominant "biblical ethic" and insisted on the varieties of moral discourse in Scripture (e.g., prophetic, narrative, ethical).[4] Attending to a variety of uses, as well as avoiding a reduction in "form," is basic to pluralistic accounts of Scripture. I propose a pluralistic position as well. My concern is not only with the Bible as a classic, as Tracy puts it, but also with its multiple uses in ethics, as Gustafson stresses. Granting those claims, I judge that in our situation we need another account of Scripture. This account must focus on human beings as travelers between "worlds," real and imaginary, who face the demand to live truthfully and responsibly. In the final step of the argument, I present a picture of the Bible embedded in pre-textual social and historical conditions (e.g., ancient patriarchal, economic, and social systems; say, the temple-state), yet (partially) freed from those conditions when read in light of the demands of present life. This account of Scripture is meant to draw from but move beyond the obvious insights of narrative and encounter ethics.

The closest historical analogy for the picture of Scripture offered below is the ancient conception of allegory. Recall that for allegory any "text" had a multiplicity of levels of meaning (literal, moral, spiritual) that the reader traversed and in doing so formed her or his own soul. There was no need to reduce the text to one conceptual or linguistic form (e.g., narrative or command), but, rather, to envision it as having interlocking meanings. Reading the text was a journey through dimensions of meaning in order to educate the soul. The problem with allegory, as the Protestant Reformers noted, was that the hermeneutic provided little check on the free play of interpretation aimed at reaching great truths. In practice, the allegorical method too easily escaped the control of the rule of faith. But this is just the point I am making about the Bible and the global explosion of the imaginary. The imaginary is a free play of images in which persons and communities fashion their world and lives. Texts, images, symbols, and narratives are swept up into the global flow of the imagi-

---

4. See David Tracy, *Plurality and Ambiguity: Hermeneutics, Religion, Hope* (New York: Harper & Row, 1986), and James M. Gustafson, *Varieties of Moral Discourse* (Grand Rapids: Calvin College and Seminary, 1988).

nary beyond the control of any community's rule of faith or canon. The problems of allegory are as important for theological ethics as its attempt to provide an education of the "soul."[5]

Obviously we cannot adopt classic allegory without revision. We do not live in any clear way in a many-storied universe where everything is (ontologically) symbolic of another level of reality. Our lives are more a matter of moving between "worlds" in a global scene. In light of our situation, my proposal is to construe Scripture as a media space. A "media space" — whether enacted in texts or television or cinema — is a means of communication through the creation of an imaginary environment of possible lives. This environment or imagined world has complex connections to the "real" world of human interaction. How then to understand the moral life? The movement between linguistically and imaginatively donated worlds and responsibility for life is in part made possible through conscience. Conscience, as a metaphor for our existence as moral creatures, is educated by navigating complex media spaces, like Scripture. When we have reached that insight, it should be clear that the essay has moved between poles of reflection (account of text, a normative outlook) on a journey from shared moral concerns, through a comparison of kinds of ethics (narrative, encounter), to, at its far end, an account of Scripture and conscience.

Consensus in Concerns

Work on the Bible and ethics has focused on some very broad and related questions.[6] Specifically, scholarship has centered on the authority of Scripture

---

5. For a classical discussion, see Thomas Aquinas, *Summa Theologiae* I, q. 1, aa. 9-10, and Augustine, *On Christian Doctrine*. For the roots of allegory, see Werner Jaeger, *Early Christianity and Greek Paideia* (Oxford: Oxford University Press, 1961).

6. See, for example, William C. Spohn, *What Are They Saying about Scripture and Ethics?* rev. ed. (New York: Paulist, 1995); Richard B. Hays, *The Moral Vision of the New Testament: A Contemporary Introduction to New Testament Ethics* (San Francisco: HarperSanFrancisco, 1996); Lisa Sowle Cahill, "The Bible and Christian Moral Practice," in *Christian Ethics: Problems and Prospects,* ed. Lisa Sowle Cahill and James F. Childress (Cleveland: Pilgrim Press, 1996), pp. 3-17; and Allen Verhey, "Scripture and Ethics: Practices, Performances, and Prescriptions," in *Christian Ethics: Problems and Prospects,* ed. Lisa Sowle Cahill and James F. Childress (Cleveland: Pilgrim Press, 1996), pp. 18-45. See also James M. Gustafson, "The Place of Scripture in Christian Ethics: A Methodological Study," *Int* 24 (1970): 430-55; idem, "The Use of Scripture in Christian Ethics," *Studia Theologica: Scandinavian Journal of Theology* 51 (1977): 15-29; Sharon D. Welch, "Biblical Interpretation in Christian Feminist Ethics" *Studia Theologica: Scandinavian Journal of Theology* 51 (1977): 30-42; and William Schweiker, "Iconoclasts, Builders and Dramatists: The

and also its application in moral judgments. With respect to authority, theologians have been led into debates about the nature and status of moral knowledge. Does Scripture — or any putative sacred text — supply true moral knowledge unavailable to common reflection? Does Scripture confirm, invigorate, or, perhaps, deepen, natural moral knowledge? Is moral reason tradition-constituted? Can we isolate a shared structure to moral reason? How does Scripture, or any appeal to "revelation," relate to valid sanctions for moral norms? Problems also surround the application of scriptural claims to the moral life. These center on the logic of moral reasoning, the nature of judgments, and the applicability of norms from one situation to another, that is, generalizability in casuistic thinking.

When thinkers turn to Bible and ethics, they address issues ranging from epistemology to theory of judgment and even to the validity of a biblical ethics. What is not often noted is that a picture of Scripture (e.g., deposit of truths, story of redemption) is intrinsically bound to some normative moral or religious outlook. This is important since, as we will see, different "images" of Scripture are actually trying to address shared concerns. Clarity about those concerns can serve as a guide through the thicket of images of Scripture in contemporary theological ethics.

First, most current thinkers insist on the need to move beyond modern accounts of the self. Descartes's maxim, "I think, therefore I am," correctly asserts a principle of identity basic to human subjectivity enacted in thinking (If I am not me in my act of thinking, then who am I?), but it wrongly assumes that we come to ourselves directly in the immediacy of thinking. After Freud, Nietzsche, and many others, it is hard to imagine a simple transparency of the self to itself. The route to self-understanding is never simply inward; it always involves relating to and understanding what is other than self (another person, a history of which we are part, beliefs about the world, etc.). Insisting on the entanglement of self and other means that the moral problem is not, as it was for thinkers like Descartes, Kant, and especially Fichte, how to get from the ego to the other in a way consistent with self-determination. We necessarily exist with others in some moral space and thus must make judgments about how to orient our lives responsibly.

Contemporary (Western) moral theory has apparently rejected the modern idealistic account of immediate self-relation, the Cartesian legacy. Many believe that in order to escape modern subjectivism we must forgo all claims about "self-consciousness" as a hopelessly opaque idea. As Seyla Ben-

---

Use of Scripture in Theological Ethics," *Annual of the Society of Christian Ethics* (1986): 129-62. Also consider the issue on the Bible and Christian theology in *JR* 76/2 (1996).

habib has noted, postmodern thought is characterized by the fact that "the paradigm of language has replaced the [modern] paradigm of consciousness."[7] The triumph of language has meant that narrative, tradition, and discourse — not the consciousness of persons — is the focus of moral consideration. We will see this shift in both narrative and encounter ethics. Granting the importance of language to consciousness, I intend to hold fast to the importance of self-understanding in ethics.[8] The distinctly moral shape of consciousness is called conscience.

Second, most forms of current thought are trying to find a way beyond the kinds of systemic violence that scarred the twentieth century. Sometimes the roots of violence are located in religious beliefs. The equation, for instance, of one God = one Ruler = one People does violence to what is other. That equation is, of course, a particular view of Western history, theistic belief, and the problem of evil. More often, the challenge of violence is linked to the point about the "modern" self. The "I" can relate to its world and others only as "not-I" (Fichte) or through some abstract idea of humanity (Kant), or one must connect mind and body via the pineal gland, as Descartes quaintly put it. Sartre, in *No Exit*, drew the conclusion to this legacy of thought: "Hell is other people." The move beyond the connection between self-immediacy and violence — and thus damnation of the other — is the enterprise of much postmodern ethics.

These points about identity and violence form a shared point of reference for exploring certain kinds of current ethics. Yet one must connect this with an idea of the imagination. Mark Johnson has stated matters well:

> We human beings are imaginative creatures, from our most mundane, automatic acts of perception all the way up to our most abstract conceptualization and reasoning. Consequently, our moral understanding depends in large measure on various structures of imagination such as images, image schema, metaphors, narratives and so forth.[9]

---

7. Seyla Benhabib, *Situating the Self: Gender, Community and Postmodernism in Contemporary Ethics* (New York: Routledge, 1992), p. 208.

8. See William Schweiker, *Power, Value and Conviction: Theological Ethics in the Postmodern Age* (Cleveland: Pilgrim Press, 1998); James M. Gustafson, *Ethics from a Theocentric Perspective*, 2 vols. (Chicago: The University of Chicago Press, 1981, 1984); Iris Murdoch, *Metaphysics as a Guide to Morals* (London: Penguin and Allen Lane, 1992); Charles Taylor, *Sources of the Self: The Making of Modern Identity* (Cambridge, Mass.: Harvard University Press, 1989); and Maria Antonaccio, *Picturing the Human: The Moral Thought of Iris Murdoch* (Oxford: Oxford University Press, 2000).

9. Mark Johnson, *Moral Imagination* (Chicago: University of Chicago Press, 1993), p. ix.

Moral rationality is never devoid of image schema. These schema are not only the furniture of the individual mind; they entail the linguistic and practical resources of communities and traditions. All contemporary ethics grant this point. Where thinkers differ is the extent to which an image schema must pay a debt to nonlinguistic reality. Narrative ethics, we will see, insists that the semantic power or intentionality of the Bible is to swallow the world of lived experience and saturate it with new meaning. Encounter ethics, conversely, insists on an "other," God or other people, never reducible to our cognitive and evaluative schema. The challenge, I believe, is to seek an image scheme that enables us to apprehend concrete others and the realities of life not reducible to, but factored through, the labors of the imagination and understanding. Can Scripture play that role?

We now have before us some of the complexity of the poles of reflection in thinking about Scripture and ethics: how to picture Scripture mindful of the place of image schema in moral understanding and how to overcome a modernist vision of moral identity and its (real or possible) connection to systematic violence. We can bring these points together by examining accounts of Scripture in current theological ethics.

Narrative and Character

Narrative ethics holds that the moral life centers on the formation of personal and communal character, and, further, character is formed by adopted stories. This ethics rightly insists on an undeniable feature of the moral life: the task of human existence is to give form to one's life. As Iris Murdoch noted, "I can only choose within the world that I can see, in the moral sense of 'see' which implies that clear vision is a result of moral imagination and moral effort."[10] What provides moral substance is the specific view of life one seeks to embody in exis-

---

10. Iris Murdoch, *The Sovereignty of Good* (New York: Routledge & Kegan Paul, 1970), p. 37. On responses to this idea, see Maria Antonaccio and William Schweiker, eds., *Iris Murdoch and the Search for Human Goodness* (Chicago: University of Chicago Press, 1996). There is also much work conducted in feminist ethics: see Martha C. Nussbaum, *Love's Knowledge: Essays on Philosophy and Literature* (New York: Oxford University Press, 1990); Elisabeth Schüssler Fiorenza, *Bread Not Stone: The Challenge of Feminist Biblical Interpretation* (Boston: Beacon, 1984); idem, *But She Said: Feminist Practices of Biblical Interpretation* (Boston: Beacon, 1992); A. Yarbro Collins, ed., *Feminist Perspectives on Biblical Scholarship*, BSNA 10 (Chico, Calif.: Scholars Press, 1984); Katie G. Cannon, *Black Womanist Ethics*, AARS 60 (Atlanta: Scholars Press, 1988); and R. S. Sugirtharajah, ed., *Voices from the Margins: Interpreting the Bible in the Third World* (Maryknoll: Orbis, 1995).

tence. How ought we to form our lives? Narrative ethics has rejected two possible answers to this question.

First, advocates of narrative ethics reject any attempt to specify moral norms from the workings of pure practical reason. The problem with so-called "Enlightenment" ethics, especially in Kantian form, is that it tries to generate universal moral norms from self-relation in thinking and willing. But we are social animals; accordingly, moral norms are rooted in traditions and not in the immediacy of reason. Second, proponents of narrative ethics jettison an assumption of traditional virtue theory. Classical Western ethics explored human nature to specify the kinds of lives we ought to live. Plato and Aristotle thought we naturally seek happiness *(eudaimonia)*; Augustine insisted that we seek after God; the Stoics spoke of the "logos" and moral choice *(proairesis)* as a distinctly human good. Ancient thinkers examined the real to generate ideas of possible lives. Ethics presented a theory of *human nature* and not simply an account of moral formation.

Despite its love of Aristotle, moral naturalism has been rejected in narrative ethics. The reasons for this rejection are beyond the scope of this inquiry, but the main one is that "nature" for moderns is purposeless, without goal or good.[11] Insofar as that rejection is accomplished, where does one look to develop ideas of morally possible lives? One turns to narratives that constitute a vision of reality for the reading community. The paradigm of language, to recall Benhabib's words, has replaced consciousness (Kant) and nature as well (classical ethics). This shift means, for theologians Stanley Hauerwas, James McClendon, and John Howard Yoder, a politicization of the text. The church as a cultural/political reality reads Scripture to envision possible lives beyond the violence of the world.[12] The activity basic to character formation is the performative practice of "reading" in communion with other Christians.[13] The insight in this position is that we develop character by appropriating what is

---

11. On the need to reject Aristotle's metaphysical biology, see Alasdair MacIntyre, *After Virtue: A Study in Moral Theory*, 2nd ed. (Notre Dame, Ind.: University of Notre Dame Press, 1984). For a challenge to the modern rejection of teleology, see Franklin I. Gamwell, *The Divine Good: Modern Moral Theory and the Necessity of God* (San Francisco, Calif.: HarperCollins, 1990).

12. Stanley Hauerwas and William H. Willimon, *Resident Aliens* (Nashville: Abingdon, 1989). Also see James McClendon, *Ethics: Systematic Theology*, vol. 1 (Nashville: Abingdon, 1986); and John Howard Yoder, *The Priestly Kingdom: Social Ethics as Gospel* (Notre Dame, Ind.: University of Notre Dame Press, 1984).

13. Stephen E. Fowl and L. Gregory Jones, *Reading in Communion: Scripture and Ethics in Christian Life* (Grand Rapids: Eerdmans, 1991). See also Michael G. Cartwright, "The Practice and Performance of Scripture: Grounding Christian Ethics in a Communal Hermeneutic," *The Annual of the Society of Christian Ethics* (1988): 31-54.

other than ourselves, specifically, the vision of human life presented in Scripture. Yet the "biblical world," in honesty, is an abstraction created by encoding within Christian doctrine quite diverse strata of texts from divergent historical contexts, social life-worlds, and ideologies. To speak of "the" Bible or "the" Christian story as a seamless whole is a doctrinal and not textual claim.[14] This is why ethicists like Hauerwas insist that the Bible is the "church's book": the faith and doctrines of the church determine the meaning and coherence of Scripture; the vision of life presented by the text is to form and test the lives of Christians. Narrative is the reduction of these texts to one form.

Narrative ethics, despite claims to be in continuity with classical virtue theory, presents an image of Scripture tailored to a media age of cultural flows. The moral life is not grounded in reason or reality. It is about how we (whoever this "we" happens to be) fashion concrete moral existence in the light of the multiplicity of possible lives mediated to us through culturally or ecclesially constructed and interpreted images, stories, metaphors, and narratives. For most (but not all) narrative ethicists, the central possibility for human life presented in Scripture is peaceableness. The church is to be a community that lives out a story of peace not available to the "world."[15] Narrative ethics responds to the problem of self-formation and the social imaginary, and it does so around a moral norm (peaceableness) necessary to keep radically diverse communities and belief systems from falling into violence.

Any adequate ethics for our time must take seriously the question of character formation simply because of the challenge that cultural flows present to coherent lives. Oddly, this ethics does not grasp how the idea of "narrative world" as a unitary form might actually warrant violence in terms of enfolding the other into the community's vision. Those outside the church are defined as simply not-church; call it the "world" or, worse yet, the Enlightenment! Christian narrative ethics, ironically, continues the idealist, Fichtean dyad of "I and not-I," but at the level of communal image schema (church and not-church). The ethics risks a loss of reality within the narrative world.

---

14. See George Lindbeck, *The Nature of Doctrine: Religion and Theology in a Postliberal Age* (Philadelphia: Westminster, 1984). For a different account, see William Schweiker and Michael Welker, "A New Paradigm of Theological and Biblical Inquiry," in *Power, Powerlessness and the Divine: New Inquiries in Bible and Theology,* ed. Cynthia L. Rigby (Atlanta: Scholars Press, 1997), pp. 3-20.

15. See René Girard, *The Scapegoat,* trans. Yvonne Freccero (Baltimore: The Johns Hopkins University Press, 1986); Mark I. Wallace and Theophus H. Smith, eds., *Curing Violence* (Sonoma, Calif.: Polebridge, 1994); and John Milbank, *Theology and Social Theory* (Oxford: Basil Blackwell, 1990).

Encounter and Command

Narrative ethics can easily slide into a postmodern version of modern moral idealism. What is real are the "ideas," the narratives or image schema, we use to see the world. An ethics of encounter is a challenge to all forms of thought that focus on acts of imagination and meaning-making by self, culture, or the "church." Versions of "encounter ethics" are found in thinkers like Karl Barth, Abraham Heschel, and Martin Buber; there are also more recent exponents such as Emmanuel Levinas.[16] The basic feature of the moral life is that we are addressed by something or someone that makes an unquestionable claim for recognition. According to Levinas, the Other utters a primal command: "Do not murder me." If I begin to approach life from the perspective of, say, the search for happiness, the demands of social justice, or even the church as a peaceable community, I will never escape the ambit of the personal or communal ego; ethics is caught in a kind of moral solipsism. This entrapment of the Other within our projects Levinas calls "totality": it is the murder of the Other. Karl Barth called it sin: the attempt to define the good outside of God's commands. The command of God shatters the totalizing drive of cultural production.

For encounter ethics, there is no morally valid perspective outside of the command of the Other. I am commanded by the Word of God, the Thou, the face of the Other. The command does not issue forth from nature or reason. In this respect, advocates of encounter ethics join the paradigm shift to language, or word-event. In that event, the reality of the Other and my own moral being are given. Yet in distinction from narrative ethics, the basic moral act is not moral formation; it is obedience. The moral ought is the key to self and reality. Put in Levinas's terms, ethics, not ontology, is philosophically basic. Barth insists God is and is known in the command that is Jesus Christ. Law is the form of the gospel.

Levinas, Barth, Heschel, and others do not deny that communities generate moral laws from the immanent structures of reason, tradition, or nature. They are claiming that insofar as distinctly "moral" action concerns how one responds to the other — a person or the Other who is God — then a valid moral command must instantiate the responsive dynamic of the moral relation. Moral commands "supervene" on nonmoral relations. The command of

16. See Karl Barth, *Church Dogmatics*, ed. G. W. Bromiley and T. F. Torrance (Edinburgh: T. & T. Clark, 1957-70); Abraham J. Heschel, *Who Is Man?* (Stanford: Stanford University Press, 1965); Martin Buber, *I and Thou* (Edinburgh: T. & T. Clark, 1937); and Emmanuel Levinas, *Totality and Infinity: An Essay in Exteriority,* trans. Alphonso Lingus (Pittsburgh: Duquesne University Press, 1969). Also see Paul Ricoeur, *Oneself as Another,* trans. Kathleen Blamey (Chicago: University of Chicago Press, 1992).

God, Barth would contend, neither destroys the natural spheres of life nor contravenes natural moral knowledge even as it is not reducible to them. The command allows for an evaluative redescription of normal relations in order to understand them in distinctly moral terms.[17]

What does this mean for the image and use of Scripture? For Levinas, language itself, and thus the medium of any narrative world, is not prior to my encounter with the Other. Language is created in the event of encounter. In a similar way, Barth insists that Scripture witnesses to the command of God who is Jesus Christ. This command is linked to, but not bound by, the biblical texts. The Bible, preaching, and theology become the Word of God if and only if God freely chooses to speak in and through them. This is what enabled Barth to use biblical criticism while insisting on the Word. The text is a witness to what God has graciously done for us and to what is required of us.

An ethics of encounter is a powerful counter-voice to the celebration of the imaginary. By insisting on the "reality" of the command of the Other, this outlook focuses the moral life on an either-or level: either I am obedient to the command of God or I am in sin; either I respond to the face of the Other or not. And that is the problem. While encounter ethics insists on the intersubjective character of moral identity, and thereby escapes solipsism, it still understands, as did modern idealists, the moral "ought" in terms of an indubitable immediacy that founds subjectivity, the immediacy of the command of God or the face of the Other. As Heschel pointedly put it: "I am commanded — therefore I am."[18] By insisting on the immediacy of the ought at the birth of moral subjectivity, this ethics reduces the complexity of existence and risks undercutting the demand to assess all claims upon us. As Levinas puts it, the self is under a demand of infinite responsibility to the Other. This has led some thinkers, especially feminist theologians, rightly to note that an unquestioned claim of the Other can enact violence to self.

Conscience and Media Space

Noting the dissemination of images within cultural flows and shared concerns in current thought, I have tried to show how in narrative ethics the connection

---

17. See William Schweiker, "Divine Command Ethics and the Otherness of God," in *The Otherness of God*, ed. Orrin F. Summerell (Charlottesville: University Press of Virginia, 1998), pp. 246-65. See also R. M. Adams, *The Virtue of Faith and Other Essays in Philosophical Theology* (New York: Oxford University Press, 1987); and R. J. Mouw, *The God Who Commands* (Notre Dame, Ind.: University of Notre Dame Press, 1990).

18. Heschel, *Who Is Man?* p. iii.

between subjectivity and violence is broken if and only if Christian life is shaped by the church through the story of Jesus. Yet in its account of Scripture, the actual world of human joy and travail is oddly engulfed by the intentionality of the narrative world. The ethics of encounter holds fast to the claim of the living God and persons on the self. This outlook breaks the connection between subjectivity and violence by attending to the event of encounter. It makes this point in a way that seems to disallow critical assessment of the validity of that demand in any concrete situation. While enacting the postmodern shift to the paradigm of language, encounter and narrative ethics preserve, ironically, aspects of the Cartesian legacy, either in the immediacy of the "ought" in the constitution of subjectivity or in a dualistic view of identity construction (church and not-church).

A pluralistic approach to Scripture and ethics requires moving between the poles of reflection, namely, a construal of text and an account of the moral outlook infusing that construal. I propose that we picture Scripture as a media space rooted in but also free from pre-textual social and historical conditions. Relatedly, the moral life involves moving between and rightly orienting life within situations or worlds, real and imaginary. My most radical claim is that Scripture as media space articulates in textual form the shape, intentionality, and task of conscience. I will make this argument by moving from simple formal features of media space and conscience to a more substantive account of each. In doing so, I will draw from, yet move beyond, narrative and encounter ethics.

Formal Features

A media space is a complex, but structured, flow of images that shapes perception by imaginatively configuring an intelligible world of possibilities and limits. As noted above, a "media space" can take various — even interwoven — forms: written texts, oral presentation, cinema, and the like. Scripture as a media space presents a bewildering multidimensional vision of reality (e.g., heaven and earth, eschaton and present, demonic powers and political forces) within which historical and fictive characters live and act. This implies an anthropological fact: human life is always situated somewhere, in some sociohistorical and value-laden context, in which persons must orient their lives with and for others. The "space" of human existence is never simply given nor one-dimensional; it is always configured imaginatively in beliefs, values, image schema, practices, and so on. It is culturally saturated with meaning. The space of human existence is thus a "world." The situatedness of life and the culturally shaped nature of any human space mean that forms of cultural saturation, including Scripture, are open to assessment, appropriation, and transformation with respect to the perplexity of living.

What does Scripture "intend" and how ought we to dwell in that vision of the world? As we have seen, it is about the "intentionality" of Scripture that theological and ethical positions differ. Does the text intend to swallow the world of lived experience, saturating it with a distinctively new vision? Does the text witness to what is other and encounter the reader? Picturing Scripture as media space means insisting on an important reflexive relation between "text" and interpreter. The interpretive community mimetically participates in the enactment of meanings even as this shapes the lives of that community.[19] What texts "mean," their semantic intentionality, is intimately related to the world of the interpreters; it is, in fact, a fusion of worlds. How first-century Roman Christians read Scripture is related to but decidedly different from late-twentieth-century Korean Christians! That difference, so a pluralist account goes, is not something to bemoan; it bespeaks the richness but also the ambiguity of meanings. Beyond the austere demands of encounter ethics and the clean story line of narrative, Scripture as a media space is more chaotic and participatory.

Scripture as a media space entails, then, a distinctive claim about the semantic power or intentionality of a text. Any text, as Paul Ricoeur notes, presents a world in front of itself in which can be found one's own most possibility.[20] Reading helps donate possibilities and thereby discloses our freedom to live in various ways: we can adopt, modify, or negate the kind of life presented by a text. On Ricoeur's account, semantic power is uniquely related to the temporal, especially futural, dynamic of human existence: as beings who struggle for wholeness, creatures who hope, we are always projecting possible courses of action and ways of life. Yet the intentionality of Scripture, I contend, is to be defined not only in terms of the opening of future possibilities. The idea of media space is also meant to signify the presentation of a "world" in which persons and communities must orient life. The intentionality of Scripture — or any media, imaginative space — is not only temporal but also spatial and thus contextual.

This account of the semantic power of a media space moves us another step into the density of our being as conscience. Part of the enduring challenge of life is rooted in the all-too-human capacity to imagine and to confuse real and fictive worlds in directing conduct and shaping character. One can imagi-

19. See William Schweiker, *Mimetic Reflection: A Study in Hermeneutics, Theology and Ethics* (New York: Fordham University Press, 1990).

20. Paul Ricoeur, *Essays on Biblical Interpretation*, ed. Lewis S. Mudge (Philadelphia: Fortress, 1981).

natively enter the world of, say, the prophet Micah, the latest movie, or a lover's heart. Fanatics throughout the ages have imaginatively entered the world of St. John's revelation, often to destructive ends. Scripture, no less than advanced media cultures, circulates textually a host of lives that saturate moral sensibilities. Possibilities for life range from the Song of Songs to the letter to James, from God's command to Abraham to sacrifice his son to the gospel vision of love. Which orientations ought we morally to embody in our lives? How should we responsibly inhabit and traverse the worlds that are the environments for our existence?

Precisely as imaginative, fanciful creatures who move with dread and delight between "worlds," we can never — within this life — be utterly at one with ourselves. Descartes's dream of absolute, immediate identity ("I" am "I") misses the tragedy and task of life, that is, our incompleteness and struggle for communion with ourselves, others, the world, and God. The intentionality of the moral life pictured through conscience is "integrity" and not rock-hard self-relatedness. Integrity is about right orientation within complex relations as well as the proper coherence of a life. The deep epistemic and moral question is, therefore, the relation between media "worlds," actual life in all its complexity, and the moral intentionality of integrity.

Dimensions and Rules

Thus far, I have correlatively outlined both the image of Scripture as media space and the conscience in terms of their most formal features (imaginative space, existential orientations) and intentionalities (world, integrity). With further reflection, we can see that a media space, especially Scripture, has dimensions and constitutive rules. First, a media space is not easily plotted as having a "beginning, middle, and end"; it is not a simple unified whole. Unless submitted to doctrine, Scripture — with sayings, parables, proverbs, visions, narratives, etc. — exceeds reduction to narrative form. It is the home or site of many forms, as Gustafson noted. Nonetheless, narrative ethics is right that a constitutive rule of any "text" is followability: it must (whether narratively or not) make sense and be sense-making. Yet "followability" also means that the lives of specific characters in the text offer moral examples; they can be "followed" or imitated. Indeed, the call of Jesus to "follow me" may instigate a novel form of reason.[21] The rule of "followability" requires that one attend not

---

21. See Robert Scharlemann, *The Reason of Following: Christology and the Ecstatic I* (Chicago: University of Chicago Press, 1991).

only to possible lives but also the actual characters and operative ideas presented in the various strata, forms, and *Sitze im Leben* of biblical texts. Thanks to global cultural flows, these lives (consider Moses in Dreamworks's movie *The Prince of Egypt*) saturate moral sensibilities and spark the social imaginary. The duplicity of Judas, no less than the faithfulness of Sarah, sharpens and refines moral sensibilities. By insisting on the actualized lives presented in the texts, we are avoiding a reduction of those individuals to the intricate and often tacit logic of canon. The rule of "followability" demands attention to the lives of characters (e.g., Judas), ideas (e.g., justice), and beliefs (e.g., apocalypses), as these move in and through the complex intersection of layers of Scripture and then out to the global media. In this way, "Judas," to take a previous example, has saturated the Western moral imagination with beliefs about and evaluations of betrayal.

For Christians and Jews, Scripture articulates a "sacred" space. The biblical texts present lives in relation to and contention with the living God. This allows us to identify a second constitutive rule. Sacred media space is constituted by a decidedly theocentric vision of reality, something encounter ethics surely has right. God is pictured in radically diverse ways: creator and destroyer, lover and lord, redeemer and judge. The polysemic ways of naming God need to be considered in terms of their moral meanings.[22] By various strategies — ranging from covenantal fidelity to discipleship, from conquest to resurrection — the plethora of images sets human life within the domain of highly differentiated divine activity. This enables us to isolate two things: (1) a constitutive rule of theocentricity, that is, Scripture as media space, sets human life amid God's complex workings; and (2) the dimensionality of this "space" is conceivable in terms of foreground and horizon. In the foreground are the actual lives of characters (Judas no less than Sarah, Job and Satan, Christ and Peter) that can be morally engaged under the rule of followability. The horizon is a claim about the theocentric shape of reality presented in namings of God and God's activity (e.g., creation, judgment, heaven and earth, eschatological kingdom, liberation, covenant, etc.).

The next task is to articulate the relation of foreground to horizon and the rule of followability to theocentricity. First John 4:20 gives, intertextually, a third constitutive rule: "Those who say, 'I love God,' and hate their brothers or sisters, are liars; for those who do not love a brother or sister whom they have seen, cannot love God whom they have not seen." This presents a religious-

---

22. See Sallie McFague, *Models of God: A Theology for an Ecological, Nuclear Age* (Philadelphia: Fortress, 1987); and David Tracy, "Literary Theory and Return of the Forms for Naming and Thinking God in Theology," *JR* 74 (1994): 302-19.

moral rule — built on the double love command — beyond the demands of intelligibility (followability) and sacredness (theocentricity). Let us call it the rule of iconicity; that is, relations to actual others ought to be "images" for apprehending the divine. Under this rule, the complex relation between the claims of responsibility and engaging the text is such that we come to understand rightly the horizon of the moral life as divine goodness only from the extent of relations among concrete, actual individuals. The many ways of knowing God are tested by responsiveness to others. Scripture is not only a sacred but also a profoundly moral space.

We have now returned to a basic problem facing theological ethics. As noted, one challenge of postmodern times is that persons and communities must assess the images, symbols, and narratives that work through the imaginary to saturate consciousness and thus form existence and moral outlooks. By isolating some of the dimensions and constitutive rules of scriptural "space," we have the conceptual tools to decode the social imaginary. What is the horizon of that "space"? How do persons fare within it? Does it have, beyond the maximization of power, any moral rule? Does the media enhance or impede perception of the depth of goodness in and through moral relations? By way of such questions, what is examined in theological ethics is not simply the "depth" of culture or the "culture" of Christian community but the working of scriptural images within the moral imagination of cultures. The aim is to check vicious "images" that saturate experience and legitimate violence. One seeks to transform the rules and dimensions of the social imaginary via scriptural space in order to respect and enhance the integrity of life before God.

What then is an account of the moral life that is consistent with the task of theological ethics and picture of Scripture? To answer this question we must shift to the second pole of reflection and a richer account of conscience.

Presenting Conscience

Picturing Scripture as media space articulates the shape, intentionality, and task of Christian conscience. Laboring to understand and assess the flow of images of possible and actual lives that run through Scripture helps to form (or deform) our capacity to respond to others and be responsible for the self. Conscience is a way to speak of this "capacity" and its formation. But in order to see this, we have to escape the idealist captivity of "conscience" as the self's moral immediacy. Conscience is not simply authentic human being calling to itself; it is not an inner, psychic tribunal where the self stands nakedly before a divine judge; it is not the sovereign voice of truth.[23] Rather, conscience is the inwardness of our whole being as creatures with the power to move between, examine, and respond rightly to others and complex situations called moral spaces or worlds. For the Christian, conscience is always challenged to traverse responsibly biblical spaces and lived worlds. This is consistent with the multidimensional vision of reality seen in Scripture as a media space and the social imaginary.

The idea of conscience enables one to draw upon insights of narrative and encounter ethics but within a pluralist conception of Scripture. It parallels the image of Scripture as media space that, we have seen, draws together ideas of "encounter" (theocentricity, iconicity) and "narrative" (followability). Like advocates of encounter ethics, conscience manifests a form of moral realism. The point of every kind of moral realism is that there is an "outside" to our acts of meaning-making. This "outside" is represented biblically in terms of the divine and the claims of the neighbor (hence, theocentricity and iconicity, not just followability). The norm of moral perception cannot be one's own image schema but what we are trying to see — the reality and worth of actual others. The most basic delivery of conscience is the sense of responsibility, that is, the sense that we ought to respect and enhance the integrity of life. However, we must assess the claims of others with respect to possible lives. Not all commands are valid; not every summons ought to be heeded. Attention to the place of image schema in the moral life — and so the social imaginary — means that only those demands that open real possibilities for the integrity of life are valid. On this point narrative ethics is right. Becoming responsible persons and communities is a more arduous task than simply being encountered with the claim of the Other. One must speak of moral formation, even spiritual discipline, in ways too often missing within the ethics of encounter. The rule of followability asserts this with respect to Scripture as a media space.

23. Thomas Aquinas speaks of conscience with respect to the first precept of natural law (seek good, avoid evil) and also as a habit. See *Summa Theologiae* I/II, q. 94, a. 1, ad. 2; I, q. 79, a. 13. Paul Tillich and Martin Heidegger understood "conscience" as the human claim on itself. See Paul Tillich, *Morality and Beyond,* Library of Theological Ethics (Louisville: Westminster/John Knox, 1995 [1963]); and Martin Heidegger, *Being and Time,* trans. John Macquarrie and Edward Robinson (New York: Harper & Row, 1962). Still others understood conscience with respect to a social practice. See H. Richard Niebuhr, *The Responsible Self: An Essay in Christian Moral Philosophy,* Library of Theological Ethics (Louisville: Westminster/John Knox, 1999 [1963]); Anne Patrick, *Liberating Conscience: Feminist Explorations in Catholic Moral Theology* (New York: Continuum, 1997); and Kenneth E. Kirk, *Conscience and Its Problems: An Introduction to Casuistry,* Library of Theological Ethics (Louisville: Westminster/John Knox, 1999 [1927]). For further discussion, see William Schweiker, *Responsibility and Christian Ethics* (Cambridge: Cambridge University Press, 1995).

The moral life is about the claim of others (human and nonhuman) on the self and community (the sense of responsibility) and the right formation of character and perception. We can capture this dual fact by saying that conscience is the central virtue of responsibility. Engaging Scripture in light of the demand to respect and enhance the integrity of life is part of the practice of forming and sharpening our being as conscience. But this means — and here is the point of our inquiry — that the use of Scripture in ethics is finally and ultimately bound to the question of how the sense of responsibility — the claim of conscience — can be tutored so that the dignity and worth of the integrity of life can be rightly apprehended. Undertaking that education is the work of the Christian life. It is how the connection between identity and violence can and must be broken.

What theological ethics now faces in new and radical ways is how deeply moral sensibility is saturated by the whirl and consumption of images. The moral paradox of our lives as creatures endowed with imagination is that we must create and yet struggle to exceed image schema needed to apprehend the world. In order to escape the seduction of the giant mall of cultural flows, the Christian conscience must use and break, create and shatter, the very cultural and scriptural images used to "see" the world in order to understand, respect, and enhance the integrity of life before God. Perhaps the way best to use Scripture in ethics is not to allow it or any image schema to become an idol. Is this not the freedom of Christian conscience in an age of global cultural flows?

Conclusion

To summarize: we need, first, to understand Scripture within cultural flows, but also as a complex media space in which images, characters, and ideas circulate to shape people's lives. I have tried, second, to isolate some of the dimensions (horizon, foreground) and constitutive rules (followability, theocentricity, iconicity) of "biblical space" that find analogues within the social imaginary. Third, I insisted that in our age an ethics must connect a claim about the generative power of texts to present possible lives — a claim about the social imaginary — with the demand of responsibility. Finally, I have designated that connection not in terms of the church or in the command of the Other, but, more modestly and humanistically, by means of a form of human self-understanding, that is, conscience.

In its complexity and ambiguity, Scripture is a trove of possible and actual lives that impacts the social imaginary, a school in which a distinctly Christian conscience is forged and formed. The use of Scripture in ethics, then, is not simply to form Christian community or to witness to God's claim on our lives, although it includes those facts. Much more, we interpret Scripture in the struggle to navigate worlds in truth and responsibility. The conscientious life is neither as direct as adopting biblical narratives nor as immediate as responding to the Other. Yet it might well be for all of that a life worth living.

BIBLICAL INTERPRETATION

The Good Neighborhood:
Identity and Community
through the Commandments

Patrick D. Miller

One of the contemporary cultural definitions of desire and well-being is the "good neighborhood."[1] Without a lot of analysis or argument, the culture generally presumes that life is best in a good neighborhood and problematic to a high degree in a bad one. In most popular or implicit understandings of what constitutes a good neighborhood, it is clear that there are highly tangible dimensions and many intangibles. One can intuitively recognize a good neighborhood when one sees it; there are physical characteristics that belong to the image of desire and well-being, such as nice and decent houses of varying sizes, attractive gardens and lawns, calm streets, persons getting along with one another, playing, talking, and the like. But there are also less tangible dimensions that have to do with the character of the persons who live there, how they understand themselves, what they are about in their lives, and how they relate to others in the neighborhood. By definition, at least according to the dictionary, a neighborhood customarily involves a permanent gathering of persons in proximity to each other, usually with distinguishing characteristics.

From two directions, "neighborhood" presents itself as an image for rich thinking about moral community in relation to the Commandments. The more obvious is the use of the "neighbor" as a defining moral category in the Commandments. The other impetus for appropriating this image is the way in which

---

1. While this term has no particular identifiable source, I am indebted to Walter Brueggemann for prompting my thinking about this as a way of speaking about the moral space in which the Commandments operate. While it is the case that the term "good neighborhood" can be a code word for identifying a racially exclusive neighborhood safe from the encroachments of impoverished or "different" folks, my aim is precisely to counter such misuses of the term by drawing from an understanding of community that has shaped the Judaic and Christian communities of faith from the beginning.

spatial notions, language, and imagery have come into play for both moral reflection in general and speaking about the Commandments. Acknowledging his indebtedness to Charles Taylor's *Sources of the Self*,[2] William Schweiker has argued that human beings exist in a "moral space" that "confronts us with questions about how to orient our lives and also provides a background of distinctions of worth that persons use to guide their lives."[3] He suggests: "The place of human existence is always a space defined by questions about how to live and commitments to what is and ought to be valued in human life."[4]

In this context, therefore, I am appropriating this insight and image to argue that the Commandments offer an inviting place to live, a locus for human existence that is defined in ways that make the space and existence within its bounds desirable and good. That such a spatial metaphor may be appropriate for speaking about the moral dimensions of the Decalogue is further indicated by the frequent spatial images that have been drawn into interpretation and analysis of the Commandments.[5] Thus one of the books on the Decalogue is titled *Signposts to Freedom*.[6] And when others speak about the Commandments, they may speak about the Commandments as marking the "boundaries" of life under God, providing "fenceposts" for direction, marking out the "area" of freedom and responsibility, giving much "latitude" in the moral life. The notion of the "good neighborhood" is a way of claiming such spatial language but giving some *specificity* and *valuation* to moral space. My contention in this essay, therefore, is that the Commandments, as presented in their context and in view of their continuing force among later generations, serve to define the good neighborhood, the formation of a community that is the desirable locus of well-being, the place to live the good life, a place to call home and feel at home. In other words, the Commandments present themselves as a way of identifying the "distinguishing characteristics" (so the dictionary) or the marks of the good neighborhood.

2. Charles Taylor, *Sources of the Self: The Making of the Modern Identity* (Cambridge, Mass.: Harvard University Press, 1990).

3. William Schweiker, *Power, Value, and Conviction: Theological Ethics in the Postmodern Age* (Cleveland: Pilgrim, 1998), p. 5.

4. Schweiker, *Power, Value, and Conviction*, p. 34.

5. For further discussion of the significance of space as a category for conceptual and moral thinking, see James W. Flanagan, "Space," in *Handbook of Postmodern Biblical Interpretation*, ed. A. K. M. Adam (St. Louis: Chalice, 2000), pp. 232-37; Edward S. Casey, *Getting Back into Place: Toward a Renewed Understanding of the Place-World* (Bloomington: Indiana University Press, 1993); and idem, *The Fate of Place: A Philosophical History* (Berkeley: University of California Press, 1997). See also the review of both books by Robert McCarter in *ThT* 56 (1999): 139-43.

6. Jan M. Lochman, *Signposts to Freedom: The Ten Commandments and Christian Ethics* (Minneapolis, Minn.: Augsburg, 1982).

Identity and Community

This assumption arises out of indications in the text that the giving of the Commandments served as the *constitution* of a community and a definition of how it was to live out its life. That the story presents the proclamation of the Commandments at the beginning of the sojourn of the people after their delivery from Egypt and then reiterates them as they are poised to enter the land that will be the space of the good neighborhood suggests the definitive character of the Commandments for this community. The formality of the constitution of the community is marked in the text to a high degree with the gathering of the people at the "mountain of God" (Exod 3:1; 4:27; 18:5; 19:3 [LXX]; 24:13) and the various preparatory acts to get ready for the divine word.

The Decalogue begins with "I am the Lord your God" and closes with "your neighbor." Within those borders, identity is given or made known and a community is formed. This community does not constitute itself, nor does it evolve. It is created in the formality of a covenant agreement between YHWH, the Lord, and the people. In this agreement, each party becomes forever defined in relation to the other. Thus the Hebrews, the children of Jacob, are in effect given a new name, "the people of YHWH." Whatever acts stand in tension with that definition become problematic henceforth. Conversely, this deity is permanently defined as "your God" or "our God." The expression "YHWH your/our God" is ubiquitous in the literature, grounded in the Prologue to the Commandments and the Shema (Deut 6:4-9), where the divine declaration of the Commandments is turned into a confessional claim of the people. At times, certainly in the Deuteronomic material, it seems impossible to name this deity without the epithet that connects the deity to the community.[7] In effect, neither community nor deity has a separate existence once the covenant is established.[8]

---

7. In Deuteronomy alone, the expression "the Lord our/your God" appears over three hundred times.

8. Such a claim cannot be read so as to exclude the Lord of Israel from having other stories, redemptive or otherwise, with other peoples, for there is inner-biblical testimony to such relationships (e.g., Amos 9:7). The weight of the claim is on the exclusion of Israel from having stories with other deities, as the First Commandment so indicates. Yet the connection is so tight that it is difficult to imagine a way of understanding YHWH that would not always include the relationship to Israel. At least, those who find the biblical story identifying have only that lens through which to view the character of both deity and community. On this issue, see Patrick D. Miller, "God's Other Stories: On the Margins of Deuteronomic Theology," in *Realia Dei: Essays in Archaeology and Biblical Interpretation in Honor of Edward F. Campbell, Jr. at His Retirement*, ed. Prescott H. Williams, Jr. and Theodore Hiebert (Atlanta: Scholars Press, 1999), pp. 185-94.

Even though both may experience real abandonment on the part of the other for a time, they are forever linked.[9]

Implications for Community

The implications that the Commandments bear on the moral shape of community are significant and can be briefly delineated.

Formation of a Particular Community

The texts of Exodus and Deuteronomy do not speak about a *general* understanding of community but of the formation of a *particular* community whose identity as a people is evoked by their inextricable relationship to the LORD. There is a logically prior relationship to those of kinship, geographical proximity, shared experience, and the like — though these are also dimensions of this particular neighborhood as often of others — that constitutes this community. That is the relationship articulated in the initial words of the community-constituting act: "I am the LORD your God, who brought you out of the land of Egypt, out of the house of slavery" (Exod 20:2; Deut 5:6).

Transcendent Ground

The community so constituted is "a more than human fellowship."[10] It has a transcendent ground. Whether or not there is any historical connection between the apparently early name for this community, *'am yhwh* (e.g., Num 11:29; Judg 5:11, 13; 20:2; 1 Sam 2:24; 2 Sam 1:12), and the Decalogue, that identification or characterization is fully in conformity with the Commandments and the Shema. As such, this community is not self-defining but other-defined. The degree to which that is the case is indicated in the first set of Commandments, where the focus is on the relationship to the deity. This is the ground for the rest of the Commandments, the neighborly ones.[11] The rules for the neighborhood

9. The many references to Israel "abandoning" the LORD in Jeremiah and elsewhere do not need enumerating, but there is also a tradition about the LORD abandoning the people (e.g., Isa 54:7-8).

10. I am conscious of the appropriation of a term that was, in effect, the motto of the World Student Christian Federation.

11. If it is the case that one should read from the Prologue into the First Commandment

are not confined to the neighborly relationship; they do not begin there, but they do end up there. The neighborhood or space of the Commandments is thus countercultural, at least to the extent that the culture operates as if God did not exist.[12] It is a place where the primary practice is the love of God as a character-forming enterprise, or, to use both the biblical language and that of Martin Luther, learning "how to trust completely in God as our ultimate good."[13] Even the Commandments in behalf of the neighbor's well-being serve this character-forming enterprise, particularly the prohibition of coveting the things that belong to one's neighbor (see below on human desires). The transcendent ground of the community also implies something about the source of moral identity and how it may be possible for the community — both individually and communally — to act morally (see below).

Morally Constituted Community

The formation of a moral community is not the by-product of the formation of community. This community is *constituted* around the issue of relationships and how it is that members of the community are to live their lives together, their conduct toward one another. The moral character of the community is inherent, constitutive of its being as a community. The way in which and the degree to which the Pentateuch is *tôrâ*, and the degree to which the Torah flows out of the Commandments and the giving of the Commandments, are indicators that the community formed at Sinai is to be a neighborhood and not only a people. In fact, the giving of the Commandments begins a process of transforming a people into a neighborhood without relinquishing its character as a particular community whose unity is a matter of kinship as well as proximity. One of the clearest indications of this is that while the kinship relationship remains definitive, the instruction about how to live in the neighborhood affects all who live there,

---

in a causal way, that is, "because I am the LORD your God . . . , you shall have no other gods before me," such a syntactical connection carries over implicitly into the other Commandments. That is obviously the case for the first three, but there is no reason for assuming the connection is dropped as one moves into the rest of the Commandments.

12. See Reinhard Hütter, "The Twofold Center of Lutheran Ethics: Christian Freedom and God's Commandments, in *The Promise of Lutheran Ethics*, ed. Karen L. Bloomquist and John R. Stumme (Minneapolis, Minn.: Fortress, 1998), p. 44. On the presupposition of God's nonexistence or the indifference to the question as a feature of the modern consciousness, see, for example, Emmanuel Levinas, *Entre Nous: On Thinking of the Other* (New York: Columbia University Press, 1998), pp. 18-19.

13. Hütter, "The Twofold Center of Lutheran Ethics," p. 44.

all who are neighbors, including the *gēr*, persons who move into the neighborhood but do not belong to the family, the clan, the ethnic community (e.g. Exod 20:10 [cf. 23:12]; Deut 5:14; Exod 12:49;[14] Lev 24:22; Num 9:14; 15:15-16;[15] 15:29-30; Lev 19:33-34;[16] cf. Exod 12:19; Lev 16:29; 17:8, 10, 12, 13, 15; 18:26; Num 35:15). This people have become a moral community, and the prospect of living as a good neighborhood depends henceforth not upon their membership in the family but upon their willingness and ability to be moral. That orientation toward the

14. "There shall be one law *(tôrâ)* for the native *('ezrāḥ)* and for the alien *(gēr)* who resides among you."

15. "You and the alien shall be alike before the Lᴏʀᴅ."

16. "The alien who resides with you shall be to you as the citizen among you; you shall love him as yourself." It is not clear whether the terms *'āḥ* or *rēaʿ* ever include the *gēr* in their frame of reference. In fact the many references to treating the resident alien and the native/citizen (*'ezrāḥ* in Exodus — Numbers, but *'āḥ* in Deuteronomy [e.g., 1:16]) alike suggest that may not be the case. But the very presence of these references indicates that the resident alien is to be treated as a member of the neighborhood, that the rules apply to him/her as well as to the native/citizen/brother. Leviticus 19:18 and 34, with their calls to "love your neighbor as yourself" and "love the resident alien as yourself," serve to identify the resident alien as the recipient of exactly the same moral treatment as the neighbor (cf. Deut 10:19). The alien is to be regarded as "like yourself," with the same needs and endangerments. (On the meaning of the construction here, particularly the term *kāmôkā*, "like yourself," see the forthcoming essay by Andreas Schüle, "'Denn er ist wie Du.' Zu Übersetzung und Verständnis des alttestamentlichen Liebesgebots Lev 19,18," *ZAW* 113 [2001]: 315-34.)

The brother/sister/neighbor and the alien are bound together morally even if they are not the same categories. Both are members of the good neighborhood. The references in Leviticus to "anyone *('îš)* of the people of Israel or any resident alien residing in Israel" (Lev 20:2; cf. Num 19:10; 35:15) and to "anyone of the house of Israel or any resident alien residing in Israel" (Lev 22:18) serve to preserve the ethnic differentiation apart from the proximity designation but insist that the proximity relationship works in the same way. That some differentiation is made within the statutes is indicated in Leviticus 25 where, for example, if a "brother" falls into difficulty, you treat him like a resident alien (v. 35). But the stipulations that follow describing the appropriate treatment indicate how one treats a neighbor/brother in Israel, that is, not taking interest in advance, not lending money with interest, and not providing food at a profit. The most extensive difference is also found in this chapter: slaves may be acquired from the surrounding nations and also from the resident aliens residing with you (vv. 44-46). Deuteronomy makes a single differentiation between the resident aliens and the Israelites as members of the sacral community by indicating that meat that dies of itself may not be eaten by Israelites but may be given to aliens (14:21). At the same time, Deuteronomy is explicit about including the resident aliens in the gathering of the people to hear the terms of the covenant and to be instructed about the rules of the neighborhood in which they are going to live (29:11; 31:12) and about accepting them by entering into covenant. On the *gēr*, see now Christiana van Houten, *The Alien in Israelite Law*, JSOTSup 107 (Sheffield: JSOT, 1991); and José E. Ramírez Kidd, *Alterity and Identity in Israel*, BZAW 283 (Berlin: Walter de Gruyter, 1999).

moral, however, is derivative from their identity and self-knowledge as slaves redeemed by YHWH, who is their God.

Time and Space

The community is one that exists in time and space. It assumes a conventional locale, proximate relationships, place to live, and the provisions for life. But the community so defined and constituted by the Commandments is not fixed in a *particular* time and space. It may be constituted at different times and places. It is assumed that the community created by this formal covenantal act and given definition of the character of its life together is a *continuing* community. The assumption of that continuity is tied to kinship relationships, to successive generations, whose instruction in the moral character of the community is a prime concern.[17] Kinship relationship is critical and later shows itself not only within Judaism (and even among those hostile to Judaism) by the question of what determines who is a Jew but also within Christianity, for which it is critical that its messianic figure is a Jew and its earliest leader insists on viewing the church as grafted onto the tree that is Israel (Romans 9–11). In other words, the particularity of this community never disappears. So matters of kinship and election are never off the table, and it is difficult to submerge them, as if the community so defined by this formal covenantal act could transcend its character as a people and its particular election into a community whose very character is dependent upon the relationship to the LORD of Israel and the way that neighborly life is defined in the community-constituting act.[18]

Voluntary Association

The moral community constituted in relation to "the LORD your God" and in relation to "your neighbor" is a voluntary association. That is, those who live in this community and by this definition of community do so because they wish to, voluntarily (Exod 19:3-8). But the inherent notion of voluntary association is complex. It is not as if persons wander in off the street and decide to hook up

17. That is particularly evident in the way that the biblical book most shaped by the Commandments, Deuteronomy, places heavy stress on teaching the next generations the way of the LORD.

18. For a treatment of the Decalogue in relation to family and kinship issues, see now the two essays by Ron E. Tappy, "Lineage and Law in Pre-Exilic Israel" and "The Code of Kinship in the Ten Commandments," in *RB* 107 (2000): 175-204, 321-37.

with the persons who are there, with like-minded people, and so on. If the covenantal moment is a constituting moment and one that depends upon the community's agreement, upon the decision of individual members that they choose this neighborhood — as it does — the community has a prior history that is also determinative of its makeup and brings them together. History and kinship, election and deliverance bring this community into being. It is not, however, formally constituted as a neighborhood for living together apart from the willing decision of one and all, of all as one (Exod 19:8), to live by the constituting rules, by the polity set forth in the divine revelation of the Commandments and the Mosaic teaching. That decision is not only voluntary; it is one that is taken up as a *welcome obligation,* as an appropriate response to the experience of deliverance from slavery. Obligation is not imposed (though it is certainly expected by the deity — see next item) but assumed.

The fact that the community readily disobeys the moral obligations it has taken upon itself does not vitiate the voluntary and welcome assumption of the obligation as a mark of the good neighborhood. But it does identify the reality of sin as something that comes into the neighborhood and has to be dealt with. The moral problematic between the willing acceptance (Exodus 19) and the immediate disobedience (Exodus 32–33) has been examined in a helpful way by Jacqueline Lapsley in a study of the problem of the moral self in the Book of Ezekiel. She uncovers a conflict between different moral anthropologies, one of virtuous moral selfhood and another more deterministic one, suggesting that the people of this neighborhood as they lived out their lives were "inherently incapable of acting in accord with the good (they possess a neutral moral self)."[19] Ezekiel offers a solution: a new moral identity is given in the knowledge of God and the knowledge of self, so that "character displaces action as the central component of the moral self."[20] Or at least the new moral identity becomes the source of actions, and the focus of the book in its final chapters is more on the divinely given identity than upon the actions of the community. The move from virtuous selfhood to the gift of a new being, that is, "a moral identity formed and sustained by a transcendent God" that makes possible a new mode of action, is also a dimension of the decalogical tradition, as indicated by the movement in Moses' speeches from the injunction to Israel to "circumcise the foreskin of your heart, and do not be stubborn any longer" (Deut 10:16) to Moses' final climactic declaration:

19. Jacqueline E. Lapsley, *Can These Bones Live? The Problem of the Moral Self in the Book of Ezekiel,* BZAW 301 (Berlin: Walter de Gruyter, 2000), pp. 185-86.

20. Lapsley, *Can These Bones Live?* p. 186.

> Moreover the LORD your God will circumcise your heart and the heart of
> your descendants, so that you will love the LORD your God with all your
> heart and with all your soul, in order that you may live. . . . Then you shall
> again obey the LORD, observing all his commandments that I am com-
> manding you today, and the LORD your God will make you abundantly
> prosperous in all your undertakings, in the fruit of your body, in the fruit of
> your livestock, and in the fruit of your soil. (Deut 30:6, 8)

Deuteronomy reinforces this word with its consequent indication that the commandment is neither too difficult nor too far away. It is at hand and accessible
(30:11-14). The final Mosaic speech holds the gift of a new identity, a new character, and the capacity to carry out the right action in a realistic tension appropriate to the complexity of the moral self as it is actually lived out.

Sanctions and Rationalities

Participation in the moral community is both sanctioned and rationalized. The
motivation clauses of the Decalogue and their counterparts in the various legal
codes serve to do both. Negative outcomes for failure to conform to the stipulated marks of the neighborhood or, in more traditional language, to keep the
Commandments are made explicit, but the rationalization is not purely negative. Throughout the first half of the Decalogue, various reasons are given why
the particular prohibitions or Commandments should be kept and observed.
These include not only sanctions for disobedience (as in the prohibition of
idolatry and against misuse of the divine name) but also visions of the good (as
in the prohibition of idolatry and the commandment to honor parents), as well
as appeals to experience and memory as a way of encouraging conformity to
the stipulations laid out in the covenant (the Sabbath commandment). In all of
this, one perceives a way of effecting moral community that makes attention to
the distinguishing characteristics a highly desirable commitment, the reasonable thing to do.

Obedience to God

Obedience to God, rather than to human beings, defines this moral community. That is seen not only in the emphasis placed upon loyalty to the LORD of
Israel but also in comparison with similar ethnic and national communities
contemporary with Israel. This is a point that Eckart Otto has made strongly in

recent writings.[21] It is exemplified in the loyalty oath of Deuteronomy 13:1-11, a negative reflex of the commandments prohibiting the worship of other gods and the making of images, as well as in the positive reflex of these in the commandment calling for the exclusive love of the LORD of Israel in the Shema.[22] Otto has noted that Deuteronomy 13:1-11 is a translated version of Esarhaddon's loyalty oath. In the Assyrian version, any criticism of the king, any suggestion of rebellion or insurrection, whether from prophets, members of one's own family, or members of the royal family, was to be reported to the king, and the one who spoke of rebellion was to be executed. The good neighborhood constituted out of the Commandments knows such loyalty oaths and places them prominently to the fore. But they require loyalty to the redeeming God, not to any member of the neighborhood or any ruling figure. There is no ultimate authoritative[23] claim in this neighborhood except that of the deity. The relationship to the neighbor is not ultimate and not one of obedience. The only other relationship in the neighborhood that comes close to this is not a political one. It is a kinship one and has to do with the way that children relate to their parents. The language there is comparable to the way in which the community is to relate to God: honor (see the Fifth Commandment to honor father and mother). The good neighborhood, the moral community defined at Sinai, is a political community (see below on Levinas and *le tiers*), and in its history rulers are present and act. But what the Torah does is to set the king not as equivalent to the parent but on a par with every other member of the community in that his primary responsibility is to live by the moral definition that is given in the constituting of the community, in the creation of the good neighborhood

---

21. See, for example, E. Otto, "Human Rights: The Influence of the Hebrew Bible," *JNSL* 25 (1999): 1-20.

22. At this point, the distinction between the prohibition of other gods and the prohibition of images of either YHWH or the other gods does not make a difference. Deuteronomy 13 has both in mind. The First Commandment is clearly in view, for the issue is going after "other gods" (the language of the First Commandment) versus the worship of "the LORD your God . . . alone" (the Shema). Whether or not idolatry per se is in the picture, the language of the Second Commandment is present also in the double reference to "serving" other gods (vv. 2, 6) and the testing to see whether "you indeed love the LORD your God with all your heart and soul" (v. 3). The language of "loving" God comes in the Second Commandment in the Decalogue (5:10), but it is associated with the First Commandment by its presence in the positive form of the First Commandment, the Shema (6:5).

23. On the distinction between authoritative and authoritarian, see J. Vining, *The Authoritative and the Authoritarian* (Chicago: University of Chicago Press, 1986). The distinction is between "willing obedience and obedience for its own sake" (p. 77). I am indebted to Jeffries Hamilton's unpublished paper, "How to Read an Abhorrent Text: Deuteronomy 13 and the Nature of Authority," for this reference.

(Deut 17:18-20). Nothing is said about the members of the community being obedient to the king but only about the king not being outside the membership of the community and being under the same moral code as they are.

Human Desire

In the movement from the first Commandments, which have to do with the locus of one's ultimate trust, to the final Commandment, which has to do with the control of our desire for the goods of our neighbor, the Commandments inscribe an approach to human desires as an aspect of the good neighborhood. In Reinhard Hütter's succinct appropriation of Luther's conviction as expressed in his Large Catechism, "They stubbornly keep our desires directed toward God."[24] To that end, Luther proposed to weave the Ten Commandments into a mode of prayer, serving to form the desires of the members of the community toward God. He saw in the regular study, meditation, and reflection upon the Commandments a combination of instruction, thanksgiving, confession, and petition that can shape human desires toward their true object, which is the starting point of the Commandments (the prohibitions of the worship of other gods and the making and worshipping of idols).[25]

Outside Recognition

Persons outside the neighborhood are able to recognize the quality of life within this neighborhood and identify it as desirable. Their grounds for doing so are precisely the norms that have been set forth, the constituting rules and polity for the life together (Deut 4:6, 8), as well as the transcendent ground of the community's life (v. 7). This neighborhood is easily recognizable as a good place to live. Both grounds for that recognition — "What nation has a god so near to it as the LORD our God is whenever we call to him? And what other great nation has statutes and ordinances as just as this entire law . . . ?" — are at the center of the con-

---

24. Hütter, "The Twofold Center of Lutheran Ethics," p. 47.

25. See Martha Ellen Stortz, "Practicing Christians: Prayer as Formation," in *The Promise of Lutheran Ethics,* ed. Karen L. Bloomquist and John R. Stumme (Minneapolis, Minn.: Fortress, 1998), p. 67. That the inclination toward idols has to do with human desires and is to be connected with the last Commandment(s) is well illustrated in the Deuteronomic instruction to the Israelites to burn the idols of the nations around them when they enter the land: "Do not covet the silver or the gold that is on them and take it for yourself, because you could be ensnared by it; for it is abhorrent to the LORD your God" (Deut 7:25).

stituting covenantal act: the relationship with "the Lord your God," which is defined by the deity's act of compassionate deliverance,[26] and the relationship to the neighbor, whose just character is determined and defined by the Commandments and their elaboration in the statutes and ordinances.

Order and Freedom

Both order and freedom are built into the moral community shaped by the Commandments. The Commandments take the community from disorder and slavery (Egypt) to order and freedom (the good neighborhood of the Commandments, a community of time and place). The focus of attention is customarily on effecting an order as the Commandments are understood prescriptively. Whether prescriptively or descriptively interpreted, they clearly function to lay out guidelines, directions, and parameters that give structure to the life of the community formed and directed by them. But as is often noted, the Commandments leave much open; they provide a lot of elbow room, as it were, in the moral space they create. There are wide realms of human life and conduct left without moral requirement, although it may be possible to infer from what is given how one might act and what the character of community life would be like on other issues. Furthermore, the direction that is given through the Commandments needs much fleshing out and receives it in the statutes and ordinances, which identify the long and often complex trajectory of meaning, action, and effects that extends out of each of the Commandments and the Decalogue as a whole. Indeed, there is much to be spelled out in cases that, even if more time and circumstance controlled, nevertheless, give much direction for the life of the neighborhood, particularly as it tries to unpack the moral formation the Commandments evoke. As the Commandments are indeed unpacked through the statutes and ordinances, the case law and other legal formulations in the Pentateuch, they are revealed to encompass a rich, detailed, and coherent sense of how to live in a structured, free moral space. Freedom has limits and direction; it is not constricted or chaotic.

More specifically, the order and freedom of this moral community are experienced in *time* and *place*. That is, the order of *time*, exemplified particularly

---

26. See the Exodus story and note the linguistic argument of Norbert Lohfink that the calling to the deity referred to in Deut 4:7 is the cry of the oppressed and the poor. The laws build into the system the compassionate divine response that evoked the divine deliverance, the deity's hearing the cry of distress and coming to deliver. See N. Lohfink, "Poverty in the Laws of the Ancient Near East and of the Bible," *TS* 52 (1991): 34-50.

in the seven-day cycle, is in behalf of freedom from the oppressive potential of work or labor (the Sabbath commandment). The primary form of freedom is found in the regularity of time, which guarantees release from hard labor. It is no accident that this order in behalf of freedom is undergirded in the Deuteronomic form of the Decalogue by a recollection of the Exodus deliverance (Deut 5:15), for the experience of slavery and nonfreedom in Egypt was the experience of unrelenting and oppressive work. This freedom in time is then extended into a sabbatical principle that operates to bring release from all forms of economic bondage (Deuteronomy 15).

The order of *place* is the realm of freedom. It is identified only at one point in the Decalogue, specifically the commandment to honor one's parents. But the movement from the giving of the Commandments (Exodus) to the recollection of their giving (Deuteronomy) enhances the way in which the neighborhood is marked out as a space for life. It is in the commandment regarding the honor of parents that the community hears that its life is in a gifted place, "the land that the LORD your God is giving you." This order of space is marked not so much by substantive freedom as it is by substantive goodness.[27] It is a place of blessing, articulated in the provision of life and the provision of good. The neighborhood is marked specifically as a *good* neighborhood in two ways: it is gifted space and it is a place where good can happen ("that your days may be long and that it may go well with you"). But the latter is effected precisely as the community constitutes itself by this covenant and makes its space one that is marked by the distinguishing characteristics embodied in the Commandments as specified, particularized, and exemplified in the statutes and ordinances.

The Other and Others

It is not possible to talk about either the order or the freedom without a large sense of the Other and others. The moral community effected by the Commandments is one in which human self-understanding is found in an encounter with the Other. In this sense, they offer an example of the concern for the Other that is accentuated in the ethics of Emmanuel Levinas.[28] The Other is found not only in the neighbor but in the relationship between God and the

---

27. In the divine allotment of land for the various members of the community, there is a precise order whose purpose is to provide the freedom for life on the land and access to its productivity without restriction except the restriction that keeps each member or family from undercutting the freedom of the neighbor for life on the land (Joshua 13–22).

28. E.g., Levinas, *Entre Nous.*

community. Each comprehends moral purpose in relation to the Other. That relationality is definitive of human existence and experience but also determinative of who God is. This is not, however, a Buberian "I-Thou" relationship, which is too reductionistic a way of viewing the moral community. Here Levinas is helpful with his insistence that in the moral community there is always "the third party" *(le tiers)*. In the Decalogue, the third party is the neighbor. In Frank Yamada's helpful interpretation of Levinas's ethics, he summarizes as follows: "Encountering the Other is the primary experience that makes possible the working out of ethical acting and thinking. The realization of a third party, however, disrupts my bi-symmetrical relation to the Other and thus forms the basis for society. *Le tiers* requires me to think about issues that are larger than my own relation to the Other. It creates the necessity for talking about justice for other human beings and the world."[29] The moral community is a fully social one precisely because it is a neighborhood in which the definitive relationship includes the third party from the start.

Relationships

The structure of order and freedom, therefore, has to do with relationships. Such relational order is not primarily oriented toward a broad hierarchy of human relationships, though some hierarchy is assumed (for example, in the commandment having to do with Sabbath rest and the prohibition of coveting). Alongside certain *assumed* relationships, there are those that are explicitly *effected, nurtured, or protected in the Commandments*. The latter are several:

1. The *sovereign deity and the redeemed community*, a relationship that is both personal/individual and corporate/communal in that, according to the narrative, the community as a whole is explicitly addressed by the Commandments, while the form of address ("you") is regularly cast in the singular. Each individual member of the community is addressed by the obligations and possibilities of the Commandments but only as part of the whole community. This is not an individual ethic; it is communal from the start and applies to the community. Yet the ethic is individual insofar as the directions and structure apply to each member of the community. This is one of the many ways in which the ethics of the Bible function to keep a complex but coherent relationship between the part and the whole, between individual and society, the one and the many.

---

29. Frank Yamada, "Ethics," in *Handbook of Postmodern Interpretation*, ed. A. K. M. Adam (St. Louis: Chalice, 2000), p. 81.

The initial encounter with the other is found in the community's call to the worship and service of "the LORD your God," so that the Other with whom it deals first and always is the sovereign and redeeming God, whose actions have made possible the formation of this particular moral community. But it is just as true that the deity also deals first and always with the other who is discerned in the community, both in its corporate expression and in its individual lives. The way in which that relationship constantly slides back and forth between individual and community is evident in large measure in the oracles of the prophets.

2. *Member of the community and neighbor,* a relationship that is made explicit in the last two (or three) Commandments with the prohibitions against false witness "against your neighbor" and against coveting the wife of "your neighbor" or the house of "your neighbor," or, for that matter, anything that belongs to "your neighbor" (Exod 20:16-17 ; Deut 5:20-21). There is a structured moral movement from the encounter with the Other as deity to the encounter with the other as neighbor.[30]

There is some danger that *the neighbor may disappear* from the picture as the community interprets the moral space of the Commandments. That is, it is possible to turn the moral direction of the Commandments inward so that they have to do with the individual's life apart from the neighborhood and thus no longer become crucial for life in the good neighborhood. They are seen to have to do with personal attitudes and actions that might indirectly affect the neighbor but are not primarily oriented toward the well-being of the compatriot in the neighborhood.

There is little danger that the prohibition against *killing/murder* would be viewed as not having to do first of all, if not only, with the protection of the life of the neighbor. And it is highly likely that the prohibition of *stealing* will regularly be perceived as protecting the property of the neighbor. Even there, however, it is easy to miss the fact that the first protection is not the property of the neighbor but the neighbor herself or himself, that is, protection of the life of the neighbor from being stolen or *kidnapped* for personal gain and profit (see Exod 21:16).[31]

A more common disappearance of the neighbor is found in the Commandment against *adultery.* It is easy and commonplace to interpret the prohibition of adultery as restricted to "my" marriage relationship, even though the context clearly indicates that the marriage of "my" neighbor falls under the

---

30. On the relation of the resident alien (*gēr*) to the neighbor, see above.

31. A. Alt, "Das Verbot des Diebstahls im Dekalog," in *Kleine Schriften zur Geschichte des Volkes Israels,* vol. 1 (Munich: C. H. Beck, 1953), pp. 333-40.

protection in this Commandment. To be sure, adultery has terrible effects upon the marriage of the one who commits adultery, which merit attention in the moral discussion about adultery. But the Commandment does not have its primary aim at the spouse of the violator (whether male or female) but at the damage done to the neighbor and the marriage relationship of the neighbor. Insofar as the neighborhood defined by the Commandments deals with issues of sexual relationships, the starting point is the way in which neighbor relations are endangered by violating the marriage relationship of the other.

Even Commandments with explicit reference to the neighbor may be interpreted in such a way that the neighbor and his or her well-being disappear as the primary concern of the Commandment. This is evident in the way in which the Commandment against *false witness* is often turned into a general prohibition against *lying*. It is certainly possible to see deceit in general as coming into play in this Commandment. In the Psalter, no commandment is set more prominently to the fore, often in relation to deceit broadly understood. But even there, the primary reference and context in which the concern for lying arises is in the way in which the *neighbor* is harmed by false witness, whether through gossip, rumor, or the more technical case of judicial perjury (e.g., Amos 5:10). So also the prohibition against *coveting,* where the neighbor is mentioned *three* times, may be turned into a resistance to *greed and consumerism,* phenomena that indeed may belong to the trajectory of the Commandment but should not displace the primary concern of the Commandment, which reflects the attitude of a member of the neighborhood *not as a personal stance* but as it leads to actions *detrimental to the other.* Lodged within the moral space of the last Commandment, greed has to do with its effects against the neighbor, not so much with a generally inordinate love of things or desire of things as with a desire for the things of the neighbor that leads to other acts against the neighbor — killing, adultery, stealing, false witness, and so forth. To the extent, then, that broader matters come in view, for example, greed and consumerism, they do so as neighbor concerns for the good of the neighborhood.

3. *Member of the community and slave,* the starting point in the Decalogue for the relationship with the neighbor as other. The Sabbath Commandment in its Deuteronomic form sets the rest of the male and female slave as its particular objective. It presumes the capacity of the members of the community to find and provide for rest and relaxation, but it fixes a time for such rest specifically so that the members of the community who are not free — and one presumes that the slave meant in this instance is first of all a Hebrew, that is, a neighbor who is now in a situation of economic endangerment and so forced into bonded service — may find the rest that is necessary for human life. So the neighbor is first encountered in a way that is problematic, that is, as slave, but the encounter is sub-

versive in that it is set to provide release for the slave. That such release is meant to be a foretaste of ultimate release is clearly indicated by the laws bringing about permanent release of debts and slaves in the seventh year (Deuteronomy 15). The relationship to the other as a member of the neighborhood who is economically threatened is opened by creating characteristics that will serve to resist economic oppression and bring about economic restoration.

4. *Member of the community and family,* the primary relationship within the kinship ethos and, more generally, the primary relationship within a neighborhood. It is characteristic of the moral space filled by these guidelines and distinguished by this way of living that the family is undergirded precisely where it is most vulnerable, the breakdown of the care and respect of adult children for their parents. The protection of the parents by ensuring their honor and respect is a protection of the family.

5. *Member of the community and nature,* a subdued but present association in the Commandments as the Sabbath Commandment and the coveting Commandment lift up cattle, the ox, and the ass as being provided rest and protection (cf. Exod 23:12; Lev 25:3-4). The significance of this should not be overlooked. These are work animals, and so there is self-interest in providing for their rest. But the Sabbath Commandment cannot be seen simply as a self-interested statute. It rather seeks to be comprehensive in setting aside the rest time. That includes the natural world. That such a broader relationship to nature is envisioned is underscored when the sabbatical principle is carried over in the statutes to include the land and fields. Again, self-interest may be a part of this because the land that lies fallow is renourished, but the harmonious interface of people and land is evident in the fact that the time of rest is beneficial to both parties in the relationship. A further dimension of the relationship between the community and nature in the Sabbath rest is seen in the indication that such rest for the land envisions accessibility to its produce as available to the *wild animals* as well as to the poor (Exod 23:11).[32]

Memory and Experience

Morality is rooted in memory and shared experience. Both the Prologue, which recalls the redemptive work of God that created the possibility of a moral community, and the Deuteronomic Sabbath Commandment, which recalls the ex-

---

32. The inclusion of nature in one's definition of community has been especially argued by Wendell Berry in various works, e.g., *Sex, Economy, Freedom, and Community* (New York: Pantheon, 1993).

perience of slavery and redemption either as the goal of the Sabbath observance or its impetus, mark this community as one whose identity is constitutive of moral possibility. The memory of God's redemptive work on their behalf brings the knowledge of God to life and becomes the ground of the moral life. That this memory is a shared one means that the neighbors have a common ground for the moral life. It is in the act of remembering that the community discovers its ground and finds the source of the moral life outside itself but rooted in its experience, an experience available in memory. That memory may be actualized by later generations for whom the experience of the LORD's redemption is indirect, that is, available only in the memory as the story is told and retold. In that process, new generations are given a memory (Deut 11:1-7)[33] and the covenant is made afresh with each new generation (5:3). Moral obligation and moral identity, action and character, come together as the community remembers what God has done and places its trust in the redeeming LORD.[34] That such self-understanding erupts in moral action is precisely the point of the Sabbath Commandment, as the provision of rest for bonded slaves is grounded in the experience of God's provision of rest and freedom from slavery for the community. The self receives its identity out of this shared experience that is recalled in memory: the memory of Pharaonic oppression, the LORD's liberating act and its revelation of the character of the source of moral understanding, and the connection to the neighbor who is "like yourself" in memory and in present reality.

33. See Patrick D. Miller, *Deuteronomy* (Louisville: John Knox, 1990), loc. cit.

34. As Jacqueline Lapsley has reminded me, such memory may be a *negative* memory of the people's sinfulness, as in the case of Ezekiel. One may also cite the way in which Psalms 105 and 106 preserve the story of God's faithfulness in Israel's history as a character-forming memory (Psalm 105) but also the story of Israel's sinfulness in that same history (Psalm 106). Both positive and negative memories are crucial to authentic self-understanding and identity, as well as to the shaping and reshaping of community.

The Complexity of Character
and the Ethics of Complexity:
The Case of King David

Richard G. Bowman

The tellers of the tale about biblical Israel's monarchy routinely praised King David for his integrity. Following a lengthy account of how David consolidated his kingdom and unified his people, one narrator evaluates his administration: "David administered justice and equity to all his people" (2 Sam 8:15). In assessing the reigns of subsequent kings, the Deuteronomic chroniclers repeatedly use David as a role model,[1] noting that while "David did what was right in the sight of the Lord" (1 Kgs 15:5) his successors did not, as, for example, in the case of Ahaz: "He did not do what was right in the sight of the Lord his God, as his ancestor David had done" (2 Kgs 16:2). Such comments suggest that the narrative of King David may have functioned as a "normative story," a compelling narrative that imparts acceptable community virtues and values.[2] Yet many of the narrated episodes conflict with this positive ethical assessment of David's character.

Violence and estrangement are repeated themes throughout the larger narrative. David's use of violence to defeat the Philistines wins him fame and acclaim; but it also alienates him from Saul, thereby forcing him into exile. Estranged also from his supporters, David seeks refuge with his former Philistine foes. As the eventual successor to a defeated Saul, David presides over a monarchy consolidated through a violent purge that eliminates all rivals. Even though David is not an active participant in the violence, he is its direct beneficiary.

Once David's political problems have been resolved, the storyteller focuses on David's personal and familial life. Violence and estrangement erupt again. David sexually assaults Bathsheba and orders the murder of her husband

---

1. See 1 Kgs 14:8; 15:3-5; 2 Kgs 8:19; 14:3; 16:2; 18:3; 21:7; 22:2.
2. See Richard Bondi, "The Elements of Character," *JRE* 12 (1984): 209, 213.

in a failed attempt to cover up his transgression. His behavior is then mirrored in the behavior of his sons. Amnon rapes his half sister Tamar and is then murdered by her brother Absalom. Exiled by David, Absalom eventually returns to initiate a revolution against his father. Even though the revolt fails and ends with the execution of Absalom, David's legacy of violence and estrangement is passed on to his son Solomon. On his deathbed, David instructs Solomon to consolidate his own power by executing all personal and political rivals.

Biblical Character Ethics Considered

This summary suggests a high degree of complexity in the portrayal of David, resulting by and large from a discontinuity between the various narrators' *assessments* of David and his narrated *actions*. These complexities and apparent contradictions make it difficult to construe the David story as a typical "normative story" that is used to shape the ethical character of a community and its leaders. This challenging story dramatizes the seven deadly sins more than the four cardinal virtues. Thus it is more a counter-story than a normative, confessing one.

Yet such counter-stories also have a function within the confessing community. As the novelist Salmon Rushdie notes: "Impossible stories, stories with No Entry signs on them, change our lives, and our minds, as often as the authorized versions, the stories we are expected to trust, upon which we are asked, or told, to build our judgments, and our lives."[3] Significantly, the tellers and redactors of Israel's story seem to recognize and accept the validity of Rushdie's claim. Instead of neglecting or even suppressing counter-stories, these perceptive chroniclers include them within the confessing story.[4] They not only include them but co-opt them so that the counter-story constitutes an integral part of the confessing story. This encompassing of counter-stories within the confessing story is perhaps the genius of the biblical witness. The "shadow" side of character is acknowledged, and an overall complexity of character is accepted. Counter-narratives thus offer a confessing community not so much ideals to emulate as complexities to ponder. They present a mirror of ourselves.

If one accepts Rushdie's notion that lives can be changed even through counter-stories just as they can be shaped by normative stories, and if one seeks thereby to interpret the counter-narratives included within the biblical confess-

---

3. Salman Rushdie, *The Ground Beneath Her Feet* (New York: Henry Holt, 1999), p. 199.

4. On the hazards of neglecting and suppressing counter-stories, see Chinua Achebe, *Home and Exile* (New York: Oxford University Press, 2000).

ing narrative, then a character ethics discussion must focus on what exactly is learned from these counter-stories and on how they change our lives. If they do not overtly cultivate virtues and inculcate character, then what do they do? How are such stories useful for the doing of character ethics, especially a character ethics constructed from biblical counter-narratives?

Contemporary cultural critic Terrence Rafferty provides a suggestion through his reflections on the elusive quest for the Great American Novel. The Great American Novel, he writes, "had to be one that would, comprehensively and definitively, explain us to ourselves, that would make sense of our senseless sprawl and contradictions — that would show us who we are and were and will be."[5] This is perhaps how counter-narratives can function for a biblically based character ethics: through the story of King David, we gain an enhanced sense "of who we are and were and will be." Perhaps better than normative stories, counter-stories "explain us to ourselves." Rather than catalog virtues, condemn vices, and commend a vision of the good life, a biblical character ethics may be limited by the nature of the stories themselves to explain us to ourselves.[6] Narratives, after all, are not discursive reflections on character and the nature of community but stories about people who live in communities, struggle with each other, themselves, and even God, and attempt in some way to prosper.

Characters and Character: A Point of Entry

King David, as he is portrayed in 1 and 2 Samuel, is primarily a literary creation.[7] He is a character in a narrative, the protagonist of a story about the ac-

5. Terrence Rafferty, "Ralph Ellison's Unfinished Business," *GQ* (July, 1999): 46.

6. This is, I realize, not how Aristotle envisioned character ethics. Nor is it consistent with the practice of this discipline by Stanley Hauerwas in, for example, *Character and the Christian Life* (Notre Dame, Ind.: Notre Dame University Press, 1994); and idem, *A Community of Character* (Notre Dame, Ind.: Notre Dame University Press, 1981). Yet biblical scholars typically misuse and abuse the conventions of other disciplines to suit their own purposes.

7. For other literary interpretations of the David story see, for example, Robert Polzin, *Samuel and the Deuteronomist*, ISBL (San Francisco: Harper & Row, 1989); idem, *David and the Deuteronomist*, ISBL (Bloomington: Indiana University Press, 1993); David Gunn, *The Fate of King Saul*, JSOTSup 14 (Sheffield: JSOT Press, 1980); idem, *The Story of King David*, JSOTSup 6 (Sheffield: JSOT Press, 1976); Peter Miscall, *1 Samuel: A Literary Reading*, ISBL (Bloomington: Indiana University Press, 1986); J. Cheryl Exum, *Tragedy and Biblical Narrative: Arrows of the Almighty* (Cambridge: Cambridge University Press, 1992); J. P. Fokkelman, *Narrative Art and Poetry in the Books of Samuel: A Full Interpretation Based on Stylistic and Structural Analyses*, 4 vols., SSN 20, 23, 27, 31 (Assen: Van Gorcum, 1981-93); and Marti Steussy, *David: Biblical Portraits of Power*, SPOT (Columbia: University of South Carolina Press, 1999). For historical analy-

quisition, administration, and abdication of political power. As such, an analysis of the ethical character of David merges with and emerges from reflections about the portrayal of his literary character and the characteristics attributed to him. As a character in a narrative, David is typically portrayed through his actions and speeches along with evaluative comments from both the narrator and other characters.

Significantly, however, David is initially introduced and characterized not by reports of his actions or even by citations of his speech but through descriptions and discussions of his physical appearance. Even before David appears as a dramatized presence, his physical appearance becomes an issue. As Samuel prepares to anoint Saul's successor from among the sons of Jesse, the narrator reports that he "looked on Eliab and thought, 'Surely the LORD's anointed is now before the LORD'" (1 Sam 16:6). The criterion for this assessment of Eliab's leadership potential seems to be physical appearance, for which God subsequently rebukes Samuel: "Do not look upon his appearance or on the height of his stature, because I have rejected him" (v. 7). God then instructs Samuel on the divine criterion: "The LORD does not see as humans see; for humans see the eyes, but the LORD sees the heart" (v. 7).[8]

Having stated the divine criterion, God proceeds to reject six other sons of Jesse. After querying Jesse about further possibilities, Samuel instructs him to send for David, the remaining and youngest son. Yet before recounting the selection and anointing of David, the storyteller interrupts the action to describe David's physical appearance: "He was ruddy with beautiful eyes and a good appearance" (v. 12).[9] After suggesting that God does not assess leadership potential on the basis of physical appearance, the inclusion of this description of David's appearance is curious. That David bears a commanding physical presence with "beautiful eyes" is especially significant, since the divine speech specifically rejects "seeing the eyes." Contrary to divine preference, David's physical appearance seems important for both Samuel and the narrator.

Nevertheless, the divine criterion of "seeing the heart" remains decisive for the narrative. What exactly God sees in David is not revealed. God does not justify the choice further but instead instructs Samuel to "rise and anoint" David (v. 12). However, two incidents in the larger narrative context about the rejection of Saul suggest possible assets lacked by Saul but possessed by David. At

---

ses see, e.g., P. Kyle McCarter, Jr., *1 Samuel*, AB 8 (Garden City, N.Y.: Doubleday, 1980); idem, *2 Samuel*, AB 9 (Garden City, N.Y.: Doubleday, 1984); Ralph Klein, *1 Samuel*, WBC 10 (Waco, Tex.: Word Books, 1983); A. A. Anderson, *2 Samuel*, WBC 11 (Waco, Tex.: Word Books, 1989).

8. My translation.

9. My translation.

Gilgal, Saul offers sacrifices, thereby violating Samuel's instructions to wait for him seven days. When Samuel confronts Saul, he informs him that God would have given him an eternal dynasty if it were not for his disobedience. Consequently, "the LORD has sought out a man after his own heart; and the LORD has appointed him to be ruler over his people, because you have not kept what the LORD has commanded you" (1 Sam 13:14). This speech suggests not only that David is a man after God's own heart but also that what God sees in David's heart is obedience to divine commands, or at least the potential for obedience.

A second incident suggests that the capacity to exercise violence is also expected of David. Before instructing Saul to attack the Amalekites and "utterly destroy all that they have" (1 Sam 15:3), Samuel admonishes him: "Now therefore listen to the word of the LORD" (v. 1). Lest Saul misunderstand the expectations that he is to fulfill obediently, Samuel specifies the kind and degree of violence expected: "Kill both man and woman, child and infant, ox and sheep, camel and donkey" (v. 3).

The narrator then reports that although Saul "utterly destroyed all the people with the edge of the sword" and "all that was despised and worthless," he "spared Agag and the best of the sheep and of the cattle and of the fatlings, and the lambs and all that was valuable and would not utterly destroy them" (vv. 8-9). Saul was not only disobedient; he also apparently lacked the capacity for an adequate level of violence: "He has turned back from following me, and has not carried out my commandments" (v. 11). When Samuel reports the divine displeasure to Saul, he specifies the disobedient act as the failure to exercise violence, reminding Saul that in his capacity as the LORD's anointed God sent him to "utterly destroy the sinners . . . and fight against them until they [were] consumed" (v. 18).

Samuel then informs Saul that God has given his kingdom to a neighbor "who is better than you" (1 Sam 15:28). What makes David better than Saul? Why is David a man after God's own heart? What does God see in David's heart that is not in those of his older brothers? The narrative context of the stories about Saul's rejection suggests a twofold answer: (1) obedience to the divine command and (2) a capacity for and ability to exercise violence in executing the divine agenda.

Although these are not necessarily the attributes typically promoted by character ethicists, they are the characteristics seemingly favored by God in the narrative. As God attempts to establish a sovereign nation, obedience to the divine agenda of violent subjugation takes precedence over faithfulness to a personal moral code. Obedience, not moral character as it is usually defined, is the divine priority.

Even though the narrator may subtly attempt to subvert or at least call into question God's selection of David through repeated references to physical characteristics, the teller of the tale must finally acknowledge that divine sovereignty prevails over human rationalizations and reservations. God ultimately rejects Saul's reasons for disobedience, overrules Samuel's choices for the ideal king, and selects David as the future monarch. The introductory anointing scene thus concludes with a powerful reminder that God, not humans, is sovereign: "the spirit of the LORD came mightily upon David from that day forward" (1 Sam 16:13).

Varying Perspectives on David's Character

David's physical appearance continues to play a significant role in the unfolding of his character, as does the sovereignty of God. David's introduction into the story prepares not for a future philosopher king but for an anticipated warrior king. Yet before David gains a reputation as a warrior, he is portrayed as Saul's personal comforter. In response to God's ongoing affliction of Saul with "an evil spirit," Saul's courtiers propose music therapy and suggest that the afflicted monarch "look for someone who is skillful in playing the lyre," someone who will play for the suffering king and make him "feel better" (1 Sam 16:16). That someone is, of course, David. A warrior is anticipated, but a healer arrives.

A recitation of David's credentials by one of Saul's courtiers blurs the contrast between anticipation and actuality. He tells Saul that David "is skillful in playing, a man of valor, a warrior, prudent in speech, and a man of good presence; and the LORD is with him" (1 Sam 16:18). On the one hand, David is a talented musician and a skilled speaker. On the other hand, he is a courageous warrior and a man of battle. In addition to being a man of war, he is a man of good presence. Significantly, the Hebrew word translated "good presence" is frequently used with reference to women.[10]

This reference to David's appearance recalls the story of his selection by Samuel as king. The courtier's speech hints that David does not have the physique of a warrior, though he is described as one and is expected to be one. Implied is something unmasculine or even effeminate about David's physical appearance. On the one hand, this perspective makes explicit what was implicit in the previous episode: David is a warrior. On the other hand, it specifies Samuel's apparent reservations about David's warrior physique or lack thereof.

The characterization of David in this scene, juxtaposed with that of the previous scene, suggests an emerging complexity in his portrayal. David is ex-

---

10. Gen 29:17; Deut 21:11; 1 Sam 25:3; and Esth 2:7.

pected to be a warrior, yet he functions as a musician; violence is anticipated, but tranquility prevails as he soothes Saul's troubled spirit. A masculine physique is assumed; however, a less than macho appearance is described. As a complex character, David defies easy classification.

Yet one aspect of David's résumé as recounted by the courtier remains consistent with his portrayal in the rest of the story, namely, the perception that "the LORD is with him" (1 Sam 16:18). As the larger story develops, the presence of God with David is not only perceived by other characters in the story and reported by the narrator but also experienced by David himself. David's concomitant success is not only implied by the narrative juxtaposition of assessments and incidents but also explicitly stated by David himself. Notwithstanding the inclusion of alternate perspectives, the narrative of King David unfolds with divine sovereignty trumping human expectations and desires. David is clearly the chosen monarch.

Divine perceptions and pronouncements define the parameters of David's character. Yet within these divinely established expectations, David will assert his human freedom to defy and disobey, as well as to consent and comply. He will respect the divine expectations, and he will repent of his human infractions. As a result, David will approach life from a perspective best described as pragmatic pietism or pietistic pragmatism. This theological position contributes to an evolving complexity in the portrayal of David that ultimately defines his humanly flawed but divinely favored character.

This character dynamic begins to emerge through a second perspective on David's introduction into Saul's court. The episode begins by sketching a political rather than personal affliction for Saul and the Israelites. A confrontation between the Philistine and Israelite armies begins when the Philistine warrior Goliath challenges the Israelite army presided over by Saul. Goliath mocks the Hebrew army — "Why have you come out to draw up for battle?" — and challenges them to battle — "Choose a man for yourselves, and let him come down to me" (1 Sam 17:8).

The challenge is typically masculine: it casts aspersions on the masculinity of the opponent and provokes a confrontation that will be resolved by combat. At stake is a life of either domination or domestication, honor or humiliation. As if to emphasize his own hegemonic masculinity, Goliath concludes his challenge: "Give me a man (*'îš*), that we may fight together" (v. 10). This assertion of masculine prowess and bravado contrasts sharply with the timidity of a frightened Israel whom the narrator assesses as "dismayed and greatly afraid" (v. 11).

The focus of the narrative then shifts to an introduction of David as an unlikely opponent for Goliath. As the youngest son of Jesse, David tends his fa-

ther's sheep and runs supplies to his three older brothers who have followed
Saul to the battlefield. In the ensuing narrative, David, the emerging warrior, is
variously evaluated by other characters: (1) Eliab, his brother, considers him irresponsible, (2) Saul regards him as immature, and (3) Goliath impugns his
masculinity.

Arriving on the battlefield, David asserts his presence with a twofold response. Even though he has presumably heard conjectures about the reward for
killing Goliath, he initially asks: "What shall be done for the man who kills this
Philistine and takes away the reproach of Israel?" (v. 26). He then expresses his
political patriotism and religious indignation over the Philistine challenge:
"For who is this uncircumcised Philistine, that he should defy the armies of the
living God?" (v. 26)

The speech shows that David is concerned about what is in his own best
interest as well as what is in the best interest of Israel. He sees the situation as an
opportunity for personal advancement, but he is also loyal to his people and
faithful to his God. As he perceives it, the Philistine challenge is not merely a
challenge to "the armies of Israel" but to the "armies of the living God." It is also
not simply a Philistine challenge but an "uncircumcised Philistine" challenge.
The additional adjective, along with the characterization of the Hebrew army,
emphasizes David's theological allegiance to the chosen people of Israel and his
abhorrence of the pagans of Philistia.

That David expresses his concern about this conflict in terms of personal
priority and national prestige and that he is politically and theologically
shocked by Goliath's challenge and yet is able to consider it an occasion for personal advancement suggest a complex character, a distinctive mix of egoism
and altruism. Such complexity exemplifies David's stance of *pietistic pragmatism:* his commitment to God occasions opportunities for personal advancement, and occasions for personal advancement offer opportunities to advance
the agenda of God.

Such subtleties, however, are lost upon David's older brother Eliab whom
he supplanted as the heir apparent to King Saul, for the narrator reports that
"Eliab's anger was kindled against David" (1 Sam 17:28). He questions why David has come to the battlefield and suggests that in doing so he is acting irre-
sponsibly, leaving the sheep alone in the wilderness. Having thus accused David, he concludes his speech: "I know your presumption, and the evil of your
heart; for you have come down just to see the battle" (1 Sam 17:28).

Through this reintroduction of the "heart" motif, the narrator may again
be implicitly subverting God's assessment of David, suggesting that the
evaluative criterion for divine and human character ethics differ significantly.
Whereas David was earlier considered a warrior after God's own heart, his

brother now maintains that David's heart is "evil," though "evil" seems to be associated with an irresponsible understanding of the battle as entertainment, not politics.

Flippantly dismissing Eliab's hostile accusations with two dismissive questions ("What have I done now? Was it not but a word?" [v. 29]), David next faces Saul's more cautionary assessment of his youthful immaturity in which his physical appearance is again an issue. Summoned by Saul, David boasts with the aggressive bravado of a warrior: "Let no one's heart fail because of him; your servant will go and fight with the Philistine" (v. 32). After assessing his physical appearance, Saul counters: "You are not able to go against this Philistine to fight with him; for you are just a boy, and he has been warrior since his boyhood" (v. 33).[11] David is just a boy, as opposed to a man, and Goliath has been a warrior, that is, a man, *even* in his boyhood.

Responding to Saul's critique, David asserts his requisite maturity by citing at some length and in considerable detail his credentials as a shepherd who has successfully protected his flock from lions and bears. That he has killed predators supports his contention that he can kill Goliath. However, his ability to protect his flock is not just a secular enterprise; it is also a theological one. David acknowledges that his success is not the result of his own prowess but the result of his protection by God. He argues: "God who saved me from the paw of the lion and from the paw of the bear will save me from the hand of this Philistine" (v. 37). Pragmatically, David is aware that to be successful in his world he needs to acquire and develop survival skills, survival skills involving the implementation of violence. Yet, pietistically, he attributes his survival to divine agency.

In granting David's request to prove himself against the Philistine, Saul also invokes divine protection: "Go, and may the LORD be with you" (1 Sam 17:37). Saul then proceeds to hedge his bet and outfit David in the garb of a traditional warrior, giving him his own armor, helmet, and sword. Yet David's youth and inexperience are again underscored through the narrator's observation that the armed, armored, and helmeted David "tried in vain to walk, for he was not used to them" (1 Sam 17:39). In a speech repeating the same information, David acknowledges both his immobility and his inexperience: "I cannot walk with these; for I am not used to them" (1 Sam 17:39). That these accessories to warfare will not work for David also suggests the complexity of David's character. David will not be garbed as a warrior, but neither will he be deterred from his mission; he may not be skilled with the usual weapons of a warrior, but neither does he approach his opponent unarmed. Accordingly, the narrator relates

---

11. My adaptation of the NRSV translation to reflect more literally the Hebrew.

that David prepared for combat by selecting "five smooth stones" and "drew near to the Philistine" with "his sling in his hand" (1 Sam 17:40).

So armed, David meets the third challenge: Goliath's hegemonic deprecation of David's masculinity. The narrator observes that when Goliath saw David, "he disdained him, for he was only a youth, ruddy and handsome in appearance" (1 Sam 17:42). Goliath rejects David as a worthy opponent both because he is a boy and not a man and because his physical appearance seems unmasculine.

Once again, David's physical appearance becomes a character issue. From Goliath's perspective, David is "ruddy and handsome in appearance." Similar features were cited by the narrator prior to God's designating David as the one whom Samuel should anoint as king. David is described as "ruddy with beautiful eyes and a good appearance" (1 Sam 16:12). Prior to David's employment as Saul's music therapist, a courtier also describes David as "a man of good presence" (v. 18). Whatever specific attributes these descriptors suggest, they apparently are not characteristic of warrior masculinity. God has not selected as future monarch a man with a traditionally masculine and presumably warrior-like appearance. Hence, David is despised by Goliath.

The challenge by a man of subordinate masculinity is an insult to Goliath's hegemonic masculinity. Goliath states the offense: "Am I a dog, that you have come to me with sticks?" (1 Sam 17:43). He then counters with an assertion of his own virulent warrior masculinity: "Come to me, and I will give your flesh to the birds of the air and to the wild animals of the field" (v. 44). David's response to the challenge acknowledges Goliath's own warrior masculinity along with its weapons — "You come at me with sword and spear and javelin" — which he contrasts with his own nontraditional masculinity and its weapons — "But I come to you in the name of the LORD of hosts, the God of the armies of Israel, whom you have defied" (v. 45). He then invokes his own masculine prowess: "This very day the LORD will deliver you into my hand, and I will strike you down and cut off your head" (v. 46). Appearances aside, David can and will engage in aggressive, hostile actions. Confessing confidence in God's ability to work through his human skill with a sling to defeat Goliath, David's speech is yet another expression of his pietistic pragmatism.

At the conclusion of the combatants' preliminary and obligatory verbal encounter, complete with boasts and taunts, the narrator summarizes the actual physical battle. David kills the Philistine giant, striking him in the head with a stone from his sling, and in the time-honored fashion of warriors severs Goliath's head. Thus David begins to fulfill the divine mandate to conduct policy through the politics of violence.

Throughout the ensuing story of David's continuing success against the

Philistines, the storyteller insistently, persistently, and consistently asserts divine presence with David. The narrator relates that Saul feared David "because the LORD was with him [and] had departed from Saul" (1 Sam 18:12). Summarizing David's campaigns against the Philistines, the narrator notes: "David had success in all his undertakings; for the LORD was with him" (1 Sam 18:14). As if to reinforce the storyteller's own perceptions, the narrator reports Saul's awareness: "But when Saul realized that the LORD was with David, . . . Saul was still more afraid of David" (1 Sam 18:28-29). Whatever human skill and appearance David possesses, he is ultimately successful because of divine favor.

Thus far, the narrative offers several portrayals of David and assessments of his character. God regards him as a worthy successor to Saul, a man after God's own heart. Yet as chair of the search committee, Samuel finds it difficult to select David because he lacks the requisite royal physique. Saul's courtiers offer him as a music therapist. His brother considers him irresponsible. Saul regards him as immature. Goliath rejects him as less than masculine. David sees himself as a well-prepared, though unconventional, opportunistic warrior who lives faithfully in relationship with God. In addition, the narrator repeatedly notes that God was with David and concludes that whatever else he was, David was successful. The portrayal of David is nothing if not complex.

The Ambiguous Consequences of Obedience

Not only is David's character portrayed as complex, but the consequences of actions emerging from this character are not unambiguous. David's successful campaigns against the Philistines indicate his fulfillment of and commitment to divine expectations of a warrior. His successes also earn him the "love" of first one and then another member of the royal family, in addition to the Hebrew people: (1) "Saul loved him greatly" (1 Sam 16:21), (2) Jonathan "loved him as his own soul" (1 Sam 18:3), (3) "All Israel and Judah loved David" (1 Sam 18:16), and (4) "Saul's daughter Michal loved David" (1 Sam 18:20).

However, the violence that brings David fame and acclaim soon jeopardizes these relationships. David as the warrior inspires the women of Israel to herald him with the following refrain: "Saul has slain his thousands, and David his ten thousands" (1 Sam 18:7). The narrator tersely reports Saul's response to this accolade: "Saul was very angry" (1 Sam 18:8). Perceiving David as a threat to his monarchy, Saul acts on his anger and attempts to assassinate David.

These unsuccessful attempts on David's life necessitate a temporary exile from his kingdom. With the help of two of Saul's children, David escapes from Saul, but his safe passage also separates him from Jonathan and Michal. David subsequently seeks refuge among the Philistines, thereby separating him from the final member of the original quartet who "loved" him: the Hebrew people. The violence that initially gained David both divine and human favor has now alienated and separated him from all but God, with whom he presumably continues to find favor.

Obedience and the Character of David

Rejecting Saul, God commits to David. However, at this juncture in the story the divine commitment is provisional, not unconditional. Before the commitment is made irrevocable in 2 Samuel 7, David must reciprocate and demonstrate both his obedience to God and his commitment to exercise violence vis-à-vis Israel's enemies.

Once Saul is defeated by the Philistine army, David initiates measures to assume the monarchy for which he was anointed. In so doing, he confronts three critical situations: internal, external, and theological. Internally, he must consolidate his power base and unite a divided people. Externally, he must decisively defeat the Philistine menace. Theologically, he must legitimize his reign. On these three fronts, David receives numerous opportunities to demonstrate his obedience.

As David seeks to consolidate his monarchy, his first reported act is to inquire about the divine agenda. Before making overtures to Judah, David asks God: "Shall I go up into any of the cities of Judah?" (2 Sam 2:1). After receiving a favorable reply, he presses for specifics and is told to go to Hebron. Once he has established residency there, he is approached by the people of Judah, who anoint him as king over the house of Judah. The episode shows David respecting the divine prerogative and receiving the monarchy of Judah.

The following episode, however, shows David attempting to negotiate a similar arrangement with survivors from Saul's supporters. David initially praises the people of Jabesh-gilead for their loyalty in burying Saul and invokes a blessing upon them. He then promises loyalty from both God and himself: "Now may the LORD show steadfast love and faithfulness to you. And I too will reward you because you have done this thing" (2 Sam 2:6). On the basis of these divine and human promises, David makes his appeal: "Therefore let your hands be strong, and be valiant; for Saul your lord is dead, and the house of Judah has anointed me king over them" (v. 7). He implies that the courageous response to the death of their king would be to anoint him king as the people of Judah have done. They refuse. Abner "made," rather than "anointed," Ishbaal, the only surviving son of Saul, king over "all Israel" (v. 8).

Significantly, David is portrayed in this episode as invoking divine favor without first seeking it. The previous episode showed David initiating measures that would result in his being anointed king of Judah by seeking and receiving divine authorization. By way of contrast, this episode shows him taking action without first securing divine approval. He does, however, assume divine favor, since he promises it to Jabesh-gilead in return for their support. The error of David's assumption is revealed by the report of Ishbaal's coronation.

These episodes are significant for what they reveal about David's character and about the divine constraints placed upon the free exercise of that character. Once again the narrator portrays an assertive David who is willing to take advantage of situations and use them for his own benefit, as well as that of others and even God. Yet David's success depends on divine approval. When he acts assertively after securing divine authorization, he succeeds. When he acts without it, he fails.

Only after a "long war between the house of Saul and the house of David" (2 Sam 3:1) and after the assassination of Abner and Ishbaal does David succeed. On this occasion, David does not make a direct appeal for support. He merely makes himself available as a viable alternative to the existing situation. Just as the people of Judah "came" to David at Hebron and "anointed" him king after the death of Saul, all the tribes of Israel "came" to David at Hebron and "anointed" (not "made") him king after the death of Ishbaal (2 Sam 5:1-3). After establishing kinship ("Look, we are your bone and flesh"), they acknowledge David's personal accomplishments as well as his providential favor: "While Saul was king over us, it was you who led out Israel and brought us in. The Lord said to you: It is you who shall be shepherd over my people Israel, you who shall be king over Israel" (vv. 1-2). Thus, the supporters of Saul concede divine favor and cede David the monarchy. David is successful not because he seized or even negotiated power but because his opponents realized the involvement of God and acquiesced to God's demands.

Following the accounts of how David became king over all Israel and Judah, the narrator uses the story about David's capture of Jerusalem to reinforce the notion of David's divine favor. After noting that David renamed the fortress the "city of David," the narrator comments that "David became greater and greater, for the Lord, the God of hosts, was with him" (2 Sam 5:10). The narrator also climactically reports David's own awareness of divine favor: "David then perceived that the Lord had established him king over Israel, and that he had exalted his kingdom for the sake of his people Israel" (2 Sam 5:12). As he resolves his internal political crisis, David realizes that his success is the result of divine favor and that this favor is bestowed not for his own sake but for the benefit of all Israel.

Having attributed the resolution of David's internal political crises to divine favor, the narrator turns to David's external political crisis: eliminating the Philistine menace that had plagued Saul's reign and eventually led to his demise. Having learned of David's acquisition of Israel's monarchy, the Philistines launch an attack. David does not reflexively respond but obediently inquires of God: "Shall I go up against the Philistines? Will you give them into my hand?" (2 Sam 5:19). Only after receiving the divine command to "Go up" and assurances that God "will certainly give the Philistines into your hand" (2 Sam 5:19) does David counterattack. Once successful, David does not claim credit but acknowledges God's involvement: "The LORD has burst forth against my enemies before me, like a bursting flood" (2 Sam 5:20).

Unlike his strategy for dealing with internal political problems, David does not proceed on his own initiative. When the Philistines resume their attack, David does not presume continuing divine favor but again consults God. This time God does not instruct David to "go up" but devises an alternative strategy and accordingly directs him to "go around to their rear" (2 Sam 5:23). Even then God reminds David that "the LORD has gone out before you to strike down the army of the Philistines" (2 Sam 5:24). In reporting David's success, the narrator states that "David did just as the LORD commanded him" (2 Sam 5:25). Thus, the resolution of David's external crises, like the resolution of David's internal crises, depends on David's respect for and obedience to the divine prerogative.

Having secured the throne of Judah and Israel, David attempts to secure the legitimization of his reign by obtaining possession of the ark of God and transferring it to Jerusalem. In initiating such action, however, David once again presumes divine favor without necessarily securing it. The narrator reports only that "David and all the people of Israel with him set out and went from Baale-judah, to bring up from there the ark of God" (2 Sam 6:2). But as previous episodes have shown, favor presumed is not favor granted.

The procession is abruptly halted when it reaches the threshing floor of Nacon where the oxen stumble and Uzzah, one of the ark's attendants, touches the ark to steady it. The narrator uses this occasion to report God's anger: "And the anger of the LORD was kindled against Uzzah; and God struck him there because he reached out his hand to the ark" (2 Sam 6:7). This episode shows David in opposition to God. God is angry at David because he has again acted without authorization. Yet God's anger is matched by David's anger. The narrator reveals that "David was angry because the LORD had burst forth with an outburst upon Uzzah" (2 Sam 6:8). Unlike God, David cannot act upon his anger; he can only acquiesce, for the narrator further discloses that "David was afraid of the LORD that day" (2 Sam 6:9). David therefore stops the procession and leaves the ark in the house of Obed-edom. His submission, though, is not without insight. That David realizes he has acted without divine authorization is indicated when he rhetorically asks: "How can the ark of the LORD come into my care?" (2 Sam 6:9).

David resumes the procession of the ark to Jerusalem only after a sign of divine approval. When a report that God had blessed Obed-edom and all his household reaches David, he correctly interprets this as a sign of renewed divine favor. Having learned God's intentions and received the authorization he previously lacked, David resumes and completes the transfer of the ark to Jerusalem.

As David seeks to resolve the internal, external, and theological crises facing his administration, his personal ambition conflicts with his commitment to God. At times, he assumes favor without first securing it. Yet he will not acquire the thrones of Judah or Israel without an acknowledgment of divine sovereignty. Nor will he protect their autonomy from Philistine attacks without divine involvement. Not through his own initiative will he legitimate his reign.

Davidic Character and Covenant

Ultimately, David's monarchy will be legitimated in ways David could not anticipate. Unprecedented divine initiative, not human effort, guarantees the Davidic monarchy. The Davidic dynasty will be secured through a divinely initiated covenant rather than through human possession of the ark. The account in 2 Samuel 7 begins with a reminder of God's sovereignty. The narrator characterizes the setting as a time when David "was settled in his house" and God "had given him rest from all his enemies around him" (v. 1). David again mistakenly interprets the situation and seeks to use the internal and external peace to build a house for God.

Through the prophet Nathan, God informs David that the deity did not then and never had desired a house. God reminds the former shepherd that he was designated as ruler over Israel, identified not as David's people but as "my [i.e., God's] people." Furthermore, God affirms the agenda of violent conquest and God's solidarity with David: "I have been with you wherever you went, and have cut off all your enemies from before you" (v. 9). The affirmation asserts that David's success, however attributable to his own political and military skill, ultimately derives from God.

Having confronted the present and reviewed the past, God promises David a future, a future again contingent upon divine involvement: "I will make you a great name, like the name of the great ones of the earth" (v. 9). Not only will David's political legacy be secure, but Israel's future will be guaranteed: "I will appoint a place for my people Israel and will plant them, so that they may live in their own place, and be disturbed no more" (v. 10).

Preliminaries aside, God then comes to the point of this new revelation to David: instead of David building a "house" (i.e., a temple) for God, God will establish a "house" (i.e., a dynasty) for David. "The LORD will make you a house. When your days are fulfilled and you lie down with your ancestors, I will raise up your offspring after you, . . . and I will establish his kingdom" (v. 12). God promises David, "Your house and your kingdom shall be made sure forever before me; your throne shall be established forever" (v. 16).

The promises to David, though unconditional, are qualified by the familial nature of the relationship: "I will be a father to him, and he shall be a son to me. When he commits iniquity I will punish him with a rod such as mortals use, with blows inflicted by human beings" (v. 14). David and his dynastic descendants will be punished for transgression, but the punishment will not involve the loss of the kingdom: "But I will not take my steadfast love from him, as I took it from Saul" (v. 15).

The divine commitment to David in the form of a royal grant signals a new phase in the relationship between God and David. God previously required of Saul both obedience and the implementation of a violent agenda against Israel's enemies. When Saul was unable to fulfill either requirement, God provisionally turned to David. That David was able to implement the divine agenda is uncontested. That he was consistently obedient is problematic. That David is willing to take risks, willing to fill leadership vacuums, and willing to take advantage of critical situations and turn them to his own (and God's) advantage is also uncontested. Such assertiveness and confidence find favor with God despite their potential for occasional disobedience. Making allowances for such lapses, God affirms David and rejects Saul. God apparently approves of David's brand of pietistic pragmatism even with its potential for transgression.

Indeed, David's response to the covenant is a typical example of pietistic pragmatism. He is initially awed that someone as insignificant as he should receive such divine favor. He wonders: "Who am I, O Lord GOD, and what is my house, that you have brought me thus far?" (2 Sam 7:18). He realizes: "this was a small thing in your eyes, O Lord GOD" (v. 19). He acknowledges: "according to your own heart, you have wrought all this greatness" (v. 21). And he praises: "Therefore you are great, O LORD God" (v. 22).

David's pietistic response resonates with previous narrative themes. God rejected Saul because the deity wanted "a man after his own heart." God selected David over his brothers because the deity looked at "the heart" of David instead of "the eyes." Now David verbalizes the congruence between the divine heart and his own and acknowledges that "this small thing" has been brought about "according to [God's] own heart" and that this small thing in God's eyes is perceived as "great" by humans (vv. 18-21).

David's pragmatic response dictates a series of imperatives. He begins demanding assurances that the divine promises will be fulfilled: "And now, O LORD God, as for the word that you have spoken concerning your servant and concerning his house, confirm it forever; do as you have promised" (v. 25). He concludes by requesting a confirming blessing: "Now therefore may it please you to bless the house of your servant forever, so that it may continue forever before you" (v. 29).

The report of the Davidic Covenant offers a quintessential example of David's pragmatic pietism. On the one hand, he pietistically receives the gift of the dynasty praising God's greatness, and, on the other hand, he pragmatically presses God to fulfill the promise.

The Character of David and the Divine Agenda

As if to reinforce the violent nature through which David's throne was established in perpetuity and David's obedient implementation of that divine agenda, the narrator follows the report of the Davidic Covenant with a summary of David's conquests (2 Samuel 8). Thematically uniting the catalog of David's victories is the sevenfold repetition of the verb "to strike down" (2 Sam 8:1, 2, 3, 5, 9, 10, 13). Divine involvement in these bloody defeats is also emphasized by a twofold repetition of the phrase: "the LORD gave victory to David wherever he went" (2 Sam 8:6, 14). The summary clearly indicates David's obedience to the divine command to execute violence. Again, the narrator emphasizes that David's success as monarch does not result solely from his own skill but rather from his being the recipient of divine favor and, as such, the chosen implementer of a divine agenda of violent subjugation of opponents, both internal and external.

Once David is established as monarch and his kingdom is consolidated, the critical issue becomes: How will the warrior king govern? Can a life-long man of violence rule in times of peace, in times of "rest from all his enemies around him" (2 Sam 7:1)? The answers to these questions come quickly and provide an additional perspective on David's character. The warrior king cannot easily preside over a kingdom at peace. David's divinely approved obedience to an agenda of violence compromises his ability to rule effectively and justly.

As the incident preceding the Ammonite war shows, his reputation for violence jeopardizes his offering of condolences upon the death of the Ammonite king. Accordingly, David's benevolent actions are viewed with suspicion by his former foes, who provoke a conflict, during which the warrior king stays in Jerusalem while his armies fight on the battlefield. Yet violence manifests itself in personal rather than political ways. However the story of David and Bathsheba is read, whether constructively, deconstructively, or reconstructively, David is guilty of an abuse of power. Neither contentious nor conscientious parsing of the narrative will alter the situation: David wields his political power for personal gain.

The portrayal of David's use and abuse of this power focuses on several repetitions of the verb "to send." As the episode begins, he *sends* his army to battle the Ammonites. Later when David sees Bathsheba bathing, he *sends* for information about her. Even after learning she is the wife of one of his soldiers, Uriah the Hittite, he *sends* for her. Upon learning that she is pregnant, he *sends* a message to his general Joab requesting that Uriah be *sent* to him. When Uriah refuses to cooperate and spend the night with his wife, David *sends* him back to the front with a letter commissioning his own death. When the deed is done, David again *sends* for Bathsheba, who is specifically identified as the wife of Uriah; she then becomes David's wife and bears him a son.

Whereas God previously looked with favor upon the heart of David, God now looks upon the deeds of David and is displeased. In response, God "sent Nathan to David" (2 Sam 12:1). The balance of power has shifted. God, not David, now exercises the authority "to send," that is, the power to initiate, alter, and control the course of events.

Through the fictive tale of the rich man and the poor man, Nathan manipulates David to pronounce judgment upon an abuser of power. Through the words "You are that man" (2 Sam 12:7), Nathan forces the identification of David with the offender. With characteristic piety, David seems to accept the identification, acknowledging: "I have sinned against the LORD" (2 Sam 12:13).

Consistent with previous value judgments, "evil" is defined in relation to divine perception. Evil is evil done "in the eyes of the LORD." The phrase "to do evil in the eyes of . . ." is repeated three times in this episode. Initially when David counsels Joab not to be concerned about the excessive casualties incurred in the assassination of Uriah, he instructs him: "Do not let this thing be evil in your eyes, for the sword devours now one and now another"[12] (2 Sam 11:25). The matter was, nonetheless, evil in the sight of God, and the narrator tersely reports: "The thing that David did was evil in the eyes of the LORD" (v. 27).[13]

---

12. My more literal adaptation of the NRSV translation.
13. My translation.

Finally, Nathan questions: "Why have you despised the word of the LORD, to do what is evil in his eyes?" (2 Sam 12:9).[14]

The threefold repetition of the phrase suggests the difference between divine and human perceptions regarding the use of violence, a difference in which divine sovereignty prevails over David's human hegemony of power. God can authorize violence, but David cannot. David can implement a divinely authorized agenda of violence, but he cannot initiate his own. As consequence of David's striking Uriah, God strikes David's son. Furthermore, as a consequence of committing murder with the sword, the sword is destined to remain in David's house.

Although David's response to his son's death confuses his courtiers, it is typical of the pietistic pragmatism that circumscribes his character. In an apparent reversal of custom, David pietistically enacts the mourning rituals for his son as long as the child is alive. Pragmatically, he resumes normal life once the child has died. His explanation is again both theological and realistic: "While the child was still alive, I fasted and wept; for I said, 'Who knows? The LORD may be gracious to me, and the child may live.' But now he is dead; why should I fast? Can I bring him back again? I shall go to him, but he will not return to me" (2 Sam 12:22-23).

Years of political violence have infected David's moral character. Violence divinely sanctioned and executed in pursuit of military objectives yields violence exercised in the quest to fulfill individual desires. The victims of interpersonal crimes — sexual assault and murder — replace the casualties of war and civil unrest.

Nevertheless, this infection does not jeopardize David's piety and respect for God's sovereignty. Though blind to his own character flaws, David recognizes and condemns moral failure in others; once he recognizes his own transgressions, David readily confesses and repents. His anguished response to the illness of his son and his intercession on his behalf are further expressions of his repentance and remorse, reflections of a genuine and renewed piety.

David seems to have learned from the incident a new respect not only for God but also for the nature of human relationships. Following the death of the child, he did not "send" for Bathsheba, but he "went to her" and "consoled" her (2 Sam 12:24). In this instance, Bathsheba is specifically and more intimately identified as "his wife" (2 Sam 12:24). From this relationship, Solomon is born. David's repentance and acts of contrition earn him renewed favor from God. Following the birth of Solomon, the narrator informs us that God "sent a message by the prophet Nathan" (2 Sam 12:25). This time the message

14. My more literal adaptation of the NRSV translation.

does not result in the death of the child but in naming him Jedidiah, "Beloved of the LORD."

Pragmatic Pietism

Favor restored does not mean punishment revoked. Nathan's judgment that "the sword shall never depart from your house" (2 Sam 12:10) describes the situation in which David must live the remainder of his life. David responds to the ultimate consequences of his disobedience with a typical pragmatic pietism.

David's children adopt various forms of their father's violent behavior. Amnon rapes his half-sister Tamar. Her brother Absalom then murders Amnon. Exiled to Geshur, Absalom lives estranged from his father for several years. After an uneasy return and superficial reunion, Absalom instigates a rebellion. In a reprise of the "heart" theme, the narrator notes that "Absalom stole the hearts of the people of Israel" (2 Sam 15:6), thereby providing him with the constituency necessary to initiate a coup. When a messenger informs David that "the hearts of the Israelites have gone after Absalom" (v. 13), he responds by instructing his servant: "Get up! Let us flee, or there will be no escape for us from Absalom. Hurry, or he will soon overtake us, and bring disaster down upon us and attack the city with the edge of the sword" (v. 14). These instructions portray a submissive David who takes flight instead of launching his own aggressive counterattack.

As David leaves Jerusalem, he encounters a variety of supporters among whom are Zadok and Abiathar, two loyal priests. They bring with them the ark of God, the traditional sign of God's presence and protection. David responds to the situation with characteristic pragmatic pietism as reflected in two speeches.

In the first speech, he instructs the two priests: "Carry the ark of God back into the city. If I find favor in the eyes of the LORD, he will bring me back and let me see both it and the place where it stays. But if he says, 'I take no pleasure in you,' here I am, let him do to me what seems good in his eyes"[15] (vv. 25-26). The reintroduction of the "ark" motif and the "eyes" motif at this juncture in the story is significant, for it suggests that David has learned from his previous experiences of trying to manipulate the location of the ark in order to secure favor for himself. By sending the ark back, David is implicitly refusing to accept the protection guaranteed by its presence. Instead, David will rely on God alone to determine the outcome of Absalom's rebellion rather than on the tactical maneuvering of symbols representing God's presence. David has

---

15. My more literal adaptation of the NRSV translation.

learned not only to respect the sovereignty of divine prerogative but also to honor the unequivocal authority of divine perception. Hence, he begins and ends his speech with the phrases "in the eyes of God" and "in his eyes."

Even though David pietistically places his trust in divine justice, his pragmatic realism does not allow him to wait complacently for God's intervention. His second speech suggests that his theological commitments are coupled with practical, assertive human action. He further instructs Zadok: "Look, go back to the city in peace. . . . See, I will wait at the fords of the wilderness until word comes from you to inform me" (vv. 27-28). The loyal priest will act as David's spy within the city and report to him on Absalom's activity. David thus begins to formulate and implement the pragmatic component of his counter strategy against Absalom's rebellion.

Having both rejected the traditional guarantee of divine presence in favor of God's immediate involvement and having initiated human counteraction, David ascends the Mount of Olives, a peak specifically identified as a place "where God is worshipped" (v. 32). As David ascends, the narrator reveals David's emotional response to the situation: David climbed, "weeping as he went, with his head covered and walking barefoot" (v. 30). As he retreats from Jerusalem, David adopts the signs of mourning, mourning not the death of others but the potential loss of his kingdom.

David's ascent is interrupted by a messenger who informs him that "Ahithophel [is] among the conspirators with Absalom" (v. 31). Not only has Absalom initiated a revolt, but he has also recruited David's personal counselor. David knows that the outcome of the attempted coup may well depend upon the wise counsel of the defector Ahithophel, but he also knows that the purposes of God will ultimately determine the course of events. In his response to this situation, David is again portrayed as pietistically trusting in God but at the same time pragmatically aware that God's purposes are worked out through humans.

To the immediate report of Ahithophel's defection David responds by praying: "O LORD, I pray you, turn the counsel of Ahithophel into foolishness" (v. 31). Yet once David reaches the summit of the Mount of Olives, where he fortuitously meets Hushai the Archite, he resumes assertive, pragmatic action against Absalom. Employing Hushai as a double agent, David instructs him: "If you return to the city and say to Absalom, 'I will be your servant, O king; as I have been your father's servant in time past, so now will I be your servant,' then you will defeat for me the counsel of Ahithophel" (v. 34).

As the pieces of David's counter strategy to defeat Absalom come together, Hushai appears as the human answer to David's prayer. After gaining Absalom's trust, Hushai so persuasively opposes Ahithophel that Absalom accepts Hushai's David-friendly counsel rather than Ahithophel's Absalom-friendly advice. Pietistic in conception, pragmatic in implementation, David's plan succeeds. Yet it succeeds, as the narrator notes, because of divine favor: "For the LORD had ordained to defeat the good counsel of Ahithophel, so that the LORD might bring evil upon Absalom" (2 Sam 17:14).[16]

In the End, the Beginning

The final scenes of the David story mirror its initial episode, concluding as it began with a recounting of the violent acquisition of power, transferred on this occasion from father to son, from an aging and impotent David to a more youthful and opportunistic Solomon. However, the feats recounted are more Machiavellian than heroic. Pious words are again invoked to support violence. Yet the enacted violence is not defensive but offensive; it does not so much preserve national security as justify personal vengeance. Divine favor is presumed but not confirmed, though it seems to be implicitly granted through the successful succession of Solomon to the throne of David.

The transfer is prematurely occasioned by yet another rebellion. Initiated by Adonijah, alliances are quickly formed: two generals, two priests, and one prophet. Adonijah's key supporters include David's general Joab and his priest Abiathar. Remaining loyal to David are his general Benaiah, his priest Zadok, and the prophet Nathan.

Strategically the balance of power resides with Nathan the prophet, who previously announced David's divine favor in covenantal terms. Were it not for Nathan's intervention persuading David to name Solomon as king, Adonijah might have been successful. After Solomon is anointed king, he pardons Adonijah, and violence appears to have been averted.

On his deathbed, David counsels Solomon on the pragmatic actions needed to be a successful monarch. In so doing, he bequeaths to Solomon a legacy of violence, a legacy introduced with pietistic admonitions. David instructs Solomon not only to be strong and courageous but also to "keep the charge of the LORD your God, walking in his ways and keeping his commandments, his ordinances, and his testimonies" so that Solomon "may prosper in all that [he does] and wherever [he] turn[s]" (1 Kgs 2:3). Having indoctrinated his son, David then instructs Solomon to execute the general Joab, who often disobeyed his orders and finally betrayed him. He further orders the execution of Shimei, who also betrayed him during Absalom's rebellion.

Having learned from David's tactics of violence, Solomon not only im-

---

16. My more literal adaptation of the NRSV translation.

plements David's hit list but adds to it. His bloody purge is sparked when Adonijah requests through Bathsheba the services of David's final concubine Abishag. Solomon then commissions Benaiah to execute Adonijah, as well as Joab and Shimei. With each execution order, Solomon assumes the divine favor once bestowed upon his father David and accordingly invokes a divine mandate: "Now therefore as the LORD lives, who has established me and placed me on the throne of my father David, and who has made me a house as he promised, today Adonijah shall be put to death" (vv. 22-24); "So their blood shall come back on the head of Joab and on the head of his descendants forever; but to David, and to his descendants, and to his house, and to his throne, there shall be peace from the LORD forevermore" (v. 33); and "You [Shemei] know in your own heart all the evil that you did to my father David; so the LORD will bring back your evil on your own head. But King Solomon shall be blessed, and the throne of the LORD shall be established before the LORD forever" (v. 44).

This report of Solomon's executions recalls 2 Sam 8:1-14, a catalog of violent conquests by which David established his kingdom, and suggests that Solomon's kingdom was established through violence just as David's was. Obedience to a divinely sanctioned agenda of violence has shown itself to be an ambiguous virtue. Through various exercises of violence, David secured and consolidated power. Yet David was not able to control, confine, or constrain the violence. Violence consequentially contributed to the disintegration of his coalition and led to several direct challenges of his authority. Through the story of the generational transfer of pietistically pragmatic violence, the narrator suggests, perhaps again subversively, that the future does not bode well for a dynasty so founded and grounded.

Biblical Character Ethics Reconsidered

Almost every character in the David story has an opinion about David, everyone from Eliab to Absalom, from Goliath to Joab, from Saul to Michal, and from Abner to Nathan. Irrespective of the various human perceptions about David, the narrator continually reminds us of the sovereignty of God's perception. The variety of perspectives reveals the complexity of David's character. Although other characters in the narrative embody single traits, the narrator includes all of these perspectives. By acknowledging David's complexity, the narrative presentation rejects the reductionistic simplicity of any single perspective.

God chose David, a man after God's own heart, to implement the divine agenda of establishing an autonomous nation. Although David is often obedient to this agenda, he is not without self-interest as he executes it. Indeed, the entangling of divine expectations and personal ambitions often results in disobedience. Although divine commitment preserves the Davidic monarchy, it does not protect David from experiencing the frequently devastating consequences of his transgressions.

David is therefore not merely a purely "good" or "bad" character who must, in turn, be either admired or despised. Yet accepting complexity does not mean an indiscriminate endorsement of David's behavior. Nor does it encourage acquiescence toward an enigmatic portrayal of character whose very ambiguity silences all attempts at evaluation.

Although the narrative of King David is not the great American novel or even the great Hebrew epic, it is a candidate for the great human story in that it seeks to explain us to ourselves. It seeks, in novelist Philip Roth's earthy term, to present the human "stain":

> We leave a stain, we leave a trail, we leave our imprint. Impurity, cruelty, abuse, error, excrement, semen — there's no other way to be here. Nothing to do with disobedience. Nothing to do with grace or salvation or redemption. It's in everyone. Indwelling. Inherent. Defining. The stain that is there before its mark. Without the sign it is there. The stain so intrinsic it doesn't require a mark. The stain that *precedes* disobedience, that *encompasses* disobedience and perplexes all explanation and understanding.[17]

Dramatizing so effectively the human stain, the David story functions more as a counter-narrative than as a typical, normative story. The biblical tale poignantly recognizes that desired behaviors often cannot be separated from undesirable actions, and that acceptable accomplishments and achievements cannot readily be extracted from unacceptable consequences and calamities. David implements the divine agenda of violence and secures the autonomy of a new nation. Yet violence continues to plague both his personal and political life. Similarly, the nation born in violence matures into a nation that must live with the consequences of escalating violence.

Unlike the secular counter-stories of Rushdie and Roth, the biblical counter-story of David's human stain is also a confessing story. David's character is not just stamped with the human stain of self-interested pragmatism; it is also marked with a genuine piety that respects the sovereign righteousness of God. Throughout this confessing counter-story, David emerges as a pietistic pragmatist. He respects the divine favor granted him yet knows the limits of God's involvement. God provides him with opportunities that he must use to both his

---

17. Philip Roth, *The Human Stain* (New York: Houghton Mifflin Company, 2000), p. 242.

and God's advantage. That he fails to do so consistently indicates his human failings. That he repents of his sins, learns from his transgressions, and resumes his implementation of the divine agenda shows his reverent respect for divine authority. Flawed though he is, David is more importantly divinely favored.

That this confessing counter-narrative presents David as favored by God despite his flaws, that God accepts David's piety despite his pragmatism, reveals the limits of a traditional, normative character ethics approach. God chooses to implement through a humanly stained person the divine agenda of establishing an independent nation through violence. The limits of a traditional character ethics approach are further revealed in that the responsibility for the specter of violence that continues to haunt the nation and its founder must ultimately be shared by God, even though David is also held accountable for its misuse and abuse. Although David's dual nature, flawed but favored, may offend contemporary sensibilities, such complexity is preserved by the ancient storyteller. Although David's pietistic opportunism may distress modern ethicists, the often subversive biblical narrator offers the information without either implicit or explicit evaluative judgment.

A biblical character ethics based on confessing counter-narratives suggests an acceptance of complexity as an essential element of the human character and a recognition of the inability to isolate *beneficial* traits from *detrimental* ones, or even to identify the degree to which a given characteristic is helpful or harmful. As a result, the complexity and consequent ambiguity of biblical characters itself becomes the source for ethical *and* theological reflection.

What emerges then from a biblical character ethics is not a catalog of virtues and vices but a consideration of what it means to be human *coram deo*. What emerges is not so much a recommendation for constructive community action as a reconsideration of how to live within the ambiguity of human community. What emerges is not an admonition against destructive behavior but an affirmation of the equivocal nature of human beings. A biblical character ethics provides us neither with dogmatic assurance nor with problematic skepticism but with an enhanced understanding of the flaws and fecundities, the problems and possibilities, of human character. What emerges, finally, is a reflection of who we are and were and who we will certainly remain: complex, pietistic but pragmatic, humanly flawed individuals who are also the beneficiaries of divine favor.

A Character Ethics Reading of 1 Chronicles 29:1-25

M. Patrick Graham

To describe the present study in view of its title is not to claim a fully developed critical method for biblical interpretation called "character ethics criticism." To be sure, Stanley Hauerwas and others have crafted various approaches to Christian ethics that have as a central concern the formation of Christian character and community. In the case of Hauerwas, this focus on character has been closely linked with narrative and the importance of the biblical story for character formation.[1] Two assumptions that have proven critical for this work are "that human beings are creatures formed in communities marked by allegiance to a normative story, and that this formation can best be discussed in the language of character."[2] As far as the study of the Hebrew Bible is concerned, Bruce Birch has shown how questions related to "character" and "narrative" can illuminate Scripture.[3] Others have explored the Bible by means of these and related

---

1. Among the long list of works by Stanley Hauerwas, see especially "Toward an Ethics of Character," *TS* 33 (1972): 698-715; *A Community of Character: Toward a Constructive Christian Social Ethic* (Notre Dame, Ind.: University of Notre Dame Press, 1981); and *The Peaceable Kingdom: A Primer in Christian Ethics* (Notre Dame, Ind.: University of Notre Dame Press, 1983). From among those who have responded to Hauerwas, see especially Richard Bondi, "The Elements of Character," *JRE* 12 (1984): 201-18. Closely related to the subject of character is virtue. In this connection, Alasdair C. MacIntyre's *After Virtue: A Study in Moral Theory* (Notre Dame, Ind.: University of Notre Dame Press, 1981) has been most significant for Hauerwas.

2. Bondi, "Elements of Character," p. 201.

3. See, e.g., Bruce C. Birch and Larry L. Rasmussen, *Bible and Ethics in the Christian Life* (Minneapolis, Minn.: Augsburg, 1976; rev. ed., 1989); Bruce C. Birch, "Old Testament Narrative and Moral Address," in *Canon, Theology, and Old Testament Interpretation: Essays in Honor of Brevard S. Childs*, ed. G. M. Tucker, D. L. Petersen, and R. R. Wilson (Philadelphia: Fortress, 1988), pp. 75-91; idem, "Moral Agency, Community, and the Character of God in the Hebrew Bi-

categories,[4] but there is still no established approach to Scripture that can be isolated as "character ethics criticism."

This article has the modest aim of attempting a theological reading of 1 Chronicles 29:1-25 on the basis of the assumptions that Richard Bondi has identified as central to a character ethics approach to theology and ethics. Although it is not necessary to presume that the author of Chronicles self-consciously set out to write his narrative on the basis of these assumptions, it seems obvious that the Chronicler[5] had an appreciation for the role of community in the spiritual formation of persons and regarded the story of God's dealings with Israel and the nation's ancestors as in some way normative for the life of God's people. Therefore, it is hoped that by means of this approach additional insight will be offered on the biblical text and a way will be found to help the contemporary church hear anew the voices of the biblical writers — even that writer responsible for a much neglected part of the biblical canon.[6]

The analysis will begin with comments on the narrative setting of 1 Chronicles 29:1-25 within Chronicles as a whole, and especially its relation to 1 Chronicles 28. This will be followed by a narrative overview of 1 Chronicles 29:1-25, with attention given to some basic exegetical issues that lay the groundwork for the character ethics observations that will follow. Such a reading will consist of five parts: (1) a brief description of the assumptions of the approach, (2) analysis related to community, (3) analysis related to narrative, (4) analysis related to character in terms of four elements identified by Bondi, and (5) a theological summary.

---

ble," *Semeia* 66 (1995): 23-41; and idem, "Divine Character and the Formation of Moral Community in the Book of Exodus," *Journal of Korean Old Testament Society* 8 (2000): 281-301.

4. See, e.g., Gordon Matties, *Ezekiel 18 and the Rhetoric of Moral Discourse*, SBLDS 126 (Atlanta: Scholars Press, 1990); and William P. Brown, *Character in Crisis: A Fresh Approach to the Wisdom Literature of the Old Testament* (Grand Rapids: Eerdmans, 1996).

5. "Chronicler" will be used here to designate the anonymous author of Chronicles, a work composed in Jerusalem in the last half of the fourth century. Ezra-Nehemiah was produced at a different time and by another author. For a concise treatment on these matters, see R. W. Klein, "Chronicles, Book of 1-2," *ABD* 1: 992-1002.

6. On the modern neglect of Chronicles, see M. Patrick Graham, "Setting the Heart to Seek God: Worship in 2 Chronicles 30.1–31.1," in *Worship and the Hebrew Bible: Essays in Honor of John T. Willis*, ed. M. P. Graham, R. R. Marrs, and S. L. McKenzie, JSOTSup 284 (Sheffield: JSOT Press, 1998), pp. 124-26, and the literature cited there.

Narrative Setting of 1 Chronicles 29

Chronicles may be divided into four parts: 1 Chronicles 1–9 consists of a series of genealogies; 1 Chronicles 10–29 reports on the reign of David; 2 Chronicles 1–9 treats the reign of Solomon; and 2 Chronicles 10–36 covers the reigns of the kings of Judah from Rehoboam to Zedekiah.[7] 1 Chronicles 29, therefore, forms the capstone of the Chronicler's treatment of David's reign, coming at the end of the final unit (chs. 21–29) that describes David's preparations for the construction of the temple,[8] and, appropriately enough, concludes with the sort of "Regnal Résumé" found in Samuel-Kings and later in 2 Chronicles.[9] Most of this final unit (chs. 21–29) is without parallel in the Deuteronomistic History. With the exception of verses 20-30, 1 Chronicles 29 is without parallel in the Hebrew Bible.

David summons an assembly of Israelite leaders in 1 Chronicles 28–29 in order to prepare for the construction of the temple and the succession of Solomon to the throne. These chapters form, therefore, a single unit that serves a transitional function: they conclude the Chronicler's account of David's reign and prepare for the description of Solomon's in 2 Chronicles 1–9.[10] Moreover, the chapters pick up the narrative of 1 Chronicles 22, with which they have many connections,[11] and the Davidic prayer in 29:10-19 may even function with

---

7. Alternatively, the two central sections (1 Chronicles 10–2 Chronicles 9) may be viewed as a single unit: Israel under David and Solomon. Sara Japhet, *I & II Chronicles: A Commentary*, OTL (Louisville: Westminster/John Knox, 1993), pp. 8-9.

8. First Chronicles 10–12 describes David's ascension to the throne; chs. 13–17 record his effort to establish the worship of Yahweh in Jerusalem; chs. 18–20 report David's wars. See Japhet, *I & II Chronicles*, pp. 10-11.

9. Simon J. De Vries, *1 and 2 Chronicles*, FOTL 11 (Grand Rapids: Eerdmans, 1989), p. 231.

10. Japhet, *I & II Chronicles*, p. 482; De Vries, *1 and 2 Chronicles*, p. 215.

11. 1 Chronicles 22 and 28–29 both report David's speeches that exhort Solomon to the faithful discharge of his royal duties, offer a historical retrospective that rehearses God's promise to David, and describe David's preparations for the construction of the temple. Cf. esp. Roddy L. Braun, *1 Chronicles*, WBC 14 (Waco, Tex.: Word Books, 1986), pp. 267, 279. On the function of 1 Chronicles 23–27 and its position between chs. 22 and 28–29, see Japhet, *I & II Chronicles*, pp. 406-10, who makes a convincing case for all these chapters deriving from the Chronicler. Rudolph Mosis (*Untersuchungen zur Theologie des chronistischen Geschichtswerkes*, FTS 92 [Freiburg: Herder, 1972], pp. 105-7) has challenged the authenticity of 1 Chr 29:1-19, and Mark A. Throntveit (*When Kings Speak: Royal Speech and Royal Prayer in Chronicles*, SBLDS 93 [Atlanta: Scholars Press, 1987], pp. 89-96) has modified his analysis at certain points, agreeing that vv. 1-9, 14b, and 16-17 are secondary, but holding that vv. 10-14a, 15, and 18 are "the original creation of the Chronicler" (p. 94). While this part of ch. 29 does indeed offer certain repetitions and creates tensions with the narrative (e.g., two coronations for Solomon), vv. 1-9 fit well within the context structurally and with regard to content, as well as reflect the language and

the anthology of psalmic material in 1 Chronicles 16:8-36 to "provide a framework to the whole section of chs. 17–29, which has been totally dominated by David's preparations for building the temple."[12]

While the narrative divisions within chs. 28–29 are generally clear and scholars have noted the important role that David's addresses play in this material, what has not been given adequate attention is the way the narrative progresses by means of a chiastic arrangement of an equal number of speeches and reports.

A.   **Report** that David assembles the people in Jerusalem (the presence of Solomon is unmentioned — though assumed — in all this) (28:1)

B.   **Speech** of David to the assembly and then to Solomon (28:2-10)

C.   **Report** that David gives God's temple plan to Solomon (28:11-19)

D.   **Speech** of David that exhorts Solomon to build the temple and promises the people's help (28:20-21)

D′.   **Speech** of David to the assembly, ending with an appeal (29:1-5)[13]

C′.   **Report** of the people's generous gifts and joy (29:6-9)

B′.   **Speech/Prayer** of David regarding the people's response, ending with an appeal to God (29:10-19)

A′.   **Report** of the people's response: worship and coronation of Solomon (29:20-25)

Such careful arrangement, in which reports largely alternate with speeches/addresses, creates balance and internal cohesion. This alternation of address and report also allows the Chronicler to use the former both to provide the rationale for the actions reported and to offer theological commentary on the actions. (Note especially in this connection the role that David's prayer in 29:10-19 plays in connection with the report of the people's gifts in vv. 6-9.) The central pair of units in this chiasm are both speeches by David to the other two parties in the narrative — Solomon and the assembly — and serve to highlight

---

ideas found elsewhere in Chronicles. The linguistic features indicating that both of David's addresses in 1 Chronicles 29 derive from the Chronicler were identified by S. R. Driver a century ago in "The Speeches in Chronicles," *The Expositor*, 5th ser., 1 (1895): 241-56; and "The Speeches in the Chronicles," *The Expositor*, 5th ser., 2 (1895): 286-308 (the second of these articles was written against Valpy French's contention that the Chronicler derived speech material from his sources ["The Speeches in Chronicles," *The Expositor*, 5th ser., 2 (1895): 140-52]).

12. H. G. M. Williamson, *1 and 2 Chronicles*, NCB (Grand Rapids: Eerdmans, 1982), pp. 185-86; De Vries, *1 and 2 Chronicles*, p. 222.

13. That the speeches D and D′ are separate and not a single address (like 28:2-10) is indicated by the narrative transition in 29:1a.

the two burdens of the narrative: the exhortation to Solomon to discharge his royal duty to build the temple and the exhortation to the leaders of Israel to support him in this effort.

The parties involved in these chapters are David, the assembly of Israelite leaders, and Solomon. David is the king, the recipient of God's promise and the one charged with conveying it to the next generation.[14] Solomon is passive and has little to do at this point: he receives the plan for the temple from David (28:11-19) and later the crown from the people (29:22b). The assembly plays a more important role immediately through their contributions for the construction of the temple and their acclamation of Solomon as king. In these ways, they serve as the intermediary between David and Solomon and between the plan for the temple and its construction.

Finally, it should be noted that throughout the narrative of reports and addresses — even with their historical retrospectives — there is a critical orientation to the future, to the *telos* of David's reign, the construction of the temple by Solomon.

Narrative Overview

Chapter 29 begins with David's address to the assembly (vv. 1-5), in which he appeals to the leaders to assist Solomon with the construction of the temple.[15] Rhetorically, the speech is crafted in three parts, with the first and the third forming an inclusio. First, there is the appeal to the assembly to help Solomon by contrasting the greatness of the project with the youth and inexperience of Solomon and the difference between building a house for God and one for humans. The second and central part of the speech is an account by David of what he has done by way of assistance for the project: he has contributed enormous amounts of precious metals and stones, as well as other building materials, for the construction of the temple.[16] The final element in this address is David's in-

---

14. David's importance is further underscored by the fact that while others spoke, it is only the addresses of David that are reported by the Chronicler.

15. On the role of the king in temple building, see Arvid S. Kapelrud, "Temple Building, a Task for Gods and Kings," *Or* 32 (1963): 56-62. While Samuel-Kings makes Solomon the temple builder, the Chronicler divides this responsibility between David and Solomon but highlights David's role as the true cult-founder. See William Riley, *King and Cultus in Chronicles: Worship and the Reinterpretation of History*, JSOTSup 160 (Sheffield: Sheffield Academic Press, 1993), pp. 58-66.

16. It appears that David made contributions from the state treasury (v. 2) and from his own private resources (vv. 3-5a). On the problems associated with this list, see Japhet, *I & II*

vitation to the assembly to follow his own example,[17] phrased in terms of a question: "Who then will offer willingly, consecrating himself today to the LORD?" The appeal is a powerful summons for immediate action ("today") that must be generous (hithpael of √*ndb*, "to offer freewill offerings")[18] and directed toward God ("to the LORD") rather than toward the king, resulting in the consecration[19] of those who give. Such a characterization of Israelite laity with priestly terminology is especially striking in Chronicles, and yet it is precisely this striking usage that energizes and ennobles the Chronicler's account of David's appeal.

In response to David's challenge, the assembly gives freely (√*ndb*, as in v. 5) for the building of the temple an enormous sum of precious metal[20] and stones, as well as other building materials (vv. 6-8). The consequence of their great generosity is joy (√*śmḥ*) — joy for the people and for the king, because it was "with a whole *(šlm)* heart they had given freely to Yahweh" (v. 9). The theme of cultic joy is characteristic in Chronicles,[21] and in the present context it serves to indicate the willingness of the assembly to offer their gifts; that is, they were not given under compulsion.[22] The use of the phrase *blb šlm*, "with a whole (complete/per-

---

Chronicles, pp. 506-7. Gary N. Knoppers has shown that by means of contributions to or despoliations of Israel's treasuries, the Chronicler intends to indicate the nation's growth and prosperity or its destruction and decline, respectively. "Whereas Chr. relegates despoliations to negative phases in royal careers, he promotes dedications as illustrative of loyal conduct" ("Treasures Won and Lost: Royal [Mis]Appropriations in Kings and Chronicles," in *The Chronicler as Author: Studies in Text and Texture*, ed. M. P. Graham and S. L. McKenzie, JSOTSup 263 [Sheffield: Sheffield Academic Press, 1999], p. 205).

17. On David's paradigmatic function in Chronicles as an example of piety, see, e.g., Gary N. Knoppers, "Images of David in Early Judaism; David as Repentant Sinner in Chronicles," *Bib* 76 (1995): 449-70; and Howard N. Wallace, "What Chronicles Has to Say About Psalms," in *The Chronicler as Author: Studies in Text and Texture*, ed. M. P. Graham and S. L. McKenzie, JSOTSup 263 (Sheffield: Sheffield Academic Press, 1999), pp. 290-91.

18. See J. Conrad, "*ndb*," *TDOT* 9:219-26 (esp. pp. 222-23). The verb occurs in 1 Chr 29:5, 6, 9 (twice), 14, 17 (twice); 2 Chr 17:16.

19. The RSV's "consecrating himself" translates the Hebrew expression "to fill his hand," an expression that is used sixteen times elsewhere in the Hebrew Bible to refer to the consecration to priestly office (e.g., Exod 28:41; Lev 8:33; Num 3:3; Judg 17:5; 2 Chr 13:9; 29:31). See L. A. Snijders, "*ml'*," *TDOT* 8:301-6 (esp. p. 305).

20. The anachronistic use of the term "darics" (*'drknym*) in v. 7 provides one of the arguments for the dating of Chronicles in the Persian period or later, since these gold coins were first minted by Darius I in the late sixth century B.C.E. (Japhet, *I & II Chronicles*, p. 508).

21. See also in this chapter vv. 17, 22 and 2 Chr 15:15; 24:10. S. Japhet, *The Ideology of the Book of Chronicles and Its Place in Biblical Thought*, BEATJ 9 (Frankfurt: Peter Lang, 1989), p. 253.

22. On this point, see Yochanan Muffs, "Joy and Love as Metaphorical Expressions of

fect/peaceful?) heart," indicates that the assembly acted with singleness of purpose and without reservation.[23] This focus on the human heart in the context of a discussion of God's relationship with humans is found earlier in 1 Chronicles 28:9, when Solomon was urged by David to serve God with a "whole heart and with a willing mind" and was reminded that God searches every heart. It occurs later in chapter 29 in David's prayer. In all this, it is clear that the Chronicler is concerned not only about overt human actions but also about a spiritual issue, the disposition of the human heart toward God.[24]

David's prayer in verses 10-19[25] praises God for the successful efforts by king and people to provide for the construction of the temple and in the process offers theological commentary on those efforts.[26] Verses 10-13 praise the majesty, power, and sovereignty of God and offer thanksgiving.[27] The implication, of course, is that God is the source of all wealth and bestows it freely, a point that is critical for David's remarks that follow. Verses 14-16 make this

---

Willingness and Spontaneity in Cuneiform, Ancient Hebrew, and Related Literatures," in *Christianity, Judaism and Other Greco-Roman Cults: Studies for Morton Smith at Sixty,* ed. Jacob Neusner, SJLA 12/3 (Leiden: E. J. Brill, 1975), pp. 1-36; idem, "Love and Joy as Metaphors of Volition in Hebrew and Related Literatures, Part II: The Joy of Giving," *JANES* 11 (1979): 91-111, esp. pp. 108-11.

23. Similar collocations occur in 1 Chr 12:38-39; 28:9; 2 Chr 15:17; 16:9; 25:2. On the use of *lb, lbb* in the Hebrew Bible generally, see H. W. Wolff, *Anthropology of the Old Testament* (Philadelphia: Fortress, 1974), pp. 40-58, and for the debate about differences between Deuteronomistic and Chronistic usage, see H.-J. Fabry, *"lb, lbb," TDOT* 7:431-32.

24. See esp. Japhet, *Ideology,* pp. 250-53.

25. Samuel E. Ballentine ("'You Can't Pray a Lie': Truth *and* Fiction in the Prayers of Chronicles," in *The Chronicler as Historian,* ed. M. P. Graham, K. G. Hoglund, and S. L. McKenzie, JSOTSup 238 [Sheffield: Sheffield Academic Press, 1997], p. 262) points out that the Chronicler "has surrounded the Davidic-Solomonic concern for the temple with the most concentrated collection of prayers in the entire composition" (1 Chr 14:10; 16:8-36; 17:16-27; 21:8, 17; 29:10-19; 2 Chr 1:8-10; 5:13; 6:14-42 [cf. 7:3, 6]). Similarly, Mark A. Throntveit maintains that David's prayers in 1 Chr 17:16-27 and 29:10-19 "effectively frame David's participation in the process of planning for the building of the temple" and so highlight the event ("The Chronicler's Speeches and Historical Reconstruction," in *The Chronicler as Historian,* ed. M. P. Graham, K. G. Hoglund, and S. L. McKenzie, JSOTSup 238 [Sheffield: Sheffield Academic Press, 1997], p. 232), thus drawing on Otto Plöger's "Reden und Gebete im deuteronomistischen und chronistischen Geschichtswerk," in *Festschrift für Günther Dehn. Zum 75. Geburtstag am 18. April 1957 dargebracht von der Evangelisch-Theologischen Fakultät der Rheinischen Friedrich Wilhelms-Universität zu Bonn,* ed. Wilhelm Schneemelcher (Neukirchen: Kreis Moers, 1957), pp. 35-49.

26. Japhet (*I & II Chronicles,* p. 504) analyzes it into three parts: doxology (10b-13), presentation and dedication to God of the freewill offering (14-17), and supplication (18-19).

27. On the Chronicler's view of God's dominion over the world, based on the idea of his ownership and providential rule, see esp. Japhet, *Ideology,* pp. 54-55.

point, contrasting the eternity of God ("Blessed art thou . . . for ever and ever," v. 10) with the transience of humans ("as a shadow are our days on the earth," v. 15)[28] and affirming that all the wealth given for the construction of the temple by David and the assembly is simply wealth that God had already given to Israel — the people take from one of God's hands, as it were, and return a portion to God's other hand. The effect of such affirmations is to undercut any basis for human pride in religious achievement that might arise from the gifts contributed to God. In addition, while the rhetorical question of verse 14 has an obvious import, it may suggest another as well. First, it asks, "How is Israel able [i.e., wealthy enough] to offer such gifts to God?" The answer follows immediately in verse 14b, "Because God has blessed Israel." The question may also, though, be intended to hint at another consideration (to be raised later): "How is Israel able [i.e., generous enough] to offer such gifts to God?" The answer that comes in verses 18-19 is, "Because God has directed the hearts of David and his people to God." In verses 17-18, David moves on to the issue of the motivation of such gifts, asserting that God's concern with the human heart is welcomed in this case, because just as David has made his contributions in "uprightness of heart," so the assembly has offered their gifts freely ("with joy"). Then he looks to the future and asks that God preserve such motivations and dispositions of the heart (v. 18). This last petition in David's prayer serves to undermine further any human pride before God because of the contributions. Even the motivation to give to God is not entirely within human power; God's grace is necessary here as well.[29] Finally, David's attention turns to Solomon once more, and he asks that God give a "whole heart" to this future king of Israel so that he will obey God in every way and build the temple.

The final report of the chapter (vv. 20-25) describes the activities that bring the gathering to a close.[30] First, the people bless God[31] and then bow and

---

28. On the use of contrast as a rhetorical technique in the prayer generally, see Japhet, *I & II Chronicles*, p. 505. On this metaphorical use of sojourning and its sociopolitical connections, see Daniel J. Estes, "Metaphorical Sojourning in 1 Chronicles 29:15," *CBQ* 53 (1991): 45-49.

29. Cf. also 2 Chr 29:36; 30:12; and Japhet, *Ideology*, pp. 254-55, esp. n. 182 regarding the Targum and Pseudo-Rashi.

30. On this pericope, see esp. William Johnstone, *1 Chronicles 1–2 Chronicles 9: Israel's Place among the Nations*, vol. 1 of *1 and 2 Chronicles*; JSOTSup 253 (Sheffield: Sheffield Academic Press, 1997), p. 289.

31. The verb √*brk* occurs four times in ch. 29, twice in v. 10, where David blesses God, and twice in v. 20, where the assembly blesses God in response to David's command to do so. David appears in this (as with the gifts for the temple) as one who does first what he summons the people to do. David's position takes on priestly overtones: he has summoned the people to assemble, exhorted them to make freewill offerings, and then called upon them to bless God.

prostrate themselves before both God and King David (v. 20), an extraordinary statement of reverence connecting God and David, but one that illustrates the high regard of the Chronicler for David.[32] Then the people offer sacrifices, eating and drinking "with great gladness" *(śmḥ),* and crown Solomon king, anointing him as prince and Zadok as priest.[33] Culminating his coronation, Solomon receives the pledges of loyalty from those assembled (vv. 21-25).[34]

Character Ethics Analysis of 1 Chronicles 29

Though the focus of chapters 28–29 is on the building of the temple, the Chronicler's real interest is in the instruction of later generations about how to live before God and secure God's blessings.[35] In this way, the Chronicler was doing "ethics" of a sort, and he rooted this firmly in the narrative of God's dealings with Israel. He was interested not only in offering models of virtue and vice for later generations[36] but also in motivation (why did this or that ruler act as he did?)[37] and in issues related to spirituality (was this one's heart directed toward God or not?).[38] In this regard, the Chronicler identifies a critical element in the evaluation of human behavior, namely, the relation of humans to God.[39] He insists on considering human virtue and behavior in relation to God

32. Such a statement is not found elsewhere in the Hebrew Bible. Japhet, *I & II Chronicles,* p. 512; Wilhelm Rudolph, *Chronikbücher,* Handbuch zum Alten Testament 1, 21 (Tübingen: J. C. B. Mohr, 1955), pp. 191-92.

33. The reference to this coronation as "a second time" for Solomon (v. 22) seems to be a later gloss (it is lacking in the LXX and in the Syriac, perhaps influenced by 1 Chr 23:1 or 1 Kings 1–2). Japhet, *I & II Chronicles,* p. 514; cf. Williamson, *1 and 2 Chronicles,* p. 187. On the relation of v. 22 to 1 Chr 23:1, see Braun, *1 Chronicles,* p. 288.

34. For the chronology of these events — i.e., whether "on the next day" (v. 21) should be understood as a gloss (Japhet) or to mean that the sacrifices took place over two days (Braun) — see Japhet, *I & II Chronicles,* p. 513; Braun, *1 Chronicles,* p. 287.

35. See esp. Rodney K. Duke, *The Persuasive Appeal of the Chronicler: A Rhetorical Analysis,* JSOTSup 88, BLS 25 (Sheffield: Almond, 1990), pp. 47-51.

36. The Chronicler follows the practice of the Deuteronomistic Historian, placing evaluative summary statements — typically at the beginning or end of a regnal account — that often compare kings to David or other exemplary rulers (e.g., 2 Chr 29:2).

37. See, e.g., Amaziah's pride in 2 Chr 25:17-19 and Uzziah's in 2 Chr 26:16-21.

38. See, e.g., 1 Chr 29:17-19; 2 Chr 30:18-19.

39. Such a theological perspective radically transforms an anthropocentric ethics concerned just about the development of human virtue (is this person generous, just, etc.?). Drawing from Calvin, Hauerwas writes, "[K]nowledge of self [is] tied to knowledge of God . . . we know ourselves truthfully only when we know ourselves in relation to God" (*Peaceable Kingdom,* p. 27).

and within the context of the story of God's dealings with humanity through Israel.[40] All this, of course, robs human ethical achievement of its standing before God and introduces further complexity by challenging absolute claims of self-mastery over human behaviors and dispositions.[41]

In the character ethics approach, it is assumed "that human beings are creatures formed in communities marked by allegiance to a normative story, and that this formation can best be discussed in the language of character."[42] The idea that humans are formed in communities is generally recognized and undergirds the narratives of both the Hebrew Bible and the New Testament.[43] Similarly, the importance of normative stories for the formation of humans in community is widely accepted, both for communities described in Scripture and for those outside it.[44] Whether "the language of character" is the best strategy for discussing this formation is debatable, but for the purposes of this paper it will be assumed to be the case. To study character is to study "the self in relation,"[45] and the four elements of character that Bondi has identified ("capacity for intentional action," "involvement with the affections and passions," "subjection to the accidents of history," and "capacity of the heart")[46] are "fundamental aspects of human existence which are formed or combined in a characteristic way of being in the world."[47] These elements assume a unique configuration with each person and are subject to change over time.[48]

So, we will begin the treatment of 1 Chronicles 29 by taking up the role of community, move to the topic of narrative, and then conclude with a discussion of character under Bondi's four rubrics noted above.

40. Chronicles begins with the creation of *Adam* and establishes a creation-wide concern in the first chapter of 1 Chronicles. In addition, the Chronicler shows a concern for Gentiles later on. Hezekiah includes them in his Passover observance (2 Chr 30:25), and it is Pharaoh Neco who delivers the word of God to King Josiah (2 Chr 35:22). See Japhet, *Ideology*, p. 351.

41. On this point, see Japhet, *Ideology*, pp. 254-55.

42. Bondi, "Elements of Character," p. 201.

43. See most recently, Birch, "Divine Character," pp. 285-88; idem, "Moral Agency," pp. 24-29.

44. Hauerwas, *Community of Character*, pp. 9-86, esp. pp. 9-12. From a comparativist perspective, myths or traditional stories have been held to serve the function of establishing social bonds. See, e.g., Robert A. Oden, Jr., "Myth and Mythology," *ABD* 4:946-56, esp. p. 952.

45. Bondi, "Elements of Character," p. 204.

46. Bondi, "Elements of Character," pp. 204-5.

47. Bondi, "Elements of Character," p. 204.

48. Bondi, "Elements of Character," p. 204.

Community

While the Chronicler appreciates and even champions individual examples of virtue or faithfulness to God (e.g., Solomon, 2 Chr 30:26; prophets who resisted evil kings, 2 Chr 24:20-22; etc.), the real focus of his narrative is on the larger community — the people of Israel.[49]

Although David's generous support for the building of the temple was laudable, it was incomplete until the assembly joined him in this. Similarly, his support for Solomon as king required the acclamation of the people. Therefore, while the Chronicler had something to offer individual readers, the author's primary focus was on the creation of a community that was faithful to God, that is, a community of a certain kind of character.[50] Hence, it is a unified community, supporting its leaders and acting together, that is nurtured, and the Chronicler's interest was in the formation and strengthening of its identity.[51] This was to be accomplished through the telling of the people's story (hence, the Chronicler produced his own version of Israel's story) and — particularly germane for a consideration of 1 Chronicles 29 — through the creation and maintenance of institutions, such as the temple and its staff, to support that identity.[52] In this connection, it is worth noting that the story about the building of a temple becomes in Chronicles a story about the building of a community. In Chronicles, the temple "is not a litmus test of an orthodoxy that would exclude the nonconformist but rather a focus of unity for the people of Israel as a whole."[53]

---

49. "[T]he Chronicler sought to redress the balance with those who, concerned to avoid the dangers of syncretism and assimilation, had allowed the Jerusalem community so to close in on itself as even to exclude some who had a rightful claim to participation. He achieved this by demonstrating from the history of the divided monarchy that a faithful nucleus does not exclude others, but is a representative centre to which all the children of Israel may be welcomed if they will return" (H. G. M. Williamson, *Israel in the Books of Chronicles* [Cambridge: Cambridge University Press, 1977], p. 140).

50. "Throughout the Hebrew Bible Israel is understood and presented as a moral community" that "serves as the shaper of moral identity, the bearer of moral tradition, the locus of moral deliberation and the agent of moral action" (Birch, "Divine Character," p. 281).

51. See Jonathan E. Dyck, *The Theocratic Ideology of the Chronicler,* Biblical Interpretation Series 33 (Leiden: Brill, 1998), p. 226.

52. On the role of institutions in the formation — and sometimes, corruption — of identity, character, or virtue, see esp. MacIntyre, *After Virtue,* pp. 194-96.

53. H. G. M. Williamson, "The Temple in the Books of Chronicles," in *Templum Amicitiae: Essays on the Second Temple Presented to Ernst Bammel,* ed. William Horbury, JSNTSup 48 (Sheffield: JSOT Press, 1991), p. 19. By associating the temple with Israel's earlier traditions (e.g., the temple site with Abraham and the cave of Machpelah [1 Chr 21:22-25; Genesis 22–23] and its

In addition, the assembly of political, military, and economic leaders that is called together in 1 Chronicles 28:1 is seen as representative of the larger community. As they listened and responded to David, so the reader sees "all Israel" following its king. Such descriptions of leaders coming together at important junctures in the nation's history is typical in Chronicles and serves an important rhetorical and theological purpose. It shows the people united — with "one heart" (2 Chr 30:12) — in their activity and following the leadership of God's anointed, the king (1 Chr 29:22-23), who regards himself as part of the community and counts himself among them as they stand before God.[54] As the assembly engages in these activities under David's direction, they represent all the people, and thus all Israel is involved. In such a setting, the community of Israel receives religious instruction from its leaders so that it can be faithful to God, and thereby becomes the source of the blessing and praise offered to God.

Finally, as the assembly engages in cultic ritual together in their contributions, blessing of God, and sacrifices, they also engage in a political event, the coronation of Solomon. In fact, one could argue that all the activity described in chapter 29 has as its *telos* the construction of the temple, an external good that will glorify God, be the place where Israel's story is proclaimed, celebrated, and memorialized in religious ritual, and sustain the worship of God by Israel. Such worship, of course, is the outward expression of an internal good, faith in God — their wholehearted commitment to God, which pleases God (as one who tests hearts and has pleasure in uprightness, v. 17) — and this faith finds expression in certain practices: obedience to God's commandments, testimonies, and statutes (v. 19). There is, thus, a dialectical relation between external and internal goods, and the Chronicler's immediate focus is an external good (the temple) that will support institutionally certain practices (prayer, sacrifice, praise of God) that will in turn nurture the internal goods of faith and devotion to God.[55] Accordingly, the vision of David (and the *telos* of his efforts) does not end with the completion of the temple. Rather, David is concerned about the future disposition of Israel's heart: Will it be directed toward God or elsewhere (see v. 18)? Such a question speaks to the issue of *telos* in terms of both chronology ("forever") and destination or loyalty ("toward you [God]"). Through these practices David and the assembly affirmed their relationship with the

---

design with the tabernacle of Moses [1 Chronicles 21]), the Chronicler takes pains to link the temple "back by physical ties of unbroken continuity with institutions or settings of far earlier days, before the divisions of the monarchical period, let alone his own much later time, had surfaced" (Williamson, "The Temple in the Books of Chronicles," pp. 19-20).

54. Note the use of the first person plural in David's prayer (1 Chr 29:13, 15, 16, etc.).

55. For a description of the inherent conflict between institutions and the practices they are intended to support, see MacIntyre, *After Virtue,* pp. 194-96.

wider community of Israel that served God in such ways, but also with those earlier generations that had served YHWH similarly.[56]

Narrative

As mentioned earlier, one of the critical assumptions of Hauerwas's character ethics approach is "that human beings are creatures formed in communities marked by allegiance to a normative story."[57] That a normative story played a central role in the formation of the people of Israel is commonly acknowledged by students of the Hebrew Bible,[58] and in the case of Chronicles, the author's commitment to a normative story is obvious. Sometimes this is conveyed through references to the patriarchs Abraham, Isaac, and Israel or other persons, but on other occasions through references to specific events.[59] In addition, it is clear that the Chronicler has based his narrative not just on stories that were commonly known and retold in Israel but also on earlier compositions.[60] Finally, it is clear that the narrative of Chronicles is itself an attempt to instruct later generations by retelling a story that has been told many times before and that has become normative for Israel.[61] In the process of this ethical

56. "To enter into a practice is to enter into a relationship not only with its contemporary practitioners, but also with those who have preceded us in the practice, particularly those whose achievements extended the reach of the practice to its present point" (MacIntyre, *After Virtue*, p. 194).

57. See above, especially Birch, "Old Testament Narrative." The observations of Stephen Crites on the essentially narrative form of human experience have become foundational for character ethics ("The Narrative Quality of Experience," *JAAR* 39 [1971]: 291-311).

58. See, e.g., Birch, "Divine Character," pp. 281-82; and more generally, the anthology gathered in Stanley Hauerwas and L. Gregory Jones, eds., *Why Narrative? Readings in Narrative Theology* (Grand Rapids: Eerdmans, 1989).

59. See, e.g., the genealogies in 1 Chronicles 1–9, often with their narrative expansions (e.g., 1 Chr 6:49).

60. On the Chronicler as an interpreter of traditions, see the enormously influential work of Thomas Willi, *Die Chronik als Auslegung: Untersuchungen zur literarischen Gestaltung der historischen Überlieferung Israels*, FRLANT 106 (Göttingen: Vandenhoeck & Ruprecht, 1972); the thorough study by Kim Strübind of the Chronicler's treatment of Jehoshaphat, *Tradition als Interpretation in der Chronik. König Josaphat als Paradigma chronistischer Hermeneutik und Theologie*, BZAW 201 (Berlin: Walter de Gruyter, 1991); and, most recently, the work of William M. Schniedewind, "The Chronicler as an Interpreter of Scripture," in *The Chronicler as Author: Studies in Text and Texture*, ed. M. P. Graham and S. L. McKenzie, JSOTSup 263 (Sheffield: Sheffield Academic Press, 1999), pp. 158-80.

61. On the nature of Chronicles as a history, see Isaac Kalimi, "Was the Chronicler a Historian?" in *The Chronicler as Historian*, ed. M. P. Graham, K. G. Hoglund, and S. L. McKenzie,

reflection and instruction by means of narrative, the Chronicler has also incorporated psalmic material, genealogies, speeches, and other genres into his work.[62]

As for 1 Chronicles 29, one finds the Chronicler keeping before his readers the broader narrative context for events that unfold. This is often done through references to God as the "God of Abraham, Isaac, and Israel, our fathers" (1 Chr 29:18) or simply as the "God of our fathers" (1 Chr 29:20), which remind his readers of the enduring faithfulness of God to the promises made to the patriarchs.[63] This larger effort is also aided by repeated references to other events in the story (e.g., God's promise to David and denial of his request to build the temple in 1 Chr 28:3-7), thus articulating a narrative that is infused with the constancy of God's faithfulness and is always related to the whole. Moreover, as the reader will find in the narrative of 2 Chronicles, the events of 1 Chronicles 28–29 provide the basis for all that follows concerning the temple and the worship of God in Israel. All this creates a web of connectedness, coherence, and wholeness for his literary production.

Character

While the Chronicler pays careful attention to what people do,[64] he is also concerned about motivation and issues of faith and character. The regnal summaries in Chronicles, for example, attend not just to issues of parentage, chronology, and succession, but also to ethical and religious characterizations or summaries for the kings. The latter assume a certain constancy or character for each king (Hezekiah "did what was right in the eyes of the LORD, according to all that David his father had done" [2 Chr 29:2]), allow for changes in this character to occur in the course of a reign (Joash was faithful to God in the first part of his reign but succumbed to the influence of evil advisors later on [2 Chronicles 24]), and recognize the ambiguities of human existence (Amaziah "did

---

JSOTSup 238 (Sheffield: Sheffield Academic Press, 1997), pp. 73-89; Japhet, *I & II Chronicles*, pp. 31-41.

62. On the Chronicler's use of various genres in his composition, see esp. the commentary by De Vries, *1 and 2 Chronicles*.

63. "The epithet 'God of the fathers' . . . in a variety of forms appears twenty-seven times in Chronicles. None of these instances is taken from the parallel source in Samuel-Kings. . . . The link between YHWH and the people is continuous and abiding; in every generation Israel's God is YHWH" (Japhet, *Ideology*, pp. 14-19).

64. The Chronicler's idea of divine retribution illustrates this especially well (Japhet, *Ideology*, pp. 165-76).

what was right in the eyes of the LORD, yet not with a blameless heart" [2 Chr 25:2]). In addition, the rest of the Chronicler's narrative richly illustrates these attempts to deal with human character.

As noted above, Bondi has analyzed character into four elements. Each will be taken up as a rubric for the reading of 1 Chronicles 29. It will come as no surprise, of course, that the yield will be greater in some cases than in others.

Capacity for Intentional Action

The first element of character that Bondi proposes is "the capacity of the self for intentional action," something that preserves "the notion of moral agency."[65] As is the case with other writers in the Hebrew Bible,[66] the Chronicler assumes generally that people are responsible for their actions. They choose their course of life and are capable of repenting from evil and turning to God.[67] The rhetoric of David's appeal to the leaders of Israel (29:1-5) assumes this capacity and is based on David's conviction that the character of the people is sufficiently well formed and devoted to God that they will respond positively to his challenge. Similarly, when David mentions that God tries the human heart and has pleasure in uprightness (29:17), the presumption is likely that humans are responsible for the disposition of their hearts and can determine whether uprightness will be found.

Nevertheless, the Chronicler seems to hold this assumption in tension with another one: God's grace is necessary for people to respond properly.[68] God is called upon to direct Israel's heart toward God (29:18) and to give to Solomon the disposition to serve and obey God wholeheartedly (29:19).[69] How these two conflicting principles are to be adjudicated is not addressed by the Chronicler.

---

65. Bondi, "Elements of Character," p. 205.

66. "From first page to last the Hebrew Bible assumes that all persons are moral agents. Who we are and how we act as individuals and as communities are considered by the Scriptures to be matters of moral accountability" (Birch, "Moral Agency," p. 23).

67. These ideas are worked out typically and most obviously in Chronicles by means of the author's "short-range retribution" theology, by which God punishes sin immediately. Robert North, "Theology of the Chronicler," *JBL* 82 (1963): 372-74. On the role of the prophets in this theological affirmation, especially as it relates to the later rabbinic idea of warning, see Japhet, *Ideology*, pp. 176-91.

68. It may not be the case that the Chronicler assumes that proper human response requires divine assistance, but there are instances in which the response is so exceptional (e.g., the extreme generosity of the people in 1 Chronicles 29; the rapidity with which events take place in 2 Chronicles 30) that divine assistance is firmly presupposed (cf. 2 Chr 30:12).

69. See the comments above in the "Narrative Overview" section on David's prayer.

So, what is one to make of all this? David calls on the people for *freewill* offerings, and when such are forthcoming, David responds with a prayer that thanks God for God's beneficence, which has made the people's offerings possible. Then David comments on God's role in disposing the human heart toward God. All this suggests that "freewill" is somewhat of an illusion: whenever one is devoted to God and expresses it in practices, God is to be thanked for having made that disposition possible. The reader, thus, is seduced by the narrative into congratulating David and the leaders of Israel for their generous gifts to God for the temple, only to have this subverted by David's declarations in prayer. We are first alerted to this issue in v. 14, when David asks God, "Who am I, and what is my people, that we should be able thus to offer willingly?" It seems reasonable to interpret David's rhetorical question as speaking only of the human ability (to give) that has been made possible by God's blessing of Israel with possessions from which they could offer gifts to God (although even here, the reference may include the matter of the disposition of the heart). In verses 15-16, though, David takes a more profound and spiritual step, declaring that even with God's provision of wealth for Israel, human beings require the grace of God to direct their hearts toward God. The mystery of human and divine interaction in repentance and devotion to God is never explained, and such ambiguity is not allowed by the Chronicler to dissuade him from holding the people of Israel absolutely responsible for their actions and for the dispositions of their hearts.

Involvement with the Affections and Passions

The second element of character that Bondi proposes is "involvement with the affections and passions." He elaborates, "If character is the language of the self in relation, then it must speak of feelings, for these are often the most telling features of personal and social relations. . . . Emotions and feelings . . . are sensors relating us to the world. . . ."[70] "*Affections* refer to those feelings which nurture, focus, express, or are consonant with deeply held apprehensions of the good life. *Passions* are those feelings which disrupt our apprehension of goodness and which, were we habitually to act on them, would be destructive of self and others and subversive of the character we seek to form."[71]

This element of character appears in a variety of forms in Chronicles,[72]

---

70. Bondi, "Elements of Character," p. 206.

71. Bondi, "Elements of Character," p. 207.

72. E.g., Rehoboam's love for his wife Maacah (2 Chr 11:21a); Jehoshaphat's fear of a large enemy army (2 Chr 20:3); and Uzziah's anger at the priests who opposed him (2 Chr 26:19a; etc.).

but in the text at hand it is encountered predominantly in one affection, the joy of David and the people.[73] It is only after the people bring their generous gifts for the building project that they rejoice, because they gave to God willingly and with a whole heart, and David joined them in their joy (v. 9). This joy is followed by David's prayer (vv. 10-19), by the assembly's blessing of God, and, finally, by sacrifices that they "ate and drank before the LORD on that day with great gladness" (v. 22a). This joy finds public expression and is related to external objects: other people, corporate activities by the assembly, and even God.[74] In addition, it adds to the richness of the narrative since it directs the eyes of the reader to something more profound and mysterious than the *realia* of history. Such indications attest the energy and emotional power of the actors in the narrative and, in turn, engage the emotions and feelings of the readers, inviting them to join king and assembly in their joy before God.

As testimony that the people's gifts were not coerced, this expression of communal joy by king and people is significant, as has been noted already. Their joy attests the sincerity of their acts of religious devotion to God. They had indeed consecrated themselves to God (v. 5b), and it was in uprightness of heart that both king and people had made their contributions to God (v. 17). Their joy is indeed presented as a positive element in the narrative, an affection that is consistent with the Chronicler's portrayal of the "good life" that is lived in fellowship with God. In light of Chronicles as a whole, one might even argue that such joy is characteristic of Israel when its heart is directed toward God.[75]

---

73. The Chronicler makes a certain rhetorical use of this emotion here and elsewhere. "[A]lthough on the whole Chr. rarely portrays the inner feelings of his characters, he frequently paints them as carrying out cultic activities with joy and singing. Such pleasant associations draw the audience toward proper cultic participation" (Rodney K. Duke, "A Rhetorical Approach to Appreciating the Book of Chronicles," in *The Chronicler as Author: Studies in Text and Texture*, ed. M. P. Graham and S. L. McKenzie, JSOTSup 263 [Sheffield: Sheffield Academic Press, 1999], pp. 132-33). In addition, Duke notes that the use of the speech genre creates an emotional appeal (p. 134). For a more general treatment of the Chronicler's appeal to the emotions of the readers, see Duke, *Persuasive Appeal*, pp. 139-47.

74. Bondi comments on the privatization of emotions and feelings and the moral problem that this raises: "Emotions and feelings can be privately experienced yet not significantly privatized, for though we do experience them inwardly, they by necessity have external objects in people, situations, symbols, or the natural world. We allow emotions to become merely private and thus open the way to the tyranny of fantastic desires when we discount the connection between feelings and the world so as to dismiss its moral relevancy, when we fail to heed what it might be that our anger, sympathy, depression, or lust is telling us about the way we are relating to our world" ("Elements of Character," p. 206).

75. See n. 22 above.

Such affections are to be nurtured and contrasted with the passion of greed and the unwillingness of people to give freely to God.[76] This contrast is suggested when David raises the issue of uprightness of heart and the motive for the giving that has taken place (v. 17).

In addition, the joy of David and the assembly is important for its role in portraying a coherent and unified *(šlm)* response of the people to God.[77] In this respect, it attests the unity of the community, something that was fractured when Rehoboam assumed the throne (2 Chronicles 10), was restored to a certain degree during Hezekiah's celebration of the Passover in Jerusalem (2 Chronicles 30), but essentially was continued to the Chronicler's day.[78]

Subjection to the Accidents of History

People are subject to the accidents of history "in three ways: (1) events which are beyond the control of any individual or group, (2) circumstances in which we simply find ourselves, and (3) the past, insofar as we cannot change what has already occurred."[79] By way of elaboration, it should be explained that the "circumstances in which we simply find ourselves" include the "givenness of our social, cultural, and temporal setting, as well as the beliefs, convictions, symbols, and stories which a given culture employs to understand itself and the world."[80] All these combine to constitute the dynamic context for character and its development. They cannot be separated from character, but they do not determine it in any absolute or mechanical way. Rather they are dynamically and intimately involved in the formation of character and have a substantial impact on its interpretation.

From the perspective of the Chronicler, there are several critical aspects of historical circumstance that have shaped the lives of the actors and continue to influence their behavior in 1 Chronicles 29. First, Israel's identity flows from its position as the people of God, who have inhabited the land since the time of

---

76. In Chronicles the issue of human greed vis-à-vis God is typically only hinted at, instead of overtly expressed, as in Neh 13:10-14 or Mal 1:6-14.

77. The references in Chronicles to a "whole heart" *(šlm lb, šlm lbb;* 1 Chr 12:38-39; 28:9; 29:19; 2 Chr 15:17; 16:9; 25:2) are suggestive. They appear to signify a disposition that is unified, and in 1 Chr 28:9 and 29:19, e.g., the expression is used to characterize an entire life. Perhaps this should be understood as the virtue of integrity or constancy that MacIntyre describes as "singleness of purpose in a whole life" and associates with Kierkegaard's statement that "purity of heart is to will one thing" *(After Virtue,* p. 203).

78. See n. 49 above.

79. Bondi, "Elements of Character," p. 207.

80. Bondi, "Elements of Character," p. 208.

Jacob.[81] They include not only those whose lineage can be traced to the patriarch Jacob/Israel but also others who now dwell in the land with them.[82] In addition, the centerpiece of the cult that David and his people had inherited, according to the Chronicler, was the tabernacle, and so it comes as little surprise that the cultic center that David seeks to establish is modeled on the tabernacle, and that the events of 1 Chronicles 28–29 parallel those of Exodus that describe the construction of the tabernacle. Just as God supplied Moses with the plans for the tabernacle, so David receives the plan for the temple from God in Chronicles, and just as Israel's freewill offering supplied materials for the tabernacle (Exod 36:2-7),[83] so the freewill offerings of the assembly of Israel provided materials for the temple (1 Chr 29:1-9).[84] The chronological setting for 1 Chronicles 29 is the transition from David's reign to that of Solomon and is absolutely critical to the narrative of the temple since the king who prepared for its construction will not live to see it through. Thus, this chapter adds to the narrative an element of suspense and tension. Will the people accept Solomon as their king? Will Solomon prove equal to the task of building the temple? Will people and king prove faithful to God in the days that lie ahead? The answers to these questions will prove crucial for the future of Israel and for its possession of the land (cf. 1 Chr 28:8). Finally, David is the recipient of God's promises (1 Chr 28:2-7), and Solomon has been chosen by God to succeed him and to build the temple (1 Chr 28:9-10).

All these factors of historical circumstance, of course, have their impact on the character of David and Israel, the primary human actors in the chapter at hand. Both have a clear identity as part of the people of Israel and stand squarely in the religious traditions of that people. David shows himself at the end of life fully engaged in the acceptance of God's promises and the comple-

---

81. The bond between the people and the land existed from the beginning and is continuous, as is the bond between a people and its god. See Japhet, *Ideology*, p. 386.

82. "According to the Chronicler's portrayal, there are no Gentiles in the land of Israel; all its dwellers are 'Israel,' either through their affiliation with the tribes, or as the attached 'sojourners'" (Japhet, *I & II Chronicles*, p. 46). See also Japhet, *Ideology*, pp. 267-351.

83. In the Exodus story, Moses had to restrain the people from contributing too much material for the tabernacle, so overwhelming was their generosity.

84. Some have called attention to the fact that the Chronicler has patterned some of his characters after notable figures in the traditions of Israel. Solomon's succession to David is cast so as to resemble Joshua's succession of Moses (Braun, *1 Chronicles*, p. 227; see also idem, "The Significance of 1 Chronicles 22, 28 and 29 for the Structure and Theology of the Chronicler" [Th.D. diss., Concordia Seminary, St. Louis, 1971], pp. 30-34; and H. G. M. Williamson, "The Accession of Solomon in the Books of Chronicles," *VT* 26 [1976]: 351-61). Solomon and Hiram's roles in the construction of the temple remind the reader of Bezalel and Oholiab in connection with the tabernacle (Raymond B. Dillard, "The Chronicler's Solomon," *WTJ* 43 [1980]: 296-99).

tion of all the tasks that God has entrusted to him. He is the model of obedience and energetic service to God, and he offers an example for all later kings in the leadership that he provides. The people, for their part, also offer later generations a worthy example of how Israel should follow their king wholeheartedly in service to God.[85] Their response to the needs of the temple and the approaching demise of David affirms and further establishes their character as a faithful community that can pass along its faith in God to the next generation by means of its exemplary conduct and strong religious institutions. Although Solomon plays a passive role in 1 Chronicles 28–29, and concern is expressed about his ability to follow David as king (29:1, 19), the Chronicler will show in the chapters that follow (see, e.g., 2 Chronicles 6–7) that David's prayers for Solomon were answered by God, and Solomon proved fully equal to the tasks set before him. In this way, through the later developments in his story, the Chronicler answers the questions raised above and shows the development of character.

Capacity of the Heart

Bondi designates the fourth element of character as "the capacity of the heart" and in doing so self-consciously draws

> on a longstanding metaphor which uses the heart to describe the center of our being, that about us which unites intellect and feeling on a fundamental and telling level. The heart is the seat of our deepest memories, of our imaginative exploration of other lives and times, of our yearning for union both of the self and with other people, ideals, and possible ways of life. I am suggesting we can also use the heart to describe the way stories offer us the symbolic language to ponder who we are, who we have been, and who we might become in the possible worlds of the future. Character and story are inherently connected because stories beckon the heart. . . . [Therefore] in our hearts we ponder ourselves and the world through memory and imagination, but we are also moved and drawn out by a desire for union with stories and their visions, a desire to become the sort of person envisaged in the story. We reach out, and in this reaching acknowledge we are drawn out.[86]

---

85. On this topic of characters in the Hebrew Bible offering examples for imitation by later generations, Birch observes, "None of the OT characters model moral behavior in such a consistent and intentional way [as Jesus]. Their stories reflect all the ambiguities and complexities of human experience and the struggle to find and live out faith relationships to God in the midst of life" ("Old Testament Narrative," p. 77).

86. Bondi, "Elements of Character," p. 210.

Bondi's usage of the term "heart" resonates well with the usage in the Hebrew Bible, where the focus is on the rational and volitional aspects of human life (planning, willing, etc.) rather than on the emotive or affective aspects.[87] In Chronicles, this is the case when "heart" language is used to indicate someone's intentions by noting that a king had something in his heart (1 Chr 22:7; 28:2; 29:17; 2 Chr 1:11; 24:4; 29:10) or that certain ones established their heart toward someone or a specific course of action (1 Chr 22:19; 29:8; 2 Chr 11:16; 12:14; 19:3; 20:33; 30:19) or that one acts with all the heart (2 Chr 15:12, 15; 22:9; 31:21). Similarly, God tests the human heart (1 Chr 28:9;[88] 29:17; 2 Chr 32:31). Elsewhere, there are references to kings' hearts being exalted in pride (2 Chr 26:16; 32:25, 26) or in God's ways (2 Chr 17:6) and to the heart being hardened (2 Chr 36:13). Hearts are also described as glad (2 Chr 7:10), generous (2 Chr 29:31), irresolute (2 Chr 13:7), upright (1 Chr 29:17; 2 Chr 29:34), one (2 Chr 30:12), and perfect or whole (*šlm;* 1 Chr 12:38-39; 28:9; 29:19; 2 Chr 15:17; 16:9; 25:2).

In 1 Chronicles 29, the people offered their gifts to God with a whole heart (v. 9), and David offered his in the uprightness of his heart (v. 17b); God is said to test the heart (v. 17a); and David prays that God will keep upright thoughts in his people's hearts (v. 18b), direct the people's hearts toward him in the future (v. 18b), and grant Solomon to serve him with a whole heart (v. 19a). This usage indicates the deepest engagement of David and Israel with God, that they have in fact committed themselves to God with sincere devotion, as is indicated by the generosity of their gifts, their joy in giving, and their worship. It is this sort of complete and wholehearted engagement and sincere devotion that God seeks, and so the people become the model for future generations — those for whom David prays in verse 18. Their commitment encompasses their memory of the ancestral tradition, their inner resolve and intentions, and their corporate economic, political, and religious activities. Through collaborative public actions, they find and confess their unity with one another, with their king, and with God. Their worship, in the end, defines their relationship to God and king, as well as their commitment to follow divine and royal leadership. The Chronicler has used language of the heart in a concentrated and powerful way in this chapter to signal God's concern about the disposition of the inner person and to indicate the completeness of Israel's devotion to God. This same concern is acted out in paradigmatic fashion in the giving of David and his people. In-

87. See the discussion in Wolff, *Anthropology of the Old Testament*, pp. 40-58, who designates *lb, lbb* "the most important word in the vocabulary of Old Testament anthropology" (p. 40), and that of Fabry, *"lb, lbb,"* pp. 399-437.

88. This text has been understood to indicate that God "searches all hearts," but J. G. McConville has proposed that it means that God seeks out (i.e., longs for) all hearts ("I Chronicles 28:9: Yahweh 'Seeks Out' Solomon," *JTS* n.s. 37 [1986]: 105-8).

deed, there is a consistent and integral relation between the people's actions and their dispositions. Through their gifts, they indicate their loyalties, and who they are is shown by what they do.

Theological Summary

The story of the building of the temple is a story of dedication to God and the building of a community of character.[89] The concern is not with the development of individual character — except perhaps in the case of David, where he becomes a model of devotion and godly leadership — but with the development of a community's character. And the character that is developed is not defined as generous, loving, just, or with any of the other virtues that might come to mind to characterize a people who have achieved moral perfection. Rather, the concern is defined in terms of the people in relation — to God and to God's anointed, the king.

The events of 1 Chronicles 29:1-25 occur at an important political and religious juncture in Israel's history. These two concerns merge in David's effort to enlist public support for the accession of Solomon and his most important task, the construction of the temple in Jerusalem. David models the character of a devoted servant of God who invests his energies and fortunes in an institution that will support the service of God for generations to come. As the chapter ends, the representatives of the people of Israel have accepted David's challenge to follow him in this commitment and so come to model the character that God's seeks in God's people: they are unified in their devotion to God and commitment to God's anointed. They have demonstrated their ability to decide, act, and invest their affections in a course of life that is consistent with the normative story they have received and that is responsive to the demands of

---

89. 1 Chronicles 29 has been an obvious text for sermons devoted to Christian giving (e.g., John Bonar, *A Sermon Preached at New-house in the West End of the Parish of Livingstoun* . . . [Edinburgh: John Reid, 1719]; Charles Burroughs, *A Sermon, Delivered in St. Paul's Chapel, New-York* . . . [New York: Protestant Episcopal Press, 1830]), but the most skillful preachers have been able to weave the theme of giving with that of the importance of a building for worship and with that of spiritual commitment to God. In his sermon for the dedication of the Harriet Holland Memorial Chapel in Philadelphia, for example, Henry A. Boardman elaborated on the importance of the structure for instruction in the Christian faith, noted its significance as "a Memorial of your Christian liberality, piety, and zeal," but then called on those assembled: "With the dedication of your chapel, dedicate yourself afresh to God" (*What Christ, the Anointed of God, Has Done for Woman; What Woman Has Done for Christ* [Philadelphia: Samuel A. Loag, 1874], p. 28).

their circumstances. It is their devotion and submission to God, their commitment of life and fortune to a relationship with God and to God's future for Israel, that is the subtext of the Chronicler's narrative. Consequently, just as David becomes the standard that the Chronicler uses to judge later kings, so the
example of the people in this chapter offers a model for later generations.[90]

90. On this issue of characters in the Hebrew Bible modeling moral behavior, see Birch,
"Old Testament Narrative," p. 77. In terms of the macro-picture of the Chronicler's message, one
could do worse than the summary offered by Adam C. Welch: "Through C's account of David's
life we can hear an authentic voice speaking from the period after the Return. What he had it in
his heart to say was that David gave Israel two great gifts, the kingdom and the temple, the two
institutions which dominated and coloured the national life in Palestine. The one had gone
down the wind and could never return. It was conditioned by faithfulness on the part of its
kings to the purpose which brought it into being. . . . But David's other gift of the temple remained, and in it and its worship was the hope for the future of Israel" (*The Work of the Chronicler: Its Purpose and Its Date*, Schweich Lectures 1938 [London: Oxford University Press, 1939],
p. 29).

Narrative Ethics, Character,
and the Prose Tale of Job

Carol A. Newsom

One of the emerging areas of interest in literary studies and in biblical studies in recent years has been that of "narrative ethics." This term actually covers a wide range of interests, questions, and perspectives, not all of which I will address.[1] My own concern with this topic emerged out of my work with the prose tale of Job. I take that narrative to be, generically, a kind of didactic tale or example story.[2] As such, it is self-consciously concerned with the moral formation of its readers or hearers. But anyone who has looked at the history of reception of the prose tale knows that it has elicited the most astonishing variety of responses, from deep admiration to utter revulsion. Consequently, I wanted to find a way of thinking systematically about the moral claims of this text, the

1. Major works include J. Hillis Miller, *The Ethics of Reading* (New York: Columbia University Press, 1987); Wayne Booth, *The Company We Keep: An Ethics of Fiction* (Berkeley: University of California Press, 1988); Martha Nussbaum, *Love's Knowledge: Essays on Philosophy and Literature* (New York: Oxford University Press, 1990); Tobin Siebers, *Morals and Stories* (New York: Columbia University Press, 1992); David Parker, *Ethics, Theory, and the Novel* (Cambridge: Cambridge University Press, 1994); Adam Zachary Newton, *Narrative Ethics* (Cambridge, Mass.: Harvard University Press, 1995); Robert Eaglestone, *Reading After Levinas* (Edinburgh: Edinburgh University Press, 1997); Jane Adamson, Richard Freadman, and David Parker, eds., *Renegotiating Ethics in Literature, Philosophy, and Theory* (Cambridge: Cambridge University Press, 1998). In biblical studies, see Gary A. Phillips and Danna Nolan Fewell, eds., *Bible and Ethics of Reading, Semeia* 77 (1997).

2. My analysis of the genre of the prose tale, part of a forthcoming book, is based in part on the studies of Hans-Peter Müller, "Die weisheitliche Lehrerzählung im Alten Testament und seiner Umwelt," *WO* 9 (1977): 77-98. See also his "Die Hiobrahmenerzählung und ihre altorientalischen Parallelen als Paradigmen einer weisheitlichen Wirklichkeitswahrnahme," in *The Book of Job*, ed. W. A. M. Beuken, BETL 114 (Leuven: Leuven University Press and Uitgeverij Peeters, 1994), pp. 21-39.

way in which those claims are inextricably bound to its particular narrative form and style, and the nature of the relationship between the text and its readers as itself a form of ethical relation.

Two different strands of thought in recent narrative ethics seemed to offer congenial ways of exploring the ethical dimensions of the prose tale. Yet to my bemusement and perplexity, when each approach was followed to its conclusions, I found myself faced with sharply contrasting evaluations of the ethical significance of the prose tale. The debate about the story that was implicitly present in its reception history did not go away when examined in more self-consciously theoretical fashion. If anything, it was intensified. The value of the exercise thus lies not in resolving once and for all the "right" way to evaluate the prose tale but in bringing to light how different aspects of narrative and different modes of ethical analysis can help to clarify why certain stories continue to provoke ambivalent or contradictory responses in readers and reading communities.

The two theories of narrative ethics I work with here are those represented, on the one hand, by Wayne Booth and Martha Nussbaum and, on the other hand, by Adam Zachary Newton.[3] Wayne Booth more or less reintroduced self-conscious ethical criticism into the study of narrative in 1988 with his wonderfully idiosyncratic book, *The Company We Keep: An Ethics of Fiction.* As the title suggests, Booth's governing trope is that narratives are analogous to friends with whom we keep company. Or, more properly speaking, the implied author of a narrative is the friend, and the story that is told is a friendship offering. The moral framework within which Booth situates his understanding of the effects of narrative is that of the formation of character. It is a simple theory and one that is intuitively appealing. Booth's understanding of the human self is that it is not "an atomic unit bumping other atoms"[4] but is dialogically constructed, composed of many internalized and semi-internalized voices (a notion adopted from Mikhail Bakhtin). Thus, with this fluid and mobile understanding of the self, it is easy to grasp how character can be formed (or deformed) by keeping company with good or bad friends, whose influence registers to some degree in the type of person we become. We "try out" different ways of being and different characters for ourselves, depending on the company we keep.

Perhaps the most useful part of Booth's discussion, however, is his analysis of desire in reading and in the formation of character.[5] Narrative interest de-

3. See n. 1 for bibliographic information.
4. Booth, *The Company We Keep*, p. 239.
5. Booth, *The Company We Keep*, pp. 201-23.

pends on desire. Except for students who are forced to read certain texts, narratives can secure our continuing presence with them only by stimulating and offering to satisfy some desire. It may be a simple desire to know what comes next, or a desire to get to know more about a character, or a desire to imagine ourselves in a certain kind of world, and so forth. But if we turn the page, it is only because we desire more of what we have been offered. Thus narratives "pattern" our desire and induce us to become "that kind of desirer," at least provisionally and for the duration of the reading experience. That is not to say, of course, that one cannot be a resisting reader or that, after reading, one might not throw aside the book in disgust. But such resistance is itself predicated on a recognition of a desire that has been entertained at least sufficiently to alarm us. Although Booth's work actually has a considerable theoretical and even philosophical underpinning, he presents it only incidentally.[6] In contrast, Martha Nussbaum, whose perspective is in many respects close to that of Booth's, is explicit about the philosophical perspectives that direct her interest in the moral effects of literature. Trained as a philosopher and frustrated by contemporary philosophy's difficulty in dealing adequately with the ethical dimensions of human experience, Nussbaum is one of the leading figures in the philosophy and literature movement. Nussbaum locates herself within the Aristotelian tradition of moral philosophy and practical reasoning.[7] In attempting to answer the fundamental question, "How should one live?" this tradition insists on the incommensurability of values, on the priority of particular judgments over universal ones, and on the central role of the emotions and of the imagination in rational choice. Thus it is not surprising that Nussbaum turns to literature as a form of discourse particularly suited to the exploration of ethical choices.

> As Aristotle observed, [literature] is deep, and conducive to our inquiry about how to live, because it does not simply (as history does) record that this or that event happened; it searches for patterns of possibility — of choice, and circumstance, and the interaction between choice and circumstance — that turn up in human lives with such a persistence that they must be regarded as our possibilities. And so our interest in literature becomes . . . cognitive: an interest in finding out (by seeing and feeling the otherwise perceiving) what possibilities (and tragic impossibilities) life offers to us, what hopes and fears for ourselves it underwrites or subverts.[8]

6. Newton (*Narrative Ethics*, p. 308, n. 58) situates Booth's focus on friendship in relation to Aristotle's discussion on friendship in *Nicomachean Ethics* and *Eudemian Ethics* and to Jacques Derrida's "The Politics of Friendship," *Journal of Philosophy* 35 (1988): 632-44.

7. Nussbaum, *Love's Knowledge*, pp. 3-53.

8. Nussbaum, *Love's Knowledge*, p. 171.

With this brief and all too inadequate sketch, I would like to explore what a "Boothian" and "Nussbaumian" approach to the prose tale of Job might look like. Since I am not here engaging in an argument about the redaction history of the book of Job but simply trying to illustrate two approaches to narrative ethics, I will do a bit of reconstructive surgery on the prose tale. For present purposes, I wish to take the prose tale as consisting of the introduction (1:1-5), the conclusion (42:11-17), and the two tests of Job (1:6–2:10), each of which takes place in two scenes, one in heaven (1:6-12; 2:1-7) and one on earth (1:13-21; 2:7-10). That is to say, I leave out the friends entirely. As Robert Gordis has suggested, the passages introducing them in 2:11-13 and dealing with them in 42:7-10 are simply "hinge" passages that serve to integrate the poetic dialogue.[9] In my re-sutured account, one would proceed directly from the narrator's comment in 2:10 ("[i]n all this Job did not sin with his lips") directly to the conclusion in 42:10 (*sans* the reference to the friends): "And the LORD restored the fortunes of Job . . . and the LORD gave Job twice as much as he had before," and so forth. The advantage of this reconstruction is that I do not have to make up a part of the story that is purportedly missing. It is coherent as is.

Both Booth and Nussbaum pay particular attention to the way a story begins, for that is what first indicates the type of friendship offering it will be, the nature of the desires it will offer to stimulate and satisfy, and what perspectives on how one should live are embedded in the story's point of view, tone, and genre.[10] The opening of Job is well known:

> A man there was in the land of Uz; Job was his name. That man was blameless and upright, one who feared God and turned from evil. And there were born to him seven sons and three daughters. (Author's trans.)

The immediate foregrounding of a character and his virtues appears to establish the prose tale as a story that attempts to do us good by providing a model or example. In part, that is correct, but Booth's question about desires addressed by the text requires a more nuanced reading of these verses. Not only the content of the story but also the textures of the language attempt to awaken the reader's desire. The language of the narrative is simple and accessible, but also beautiful in its balance and symmetry. The short and rhythmic phrases of

---

9. Robert Gordis, *The Book of Job: Commentary, New Translation, and Special Studies* (New York: Jewish Theological Seminary, 1978), pp. 573-75. Albrecht Alt ("Zur Vorgeschichte des Buches Hiob," *ZAW* 55 [1937]: 265) made a similar suggestion concerning the relationship of chapter 1 and 42:11-17, though his proposal also included a hypothesis about the secondary nature of chapter 2.

10. See Booth, *The Company We Keep*, pp. 175-79; Nussbaum, *Love's Knowledge*, pp. 30-35.

the first verse in Hebrew beg to be read aloud (*’îš hāyâ bĕ’ereṣ-‘ûṣ ’îyôb šĕmô wĕhāyâ hā’îš hahû’ tām wĕyāšār wîrē’ ’ĕlōhîm wĕsār mērā‘*). The patterned repetition and parallelism is pleasurable — three two-word phrases, a three-word phrase, then again three two-word phrases. Job's virtues are represented in two neatly balanced pairs of parallel terms ("blameless and upright, fearing God and turning from evil"). Such linguistic textures do not of themselves have meaning, yet they can acquire a sort of iconic significance in context. That significance is partly clarified in the following verse by the round numbers used to describe Job's children and animals, numbers that, as so often noted, add up to ten and multiples of ten. What these stylistic features suggest, at least initially, is a world of coherency and wholeness. This, I would argue, is the desire that the prose tale addresses and offers to satisfy, the desire for a world that can be experienced as supremely coherent, a world of utterly unbreachable wholeness.

These stylistic traits not only characterize the beginning but also pervade the entire story. The tale is structured in mirroring sections that make use of extensive patterns of internal repetition and correspondence. Characters are aligned in contrasting pairs of positive and trustworthy characters (God, Job) and negative and untrustworthy ones (the *satan* and Job's wife). One should not be surprised that disasters, as well as blessings, are also described with imagery of completeness (four messenger reports, signifying total destruction, 1:13-19; disease that reaches "from the sole of his foot to the top of his head," 2:7). The point is not that good things are represented symmetrically and bad things are not. The stylistic features are not allegorical but iconic of an aesthetic imagination that operates — all the way down — with categories of completeness. Yet, though disaster may be recounted, both the aesthetics of the text and the moral imagination with which it correlates cannot end with disaster but must encompass the reassertion of wholeness, as accomplished in the resolution of the plot and the idyllic conclusion (42:11-17). What is iconically represented in the syntax, numerical patterns, and various other formal features has to be related to the substantive claims that the text makes by means of the plot and by thematic statements.

The world described in the first scene of the prose tale is so orderly and stable that one can scarcely imagine its giving rise to the conflict — the brokenness — required to sustain a plot. There are no unhappy families, megalomaniac kings, or jealous rivals to get the story moving. The conflict, of course, will be provided by the conflict between God and the *satan*. Though his official function, as is often noted, is to identify disloyalty or falsity and so to maintain the good order and thus the wholeness of the world, the *satan* actually embodies a profoundly destabilizing force. The *satan* is the narrative embodiment of a hermeneutic of suspicion. For the *satan*, the ostensible coherency that is at the heart of the moral imagination of the story is an illusion he is pre-pared to demystify. The *satan* has uncovered an ideological contradiction in the religious discourse that, when brought to light, threatens to render meaningless the fundamental category of that discourse. As this proto-Nietzschean figure says in his clever genealogy of piety, "Does Job fear God for nothing? Have you not hedged him about . . . ?" (1:9-10). Fear of God as an absolute value is contra-dicted by the practice of blessing. What had been represented as the very image of a coherent and meaningful world in 1:1-3 (a blessed existence) is now argued to be a kind of false consciousness. A hermeneutics of suspicion, if persuasive, performs an unmasking, displacing the false consciousness of ideology with an account that claims to be the real truth. Once exposed, the old categories are emptied of meaning, and a world is destroyed.

In this surprisingly philosophical little didactic tale, what is at stake is not simply the testing of a virtue but the testing of the conditions that make virtue itself possible. As compelling as the *satan*'s challenge appears to be, the conven-tions of the didactic story ensure that the hero will meet the challenge and the threat will be discharged. The interest thus turns to *how* Job will articulate a form of piety that persuasively resolves the threat of contradiction and inco-herency and so restores the conceptual and experiential wholeness of the moral world.

This reformulation is articulated in the words that Job speaks in response to his first loss. To grasp the moral imagination that these words embody, a "Boothian" or "Nussbaumian" approach would direct us to attend carefully to the rhetoric: the formal qualities of speech, the embedded metaphors, the se-mantic framing they enact, the schematic narrative they imply, and so forth. One may begin with metaphor: "Naked I came from my mother's womb" (1:21a) appears to be a literal statement, but the following "and naked I will re-turn there" is clearly metaphorical. Moreover, it retrospectively metaphorizes the first part. "Mother's womb" now figures the tomb and Sheol, but also the earth as the mythic origin of all humanity (cf. Gen 3:19). Through this meta-phoric interaction of meaning, a single human being's experience is framed within the common condition of humanity.

The metaphor may be understood on its own, but within the narrative it is a response to a situation, and so a way of mapping that situation. "Naked" is the key word. Though it is literally true that one comes naked from the womb, metaphorically the saying analogizes both property and human relationships to clothes. They are put on, yet they must be taken off again. Just as clothes are not part of the "naked self," so property and even relationships are not inalienable possessions but must be relinquished. "Naked" also connotes the vulnerability of exposure. Job's words refer himself to images of vulnerability and utter dependency, the naked body of the just birthed infant and the powerless naked corpse. The metaphorical statement names his present experience of loss as like death itself, for he has been stripped of all that clothes a human life.

The rudimentary narrative structure of the metaphor also signifies. In it, existence is construed as a story of leaving and returning, a narrative schema rooted deeply in the human psyche. To apply the schema of departure and return to life itself is to give life a unity and sense of completeness it does not self-evidently possess. To unite this narrative structure with the emotionally charged image of the mother incorporates death (and the losses that are likened to it) within a symbolics of security and protection.

This metaphoric statement by itself does not explain how Job brings together gestures of grief with gestures of worship. The first statement, however, is followed by a second, which parallels it both formally and grammatically: "Adonai has given and Adonai has taken." In both statements, the noun (Adonai) or predicate complement (naked; mother's womb/there) remains the same in each half, whereas the verbs are binary opposites (come forth/return; give/take). The grammatical parallelism invites one to treat the two statements as part of a paradigmatic set, both describing the same thing. One is naked, and Adonai gives those things that clothe life; Adonai takes those things back, and one returns naked to death. Adonai is represented as the horizon of experience. That sense of Adonai as ultimate horizon underwrites the parallel between Adonai and the mother's womb from which one departs and to which one returns. It is not the abyss but something that is experienced as protective and loving that frames existence. If it were not so, one could not endure the burden of the gift that cannot be possessed but must inevitably be relinquished. But because Job understands it to be so, he blesses the name of Adonai. Through the work of metaphor and narrative, symmetry and contrast, Job's moral imagination establishes a context within which the connection of grief and of doxology is not merely comprehensible but profound.

The second episode does not merely repeat but also extends the argument. As the metaphor with which Job had comprehended his situation in the first episode drew upon imagery of the body and its nakedness, and thus highlighted the intimate relationship between body and meaning, so the *satan* shifts the locus of the test to Job's body. In contrast to the first episode, where the messengers simply reported the events of destruction but did not attempt to construct an interpretive framework or suggest a response, the words of Job's wife in the second episode are explicitly directive and implicitly gesture toward a moral framework that contrasts with Job's: "Do you still hold fast to your integrity? Curse God and die" (2:9). Her words, which echo phrases from the heavenly debate (2:3b, 5b), are not, however, accompanied by any interpretive imagery that would explicate the moral framework from which she arrives at the conclusion that curse, rather than doxology, is the appropriate response. Suffice it to say that Job's wife reads his situation as a sign of alienation, of a brokenness in the world to which the appropriate response is an answering act of alienation. The narrative is not interested in making a plausible case for her viewpoint, however, but simply in discrediting her through her alignment with the *satan* and her opposition to God and to Job. The nihilism of the position that she and the *satan* embrace is evident from the one word in her speech that is not an implicit quotation of the heavenly voices: "die." According to the perspective of the narrative, the values shared by the *satan* and Job's wife cannot sustain life in the face of catastrophe and acute suffering.

Yet what, if anything, do Job's words in the second episode add to his previous statement? Certain syntactical elements that are similar yet not identical to his previous statements invite one to draw the sentences together for comparison. In the sayings in the first episode, the verbs formed contrasting pairs, whereas the other terms were the stable elements. Here the verb ("receive") is the repeated term, whereas the contrast comes with the object, "good" and "trouble" (lit. "bad" [*rāʿ*]). Moreover, the verb "receive" belongs to the same semantic field as the verbs of 1:21b ("give" and "take") and so facilitates reading 2:10b in light of that earlier statement. In those sentences, Job had dealt with the horizons of existence but not with the more particular content of life. Here he supplies that lack. What Adonai gives and human beings receive is not simply life but life inevitably characterized by both "good" and "trouble." Such a claim would not be meaningful as a reply to his wife except in the context of Job's earlier statements identifying Adonai as the horizon of all existence. However, within such a context, the occurrence of trouble cannot break the stance of radical acceptance modeled by Job.

That Job has reestablished the moral vision that undergirds an unbreakable wholeness of being is evident in the further echo of the word "trouble" in the final scene, and in the contrasting parallel between Job's wife and his sisters and brothers. They come to console him "concerning all the trouble that Adonai had brought upon him" (42:11). That is to say, they act out of an understanding like that of Job. They do not see his situation as an occasion of and for alienation, but rather one that calls forth an ethic of solidarity and compassion (their presence, sharing of food, giving of gifts). Like Job sacrificing for his children (1:5), their presence is an emblem of the wholeness available to and embodied by those whose virtue is grounded in the perspective Job has articulated.

There is much more that could be said, but this brief sketch suggests one way of reading the narrative as a simple but profound response to the question, "How should one live?" It embodies a representation in aesthetic form of the wholeness and fundamental goodness that can be experienced if one embraces the radical values and perspectives it champions. Thus this kind of narrative ethical criticism is one that highlights what Nussbaum called the "cognitive interest" in literature, the interest in discerning the possibilities and tragic impossibilities life offers. In that sense, the analysis highlights the thematics of narrative, the meaning communicated both by aesthetic form and by propositional statement.

And yet there is something that escapes this sort of cognitive approach, something that has to do with the nature of narrative itself. Narrative "happens." It has the structure of an event, and there is something irreducibly nonpropositional about events. Even though an example story may attempt to minimize this "event" quality, it remains an element that resists reduction to the propositional and, thus, eludes an analysis of meaning. This immediacy of narrative is the area that Adam Zachary Newton has staked out as the overlooked space for narrative ethics. Drawing on the categories of Emmanuel Levinas, Newton identifies the two dimensions of narrative as the "Saying" and the "Said."[11] The "Said" refers to the propositional content, that is, to the thematics of a narrative and its moral prescriptiveness. The "Saying" refers to the intersubjective relationships established in narrative through its performative aspect. Both aspects make moral claims on readers, but these claims are of different orders. The prescriptive claims of the Said invite agreement or disagreement with the text's construction of value. The claims of the Saying require a bit more explanation. This mode of reading and the claims that arise from it are based on the analogy, as Newton puts it, "that one faces a text as one might face a person."[12] The encounter with the text is one of immediacy, an immediacy of contact that is *prior to meaning.*

The analogy between text and person, of course, has obvious limits. One does not owe to texts or their characters all the same kinds of ethical obligations that one owes to actual persons. Nor is one related to the world of fictional characters in all the same ways one is related to the world of persons. Yet the divide between the fictional and the real may not be so sharp as first appears. Many of the ethical issues raised both by the content and by the

11. Newton's work incorporates three philosophical perspectives, including not only that of Emmanuel Levinas but also that of Stanley Cavell and the early writings of Mikhail Bakhtin. Levinas develops the categories of "the Saying" and "the Said" in *Otherwise Than Being: or, Beyond Essence,* trans. Alphonso Lingis (The Hague: Martinus Nijhoff, 1981). For a discussion of these categories more accessible than that found in Levinas himself, see Eaglestone, *Reading After Levinas,* pp. 137-46, or Colin Davis, *Levinas: An Introduction* (Notre Dame, Ind.: University of Notre Dame Press, 1996), pp. 74-79.

12. Newton, *Narrative Ethics,* p. 11.

performative aspects of the virtual world of narrative are continuous with issues encountered in the world of everyday experience. The situations that move us in narrative, even in nonrealist narrative, are recognizably the kinds of events and situations that may also occur in the world. Newton's analogy, which is a tacit assumption of much reading practice, thus accounts for certain important phenomena, such as the emotional reactions that readers experience when they read: one may weep for characters, feel joy for them, be angry at them or on their behalf. Behind such emotions stand normative judgments about what is deserved or undeserved, good or bad, worthy or unworthy.[13] To be sure, one cannot intervene in the world of fictional characters, but ethical relations, even among actual persons, are not all about interventions. Many of our ethical relations with other persons involve listening to their stories, relating their stories to others, and forming evaluative judgments about those narratives. Thus the analogy that Newton claims, "that one faces a text as one might face a person," may be illuminating in both directions.

For the approach championed by Newton, ethical reflection begins with the relation of addressivity established in the very act of storytelling. In this regard, Newton stakes out a position even more calculatedly naive than that of Booth. Whereas Booth's model of a story as a "friendship offering" between implied author and reader draws attention to the status of the story as a thing made and shared between two friends external to the story, Newton's model tends to dissolve the boundaries between story and reader. For Newton, it is the narrator, not the author, with whom we have to do. Like the ancient mariner who seizes the wedding guest in Coleridge's poem,[14] the narrator of the prose tale stops us, arrests us in our activity, when we pause and listen to the story of Job. The ethical relations established in this configuration are multiple. In telling the story, the narrator assumes a responsibility toward the one whose story is told, for the narrator undertakes to relate the life of another. In the reader's act of submitting to the story, the reader also becomes in some sense "answerable." Long before issues of meaning arise, the immediacy of the encounter with the character, as well as with the narrator, makes a claim upon the reader. Via Levinas, Newton argues that the character whose story is told confronts the reader as a "face." And a face always makes a claim upon another face. Though it is true that a reader cannot intervene in a story, the reader becomes a witness with at least a witness's responsibility.

13. See the similar analysis of Eva M. Dadlez, *What's Hecuba to Him? Fictional Events and Actual Emotions*, Literature and Philosophy (University Park, Pa.: Pennsylvania State University Press, 1997).

14. Newton, *Narrative Ethics*, pp. 3-8.

Newton's account of the dynamics of immediacy in reading helps explain the ethical discomfort of many allegedly naive readers of the prose tale, who respond with distress and anger to the mistreatment of Job and his family. It also leads one to note other areas of ethical discomfort with the narrative besides the physical abuse it recounts.

From this perspective then, what are the relations of narrator, character, and reader? As noted earlier, the focus of the story is on character, and the narrator arrests our attention from the very first words of the story with praise for Job's character. Yet there is room even here for ethical disquiet, for the narrator's relation to Job is one of utter transcendence. The narrator needs Job as example, not as person, as one whose character can be fixed, summed-up, or, in Bakhtin's expression, "finalized." The narrator's claim on the reader is that the reader join in contemplating Job. Thus Job becomes a spectacle as the narrator brings Job onstage and positions the reader where she can eavesdrop, overhearing Job's words and watching his actions. This status of Job as spectacle is not just a narrative device to get the story started but rather is intrinsic to the character relations within the story as well. God's first words concerning Job also cast him as an object of "speculation" (in both senses of the word), for God says to the *satan*, "have you directed your attention to my servant Job?" (1:8a). God's words are words of praise for Job, echoing those of the narrator (1:8b), but the discomfort that some readers experience even at this point in the narrative can perhaps be illumined by a comment from Bakhtin: "The truth about a man in the mouths of others, not directed to him dialogically and therefore a *second-hand* truth, becomes a *lie* degrading and deadening him, if it touches upon his 'holy of holies,' that is, 'the man in man'. . . . Truth is unjust when it concerns the depths of *someone else's* personality."[15] God's "summing up" of Job, like the narrator's, already includes an element of injustice, even though what they say *is* true, because it renders Job simply as object and as example.

Oddly, it is the *satan* who speaks of Job in a way that appears to acknowledge his subjectivity. The *satan* perceives Job as one who may have a complex interiority and levels of motivation that are not so easily identified. The *satan* sees Job as possessing implicit values, values that Job himself may not even be aware that he holds. Yet despite this ostensibly richer view of Job as complex subject, the *satan*'s perception is no less reductive, for with his hermeneutic of suspicion he claims already to know about Job what Job does not even know about himself. Both God and the *satan* seek to "narrate" Job. They differ only in

---

15. Mikhail Bakhtin, *Problems of Dostoevsky's Poetics*, ed. and trans. C. Emerson, Theory and History of Literature 8 (Minneapolis: University of Minnesota Press, 1984), pp. 59-60 (italics in original).

laying claim to incompatible narratives, but they are equally certain that they know the truth about him and that they can state it in a single sentence. The violence that will erupt upon Job is already anticipated in the violence done in these attempts to define him.

The violence has another, related source as well. Didactic stories, by the very nature of the genre, have a passion for unitary truth. That passion for displaying the truth works itself out in the performative dimensions of the text as a kind of narrative necessity to know. Once doubt has been cast upon Job, that doubt must be resolved. Within such a story, one cannot imagine God, upon hearing the *satan*'s counterclaims about the true moral character of Job, saying in reply, "Well, I don't think you are right, but I guess we will never know." For this narrative, the compelling desire to establish the truth about a person trumps all other values. It permits everything. To the extent that the storyteller succeeds in communicating to the reader the desire for such knowledge, the reader is complicit in the violence against Job. Even the reader who deplores the test of Job but desires the rest of the story is not innocent. The reader who turns the page stands in an ethical relation to Job not so different from God who says, "Very well, he is in your hands."[16]

In this story, the Other who is Job is not allowed to remain undisclosed. He must be rendered transparent. Not all seeking of knowledge about another is abusive, of course. There are modes that are just, modes that enact solidarity, modes that are generous, modes that heal or redeem. Yet in this story, the ethical relations governing such knowledge of another are deeply perverse. For the truth to be disclosed, Job must indeed "speak his own word," but the conditions for truth are not dialogical.[17] Instead, the crucial speech act will be a form of coerced speech. This coerced speech differs from torture, where pain is inflicted to elicit a truth someone wishes to withhold. It differs also from the ordeal, where a nonhuman entity "speaks" to disclose a truth that the accused cannot be trusted to speak. The speech forcing in Job has more the structure of the scientific experiment in which a subject must be manipulated into a predetermined set of circumstances, disclosing the desired information unwittingly, without ever knowing the real conditions of his own speech. Thus, ironically, in

16. One should not be too smugly condescending toward the character God. Deciding whether to live without knowledge of the basis upon which an intimate relationship is grounded presents one of the most difficult moral dilemmas. Yet, as this story shows, there may be a tremendous price — physically, psychically, and ethically — to be paid by both parties for such knowledge.

17. For a study that explores the limits of Bakhtin's notion of dialogic speech see Aaron Fogel, *Coercion to Speak: Conrad's Poetics of Dialogue* (Cambridge, Mass.: Harvard University Press, 1985).

such experiments deception becomes the essential precondition of truth, and the one whose speech is necessary is never directly addressed by those who desire to know.

The scenes in which Job speaks have an intensely voyeuristic quality to them. God watches Job, the *satan* watches Job, and the reader watches Job. Just as we had watched Job in an intimate moment of anxiety and piety as he explained to himself why he sacrificed on behalf of his children (1:5), so now we watch him in the intensity of grief and in deep physical pain. Yet the kind of watching to which the story invites and incites is an objectified watching. We are encouraged to watch and see what he will do and say. Such focused, "scientific" watching is the antithesis of the compassionate gaze.

Read with attention to the performative aspects of the narrative and the ethical relations established among the characters, Job's words take on a different resonance than they do when one is simply asking about the moral imagination they embody. From this perspective, one is drawn to a sense of the disjunction between the relationship with God as Job assumes it to be and that relationship as it has been portrayed in the narrative. Job makes no claim upon God for protection from the contingencies of human existence and even identifies God as the agent who both gives and takes life, who sends both good and trouble. That relationship is one of utter and complete trust. Yet trust is precisely what is sacrificed to knowledge in the hierarchy of values enacted by the prose tale.

The horrific suffering inflicted on Job, culminating in the death of his children and the savaging of his own skin, is the unjustified violence that many readers find so disturbing. Yet as this brief analysis has argued, those acts are but the ultimate manifestation of a more pervasive ethical dislocation, which becomes apparent when one examines the communicative relations within the narrative. Some readers have attempted to find a trace of a guilty conscience or sense of shame in the narrative by pointing to God's remark to the *satan* in 2:3 that the *satan* incited God to destroy Job "for no reason" *(ḥinnām)*, or by observing that the doubling of Job's possessions echoes the law of restitution for stolen property (Exod 22:7). Even if that is so, the narrative does not move to address what many readers consider to be the crowning injustice, that Job is not entrusted with the truth about what has happened. Thus, to its very end, the narrative continues to deprive Job of his subjectivity. He remains simply the objectified, finalized, utterly narrated example that serves the purposes of the didactic narrator. The reader, who has been the recipient of this act of narration at the expense of Job, may well feel implicated in and contaminated by the abuse it enacts.

I am not arguing that one or another of these approaches to the moral and ethical dimensions of the prose tale — the approach that focuses on the moral imagination of the didactic story or the approach that focuses on the performative elements of the narrative — is superior to the other. Both are valid and capable of illumining aspects of the tale that the other has difficulty in perceiving. Although these two approaches are not theoretically contradictory, at least in the case of this narrative, the different ways in which they focus attention are difficult to hold together. It may be that one must temporarily bracket attending to the performative aspects of the text, the "Saying," in order to hear the "Said," the particular claim the text makes about the world. To attend only to the ethical issues raised by the performative aspects of the text is to evade its propositional claim. Yet by the same token, to refuse to acknowledge the disturbing issues implicit in the performative aspects of the text is to impoverish the scope of narrative ethics.

Both approaches are also important for clarifying ethical implications of the structure as a whole, which can be thought of in terms of both a Bakhtinian dialogism and a Levinasian interruption. Attending to the propositional claims of the prose tale and the moral imagination that gives rise to them allows one to hear an important and provocative word about the world. But the closed and monologic form of the didactic genre presents itself as though it were the only word that could be spoken. How can that assumption of super-adequacy be challenged, be required to make space for another word? How can it be shown that although the prose tale may speak truth, it cannot speak the whole truth? It could be challenged by the telling of a rival story, but the author of the book of Job as a whole chooses another strategy, breaking into its closed discourse of the didactic tale to insert another, alien genre, that of the wisdom dialogue whose language, values, and moral perspectives are radically different from those of the prose tale. Thus, by this juxtaposition of genres, ideas and moral imaginations that may have been isolated from one another in the social and cultural world of ancient Israel were brought together and "forced to quarrel," as Bakhtin puts it.

Attending to the performative aspects of the prose tale also generates an urgency that motivates and is answered by the structure of the book as whole. Job in the prose tale is a character who has become an instrument in the disagreement between God and the *satan*, a mere illustration in the discourse of the narrative. By interrupting the story in which Job is narrated in such a diminished fashion, the author of the whole book challenges the adequacy of that narration. By interrupting with a wisdom dialogue, in which characters speak without significant narration, the author gives back to the character Job his subjectivity, the unfinalized presence of a person whose last word is not yet spoken.

"The Way of the Righteous" in the Psalms: Character Formation and Cultural Crisis

J. Clinton McCann, Jr.

Whom are we talking about when we refer to "the psalmist" or "the psalmists"? It depends, of course, upon who is doing the talking. For many readers of the Psalms, "the psalmist" is David, unless the heading of a particular psalm mentions someone else, in which case this other person is "the psalmist" (e.g., Asaph for Psalms 50, 73–83; Ethan for Psalm 89; Moses for Psalm 90; Solomon for Psalms 72, 127; Heman for Psalm 88; or some unspecified individual among the sons of Korah for Psalms 42–49, 84–85, 87).

Students trained in historical criticism have a different view. In their view, the Psalms are the result of many years of liturgical and devotional use, and it is simply impossible to know who wrote them. So, when historical critics refer to "the psalmist" or "the psalmists," it is simply a convenient way of referring to whatever individual or group may have been responsible for a particular psalm or certain psalms.

While the conventional scholarly practice of referring to "the psalmist(s)" is convenient and helpful, it raises another interesting possibility. Suspending or at least bracketing out historical questions like authorship, one could seek to draw on the basis of the Psalms themselves a portrait of what "the psalmist" would look like. To be sure, this is a synchronic rather than a diachronic approach; or, to put it differently, it is a canonical rather than a simply historical approach. It is the primary purpose of this essay to construct such a portrait. On the basis of the Psalms themselves, I shall attempt to describe what Psalm 1:6 calls "the way of the righteous" — that is, the lifestyle of "the righteous" or the character of the faithful life.

There is some precedent for this attempt.[1] It is easier, however, to articu-

---

1. See, for instance, James L. Mays, *The Lord Reigns: A Theological Handbook to the Psalms* (Louisville: Westminster/John Knox, 1994), pp. 87-107. My attempt is more broadly focused.

late *what* I am attempting than it is to cite any *particular method* by which I shall proceed. I shall begin with Psalms 1–2 and then proceed to Psalm 3 and the prayers in the Psalter. Because the prayers generally end with praise and/or trust, I shall then turn to these voices in the Psalms. Thus, while I shall depend on form-critical work on the Psalms, the agenda that I shall pursue will not be the traditional one of attempting to locate particular types of Psalms within the life of ancient Israel or Judah. Rather, I shall ask what kind of faithful lifestyle or character is implied by way of the portrayal of "the psalmist" who prays, praises, and professes her or his trust in God alone.

This approach to biblical material — that is, the reading of the Bible with an eye toward character and character formation — was initiated by scholars who were and are concerned about the contemporary debate in North American society about character, virtue, "family values," and ethics.[2] Consequently, not only shall I construct a sort of composite character sketch of "the psalmist," but I shall also suggest ways in which this portrait might address what many persons, including myself, consider to be the current crisis in North American culture. My attempts in this regard are heavily indebted to the incisive cultural critique offered by therapist Mary Pipher, especially in her book, *The Shelter of Each Other: Rebuilding Our Families.*[3]

Psalms 1–2

Scholars almost unanimously agree that Psalm 1 was placed at the beginning of the Psalter to orient the reader on how to approach the entire collection. Thus, it is initially important that one of the key words in the psalm is *derek* ("path" in v. 1, and "way" twice in v. 6), which in modern parlance might be translated "lifestyle." Furthermore, the first verb in Psalm 1 is literally "walk" (NRSV "follow" in v. 1); and its sense could be captured in the modern idiom, "walk of life," or again, "lifestyle." The next verb is "stand" (NRSV "tread"), followed by "sit." In short, from the beginning, the psalm is concerned about how a person is positioned. This concern continues in verses 3-5, where the "happy" person is "planted by streams of water" — that is, positioned where she or he can put down firm, stable roots. The wicked, by contrast, have no stable rootedness and

---

2. See especially William P. Brown, *Character in Crisis: A Fresh Approach to the Wisdom Literature of the Old Testament* (Grand Rapids: Eerdmans, 1996), pp. vii-ix.

3. Mary Pipher, *The Shelter of Each Other: Rebuilding Our Families* (New York: G. P. Putnam's Sons, 1996). See also Mary Pipher, *Reviving Ophelia: Saving the Selves of Adolescent Girls* (New York: Balantine Books, 1994).

are blown away; that is, they have no solid position and thus "will not stand" (v. 5).

The dominant concern with lifestyle or "walk of life," expressed with images of motion or stability that suggest the importance of life position, actually invites readers to approach the Psalms seeking instruction about what today we might call character or character formation. This orientation is reinforced by the repetition of the word *tôrâ* in verse 2, which should be translated as "teaching" or "instruction" instead of "law." In short, Psalm 1 and the Psalter as a whole aim at teaching people how to live.[4] Learning this lesson is crucial, for it means the difference between happiness or prosperity (vv. 1, 3), on the one hand, and death (v. 6), on the other.

Yet what is "the way of the righteous" (v. 6)? Commentators have often viewed the lifestyle of "the righteous" in Psalm 1 as anything but commendable. Psalm 1 has frequently been interpreted to advocate a sort of self-righteous legalism that frets constantly over rules and regulations that must be obeyed in order to earn God's attention and favor. But this is a gross misreading. To be sure, the word can more narrowly designate legal stipulations, but it can also suggest something as broad as "unmediated divine teaching."[5] Especially if the word is heard in this broader sense, the righteous person is not being portrayed as a pedantic, self-righteous legalist but rather as one who is remarkably open to God and God's instruction, constantly awaiting what God might say next.

Indeed, it is precisely this complete orientation to God and openness to God's instruction that define what it means to be "happy" (v. 1) and to "prosper" (v. 3). Unfortunately, the translation "prosper" seems to suggest a retributive scheme, and North American readers almost inevitably hear "prosper" in terms of material wealth or reward. But that is not the point. Rather, as James L. Mays suggests, to "prosper" describes the "result of life's connection with the source of life" — God.[6] For trees with deep roots, even bad times such as drought are not deadly. The point of the simile is *not* that the righteous will not suffer, but rather that the righteous will always have in God a reliable resource to face and endure life's worst. Or, as the conclusion to Psalm 2 puts it, "Happy are all who take refuge in God" (v. 12). The affirmation of God as "refuge" will

4. For a more extensive explanation of this interpretive direction, see J. Clinton McCann, Jr., *A Theological Introduction to the Book of Psalms: The Psalms as Torah* (Nashville: Abingdon, 1993), pp. 13-40; idem, "The Book of Psalms: Introductory Commentary and Reflections," in *The New Interpreter's Bible*, vol. 4 (Nashville: Abingdon, 1996), pp. 641-75.

5. Jon Levenson, "The Sources of Torah: Psalm 119 and the Modes of Revelation in Second Temple Judaism," in *Ancient Israelite Religion*, ed. P. D. Miller, Jr., P. D. Hanson, and S. D. McBride (Philadelphia: Fortress, 1987), p. 568.

6. James L. Mays, *Psalms*, Interpretation (Louisville: John Knox, 1994), p. 44.

remain a central theme in the psalmic prayers.[7] What is commended is a life of fundamental dependence upon God rather than upon the self.

While the final line of Psalm 2 clearly commends dependence upon God, so does the rest of the psalm. From a form-critical perspective, it makes sense to hear Psalm 2 as an artifact of an ancient Judean coronation liturgy. For the purpose of this essay, however, it is crucial to note that Psalm 2 ultimately calls all the earth's most powerful people — "kings" and "rulers" — to submit themselves to God: "Serve the LORD with fear" (v. 11). Not surprisingly, the only other direct invitation in the Psalms to "serve the LORD" is Psalm 100:2 (NRSV "worship"), which immediately follows a collection of psalms that have explicitly proclaimed God's universal sovereignty and intent to establish justice and righteousness among all peoples (Psalms 93, 95–99). Thus, Psalm 2 joins Psalm 1 in portraying "the way of the righteous" as a life oriented completely to God. Happiness derives from being constantly attentive to God's instruction and constantly intent upon submission to God and God's will for justice and righteousness.

One crucial point remains to be made. If "complete orientation" to God characterizes "the way of the righteous," then what about "the way of the wicked" (1:6)? In a word, to be wicked is to be selfish. Whereas the righteous, happy, and prosperous attend to God and God's instruction, the wicked attend only to themselves. Their creed is found in their words to "the psalmist" in Psalm 3:2: "There is no help for you in God."[8] To adopt the NRSV's translation of *tôrâ* for a moment, if we say that the righteous are characterized by openness to God's "law," then by contrast the wicked are a "law unto themselves." The English word that captures this precisely is "autonomy" (which, if the Greek components are translated literally, means "self-law"). "Autonomy" is nearly always considered to be a virtue in contemporary North American society, and herein lies a major clue to our contemporary cultural crisis.

The Pursuit of Happiness:
The Contemporary Challenge of Psalms 1–2

In her book, *The Shelter of Each Other,* Mary Pipher suggests that one symptom of our cultural crisis is that a word like "autonomy" is viewed as unambiguously positive. As she puts it:

---

7. See Jerome F. D. Creach, *Yahweh as Refuge and the Editing of the Hebrew Psalter,* JSOTSup 217 (Sheffield: Sheffield Academic Press, 1996).

8. Notice that it is the precise opposite of the conclusion of Psalm 2.

Our words for distance tend to be positive — autonomy and independence. Our words for closeness tend to be negative — enmeshed, overprotective and dependent.[9]

Most troubling perhaps, Pipher points out that what we now often call co-dependence we used to call love![10]

In other words, the frightening reality is that what the Psalms call wickedness is what we routinely and systematically promote as virtues — autonomy, independence, self-reliance, self-sufficiency, and self-actualization. To be sure, if persons or groups of people are subjugated or oppressed, then they may legitimately seek more autonomy in the sense of independence or self-determination. Yet for many, indeed for most North Americans, the problem is not too little self-determination but rather too much. Consequently, we have created what singer and songwriter Iris DeMent calls the "Wasteland of the Free,"[11] or what Robert Putnam identifies as "America's declining social capital."[12] In short, we are so good at being autonomous that communal life at every level is suffering — family, neighborhood, town, city, school, church, and more.

It is no exaggeration to call our current situation a cultural crisis. As writer Anne Lamott points out, it is very much upon us:

> We are all in danger now and have a new everything to face. . . . My friend Carpenter says we no longer need Chicken Little to tell us the sky is falling, because it already has. The issue now is how to take care of one another.[13]

Or, to put it in terms of the Psalms, the issue now is how to pursue happiness differently.

Interestingly, Mary Pipher defines the current crisis both in Lamott's terms of caring for each other and in psalmic terms of happiness. In Lamott's terms, Pipher asserts the following:

> Our land of opportunity has become a land of opportunists. Our most organized religion is capitalism, which at its meanest turns virtue upside down. Predators become heroes, selfishness is smart and compassion is

9. Pipher, *The Shelter of Each Other*, p. 113.

10. Pipher, *The Shelter of Each Other*, pp. 137-38.

11. Iris DeMent, "Wasteland of the Free" on the CD entitled "The Way I Should" (Warner Brothers Records, Inc., 1996).

12. Robert D. Putnam, "Bowling Alone: America's Declining Social Capital," *Journal of Democracy* (January 1995): 65-78.

13. Anne Lamott, *Bird by Bird: Some Instructions on Writing and Life* (New York: Anchor Books, 1994), p. 108.

softheaded. Capitalism favors what's called survival of the fittest, but really it's survival of the greediest, most driven and most ruthless. We have cared more about selling things to our neighbors than we've cared for our neighbors. The deck is stacked all wrong and ultimately we will all lose.[14]

In terms that overlap with the language of Psalms 1–2, Pipher puts it this way:

We have a crisis of meaning in our culture. The crisis comes from our isolation from each other, from the values we learn in a culture of consumption and from the fuzzy, self-help message that the only commitment is to the self and the only important question is — Am I happy? We learn that we are number one and that our own immediate needs are the most important ones. The crisis comes from the message that products satisfy and that happiness can be purchased.[15]

In sharp contrast to a capitalistic society that teaches us systematically to be autonomous, selfish, and greedy, the Psalms (beginning with Psalms 1–2) offer a different teaching — God's *tôrâ*. This alternative way, "the way of the righteous," commends the pursuit of happiness not in terms of the self and its desires but in terms of God and God's desires, which always involve justice, righteousness, and equity (see Ps 96:13; 98:9, where "judgment" should be understood in the positive sense of establishing justice in the world). The selfishness taught by society produces both isolation and greed, and greed ultimately yields the violence among us that is now so routine that we take it for granted. We are discovering the truth contained in the final line of Psalm 1: "but an evil life leads only to ruin."[16] By contrast, the other-directedness taught by the Psalms produces the communal virtues of justice and righteousness — that is, the caring for one another that is so desperately lacking among us, so much so that we find ourselves confronted with a crisis. Or, as "the psalmist" puts it at the beginning of Psalm 41, in what forms a revealing inclusio for Book 1 of the Psalter: "Happy are those who consider the poor" (v. 1). For those shaped by the Psalms, openness to God's teaching and consideration of the poor go hand in hand, for the God of the Psalms, indeed the God of the whole Bible, wills the creation of conditions that sustain life for all people, all creatures, and all creation — in a word, justice.

---

14. Pipher, *The Shelter of Each Other*, p. 94.

15. Pipher, *The Shelter of Each Other*, p. 26.

16. The translation is that of Gary Chamberlain, *The Psalms: A New Translation for Prayer and Worship* (Nashville: Upper Room, 1984), p. 26.

Psalm 3 and the Psalmic Prayers

If there is any tendency for the reader of the Psalms to conclude that Psalm 1 commends a mechanistic reward-punishment scheme — that is, if there is any tendency to conclude that divine justice is distributive or retributive justice — then Psalm 3 and the subsequent psalmic prayers make this conclusion impossible! The situation of "the psalmist" at the beginning of Psalm 3 is entirely typical. In the psalmic prayers, which account for the majority of the Psalms (especially in Books 1-2, Psalms 1–72), "the psalmist" is constantly opposed. In his comment on Psalm 3, Eugene Peterson cites Isaac Bashevis Singer, who once said, "I only pray when I am in trouble, but I'm in trouble all the time."[17] Singer captures precisely the normal situation of "the psalmists"; they are in trouble all the time. For exactly this reason, of course, the psalmic prayers are usually known among scholars as laments or complaints.

The three two-verse sections of Psalm 13 illustrate the typical elements of the psalmic prayers: (1) verses 1-2: the complaint proper; (2) verses 3-4: request for God's help; and (3) verses 5-6: expression of trust and/or praise. The first two of these elements fit together well; a troubled person naturally asks for help. The sudden shift to trust and/or praise is not expected, however, and the primary interpretive issue for students of the psalmic prayers has been how to explain this remarkable transition. Scholars have proposed a variety of explanations; but for the purposes of this essay, the literary-theological approach offered by James L. Mays is the most helpful. Mays finds in Psalm 13 a lesson about identity or, one might say, character formation:

> So in taking up the Psalm as our prayer, we are shown who we are when we pray. We are taught our true identity as mortals who stand on the earth and speak to a God who is ours but never owned. Agony and adoration hang together by a cry for life — this is the truth about us as people of faith. . . . The Psalm is not given us to use on the rare occasions when some trouble seems to make it appropriate. It is forever appropriate as long as life shall last. We do not begin at one end and come out at the other. The agony and the ecstasy belong together as the secret of our identity.[18]

This insight has profound and far-reaching implications. Prime among them is the conclusion that suffering cannot and should not be interpreted as punishment from God. Rather, it is one of the conditions of being mortal, or, as

---

17. Eugene Peterson, *Answering God: The Psalms as Tools for Prayer* (San Francisco: Harper and Row, 1989), p. 36.

18. James L. Mays, "Psalm 13," *Int* 34 (1980): 282.

some psalms make clear, it is a result of being faithful to God and thus incurring the wrath of persons who oppose God and God's purposes (see Ps 10:2-4, 10-11; 69:7-12). In any case, those identified in Psalms 1–2 as "happy" and "the righteous" are the ones in the psalmic prayers who are regularly identified with words like "poor," "helpless," "oppressed," "meek," "persecuted," "afflicted," and so on. Again, the righteous are in trouble all the time. Thus, the psalmic prayers, even though they sometimes suggest that God is the problem (see Ps 6:1; 13:1; 38:1), serve finally to obliterate any mechanistic doctrine of retribution that would allow suffering to be explained as divine punishment (see also the book of Job).

This conclusion is crucial because only the obliteration of a doctrine of retribution allows for the logical possibility of grace. In other words, if God or divine justice operates only to give people what they deserve, then "grace" is a meaningless concept. In this regard, it is important to notice that several of the psalmic prayers make it clear that "the righteous" are not the morally meritorious. In fact, Psalm 32:1 addresses the issue explicitly in terms of happiness, recalling Psalms 1–2. To be "happy" is a matter of grace: "Happy are those whose transgression is forgiven, whose sin is covered." Psalm 51 makes the same affirmation.

Because "the psalmist" knows that he or she has been treated graciously, "the psalmist" is free to treat others graciously. Although "the psalmist" is regularly shunned, even by friends who apparently interpret his or her suffering as evidence of divine punishment (see Ps 38:11; 41:9; 55:20-21; 88:8, 18), "the psalmist" refuses to victimize further those who are suffering. As "the psalmist" puts it in 35:13-14:

> But as for me, when they were sick,
>   I wore sackcloth;
> I afflicted myself with fasting.
> I prayed with head bowed on my bosom,
>   as though I grieved for a friend or brother;
> I went about as one who laments for a mother,
>   bowed down and in mourning.

In short, "the psalmist" refuses to blame victims. Shunning distributive or retributive justice, "the psalmist" embodies what might be called restorative justice, the pursuit of happiness by caring for others (see Ps 41:1).[19] This kind of justice is possible only by grace. At this point, the psalmic prayers converge with Psalms 1–2. Both command an other-directedness that impels people into a community of justice, righteousness, and equity that is grounded in grace.

19. See Desmond Tutu, *No Future Without Forgiveness* (New York: Image Doubleday, 1999), pp. 49-64, esp. 54-55.

The Psalmic Prayers and the Craziness
of Contemporary Culture

According to Mary Pipher, a major aspect of our contemporary cultural crisis is our inability to deal realistically, much less constructively, with suffering. What therapists, as well as parents and others, can do to address this aspect of the crisis is this: "We can teach that almost all the craziness in the world comes from running from pain."[20] This lesson, as suggested above, is one that is also taught by the psalmic prayers. Because "the psalmist" is in trouble all the time, the psalmic prayers teach us that to be human, and indeed to be faithful to the God of the Bible, means inevitably to suffer. To be sure, this lesson must be communicated carefully lest we teach that suffering itself is a positive virtue. The point is not that suffering is good, but rather that community formed by justice, righteousness, and equity is good. In short, the point is love, but to love means inevitably to suffer because it means that we take upon ourselves the hurt and the brokenness of others. While suffering is natural and while suffering for love's sake is to be embraced, this does not mean that we commend suffering itself as inherently virtuous, nor does it imply that suffering is to be tolerated when it perpetuates injustice.

Failing to learn the lesson that suffering is normal, we will fall prey to nearly any ideology that promises an easier way. In our culture, it is primarily the ideology of consumerism that is proclaimed incessantly by advertisers. As Pipher puts it:

> Advertising teaches that people shouldn't have to suffer, that pain is unnatural and can be cured. . . . Over and over again people hear that their needs for love, security and variety can be met with products. . . . When we suggest that suffering can be avoided, we foster unreasonable expectations. We are sending the same message that advertisers send. Advertisers imply that suffering is unnatural, shouldn't be tolerated and can be avoided with the right products. Psychologists sometimes imply that stress-free living is possible if only we have the right tools. But in fact, all our stories have sad endings. We all die in the last act.[21]

As Pipher suggests, what we need to learn in order to avoid the craziness of our culture is that suffering is normal because all human beings are fallible and finite. This is precisely the message of the psalmic prayers. Persons formed by the psalmic prayers know that they are in trouble all the time, but they also

20. Pipher, *The Shelter of Each Other*, p. 143.
21. Pipher, *The Shelter of Each Other*, pp. 93, 119.

know that the agony and the ecstasy of human life belong together. Or, in short, they will know finally that they live not by the sufficiency of their own resources or purchasing power but by the grace that invites them into a community characterized by caring for others — a community of restorative justice.

Persons who know that they live by grace will in turn be gracious (see above on Ps 35:13-14; see also Ps 112:4, especially in comparison to Ps 111:4). In contrast, persons who buy the message of the advertisers, and who in turn buy their products in an attempt to satisfy emotional and spiritual needs, will deny the reality of suffering. They see themselves as autonomous and conclude that they deserve the best. At best, this logic destroys any overarching sense of community with or accountability to other people — that is, it is unloving. At worst, this logic directly issues in violence. It is no wonder that a major aspect of our current cultural crisis is the rapidly increasing extremes of wealth and poverty among us, and it is no mere coincidence that the United States of America at the beginning of the twenty-first century is simultaneously the wealthiest and the most violent society in the world. Failing to learn to live by grace, the proud and the powerful will continue to perpetuate the violent cycle of blaming victims — for instance, the poor for being poor — conveniently absolving themselves of any responsibility for restorative justice. To borrow Mary Pipher's words again, by failing to live by the grace that impels us toward community, "ultimately we will all lose." Or, to paraphrase the conclusion of Psalm 1, while the "way of the righteous" leads to life, the preeminence of the autonomous self leads only to ruin.

Psalm 100 and the Songs of Praise

As noted above, the psalmic prayers (with the exception of Psalm 88) juxtapose complaint and request for help with praise and/or assurance, and it is crucial not to ignore this juxtaposition. As Walter Brueggemann warns, praise and assurance separated from complaint are dangerous. Praise in isolation easily becomes the ideology of the proud, the prosperous, and the powerful, reinforcing a status quo that benefits some people at the expense of others.[22]

However, when praise and pain, agony and ecstasy, are held together, then the songs of praise in the Psalter offer powerful reinforcement to the messages of Psalms 1–2 and the psalmic prayers. Psalm 100 is a helpful example because it makes explicit what all the songs of praise imply. It invites people: "Serve the

---

22. Walter Brueggemann, *Israel's Praise: Doxology against Idolatry and Ideology* (Philadelphia: Fortress, 1988).

LORD with gladness" (v. 2; NRSV "Worship"). Especially since it follows Psalms 93, 95–99, explicit celebrations of God's sovereignty, Psalm 100 invites submission of the self to God and God's claim upon human life and the life of the world. Verse 3, beginning with the invitation to "know," states explicitly what this means for human beings. In essence, we are not our own because we belong to God.[23] From this perspective, there can be no legitimate human claim to autonomy. Human life cannot be self-grounded, and human beings cannot be self-sufficient. To know these things and to live accordingly constitute "the way of the righteous." Thus, the songs of praise reinforce the claim of Psalms 1–2.

Both on the basis of Psalms 1–2 and the psalmic prayers, "the way of the righteous" involves the pursuit of happiness in a community of justice, righteousness, and equity. The songs of praise that proclaim God's sovereignty (Psalms 93, 95–99) most explicitly proclaim God's will for justice, righteousness, and equity.[24] Beyond this, many of the songs of praise point toward God's desire to bring people, indeed all people, together. This communal thrust is communicated by the invitation to praise, which includes "all the earth" (Ps 100:1), "all you nations" and "all you peoples" (Ps 117:1), and ultimately "everything that breathes" (Ps 150:6; see also Psalm 148). Even the psalms that request God's vengeance upon enemies (see Ps 109:6-19, which, contra NRSV, are the words of "the psalmist") or "on the nations" (Ps 109:7) should be understood as the victims' requests that things be set right. The point is not so much revenge as the establishment of justice and righteousness, inherently communal virtues.[25]

The Songs of Praise as Acts of Sanity

Walter Brueggemann calls Psalm 100 an "act of sanity," explaining what he means as follows:

> Obviously our world is at the edge of insanity and we with it. Inhumaneness is developed as a scientific enterprise. Greed is celebrated as economic advance. Power runs unbridled to destructiveness. . . . In a world like this one, our psalm is an act of sanity, whereby we may be "reclothed in

23. See the hymn by Brian Wren, "We Are Not Our Own," in *The New Century Hymnal* (Cleveland: Pilgrim Press, 1995), no. 564.

24. See especially Pss 96:13; 98:9; 99:4, as well as Psalms 82 and 72, which suggest that God wills human institutions like the monarchy to embody and enact justice and righteousness.

25. See Erich Zenger, *A God of Vengeance? Understanding the Psalms of Divine Wrath*, trans. Linda M. Maloney (Louisville: Westminster/John Knox, 1996), pp. 80-86.

our rightful minds" (cf. Mark 5:15). . . . Life is no longer self-grounded without thanks but rooted in thanks.[26]

More broadly, all the songs of praise may be considered acts of sanity addressed
to a culture of craziness, as they call us away from the temptation to be autonomous selves and invite us into a worldwide community of justice, righteousness, and equity.

That the songs of praise envision nothing short of a worldwide community is especially noteworthy because it suggests that the God of the Bible cannot
properly be worshipped until *everyone* is welcome. This perspective is especially
timely, since we are currently experiencing incredibly rapid globalization. At the
same time, there is a resurgence of tribalism — renewed commitment to national and ethnic identity. Although the two trends seem contradictory, they are
in fact related. As Thomas Friedman points out, the globalization we are experiencing is essentially driven by economics. North American and Western European capitalism is spreading around the world. As capitalism spreads, it tends to
take Western-style institutions with it, thus threatening national identities and
native cultures around the world. To be sure, poorer nations seem to welcome
the promise of increased economic prosperity, but the promise has a price. Even
experts on international economics and politics, like Friedman, are calling for a
form of globalization that will be driven by something other than just money.[27]
In any case, as the world grows smaller, for whatever reasons, the issue of the
twenty-first century is likely to be how persons confront "the other." The songs
of praise, of course, offer no easy or simple solutions to this complex issue. They
do, however, offer an alternative vision of globalization — one based on gratitude rather than greed, and one that calls for the valuing of all nations and all
peoples simply as children of a God who calls the whole world together.

Psalm 23 and the Psalms of Trust

If there is a third primary voice in the Psalms, besides prayer and praise, it is the
voice of trust. In keeping with what was said above concerning the holding together of complaint and praise, it is important, also, not to separate threat and
trust. Psalm 23, for instance, does not promise uninterrupted good times, but
rather God's provision and presence even in "the darkest valley" (v. 4).

---

26. Walter Brueggemann, "Psalm 100," *Int* 39 (1985): 67.

27. Thomas L. Friedman, *The Lexus and the Olive Tree: Understanding Globalization*
(New York: Farrar, Straus, Giroux, 1999), pp. 350-78, esp. pp. 376-78.

Like Psalms 1–2, the psalmic prayers, and the songs of praise, Psalm 23 and the other psalms of trust commend utter dependence upon God. In Psalm 23, "the psalmist" earns nothing, achieves nothing, deserves nothing. Rather, everything is a gift, motivated only by who God is.[28] Because all is grace, Psalm 23 leaves absolutely no room for autonomy.

Also like Psalms 1–2, the psalmic prayers, and the songs of praise, Psalm 23 invites people into a community of justice, righteousness, and equity. The controlling metaphor for God is "shepherd," a royal title, which thus calls to mind the divine will for justice, righteousness, and equity. The work of the shepherd in Psalm 23 is the work of restorative justice, the provision of resources that make life possible — the necessities of food, water, and shelter or protection. When the metaphor shifts in verses 5-6 to gracious host, the same sort of provision is made. God not only gathers in God's "house" (v. 6) a family that includes "the psalmist" but also brings his or her "enemies" to the table (v. 5). To be sure, some scholars have argued that the enemies are there just so that they can be taunted by the psalmist as he or she eats, but this is unlikely, especially in light of the conclusion of Psalm 22, which also includes a meal at which "the poor shall eat and be satisfied" (v. 26). Moreover, Psalm 22 suggests that the dimensions of God's family are unbounded: everyone, even the dead (v. 29), and "people yet unborn," are part of God's household. Psalm 23, like Psalm 22, ultimately envisions a community of restorative justice.

Psalm 23: An American Secular Icon?

William L. Holladay has suggested that Psalm 23 has become "an American Secular Icon," meaning that the psalm is widely known and used in the United States, especially in popular culture influenced by American Protestantism. As Holladay points out, Psalm 23 has achieved such popularity only because of a "process of sentimentalization" and "an overindividualized interpretation of the psalm."[29] He is undoubtedly correct. As suggested above, Psalm 23 offers a sharp criticism of the preeminence of the autonomous self, as well as an invitation to find one's primary identity as a member of a family that knows no bounds. Both the criticism and the invitation are, of course, profoundly un-American, at least in the minds and hearts of most citizens of the United States

28. See "for his name's sake" in v. 3, as well as the word *ḥesed* (NRSV "mercy") in v. 6, a sort of one-word summary of the character of God; see Exod 34:6-7.

29. William Holladay, *The Psalms through Three Thousand Years: Prayerbook of a Cloud of Witnesses* (Minneapolis, Minn.: Fortress, 1993), p. 368; see also pp. 359-71.

of America. By and large, most of us pursue happiness, as Mary Pipher suggests, with an unrelenting focus on ourselves and on what we can achieve or purchase, and we believe the advertisers when they tell us that we deserve the best, even if it is at the expense of our neighbors or of the rest of the world.

If Psalm 23 has become "an American Secular Icon," what is needed now is a process of recovery and a thoroughly communal interpretation of the psalm. Mary Pipher's designation for us contemporary North Americans is "the 'I want' generation."[30] Perhaps if we could recover a thoroughly communal interpretation of Psalm 23, we might actually discern its profoundly formative message. Indeed, we might even be able to say (and to mean it rather literally) what is nearly unthinkable for most North Americans, "I shall not want."

Conclusion

By way of its beginning with Psalms 1–2 and by way of each of its major voices — prayer, praise, and profession of trust — the Psalter portrays "the psalmist" as one who is constantly and completely attentive to God and God's purposes. From the beginning and throughout the Psalms, "the way of the righteous" means the pursuit of happiness by way of openness to God's teaching, God's protection, presence, provision, and forgiveness. In other words, "the way of the righteous" is submission of the self to God's sovereign claim upon the life of the world, and it is the commitment of the self to the embodiment of the divine will for justice, righteousness, and equity. What this will mean in practice is the acceptance of suffering that derives from human finitude and fallibility, as well as the anticipation of suffering that derives from those who oppose God and God's purposes. In short, "the way of the righteous" is finally to live by grace, accepting God's forgiveness and, in gratitude, extending forgiveness to others. This means the refusal to blame apparent victims, and it opens the way for the formation of a community that is open to the world. Thus, ultimately, the world-encompassing justice that God wills is founded on grace.

As suggested above, the kind of character formed by the Psalms is a significant challenge to the formative influences of North American culture, which systematically teaches us to pursue happiness by being self-centered. The result is greed rather than gratitude; a sense of entitlement rather than a spirit of generosity; and the formation of exclusive enclaves of wealth, power, and privilege rather than the formation of a world-encompassing community of restorative justice for all. In short, the result is violence rather than love.

30. Pipher, *The Shelter of Each Other,* p. 180.

It may occur to Christian readers of the Psalms that the composite portrait of "the psalmist" looks a lot like the portrayal of Jesus in the Gospels. According to the Gospel of Matthew, for instance, Jesus claimed to live by God's word alone (4:4); he announced God's sovereign claim on the world and invited people to respond (4:17); he pronounced "blessed" or "happy" those people who are in trouble all the time (5:1-11); and he invited them to "rejoice and be glad" (5:12), thus holding together the agony and ecstasy. Jesus obliterated the doctrine of retribution, telling his followers to give freely (5:42) and to "love your enemies" (5:44). By such grace, Jesus claimed to be striving for a greater "righteousness" (5:17; see 6:33), for justice that is restorative rather than retributive. And, of course, for God's sake and love's sake, Jesus suffered; and he invited others to follow in his path of self-denial and suffering (16:24). The pattern of Jesus' death and resurrection holds together agony and ecstasy, and it communicates the divine acceptance of a sinful world that formed the foundation for the gathering of a community "of all nations" (28:19). It would fall to the Apostle Paul to pursue the structural embodiment of such a new community of Jews and Gentiles (= the nations), a task Paul supported by the announcement of the establishment of God's justice (justification) by grace alone.

Given these congruencies between "the psalmist" and Jesus, it is not surprising to discover that Matthew and the other Gospels cannot tell the story of Jesus, especially the story of Jesus' passion, without recourse to the Psalms — especially Psalms 22 (Ps 22:1 and Matt 27:46; Mark 15:34), 31 (Ps 31:5 and Luke 23:46), and 69 (Ps 69:21 and Matt 27:48; Ps 69:9 and John 2:17), the longest and most intense of the psalmic prayers. We cannot explore in this essay all the complexities involved in the relationship between these psalms and the Gospels. Suffice it to say that the Gospel-writers saw embodied in Jesus the fullest expression of the character of "the psalmist," the ultimate expression of "the way of the righteous."

The Pedagogy of Proverbs 10:1–31:9

William P. Brown

With the exception of specific vocational training, education in ancient Israel and throughout the ancient Near East was devoted primarily to the task of "moral formation" or "the building of character."[1] It is often noted that much of the wisdom literature (i.e., Proverbs, Job, and Ecclesiastes, as well as the extracanonical books of Sirach and the Wisdom of Solomon) shares this aim.[2] Consonant with this purpose, the sapiential material of the Hebrew canon is by nature open-ended and dynamic, as opposed to dogmatic, in its scope.[3] Like the divergent psalms of the Psalter, the wisdom corpus contains its share of orienting and disorienting elements.[4] Scholars most typically discern such variety of material either from the broadest possible perspective, that is, by highlight-

1. James L. Crenshaw, *Education in Ancient Israel: Across the Deadening Silence,* ABRL (New York: Doubleday, 1998), p. 1; see also pp. 58, 158. For an analysis of the wisdom corpus from a character ethics perspective, see William P. Brown, *Character in Crisis: A Fresh Approach to the Wisdom Literature of the Old Testament* (Grand Rapids: Eerdmans, 1996).

2. For an analysis of Sirach from a character formation perspective, see Roland E. Murphy, "Sin, Repentance, and Forgiveness in Sirach," in *Der Einzelne und seine Gemeinschaft bei Ben Sira,* ed. Renate Egger-Wenzel and Ingrid Krammer (Berlin and New York: Walter de Gruyter, 1998), pp. 261-70.

3. See, in particular, Roland E. Murphy's pronouncement, "Any gnomic conclusion relative to God, world, and man needs a balancing corrective" ("The Hebrew Sage and Openness to the World," in *Christian Action and Openness to the World,* ed. J. Papin [Villanova, Pa.: Villanova University Press, 1970], p. 229). See also the discussion of this "axiom" in James L. Crenshaw, "Murphy's Axiom: Every Gnomic Saying Needs a Balancing Corrective," in *The Listening Heart: Essays in Wisdom and the Psalms in Honor of Roland E. Murphy, O.Carm.,* ed. K. G. Hoglund et al., JSOTSup 58 (Sheffield: JSOT Press, 1987), pp. 1-17.

4. See the terminology used by Walter Brueggemann in his functional analysis of the psalms in *The Message of the Psalms,* AOTS (Minneapolis, Minn.: Augsburg, 1984).

ing the formal or content-oriented characteristics that distinguish the various wisdom books from each other, or in piecemeal fashion by analyzing discrete groupings of proverbial or instructional material around certain themes and catchwords. Regarding the former, it is commonly observed that Job and Ecclesiastes feature radical, even subversive, forms of sapiential reflection, much in contrast to what is frequently considered "traditional" or conventional wisdom, as found throughout much of Proverbs.[5] Matching this contrast are two modes of understanding reality, James L. Crenshaw claims, "one firmly grounded in experience, the other abstract and philosophical."[6] Such differing epistemological orientations help to define various teaching modes as well. Crenshaw identifies the expository mode, conveyed through aphorisms and instructions, which "emphasizes the teacher's authority and depends heavily on the power of example," and the hypothetical mode, which "shifts the focus to students, who are challenged to engage in an exciting quest to discover answers to intriguing questions."[7]

Such analysis esteems Job and Ecclesiastes as "highly reflective" works, in contrast to Proverbs, whose "vast majority of proverbial sayings," Crenshaw submits, "tends toward the banal, hardly commending themselves as worthy of careful study by serious students."[8] This, however, is a gross overstatement. Regardless of whether a formal educational context can be demonstrated in the case of Proverbs, as Crenshaw argues for Job and Ecclesiastes, one cannot deny the book's didactic value. Proverbs bears the expressed aim to teach and embodies or commends certain teaching methods and techniques, some of them quite sophisticated, such as recitation, reproof, indirection, disputation, learning by analogy, and metaphorical teasing.[9]

The tendency to view the proverbial as pedagogically simplistic is inaccurate, if not prejudicial. For all the careful attention given to identifying the vari-

---

5. As a parallel movement, mention is frequently made of the striking progression of thought in Egyptian wisdom literature from Old Kingdom confidence to Middle Kingdom disillusionment and New Kingdom skepticism (Crenshaw, *Education in Ancient Israel*, pp. 24-25).

6. Crenshaw, *Education in Ancient Israel*, p. 51.

7. Crenshaw, *Education in Ancient Israel*, p. 27. It is difficult to see how either Job or Ecclesiastes fits into Crenshaw's "hypothetical mode" as he has defined it. Neither book conveys much excitement in the "quest" of discovery, as if the journey of wisdom were simply a felicitous academic exercise. I find Crenshaw's observation ironic in light of his studies that stress the agonizing pathos of Job and Ecclesiastes (see, e.g., *A Whirlpool of Torment: Israelite Traditions of God as an Oppressive Presence*, OBT 12 [Philadelphia: Fortress, 1984], pp. 57-92).

8. Crenshaw, *Education in Ancient Israel*, pp. 27, 232.

9. See Charles F. Melchert, *Wise Teaching: Biblical Wisdom and Educational Ministry* (Harrisburg, Pa.: Trinity Press International, 1998), pp. 47-58, 71-72.

ous literary forms contained in Proverbs, from the terse sentence to the extended instruction, largely overlooked is the overarching editorial arrangement and pedagogical movement the book exhibits as a whole. Crenshaw, along with many others, notes only a "haphazard arrangement, with a few notable exceptions."[10] Those "few" exceptions include certain formal patterns of arrangement. It is recognized, for example, that the sayings in Proverbs 10–15 are largely cast in antithetical parallelism, whereas chapters 16–22 exhibit primarily synonymous parallelism. In addition, paronomasia, catchwords, synonym sequences, wordplays, and repetitions serve as mnemonic devices linking halves of verses or associating one verse with the next.[11] Yet beyond these stylistic features, most interpreters see little evidence of broader formal and content-related principles of arrangement that would suggest an overarching advancement of instruction from beginning to end.[12]

There is more than meets the form-critically trained eye. It is commonly suggested that Proverbs 1–9, which acknowledges that wisdom's scope

10. Crenshaw, *Education in Ancient Israel*, p. 230.

11. See Harold C. Washington's discussion in *Wealth and Poverty in the Instruction of Amenemope and the Hebrew Proverbs*, SBLDS 142 (Atlanta: Scholars Press, 1994), p. 191; Ted Hildebrandt, "Proverbial Pairs: Compositional Units in Proverbs 10–29," *JBL* 107 (1988): 207-24; Raymond C. Van Leeuwen, *Context and Meaning in Proverbs 25–27*, SBLDS 96 (Atlanta: Scholars Press, 1988). See also Daniel C. Snell, *Twice-Told Proverbs and the Composition of the Book of Proverbs* (Winona Lake, Ind.: Eisenbrauns, 1993), who examines the proverbial repetitions to determine the book's compositional history but refrains from speculating on "ideological development" (p. 61).

12. Raymond C. Van Leeuwen has noted that the Solomonic "subcollections" indicate a move from a simple to a "more complex view of acts and consequences" ("Proverbs — An Introduction," in *The New Interpreter's Bible*, vol. 5 [Nashville: Abingdon, 1997], p. 23). Also of note is the work of Patrick Skehan, who has sought to discern the book's architectural contours through numerical analysis (*Studies in Ancient Israelite Poetry and Wisdom*, CBQMS 1 [Washington, D.C.: Catholic Biblical Association, 1971], pp. 9-45, which contains the following revised studies: "The Seven Columns of Wisdom's House in Proverbs 1–9," *CBQ* 9 [1947]: 190-98; "A Single Editor for the Whole Book of Proverbs," *CBQ* 10 [1948]: 115-30; "Wisdom's House," *CBQ* 29 [1967]: 468-86). Such an analysis, however, has little to do with the content and message of the book, except that Skehan sees an architectonic structure behind the tripartite division of Proverbs that is proportioned to the dimensions of the Solomonic Temple, which in the context of the book corresponds to Wisdom's House referenced in 9:1 (Skehan, *Studies in Ancient Israelite Poetry and Wisdom*, p. 27). Unfortunately, Skehan's architectural plan for Proverbs rests more on speculation than on hard evidence to support his numerical analysis since his architectural argument requires certain rearrangements of the MT (*Studies in Ancient Israelite Poetry and Wisdom*, p. 29). But even granting his argument would simply suggest that the final editor of Proverbs envisioned the book as a literary replacement of the temple, a formalized and abstract function that lacks concrete reference to the book's content.

includes *both* the young and the wise,[13] serves as the formal introduction to the book and, thus, as a guide to how it is to be read and used. Indeed, Proverbs 1–9 and 31:10-31 have been deliberately placed to *exemplify* the formation of moral character. The development of Wisdom's character, for example, from irritated teacher in 1:20-33 to child of God and hostess in chapters 8 and 9, and ultimately her association with the *'ēšet ḥayil* ("woman of strength") in the concluding acrostic poem of 31:10-31, suggests an overarching movement from beginning to end. Not unrelated is the development of the implied or "interpellated" reader of Proverbs,[14] from the figure of the silent son in the first nine chapters to his mature counterpart, the esteemed spouse of the "woman of strength," profiled at the conclusion. Whereas Proverbs opens with a crisis situation painted by a father's urgent warning to his son about the dangers of violence and greed (Prov 1:8-19), the book concludes with the climactic, irenic scene of the productive and generous household. In short, the bookends of Proverbs trace the formation of moral character that culminates in the union between Wisdom and her student, a movement that spans the process of maturation from receptive child to responsible adult, from dependent to patriarch. It would be reasonable, then, to expect a compatible development within the intervening material (10:1–31:9) that would sustain this overall movement.

If there is evidence of pedagogical movement in the compositional units of Proverbs 1–9 and 31:10-31, what place, then, do the collections that are bracketed by them have? Specifically, why are the various collections of sayings arranged in their present order in the MT?[15] Is there a logical, indeed pedagogical, rationale behind their arrangement? One possible clue is to be found in the superscriptions that introduce the various collections.

---

13. See 1:5. In 9:9, the reader is exhorted to "give instruction to the wise" and the "righteous." Proverbs, thus, acknowledges an *advanced* quality to much of the wisdom it has to offer.

14. See the notion of "interpellation" by Louis Althusser as discussed by Carol A. Newsom, "Woman and the Discourse of Patriarchal Wisdom: A Study of Proverbs 1–9," in *Gender and Difference in Ancient Israel*, ed. Peggy L. Day (Minneapolis, Minn.: Fortress, 1989), pp. 143-44.

15. The LXX features the "words of Agur" immediately following "words of the wise" and places the Hezekian collection immediately prior to the acrostic poem. The Masoretic arrangement, however, is to be preferred over the LXX because the arrangement and editorial work featured in the LXX can be attributed to a concern to strengthen the Solomonic authorship of the book as a whole (see Washington, *Wealth and Poverty*, pp. 126-27; H. Gese, "Wisdom Literature in the Persian Period," in *The Cambridge History of Judaism*, vol. 1: *Introduction: The Persian Period*, ed. W. D. Davies and L. Finkelstein [Cambridge: Cambridge University Press, 1984], pp. 200-201).

I. Proverbs of Solomon	10:1–22:16
II. The words of the wise	22:17–24:22
III. Additional sayings of the wise	24:23-34
IV. These are Solomon's other proverbs that the officials of King Hezekiah of Judah copied	25:1–29:27
V. The words of Agur son of Jakeh	30:1-33
VI. The words of King Lemuel, an oracle that his mother taught him	31:1-9

Those proverbs that are directly attributed to Solomon assume pride of place, followed by two small groups of anonymous wisdom sayings and the more substantial Hezekian collection. Sayings attributed to foreign figures are grouped at the end of the corpus. This extensive collection of collections begins and ends with a royal figure and moves, in terms of attribution, from specifically Israelite to international wisdom.

There is, however, much more to this arrangement than simply the matter of attributed sources. Curious is the fact that the anonymous "words of the wise" and the "additional sayings of the wise" are located between two substantial collections attributed to Solomon, the latter purportedly transmitted by the "men of Hezekiah." The possibility remains that certain formal and content-related features help to account for the present arrangement in Prov 10:1–31:9, factors that profile a certain direction of moral formation consonant with the pedagogical contours of the book as a whole.

Initial Context

The placement of these collections between the instructional material of Proverbs 1–9 and the acrostic in chapter 31 is telling. Many have noted that the concluding acrostic, which depicts the household of the "woman of strength," has its negative counterpart in 7:6-27, which takes the reader into the domicile of the "strange woman" (ʾiššâ zārâ / nokrîyâ). These two contrasting domiciles and their respective managers are virtual mirror images of each other: one embodies wisdom and life, the other, waywardness and death. Whereas the "strange woman" imports linens from Egypt (7:16), the "woman of strength" produces her own textiles (31:13, 19, 22). That they are not tightly juxtaposed but separated at a considerable literary distance in part by six collections of sapiential material is significant. The household setting of chapter 9 serves as a transition to the collections that begin in chapter 10. In addition to building her home of "seven pillars," Wisdom invites her guests to a lavish banquet: "Come, eat my bread and drink the wine I have mixed," she declares (9:5).[16] The "foolish woman," Wisdom's nemesis, also issues an invitation: "Stolen water is sweet, and bread secretly eaten is pleasant" (9:17). Unlike her offer, Wisdom's lavish banquet is distinctly fraught with sapiential background.[17]

Eating and appropriating wisdom are, in fact, intimately associated throughout Proverbs and elsewhere in the wisdom corpus: "Does not the ear test words as the palate tastes food?" asks Job (12:11). "The lips of the righteous nourish many, but fools die for lack of sense" (Prov 10:21); "From the fruit of the mouth one is satisfied with good things" (12:14a); "From the fruit of the mouth good persons eat good things" (13:2a); "Pleasant words are a honeycomb, sweetness to the palate and health to the body" (16:24); "My son, eat honey, for it is good . . . know that wisdom is such to your *nepeš*" (24:13-14; see also 13:4, 25; 17:1). The association of food with wisdom establishes a suggestive meta-context for the sapiential collections that follow chapter 9. Wisdom's banquet is a feast of insight (9:6), a veritable smorgasbord of sapiential thought with each proverb and poem constituting an edifying morsel to be savored and digested. As food is to be tasted and consumed, so wisdom's discourse is to be heard and appropriated. It all begins with a diet of discipline in small, discrete doses.

The Solomonic Collection (10:1–22:16)

To state the obvious, Prov 10:1–31:9 presents a bewildering array of literary forms, from the terse antithetical proverb, which contrasts two thematic elements, to the extensive instruction, in which direct address predominates, as well as lament, petition, and the graded numerical proverb. Yet, for all of its variety, certain hints of pedagogical movement can be discerned by attending to both the formal and content-oriented features of each collection. The first collection is telling.

Literary Form

It is commonly suggested that the "Proverbs of Solomon" (10:1–22:16) is divisible into two discrete collections characterized by a preponderance of antitheti-

---

16. Unless otherwise indicated, all translations are the author's.

17. See the guarded analysis in Karl-Gustav Sandelin, *Wisdom as Nourisher: A Study of an Old Testament Theme, Its Development within Early Judaism and Its Impact on Early Christianity*, Acta Academiae Aboensis, Ser. A, 64/3 (Åbo: Åbo Akademi, 1987), pp. 19-26.

cal sayings in roughly the first six chapters and a predominance of non-antithetical or synonymously paralleled sayings that follow.[18] Typical of the first "collection" is the first proverb:

> A wise son makes a glad father;
>> but a foolish son is a mother's grief.   (10:1)

This opening proverb contrasts the wise son with the foolish and notes the effects of his character upon the parents' disposition. In addition to the wise and the foolish (see also 10:8), numerous moral polarities dominate this first section: the wicked versus the righteous (10:2, 3, 6), the lazy versus the diligent (10:4), love versus hatred (10:12), integrity versus crookedness (11:3), curse versus blessing (11:26), faithfulness versus deceit (12:22), restrained versus rash speech (10:19; 12:18), and to some degree wealth versus poverty (10:15). The accumulation of such antithetical sayings paints a morally dualistic world largely devoid of ambiguity or compromise: one is either wise or foolish, righteous or wicked. Except for 14:7, absent is any instruction or direct address. Rather, the mood is predominantly indicative and observational, though far from neutral: the tone is clearly prescriptive. Careful delineation is made, for example, of how the righteous conduct themselves and what benefits can be expected from such conduct.

Antithetical parallelism, however, does not exhaust the poetic forms employed in this first so-called "collection." Nonantithetical or positive parallelism can also be found sprinkled liberally throughout this first collection, tending to occur in loose clusters: 10:18, 22, 26, 28; 11:7, 10, 25, 29; 12:14, 29; 13:14; 14:13, 17, 19, 26; 15:3, 11, 12, 23, 24, 30, 31. Moreover, three *ṭôb* or "better-than sayings" (12:9; 15:16, 17) and two (explicit or implied) similes (10:26; 11:22) appear. Of the nonantithetical forms (excluding the *ṭôb* sayings), ten are cast negatively and twelve are conveyed positively, a symmetrical presentation in keeping with the overall tenor of the antithetical proverbs, each of which comprises a negative and positive component.

It is not fortuitous, perhaps, that a cluster of positively paralleled or synonymous sayings concludes the "antithetical" section, for the next section — typically called the "royal collection" (15:33–22:16) — contains a significantly higher percentage of nonantithetically paralleled bicola, even though antithetical proverbs still occur frequently, beginning with 16:1-2. Indeed, antithetical proverbs comprise 21.5 percent of this corpus (forty-one total), whereas they constitute 84 percent in the first "collection." In addition, a greater number of

---

18. I use the terms "antithetical" and "synonymous" parallelism out of convenience but with some reservation in light of James L. Kugel's critique in *The Idea of Biblical Poetry* (New Haven, Conn.: Yale University Press, 1981), pp. 49-58.

ṭôb sayings (nine) and instructions (eight) are featured in this "collection." The majority of the sayings, however, are cast in nonantithetical parallelism, but similar to the previous "collection," the proverbs of 15:33–22:16 also convey a morally bifurcated worldview: fifty-eight are cast positively; eighty-four are cast negatively. Evident is a greater variety of form in this second half of the Solomonic collection.

The so-called "royal collection" continues many of the themes treated in the first "collection," so much so that an originally discrete compilation is difficult to discern. Such evidence suggests that these so-called "collections" did not exist independently.[19] More likely, they constituted the two related halves of a larger collection that exhibits a certain didactic progression of content and form. Hence, I shall refer to these "collections" as the first and second halves or sections of the larger Solomonic collection of 10:1–22:16.

The prominence of synonymous parallelism in the second half of the Solomonic collection serves to expand and thereby reinforce numerous themes and values conveyed in the first half. Compare, for example, the following sayings on a common theme:

A false balance is an abomination to YHWH,
  but an accurate weight is his delight.   (11:1)

Valid balances and scales are YHWH's;
  all the weights in the bag are his work.   (16:11)

Discrepant weights and measures
  are both an abomination to YHWH.   (20:10)

Discrepant weights are an abomination to YHWH,
  and false scales are not good.   (20:23)

The three proverbs of the second half of the Solomonic collection expand upon what is encapsulated antithetically in the first proverb. One can find a similar dynamic at work on the theme of bearing truthful witness, which is treated only once in the antithetical half of the collection (12:17) and subsequently expanded in four proverbs in the so-called "royal collection" or second half (19:5,

---

19. Cf. Snell, *Twice-Told Proverbs*, p. 61, who rejects the common division in favor of Skehan's suggestion that 14:26–16:15 constitutes a later subdivision. See, most recently, Andreas Scherer, *Das weise Wort und seine Wirkung: Eine Untersuchung zur Komposition und Redaktion von Proverbia 10,1–22,16*, WMANT 83 (Neukirchen-Vluyn: Neukirchener Verlag, 1999), pp. 190-202, who identifies the unit 15:33–16:15 as a *Sammlungskern* for 10:1–22:16. Hence, I include 15:33 in the "second half."

9, 28; 21:28). Finally, the theme of child rearing is addressed five times antithetically in the first half (10:1; 13:1, 24; 15:5, 20) but expanded almost twofold in the second half in nonantithetical fashion (17:21, 25; 19:13, 18, 26, 27; 20:11; 22:6, 15).

While one can generalize that much of the second half of the Solomonic collection advances the themes presented by the first section, other sayings in the second section do not find precedent in the first half. Numerous proverbs of the second half exhibit greater flexibility in form, as well as theme. Such is the case with the YHWH sayings (e.g., 16:1, 2, 9; 17:3; 20:24, 27; 21:31), which frequently emphasize the inefficacy of human activity in the face of divine providence (see below).

Thematic Movement in the Solomonic Collection

Along with the increasing variety of poetic forms found in the latter half of the Solomonic collection, a number of thematic or content-oriented trajectories can be traced from the first to the second half of the Solomonic collection. The progression of various themes suggests a "curricular" advancement in such areas as human relations, communication, ethics, money, governance, and theology.

From Family to Friendship

The two halves of this extensive collection of sayings exhibit distinctive emphases in terms of moral scope and message. Held in common throughout the Solomonic proverbs is the value of heeding instruction and wise advice (e.g., 10:17; 13:10; 16:20; 19:20, 23; 20:30; 22:15). In 10:1–15:32, the predominant social setting is that of the family. The child's success in appropriating wisdom is shared by the entire household, including in particular the parents (10:1; 13:1; 15:20). The language of discipline and rebuke emerges directly from the familial setting: "A fool despises his father's instruction, but the one who heeds admonition is prudent" (15:5). A functional household is marked by strict discipline and fulfilled needs. Wisdom upholds the household: "The wisest of women builds her house, but the foolish woman tears it down with her own hands" (14:1).[20] Character types are even distinguished by their respective households: the household of the wicked meets destruction (14:11) and is to be torn down by YHWH (15:25). The greedy "make trouble for their households" (15:27; see also

20. See Clifford's translation (*Proverbs*, OTL [Louisville: Westminster John Knox, 1999], pp. 141, 143).

11:29a). In contrast, the house of the righteous will endure (12:7b) and is filled with treasure (15:6). Perhaps it is no coincidence that "the ear that heeds wholesome admonition *lodges (tâlîn)* among the wise," as if the ear were a welcomed guest in an accommodating household (15:31). Moreover, wisdom finds itself "at rest" *(tânûaḥ)* in the heart of the discerning individual (14:33a).

In short, a familial ethos pervades this initial half of the collection. The family serves as the primary means by which wisdom is successfully appropriated. The cultivation of right character begins in the home, in which the principal characters are the parents and the child. Wider social contexts, such as the city and nation, are relatively peripheral by comparison (see 11:10-11, 14).

The household setting is maintained in the second half of the collection, which includes advice on child training and discipline (17:21, 25; 19:13, 18, 26, 27; 20:11, 20), identifying the ideal wife (18:22; 21:9, 19), and establishing the functional household (17:1, 13; 21:12). Yet a new relational dimension is introduced. Extending the scope of the predominantly familial context of the first half, the second half of the collection devotes considerable attention to matters of friendship, occasionally at the expense of familial relations: "A friend loves *('ōhēb hārēa')* at all times, but kinsfolk *('āḥ)* are born to strife" (17:17); "A friend *('ōhēb)* sticks closer than one's kin" (18:24b). Friendship is the central focus of six proverbs (16:28; 17:9, 17; 18:24; 19:6, 7) and is associated with harmonious relationships that reach beyond the familial sphere (16:28; 17:9, 17). Indeed, it is among friends (rather than among relatives?) that forgiveness is highlighted as a virtue (17:9). Even the king can be counted as friend, depending on the moral status of one's character (22:11). Consonant with this focus, the dangers of strife and quarreling receive more attention in the second half (16:28; 17:14, 17, 19; 18:6, 18, 19; 20:3; cf. only 10:12 in the first half). In sum, the familial context that pervades the first half of the Solomonic collection is significantly widened in the second.

From Character to Concept

Along with its focus on the household, the first half of the Solomonic collection also gives pride of place to the individual, frequently referenced in terms of the physical body. The eye (15:30), the ear (15:31), and the hand (10:4) all receive due attention as instruments for appropriating wisdom and exercising right conduct. In addition to the physical body, the virtues of righteousness and wickedness are denoted largely by individual character types (see, e.g., 11:10-11). The "righteous person" *(ṣaddîq)* endures, while the wicked individual will disappear off the land (10:30; cf. 13:9). The abstract term "righteousness" *(ṣĕdāqâ or ṣedeq)* is found in only eleven cases, sometimes grouped together (11:4-6, 18-19), and only in three instances is it referenced apart from individual character (10:2; 11:4; 12:28) in order to stress the salvific efficacy of this moral category.[21] However, such abstract language is considerably less common than the use of the concrete adjectival form *ṣaddîq*, which occurs no less than thirty-nine times. Abstract terminology, thus, constitutes only 22 percent of all sayings in which the root for "righteous" is attested. Wickedness, too, is also defined predominantly by individual character and action: whereas the adjective *rāšāʿ* occurs twenty-eight times, the abstract form *rešaʿ* is attested only twice (10:2; 12:3) in the first half (6.7 percent). In general, individual character is placed in the foreground relative to abstract categories of virtue. Prominent focus, thus, is given to the *conduct and consequence* of the wicked and the righteous individual.

Such references to individual character types are less attested in the second half of the collection. Reference to the "righteous individual" (*ṣaddîq*) occurs only ten times, compared to thirty-nine times in the first half. The corresponding abstract category, "righteousness," is attested at a significantly higher percentage in the second half (37.5 percent, compared to 22 percent in the first half). Relatedly, the theme of justice (*mišpāṭ*) commands greater attention in the latter half of the collection. Whereas *mišpāṭ* is attested only twice in the first half (12:5; 13:23),[22] it is found no less than ten times in the second (16:8, 10, 11, 33; 17:23; 18:5; 19:28; 21:3, 7, 15). Justice, for example, holds sway when the innocent are acquitted and the guilty are condemned (17:15, 26; 18:5), and when truthful witness is given (19:28) and impartiality reigns (17:23; 18:5). Echoing a theme from the Psalter and the prophets is the summary statement in 21:3 ("To do righteousness and justice is more acceptable to YHWH than sacrifice"),[23] which can be compared to the only reference to sacrifice in the first half of the Solomonic collection: "The sacrifice of the wicked is an abomination to YHWH, but the prayer of the upright is his delight" (15:8). Whereas the latter saying focuses on individual character in relation to worship, the former compares the cultic context to the judicial sphere. In short, the Solomonic collection marks a gradual move from individual character types to the abstract conceptions they embody.

From Silence to Elocution

Among the parts of the body that are instrumental in embodying wisdom, most critical is the mouth, the organ of discourse. Typical is 10:11: "The foun-

---

21. In 14:34, the efficacy of righteousness is described from a collective perspective.

22. Prov 12:5 contextualizes the term on the individual level, and 13:23 invokes the term in the context of oppression-induced poverty.

23. Cf. Ps 50:8-18; Mic 6:6-8; Isa 1:12-17; Prov 1:3.

tain of life is the mouth of the righteous, but the mouth of the wicked conceals violence." More hyperbolic is 15:4a: "A healing tongue is a tree of life." In proverbial wisdom, the edifying mouth can not be overestimated: "The lips of the righteous nourish many" (10:21a). The mouth or discourse of the wicked or fool, in contrast, produces incoherent babbling, sets a deadly ambush, conceals violence, and destroys neighbors (10:6b, 8; 12:6; 11:9). At the opposite extreme, the tongue of the wise or righteous brings healing (12:18b), is truthful (12:19), provides an apt answer (15:23), and, most importantly, is silent (11:12; 12:23; 13:3). Silence is a theme that also pervades much Egyptian instruction and is also attested in Sumerian sources, as in the proverb: "An open mouth draws flies."[24]

In short, the mouth must be guarded carefully (13:3). Sagacious discourse is marked by restraint, gentleness, and silence (10:19; 11:12; 15:1; see also 17:28). As "the mouth of the wicked conceals violence" (10:6b), so the "one who is clever conceals knowledge" (12:23a). Yet "the lips of the righteous know what is acceptable" (10:32), and "the tongue of the wise improves[25] knowledge, whereas the mouths of fools spew out folly" (15:2). Inextricably connected to the mind or heart *(lēb)*, the seat of intelligence (15:7, 28), the mouth is the organ of wisdom and folly; it wields the power of life or death, depending on the speaker's character, and the less it imparts, the better.

Thematically continuous with the first half, the integrity of discourse is heavily underscored in the latter half of the Solomonic collection: "Death and life are in the power of the tongue, and those who love it will consume its fruits" (18:21).[26] Striking, however, is that the virtues of silence and listening, dominant themes in the first half, are scarcely mentioned in the second half (only 17:28).[27] While the importance of listening is occasionally highlighted, honesty and elocution command greater attention in the second half. The art of elocution is emphasized in 16:21 ("Pleasant speech increases learning"), 16:24 ("Pleasant words are like a honeycomb, sweetness to the palate and health to the body"), and 16:23 ("The heart of the wise makes his mouth judicious and adds learning to his lips"). In addition, telling the truth, as opposed to bearing false witness, is explicitly placed on the level of jurisprudence: "A worthless witness scoffs at justice, and the mouth of the wicked swallows iniquity" (19:28; cf. 17:7; 19:5, 9; 21:28, as well as 12:17; 14:25). In short, the virtue of silence or reserved speech is extolled in the first half as the beginning point of sagacious discourse, while the

---

24. Bendt Alster, *Proverbs of Ancient Sumer: The World's Earliest Proverb Collections*, vol. 1 (Bethesda, Md.: CDL Press, 1997), 3.119 (p. 100).

25. So MT *(têṭîb)*.

26. See also 16:21, 24, 27, 30; 17:4, 7, 27; 18:4, 6, 7, 13, 20; 19:5, 9, 28; 21:23, 28.

27. Cf. 10:19; 11:12; 12:8, 15; 15:1.

art of elocution and its forensic implications are laid out in the second. From this, one can discern a prescribed movement from discursive restraint to persuasive speech, from silence to elocution.

Wealth and Poverty

Another major theme addressed in the first half of the collection is the theme of wealth and poverty. While wealth is treated with a degree of suspicion, poverty is considered anathema. Riches demonstrate either YHWH's blessing (10:22) or a person's greed and wickedness (10:2; 11:16b; 13:11). The distinction turns on how wealth is acquired. Poverty, by contrast, must be avoided at all costs and is attributable primarily to character deficiencies, such as laziness and intransigence (e.g., 10:4; 12:24; 13:18; 14:23). In only one instance is there any recognition that a systemic condition is to blame (13:23). Only two proverbs in the first half of the collection encourage charity: "How fortunate is the one who is kind to the poor" (14:21); and "Whoever oppresses the poor insults his Maker, but whoever is kind to the needy honors him" (14:31).

As in the first half, poverty is described in the second half as both a culpable and tragic condition. On the one hand, wealth offers protection (18:11) and is intimately related to wisdom (19:10a; 21:20). On the other hand, amassing wealth at the expense of the poor is roundly condemned (22:16). The quick acquisition of property will not deliver in the end (20:21). Treasure acquired by lying is a "fleeting vapor" *(hebel niddāp)*, if not fatal (21:6).

More striking in the second half is a relatively positive estimation of poverty found in three *ṭôb* sayings: poverty is morally preferable over pride (16:19), foolish or perverse speech (19:1), and lying (19:22). Poverty, here, serves as a point of *comparison* that underscores the gravity of certain flaws in conduct or character. Also unique to the second half is the prescribed conduct of generosity to the poor (21:13; 22:9, 16). The sages note that while "the rich rules over the poor" (22:7a), the poor and the rich have in common their creator, YHWH (22:2; cf. 14:31; 17:5). Consequently, wealth and poverty, as in the first half, send mixed yet moderating signals: wealth is a desideratum but not an object of obsession; poverty is undesirable but not necessarily a culpable condition. Taken together, the various sayings, *particularly in the second half,* temper both the efficacy of wealth and the culpability typically associated elsewhere with poverty.[28]

---

28. See the important study of Raymond C. Van Leeuwen, "Wealth and Poverty: System and Contradiction in Proverbs," *Hebrew Studies* 33 (1992): 25-36, in which the contradictory stance in Proverbs on this issue is examined. Also significant to such an analysis is the *order* of presentation in the Solomonic collection (see below).

Kingship

More fully developed in the latter half of the Solomonic collection is the royal context, which commands only two proverbs in the first half (14:28, 35), whereas twelve in the second half explicitly address royal character and office, all concentrated at the beginning and the end of this section.[28] The king is regarded as perfect in judgment (16:10); his eyes winnow out the evil and the wicked (20:8, 26). The king's favor is conferred on those who speak rightly (16:13); his wrath is appeased by wisdom (16:14). The two themes of royal favor and wrath dominate the royal proverbs of this section: a growling lion serves as an apt metaphor for the king's wrath (19:12a; 20:2); royal favor, in contrast, is likened to fresh dew (19:12b) and spring rain (16:15b), similar to David's testimony in 2 Samuel 23:4. Such poetic imagery, as applied to the king, echoes language associated with the deity in the first half: "The good man obtains favor from YHWH, but the man of machinations he condemns" (12:2). One finds, moreover, in the second half of this collection language reminiscent of the divine countenance, as found in many psalms and the Aaronic blessing: "In the light of a king's face is life" (16:15a).[29] Elsewhere, the king's heart is considered an instrument of the divine will, literally a "stream of water" directed by the deity's "hand" (21:1). Finally, "steadfast faithfulness" (*ḥesed we'ĕmet*), along with righteousness, constitutes the moral foundation of kingship (16:12; 20:28). Such language is applied only generally in the first half to those who "plan good" (14:22), whereas in the second half it is directly related to the royal office. As profiled in the second half, the ideal king, like God, judges rightly and commands estimable character among his subjects.

God

The role of the deity also receives attention in the first half of the Solomonic collection. The expression "fear of YHWH" is frequently attested (10:27; 14:2, 26-27; 15:16). Such reverence "prolongs life" (10:27), instills confidence, provides protection (14:26; cf. 10:29), promotes life over death (14:27), and exceeds material treasure (15:16). Divine reverence is inseparable from righteousness. Anything associated with wickedness is considered an "abomination to YHWH," such as "crooked minds" (11:20), the "sacrifice of the wicked" (15:8), the "way of the wicked" (15:9; cf. v. 29), and "evil plans" (15:26). YHWH ensures the welfare of

29. Perhaps it is not accidental that the two earlier proverbs on the king are grouped near the end of the first half (14:28, 35).

30. Cf. Pss 4:6; 44:3b; 80:3; 89:15; Num 6:24-26.

the righteous and the demise of the wicked (10:3): "YHWH demolishes the house of the proud, but maintains the widow's boundaries" (15:25; see also vv. 3, 29).

In the second half of the collection, the YHWH sayings are even more pronounced than the royal references. A common theme, distinct from the first half, is the primacy of the divine will over and against human resolve: "The plans of the mind belong to mortals, but the answer of the tongue comes from YHWH" (16:1); "The human mind plans the way, but YHWH secures the steps" (16:9). For all the deliberate planning and wise counsel of human beings, the outcome is divinely determined. Human plans can be overruled by divine providence (19:21), to which all events are related (16:4). "The horse is prepared for the day of battle, but the victory belongs to YHWH" (21:31). The decision in all matters, from the mundane to those of national interest, "is YHWH's alone" (16:33). Taken together, these sayings give wisdom an explicitly theocentric orientation and at the same time reveal wisdom's limitations. On the one hand, the sages exhort the reader to "commit your work to YHWH, so that your plans may be established" (16:3). On the other hand, "neither wisdom, nor understanding, nor counsel can avail against YHWH" (21:30). Such sayings stand in marked contrast to the advice given in the first half, which lodges the success of one's plans in the abundance of counsel (11:14; 15:22). Indeed, a concomitant move is made regarding how the "fear of YHWH" is appropriated. In the earlier sayings, reverence of God is directly related to "strong confidence" (14:26), whereas such reverence is associated more intimately with humility in the second half (15:33; 22:4).

Summary

As a whole, the so-called "antithetical" and "royal" collections share much in common. Nevertheless, each has its distinctive rhetorical characteristics and thematic emphases that, taken together, give indication of didactic movement. Pedagogically, subsequent themes and rhetorical forms progressively build upon previous material. The move from terse antithetical sayings to more diverse poetic forms *may* indicate greater complexity of learning, particularly a move from a strictly binary mode of moral understanding to more synthetic modes. This can also be confirmed thematically. Numerous proverbs examine issues such as wealth and poverty from various angles rather than promulgate a homogeneous message that vilifies the poor and esteems the wealthy. More pronounced in the latter half, such sayings have the cumulative effect of mitigating powerful stereotypes, while also holding the reader morally accountable for actions that would lead to easy or ill-gotten wealth (cf. 1:19), on the one hand, and self-induced poverty, on the other. More obvious is the expanding moral purview indicated by the various sayings. There is a general progression from the predominantly familial and individual contexts to a more encompassing scope that includes neighbor, friend, and king. Finally, in the latter half of the collection, wisdom's limitations are divulged in relation to an increasing theocentric orientation.

The "Words of the Wise" (22:17–24:22; 24:23-34)

In Proverbs 22:17–24:22, entitled "words of the wise,"[31] and its appendix (24:23-34), instructional language, specifically that of direct address, comes to the fore. The implied speaker of the first, more extensive section describes the content of his discourse as containing "thirty [sayings] of admonition *(mô'ēṣôt)* and knowledge" (22:20), which refer generically to direct instruction. Virtually absent are the antithetically structured proverbs (cf. 23:17), and only a smattering of synonymously paralleled sayings are attested (23:23; 24:3-7, 9). In their place is a mixture of positive and negative commands (seventeen versus twenty-five, respectively). By contrast, the language of direct address is largely lacking in the Solomonic collection, except in several isolated cases (14:7; 19:19b, 27; 20:20; 22:10). Moreover, literary units can extend beyond the single bicolon to encompass several lines (23:29-35; 24:30-34). Not unrelated to the extension of rhetorical units and the predominance of direct address, self-reference is heavily featured for the first time. "My words" and "my teaching" open this first section, and scattered throughout are references to the first person (22:20; 23:15-16, 26). The parental figure of an instructor emerges from the morass of proverbial sayings of the previous collection, one who expresses a vested interest in the formation of the one addressed, the "son."

Whereas sagacious advice was conveyed largely through the "neutral" language of observation in the Solomonic collection, sapiential prescription in these two collections has become intensely personalized and directive. More than simply the source of imperatival address, the purveyor of wisdom in this collection is given personal definition: a pedagogue who rejoices over the implied reader's successful appropriation of wisdom (23:15b, 16), whose ways are exemplary (23:26), and who shares moral experiences (24:30-34).[32] As the pur-

---

31. That this title is incorporated into the first line of 22:17 in the MT may reflect a move toward highlighting Solomonic authorship (cf. LXX).

32. Such personalized rhetoric is particularly striking when compared to its Egyptian counterpart, *The Instructions of Amenemope*. Commonly considered the literary antecedent of Prov 22:17–24:22, this sapiential corpus of the Ramesside period is almost entirely lacking in self-reference within the body of the instructions (see only "my words" in IV.I).

veyor of wisdom is identified, so also the intended recipient of wisdom, namely, "my son" (e.g., 24:13, 21). Such rhetoric recalls the parental address that pervades chapters 1–9 (e.g., 1:8-19; 2:1-22; 3:1-18, 21-35; 4:1-9, 10-27; 5:1-23; 6:1-15, 20-35; 7:1-9; 9:7-18).[33] Compare, for example, 23:22 with 1:8 (see also 6:20):

> Pay attention to your father who begot you,
>> and do not despise your mother when she is old. (23:22)

> Hear, my child, your father's instruction,
>> and do not dismiss your mother's teaching. (1:8)

As throughout much of Proverbs 1–9, an explicitly parental relationship is established in 22:17–24:22, one that accompanies and sustains the language of instruction. In addition to parental address, other various rhetorical forms appear in much greater concentration in this section, such as conditional sentences or protases (22:27a; 23:13b, 14[?], 15; 24:10-11, 12a, 14b)[34] and rhetorical questions (22:27b, 29; 23:29; 24:12b).[35]

Despite the fact that these two collections are relatively small in volume compared to other collections, the ethos of these two collections is rich and complex. Other than delineating "what is right and true" (22:21a), the introduction identifies two other objectives behind the various sayings that follow: to encourage "trust" in YHWH (22:19) and to enable the reader to "give a true answer to those who sent you" (22:21b), in short, right faith and true discourse. The explicit theological focus of this collection builds on the various references to YHWH's activity and judgment dispersed throughout the first collection (e.g., 22:23; 23:11, 17 ["the fear of YHWH"]; 24:12, 18, 21). Unlike the royal section of the Solomonic collection, nowhere is there mention of wisdom's limitations vis-à-vis divine providence. Rather, divine activity now provides specific motivation for prescribed behavior, cast predominantly as a series of negative commands. The reader is proscribed from taking advantage of the vulnerable, being envious of sinners, neglecting the victims of society, and rejoicing over the enemies' fall. The final command of the first collection (24:21-22) pairs YHWH and the king as partners in eliciting obedience and in exacting punishment (24:21). In short, YHWH continues to serve a *limiting* role, but in a more concretely prescriptive way, relative to the Solomonic collection. The deity provides the primary reason for restraining unacceptable behavior. More broadly, divine rever-

---

33. In addition, there is one nearly identical repetition in these two sections (6:10-11; 24:33-34).

34. Cf. only 19:19b.

35. Cf. 14:22; 18:14b; 20:6, 9, 24.

ence is promoted as a personal incentive for appropriate conduct. The two references to the reader's future and hope, assured when the speaker's wisdom is successfully appropriated, suggest a constructive relationship between reverence and success (23:18; 24:14).

Specific admonitions of right discourse are found in only three sayings (23:16; 24:26, 28), each highlighting the need for truthfulness. The lips of the wicked, in contrast, utter only "mischief" (24:2) and, by implication, deceit (24:28). The art of elocution is not as urgent a concern as one finds in the Solomonic (latter half) and Hezekian collections (see below). Rather, something more basic is at stake in the exercise of discourse among the sayings of the wise, namely, honesty: "One who gives honest answers gives a kiss on the lips" (24:26).

Yet there is much more to these two short collections. The familiar themes of folly and wisdom, the wicked and the righteous, wealth and poverty, and household and kingdom in the Solomonic collection are all summarized in *instructional* form. First and foremost, the household receives prominent attention: an exhortation to heed one's parents — both father and mother — opens a unit that lodges wisdom's ethos squarely within the family (23:22-25). Indeed, wisdom is considered the means by which the proper and prosperous household is established (24:3). Another admonition highlights the need for sufficient preparation of the land before a house can be built (24:27). In contrast, the field of the lazy person is left to decay (24:30-31). In addition, the integrity of the ancestral land and of neighborly relations (22:28; 23:10; 24:28) is deemed essential for the maintenance of households, and thus the community at large. Moreover, acknowledging the established boundaries of the ancestral land prevents exploitation of those most vulnerable in the socio-economic order (23:10b).

Also related to the Solomonic collection, particularly its second half, is positive attention given to the poor, but the admonitions are given a more pronounced theological rationale. YHWH, the redeemer, assumes the role of advocate and judge on behalf of the poor and the orphan (22:23; 23:11). Nevertheless, the sages behind these collections identify three causes of poverty that are lodged in deficiencies of moral character. The drunkard, the glutton, and the lazy fool have only themselves to blame for their impoverishment (23:21; 24:33-34). On the other side of the coin, the acquisition of wealth is acknowledged to be hazardous to one's health: "Be wise enough to desist" warns the sage, acknowledging that riches can all too easily become an object of obsession (23:4). No qualification is given, as in the earlier collections (see above) to suggest that such wealth is illegitimately acquired; only blanket condemnation is given. Indeed, next to the rich are the stingy, from whom the reader is advised to part company (23:6).

The figure of the fool is given only passing reference. Since wisdom is by definition beyond their reach (24:7), fools are not worth a word of sagacious advice. Their only response is derision; hence, the reader is warned not to waste words on the fool (23:9). More attention is given to the wicked, who like the fool is irredeemable. "Their lips talk of mischief" and "their minds devise violence," hence the warning not to cavort with the wicked (24:1-2). Yet the reader is encouraged to "rebuke the wicked" (24:24-25). "Rebuke" in this case takes on a distinctly judicial nuance, tantamount to the charge of guilt and an accompanying sentence of punishment. Not unrelated is the claim that the "lamp of the wicked will go out" (24:20b). The wicked, in contrast to the student of wisdom, "have no future" (24:20a; cf. 23:18; 24:14). Given their certain demise, the reader is admonished not to fret over evildoers, let alone envy them (24:19). Moreover, one admonition goes so far as to typecast the reader among the company of the wicked: "Do not, O wicked one, lie in wait against the home of the righteous; do no violence to his place" (24:15).[36] Whereas the "wicked will be overthrown by calamity," the righteous — though vulnerable to "falling" — will "rise again," seven times no less (24:16). In contrast to the Solomonic collection, this piece of instruction acknowledges that there are those who waffle between wickedness and righteousness, including those who would appropriate the sage's advice, including the implied reader.

Last and equal to the emphasis on the household is attention given to matters of royal service. "Do you see one who is skillful in his work? He will serve kings, not common folk" (22:29). Following this example is a vivid description of proper etiquette at the royal table (23:1-3). The reader is warned that the desire for royal delicacies inexorably slides into the craving for wealth, while the delicacies of the stingy will only induce vomiting (23:4-8). Obedience to the king is required, a reverential conduct next only to the fear of God (24:21). Yet the implied reader is more than simply a lowly subject; instruction is given on the proper way of waging war, highlighting the need for an "abundance of counselors," as if the reader were a military official in training (24:5-6; cf. 15:22).

In summary, the series of admonitions that comprise these two relatively short collections are firm yet irenic in tone. The successful appropriation of wisdom is the overarching concern, so much so that the sage likens wisdom to the "drippings of the honeycomb," so delightful it is to the appetite (*nepeš*, 24:14). It is confidently assumed that the wicked and evildoers will meet their demise and the righteous will triumph, although they may temporarily stumble (24:16). The settings of these instructions presuppose both the household and

---

36. See MT, along with the versions. There is no textual reason to excise *rāšāʿ*.

the court. Wisdom is at once the foundation of the home and the basis for the royal court. Discipline and industry reign within the familial estate; restraint of desire and control of envy are requisite for dining with the king. Attention given to service in the royal court suggests an implied reader who has within the realm of vocational possibility employment under the king (22:29; 23:1-3). What is more, the sage briefly frames the reader as an official in training on the battlefield (24:5-6). To be sure, much of what is expressed within an explicitly royal context, including proper etiquette at the king's table and receiving sufficient counsel, is applicable at any social level. Nevertheless, as in the Solomonic collection, there is a thematic movement from household to court. Although nothing judgmental is said of the king, the rights of the poor are fully acknowledged in these "words of the wise."

In addition, disassociation and civility in less than ideal associations are encouraged. Fools are deemed unworthy of sapiential discourse; the wicked require rebuke within a court of law; and the demise of one's enemies is not to be met with rejoicing (24:17). All in all, society remains stratified and stable among three basic character types: the wise or righteous, the wicked, and the fool. Economic stratification is found in the contrast between the poor and the rich, as well as between the common folk and those who "will serve kings" (22:29). The implied reader of the admonitions of the wise stands liminally between the righteous and the wicked, even between the common and the royal.

The Hezekian Collection (25:1–29:27)

The following set of sayings that comprise 25:1–29:27 — ascribed to Solomon but transmitted or "copied" (*'tq*) by the "men of King Hezekiah of Judah" — is an eclectic collection from any formal point of view.[37] It opens with an antithetical saying, but one that does not embrace the moral polarity that typically characterizes the form in earlier collections. Several commands, mostly negative and frequently accompanied by a motive clause, can also be found (25:6, 8, 9; 26:4-5; 27:1, 10, 13, 23), as well as parental addresses (27:11), jussive commands (25:17; 27:2), conditional sentences (25:16, 21; 29:9, 12, 14), "better-than" sayings (25:7, 24; 27:5, 10c), rhetorical questions (26:12a; 27:4; 29:20), two *'ašrê* sayings (28:14a; 29:18b), and numerous antithetical sayings. Frequently, a proverbial

---

37. Raymond C. Van Leeuwen has discerned a subtle arrangement in chs. 25–26 that exhibits the balance between positive and negative statements and between admonitions and sayings. Chapters 27–29, however, appear to be more randomly arranged (*Context and Meaning in Proverbs 25–27*).

unit extends beyond the single bicolon, with the longest unit encompassing no less than eleven cola (27:23-27).

Relatively new from a stylistic standpoint is the preponderance and variety of poetic analogies, as conveyed by numerous metaphors and similes.[38] Some of the most evocative proverbial expressions are found in this section. For example:

> A word spoken in its turn
>   is like apples of gold on silver showpieces.
>
>   (25:11; cf. 15:23)

> Like a mace, a sword, or a sharp arrow
>   is one who bears false witness against a neighbor.   (25:18)

> With patience a ruler can be persuaded,
>   and a soft tongue will break bones.   (25:15)

> Like a dog returning to its vomit
>   is a fool who reverts to his folly.   (26:11)

> Like a madman who shoots deadly firebrands and arrows
>   is one who deceives a neighbor and says, "Just kidding!"   (26:18-19)

> Iron sharpens iron,
>   and one person sharpens the face of his partner.   (27:17)

> A ruler[39] who oppresses the poor
>   is a beating rain that leaves no food.   (28:3)

> A roaring lion or a charging bear
>   is a wicked ruler over a poor people.   (28:15)

Such evocative analogies are concentrated particularly at the beginning and middle of the Hezekian collection, beginning with 25:11, extending through

---

38. Analogical language is attested only sporadically in the Solomonic collection. Moreover, the repertoire of metaphors is relatively limited and repeated: "tree of life" (11:30; 13:12; 15:4), "crown" (14:24; 17:6), "fountain of life" (10:11; 13:14; 14:27; 16:22), "deep waters" (18:4; 20:5), "growling of a lion" (19:12; 20:2), "dripping of rain" (19:13), "fruit of the mouth" (12:14a; 13:2a; 18:20a).

39. So NRSV. Verse 3a is corrupt and requires only slight emendation to make good sense: *geber rāš > geber rōš (= rō'š),* meaning "head," hence, "leader" (so also William McKane, *Proverbs: A New Approach,* OTL [Philadelphia: Westminster, 1970], pp. 628-29).

much of chapters 26 and 27, and occurring only occasionally in the final two chapters (28:3, 15; 29:5). Indeed, there appears to be an inversely proportionate relationship between analogical and antithetical sayings: as the analogies taper off near the end of the collection, so the antithetical proverbs, reminiscent of the first collection, reemerge with greater frequency in the last two chapters. Thus, in addition to proverbial sayings that recall the proverbial forms of earlier sections, from antithetical sentences to instructional sayings, are the analogical proverbs, which revel in the use of metaphor and display a level of sophistication that is only sporadically attested in the earlier collections. More varied poetically than the previous collections, the Hezekian collection is a veritable montage of literary forms, serving not only to prescribe but also to *model* the art of elocution.

Equal to its poetic versatility, this collection covers a rich variety of topics, from the heavy heart and troubled soul (25:20; 27:9) to the wicked ruler (28:15). Predominant are references to royalty, neighborly conduct, the conflict between the righteous and the wicked, the fool, and wealth. These are familiar themes that are in some cases given new twists. For example, while the first two proverbs of this collection credit the king's sapiential quest and depth, the following sayings concerning royalty lay the grounds for a more critical perspective of those who hold positions of authority (28:3, 15-16; 29:12). The king is held accountable for his treatment of the poor. A ruler who oppresses the poor is labeled wicked (28:3, 15). The measuring stick by which to judge the king's fitness for royal office is justice, which ensures the land's stability (29:4). However, *reliable* justice comes not from any king, but from YHWH (29:26).

Despite the opening proverbs of this collection, the royal figure profiled throughout this collection is fully fallible. Indeed, the royal task of pursuing wisdom described in 25:2 ("the glory of kings is to search [that which God has concealed]"), if read in light of the subsequent royal proverbs, is equally a basis of critique and support of the royal persona. Note 28:16a: "a clueless ruler is a cruel oppressor." If the king, in accordance with 25:2, is to discern the divine order of things, then a critical aspect of this order is the bond that unites the poor and the powerful: "The poor and the oppressor share this in common: YHWH gives light to the eyes of both" (29:13). Yet far too often, the poor remain "hidden" in the socio-economic order. Hence, the king is judged in part by a policy of *discernment*, one that recognizes the voice of the voiceless (cf. 31:9), as the following proverb makes clear: "If the king judges the poor with equity, his throne will be forever established" (29:14). Also acknowledged is the king's need for guidance in such matters, requiring patience and perseverance on the part of his counselors (25:15). In short, the royal personage limned in this collection is preeminently human and frequently, at least potentially so, incapable of judicious policy. God and king part company, as it were, in this collection, much in contrast to the previous sayings in which they are paired together or virtually identified as one (e.g., 16:10, 15; 19:12; 21:1; 24:21-22). A comparison of 19:12 and 28:15 is particularly telling.

> Like the roar of a lion is the king's anger,
>   but his favor is like dew on the grass.   (19:12; see also 20:2)

> A roaring lion or a charging bear
>   is a wicked ruler over poor people.   (28:15; see also v. 3)

Invoking overlapping metaphors, the first proverb — drawn from the "royal collection" — and the following saying from the Hezekian collection diverge remarkably. The former is meant to command respect and awe for the king; the latter elicits abject condemnation. It is not accidental that they are found in their present arrangement. Given the similarity of imagery, the Hezekian proverb gives corrective balance to the first. Within the royal context, the roar of the wild can connote either woe or weal.

Not unrelated to the collection's critical tone is the prominent focus on "law" *(tôrâ)*. "Those who forsake *tôrâ* praise the wicked, but those who keep *tôrâ* struggle against them" is an antithetical proverb that follows on the heels of an indictment against the ruler who oppresses the poor (28:4; see also vv. 7, 9; 29:18; cf. Deut 17:14-20). Adherence to *tôrâ* serves as foundational support, a veritable weapon, in the struggle against the wicked. Indeed, the theme of mortal conflict between the righteous and the wicked is more pronounced in this collection than in any other. "Like a muddied spring or a polluted fountain is the righteous one who gives way before the wicked" (25:26). The point of contention is made clear in 29:2, authority: "When the righteous are great (in authority), the people rejoice; but when the wicked rule, the people groan" (see also 28:12). Indeed, the righteous appear to be beset by constant danger from the bloodthirsty wicked (29:10). Yet even in the unfortunate case of the wicked assuming authority, the righteous can look forward to their inevitable downfall (29:16). The wicked are afflicted with illusions of danger, in contrast to the righteous, who are bold as lions (28:1). The moral polarity between the wicked and the righteous is, of course, nothing new. Nevertheless, the Hezekian collection explicitly lodges the conflict within the political sphere. The issue of conflict is set no longer in the abstract but on the concrete level of social struggle over authority within and outside the royal court (see 29:12). The theme of mutual contempt between the righteous and the wicked, like opposing political parties, is acknowledged (29:27). Perhaps it is not fortuitous, then, that the Hezekian collection is the only collection that focuses on appropriate strategies against the "enemy" (25:21-22; 26:24-26). It is in the judicial sphere in which the "enemy's wickedness will be revealed" (26:26).

Related to the category of the wicked is that of the fool. Indeed, the Hezekian collection features a whole series of proverbs devoted to the character of the fool, beginning with 26:1. Honor and eloquence do not befit the fool (26:1, 7, 8, 9). Folly is an intractable quality (26:11; 27:22). Yet for all the fool's intransigence, there is a class of character that is more hopeless, and by implication more dangerous:

> Do you see someone wise in his own eyes?
> There is more hope for a fool than for him.   (26:12)

Similarly:

> Do you see someone who is hasty in speech?
> There is more hope for a fool than him.   (29:20)

The Hezekian collection paints the fool on the lower end of the sapiential scale, one who deserves rebuke and harsh discipline by the wise, akin to the intransigent student (26:3; 5, 10?). In contrast, however, there is the presumptuous individual for whom there is no hope. Hastiness in speech bespeaks deliberate deceit, which can wreak social havoc (26:20, 24, 28). There is nothing particularly fearsome about the fool, except that the fool, if left unchecked by wise rebuke, can potentially become presumptuous, as if descending on a slippery slope. As self-trust is the root of all folly (28:25-26), severe discipline is necessary in preventing a fool from becoming hopelessly "wise in his own eyes" (26:5), a phrase relatively unique to the Hezekian collection.[40] Identified with the greedy, who stir up strife (28:25), presumptuous individuals present a clear and present danger; they are beyond all hope of redemption. Compared to the sin of presumption, folly is only a relative flaw. Indeed, the two sayings in this collection that conclude with "there is more hope for a fool than . . ." are similar in rhetorical structure to the "better-than" sayings that refer to the poor in earlier collections. Such similarity militates against vilifying either the fool or the poor (16:19; 19:1). In the hands of the Hezekian scribes, the fool is given the slightest benefit of the doubt, in contrast to the earlier Solomonic collection (cf. 14:7). The presumptuous, in turn, are raised to the level of the hopelessly wicked, the antagonists of wisdom. Theologically, what fundamentally distinguishes the presumptuous from the righteous is their object of

---

40. See also 26:12, 16; 28:11. Prov 3:7 uses the expression in a general admonition.

trust: the former trust only in themselves, whereas the righteous trust in YHWH (28:25; cf. 29:25).

Another level of social relationship that gains greater currency in this collection is that of the neighbor. Extending beyond the bonds of kinship, respectful coexistence with the neighbor is highly valued. Hence, litigation and dependency upon neighbors are discouraged (25:7b-10, 17). Deceiving a neighbor is likened to mortal combat (26:18-19), so also flattery (29:5). Conversely, friendship is prized, a bond that is equal to, if not surpasses, that of kinship (27:6, 10; cf. 17:17).

Finally, the theme of wealth and poverty pervades the Hezekian collection. More than in previous sections, poverty is disassociated from character deficiencies such as laziness and sloth. Although the collection contains a series of proverbs on laziness (26:13-16), lacking is any reference to poverty as an assured outcome (cf. 24:33-34). In comparison to wealth, poverty can even be preferable:

> Better to be poor, walking in integrity
> > than to be crooked in one's ways, though rich.   (28:6)

More damning is the antithetical saying:

> The rich man is wise in his own eyes,
> > but the discerning poor person sees through him.   (28:11)

Such a remarkable observation suggests that the Hezekian sages considered a certain class of wealthy to be inimical to community life, sharing much in common with the wicked and the presumptuous. While the greedy richly deserve punishment (28:20), those who "give to the poor" find true abundance (28:27). Furthermore, a criterion for judging between the wicked and the righteous is their ability to recognize the rights of the poor (29:7). As noted above, judging the poor with equity is the mark of a good king (29:14; see 28:15). Of all the collections featured thus far in Proverbs, the Hezekian series looks most critically on wealth and most sympathetically upon the poor.

The five YHWH sayings, concentrated in chapters 28–29, reinforce two primary values conveyed in the collection. Justice comes from seeking YHWH (28:5; 29:26). In addition, true enrichment, as opposed to wealth greedily gained, is found in trusting the deity (28:25; 29:25). Curiously, the stock expression "the fear of YHWH" is not referenced in this extensive collection. Instead, "trust in YHWH" is the leitmotif, which is contrasted to "human fear" *(ḥerdat 'ādām)* in 29:25.

In summary, the Hezekian collection widens the purview of moral discourse while also achieving a higher level of discursive elocution. The family or household is no longer the central context for ethical conduct. The social world of this collection is populated with wicked and just rulers, good and deceitful neighbors, the greedy rich and the righteous poor, friends and enemies. Particular attention is given to relationships with neighbors and those who are in authority, including the king. Not unrelated, the collection highlights the character of the true witness and the faithful messenger (25:18-19, 25), recalling the profile of the implied reader of the previous section (22:21b). Deception of a neighbor is considered anathema (26:18-19, 24), and flattery directed toward a neighbor is akin to deceit (29:5). Foundational to moral living within such a conflicted community — a community in which the "upright" and the "unjust," the wicked and the righteous (including wicked and righteous kings!), are considered equally abominable from each other's point of view (29:27) — is *tôrâ*, to which recourse is gained among the righteous as a weapon against the wicked. The Hezekian collection, in short, thrusts the reader into the fray of political wrangling. The wicked and the righteous have become overtly politicized to a degree not found in the previous collections. Character, in short, has become a predominantly political construct, a necessary development in light of this collection's widened social purview.

The Words of Agur (30:1-33)

Chapter 30, labeled an "oracle" (*ně'um;* cf. Num 24:15; 2 Sam 23:1), at least for the first four verses (see v. 4), is in a class by itself. Attributed to a foreigner, Agur ben Yaqeh (a Massaite), this collection contains literary forms not found elsewhere in the book of Proverbs. It comprises a (partial) lament and response (vv. 1-6), a petition (vv. 7-8), and several catalogues of natural and social phenomena, frequently cast as graded numerical sayings (vv. 15-16, 18-19, 21-23, 24-28, 29-31). Only occasionally does a more familiar form appear, such as negative instruction (vv. 6, 10), an extended proverb cast in synonymous parallelism (v. 17), a conditional address (v. 32), and an analogical saying (v. 33).

This bizarre collection opens with an individual's confession of abject ignorance over things that pertain to wisdom, including in particular knowledge of God (vv. 1-3). The quest for wisdom has become too elusive or burdensome for the speaker to endure. Wearied and frustrated, the speaker confesses that he is a "beast" *(ba'ar)* rather than a human being (v. 2; for similar language, see Ps 73:22).[41] Perhaps the speaker is a *self-professed* "fool," who by def-

---

41. For the translation issues of v. 1, see Paul Franklyn, "The Sayings of Agur in Proverbs 30: Piety or Scepticism?" *VT* 95 (1983): 242-45.

inition lacks understanding (see 10:21, 23; 14:7; 16:22). More likely, Agur is a student of wisdom who vents his fatigue and frustration over the rigors of his discipline. In any case, here is one who is far from being "wise in his own eyes"! In response to his confession of ignorance, a barrage of questions, like those that characterize God's confrontation with Job, deliver what appears to be a stinging rebuke. Indeed, the comparison with Job is suggestive, as others have noted.[42] The rhetoric of 30:4, presumably a divine response — or at least a response given on behalf of the deity — resembles the rhetoric of the YHWH speeches in Job (e.g., Job 38:2-30). Yet whereas divine discourse in Job is intended, at least on the surface, to answer Job's litigation against God, the divine discourse of Agur's "oracle" presupposes no such act of chutzpah on the part of the lamenter. Although rhetorically cast as a rebuke, the series of questions is not meant to counter any case of presumption on the part of the lamenter. To the contrary, the questions serve to forestall the evident slide into despair over the seemingly elusive quest for wisdom. This series concludes with the contention that the lamenter, in fact, *does* know something, namely, God's activity in creation (30:4b; cf. v. 3b).[43] This is then followed by an affirmation of the veracity of the divine word and a prayer, presumably by the lamenter, for deliverance from deceitful words and for material sustenance that is neither excessive nor insufficient.

Dominating the words of Agur that follow the prayer are the numerical sayings. Such units catalogue what is despicable (vv. 11-14, 20, 21-23), awe-inspiring and edifying (vv. 18-19, 24-28, 29-31), and fearsome (vv. 15-16). Together, a veritable taxonomy of social and natural phenomena is given. Echoing the heart of Agur's confession in verse 3, awe, it is claimed, reaches beyond human understanding: "Three things are too marvelous for me; four I do not understand" (v. 18). The soaring eagle, the marching locusts, the choreography of physical intimacy, insatiable Sheol — all evoke a sense of awe over the created order, which is intimately related to the social order. For example, the eye that mocks the parent not only warrants social condemnation but also deserves to be "pecked out by the ravens . . . and devoured by vultures" (v. 17). The earth, moreover, trembles when the social order is subverted (vv. 21-23). Culture and nature are inseparably intertwined, indeed locked together in sus-

---

42. E.g., Franklyn, "The Sayings of Agur," pp. 246-48; James L. Crenshaw, "Clanging Symbols," in *Justice and the Holy,* ed. D. A. Knight and P. J. Paris (Philadelphia: Fortress, 1989), pp. 55-57 (reprinted in *Urgent Advice and Probing Questions* [Macon, Ga.: Mercer University Press, 1995], pp. 371-82).

43. The last clause of the MT of v. 4 is omitted in the LXX manuscripts Vaticanus and Sinaiticus. It was evidently added by the Masoretes to highlight the question's pedagogical value vis-à-vis Agur's lament.

taining the social order. Majesty and strength are reflected in the natural and social realms (vv. 29-31); wisdom is found in the most seemingly powerless species in the natural order (vv. 24-28) and, yes, even in someone likened to a "beast" (v. 2)!

In short, Agur's collection significantly widens the context and scope of moral discourse. To be sure, some of the familial ethos is retained, but prominently new is the ethos of creation, from the insect to the cosmos. All the world gives evidence of wisdom, sustains the social order, and decisively reacts in case folly ever gets the upper hand. Moreover, as the created order elicits a sense of *mysterium tremendum,* of awareness beyond knowledge in the heart of the discerning, so humility is lifted up as the virtue of virtues, for only through the acknowledgment of human ignorance is divine transcendence most sharply set in focus (v. 4). Humility is the necessary complement to awe, and humanity no longer holds a monopoly over wisdom within the created order. Certain activities (or "ways") in nature reflect a divinely inscribed wisdom that provokes wonder beyond reason (vv. 18-19).

Yet present in the human community are other modes of activity that counter this order: the "way of an adulteress who sees no wrong" and the overturning of certain social hierarchies (vv. 20-23). As in the Hezekian section, exalting oneself is considered a cardinal sin (26:12; 30:32a). In addition, the opposite is taken to its logical extreme: humility leads to self-abasement (30:2-3a). Thus, the collection concludes with the observation that the least, from the locust to the lizard, actually possess the lion's share of wisdom (vv. 24-28), and the lowly reader, in turn, is warned of falling into the trap of self-exaltation (v. 32).

Some continuity of themes from the previous collections is evident in this innovative collection. Once again, the quality of discourse is given significant attention, but it is focused almost exclusively on one particular vice, namely, lying, a theme that binds three units in the collection together (vv. 6, 8, 10). The gravity of the vice is highlighted in verse 10, in which slander is considered a grievous offense for which the slanderer will be held accountable by God, even if the one slandered is a slave. The integrity of discourse is rooted in the theological realm; lying, consequently, is regarded as a distortion of divine discourse (v. 6). Moreover, the petitioner pleads that God remove all temptation to lie (v. 8).

Agur's petition in verses 8-9 also mediates the issue of wealth and poverty. Both wealth and impoverishment are acknowledged to carry their share of temptations. On the one hand, an insulated sense of self-sufficiency is an ever present danger among the affluent, one that ultimately leads to a denial of dependence upon the creator, in short, a "practical atheism" (v. 9a; cf. v. 13). Indeed, the sage has the rich in mind when he refers to "those . . . who devour the poor off the earth, the needy from among mortals" (v. 14b). On the other hand, poverty leads to desperate and ultimately unscrupulous measures such as stealing and lying, which result in profanation of the divine name. In short, a life of moderation regarding material possessions is considered an ethical ideal. Also noteworthy, wealth and poverty, like the integrity of discourse, are given explicit theological reference. Nothing is said of either condition being self-made, as one finds in the earlier collections. Poverty and wealth come from the hand of God, and the petitioner prays to avoid both extremes.

Kingship also receives a measure of attention: a slave assuming the throne is one of four items that can cause upheaval in the natural, as well as social, order (v. 22a). Wisdom is embodied by the locusts, which "have no king, yet all of them march in rank" (v. 27). The lizard, though graspable by the hand, can infiltrate the royal stronghold (v. 28). Finally, while the "striding king" is a model of stately posture (v. 31b), such an observation is followed by an admonition against self-exaltation (v. 32a). With the possible exception of verse 31, whose reading is uncertain, the king is considered vulnerable to vice. Among the locusts, the king is even dispensable!

In summary, the words of Agur single out the virtue of humility in part by underscoring God's transcendence as creator. The integrity of discourse and the moderation of possessions are given theological reference. Such moral values are set in the context of creation, a purview unmatched in the previous collections except in a few isolated cases. For the first time, a virtual catalogue of examples are drawn from natural phenomena to illustrate certain moral norms and to advance the measure of wisdom, one that moves from ethically practical knowledge to wonder and mystery of the divine. As in the climax of Job, the terse taxonomies of nature expand the moral scope of the sages to include even the cosmos. Nevertheless, the cosmos is not where the sages conclude their instruction.

The Words of King Lemuel (31:1-9)

This compendium of royal instruction comprises the most extended and continuous direct address among the collections. Moreover, it is the only one that features explicit maternal instruction. The words are those of the foreign queen mother directed to her son, King Lemuel of Massa (31:1-9). While previous collections profile specific authorial sources (i.e., Solomon, the sages, the men of Hezekiah), nowhere in Proverbs is the *implied* reader given such specific reference, namely, a king's personal name. Only in this final collection does the pedagogy of instruction reveal its specific subject *and* object, a mother and her royal son, further personalizing the didactic relationship previously established in the "words of the wise."

The queen mother begins her direct parental address with a series of staccato exclamations (*mah . . . mah . . . meh . . .* ; 31:2) that serve as intensive appeals to capture the royal son's attention: "*What* are you doing, my son?"[44] Moving from negative to positive commands, a series of four impassioned admonitions are directed to Lemuel concerning just governance of his kingdom, beginning with "private" behavior and culminating with social policy (vv. 3, 4-5, 6-7, 8-9). The overarching issue is competent leadership. Negatively, she warns against illicit sexual relations and excessive drinking. Positively, she urges her son to find more constructive uses for beer *(šēkār)* and wine *(yayin)* — antidotes for those suffering from destitution — and to act as advocate on behalf of the vulnerable, namely, the weak (literally, "those passing away" [*bĕnê ḥălôp*]), the poor, and the needy. Indeed, the theme of the vulnerable links the last three admonitions (vv. 5b, 7-9).

Thematically, a maternal voice issues a royal mandate that culminates with the king's role to protect the voiceless, "those who cannot speak" (v. 8a), namely, "the poor and needy" (v. 9b). Far from the mediator of divine wrath or the embodiment of exalted power, as found in the Solomonic collection, the king himself is the object of admonishment, held accountable for his actions, both private and public. Rhetorically, the admonitions are lodged squarely in a familial setting, in the voice of a mother to her son, bringing the pedagogical movement full circle: "a foolish son is a mother's grief" (10:1b). The royal court is shown to be a home.

Conclusion

Readily discernible from Proverbs 10:1 to 31:9 is the rich variety of rhetorical forms and themes evident in sapiential discourse. Moreover, some lines of development in both content and form are evident, suggesting certain pedagogical moves by those responsible for editing and bringing these collections together. The first three collections progress from antithetical to nonantithetical bicola to extended instructional material. The Hezekian collection evinces a wider variety that comprises all forms attested in previous sections and then some, including evidence of greater artistic sophistication, as found in the evocative analogical sayings in chapters 25–28. Finally, the last two collections,

---

44. See McKane, *Proverbs*, pp. 408-9; Otto Plöger, *Sprüche Salomos (Proverbia)*, BKAT 17 (Neukirchen-Vluyn: Neukirchener Verlag, 1984), p. 369.

those of Agur and Lemuel, feature the most extensive instructional material as well as introduce new literary forms, such as disputational dialogue and the numerical sayings in the former section.

The various rhetorical forms employed in the collections are matched by a rich variety of themes and messages. Generally, the greater the variety of forms in a given collection, the more encompassing and complex the overall moral setting in which the various sentences and instructions are set. At one extreme are the Hezekian and Agur collections, which exhibit the greatest variety of literary forms, with the latter collection embracing creation for its ethos or moral setting. At the other end of the scale, as it were, are the opening antithetical half of the Solomonic collection and the concluding words of King Lemuel, both of which are fairly uniform literarily and contain a most pervasive familial ethos. Yet they could not be more different. The moral scope of the antithetical section is lodged in a familial setting in which the fates of parents and children are inextricably connected, and discipline and diligence provide the basis for moral formation. The Lemuel collection concludes the main body of Proverbs with a series of admonitions that are also situated within a familial setting, namely, a royal household, yet sets its sights outward toward the social margins of the realm.

On one level, the main body of Proverbs has come full circle, opening and concluding with the setting of the household. Yet significant shifts in focus have also occurred, which can be discerned by noting the trajectories of particular themes and how they are developed and nuanced in the course of reading and appropriating the various sayings and instructions in their codified order. Splashes of gray are in greater evidence in the moral nuances conveyed in the latter collections than in the black-and-white world of the initial antithetical section. Stereotyped polarities are tweaked and, in some cases, transformed.

One theme in particular bears further explication, kingship. The initial collections primarily profile a royal figure of distinctly mythic proportions, evoking both respect and dread for the office. The king is the earthly embodiment of divine *mysterium tremendum;* his heart is directed wholly by God (21:1). Yet the one who "loves a pure heart and is gracious in speech will have the king as a friend" (22:11), so concludes the royal section of the Solomonic collection. The following "sayings of the wise" establish a closer relationship with the king and give advice about how to be a proper royal servant even at the king's table (22:29; 23:1-2). The king and the deity are regarded as common objects of reverence and obedience (24:21).

It is not until the Hezekian collection that the royal figure becomes an object of sustained critique. Although the king's mind is unfathomable and his glory rests in discovering what God has hidden (25:2), justice holds the king morally accountable. Yet true justice comes only from YHWH (29:26). Finally, the king himself is addressed by none other than his mother, who issues a series of severe admonitions ranging from restraint in matters of sex and social carousing to the appropriate discharge of the office in behalf of the poor.

Perhaps the changing face of royalty bears some correspondence to the changing role of the implied reader. The student of wisdom progresses from child (literally "son") to king without ever losing the identity of student. The reader is addressed in the end as king, but one still in need of correction. In short, the reader, or "interpellated" subject, of the main body of Proverbs progresses toward achieving identity with the royal figure without ever losing the status of the "listening heart." And where, ultimately, is the royal reader to be found in the larger shape of Proverbs? He has returned to the household of wisdom, the rhetorical setting of the acrostic poem that concludes the book. The reader has moved from king to elder (31:23), having found the right spouse to manage his household, the familial embodiment of wisdom herself, who among her countless responsibilities "provides food for her household" (31:15; cf. 9:5). What is more, the addressed subject of the queen mother of 31:1-9 shares close affinity with the "woman of strength" profiled in the acrostic. The royal matriarch warns her son, "Do not spend your strength *(ḥayil)* on women, your ways on those who would destroy kings" (v. 3). Not fortuitously, the woman of the acrostic is a woman of *ḥayil,* one who "girds herself with strength" (v. 17a). Moreover, the king is enjoined to judge righteously and "defend the rights of the poor and needy" (*'ānî wĕ'ebyôn* [v. 9]). The *'ēšet ḥayil* in verse 20, not coincidentally, "opens her hand to the needy *('ānî)* and extends her hand to the poor" *('ebyôn).* Such shared terminology suggests an intimate link between the woman of the household who embodies wisdom and the king who judges righteously. Kingship has become domesticated, and, in turn, the household commands the community. The wisdom of the household, thus, fulfills instruction meant for the king (see 30:27).

Finally, the main body of Proverbs illustrates a certain advancement of sapiential instruction. As the king becomes an object of critique, so the reader must cultivate self-criticism, even perhaps to the point of abject self-deprecation, as in the case of Agur. The path of wisdom is well laid out at the outset, but complexities arise as the parameters of wisdom's moral purview extend beyond the household to encompass creation. Reliance upon the reader's discriminating powers of discernment are affirmed in the latter collections. The reader must decide when and how to address a fool (26:4-5), when to be bold and when to be cautious (27:12; 28:1), and to what extent to partake of wisdom's sweet honey (24:13; 25:16). The pedagogy of wisdom, in sum, begins with the basic staple and proceeds to more advanced, variegated fare.

Although many of the proverbial sayings and instructions seem simplistic in isolation, together they build up a substantive and sophisticated level of moral instruction that cannot be gainsaid or reduced as a mere foil for other books of wisdom, canonical and otherwise. Contrary to Wolfgang Mieder's observation that "the proverb in a collection is dead," in contrast to those that perform in narrative,[45] the sayings of a collection take on new life and meaning within the meta-narrative of moral formation. As a whole, the book of Proverbs, too, must be included among the ranks of sapiential works that challenge students "to engage in an exciting quest to discover answers to intriguing questions."[46] The child who would be king is cultivated to discover what God has left concealed (25:2). Such is the privilege, as well as task, of every reader of Proverbs.

45. Cited in Carol R. Fontaine, *Traditional Sayings in the Old Testament*, BLS 5 (Decatur, Ga.: Almond, 1982), p. 54.

46. Crenshaw, *Education in Ancient Israel*, p. 27.

Preserving Virtues:
Renewing the Tradition of the Sages

Ellen F. Davis

The evangelist Luke gives the earliest account of what would come to be known in church as "an inquirer's class." Paul, in custody in Caesarea, had been summoned by the Roman governor Felix, a man already "quite accurately informed concerning the Way" (Acts 24:22). Felix wanted to learn more about this new faith in Christ Jesus, but as Paul led him into a discussion of "justice, self-control, and the coming judgment, the governor, getting anxious," dismissed him: "When I have time, I'll call you back in" (v. 26). Felix did in fact renew the conversation on numerous subsequent occasions, although Luke tells us it was only because he was hoping for a bribe.

Even if Felix's motives were impure and a soul was not won for Christ, the event is worth pondering from the perspective of forming Christian character. As Luke represents it, Paul seems to have formulated his initial lesson for this sophisticated inquirer with some care. He is a skilled teacher, balancing what is new and challenging with what is familiar and unobjectionable. The form of Paul's instruction is one that an educated Roman would recognize. It is a lesson in "the virtues," a tradition of learning established in the Mediterranean world ever since Plato and Aristotle.[1] Yet the specific content of this lesson could come only from a teacher who stands within the biblical tradition and therefore is alien to Felix's way of thinking. With one sweeping gesture, Paul points to the essential three-dimensionality of the Christian life. The political, personal, and eschatological aspects of "the Way" are summed up with remarkable economy in those three immensities: "justice, self-control, and the coming judgment."

---

1. Although not presented as an innovation, the scheme of the four cardinal virtues (prudence, justice, temperance, and fortitude) finds its earliest attestation in Plato's *Symposium*. The fullest classical exposition of the virtues is found in Aristotle's *Nicomachean Ethics*.

The combination of those three dimensions is foreign, if not frightening, to Felix's understanding of religion.[2] Paul is creating a virtue tradition in a distinctly biblical mode. What makes it biblical is the fact that Paul forges the link between practice of the virtues and the judgment of God. In other words, Paul sets justice and self-control (which he himself labels "fruit of the Spirit" rather than "virtues")[3] in the context of history. Therefore, by a Jewish reading of history, practice is a matter of ultimate consequence. Doubtless this is what makes Felix anxious. Greek and Roman teachers used the virtues to school citizens for the *polis* or the empire. Paul, like other Jews before him,[4] recognizes their political function and also looks beyond it. He sees that how we live the virtues determines not only the present character of the common life but also how we will stand, individually and as a body of faith, in "the coming judgment." For Paul, then, schooling in the virtues is simply one form of the work his ancestors called "teach[ing] the fear of YHWH" (Ps 34:11; cf. Prov 1:7).

Renewing the Tradition

In this essay, I follow Paul in setting the virtues in the context of a biblically informed reading of history[5] and thus seek to demonstrate the usefulness and

2. Although the point is tangential to this essay, it could be argued that the combination of these three dimensions — political, personal, eschatological — has been enduringly problematic for those interested in or even committed to what Luke calls "the Way." Throughout history, probably most of those who have tried to walk it have not been very successful in grasping the implications of one or another of the three dimensions and shaping their lives accordingly. In light of the present religious scene, it seems that many of those who are eager to talk about the politics of Christian faith shy away from the eschaton, and vice versa. Yet a third position is taken by many mainstream North American Christians who would uphold personal virtue ("being a good person") as the great value they find in the Christian life but would draw no connection with either political responsibility or eschatological expectation.

3. "Self-control" *(enkrateia)* is among the virtues designated "fruit of the Spirit" in Gal 5:22-23.

4. Some time before Paul, the author of the Wisdom of Solomon (probably written in the latter half of the first century B.C.E.) incorporated the Platonic scheme of four cardinal virtues within the biblical tradition of praising "Lady Wisdom": "If virtue is the object of a man's affections, the fruits of wisdom's labors are the virtues; temperance and prudence, justice and fortitude, these are her teaching . . ." (Wis 8:7).

5. The necessity of speaking of virtue (or "the virtues") in the context of history has been emphasized in several recent works by Alasdair MacIntyre and Stanley Hauerwas. See especially MacIntyre, *After Virtue* (Notre Dame, Ind.: University of Notre Dame Press, 1984), and Hauerwas, *A Community of Character: Toward a Constructive Christian Social Ethic* (Notre Dame, Ind.: University of Notre Dame Press, 1981). They further emphasize that virtue is prac-

even the urgency of that approach to the formation of Christian character in our own age.[6] I focus on traits that classical philosophers and medieval Christian theologians reckoned as "cardinal virtues": prudence, justice, temperance, and fortitude. The traditional understanding of the cardinal virtues is that these four elements of human character constitute a moral unity. Each is necessary in order to support the others and render them fully efficacious. A deficiency in temperance undercuts the striving for justice. Courage (fortitude) is distinguishable from recklessness only when it is guided by prudence. In contemporary culture, however, the essential unity of the cardinal virtues is difficult to grasp: two of the virtues have been largely eclipsed as positive ways of estimating human character. Although justice and fortitude are perennially admired, prudence and temperance have fallen from favor. No one names a daughter for either of the latter virtues anymore. If ancient and medieval minds conceived of Prudentia and Temperantia as beautiful women, we are more likely to conjure up images of sour spinsters and frenetic women smashing barroom windows. This essay aims to show that prudence and temperance are fundamental to a biblically informed understanding of sound human character. Arguably, these two are what Paul calls "self-control" *(enkrateia)*.[7] Further, those virtues, far from being outmoded, are of pressing contemporary relevance. Here I suggest that failure to value them as formative elements of human character contributes significantly to the perpetuation of the ecological crisis in our lifetime — something for which, we must imagine in faith, we shall have to answer "in the coming judgment."

The need for renewed appreciation of the cardinal virtues is pressing. More than simply strengthening the common life of either state or church, these virtues are now found to be necessary for the well-being of the created or-

---

ticed within particular traditions, each of which retells history in distinctive ways. The Christian Bible (the Old and New Testaments) is one such narrative recounting of history.

6. While I confine my remarks here specifically to the church's use of the virtues, the substance of my argument about how they could be used applies equally to character formation within the Jewish community. Solomon Schimmel treats this tradition in his recent study, *The Seven Deadly Sins: Jewish, Christian, and Classical Reflections on Human Nature* (New York: The Free Press, 1992).

7. I infer this from the fact that Jewish ethical thinking in the first century was profoundly shaped by the book of Proverbs, which is to a great extent an extended exposition and illustration of prudence and temperance. Paul's own familiarity with Proverbs may be assumed. Commenting on Paul's citation of Prov 24:12 and Ps 62:12 in Rom 2:6, Richard Hays observes perceptively: "[T]he echo of Psalms and Proverbs recollects images of God that were in Paul's bones. We, belated rootless readers, can learn only through marginalia and concordances — like novice guitarists learning blues riffs from sheet music — what Paul knew by heart . . ." (*Echoes of Scripture in the Letters of Paul* [New Haven, Conn.: Yale University Press, 1989], p. 43).

der. They are "preserving virtues," which we humans must cultivate as long as history continues on this planet. Indeed, we must cultivate these virtues *in order that* history — the story of humans living before God within the created order — *may* continue on this planet. The contemporary perspective known as "deep ecology" rightly underscores the fact that the crisis itself will not be resolved primarily by technological solutions. A fundamental change in human thinking and behavior is required, at least among the economically privileged residents of the industrialized North.[8] We must cease to be willing, as we now are, to purchase our own temporary comfort at the expense of the long-term well-being of the earth and all its inhabitants. Biologist E. O. Wilson, perhaps the most widely known representative of a deep-ecology perspective, urges that we must cultivate a disposition that he calls "biophilia."[9] My own view is that the language of virtues (and corresponding vices)[10] is more adequate to the problem than such psycho-biological language. Overtly, moral discourse has the capacity to explore the subtle yet also well-documented ways in which human character becomes deformed by evil. Moreover, it exists in a tradition — namely, the religious traditions of Judaism and Christianity — that can guide and support us in making changes that are necessary, life-giving, but also painful. The traditional word for such change is, of course, "repentance."

I propose the Israelite wisdom literature, especially the book of Proverbs, as an exegetical base for renewing a biblically informed virtue tradition. This basic text of Israelite wisdom is in several ways helpful for this project. First, it seems that the Israelite sages perceive a fundamental connection between human character and creation. They begin their work of cultivating "the discipline for success" (1:3) by seeking to instill an awareness of the created order as the work of God's hands. Among the poems that preface the proverbial sayings and dispose us to understand them are two glorious lyrical recitations of the history of wisdom (3:13-26 and 8:22-36), beginning when "YHWH by wisdom founded the earth" (3:19). The earth itself is the first and greatest exemplar of practical wisdom, and those who would practice "sound judgment and prudence" are urged to keep that example ever in view (3:21). Second, while the

---

8. A good introduction to deep ecology is offered by Bill Devall and George Sessions, *Deep Ecology: Living As If Nature Mattered* (Salt Lake City, Utah: Gibbs Smith, 1985).

9. Stephen R. Kellert and Edward O. Wilson, eds., *The Biophilia Hypothesis* (Washington, D.C.: Island Press, 1993).

10. Although it goes beyond the scope of this essay, it could be argued that the dispositions known as "the seven deadly sins" are highly destructive not only of individual character and human society but also of nonhuman creation. Although there is more variation here than with the virtues, the seven sins are commonly reckoned as follows: pride, envy, anger, lust, gluttony, avarice, and sloth.

sages set forth justice as the ultimate horizon of wisdom thinking (1:3), they give more direct attention to the proximate (and less glamorous) virtues of prudence and temperance.[11] With countless short sayings, they illustrate the operation of those virtues — or the consequences of their neglect — in the life of ordinary Israelites. It is of further interest that the sages frequently use what we would call "nature imagery" to illustrate the operation of the virtues. They look to the animal kingdom for models of behavior that humans should emulate or avoid; they look to the condition of the fertile soil to show the consequences of practicing or neglecting the virtues.

By highlighting the sages' interest in creation and the nonhuman creatures, I do not mean to suggest that the Bible is an early ecological tract. Ancient Israel did not, like us, confront a profound and widespread ecological crisis of its own making. Yet the sages' attention to creation and the creatures is more than incidental. The wisdom poets of Israel devote some of their most exquisite lines to these matters in Proverbs and, most memorably, in the great divine speeches in Job. Regard for what God has done in creation is a constitutive element of biblical wisdom.

The reason for us to turn to Scripture in our present crisis is to enable a genuine renewal of the virtue tradition from a perspective that is both ancient and fresh. We must begin again, building on the foundation of Scripture, because it has been too long since the virtues (and their opposing vices) were living theological concepts.[12] From the first century to the fourteenth, the tradi-

---

11. Thomas Aquinas comments that, while justice is the appropriate focus of the commandments of "the Law" (the Ten Commandments and the books of the Torah), "so it was appropriate that later books of the Old Testament should instruct us on the activity of prudence, which is about the things serving this purpose" (*Summa Theologiae*, 2a2ae. 56, 1). Aquinas begins his extended treatment of the virtues with prudence; Proverbs is the book he cites most frequently to illustrate this virtue.

12. The virtue-and-vice tradition, a staple of medieval theology, receives very little attention among Christian theologians after 1500. Various reasons are offered for the eclipse of the tradition. Siegfried Wenzel cites "the replacement of an essentially theological system or *Weltanschauung* by various non-theological systems" for understanding human character, at the beginning of the Renaissance (*The Sin of Sloth: Acedia in Medieval Thought and Literature* [Chapel Hill: University of North Carolina Press, 1967], p. 179). Karl Olsson notes, "The Reformers were not so much interested in sins as in Sin" (*Seven Sins and Seven Virtues* [New York: Harper and Brothers, 1962], p. 9). Further, the towering emphasis on God's grace overshadowed the medieval concern with cultivating virtues. MacIntyre observes that the tradition of the virtues depended upon an understanding of the self that is foreign to "the culture of bureaucratic individualism": namely, "a concept of a self whose unity resides in the unity of a narrative which links birth to life to death as narrative beginning to middle to end" (*After Virtue*, p. 205). Hauerwas argues that neglect of the virtues in modern moral philosophy has its origin in poli-

tion was regularly invigorated by new theological work, both intellectual work and above all the daily work of prayer. For generation after generation of Christians (monks and nuns, but also lay people),[13] these were the categories by which human character was understood, by which aspirations to goodness and horror of sin (and of specific sins) were shaped. Medieval poets and artists created vivid images that showed the vices and virtues as real human possibilities, recognizable in the realm of contemporary history.

At the very end of this generative period, the Tuscan painter Giotto produced what is probably the most striking testimony extant to the vitality of the tradition, the series of personified Virtues and Vices in the Arena Chapel in Padua.[14] Among the sixty-four frescoes that cover the walls and the ceiling, the Virtues and Vices appear literally foundational for the life of faith, good or bad.[15] One passes through the sixty-seven-foot length of the chapel between two lines of frescoes. The bottom tier consists on one side of seven individual portraits of the Virtues (the cardinal virtues plus the three "theological virtues" of Faith, Hope, and Charity), with their opposing Vices on the other. The figures appear to have been caught in action. Prudentia is the first virtue portrayed, next to the altar. Seated at a study desk with a book open before her, she is just now looking reflectively in a mirror.[16] Opposite her, Stultitia

---

tics: "I suspect that it originated in a tacit fear that we lack the kind of community necessary to sustain development of people of virtue and character" (*A Community of Character*, p. 117).

13. The Christian tradition of deadly sins was first elaborated by the monastic theologians of Egypt to identify the temptations to which monks were prone. The tradition was gradually secularized and generalized to apply to all Christians. Wenzel, in his detailed history of the vice of *acedia* (sloth), comments: "The most distinctive feature of *acedia's* history between 400 and 1400 is . . . a continuing process of de-monasticization or secularization . . ." (*The Sin of Sloth*, p. 179).

14. Giotto's personifications may well have inspired his friend and fellow Tuscan Dante Alighieri, who is known to have visited him while he was working in Padua, probably between 1305 and 1308. The vividness with which the *Purgatorio* depicts those whose lives have been deformed by the vices may owe something to the work that is considered to be Giotto's greatest achievement.

15. The best guide to the overall plan of the Arena Chapel is Sarel Eimerl et al., *The World of Giotto, ca. 1267-1337* (Alexandria, Va.: Time-Life Books, 1967). This volume reproduces all the frescoes; the Virtues and the Vices (not clearly identified as such) appear inside the front and back covers. Excellent color plates of all the frescoes appear in Giuseppe Basile's *Giotto: The Arena Chapel Frescoes* (London: Thames and Hudson, 1993).

16. The mirror probably indicates familiarity with Aquinas's work on the virtues, which would have been well known to Giotto's theological advisors. In his treatment of prudence, Aquinas compares the faculty of judgment to a mirror: "[A] well-made mirror reflects the images of bodies as they really are, whereas in one poorly-made they appear distorted and crooked" (*Summa Theologiae*, 2a2ae. 51, 3).

(Folly)[17] is a fat clown in grotesquely feathered costume. Temperantia is a lovely figure, serene and strong. She stands with a sword before her, but it is sheathed; her power is fully in her command. Opposite her, Ira (Wrath), with a blinded expression, tears the clothing from her own body. Giotto graphically illustrates how someone looks and acts under the influence of these habitual dispositions.

Above the personified Virtues and Vices appear, in three additional tiers, three holy dramas: the life of Mary, the childhood and ministry of Christ, and the Passion. Sensitized by the nearly eye-level portraits of the Vices and the Virtues, we are able to read more accurately the range of human behavior displayed in the histories above. We see the hope, courage, and patient faith of Joachim and Anna in their long and humiliating infertility. The unbridled wrath of the soldiers at the Massacre of the Innocents contrasts with Jesus' prudent anger when he drives out the merchants from the temple. Even at the marriage at Cana, the porcine glutton has his place at table. Guided by the narratives of holy people confronting and enduring evil, it is not hard to apply the illustrated lessons to one's own life as the viewer makes the circuit of the chapel and goes out the door set beneath the great mural of the Last Judgment, opposite the altar. Giotto's vision bears on the work of renewing the virtue tradition. His naturalistic figures are a superb expression of what that tradition can do at its best, illumining Scripture, on the one hand, and human character, on the other.

Practicing the Virtues in the Book of Proverbs

Traditionally, the virtue of prudence is simply the steady exercise of realism in deciding what to do: "Judgment is correct when the cognitive faculty perceives a thing as it really is."[18] Aquinas identifies it as the bedrock of all moral behavior: "All sin is opposed to prudence, just as prudence participates in all virtue."[19] Justice, temperance, and fortitude are inoperative unless prudence enables us to choose, with some confidence, the right course of action. Therefore, the editors of Proverbs bring prudence to the fore, identifying it at the outset as the goal of the whole enterprise of collecting wise sayings:

---

17. The seven Vices Giotto portrays differ from the standard listing of deadly sins. They are (beginning from the altar) Folly, Inconstancy, Wrath, Injustice, Infidelity, Envy, and Despair.

18. Aquinas, *Summa Theologiae*, 2a2ae. 51, 3.

19. Aquinas, *Summa Theologiae*, 2a2ae. 55, 2.

> To give to the naïve astuteness,
>> to youth, knowledge and prudence *(mězimmâ)*.[20]   (1:4)

The exercise of prudence is so basic that to be without it is to lack the identify-ing element of humanity, namely, a "heart" or "mind" *(lēb)*:

> Folly is joy to the one who lacks a heart,
>> but the person of discernment *(tēbûnâ)* walks straight ahead.[21]   (15:21)

While the sages consistently represent prudence as a source of confidence and relative safety, it is important to distinguish their conception from the no-tion of cautious self-protection, which is our debased modern understanding of the "virtue" of prudence. (We might use the term, for example, with refer-ence to a life insurance policy or an investment portfolio.) Yet the sages' expli-cation of the prudent life proposes an entirely different orientation, not so much self-protective as self-critical. The realism that underlies good judgment begins with a rigorous attitude toward the self:

> The wisdom of the prudent is to understand one's way,
>> but the folly of fools is deception.   (14:8)

If to be without prudence is to lack a heart (15:21), then that lack can be filled only through the painful discipline of submitting to the critical judgment of others:

> The one who breaks loose from discipline despises his own self *(napšô)*,
>> but the one who listens to reproof gains a heart.   (15:32)

> A fool despises his father's discipline,
>> but the one who pays attention to reproof will be prudent.   (15:5)

The discipline of elders is a necessary help toward prudence, but a prop-erly rigorous attitude toward myself always proceeds from a realistic attitude toward God. This attitude is what the sages commonly designate "the fear of YHWH," which they identify as "the starting point for wisdom" (1:7). The follow-

20. Unless otherwise noted, the following translations are the author's.

21. Several different Hebrew words or roots as they appear in Proverbs are aptly rendered in English as "prudence" or "(be) prudent": *mězimmâ* (1:4; 2:11; 3:21; etc.), various forms of *bîn* (2:11; 10:13; 14:6; 15:21; etc.) and *'ormâ* plus cognates (1:4; 8:12; 14:8, 18; etc.). While this usage of-fers some guidance, I do not undertake a word study in this essay but rather look more broadly at how Proverbs characterizes the disposition of a person who reasons and acts on the basis of good judgment.

ing poem, which prefaces the collected sayings and disposes us to understand them rightly, is one of the clearest biblical statements of that attitude:

> Trust in YHWH with all your heart;
>> but on your own understanding do not lean.
> In all your ways, acknowledge him,
>> and he will make straight your paths.
> Do not be wise in your own eyes;
>> fear YHWH and depart from evil.
> It will be healing to your navel,
>> and moisture to your bones.   (3:5-8)

The final metaphor is meant to be startling. The sages address us as newborns, challenging us to give up our adult pretensions to know just what to do. Shockingly, prudence begins with acceptance of our own ignorance; yet ignorance itself is no virtue. The sages have no praise for the intellectually lazy; only "fools hate knowledge" (1:22). Nonetheless, genuine prudence means recognizing how much in fact we do not know, and can never know: "Do not be wise in your own eyes." The proper consequence of accepting one's own ignorance is to turn repeatedly to God in "fear." Paradoxically, "fear of YHWH" is itself a healthy form of confidence, the utter confidence with which a newborn looks to her mother. In his engaging and profound study of Aquinas's thought on the virtues, Josef Pieper asserts that prudence is impossible "without a youthful spirit of brave trust and, as it were, a reckless tossing away of anxious self-preservation, a relinquishment of all egoistic bias toward mere confirmation of the self...."[22] He perceptively contrasts prudence with the "anxious senility" of covetousness, the desperate seeking for security in material things that makes us old before our time. The Israelite sages invite us to "fear YHWH" and experience radical spiritual rejuvenation.

One aspect of prudence is especially crucial for our contemporary use of the virtue tradition. Aquinas treats as one of the special features of prudence its urgent concern *(sollicitudo)* for the future.[23] He takes his text from Proverbs:

> Go to the ant, lazy one;
>> see her ways and wise up —
> Who, having no captain, overseer, or ruler,
>> prepares in summertime her food.

---

22. Josef Pieper, *The Four Cardinal Virtues* (Notre Dame, Ind.: University of Notre Dame Press, 1965), p. 21.

23. Aquinas, *Summa Theologiae*, 2a2ae. 55, 7.

She gathers at harvest time what she will eat.
How long, lazy one, will you lie there?
When will you rise from your sleep?
A little sleeping, a little napping,
  a little folding the hands to lie down —
And your poverty will come like a highwayman,
  and your want, like a man with a shield.   (6:6-11)

The parable of the ant may (and probably should) be taken at several levels. Most obviously, it offers strong encouragement to "wise up" and make timely provision for the immediate future. The effects of laziness are soon felt in a subsistence-level agricultural economy such as ancient Israel's. Since ancient times, the parable has also been assigned a second level of meaning. It has been read as a warning against spiritual laziness, the deadly sin of sloth. In a word, sloth is the refusal to respond energetically to the new opportunities that are continually coming to us from God.[24] The third level at which the parable may be read is related to but distinct from the other two. This is an instance of nature wisdom; the sages are commending to our attention what medieval theologians called "the book of the creatures." If we can learn to "read" it accurately, then we may gain insight into God's ways and the human place in the divine economy.

Solomon himself was reputedly skilled at nature wisdom: "He would speak about the trees, from the cedar that is in Lebanon to the hyssop that grows out of the wall, and he would speak about the mammals, and about the birds, and about the reptiles, and about the fish" (1 Kgs 4:33 [MT 5:13]). Accordingly, the concluding frame of the book of Proverbs includes several short poems that draw attention to the ways of nonhuman creatures (Prov 30:15-16, 18-19, 24-31). In positive or negative ways, they enable us to see human behavior more clearly when we correlate it with the behavior of the creatures, whether the stately boldness of the lion or the insatiability of the horseleech. Further, in a saying such as the parable of the ant, the creature is more than a lens for viewing human behavior; she is a model for emulation. One might say that the ant is herself a "sage"; we can learn from her, because she still retains her original portion of the wisdom by which "yhwh founded the earth" (3:19). It is only the human creatures who have made the exercise of wisdom difficult, by separating themselves from God in willful disobedience.[25]

---

24. Perhaps the most suggestive modern treatment of sloth is that of Karl Barth in *Church Dogmatics* 4/2 (Edinburgh: T. & T. Clark, 1958), pp. 378-98.

25. For more extended treatments of the parable of the ant and other passages mentioned here, see my commentary, *Proverbs, Ecclesiastes, and the Song of Songs* (Louisville, Ky.: Westminster/John Knox, 2000).

The virtue of temperance has even less contemporary appeal than does prudence. Our culture, on the whole, admires people whose "passion" is visible; we give little attention to the difficulty of directing with care the desires that move us, and to the benefits of doing so.[26] That is what temperance is about, and because its appeal to us is not strong, it may come as a surprise to know that ancient and medieval theologians perceived that temperance has a particular affinity with beauty.[27] On the face of Temperantia, Giotto has painted a delicate jeweled chain, faintly visible as it runs across her cheeks to her mouth. It suggests a bridle,[28] yet there is no strain on her lovely face. What restrains her tongue is an ornament that only makes her lovelier. Conversely, intemperance destroys beauty. Because of the ugliness that attends the sins of intemperance, Aquinas teaches that these sins are especially painful to those who are still well enough to feel shame and desire to change.[29]

Much of the sages' positive instruction about temperance takes the form of short comparative statements:

> Better a little with fear of YHWH
>> than great treasure and turmoil with it. (15:16)

> Better a little with righteousness
>> than large profits with no justice. (16:8)

> Better to be of lowly spirit with the afflicted [or the poor]
>> than to divide spoil with the proud. (16:19)

> Better patience than being mighty,
>> and the one who governs his own spirit
>> than the conqueror of a city. (16:32)

> Better a dry morsel and ease-of-mind with it
>> than a house full of contentious feasts. (17:1)

Each saying commends to us a good that is considerably less than perfect, but that is how virtue always evidences itself. "Virtue is about what is difficult, and

---

26. One exception is ethicist James Nash, who has helpfully pointed to the contemporary relevance of "frugality," that is, temperance. See his "Toward the Revival and Reform of the Subversive Virtue: Frugality," *The Annual of the Society of Christian Ethics* (1995): 137-60.

27. Aquinas, citing Ambrose, treats the affinity between temperance and beauty in *Summa Theologiae*, 2a2ae. 141, 8.

28. The scriptural base for the image is probably the Letter of James: "Anyone who makes no mistakes in speaking is perfect, able to keep the whole body in check with a bridle" (3:2).

29. Aquinas, *Summa Theologiae*, 2a2ae. 143, 1; 2a2ae. 144, 2.

good."[30] The cumulative effect of these "better . . . than" statements is to suggest that the virtue of temperance — in the sages' terms, "governing one's own spirit" — means that one must want fewer material goods than we are generally disposed to want. The sages already anticipate the gospel imperative that we should actively choose to be lower down on the scale of acquisition and consumption. Living in the kingdom of heaven means changing our desires so that we willingly locate ourselves where the poor and oppressed are, perforce.

The sages' most forceful commendation of temperance occurs in the penultimate chapter of the book. Placed to linger in a reader's (or hearer's) memory, the prayer for sufficiency (30:7-9) stands out; these are the only words in the book that are addressed to God. After so many sayings that address us on the horizontal plane, aiming to engage us in "the discipline for success" (1:3), the switch to prayer is startling. It impresses upon us the fact that we still need God's help in order to achieve truthfulness in our economic life:

> Two things I ask of you
>   (do not deny them to me before I die!):
> Falsehood and lies take far from me;
>   poverty and riches do not give me.
> Feed me with the food allotted to me,
>   lest I be glutted and deceive,
>   and say, "Who is YHWH?"
> Or lest I be impoverished and steal,
>   and blame [literally, "seize the Name of"] my God.   (30:7-9)

It is striking that the poem speaks equally about money and about truthfulness. The immediately preceding sayings focus on true speaking (vv. 5-6). Now this prayer suggests that my income, no less than my speech, is an index of the truthfulness of my life. Both more-than-enough and less-than-enough lead directly to false speaking, but it is easy to infer which condition is more dangerous to ourselves and to others. The poor person may wrongly blame God (presumably for "making" her steal), but the one who is glutted is likely to deny God altogether, thus deceiving himself and misleading others about the Source of wealth and blessing. Furthermore, the Torah is clear that confusion about the fundament of reality will not be tolerated indefinitely:

> Look out for yourself, lest you forget YHWH your God . . . , lest you eat and
> be glutted and build good houses and settle in . . . and you say in your heart,
> "My strength and the power of my hand got me this wealth. . . ." And it shall

---

30. Aquinas, *Summa Theologiae*, 2a2ae. 141, 8.

be that if indeed you do forget YHWH your God, . . . I call you to witness against yourselves this day, that you shall surely perish. Like the nations that YHWH is making perish before your faces, so you shall perish. . . . (Deut 8:11-20)

The Torah sets the parameters by which we understand the rest of Scripture. So Deuteronomy alerts us to the fact that the prayer in Proverbs is not making an appeal about a purely personal problem. Behind that prayer stands Moses' warning to the whole people that they may become glutted, forget God, and perish from the land that is the earnest of covenant relationship. According to Israelite (particularly Deuteronomic) theology, having too much ultimately comes at the cost of being cast off the fertile soil on which the community lives solely by God's grace. That understanding is telling in light of our new awareness that the glutted condition of modern industrialized society is an insupportable burden for our groaning planet.

Character and Creation: The Great Economy

The classical and medieval schema of the cardinal virtues expresses a unitive conception of the sound moral life. Although the biblical writers are less inclined to draw fixed categories for the various dispositions they commend, they also strive to represent a moral unity. Paul in Acts speaks of "justice and self-control" and in Galatians of "the *fruit* [singular] of the Spirit"; the opening poem of Proverbs characterizes it as "the discipline for success: righteousness, justice, and equity" (1:3). But perhaps the best biblical summation of that moral unity is the portrait of "a valorous woman" with which Proverbs concludes (31:10-31). She is represented as the manager of a complex domestic economy, a prosperous village household that produces most of its own goods. Her praises are sung in an acrostic poem, a sort of "A to Z" demonstration of what the virtues look like in embodied action. Justice is evidenced when she extends her hands to "the poor and needy" (v. 20); she "acts prudently" (*zāmĕmâ*)[31] in taking a field and planting it with her own hands. Her hands, always in motion, lay hold of distaff and spindle (v. 19). Having supplied her own household with linens and clothing, she runs a small cottage industry in superior woven goods. This woman is "like merchant ships" (v. 14), but she is also a teacher: wisdom is in her mouth; on her tongue is "the teaching of *ḥesed*," the covenant virtue (v. 26). In sum, "she does not eat the bread of idleness" (v. 27); and idleness,

---

31. The rare verb √*zmm* corresponds to the more common noun *mĕzimmâ* (1:4).

from the perspective of the sages, is one of the chief causes of disaster. This busy manager of a small farm stands in complete contrast, on the one hand, to the "idle man," a farmer whose own vineyard has gone to thorns and nettles (24:30-34). On the other hand, her economic and moral life is utterly different from that of the "strange woman" of chapter 7, a city-dweller who imports *her* sheets from Egypt, the height of ancient conspicuous consumption.[32] The latter woman, who seems to take no responsibility for producing for her own house-hold, has too much time on her hands — enough to seduce "a youth lacking in heart" when her merchant-husband is away (7:7; cf. 15:21). In contrast to both negative examples, the "valorous woman" answers well and happily (31:28) to the claims laid upon her by the social and the natural orders; her reputation for building up soil, household, and community reaches even to the public square (v. 31).

It is revealing that the sages' final demonstration of the essential virtues is made in terms that are literally "economic"; wisdom manifests "herself" as a household manager *(oikonomos)*. This is the most detailed picture found in Scripture of the operation of an ordinary (albeit exemplary) Israelite household. An observation of the contemporary farmer and essayist Wendell Berry draws the connection between the virtues and concrete economic practices. He draws that connection within the context of what he calls "the Great Economy," a shorthand term for a reality that human beings did not create, within whose limits they must live, and which humans cannot fundamentally alter to the better. In other words, "the Great Economy," like the biblical phrase "the heavens and the earth," expresses the fact that the largest context of human action vastly exceeds our control; we live in and depend on a reality that God has made.

> Work that is authentically placed and understood within the Great Econ-omy moves virtue toward virtuosity — that is, toward skill or technical competence. There is no use in helping our neighbors with their work if we do not know how to work. When the virtues are rightly practiced within the Great Economy, we do not call them virtues; we call them good farm-ing, good forestry, good carpentry, good husbandry, good weaving and sewing, good homemaking, good parenthood, good neighborhood, and so on. The general principles are submerged in the particularities of their en-gagement with the world. . . .

---

32. The deliberate contrast between the two women is summed up in the single word *marbaddîm*, "bed-coverings." Whereas the valorous woman weaves her own (31:22), the strange woman entices the young man into imported sheets perfumed with exotic spices (7:16-17). These are the only occurrences of this noun in the Bible; three of four occurrences of the root occur in these two verses.

There is no "outside" to the Great Economy, no escape into either specialization or generality, no "time off." Even insignificance is no escape, for in the membership of the Great Economy everything signifies; whatever we do counts. If we do not serve what coheres and endures, we serve what disintegrates and destroys. We can *presume* that we are outside the membership that includes us, but that presumption only damages the membership — and ourselves, of course, along with it.[33]

Berry's concept of "the Great Economy" is one of the fundaments of a religious understanding of the world. As I have indicated above, it is a perspective that the sages of Israel share,[34] although they would probably call it simply the "wisdom" or "understanding" by which God established the heavens and earth. For both Berry and the sages, accepting that view means seeing that there is a connection between human character and creation, a connection that necessarily implicates our economic practices. Berry is helpful because he explicitly names creation as an Economy, an infinitely complex network of give-and-take, of exchanged life, power, and value among all the creatures of God. Therefore, sound human character (virtue) evidences itself in "little economies" that seek in various ways to imitate the patterns and submit to the limits we may discern in what we normally call nature.

Virtue, in other words, entails seeing ourselves as part of the pattern that God has woven into creation, and valuing ourselves accordingly. This way of valuing ourselves is suggested by the loveliest passage in Proverbs, where Wisdom, "the first of God's ways," recalls being at God's side when everything else was made:

> When he made firm the heavens,
>   I was there.
> When he circumscribed a vaulting on the face of the deep,
>   when he inscribed the foundations of the earth. . . .
> I was at his side as a master-worker (?),
>   and I was daily delight,
> playing before him all the time,
>   playing in his inhabited world,
> and my delight — the children of Adam!
> And now, children, listen to me:

---

33. W. Berry, *Home Economics* (New York: North Point, 1987), pp. 73-75.

34. Although Berry generally avoids specifically biblical language, he acknowledges that "the Great Economy" is otherwise known as "the Kingdom of God," and that he himself remains "under the personal necessity of Biblical reference" (*Home Economics*, p. 56).

    privileged *('ašrê)* are they who keep my ways.
Listen to discipline and be wise,
    and do not run amuck.
Privileged is the person *('ādām)* who listens to me
    in order to watch at my doors daily.   (8:27, 29-34)

"She" who was God's delight and companion in the work of creation, who has intimate knowledge of the design by which the world was made, seeks perpetual delight in Adam's children. The biblical poem urges us to esteem ourselves "privileged" precisely as those who live in lifelong discipleship to this Wisdom. What she calls "my discipline" seems to designate the way of living that Berry would consider being a member-in-good-standing of the Great Economy. Wisdom's disciples serve "what coheres and endures," for they are privileged to know that there is no life at all outside it.

    All this is a biblical commonplace. Paul's catechetical instruction about "justice, self-control, and the coming judgment" could itself be seen as a kind of economic statement about the human place in creation. Such a suggestion is plausible in light of the fact that the book of Acts shows marked interest in the economic arrangements that obtain within the new Christian community.[35] If "justice" be taken as a shorthand designation for the proper working of God's design for the world, then "self-control" is the regulation of our "little economies" in accordance with the Great Economy. Using the classical terminology of the cardinal virtues, prudence means investing ourselves properly in creation, making decisions that demonstrate steady reflection on what God has done. Temperance denotes the practice of steadily limiting our "take," which is essential if the investment is to be healthy. Together, these two elements of self-control require that our choices be guided and limited by "what coheres and endures."

    The principle of the Great Economy is simple but worth belaboring because the popular wisdom of our culture is devoted entirely to its refutation. This is evident from our advertising slogans, whose function is in some ways equivalent to that of proverbial literature in traditional cultures. In modern consumer culture, television advertisements are the "oral literature," carefully crafted and constantly repeated, that shapes our views of self and world. "Apples of gold in settings of silver," the Israelite sages called their "well-turned" rhythmic phrases (25:11). Likewise, the wisdom sayings that come from Madison Avenue are frequently something like short poems, designed to turn a profit. Consider the following advertisements for Lexus:

---

35. See Acts 4:32–5:11; 6:1-6; 20:33-35.

Follow no one,
>   because the only path to our purpose
>   is the one never taken before.
We determine our fate;
>   it has to come from within.
Yet this course demands sacrifice:
>   forsaking the certainty of the familiar to risk
>   confrontation with the inevitable.

The presupposition about reality that informs these wisdom sayings is exactly the opposite of that which informs the biblical tradition — even if the poet of Lexus does borrow a religious word like "sacrifice." Indeed, it is impossible to speak of "tradition" at all if one accepts the advice to "follow no one." There is nothing to be learned from the past, from a parent, a sage, a righteous person. Indeed, if one follows the logic, then the enterprise of learning becomes altogether doubtful. Reality begins with me; "it has to come from within." Outside me is something vaguely termed "the inevitable." If taken seriously, this is a chilling view of reality. The sages maintain that YHWH is the Author of all reality. In light of that conviction, they encourage us to embrace a life of trust, learning in community, and reverent choice. Further, they believe that such a life has the potential for bringing delight to God and to the human community. Lexus points us only toward lonely "confrontation with the inevitable."

The contrast between Israel's view and that of industrialized culture is sharpened when sayings on similar topics are compared. A Joop (jeans) advertisement counsels, "Sanity is the playground of the unimaginative." The sages of Proverbs have no enthusiasm for "imagination" untempered by reality:

Wisdom is in the presence of the one who has discernment;
>   but the eyes of the fool are at the ends of the earth.   (17:24)

Likewise, Shalimar perfume suggests, "Let the moment be your invention." To that compare:

The one who trusts to his own heart (or: mind), he is a fool;
>   but the one who walks with wisdom, he will escape.   (28:26)

In each case, the Madison Avenue proverb bespeaks a confidence in one's own judgment (or, perhaps, one's immediate desire) for which the only ground offered is the advertised product. The Israelite proverbs consistently identify confidence that is not grounded in fear of YHWH as the disposition of the fool.

All these commercial poems are designed to make us buy things we do not need. In light of the virtue tradition, it is telling that our society manufactures "wisdom" in order to market the superfluous. Aquinas makes the astute observation that covetousness, excessive desire for possessions, bears some resemblance to prudence, for it likewise involves careful use of reason. But "the folly of fools is deception" (Prov 14:8); covetousness is only mock prudence. The difference between the genuine article and its imitation lies in the fact that prudence manifests itself chiefly in justice, yet covetousness is opposed to justice.[36] The opening lines of Proverbs attest to the preeminence of justice in manifesting a life wisely lived. Thus, the Israelite teachers advertise the ultimate benefit of wisdom:

> To know wisdom and discipline,
>> to gain insight into insightful sayings;
> to acquire the discipline for success:
>> righteousness and justice and equity.   (1:2-3)

Here "success" is specified in terms of just dealing. The true measure of my success is how my talents and education work for others, whether my investments of energy and the choices I make bring improvement to the lives of those who exercise less influence in the world and less control over their own fate than I do — for in the context of the Bible, that is the only thing "righteousness and justice" can mean. In other words, my success is measured in terms of what it may mean for those whom the Bible names "the poor and needy." In contrast, consumer culture offers this depauperate definition (an advertisement for Tagheuer watches): "Success, it's a mind game."

No wonder the concepts that are the coinage of the biblical virtue tradition — wisdom and discipline, prudence and temperance — have fallen out of fashion. They are embedded in a set of assumptions about the nature of reality and the human place in the world that differs profoundly from that which sustains our economy of depredation and waste. The burden of this essay is to hold up an ancient and timely alternative to these contemporary assumptions, which are destructive precisely to the degree that they are ahistorical. We live in a culture that has no realistic connection to either the past or the future. We have in the past century used up more of the earth's wealth than the sum total consumed by everyone living on the face of the earth before us. No one has lived this way before; we are even now ensuring that no one after us will be able to live thus.

I commend the biblical tradition of the virtues because it is based upon a

---

36. Aquinas, *Summa Theologiae,* 2a2ae. 55, 8. Question 55 is entirely devoted to the phenomenon of mock prudence, its sources and various forms.

view of history stretching from the creation to the coming judgment. There-fore, it offers us the necessary scope for locating our own historical moment ac-curately. Real hope for change in this generation and realistic hope for the fu-ture lie in the possibility of engendering in ourselves and in our children a vivid and personal sense of history, strong enough to condition our economic behav-ior. For this purpose, Israel's sages offer us a poetic vision that stretches back-ward to the beginning of "heavens and earth" and forward along the way that we must go:

> YHWH by wisdom founded the earth;
>> he established the heavens by insight.
> By knowledge the deeps were broken open,
>> and the clouds dripped dew.
> My child, do not let these elude your eyes;
>> keep sound judgment and prudence;
> and they will be life's-breath to your being[37]
>> and grace about your neck.
> Then you will walk your way securely,
>> and your foot will strike nothing.
> If you lie down, you will not be afraid.
>> You will lie down, and your sleep will be sweet.
> Do not be fearful of sudden terror,
>> of the storm of the wicked when it comes.
> For YHWH will be your confidence,
>> and he will protect your foot from entrapment.   (3:19-26)

Can we accept such assurance on the terms with which it is offered and, thereby, exchange our groundless fantasies, our radically ahistorical "lifestyle," for "sound judgment and prudence"? This is perhaps the one thing most needful of the prayers of this generation.

---

37. The Hebrew wordplay connecting this and the following lines is hard to capture in English. The word translated "being" *(nepeš)* literally means "throat." The implication of the two lines is that "sound judgment and prudence" are both elemental and ornamental.

The Ethics of Narrative Wisdom:
Qoheleth as Test Case

Eric S. Christianson

Qoheleth presents a problem to anyone who attempts to formulate an ethic of character from his foreboding words. He seems, for example, not to have been deeply concerned about correcting social injustice.[1] He seems not to have any clear views about what constitutes righteous behavior. It is likely that he expressed animosity toward at least one segment of society.[2] Here is a sage who, in the course of his narrative,[3] has little qualms in informing the reader that "humanity has no advantage over the beasts; for everything is absurd" (3:19b) or that he hated life (2:17). Taken in isolation, Qoheleth's dark sayings are not unique to the Old Testament.[4] What makes his tale unique is the relative consistency of those sayings — compounded by the preponderance of the *hebel* theme — emerging as they do from a cohesive narrative voice. Indeed there is

1. For a recent expression of the problem of Qoheleth's theological ethics, see R. N. Whybray, "Qoheleth as a Theologian," in *Qohelet in the Context of Wisdom,* ed. A. Schoors, BETL 136 (Leuven: Leuven University Press, 1998), pp. 239-66 (esp. pp. 246-56). Whybray discusses the advantages of viewing Qoheleth's thought within the wider context of Old Testament thought on his themes (wisdom, fear of God, human endeavor, etc.).

2. I refer to his expressed attitude toward women (see Eric S. Christianson, "'Qoheleth the Old Boy and Qoheleth the New Man': Misogynism, the Womb and a Paradox in Ecclesiastes," in *Wisdom and Psalms: A Feminist Companion to the Bible,* ed. A. Brenner and C. Fontaine, Feminist Companion to the Bible n.s. 2 [Sheffield: Sheffield Academic Press, 1998], pp. 109-36).

3. For the argument that Ecclesiastes is expressed in a narrative, autobiographical form see Eric S. Christianson, *A Time to Tell: Narrative Strategies in Ecclesiastes,* JSOTSup 280 (Sheffield: Sheffield Academic Press, 1998), pp. 19-50.

4. See R. Murphy's helpful discussion of the commonality of some of Qoheleth's darker sayings (*Ecclesiastes,* WBC 23a [Dallas: Word Books, 1992], pp. lxvi, lxvii [esp. on the relationship between deed and consequence]).

something that rings true about Elizabeth Stone's assessment of Ecclesiastes in her 1942 essay, "Old Man Koheleth":

> [Koheleth's] book is a record of profound personal disillusionment, which has ground him until he no longer feels it as anything but a faint taste of ashes in the mouth, and the red gone out of the sunset. . . . [Yet] Koheleth has not always been bored, and he participated passionately in the life around him, but in the end he set down his pen, and was only tired with life, and frustrated in his search to see something beyond it.[5]

Given the "faint taste of ashes" Qoheleth leaves his readers, this essay seeks to answer the question, What is there for those who might look to Qoheleth for some model of how one should live? I will proceed with a model proposed by ethicist James Keenan. Keenan suggests that virtue ethicists are engaged in expanding the fundamental ethical question "What should I do?" into three related questions: "Who am I?," "Who ought I to become?," and "How am I to get there?"[6] By considering not only how Qoheleth might have answered such basic questions but also how readers of Ecclesiastes are enabled to engage with them, we will find useful points of entry.

"Who Am I?"

On one level, this would be a deceptively hard question for Qoheleth to answer. He cannot seem to make up his mind whether he is Solomon, Qoheleth, or some ghostly concoction of both. However, the more precise question virtue ethics desires to ask is, By what standard do we measure ourselves? By what standard do we measure the self and its formation in the world? This standard, according to Keenan, is revealed in the unguarded narrative of daily existence, for "we reveal ourselves to ourselves when we act in the unplanned world of ordinary life."[7] Likewise, Qoheleth reveals himself to the reader in his extraordinary narrated life that, for him, was marred by the unknown.

As soon as Qoheleth announces his quest with his programmatic statement, "I set my heart to investigate and to search out by wisdom all that has been done under the heavens" (1:13a), he introduces us to two characters: the younger, experiencing self, who is the subject of that statement, and the older

---

5. E. Stone, "Old Man Koheleth," *JBR* 10 (1942): 102.

6. James F. Keenan, "Virtue Ethics," in *Christian Ethics: An Introduction*, ed. B. Hoose (London: Cassel, 1998), p. 84.

7. Keenan, "Virtue Ethics," p. 85.

telling, relating self, who makes that statement. This is by no means a new observation. Yet we must ask of this ethical attempt at reading, With which character are we to identify? From the narrative perspective, our answer can only be the latter — the narrator Qoheleth who announces his quest. It is through those eyes that we see anything in Qoheleth's text. It is the older voice that evaluates and judges the life and soul of the younger. This is also the voice that presents character to the reader. By "character" I mean the "capacity to determine [oneself] beyond momentary excitations in the acts"[8] — it is to hold fast and not renounce oneself. It requires the possession of integrity, consistency, and reliability. At the same time, however, character is a curiously amoral qualification. It is not necessarily what makes one good.

Through the device of self-reflection, Qoheleth produces a heightened awareness of the self as subject.[9] In this sense, consciousness becomes the *enabler* of self-knowledge. As Stanley Hauerwas says of the process,

> One of the constant themes running through moral philosophy has been that the unexamined life is not worth living . . . for it is through consciousness . . . that we shape ourselves and our actions. And what else does consciousness mean but the effort to see and understand our actions in terms of their most significant moral descriptions?[10]

Qoheleth not only examines his own life, which he does with great intensity, but also is a shrewd and perceptive observer of all events that occur "under the sun"; he is dangerously open to their impact on him (cf. 1:17-18; 2:17; 8:16-17). Under his critical eye are scrutinized, among other things, all that God does (1:13-14; 3:10; 8:16-17; cf. 2:24; 3:15), a range of harmful human predicaments (2:14-16, 21-23; 4:1-3; 5:13-17; 6:1-5; 8:10-13; 9:11-12; cf. 10:5-7), and even "everything" (7:15; cf. 1:14; 4:15; 9:1).

Among Qoheleth's favorite phrases are "I observed," "I gave my heart over," "I applied myself," "I said to myself concerning," "I tested," and "I said in my heart." By thus narrating his subjective past, Qoheleth transcends it and brings it under scrutiny — the scrutiny not only of his powers of observation but of the implied positive theology of his story.[11] In other words, his withering

---

8. S. Hauerwas, *Vision and Virtue: Essays in Christian Ethical Reflection* (Notre Dame, Ind.: University of Notre Dame Press, 1986), p. 54 (cf. p. 55).

9. See Christianson, *A Time to Tell*, pp. 210-15.

10. Hauerwas, *Vision and Virtue*, p. 66.

11. I have explored this question of the testing of Qoheleth's self (and how Qoheleth broadens that test to consider what it means to be human) elsewhere and will not rehearse the arguments here (see "Qoheleth and the/his Self among the Deconstructed," in *Qoheleth in the Context of Wisdom*, ed. A. Schoors, BETL 136 [Leuven: Leuven University Press, 1998], pp. 425-33).

criticisms directed at the objects of his scrutiny (such objects prove to be fleeting or absurd) imply a deep criterion for what is meaningful and what might escape the judgment of *hebel*. As Michael V. Fox suggests, Qoheleth "posits criteria for meaningfulness so rigorous that almost nothing can meet them. Even if something is good, it can still be absurd."[12] Qoheleth is identified as the person who tests the terms by which he has measured both himself and the arena in which the formation of the self is to take place.

"Who Ought I to Become?"

Keenan's second question aims to set personal goals, "to develop a personal vision and to strive to attain it," and he identifies this as the "fundamental task of the moral life."[13] What, then, is the moral vision that Qoheleth develops? Again, from the outset of his programmatic quest, Qoheleth expresses a clear goal: the attainment of true wisdom for *better understanding* of what God does for humanity and how the world and wisdom function in relation to the self.[14] This is the goal for which he expends the lion's share of his energy. It consumes him at every turn. Doing so takes him on an unconventional route.

After the royal setting established by 1:1-2, one might rightly expect a careful and systematic approach by the king to weigh and consider what is good for humanity. To some degree this is what happens (e.g., 1:13, 16-17; 2:3), but with a difference: Qoheleth departs on a regular basis from any expectations we might reasonably construct:[15]

> I said in my heart, "Come, I will test you with mirth and enjoy good [things]." But behold, that too was absurdity. "To laugh," I said, "is madness; and to be merry, what use is it?" I set out in my heart to cheer my flesh with wine (my heart conducting itself with wisdom), and to take hold of folly until I should see what was good for human beings to do under the heavens the few days of their lives. (2:1-3)

This experiment may have been "conducted with wisdom," but it also has involved all the senses that the young Qoheleth could muster. What makes the vi-

---

12. Michael V. Fox, *A Time to Tear Down and a Time to Build Up: A Rereading of Ecclesiastes* (Grand Rapids: Eerdmans, 1999), p. 139.

13. Keenan, "Virtue Ethics," p. 85.

14. For a full discussion of those relationships, see Christianson, *A Time to Tell*, pp. 227-35.

15. All translations of the biblical text are the author's.

sion moral is Qoheleth's clear stance toward that which is under scrutiny. Yet his unorthodox route to this conclusion is what partly gives his character depth. Hauerwas's description of character "growth" applies to Qoheleth. Formation is achieved through challenging our "past determinations." It means living life in a creative mode, not limiting "our actions to a well-laid-out routine which allows a safe boredom and protects us from the ravages of the unknown."[16] This does not mean that the future holds nothing but good for us. This is where Qoheleth's express goal of becoming wise enters: the wise know the proper time, discern the moment of action, and determine "what is good for humanity to do."

At one point, Qoheleth's quest involves him in a very personal attempt at sagacious transformation: "All this I tested with wisdom. I said, 'I will become wise.' But it was far from me. What has been is far off and deep, surely deep. Who can discover it?" (7:23-24). The only first-person singular verb forms of *ḥkm* ("to be wise") in the Old Testament occur in Ecclesiastes (2:15, 19; 7:23). Only in Qoheleth's story is the notion of becoming wise related so reflexively to the speaker. In the end, Qoheleth fails to reach his goal. Nevertheless, the *pursuit* itself offers the reader a source of learning. For Qoheleth's careful student, the self must be defined by a new goal: honest confrontation with the incongruous.

The understanding Qoheleth reaches in his process of discovery constitutes a realistic assessment of his experience in relation to the world. For Qoheleth, to a large degree, this is the expressed goal of character formation: the forcible if indirect expression of "Who I Ought to Become."

"How Am I to Get There?"

Keenan's third question deals with the *enablement* of the person who has set about to achieve goals. Since Qoheleth has failed fantastically to achieve his stated goal of deeper understanding, we may put our question to him in another way: How is his "careful student" (including the reader) enabled by his narrative?

Qoheleth's attention gradually shifts from telling his own story to a more "present" concern: what his student should take from his story. In connection to that concern, novelist Doris Lessing has highlighted what I think is a fairly common experience of Qoheleth's readers:

---

16. Hauerwas, *Vision and Virtue*, pp. 63-64.

> From the very first verse of Ecclesiastes you are carried along on a running
> tide of sound, incantatory, almost hypnotic, and it is easy to imagine your-
> self sitting among this man's pupils, listening to — for instance, "Remem-
> ber now thy creator in the days of thy youth, while the evil days come not,
> nor the years draw nigh, when thou shalt say, I have no pleasure in them."
> Your ears are entranced but at the same time you are very much alert. You
> have to be old to understand that verse, to see your whole life from early
> heedlessness to present regret for heedlessness.[17]

The experience to which Lessing alludes, I suggest, is the vehicle by which *readers* attain Qoheleth's goal (which we may formulate at this stage as a truthful, if
brutal, confrontation with experience). But how is that vehicle boarded? Where
does one obtain the tickets?

It is no coincidence that most of Qoheleth's advice to his reader occurs toward the end of his narration, after the majority of his experiences have been
related. As William P. Brown states, "The bulk of the book . . . consists of a person who, like Job, shares his personal discoveries and bares his soul, but without
dialogic partners."[18] Qoheleth's strategy is to communicate through his life
story, and this provides the juncture for the reader to climb aboard. Qoheleth
moves gradually from quest to expression — from ignorance and search to
knowledge, to the dictum that knowledge is absurd. That hard-won ignorance
forms the basis of his strategy in the latter half of the book, the imparting of advice to the addressee.

The importance of advice and Qoheleth's attempt to crystallize it are reflected in the gradual change in narratorial voice — from the density of first-
person (ch. 2) to the density of second-person narration (ch. 11). The graph on
p. 208 shows the shift from first- to second-person narration.[19] The graph demonstrates well the shift from experience to advice and an overall strategy in
which readers, who comprise the audience Qoheleth addresses, are invited to
participate increasingly in the text's story world.

17. Doris Lessing, "Introduction," in *Ecclesiastes, or The Preacher* (Edinburgh: Canongate
Books, 1998), p. x.

18. William P. Brown, *Character in Crisis: A Fresh Approach to the Wisdom Literature of
the Old Testament* (Grand Rapids: Eerdmans, 1996), p. 121.

19. In various instances, the second person is indicated by the pronominal suffix, imperative verb forms (e.g., 11:1), and indirect speech (e.g., 12:1, which governs the remainder of that
poem). In the graph, I have omitted the second-person verb in 8:4, which is indirect speech at a
level removed from Qoheleth's narration ("Who may say to him [the king], 'What are you doing?'"), and also the two instances of second person as addressed to "the land" in 10:16-17. For
fuller discussion, see Christianson, *A Time to Tell*, pp. 244-46, from which this section has been
adapted.

First- and Second-Person Narration

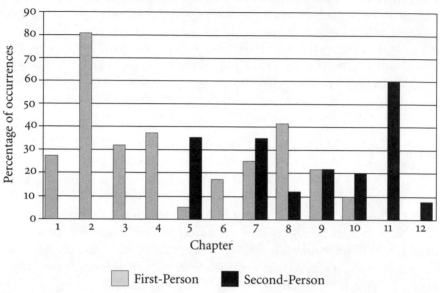

Chapter

First-Person   Second-Person

The narratee is the character who is addressed in the "space" of the text itself. At the outer level of the frame narrative, the narratee is unknown, for Qoheleth never addresses anyone by name or title. However, we can construct from "hearing one side of the conversation," so to speak, that the person Qoheleth addresses worships at the temple or "synagogue" (5:1-5), is a man (11:9), may have a wife (or "woman") whom he loves (9:9), is young (9:10; 11:9), has servants (7:21), may be a court sage by profession (8:2-4; 10:4, 20), and is inquisitive by nature (7:16b; 11:5). He is not so much a narratee as an "ideal," implied reader. That is, this addressee is able to relate perfectly to all that Qoheleth says on matters with which he too will be familiar. In him, Qoheleth would find solace, understanding, and a solid drinking partner at the local watering hole. Yet this person does not exist anymore than Qoheleth does. Any reader can, however, take the place of the implied reader and, as it were, befriend the lonely Qoheleth. This is made all the easier by the element of second-person narration, which, although the narratee has the above qualities, still does not provide a name. A name would have erected a barrier in this regard, and its absence suggests that Qoheleth desired a wide audience to identify as much as possible with his constructed narratee.

This is where readers can pick up their tickets. As Brown states, "underlying Qoheleth's reflections is an explicit awareness that the formation of personal character is a primary goal of wisdom."[20] This includes the formation not only of his own character (dealt with by the story proper of the quest) but also, and primarily, the character of the narratee, to whom his advice is given. Here is where readers can participate, as it were, in the narrative world, for they are free to suspend belief and sense this concern for character formation — which in Qoheleth's case is very appealing since it ultimately concerns living with joy — and in turn to test the conditions that Qoheleth lays down for that formation.

Qoheleth, thus, enables readers to achieve the right kind of wisdom, which enables them to take Qoheleth's extreme route to authenticity under the watchful eye of his older persona. Readers "get there" by becoming, in effect, Qoheleth's empathetic dialogue partners in his narrative world.

Conclusion: The Ethical Story

If we were to locate a paradigmatic character in Ecclesiastes, it would not be Qoheleth's younger and consumptive self, but rather the older, telling self who relates with "cold-eyed realism"[21] his journey of critical self-perspective. It is his story that delivers something of worth to the reader who will hear. In this sense, Qoheleth's story becomes a form of moral argument, and the idea of ethical discourse as story is one that is taking root in virtue ethics.[22]

Of the "classic" texts of narrative moral philosophy (e.g., Thomas à Kempis's *On the Imitation of Christ*, Nietzsche's *Thus Spake Zarathustra*, and Thoreau's *Walden Pond*), Harold Alderman suggests that we must ask "which of these narratives tells the human tale most fully? Which of them — if any — gives the truest depiction of the ways in which people of good character resolve the inevitable conflicts of human life?"[23] Qoheleth's epilogist crystallizes such a decision for the reader, and he makes his opinion clear enough; it would be better to dig your roots deeply in the fear of God and the keeping of God's commands than to confront head on the pursuit of understanding, and all the anomalies that necessarily come with it. Qoheleth's story, highlighted both by its length and its narrative structure, affirms and departs from this line. As many commentators do not allow us to forget, the fear of God indeed has its rightful place in Qoheleth's critical scheme (cf. 5:1-7; 8:12-13). Yet confrontation

20. Brown, *Character in Crisis*, p. 134.

21. Peter C. Craigie, *Psalms 1–50*, WBC 19 (Waco, Tex.: Word Books, 1983), p. 82.

22. See Harold Alderman, "By Virtue of a Virtue," in *Virtue Ethics: A Critical Reader*, ed. D. Statman (Edinburgh: Edinburgh University Press, 1997), pp. 145-64 (esp. pp. 158-59); Brown, *Character in Crisis*, pp. 16-19; Hauerwas, "The Self as Story," in his *Vision and Virtue*, pp. 68-89.

23. Alderman, "By Virtue of a Virtue," p. 159.

is a good thing if it is tempered by realism, that is, by the realization that "Just as you do not understand the way of the life-breath in the formation of bones in the womb, so too you do not understand the activity of God who does everything" (11:5).

Thus I come to the argument I hope this essay has conveyed. Qoheleth's unflinching and fulsome picture of reality, coupled with the deep joy to which he commends his readers (5:18-19 passim), wins Qoheleth's story a place among those that offer "the truest depiction of the ways in which people of good character resolve the inevitable conflicts of human life."[24]

---

24. My thanks to Andrew Dawson for his helpful comments on a draft of this essay.

The Character of God in Jeremiah

Terence E. Fretheim

How is God's character depicted in the present (MT) form of the book of Jeremiah?[1] Of what import is this portrayal for the shaping of human character? With these two questions in mind, I will treat various aspects of the character of God in Jeremiah, especially God's violent action and speech.

Point of View in Jeremiah

Various points of view on the character of God are presented in Jeremiah, and they are often difficult to assess. For example, the people's point of view is presented in various quotations.[2] To cite one instance: "My Father, you are the friend of my youth" (3:4). God is both father and friend, two metaphors juxtaposed — the subject for an intriguing exercise in metaphorical theology. Although the people's understanding of God is sometimes presented as distorted (e.g., 2:35), the theology in their laments does not seem to be so (14:7-9, 19-22). Which is the case in 3:4? The view of the false prophets (e.g., 23:16-17) is declared to be false, and the theology of many individuals (e.g., Zedekiah in 21:2) is regarded with suspicion. These and other voices present the reader with a theological cacophony. To discern the portrayal of God that the editors of the

---

1. It would be an important exercise to lay out the portrayal of God in the LXX and see the similarities and differences from that presented in the MT. More speculative would be an effort to discern differences in the portrayal of God in the various levels of redaction in the book (e.g., Deuteronomistic).

2. See T. Trapp, "Jeremiah: The Other Sides of the Story," in *Was ist der Mensch? Beiträge zur Anthropologie des AT*, ed. F. Crüsemann et al. (Munich: Kaiser, 1992), pp. 228-42.

book commend to readers in the face of falsehood becomes an important, if complicated, exercise.

Two points of view that the book presents are especially important, those of Jeremiah and God. Words placed in the mouth of God apparently have a standing in the book that Jeremiah's words do not have (see God's rebuke of Jeremiah in 15:18-19; cf. 12:5-6). Yet, certainly, when the prophet is expressly speaking the word of God, he is presented as the embodiment of God's own word.

This observation relates to another difficulty in a surprisingly large number of texts: identifying whether the speaker is God or the prophet. Their voices often "bleed" together, and scholars frequently disagree regarding the identity of the speaker. Such disagreement may be due to the personal theological perspectives of interpreters, especially when assigning speakers to texts of weeping and lamenting (e.g., 8:18–9:1 [MT 8:18-23]; 13:17; 14:17). Traditional understandings of the immutability and impassibility of God may be at work, though they are usually not explicit. One example from the NRSV is 9:10 [MT 9:9]. Is it because of the theological difficulty of having God say "I will take up weeping and wailing for the mountains and a lamentation for the pastures of the wilderness" that the translators have decided to go to the versions ("Take up weeping and wailing . . .") rather than to stay with the Hebrew?[3]

In describing the character of God in Jeremiah, it makes a difference if one usually or always assigns the texts that describe weeping to the prophet. Doing so makes the texts describing judgment even harsher and God much more removed and unmoved. Anger accompanied by weeping, while still anger, is different — in motivation, in the understanding of God, and in the relationship at stake. If these texts are, at least, sometimes assigned to God, the harsh words of judgment are not matched by an inner harshness, an important matter for exilic readers to see. Words of judgment are proclaimed reluctantly and with great anguish. The internal side of God's external word and deed of wrath is profound grief.[4]

---

3. One might ask whether this translation is testimony to an anti-anthropomorphic tendency.

4. Note that the anger of God is "provoked." This language for divine anger is common in Jeremiah (7:18; 8:19; 11:17; 25:6-7; 32:29-32; 44:3, 8) and reveals several things about God. For one, God is moved by what the people do. For another, it reveals that anger is not an attribute of God, as if anger were no different from, say, love. Rather, God's anger is contingent. If there were no sin, there would be no divine anger. To say that God is always angry, that anger, like love, is integral to the divine identity, is to fall back into a kind of dualism.

References to God's wrath being "poured out" (7:20; also 6:11; 10:25; 42:18; 44:6) provide another insight into the divine anger. While there is a personal dimension to God's anger, wrath

For some readers, it is incongruous that expressions of profound grief accompany anger and the announcement of judgment (e.g., 9:10-11 [MT 9:9-10]; see below). Yet such statements seem to be purposively interwoven. God mediates judgment so that sin and evil do not go unchecked in the life of the world, but God does so at great cost to the divine life. In terms of ethical implications, if there is no *divine* anger at sin and evil, then *human* anger toward that which is oppressive and abusive does not carry the same weight and seriousness as it would if that divine anger were present. If there is no sorrow associated with divine anger, then human anger is given a freer range regarding harshness.

Commentators increasingly assign many of these lament-filled texts to divine speech.[5] Yet this more recent willingness to speak of God as one who weeps and laments raises new theological issues that play a role in interpreting the character of God in Jeremiah. For one thing, how one speaks about the suffering of God is important.[6] For another, and more important for our purposes, it is not common for interpreters to work out the *implications* of having a God who suffers — who laments, weeps, and anguishes over decisions. Not uncommonly, alongside the acceptance of such language of suffering for God is the continued affirmation of "classical" — but now deeply problematic — understandings such as: God is immutable, "irresistible,"[7] the only "real agent,"

---

is also impersonally conceived in Jeremiah (cf. Num 1:53; 16:46). Wrath is not only "poured out" but "goes forth" because of the people's wickedness (*rōa'*, 4:4 = 21:12) like "a whirling tempest" (23:19), "is not turned away" (4:8; 23:20), "bursts upon" the head of the wicked (23:19), and is like fire that burns (4:4; 7:20; 15:14; 17:4; 21:12; 44:6). In this way of thinking, wrath is an effect that grows out of a violation of the moral order of God's creation (cf. Deut 28:15, 22, 45). God's personal anger may be said to be God's "seeing to" this movement from deed to consequence that is the moral order.

5. K. O'Connor, "The Tears of God and Divine Character in Jeremiah 2–9," in *God in the Fray*, ed. T. Linafelt and T. Beal (Minneapolis, Minn.: Fortress, 1998), pp. 172-85; M. Biddle, *Polyphony and Symphony in Prophetic Literature: Rereading Jeremiah 7–20* (Macon, Ga.: Mercer University Press, 1996); T. Fretheim, *The Suffering of God: An Old Testament Perspective*, OBT (Philadelphia: Fortress, 1984).

6. There are important differences among those who have worked with the theme of the suffering of God, a matter that needs exploration. At least three different perspectives might be examined: those of A. Heschel (*The Prophets* [San Francisco: Harper, 1962], esp. pp. 483-85), W. Brueggemann (e.g., *Theology of the Old Testament: Testimony, Dispute, Advocacy* [Minneapolis, Minn.: Fortress, 1997], pp. 267-313), and my own work, which differs in several respects from that of Heschel and Brueggemann.

7. W. Brueggemann (*A Commentary on Jeremiah: Exile and Homecoming* [Grand Rapids: Eerdmans, 1998], pp. 26, 222, 246) uses this language. Brueggemann's theological work on Jeremiah is unparalleled.

radically free, and unqualifiedly sovereign, even in "absolute control."[8] Generally, I would characterize this mixed theological situation as follows.[9]

So-Called Contradictions in Jeremiah and Theological Coherence

The claim of theological incoherence in Jeremiah is often due to the theology of interpreters; something does not make sense from within their own theological framework, which is laid over the various perspectives of God in the book. For example, Kathleen O'Connor's helpful work on the character of God claims that the book presents images for God that "contradict each other." And so, "divine tears put aside punishment . . . and characterize God in radically different terms from much of the rest of the book." These tears "provide a glimpse of another kind of deity" from that of "the divine punisher and wrathful judge."[10] To the contrary, anger and tears do go together in Jeremiah (see 8:19c in context; 9:10 with 9:11 [MT 9:9 with 9:10]; 9:17-19 with 9:22 [MT 9:16-18 with 9:21]). These emotions are held together in God, as they commonly are when speaking of people who have suffered the brokenness of intimate relationships. Anger and tears flow together. The use of marital and parental metaphors in Jeremiah suggests that such relationships inform its portrayal of the character of God.

Or, consider William Holladay on issues of agency in Jer 23:1-4; he is puzzled by the change of the subject that "drives away" *(nādaḥ)* the people in 23:2-3. In verse 2, the shepherds do so; in verse 3, *God* drives them into exile (see also v. 8; 8:3; 24:9). Holladay claims that God as the subject of the verb in verse 3 "contradicts the accusation against the shepherds in v. 2."[11] On the contrary, readers are not asked to choose between these statements. Agency is conceived in a complex sense: shepherds, Babylonians, and God are all active agents in the exiling of the people (see 50:17; see below).[12]

Or, for Walter Brueggemann, the judging God and the faithful God are

---

8. So, e.g., L. Stulman, *Order Amid Chaos: Jeremiah as Symbolic Tapestry,* The Biblical Seminar 57 (Sheffield: Sheffield Academic Press, 1998), pp. 74, 114; cf. "absolute sovereign rule of YHWH," p. 43. See Brueggemann, *Jeremiah,* p. 167.

9. The word "contradiction" (or the like) is common in Jeremiah studies and is often linked to theological matters. There may well be some contradictions, but the many claimed "contradictions" immensely exacerbate the theological cacophony in Jeremiah. At the same time, the God of the final form of Jeremiah is an immensely complex character.

10. So O'Connor, "The Tears of God," pp. 172, 184-85.

11. See W. Holladay, *Jeremiah 1,* Hermeneia (Philadelphia: Fortress, 1986), p. 615.

12. A similar complexity is evident in the other scattering verb used in these verses, *pûṣ* (cf. 23:1-2 with 9:16 [MT 9:15]; 13:24; 18:17; 30:11).

incongruous; "the completed tradition of Jeremiah makes in turn two quite different theological emphases which are impossible to coalesce," namely, judgment and promise.[13] Thus, regarding various texts in chapters 1–25, he makes the following statements: "God has withdrawn fidelity"; God "has ceased to care"; a "complete absence of fidelity on God's part."[14] I have dealt with this dimension of Brueggemann's thought elsewhere.[15] I reiterate: "Why should love be inconsistent with 'just judgment'? Why is divine judgment an act of unfaithfulness? Why cannot judgment be in the service of graciousness? Why is a word or act 'against Israel' by YHWH incongruous with God's will 'for Israel'? I would claim that divine judgment is *always* in the service of God's loving and saving purposes."

Or, for Louis Stulman, in Jeremiah "the jumbled character of God pulsates with tensions and contradictions." By way of illustration, he says that "the reader confronts in the character of God the convergence of power and vulnerability, love and wrath . . . , hope and disappointment."[16] I can accept "tensions," but the word "contradictions" is not theologically appropriate.

I suspect that the interpreters' own theological perspectives are decisively at work in claiming such incongruities (as they are in my own analysis). This point might be further illustrated with two common themes: divine sovereignty and divine freedom.

The Sovereignty of God

Stulman claims that "YHWH reigns" is "a root metaphor in the book."[17] He follows efforts to qualify the sovereignty metaphor more generally, such as "dynamic sovereignty."[18] Yet such qualification is insufficient for Jeremiah; the problem is much deeper. A definition of sovereignty must be found that allows

13. Brueggemann, *Jeremiah*, p. 270; cf. p. 283. Sometimes this issue is stated in such a way that God's judgment means the end of Israel's election! See, e.g., Stulman, *Order Amid Chaos*, pp. 46-48.

14. Brueggemann, *Jeremiah*, pp. 121, 142, 152, 278.

15. T. Fretheim, "Some Reflections on Brueggemann's God," in *God in the Fray*, ed. T. Linafelt and T. Beal (Minneapolis, Minn.: Fortress, 1998), pp. 24-37, esp. p. 30.

16. Stulman, *Order Amid Chaos*, p. 186. Regarding love and wrath, he qualifies himself by saying "or more accurately what Eichrodt called the 'wrath of love.'" One wonders why he retained the original formulation.

17. Stulman, *Order Amid Chaos*, p. 109.

18. See James L. Mays, *The Lord Reigns* (Louisville, Ky.: Westminster/John Knox, 1994), pp. 6-9.

for tears and anguish and hesitation. O'Connor broaches the issue when she claims that the tears of God "suggest a deity who vacates sovereignty and hierarchical transcendence, at least temporarily."[19] Yet this direction of reflection is not adequate either, as if God could turn sovereignty or transcendence off and on.

One could say that God's tears *recharacterize* sovereignty, say in the manner of a "crown of thorns" worn by one called "the King of the Jews" (Matt 27:29). If and when we do this, however, we should steer clear of the all too common "classical" descriptions of the God of Jeremiah noted above. Whatever the qualification, the claim that God's ruling is basic to other images for God in the book is itself problematic. Remarkably, the language of ruling is scarcely used for God in Jeremiah.[20]

Stulman's strong language that the God of Jeremiah is "in absolute control"[21] is certainly an ironic claim. He rightly warns against "confident propositional assertions about God's governance,"[22] but to say that God is "in absolute control of history" is just such a statement. If God is in "absolute control," then why is it that God is so often portrayed as one who is in anguish and sorrow? If "ruling" is a primary metaphor for God in Jeremiah, then, given how unruly Israel is, we would have to score God a crashing management failure! The divine responses to Israel in the book must mean their words and deeds stand *against* the will of God; the will of the God of Jeremiah is resistible.

With respect to ethical implications, if God is in (absolute) control, then this becomes a pattern for human activity willy-nilly. Whether God's speaking or acting *should* be a model for human conduct is in many ways besides the point; like it or not, this will happen. In the Old Testament generally, the desired character of persons who follow this God is at least in part to be explicated on the basis of an exegesis of divine action and speech. God "loves the stranger . . . you shall also love the stranger" (Deut 10:18-19). Or, "Be merciful as the Lord your God is merciful" (Luke 6:36). Be in absolute control as God is in absolute

---

19. O'Connor, "The Tears of God," p. 185.

20. None of the verbs to rule or reign (e.g., *mālak, māšal, rādāh*) are used with God as subject (cf. the future rule of the messianic king in 23:5; 30:21; 33:21). Words in this semantic field are also uncommon. For example, *kissē'* ("throne") is used four times, two regarding the future (3:17: 49:38), one by the people (14:21), and one by Jeremiah in hymnic material (17:12). The six references to God as king are in the oracles against the nations (46:18; 48:15; 51:57) or against their idols (10:7, 10) and thus have a focused point of applicability. The other reference is a quotation of the people and is suspect (8:19). Also to be noted is how rarely the word "holy" is used for God ("Holy One of Israel," 50:29; 51:5).

21. So Stulman, *Order Amid Chaos*, pp. 74, 114. The language of divine "control" appears throughout his discussion (e.g., pp. 73, 76, 96, 109-10).

22. Stulman, *Order Amid Chaos*, p. 161.

control? If monarchical images for God are the dominant ones in the book, then this invites readers to assume such images for their ways of speaking and acting. Perhaps the kings of Israel were especially fond of monarchical images for God![23]

The language of "power" is naturally drawn into any discussion of God being in control, though explicit power language is comparatively infrequent in Jeremiah (primarily with creation, 10:12 = 51:15; 27:5; 32:17). Stulman concludes at one point that "power and powerlessness embrace as divine sovereignty"; but "power," which he has just defined as being in "absolute control," empties the word "powerlessness" of any meaningful content.[24] Tears recharacterize God's power altogether.

It seems wise in the interpretation of Jeremiah to keep the language of sovereignty in reasonable proportion to its usage in the book and qualified by other pervasive images.[25] If one were to pick a "root metaphor" for God in the book of Jeremiah, and probably the Bible, it would be *relatedness*.[26] Indeed, this metaphor would constitute an essential dimension for every concrete metaphor used for God.

The Freedom of God

Talk about divine freedom is common in Jeremiah studies, but the way in which this matter is formulated is often problematic.

One distinction between true and false prophecy in Jeremiah relates to

---

23. Some statements by J. Moltmann could illustrate this point: "Since the Renaissance, God has always been understood one-sidedly as 'The Almighty.' *Omnipotence* has been valued as the superior characteristic of godliness. God is the Lord and the world is God's property to do with whatever God wills. God is the *absolute subject* and the world is the *passive object* of God's dominion. As God's likeness on earth, humans must understand themselves correspondingly as a subject . . . and the world as their passive object to be conquered. It is only through domination over the earth that humanity can correspond to God, the Lord of the world. Just as God is the Lord and owner of the whole world, so humans must work to become lords and owners of the earth and of themselves. According to this understanding, neither through goodness and truth, nor through patience and love, but through power and domination humans prove their likeness to God" ("Reconciliation with Nature," *WW* 11 [1991]: 118).

24. Stulman, *Order Amid Chaos*, p. 115.

25. For an earlier effort to qualify the language of divine sovereignty in terms of divine suffering, see T. Fretheim, "Suffering God and Sovereign God in Exodus: A Collision of Images," *HBT* 11 (1989): 31-56.

26. See, e.g., T. Fretheim, "The God Who Acts: An Old Testament Perspective," *ThT* 54 (1997): 6-18.

the preaching of peace and judgment (e.g., 6:14 = 8:11; 23:9-22; 28:1-17). The false prophets brought *only* a word of peace and assurance to an unfaithful people; Jeremiah understood that God would stand in judgment — even of the elect. One way in which this distinction has been articulated theologically is in terms of divine freedom. For example, Brueggemann asserts that "[t]he tradition of Jeremiah asserts God's freedom, even from God's partner. . . . To judge Jeremiah to be true is a theological verdict which allows for something wild, dangerous, unfettered, and free in the character of YHWH."[27] To be sure, it *is* important to affirm that God is free to judge his own people, and to affirm God's freedom more generally. At the same time, God's freedom for Jeremiah cannot be claimed in an unqualified way. For God to enter into judgment is not even fundamentally an exercise in freedom. More basically, God's judgment (or any divine action) is grounded in God's will and purpose for the world; indeed, judgment may be *necessary* if God would be faithful to that purpose. Judgment may be the only way in which God can do justice to relationships established and to a *purpose* to which he is committed (see 9:23-24 [MT 9:22-23]; 29:1-14; 31:1-6).

The immense agony of the God of Jeremiah is a demonstration that God is not truly free of his relationship with Israel. If God had "radical, unquestionable freedom,"[28] then he would not agonize so, either over the breakdown in the relationship or over decisions regarding judgment. If God were truly free, then he could just get up and leave, without hesitation, for he would have no significant commitments to this people. God agonizes over these matters precisely because he is *not* free of these people; God has long been in a committed relationship with a people whom he loves with "an everlasting love" and to whom, even in and through their pervasive infidelity, he has "continued [his] faithfulness" (31:3).

To speak of God's promises (e.g., to Noah, Abraham, David, all alluded to in 3:18; 7:7; 11:5; 30:3, 9; 31:35-37; 33:14-26; cf. 14:21) is to speak of a God who has chosen not to remain unfettered. Indeed, to speak of God's election of Israel and his promise to be their God places limits on any talk about divine freedom (see 30:22; 31:2; 32:38). God has exercised freedom in making such promises in the first place, but, having freely made them, God's freedom is thereafter truly limited by those promises. God will be faithful to his own promises. Even more, God's history with Israel through the years means that Israel has been caught

---

27. Brueggemann, *Jeremiah*, p. 138.

28. The phrase is that of L. Perdue, *The Collapse of History: Reconstructing Old Testament Theology*, OBT (Minneapolis, Minn.: Fortress, 1994), p. 216. Cf. Brueggemann, *Jeremiah*, pp. 138, 168, 215; Stulman, *Order Amid Chaos*, p. 176.

up into the divine life and has shaped the divine identity. God will *forever* be known as the God of Israel; Israel is now a part of God's identity. It is precisely because of that relationship and related commitments that God grieves. Given the Noachic covenant references, one might also speak more generally of God's relationship with the world, to which God will be true.

To speak of the freedom of God in an unqualified way has ethical implications. If God is radically free, then we who are God's followers will seek to be radically free, willy-nilly; we may even come to believe that we are not bound to our commitments and can get on with our unfettered lives. Certainly one will want to speak of the freedom of the chosen people, but not in isolation from claims regarding commitments.

To summarize, neither the language of sovereignty nor that of freedom can be used for God in an unqualified sense in Jeremiah, for these understandings have ethical implications. This point is supported further by a closer look at the means in and through which God chooses to act in the world.

God Acts through Means: Divine Dependence in Jeremiah

This section focuses on the portrayal of God in relationship to Nebuchadrezzar and Jeremiah. The general issue pertains to God's use of human beings as instruments in and through which God's purposes are carried out. The issue regarding God and Nebuchadrezzar relates to violent action; the issue regarding God and Jeremiah focuses on violent speech.

The first issue is the surprisingly common claim that the God of Jeremiah is, at least in some texts, imaged as acting in an unmediated way. For example, Robert Carroll, in connection with 13:9, claims that "YHWH does the destroying rather than Babylon."[29] Several commentators will speak of Babylon as God's "instrument," but then claim that YHWH is the only "real agent." For example, Brueggemann in a variety of contexts makes claims such as: "[t]here is no mediating agent" and "the army may be Babylonian, but the real agent is YHWH."[30] He goes on to claim that "the rule of YHWH is not done 'supernaturally,' but through historical agents."[31] Yet I cannot discern any theological space between God being the only "real agent" and God acting "supernaturally."

Such theological statements regarding agency discount the genuine role

---

29. R. Carroll, *Jeremiah: A Commentary*, OTL (Philadelphia: Westminster, 1986), p. 294.

30. E.g., Brueggemann, *Jeremiah*, pp. 54, 70, 176, 193, 428, 430, 439, 460; Stulman, *Order Amid Chaos*, p. 123.

31. Brueggemann, *Jeremiah*, p. 56; Carroll, *Jeremiah*, pp. 763-64, 811.

that the Babylonian armies play; they are no less "real" than YHWH. One must not diminish the distinction between God and his agents or discount the stature and the very real power of that human army. Just how God is involved in this activity cannot be factored out, though 51:11 may contain a clue with its reference to God as having "stirred up *('ûr)* the spirit of the kings of the Medes" (cf. Zech 1:14; Jer 6:22; 25:32; 50:9, 41; 51:1).

The second issue pertains to the *ethical implications* of God's use of creatures to act in the world in and through *violent action* and *violent speech*. God chooses to be dependent on that which is not God to carry out the divine purposes in the world. This risky move links God with the character and activities of the chosen instruments. God does not perfect people before working through them, which means that one must not necessarily confer a positive value on the results (e.g., Babylon's actions; see below).

God and Nebuchadrezzar

Note the commonality of verbs and metaphors in the chart below. Remarkable correspondences exist between God's actions and those of Nebuchadrezzar.[32]

God's Actions	Babylon's Actions
13:14 — I will dash *(npṣ)* them	48:12 — they will dash *(npṣ)* in pieces
I will not pity *(ḥml)*, or spare *(ḥûs)*,	21:7 — he will not pity *(ḥml)*, or spare *(ḥûs)*.
or have compassion *(rḥm)*,	or have compassion *(rḥm)*
when I destroy *(šḥt)* them (also 13:9).	36:29 — he will destroy *(šḥt;* also 51:25)
9:16 [MT 9:15]; 13:24; 18:17; 30:11 — I will scatter *(pûṣ)*	52:8; 23:1-2 — scattered *(pûṣ)* the flock
24:9; 27:10 — I will drive them away *(ndḥ)*	50:17; cf. 23:2 — Israel driven away *(ndḥ)*
21:5 — I will fight against you *(lḥm)*	21:2 — he is making war against us *(lḥm)*
21:6 — I will strike down *(nkh)*	21:7 — he shall strike them down *(nkh)*
21:14 — I will kindle a fire *(yṣt)*	32:29 — they will kindle *(yṣt)* a fire
49:20 — God has a plan *(y'ṣ)* and purpose *(ḥšb)*	49:30 — Nebuchadrezzar has a plan *(y'ṣ)* and purpose *(ḥšb)*
49:38 — God will set *(śym)* God's throne	43:10 — Nebuchadrezzar will set *(śym)* his throne
19:11(+) — God will break *(šbr)* the people	43:13 — Nebuchadrezzar will break *(šbr)*

32. Note the virtual absence of God talk in the descriptions of the fall of Jerusalem (39:1-14; 52:3b-30). It is also uncommon in the oracles against Babylon (chs. 50–51). Some violent actions are also ascribed to both Jeremiah and God (cf. 1:10 and 24:6; 25:15-29). For details, see T. Fretheim, *Jeremiah* (Macon, Ga.: Smyth and Helwys, 2002), pp. 35-41.

25:33 — those slain *(ḥll)* by the LORD	51:4 — Babylon must fall for the slain *(ḥll)* of Israel
27:8 — Until I have completed its destruction . . .	. . . by his [the king of Babylon's] hand.
12:12; 47:6 — sword of the LORD (also 14:12; 15:9)	20:4 — they shall fall by the sword of enemies
25:38; 49:19 — God imaged as a lion	4:7; 5:6 — foe from the north imaged as a lion
29:4, 7, 14 — God sends into exile *(glh)*	29:1(+) — Nebuchadrezzar sends into exile *(glh)*
29:17 — God will pursue *(rdp)* them	39:5; 52:8 — Chaldeans will pursue *(rdp)* them
30:3 — I will bring them back to the land	42:12b — he will bring them back to the land
31:20 — I will have mercy	42:12a — he will have mercy

What conclusions might one draw from this common fund of language? Such harsh words appear to be used for God because they are used for the actions of those in and through whom God mediates judgment. God's language in 27:8 puts the matter in a nutshell, "I have completed its destruction by his hand." In view of this mediation, God refers to Nebuchadrezzar as "my servant" (25:9; 27:6; 43:10). Others whom God designates "my servant" in Jeremiah are David, the prophets, and Israel! In some sense God has chosen to be *dependent* on Nebuchadrezzar in carrying out that judgment.[33] Note that Exodus 3:8-10, where both God and Moses (often called "my servant") bring Israel out of Egypt, could function as a paradigm for such considerations.

As Nebuchadrezzar is identified as God's servant,[34] so, at the time of the return from exile, another "pagan" king, Cyrus of Persia, is identified as God's "anointed one" (Isa 45:1-7). As with Cyrus,[35] Nebuchadrezzar does not know YHWH. The coalescence of God's actions and those of Nebuchadrezzar are abundantly clear in these texts. God will bring Babylon's armies against Israel and destroy them (and their neighbors); both God and Babylon are agents. God

33. On issues of divine dependence on the human, see T. Fretheim, "Divine Dependence on the Human: An Old Testament Perspective," *Ex Auditu* 13 (1997): 1-13. Brueggemann's perspective on this issue is stated in *Jeremiah*, p. 106 (see also p. 463): God is "not dependent on what is in the world." See also T. Fretheim, "Creator, Creature, and Co-creation in Genesis 1–2," in *All Things New: Essays in Honor of Roy A. Harrisville*, ed. A. Hultgren et al., Word and World Supplement 1 (St. Paul: Word and World, 1992): 11-20.

34. Isa 45:4. See T. Overholt, "King Nebuchadnezzar in the Jeremiah Tradition," *CBQ* 30 (1968): 39-48.

35. It is helpful to note that the granting of mercy could take place through the king of Babylon (42:11-12). Both the removal of peace and mercy (see 16:5; 21:7) and its restoration are thus related to his agency.

may be the "ultimate" agent in these events, but not in such a way that other agents are less than "real."

Importantly, in this judgmental activity the Babylonians are not puppets in God's hands. That God is not the only effective agent in these events is made clear by the divine judgment on Babylon (25:12-14; 50–51; see Isa 47:6-7; Zech 1:15, "while I [God] was only a little angry, they made the disaster worse"; note also the statement of divine regret in Jer 42:10, "I [God!] am sorry for the disaster"). In effect, Babylon exceeded its mandate, going beyond its proper judgmental activities, and committed iniquity itself in making the land an "everlasting waste." It is assumed (as with the oracles against the nations generally) that moral standards are available to which the nations are held accountable. This divine judgment on Babylonian excessiveness shows that God did not micromanage their activities; they retained the power to make decisions and execute policies that flew in the face of the will of God. Hence, the will and purpose of God, indeed the sovereignty of God, active in these events is not "irresistible."[36] In some sense God risks what the Babylonians will do with the mandate they have been given. One element of that risk is that God's name will become associated with the violence, indeed the excessive violence, of the Babylonians.[37]

Another factor to be considered here are those texts in which God calls Jeremiah to bring a word of nonviolence through Israel's submission to Babylon (see chs. 27–29; 38:17-18). This divine command, which intends to reduce the violence, was announced after Babylon's subjugation of Jerusalem in 597 B.C.E. and before the fall and destruction of 586 B.C.E. With a political realism, God announces that if Israel would not rebel against Babylon, its future would take a less violent course. In other words, Babylon would function as agent of divine judgment in different ways, depending upon how Israel responded to the call for nonviolence. Israel's own resorting to violence would lead to even greater violence and to God's association with such violence, which is in fact what happens.

To recapitulate, God is not the sole agent in this situation; God acts in and through the agency of Babylon. At the same time, the latter will certainly act as kings and armies are known to act. That is predictable, and God (and other observers) knows this from experience with conquerors such as these. So, God in judgment will not "pity, spare, or have compassion" (13:14) because that is what the Babylonians, the instruments of divine judgment, will also not do (21:7). This portrayal of God reflects an extreme realism regarding what is about to

---

36. Brueggemann, *Jeremiah*, p. 222.

37. For a comprehensive statement on divine risk taking, see John Sanders, *The God Who Risks: A Theology of Providence* (Downers Grove, Ill.: InterVarsity, 1998).

happen to the people. When the people do experience the pillaging, burning, and raping by the Babylonian armies, readers can be sure that they were real agents. Jeremiah also makes this witness when describing the actual destruction of Jerusalem (chs. 39, 52) in terms that hardly mention God.

These striking parallels suggest that *the portrayal of God's violent action in Jeremiah is conformed to the means that God uses.* God is portrayed in terms of the means available. God thereby accepts any fallout that may accrue to the divine reputation ("guilt by association").

The ethical implications of such a perspective are considerable. If God is the only "real" agent, then the humans through which God works are diminished, and, finally, they do not "count."[38] Such a perspective cheapens their creaturely status and devalues their words and deeds, making them finally inconsequential. For Jeremiah, however, both God and human agents have a crucial role to play, and their spheres of activity are interrelated in terms of function and effect. God is not only independent, and the humans involved are not only dependent. God has so shaped the created order that there are overlapping spheres of interdependence, and creative responsibility is shared with human beings.

This perspective is testimony to a fundamentally *relational* understanding of the way in which God acts in the world. There is an ordered freedom in the creation, a degree of openness and unpredictability, wherein God leaves room for genuine human decisions as they exercise their God-given power. Even more, God gives them powers and responsibilities in such a way that *commits* him to a certain kind of relationship with them. This entails a divine constraint and restraint in the exercise of power in relation to these agents (they overdid it!). These texts in Jeremiah are testimony to a divine sovereignty that gives power over to the created for the sake of a relationship of integrity.

God and Jeremiah

Jeremiah's laments often petition God to visit his enemies with various judgments (11:20; 12:3; 15:15; 17:18; 18:21-23; 20:12; also 6:11; 10:25). A comparison with God's speech shows some twenty parallels in words and phrases.

---

38. Brueggemann uses this language in *Isaiah 40–66*, Westminster Bible Companion (Louisville, Ky.: Westminster/John Knox, 1998), p. 77. My colleague Frederick Gaiser has addressed the issue of agency in response to such claims in "'To Whom Then Will You Compare Me?' Agency in Second Isaiah," *WW* 19 (1999): 141-52.

God's Speech	Jeremiah's Speech
Wrath (*ḥēmâ*, 4:4; *zʿm*, 10:10)	Filled with *God's* wrath (6:11), indignation (15:17)
— Pour out wrath (*špk*, 6:11; 14:16)	— Pour out wrath (10:25)
Slaughter (*hărēgâ*, 7:32; 19:6)	Set them apart for slaughter (12:3)
Vengeance (*nqm*, 5:9, 29; 9:9 [MT 9:8])	Let me see *your* vengeance upon them (11:20; 15:15; 20:12)
Shame (*bôš*, 2:26), dismay (*ḥtt*, 8:9)	Let my persecutors be shamed, dismayed (17:18; 20:11)
Bring evil/disaster (*rāʿâ*, 4:6; 6:19; 11:23)	Bring upon them evil/disaster (17:18)
Break this people (*šbr*, 19:11) doubly (16:18)	Break them with *double* destruction (17:18)
Give sword, famine (11:22; 14:12; 15:2, 9)	Give them sword, famine (18:21)
"Therefore" (18:13+)	Therefore + announcement of judgment (18:21)
Childless, widowed (6:11b-12; 15:7-9)	Let wives become childless and widowed (18:21)
Young men die by the sword (11:22)	Let young men die by the sword (18:21)
Terror fall[s] suddenly (*pitʾōm*, 15:8)	When you bring the marauder suddenly (18:22)
Crying out (*zʿq*, 11:11-12; 25:34)	May a cry be heard (18:22)
God will not listen after repentance (14:7-11)	Do not forgive their iniquity (18:23)
Trip up, stumble (*kšl*, 6:15, 21; 8:12)	Let them be tripped up (18:23; 20:11)
"Time" of visitation (6:15; 10:15; 11:12-14)	"Time of anger" (18:23; cf. v. 17)
Violence, destruction (6:7)	Must shout, "violence and destruction" (20:8)
Weariness (15:6)	I am weary (6:11; 20:9)
They will not prosper (*lōʾ śkl*, 10:21)	They will not succeed (20:11)

One question that arises from these comparisons is how the situation with God and Jeremiah relates to that of God and Babylon. Does God use such violent language because that is the language of God's prophet? This would be similar to what happens in any proclamation of the word of God in any age: God becomes associated with the language the preacher uses. This is certainly true at some basic level for God's words in Jeremiah; they are presented in human language. That God criticizes Jeremiah's language (15:18-19) could suggest this approach, though God never criticizes his own violent language. The task of assessing God's violent words would certainly be easier if we could say that God's language has been conformed to Jeremiah's own violent language. Perhaps one could appeal more generally to the interactive character of the God-Jeremiah relationship; identifying who learns from whom is far from clear.[39]

39. It might be suggested that Jeremiah's sharp statement to God in 20:7 constitutes, at

Another interpretation seems more likely, the upshot of which is to distinguish the character of the God-Jeremiah relationship from that of God and Babylon. An examination of Jeremiah's language reveals that he usually uses language that God has used in prior texts. Occasional parallels are found in texts subsequent to Jeremiah's speaking, but most follow the canonical order (we do not know the historical order, but God's call sets a certain agenda, 1:17-19). The canonical ordering seems decisive for interpreting the relationship between God's speech and Jeremiah's.

One example from the list is Jeremiah 6:11-12. Children (playing in the streets!) are included among those who are *objects* of God's judgment (see 6:21; 9:21 [MT 9:20]; 19:9).[40] The children will not only suffer the effects of the judgment on the community; they are *singled out* for judgment: "Pour it out on the children!" Jeremiah seems to have learned both his rhetoric and its content from God, for a comparable word is heard in his laments (18:21); he calls upon God to give the children of his adversaries over to famine and sword. This prompts the question: why should children be the *specific* object of the wrath of God, made to suffer for what adults have done? Also present in these verses is the ravishing of property, including fields and wives, a fate to which God consigns them (cf. 2 Sam 12:11). This proves to be no rhetorical flourish; the witness to the devastating effect on children, women, and the environment is clear (see Lam 1:5, 16; 2:19-21; 4:4, 10; 5:11; cf. 2 Kgs 6:28-29; Isa 49:26; Ezek 5:10). One might, of course, say that these texts were written in light of actual events; even if this were the case to a greater or lesser degree, the fact that the editors chose to ascribe such language to God remains an issue.

In thinking through these texts, the interpreter should recall that God works judgment in and through the existing moral order.[41] Generally, the Old

---

least in part, a critique of the word he was called to bring. This seems doubtful. Yes, God duped him with respect to the call, but Jeremiah recognizes that action for what it was, and he has done what he was called to do in the full knowledge of the deception. *Deception recognized* changes the equation, and Jeremiah never intimates that the word he was called to proclaim was a false word.

40. Some interpreters think that Jeremiah is the speaker of 6:11b (see NEB). Even if this were the case, the other three references noted are sufficient to ground these observations.

41. Helpful resources for this topic include Patrick D. Miller, Jr., *Sin and Judgment in the Prophets: A Stylistic and Theological Analysis*, SBLMS 27 (Chico, Calif.: Scholars Press, 1982); Klaus Koch, "Is There a Doctrine of Retribution in the Old Testament?" in *Theodicy in the Old Testament*, ed. J. Crenshaw (Philadelphia: Fortress, 1983), pp. 57-87. Most recently, see Gene Tucker, "Sin and 'Judgment' in the Prophets," in *Problems in Biblical Theology: Essays in Honor of Rolf Knierim*, ed. H. Sun et al. (Grand Rapids: Eerdmans, 1997), pp. 373-88. See also my article, "Divine Judgment and the Warming of the World: An Old Testament Perspective," in *God, Evil, and Suffering: Essays in Honor of Paul R. Sponheim*, ed. T. Fretheim and C. Thompson, Word and World Supplement 4 (St. Paul: Word and World, 2000), pp. 21-32. G. von Rad has provided a

Testament will not speak of this order in deistic ways.[42] God will see to the moral order so that sin and evil do not go unchecked in the life of the world and so that God's good order of creation (= righteousness) can be reestablished. Consistently in Jeremiah, the people's *rā'â* (= evil) will issue in their *rā'â* (= disaster; e.g., 6:19, "the fruit of their schemes"; 14:16, "I will pour out *their* wickedness upon them"; see also 21:12-14). God does not introduce anything new into the situation; he does not impose sanctions that are distinct from the violations. God's action is usually not described as forensic and external in nature; rather, he mediates the effects of the people's own wickedness, which are intrinsic to the evil deed itself.[43] This divine involvement is not conceived in terms of micro-management, as God's later judgment on the Babylonians for their overkill makes clear (see above).[44]

Readers could also recall that this is a *communal* judgment; once unleashed, Babylon's armies will cut down everything in their path. In war, everyone will suffer (cf. the effects of indiscriminate bombing in World War II). Readers might also recall this kind of rhetoric in the psalms of imprecation (Ps 109:9-10; 137:9).[45] Certainly we do not want to insist that speakers of laments to God be held to careful theological formulations; hurting persons must be allowed to pour out their anger to God regardless of the theological fallout. In this light, perhaps we should allow for such rhetoric in the laments of God as well; God is deeply pained by

---

helpful (and generally approving) look at these matters (*Old Testament Theology*, trans. D. Stalker [New York: Harper, 1962], 1:264-68, 383-87).

42. Tucker delineates several different formulations: texts that are "dynamistic" and have no explicit reference to God (e.g., Isa 3:9-11; Hos 10:13-15), those in which God makes the connection between sin and consequence (Jer 6:19; 21:14), and, least common, those that have a juridical element (e.g., Amos 4:1-3). How these "judgment" texts are to be related is best seen in the work of H. H. Schmid, who places them under the comprehensive umbrella of creation theology ("Creation, Righteousness, and Salvation: 'Creation Theology' as the Broad Horizon of Biblical Theology," in *Creation in the Old Testament*, ed. B. Anderson [Philadelphia: Fortress, 1984], pp. 102-17). See also W. Brueggemann, "The Uninflected *Therefore* of Hosea 4:1-3," in *Reading from This Place: Social Location and Biblical Interpretation in the United States*, ed. F. Segovia and M. Tolbert (Minneapolis, Minn.: Fortress, 1995), pp. 231-49.

43. Gerhard von Rad speaks of a "synthetic view of life" (*Old Testament Theology*, 1:265) in which the "retribution is not a new action which comes upon the person concerned from somewhere else; it is rather the last ripple of the act itself which attaches to its agent almost as something material. Hebrew in fact does not even have a word for punishment" (p. 385).

44. See also the statements about divine wrath in n. 4.

45. For a recent helpful study of these psalms, see E. Zenger, *A God of Vengeance? Understanding the Psalms of Divine Wrath* (German, *Feindpsalmen!*), trans. L. Maloney (Louisville, Ky.: Westminster/John Knox, 1996). These psalms are, of course, words *about* and *to* God, not words *by* God, but they may well assume an understanding of God's own words of judgment such as are found in Jeremiah and other prophets. They can speak this way because they understand God to have spoken in these terms regarding their enemies.

what has happened, expressing all the sorrow and anger that goes with the break-down of a relationship of intimacy. But if we do so, then we should seek to tell it like it is for God and not dismiss such words by (easy?) appeals to divine sovereignty or mystery. Yet, however ameliorating such comments may be, standing squarely before us is the command of God to pour out wrath on the children.

This analysis leads to the unsettling idea that, as the canonical editors present the case, Jeremiah has learned to use such violent language against his persecutors from God. In other words, the divine character has shaped Jeremiah's character. His speaking follows a pattern set by God; God's judgment has become his judgment. Jeremiah has become conformed to the wrath of God (see 6:11a; 25:15-17).

Many interpreters have had difficulty with Jeremiah's outbursts for their harsh and unforgiving nature and sought to explain them (away) in one fashion or another, usually by appealing to Jeremiah's humanity. This is a human being in deep anguish. However, these texts say more than "He's only human." However much Jeremiah's language corresponds to that of the imprecation psalms, it cannot simply be ascribed to outbursts over his suffering at the hands of his enemies. Jeremiah's language has been explicitly shaped by God's language; Jeremiah's character has been shaped by God's character.

Notably, those interpreters who seek to "explain" Jeremiah's language usually do not make a comparable judgment on God's language; God usually gets home scot-free. We would certainly be properly critical of, say, a modern general who gave his soldiers orders to kill children. Why not the God of Jeremiah? Yet on what grounds would we do so? Where does one stand in bringing such a critique? One should be guided at the least by an inner-biblical warrant, seeking to be true to the basic biblical portrayal of God (cf. the common response to patriarchy in biblical texts).[46] Even more, is not this portrayal of God deeply problematic when it comes to thinking about the development of human character? Yet again, on what grounds? One must at least be true to the basic biblical portrayal of the character of those who follow this God.[47]

One way to proceed would be that of Daniel Berrigan, whose reflections on Jeremiah are often helpful, not least on the use of the language of judgment in our own time. Yet listen to his reflections on Jeremiah 18:19-23:[48]

---

46. Criteria and texts would have to be more fully developed. For an initial attempt, see T. Fretheim and K. Froehlich, *The Bible as Word of God in a Postmodern Age* (Minneapolis, Minn.: Fortress, 1998), pp. 97-126.

47. Again, texts and criteria would need to be fully developed and issues of "canon within the canon" explored.

48. D. Berrigan, *Jeremiah: The World, the Wound of God* (Minneapolis, Minn.: Fortress, 1999), p. 84.

Who is this God anyway, the God of Jeremiah, what of his moral physiognomy? Do such oracles as are here recorded, with their summons to violent reprisal (a call taken seriously, more, initiated again and again by YHWH), offer sound insight into God, our God as well as Jeremiah's? Insight into God's hope for ourselves? Into crime (ours) and punishment (God's) — an ineluctable hyphenation, a logic of terrifying consequence? Why does the God of Jeremiah never once counsel — forgiveness? For this we are forced to turn in another direction than Jeremiah, to a later time, another seer — maligned as he is, put to scorn, murdered. And amid the infamy, a far different response is offered to his persecutors; a prayer on their behalf, an intercession (Luke 23:34). Jeremiah, we confess in confusion of heart, much resembles ourselves. And Jesus much resembles God. But not the God of Jeremiah, the God of Jesus.

But is it so simple? Is this not a return to that old saw about Jesus coming to deliver us from the abusive God of the Old Testament? Does Jesus mean that there is no place anymore for harsh, even unforgiving rhetoric? Yet, if we do not take Berrigan's route, do we simply move over to the other ditch and accept this language without evaluation? It is often argued that God's language is beyond scrutiny, or that biblical usage places an imprimatur on the (indiscriminate) use of such language by those who learn how to speak and act from such a God. However, does not this imaging of God stand for the violence that most of us would stand against?

One might seek a middle way and consider the nature of the situation into which such a word might be spoken. Upon careful discernment of a given situation of, say, the horrific abuse of human beings, one might be called upon to speak such a harsh word (though the words about children seem not to have a conceivable appropriate context). So, this language of God and Jeremiah would be placed in the same rare-use category as the psalms of imprecation and then used only by those whose personal experience calls for such rhetoric, or by those who stand in solidarity with them.

Nevertheless, however important it is to have this language available for such moments, the issue with the God of Jeremiah seems more complex. It is one thing to set a half-dozen psalms on the back burner for potential use; it is another thing to have the unrelenting harsh imagery of a major biblical book drummed into our consciousness on a regular basis. Will we not, as readers and hearers of this word, learn all too well how to speak and act from this portrayal of God?[49] This problem is at least implicitly recognized in the common

---

49. For further discussion, see Fretheim and Froehlich, *The Bible as Word of God.*

lectionary, where the only text assigned with such harsh language is Jeremiah's lament in 20:7-13 (11:18-20 is an alternate); God's use of this language is not represented. This may well be an appropriate decision regarding the public use of these Jeremiah texts, but do we leave the texts in this kind of limbo — retaining them in our printed Bibles but making no practical use of them? Several summary considerations regarding the use of these texts seem in order by way of conclusion. We also suggest further work to be done:

1. These texts remind us of the inadequacy of all of our language about God. Every image comes up short; every metaphor has its "no"; every reference to God is in some discontinuity with the reality that is God. Yet, even so, it is important to remember that these images are not "mere metaphors"; they have a great impact on our thinking, feeling, and being. Willy-nilly, they will sink deep into our selves and shape us in ways beyond our knowing. It may be that certain images for God in Jeremiah need to be set aside while retaining the "yes" of which they speak — indictment and judgment.[50]

2. By recognizing these harsh images for what they are, they can keep us alert to the fact that language about God has powerful effects upon people and world, both positive and negative, and can be used to promote ideas and practices that do not serve life and well-being. We must not be casual or indifferent about the God language we use.

3. Another approach would claim that such language about God is designed to make readers uncomfortable, to show what their sin has wrought, and to reveal the depths of their own violence. To try to escape from the force of texts such as these is a typical sinner's response. But are there no limits to such an approach? It is one thing to be told that our sin has had incredibly negative effects upon the children of the world; it is another thing to say that God directly commands that such violence be visited upon the children. Yet such effects on children are in some sense still related to God's circumstantial will,[51] and we are invited to think further of the kind of God who is often caught up in violent activities that so adversely affect children.

4. To engage texts of this kind could enhance our dialogical relationship with the biblical text more generally. The proper stance of readers in working

---

50. Zenger's comment is helpful in thinking through such issues (*A God of Vengeance*, p. 84): "[T]he history of the impact and reception of an individual text in the annals of Judaism and Christianity must also be taken into consideration when we reflect on its revelatory character. . . . [Some texts] can have been received in such a destructive way that the very knowledge of this negative history of reception becomes a constitutive part of the revelatory dimension of these texts."

51. On distinctions within the will of God, see T. Fretheim, "Will of God in the OT," *ABD* 4:914-20.

with the text is not one of passivity or submission or simply listening. As with key figures such as Abraham and Moses, the word of God calls for genuine interaction.

5. By carefully considering this language, and struggling with these texts, our imaginations may be sparked to seek ever more appropriate language for God. Certainly there are inadequacies in our present formulations that need attention, and these texts may not only remind us of this fact but also serve to generate new reflections regarding God.[52]

---

52. A postscript: I am left wondering whether much of this analysis is not too subtle for the average reader/hearer of Jeremiah. The violence of God's actions and speech in a "naked" form is what people will often take away from an encounter with these texts. They may well understand that such violent actions and language are in some sense a permitted or even mandated human response, to be exercised as they choose. Also, I am grateful to Beverly Stratton and Bruce Birch for their responses to earlier versions of this essay.

Ecumenism as the Shared Practice of a Peculiar Identity

Walter Brueggemann

Classic ecumenism in the twentieth century has had to do with partnership and cooperation among established denominational traditions. These denominational groupings have tended to reflect centrist, mainline churches that, in their own particular spheres, exercised some theological hegemony. Thus, ecumenism tended to focus upon churches finding each other in the midst of their pronounced socio-politico-economic accommodation to context. Important questions about the locus of such churches in their more or less compromised social contexts were not raised. One of the practical effects of such quests for unity and cooperation — without serious self-criticism — was the exclusion from the horizon of churches that did not participate in such centrist hegemony, for example, churches in the left-wing Reformation and Pentecostal traditions.

The ecumenical work that is now to be done is no longer among hegemonic denominations and church traditions, as though the largest animals were posturing in front of each other in the forest. Our current context requires that we recognize that unity among Christian churches is not very urgent or important unless it is unity found in an *odd identity* for an *odd vocation* in a world deeply organized against *gospel oddity*. The Lima document prepared the way for this embrace of common oddness, taking baptismal identity and vocation as the starting point for common life. But now, given where the churches find themselves, a common life in baptism is not a matter of agreeing on for-

---

The essay is reprinted (with slight editing) with permission from *Word and World* 18/2 (Spring 1998): 122-35. Its original form was presented at the SBL consultation on character ethics and biblical interpretation in November 1996 with the title "The Scandal and Liberty of Particularity."

mulae, classical or otherwise, but on *common praxis* deriving from a shared odd identity.

It is not clear in what way an Old Testament teacher can contribute to these conversations, given our propensity to traffic in old church formulae. The present essay seeks to think through Israel's odd identity in the Old Testament, an identity of course adjusted to different circumstances, but always in deep tension with hegemonic power all around. Increasingly, the church in the West is in an analogous situation to that of ancient Israel, no longer hegemonic itself but pressed by powers that are indeed hegemonic.[1] The characteristic locus of ancient Israel as a marginalized community in the midst of hegemonic power (either indifferent or hostile to that odd identity) may be a useful place from which to reread the text and rethink a shared identity in the church.

I

In the world of ancient Israel in the period of the Old Testament, it is not difficult to identify the ruling groups who we may suppose constructed and maintained dominant values. The list of superpowers that dominated the landscape of that ancient world includes, in sequence, Egypt, Assyria, Babylon, and Persia.[2] From an Israelite perspective, one can make some differentiations in their several modes of hegemony, so that it appears that Assyria was the most consistently brutal and that Persia operated in a more benign or enlightened way. But those differences likely were strategic, or at least the Israelite perception and presentation of them are likely strategic. Without fail, the impinging superpower intended to dominate the political landscape, to control military power, and to preempt the authority to tax. The control of military power, moreover, included the right to draft manpower, which issued in forced labor for state projects.

On the whole, these concentrations of power tolerated little deviation in matters of importance to them. To ensure compliance, moreover, the political-economic-military power of hegemony is paired, characteristically, with impe-

---

1. It is this awareness that has produced thinking, especially evoked by Lesslie Newbigin, that "the West" is a mission field for the church. See *Between Gospel and Culture: The Emerging Mission in North America,* ed. George R. Hunsberger and Craig van Gelder (Grand Rapids: Eerdmans, 1996).

2. I am of course aware that internally there were certainly hegemonic groups that prevailed. By focusing on the impact of the international empires, I do not overlook internal domination. I assume that patterns of domination are roughly the same, whether by external or internal agents.

rial myths and rituals, liturgical activities that legitimated power realities. It is not too much to conclude that the interface of political and liturgical efforts intended to generate a totalizing environment outside of which were permitted no political forays and, where effective, no deviant imagination. Such hegemony maintained both a monopoly of violence and a monopoly of imagination that assured privilege, certitude, and domination for its own young. It invited into its universal horizon those who stood outside the primary benefits of that monopoly, but who had come to terms with its visible and unquestioned privilege, certitude, and domination.

From an Israelite perspective, the totalizing capacity of hegemony is perceived, characteristically, as arrogant and threatening.[3] Thus, with ancient memories of oppression still palpable, Ezekiel has Pharaoh assert: "My Nile is my own, I made it for myself" (Ezek 29:3). And in the Isaiah tradition, Assyria gloats:

> Has any of the gods of the nations saved their land out of the hand of the king of Assyria? Where are the gods of Hamath and Arpad? Where are the gods of Sepharvaim? Have they delivered Samaria out of my hand? Who among all the gods of these countries have saved their countries out of my hand, that the LORD should save Jerusalem out of my hand? (Isa 36:18-20)

Babylon is no different: "I shall be mistress forever. . . . I am, and there is no one beside me. . . . No one sees me" (Isa 47:7-10).

We may register only two footnotes to this parade of totalizing superpowers. First, in the early part of the monarchic period in Jerusalem, emerging in a brief pause from imperial interference, the Davidic-Solomonic regime was not beholden to any external power. Yet the evidence we have, admittedly from a certain (Deuteronomic-prophetic) perspective, is that the Jerusalem regime practiced the same totalizing efforts, surely to be "like all the other nations."[4] Both the relentless prophetic critiques and perhaps especially the Rechabite alternative of Jeremiah 35 indicate that even this regime is no exception to the pattern of hegemonic rule.

Second, in addition to the standard lineup of imperial powers, we may mention a prophetic concern about Tyre, especially in Isaiah 23:1-18 and Ezekiel

---

3. On this motif in Israelite perspective, see Donald E. Gowan, *When Man Becomes God: Humanism and Hubris in the Old Testament*, PTMS 6 (Pittsburgh: Pickwick, 1975).

4. Norman K. Gottwald ("A Hypothesis about Social Class in Monarchic Israel in the Light of Contemporary Studies of Social Class and Social Stratification," in his *The Hebrew Bible in Its Social World and in Ours*, SBLSS [Atlanta: Scholars Press, 1993], pp. 139-64) has offered an analysis of the realities of class in the formation of the monarchy.

26–28. What interests us is that Tyre's significance is not military and political but economic. Indeed, Ezekiel suggests that Tyre is the epicenter of a world economy that features opulence, self-indulgence, and general social disregard, so that Tyre can be imagined as saying: "I am a god; I sit in the seat of the gods, in the heart of the seas" (Ezek 28:2).

This recital of hegemony, focusing on political power but ending with a recognition of commercialism, provides a window on our own current consideration of character ethics. I submit that in our time and place the hegemonic power of international corporate capitalism, driven of course by United States technological power, creates a totalizing environment that imposes its values, its field of images, and its limits of vision upon all. Theodore von Laue speaks of *The World Revolution of Westernization,* and more recently Charles Reich terms this phenomenon "the money government."[5] It is self-evident that this community of ruthless expansionism and those allied with it do not need to expend any energy in inculcating their own young into practices of privilege, certitude, and domination. I imagine, moreover, that our modest reflection upon character ethics in such a totalizing environment is not unlike that of Israel in the ancient world, deeply perplexed about how to sustain any vision or practice of life that is not swept away by the force of hegemony. This deep vexation concerns those of us who live at the center of the hegemony, who are implicated in it and benefit from it. However, there is also deep vexation among those in the less privileged places that we are pleased to term "underdeveloped," as they wonder how to maintain any local, rooted identity in the face of invasive, seemingly irresistible Coca Cola.

II

In its relentless imperial matrix, ancient Israel had only a slight chance and thin resources. It is clear, nonetheless, that a central preoccupation of the Old Testament, surely a discernment assembled and transmitted out of a passionate ideological perspective, is to maintain the scandal and liberty of particularity in the face of totalizing threat. I shall suggest that the maintenance of a self-aware, self-conscious alternative identity in the face of totalism is precisely the practice of character ethics that aims to generate and authorize liberated "agents of their own history"; such practice depends upon the great

5. Theodore H. von Laue, *The World Revolution of Westernization: The Twentieth Century in Global Perspective* (New York: Oxford University Press, 1987); Charles Reich, *Opposing the System* (New York: Random House, 1995).

"thickness" of the community that makes possible such liberated agents on a day-to-day basis.

I will organize my efforts around an easy scheme of superpowers: Egypt, Assyria, Babylon, and Persia. (I am of course aware of the historical-critical qualifications concerning the literature, but I will deal with the literature in terms of its presentation. Texts, for example, that deal with the ancient pharaoh of the Exodus period will be read without the critical qualification of later dating.)

> *As an intentional counter-community, Israel practiced relentless, dense memory as an alternative to the coopting amnesia of the empire.*

Concerning Egypt

The Exodus liturgy (Exodus 1–15) dominates the imagination of Israel and continues to be decisive for Israel's identity. Three aspects of the narrative pertain to what we may roughly regard as character formation. First, three times, the Passover provisions pay attention to intentional instructing: "When your children ask you, 'What do you mean by this observance?'" (Exod 12:26; cf. 18:8, 14). The liturgy is a launching pad for conversation. The prescribed response to the child's question is a narrative reiteration of a peculiar world with YHWH at its center.

Second, the entire Passover provision of Exodus 12–13 is quite specific and self-conscious about liturgical detail. It is clear, nonetheless, that the primary intention of the narrative and the liturgy is to construct a counterworld whereby Pharaoh's totalizing power and totalizing explanation of reality are regularly defeated. The Israelite boy or girl is invited to live in a social reality where Pharaoh's abusive power does not prevail. Third, the narrative makes clear that the recital offers a curriculum for the young:

> Go to Pharaoh; for I have hardened his heart and the heart of his officials, in order that I may show these signs [plagues] of mine among them, and that you may tell your children and grandchildren how I made fools of the Egyptians and what signs I have done among them — so that you may know that I am the LORD. (Exod 10:1-2)

The concern — to make this defining memory operative to the third and fourth generations — is crucial for our subject.

Concerning Assyria

Critical judgment suggests that the book of Deuteronomy is to be understood as an instrument of resistance against Assyrian totalism, perhaps influenced by Assyrian forms of treaty documents.[6] Pivotal to Josiah's reform is the celebration of the Passover (2 Kgs 23:21-23). The focus on Passover, of course, draws resistance to Assyria into the world of Passover resistance to Egypt found in Exodus 12–13. It is the disciplined, intentional retelling of the Exodus-seder narrative that provides ground for alternative existence outside Assyrian hegemony. The Passover festival recalls Israel's root identity of emancipation and covenant; but it also brings that counter-identity, always contemporary, into the Assyrian crisis.

Passover is one of three defining festivals that will give liturgical, dramatic, and narrative articulation to Israel's distinctiveness, the other two festivals being Weeks and Booths (Deut 16:1-8, 9-17). Thus, the danger and the rescue from Egypt are transposed into an Assyrian world. The provision of 16:1-8 mentions Egypt three times; the following provision for the festival of Weeks moves more directly to an ethical derivation: "Rejoice before the LORD your God — you and your sons and your daughters, your male and female slaves, the Levites resident in your towns, as well as the strangers, the orphans, and the widows who are among you" (16:11). Then the imperative: "Remember that you were a slave in Egypt" (16:12).

Concerning Babylon

The great danger for Jewish exiles in Babylon was assimilation into the totalizing world of Nebuchadnezzar, with the commensurate abandonment of the particular identity of Judaism. It is common to recognize that Second Isaiah is a message to Jews that they will be liberated to go home to Jerusalem. In my view, however, prior to going home geographically, Israel must go home to Jewishness, emotionally, liturgically, and imaginatively. Consider this counsel: "Look to the rock from which you were hewn, and to the quarry from which you were dug. Look to Abraham your father and to Sarah who bore you" (Isa 51:1-2).

I do not follow John van Seters in his notion that these traditions of the

---

6. See R. Frankena, "The Vassal-Treaties of Esarhaddon and the Dating of Dt," *OtSt* 14 (1965): 122-54; Dennis J. McCarthy, *Treaty and Covenant: A Study in Form in the Ancient Oriental Documents and in the Old Testament*, AnBib 21a (Rome: Biblical Institute, 1978); and Moshe Weinfeld, *Deuteronomy and the Deuteronomic School* (Oxford: Clarendon, 1972).

ancestors were first formulated in the exile.[7] Yet there is no doubt that the promissory narratives of Genesis received enormous attention and were found to be pertinent in this context. It is when all seemed lost in the face of the totalizing empire that Israel was driven deep into its narrative past, in order to have an identity apart from the offer of Babylon.

While there are important historical-critical issues, we may here mention Daniel 1, wherein the self-aware Jew Daniel negotiates his way through the civil service of Babylon by a refusal of the rich food of the empire and a reliance upon the simplicities of a Jewish diet. The refusal of junk food from the empire is linked to his being embedded in a particular sense of identity. The Daniel narrative is an echo of the challenge of exilic Isaiah:[8]

> Ho, everyone who thirsts,
>> come to the waters;
> and you that have no money,
>> come, buy and eat!
> Come, buy wine and milk
>> without money and without price.
> Why do you spend your money for that which is not bread,
>> and your labor for that which does not satisfy?   (Isa 55:1-2)

Concerning Persia

The issues with Persia are very different: antagonism has yielded to supportive imperial patronage (Neh 2:5-8). Nehemiah operates with the credentials of Persia. Nonetheless, when that community of Jews engages in an act of reconstitution, the public liturgical activity is not Persian. It is torah based, linking Jews to the oldest memories of Moses (Neh 8:1-12), and culminating in the festival of Booths, wherein Israel reengages its memory of vulnerability and inexplicable receipt of well-being (Neh 8:13-18). A primary dimension of "rebooting" is that the torah was read for seven consecutive days.

Thus in the face of every empire that sought to comprehend Jewish identity, one can see this community intentionally staking out public, liturgical space to reenact and reclaim its own distinctive identity. That liturgical act is

---

7. John van Seters, *Abraham in History and Tradition* (New Haven, Conn.: Yale University Press, 1975).

8. See Walter Brueggemann, "A Poem of Summons (Is. 55:1-3)? A Narrative of Resistance (Dan. 1:1-21)," in *Schöpfung und Befreiung*, ed. Rainer Albertz et al. (Stuttgart: Calwer Verlag, 1989), pp. 126-36.

surely an act of faith. It is at the same time an act of resistance, of propaganda, and of nurture, whereby the community asserts to its young in direct ways that its existence is not comprehended in the totalizing reality of the empire.

III

> *As an intentional counter-community, Israel practiced liberated, imaginative possibility as an alternative to the circumscribed limiting world of imperial administration.*

A totalizing empire is primarily interested in tax revenues, civil order, and due compliance with imperial expectations and quotas. Such hegemony, however, cannot be sustained unless it is supported by poetic legitimation that seeks to define appropriate social hopes and expectations and inescapable social fears and threats. The empire can never resist seeking control of the emotional life of its subjects, for in emotional life are generated dreams and visions that may be subversive of current order. Israel, as a community with a peculiar destiny, resisted the preemption of its hopes and fears by imperial confiscation. It did so by maintaining a liturgical, instructional claim that its life was not under the control of the empire but under the governance of the Holy One of Israel who rightly and with great authority denied the effectiveness and legitimacy of imperial claims. Israel's insistence upon such YHWH-driven possibility is not made on the basis of the "nuts and bolts" of political and economic life but on the basis of dramatic enactment that refuses to be domesticated by "nuts and bolts." Israel regularly invites its young into a liturgically constructed counterworld of Yahwistic possibility.

Concerning Egypt

The entire Exodus liturgy serves the sense of Israel's exceptionalism. YHWH, as a character in a narrative that Egyptian epistemology would never accept, makes possible for the slave community precisely what Pharaoh had declared impossible. The very enactment of the plagues — which make Pharaoh a fool — is the assertion that there is emancipatory power at work beyond the reach of Pharaoh.

More than that, the liturgy is replete with the protection of Israel, singled out from the massive destruction of the empire:

Thus I will make a distinction between my people and your people. (Exod 8:23)

All the livestock of the Egyptians died, but of the livestock of the Israelites, not one died. (9:6)

The hail struck down everything. . . . Only in the land of Goshen, where the Israelites were, there was no hail. (9:25-26)

There will be a loud cry throughout the whole land of Egypt . . . but not a dog shall growl at any of the Israelites . . . so that you may know that the LORD makes a distinction between Egypt and Israel. (11:6-7)

There are matters possible for Israel that Pharaoh will never permit.

Concerning Assyria

The link between liturgical reconstrual and a radical alternative ethic is most clear in Deuteronomy 15:1-18, which places next to Passover the year of release, whereby Israel resists the emergence of a permanent underclass. Both Jeffries Hamilton and Moshe Weinfeld have suggested that this provision of the torah is the quintessential mark of Israel's distinctive ethic.[9] The practice of debt cancellation stands in deep opposition to the imperial economy, which is a practice of hierarchical power and social stratification. This provision stands at the center of Deuteronomy, a script designed to distinguish Israel from Assyrian possibility.

This provision is more than simply a legal regulation. It is a remarkable exploration of a social possibility that is clearly unthinkable in the empire. The empire stands or falls with the administration of debt, for it is debt that distinguishes the powerful and the have-nots.[10]

Deuteronomic resistance to Assyrian impingement, however, is not simply liturgical. It is also the dreaming vision of an alternative economy that imagines neighbors living with generous, palpable concern for each other. The energy for such subversive activity is, predictably, grounded in memory: "Remember that you were slaves in the land of Egypt; the LORD redeemed you; for

9. Jeffries M. Hamilton, *Social Justice & Deuteronomy: The Case of Deuteronomy 15*, SBLDS 136 (Atlanta: Scholars Press, 1992); Moshe Weinfeld, *Social Justice in Ancient Israel and in the Ancient Near East* (Minneapolis, Minn.: Fortress, 1995).

10. David Daube (*The Exodus Pattern in the Bible* [Westport, Conn.: Greenwood, 1979]) has suggested links between the year of release and the Exodus narrative.

this reason I lay this command upon you today" (Deut 15:15). Assyria or any other empire would regard this social posture as impossible because Assyria has, as yet, no exodus memory.

Concerning Babylon

The challenge of Second Isaiah is to create imaginative space for Jewishness. The danger is that Israel in exile will give everything over to Babylonian definitions of the possible. So the assertion: "My thoughts are not your thoughts, nor are your ways my ways, says the LORD" (Isa 55:8). This assertion is not a generic invitation to repent of sin; it is rather a concrete assault on Jewish readiness to accept Babylonian definitions of the possible. YHWH has another way, another thought, another possibility. Babylon offered food that is not bread, and labor that does not satisfy, but YHWH offers wine and milk and bread without money and without price (55:1-2). Babylon thought to keep everything frozen and everyone in place to perpetuity. Yet YHWH anticipates in exultation: "You shall go out in joy and be led back in peace" (55:12).

Babylon had become an arena for abandonment and the absence of God, but now YHWH asserts: "With great compassion I will gather you. . . . With everlasting love I will have compassion on you" (54:7-8). The world that Second Isaiah imagines is not a world from which YHWH has been forcibly eliminated. YHWH is still there. For that reason, Babylonian designations of reality are not finally effective.

Concerning Persia

The relation between Israel and Persia is different from the relation to previous hegemonic powers. Yet even with Persia the Jews knew their life was deeply circumscribed by imperial pressures and realities. This sense of limitation and pressure is evidenced in the great prayer of Ezra in Nehemiah 9. The prayer moves between Israel's wickedness and God's mercy. The final petition, however, lets us see, beyond the intensity between YHWH and Israel, a third party:

> Here we are, slaves to this day — slaves in the land that you gave to our ancestors to enjoy its fruit and its good gifts. Its rich yield goes to the kings whom you have set over us because of our sins; they have power also over our bodies and over our livestock at their pleasure, and we are in great distress. (Neh 9:36-37)

The reality of restriction is evident. The text nonetheless suggests two facets of emancipated possibility that remained outside Persian administration. The first of these is an act of imagination in the form of prayer. The prayer is a bid for reality that lies beyond the control of Persia, a bid that shows this intentional community not yet conceding everything to hegemony. The second is the solemn community covenant that follows the prayer (Neh 9:38–10:39); the leaders of the community vow to act in solidarity concerning economic matters, a solidarity that echoes the old year of release.

The text is saturated with communal, liturgical, and imaginative practice in which a zone of social possibility, outside of imperial regimentation because it is rooted in YHWH, is maintained, celebrated, practiced, and made visible.

IV

> *As an intentional counter-community, Israel articulated a covenantal ethic of neighborliness as an alternative to the commoditization of social relationships it sensed in imperial practice.*

I do not want to overemphasize the ethical dimension here, since it seems to me that the liturgical-imaginative effort to create and protect alternative space is more important. Israel, however, cannot entertain or imagine alternative human space, sponsored as it is by YHWH, except as space that is saturated with ethical urgency, ethical possibility, and ethical requirement. Indeed, it is the practice of torah obedience to the rooted claims of the community that is the instrument and guarantee of liberated life beyond imperial reductionism: "I will keep your law continually, forever and ever. I shall walk at liberty, for I have sought your precepts. I will speak of your decrees before kings, and shall not be put to shame" (Ps 119:44-46).

Concerning Egypt

As the Exodus narrative is the paradigmatic assertion of community beyond the reality of totalizing power, so the Sinai recital is the paradigmatic articulation of neighborly ethics that counters the ethic of Pharaoh. In its completed tradition, Israel understood that emancipation from Egypt was not for the sake of autonomy but for the sake of the counter-service of YHWH. Furthermore, while we may focus on a variety of commands that epitomize such an alternative ethic rooted in liturgy, we may settle for the first command: No other gods than YHWH, the God of the Exodus, who delegitimates every other loyalty. While the commands of Sinai are demanding and abrasive, they would never be confused with Pharaoh's commands, for they are in general aimed at a communitarianism that makes "hard labor" impossible.[11]

The link between the holiness of YHWH and the concreteness of neighborliness is wondrously voiced in Deuteronomy:

> For the LORD your God is God of gods and Lord of lords, the great God, mighty and awesome, who is not partial and takes no bribe, who executes justice for the orphan and the widow, and who loves the strangers, providing them food and clothing. You shall also love the stranger, for you were strangers in the land of Egypt. (Deut 10:17-19)

It is precisely the God who commands lords, gods, and pharaohs who loves immigrants and displaced persons, who provides them food and clothing. This ethic arises from the memory and from the possibility of an alternative to Pharaoh.

Concerning Assyria

As a contrast program, Deuteronomy makes one of its foci "widows and orphans," that is, the paradigmatic powerless and vulnerable in society. The Israelite ethic urged here, alternative to imperial rapaciousness, is precisely concerned for those without resources or leverage to maintain and protect themselves:

> Every third year you shall bring out the full tithe of your produce for that year, and store it within your towns; the Levites, because they have no allotments or inheritance with you, as well as the resident aliens, the orphans and the widows in your towns may come and eat their fill. (Deut 14:28-29; cf. 16:11, 14; 24:17, 19-21; 26:12-13)

This social horizon, moreover, is rooted and made available in Exodus memories: "Remember that you were a slave in Egypt, and diligently observe these statutes" (Deut 16:12; cf. 24:18, 22). Against Assyrian amnesia, which permits ex-

11. Norman K. Gottwald ("Prolegomenon: How My Mind Has Changed or Remained the Same," in his *The Hebrew Bible in Its Social World and in Ours,* SBLSS [Atlanta: Scholars Press, 1993], p. xxv) has most recently adopted the term "communitarian" to characterize the vision of revolutionary Israel. Gottwald has employed this word after his earlier term "egalitarian" was roundly criticized.

ploitative neighborly relations, Israel's narrative embedment in the Exodus tradition will energize the radical economics of Deuteronomy.

Concerning Babylon

The vision of Second Isaiah, rooted in Exodus imagery, broadly understood Israel's life to be a practice of justice (42:1-4), light (42:6; 49:6), and covenant (42:6; 49:8) — generalities that envisioned a differently ordered economy. In Third Isaiah, however, albeit beyond the Babylonian period, the visionary ethics of Second Isaiah continued to ferment and evoke ferocious dispute in the community concerning ethical possibility. Thus, Isaiah 56:2-8 raises a powerful voice for inclusiveness, and 58:6-7 names the quintessence of covenantalism as a precondition for YHWH's presence in the community:

> Is not this the fast that I choose:
> to loose the bonds of injustice,
> to undo the thongs of the yoke,
> to let the oppressed go free,
> and to break every yoke?
> Is it not to share your bread with the hungry,
> and bring the homeless poor into your house;
> when you see the naked, to cover them,
> and not to hide yourself from your own kin?   (Isa 58:6-7)

This issue of inclusiveness is not easily settled in the years immediately after the exile. Nonetheless, the peculiar social vision of Israel continued to summon and empower even when the community had limited resources and feared for its own survival.

Concerning Persia

The lyrical anticipations of the Isaiah tradition came to concrete implementation in the reform of Nehemiah. Though authorized by the Persians, it is clear that Nehemiah and Ezra, in the reconstitution of an intentional community of the torah, had to struggle mightily for a neighborly ethic rooted in Israel's peculiar tradition.

Most spectacularly, in Nehemiah 5, Nehemiah addresses the economic crisis whereby some Jews were exploiting other Jews in a way that created a permanent underclass.[12] Nehemiah's demanding alternative vision is rooted in the Exodus memory, alludes to the old torah, is aware of Israel's distinctiveness, and requires concrete, costly economic decisions:

> As far as we were able, we have brought back our Jewish kindred who have been sold to other nations. The thing you are doing is not good. Should you not walk in the fear of our God, to prevent the taunts of the nations our enemies? . . . Let us stop this taking of interest. Restore to them this very day their fields, their vineyards, their olive orchards, and their houses, and the interest on money, grain, wine and oil, that you have been exacting from them. (Neh 5:8-11)

In every imperial context, Israel's peculiar ethic is kept alive, each time rooted in old liturgical memory, but each time brought to bear upon concrete social history in a way that requires the covenant community to act peculiarly against the common definitions of imperial social reality.

V

I want now to reflect in three ways upon this sequencing of *memory, possibility, and ethic* through the several imperial hegemonies under which ancient Israel lived.

1. The practice of an ethic rooted in *an intentional and particular communal narrative* suggests a community characteristically at risk in the face of a seemingly irresistible imperial pressure toward homogenization. The pressure of triage, of the elimination of surplus people, worked massively against the Israelites, if not in terms of physical violence then through ideological violence that sought always to eradicate Israel's sense of itself and of YHWH's reality.[13] I think it impossible to overstate the enduringly ominous threat of elimination that required a liturgy, a socialization, and an ethic that had to be understood as resistance.

a. This resistance pertains to Jewishness in a most concrete sense, for which I will cite two instances in the long history of marginality. The Macca-

---

12. See Walter Brueggemann, "Reflections on Biblical Understandings of Property," in *A Social Reading of the Old Testament: Prophetic Approaches to Israel's Communal Life*, ed. Patrick D. Miller (Minneapolis, Minn.: Fortress, 1994), pp. 276-84.

13. On the use of the term triage in such a way, see Richard L. Rubenstein, *After Auschwitz: History, Theology, and Contemporary Judaism*, 2nd ed. (Baltimore: Johns Hopkins University Press, 1992); Zygmunt Bauman (*Modernity & the Holocaust* [Ithaca, N.Y.: Cornell University Press, 1992]) has shown how the holocaust was a most modernist approach to the problem of surplus people.

bean revolt against Roman homogenization in the second century B.C.E. is of course a pivotal point for the intertestamental period. Roman triage was not directly violent but was determined to eliminate Jewish oddness. According to the brief notation in 1 Maccabees 1:11-15, "renegade Jews" sought a "covenant with the Gentiles": "So they built a gymnasium in Jerusalem, according to Gentile custom, and removed the marks of circumcision, and abandoned the holy covenant. They joined with the Gentiles and sold themselves to do evil."[14] The pressure of a "universal identity" is always a threat to a particular identity; assimilation is ever a clear and present danger.

That pressure of homogeneity and threat of triage by assimilation was directly asserted in an advertisement in the *New York Times* that took the form of a litany urging:

> We prayed for Israel when its survival was threatened in 1967 and 1973.
>   Our prayers were answered.
> We prayed for the redemption of Soviet Jewry during the
>   dark years of Communism.
>   Our prayers were answered.
> We prayed for the release of Syrian Jewry, hostages to a
>   most aggressive regime.
>   Our prayers were answered.
> Now it is time to recite a prayer for ourselves — an embattled
>   American Jewry. . . .
>   Our birthrate is too low and our rate of intermarriage too high.
>   The real question is will we survive?[15]

I make no judgment about this ad or its ideology. I simply note that the issue of a distinct community of character recurs among the heirs of ancient Israel.

b. Our ultimate concern in this essay, however, is for the distinctive ethic of the Christian church. The end of Christendom in western Europe and in the United States is likely a good thing. The question remains, however: How shall we practice a distinctive ethic of humanness in a society massively driven by the forces of the market economy toward an ethic of individualism that issues in social indifference and anti-neighborliness? It is obvious that the position of the church in the United States directly parallels neither the position in the empire of ancient Israel nor the dangerous exposure of current Judaism. Still, what might have passed for a "Christian ethic" in the period of Christendom has

14. See Robert G. Hall, "Circumcision," *ABD* 1:1028-29.
15. "A Prayer for the Continuity of American Jewish Life," *New York Times*, 6 September 1996.

now been thoroughly permeated by secularism in both its liberal and conservative modes. Therefore, attentiveness to peculiar narrative identity seems to me an urgent practical enterprise for a religious community that is often so bland that it loses its raison d'être. The issue is to practice a peculiar identity that is not craven in the face of the moralisms of the right or the left.

c. An ethic of resistance was regularly needed in ancient Israel; it is, in my judgment, needed now by a depositioned church in the West; it is also needed to combat the power of corporate capitalism, supported as that is by military and technological power as part of the Westernization of the world. Around the globe, local communities with peculiar identities and destinies are profoundly under threat from "the money government" that has no patience with or regard for rooted communities. Thus, the issue of ideological triage and the capacity for locally rooted resistance is not singularly a Jewish question or a church question; it has become a question for the shape and viability of humanness in a drastically reorganized world. For Christians and Jews who are situated in and beneficiaries of the expanding world economy, attentiveness to, appreciation for, and support of local resistance — which may take many forms — is an issue of paramount importance.

2. Because I have framed my discussion in terms of *local resistance to universalizing pressures,* a framing I think unavoidable in the Old Testament, I must also ask whether such an approach is inevitably sectarian, concerned with funding and authorizing a separatist community. In the instant, I suspect that this approach to ethics is inevitably aimed at the particularity of the community. Certainly the primary concern of the Old Testament is the assertion and maintenance of the distinctive community of Israel. Moreover, I believe that a particularistic ethic of resistance is now urgent in light of the massive power of the Coca Cola–ization of the world.

Having acknowledged that much, I must make two important qualifications: First, Israel did not live, over time, in a cultural and liturgical vacuum. It was endlessly engaged in interaction with other cultures and regularly appropriated things from the very forces it intended to critique and resist; thus, the materials for this distinctive ethic in the sixth century were very different from what purports to be thirteenth-century resistance. The process of deciding what to appropriate (and how) in the midst of resistance is completely hidden from us. The dual process of resistance and appropriation is unmistakable. Thus, for example, Hosea seems to mount a polemic against "fertility religion," but does so by a Yahwistic appeal to the modes and images of fertility.[16]

---

16. See Walter Harrelson, *From Fertility Cult to Worship: A Reassessment for the Modern Church of the Worship of Ancient Israel* (Garden City, N.Y.: Doubleday, 1969).

Second, while it is not primary, it is evident that Israel's distinctive identity and ethic are an offer, summons, and invitation to the world around it (that is, the imperial world) to share its neighbor ethic. While the texts characteristically focus on immediate concrete crises, it is equally clear that Israel's long-term hope is that the impossible possibility of covenant, rooted in the Creator's practice of steadfast love and justice, can and will be enacted everywhere. Characteristically Israel believes and trusts that an anti-neighbor ethic cannot prevail and that the gods who legitimate such an ethic will be defeated. Israel understands itself at Sinai to be at the edge of YHWH's coming rule, which will indeed reach to the ends of the earth, so that kings and princes will end their futility and join in doxological obedience — the very doxological obedience that is definitional for Israel's life. At its best (but not always), this deep hope is free from Israel's own ideological benefit. That is, the coming rule is a rule of YHWH for the benefit of all, not a rule of preference for Israel.

3. I conclude with a reference to Jacob Neusner. In his study of Jewish ritual practice, Neusner judges that the stylized gestures and words of ritual are aids in the daily work of being "Jews through the power of our imagination."[17] Indeed, Neusner opines that Jewishness is hazardous and venturesome enough that it requires a daily act of imagination, without which there would not be Jews.

I propose that in Christendom Christians needed no such effort, for identity simply came with the territory, as it always does for dominant faith. The depositioning of Christian faith in the West, however, makes the community of the baptized a community more fully dependent upon daily acts of imagination for the maintenance of identity. The daily acts evoking Christian identity are likely to be ethical as well as liturgical. The beginning point is the recognition that clear identity is not a cultural given, as it might have been in former times of domination, but is now an oddness that requires courageous intentionality.

---

17. Jacob Neusner, *The Enchantments of Judaism: Rites of Transformation from Birth through Death* (New York: Basic Books, 1987), pp. 211-16 and passim.

The Education of Human Wanting:
Formation by Pater Noster

C. Clifton Black

> *Father, may your name be hallowed,*
> *your kingdom come.*
> *Keep giving us each day our daily bread.*
> *And forgive us our sins,*
> *for we ourselves forgive everyone indebted to us.*
> *And let us not fall victim to temptation.*
>
> *(Luke 11:2b-4)*[1]

Thirty-eight simple words, translating from the Greek thirty-eight of comparable simplicity. Yet for most Christians these words set the standard for all prayer. Given by Jesus at his disciples' bidding (Luke 11:1), from its earliest utterance the Lord's Prayer has taught his followers not only how to pray but also what prayer is fundamentally about. Thus was it regarded by the church's earliest doctors, such as Tertullian (ca. 160-225 C.E.) and Cyprian (d. 258);[2] so even, in the twentieth century, Simone Weil notes: "The Our Father contains all possible petitions; we cannot conceive of any prayer not already contained in it. It is to prayer what Christ is to humanity."[3] That being so, the Lord's Prayer (hereafter, "the Prayer") is the perfect index to the human character, in all its need and desire.

"A perfect index" to the Prayer lies far beyond my competence, academic

---

1. Unless otherwise indicated, all translations in this chapter are my own.

2. St. Cyprian: "There is absolutely nothing passed over pertaining to our petitions and prayers which is not included in this compendium of heavenly teaching" (*St. Cyprian on the Lord's Prayer*, trans. T. Herbert Bindley, ECC [London: SPCK, 1914], p. 34); Tertullian: "[the Prayer] comprises a breviary of the whole Gospel" (*St. Cyprian on the Lord's Prayer*, p. 72).

3. Simone Weil, *Waiting for God*, trans. Emma Craufurd (New York: G. P. Putnam's Sons, 1951), pp. 226-27.

or spiritual.[4] The best I can offer is a meditation on the Prayer, guided by the sort of interpretation already demonstrable within Scripture and in contemporaneous works like the *Didache,* or *Teaching of the Twelve Apostles* (8.2-3).[5] Such meditation must have a focus, however. Luke has concentrated the Prayer on persistent, confident petition by Jesus' disciples (11:1-13); Matthew, on plain, reserved piety (6:1-18); the Didachist, on proper liturgical practice (*Did.* 7.1–10.7). Consonant with the present volume's aim, this essay explores some aspects of the Prayer's formation of Christian character.

A clue to my approach lies in this essay's title, derived from an offhand yet penetrating comment by Neville Ward: "The purification of desire, the education of human wanting, is one of the principal ways in which God answers prayer. It is always a reduction, which reaches its culmination in the single desire for God himself and his kingdom."[6] In that remarkably apt phrase, "the education of human wanting," Ward has crystallized much, I believe, of what the Prayer means for Christian formation. Though Ward himself does not develop their implications in this manner, he has put his finger on two basic, intersecting dimensions of the Prayer. When we pray as Jesus taught his disciples, we are enrolled in a twofold curriculum: one of *educere* ("to lead out," eliciting latent potentialities) and *educare* ("to bring up," forming habits, manners, intellectual aptitudes).[7] The Prayer draws out, or makes explicit, who we truly are: creatures made in God's image, warped by sin and restored by God's Spirit. Simulta-

---

4. Within the bottomless bibliography on the Prayer, I would highlight two scholarly treatments: Ernst Lohmeyer, *"Our Father": An Introduction to the Lord's Prayer,* trans. John Bowden (New York: Harper & Row, 1965); Daniel L. Migliore, ed., *The Lord's Prayer: The 1991 Frederick Neumann Symposium on the Theological Interpretation of Scripture,* PSB Supplementary Issue, no. 2 (1992).

5. I think it likely that Matthew and Luke, independently of each other, edited a shared source ("Q") for the Prayer. Matthew's recension (6:9b-13) appears to be more liturgically elaborate, though conceivably Luke's is a compressed version. Probably dependent on Matthew, the *Didache* (8.2) advanced the Prayer's liturgical refinement. Readers interested in finer questions of tradition and redaction may consult two technical commentaries in the Hermeneia series: Hans Dieter Betz, *The Sermon on the Mount: A Commentary on the Sermon on the Mount, including the Sermon on the Plain (Matthew 5:1–7:27 and Luke 6:20-49),* ed. Adela Y. Collins, Hermeneia (Minneapolis, Minn.: Fortress, 1995), esp. pp. 370-415; and Kurt Niederwimmer, *The Didache: A Commentary,* trans. Linda M. Maloney, ed. Harold W. Attridge, Hermeneia (Minneapolis, Minn.: Fortress, 1998), pp. 134-38. For further information, see W. D. Davies and Dale C. Allison, Jr., *The Gospel According to Saint Matthew,* ICC (Edinburgh: T. & T. Clark, 1988), 1:590-615.

6. J. Neville Ward, *The Use of Praying* (Peterborough, U.K.: Epworth, 1998), p. 57.

7. "Eduction" and "education" are derived, respectively, from the Latin cognates *ēduco* and *ēduco.*

neously, the Prayer trains what we are becoming: God's obedient children, with minds renewed in accordance with "the mind of Christ" (1 Cor 2:16). By that double-pronged education, the Prayer reforms our manifold "wanting" as human creatures: what we most profoundly *need* is evoked and exposed; what we most ardently *desire* is developed and disciplined. Each of the Prayer's petitions bears on this complex process.

Father

The Psalter reminds us of the many metaphors Israel used to address God: "our governor" (Ps 8:1, 9), "my stronghold, my crag, and my haven" (18:1), "my rock, . . . my shield, the horn of my salvation, and my refuge" (18:2), "shepherd" (23:1; 80:1), and "king" (93:1; 99:1; 145:1). Most often the psalmist cries, "O Lord" or "O God." The same images and much the same pattern persist in Jewish prayer texts of the rabbinic period.[8] By my reckoning, only three psalms describe God as "father," none of them in direct address: "the father of orphans, the champion of widows" (68:5); "You are my father, my God" (89:26, attributed to "David, my servant" in indirect discourse); "as a father has compassion for his children" (103:13).[9] Within that context, Jesus' address to God as "Our Father" (Matt 6:9) or, more simply, "Father" (Luke 11:2) offers a contrast that is distinctive though not unique (Wis 14:3; Sir 23:1, 4).[10]

What does that address evoke of our need? How does it shape our desire? In the New Testament, appeals to God as *patēr* ("father") embrace many nuances, only some of which we may consider here.

---

8. See the selections in Jakob J. Petuchowski and Michael Brocke, eds., *The Lord's Prayer and Jewish Liturgy* (New York: Seabury, 1978), pp. 21-44.

9. The later synagogue liturgy more frequently adopts paternal imagery for God. In two of the ancient Eighteen Benedictions (also known as the *Tefillah*), God is addressed as Father: 4a: "Our Father, favor us with knowledge from You"; and 6a: "Forgive us, our Father, for we have sinned against You." The great ninth-century prayer "Our Father, Our King," which introduces each of twenty-seven petitions with those vocatives, appears to have evolved from a simpler second-century prayer attributed to Rabbi Akiba: "Our Father, our King, we have no King but You; Our Father, our King, for Your sake have mercy upon us" (*b. Ta'an.* 25b). Consult Petuchowski and Brocke, *The Lord's Prayer and Jewish Liturgy,* pp. 27-30, 39-40.

10. "Father" is Jesus' customary mode of address to God in the Fourth Gospel (e.g., John 5:17; 6:32; 10:15-38; 11:41; 14:2–17:25; 20:17-21). The "Abba! Father!" outbursts (Mark 14:36; Rom 8:15; Gal 4:6) will be considered presently.

Comprehensive Authority

To attribute to God fatherhood is to acknowledge God as the one from whom our being is derived and to whom we are ultimately accountable (Matt 7:21-23; 18:23-35; Acts 17:26-28; 1 Pet 1:17). Particularly in the Gospels, God has conferred on Jesus, "[his] Son, the Beloved" (Matt 3:17; 12:18; 17:5; Mark 9:7; 12:6; Luke 20:13), faithful execution of that authority (Matt 9:6, 8; 28:18; Mark 1:22; 2:10; John 5:26-27, 30). Similarly, in Acts "times and seasons" have been set by God's own authority (1:7), even as God raised from the dead "the Author of life" (3:15). In the Fourth Gospel, Philip asks Jesus to show him and other disciples the Father; Jesus replies, "The one who has seen me has seen the Father" (John 14:8-9).

Embedded in those theological claims is a critique of both antiquity and modernity. Roman civil order, which pervaded the New Testament world, was grounded in the *patria potestas* ("fatherly potentate") or *dominium in domo* ("lordship at home"): unilateral power, accorded to the father as head of the household, to marry and to divorce, to adopt and to disown, to free and to enslave.[11] Such assumptions are undermined by Jesus, who was remembered as acknowledging women in public conversation (John 4:27), shielding them from socially devastating divorce (Mark 10:1-12), and — perhaps most brazen — esteeming children as exemplary inheritors of God's kingdom (Matt 18:1-4, 10; 19:13-15; 21:15-16). Likewise, Paul identifies Christians' inspired utterance of "Abba! Father!" as a sign of their adoption by God, right of inheritance, and emancipation from terrified slavery (Rom 8:14-17; Gal 4:3-7).[12] Abusive, deforming authority in our own day, whether patriarchal or matriarchal, falls under precisely the same critique: as formulated by James Kay, "the One in whom Jesus trusted and invited his disciples to join in calling 'Our Father' little resembles the ominous male parent of patriarchy, especially in light of subsequent trinitarian reflection."[13] Positively put, God's authority as Father resides not in bullying but in trustworthy fidelity.[14]

11. Consult Susan Treggiari, *Roman Marriage: Iusti Coniuges from the Time of Cicero to the Time of Ulpian* (Oxford: Clarendon, 1991).

12. Recent scholarship considers too extreme Joachim Jeremias's conclusions that Jesus' address to God as "Abba" was utterly unique, implying his self-consciousness as the singular "Son of God" (*The Prayers of Jesus* [Philadelphia: Fortress, 1967], pp. 11-65; cf. Mary Rose D'Angelo, "*Abba* and 'Father': Imperial Theology and the Jesus Traditions," *JBL* 111 [1992]: 611-30). As Paul and Mark testify, that address was sufficiently distinctive to have been remembered by the early church.

13. James F. Kay, "In Whose Name? Feminism and the Trinitarian Baptismal Formula," *ThT* 49 (1993): 530-31.

14. In a poignant memoir, Roberta C. Bondi describes the breakthrough that John 14:8-9

At least in the West, modernity is challenged by God's comprehensive authority in another way, scarcely imaginable by the ancients: the myth of the autonomous self. The Victorian bravado of William Ernest Henley — "I am the master of my fate, . . . the captain of my soul"[15] — appears harrowingly inane, even insane, this side of the twentieth century's bloodthirsty cruelty. Many in our culture act, nevertheless, as though they were self-created, competent to assume final responsibility for their individual and collective well-being. The Prayer exposes such belief as a lie, its performance as dangerous to ourselves and others. To pray to God as "Father" is to confess our radical contingency, our identity as children dependent on the One who has created us, chosen us for redemption, and promised never to forsake us.[16]

In Covenant with Christ

Human beings have an inbuilt pressure for companionship: "It is not good that the man should be alone; I will make for him a suitable companion" (Gen 2:18). One of the neglected yet obvious aspects of the Prayer known as "Our Father" is its *familial* tenor. "Father" does what no other available metaphor could accomplish: it identifies the one who prays as a sister or brother of Jesus, who appealed to his Father as the Son who does nothing of his own accord but only what he sees the Father doing (John 5:19; 11:41-42). Matthew (11:27) and Luke (10:22) recall a saying of Jesus that tightly forges all those linkages: "All things have been handed over to me by my Father; and no one knows the Son except the Father, and no one knows the Father except the Son and anyone to whom the Son chooses to reveal him." In the face of Christians' estrangement, for the sake of the gospel, from their blood-kin and religious homes (Mark 10:28; 13:9-13; John 9:18-23), Jesus assures his followers of their inseverable adoption into an extensive family network (Mark 10:29-31), over whom presides "my Father

---

proved for her praying to God: "Indeed, if [Jesus as portrayed in John] is who God the Father is, I discovered, to name God Father in prayer is . . . *to invoke God's fatherhood as a mighty corrective* against all the murderous images of *fallen* fatherhood that hold our hearts and persons, our churches and our world captive" (*Memories of God: Theological Reflections on a Life* [Nashville: Abingdon, 1995], p. 41, Bondi's emphasis). See also the same author's *A Place to Pray: Reflections on the Lord's Prayer* (Nashville: Abingdon, 1998).

15. "Invictus," in *The New Oxford Book of English Verse, 1250-1950*, ed. Helen Gardner (New York: Oxford University Press, 1972), p. 792.

16. In *The Promise of the Father: Jesus and God in the New Testament* (Louisville, Ky.: Westminster/John Knox, 2000), Marianne Meye Thompson underlines the irreducibly eschatological tenor of God's Fatherhood in Scripture.

and your Father" (John 20:17). That promise remains every bit as firm and valid for us — even at our most prodigal (Luke 15:11-32) — as for our ancestors, whose formation as Christians takes place in "the household of faith" (Gal 6:10). Thus, while indelibly personal, our covenant with God can never be privatist. That relationship pulls us into mutual accountability with the family of all Christians who in every time and place appeal to "*Our* Father" (Matt 6:9b) for "*our* daily bread," for release from "*our* debts" and *our* direction out of temptation (Matt 6:11-13; Luke 11:3-4). The Prayer's plural pronouns draw its pray-ers out of selfish individualism into an ever expanding generosity (compare Matt 25:31-46). "Prayer with us is public and common," as St. Cyprian reminded his listeners; "and when we pray we do not pray for one but for the whole people, because we the whole people are one."[17]

Help in Time of Need

Resonant among all three of the New Testament's "Abba! Father!" passages (Mark 14:32-42; Rom 8:12-39; Gal 4:1-20) is an important theme: an obedient child's spontaneous cry, uttered in desperate straits, to an adored parent of compassionate providence. That motif is rhymed in John's Gospel, where "[t]he more suffering enters the picture, the more Jesus is depicted . . . as the One who prays to the Father."[18] In *none* of these cases, we must carefully note, is God the cause of torment. To the contrary, God is the Father to whom tormented children flee for strength. The Epistle to the Hebrews offers, in effect, an interpretation of Gethsemane that bears on our training in prayer to "Our Father":

> In the days of his flesh, [Jesus] offered up prayers and supplications, with loud cries and tears, to the one who was able to save him from death, and he was heard because of his reverent submission. Although he was a Son, he learned obedience through what he suffered; and having been made perfect, he became the source of eternal salvation for all who obey him, having been designated by God a high priest according to the order of Melchizedek. (Heb 5:7-10; cf. Luke 22:39-46)

Notably, "the one who was able to save him from death" remains the addressee of Jesus' prayers even in the absence of rescue (so also Mark 14:36). Jesus remains a Son heard by his Father "because of his reverent submission" (so also John 10:14-18). Indestructible salvation, which trumps even the most hideous

17. *St. Cyprian on the Lord's Prayer*, p. 33.
18. Gottlob Schrenk, "*patēr, ktl*," *TDNT* 5 (1967): 1002. See John 11:41-42; 12:27 33; 17:1 26.

adversities "in the days of [our] flesh," is the property of all whose obedience to Christ corresponds with the obedience that Christ himself learned "through what he suffered." God is neither sadistic, impotent, nor indifferent. God is our refuge and strength, gracious and full of compassion (Ps 46:1; 86:15; 111:4; 112:4; 145:8; Jas 5:11). Yet the Father to whom we pray no more spares us than he spared his own Son, giving him up for us all so that he may also give us all things with him (Rom 8:32). The Prayer of our Lord disciplines us to appreciate that servants, indeed, are not greater than their master (John 13:16). If the Son — through whom creation was consummated, who bears the stamp of God's very being — grew in maturity from what he suffered, how much more shall we (Heb 1:2-3; 5:8-9; 12:3-11)?[19]

Summary

In its scriptural context, to pray to God as Father is to unite with Christ and his body, the church, in submitting ourselves to God's ultimate, trustworthy, merciful authority. That the metaphor of God's fatherhood has been perverted into an abusive patriarchy by stupid, insecure Christians can be neither denied nor justified. It is a sin of which the church should repent. That such perversion has stimulated others to find in Christianity "an abusive theology that glorifies suffering," predicated on "divine child abuse,"[20] is no less foolish or faithless. Of that, too, the church should repent. Common to both of these distortions is a sometimes unspoken anthropocentrism: the projection onto God of humanity's own puerility, injustice, and selfishness. The Gospels, however, are clear that Jesus' disciples are in no way to judge their "heavenly Father" (Matt 6:9b, 14; 7:21; Luke 11:13) by the conduct of earthly fathers, who are, in spite of all they give their children, evil (ponēroi: Matt 7:9-12; Luke 11:11-13). To the contrary: "Call no one your father on earth, for you have one Father — the one in heaven" (Matt 23:9; see also 8:21-22).[21] Even the first among Jesus'

19. Neville Ward: "For the Christian believer, in suffering, the struggle is not 'about' *enduring* the suffering but *serving God in it*. . . . We begin praying by thinking 'this is what I hope for in this situation and I trust God not to let me down'; we end by thinking 'this is how this situation looks in the light of God's purpose, this is what I must now do to serve God in it, and this is what I really want'" (*The Use of Praying*, pp. 77, 92).

20. See, for example, Joanne Carlson Browne and Rebecca Parker, "For God So Loved the World?" in *Christianity, Patriarchy, and Abuse: A Feminist Critique*, ed. Joanne Carlson Browne and Carole R. Bohn (New York: Pilgrim, 1989), p. 26.

21. A similar critique of patriarchy is suggested by Mark 10:29-30: Jesus promises that those who, for his sake and for the gospel, have left "house or brothers or sisters or mother or father or children or lands" will get back by a hundredfold all of them — *except for fathers*.

followers operates satanically when measuring God by human standards (Mark 8:33) or, as Paul would put it, proceeds *kata sarka,* "according to the flesh" (Rom 8:4-5, 12-13; 1 Cor 1:26; 2 Cor 5:16; 10:2; 11:18; Gal 5:17). Prayer to the heavenly Father enables Jesus' disciples, including earthly parents and children, to grow into the likeness and life of God (Eph 6:18; cf. 6:1-4). To devote proportionately more space to the address of the Prayer than to any of its ensuing petitions may seem odd, until we realize that the rest of the Prayer is its own commentary on what it means to pray, with wisdom and love, to God as our Father.

May Your Name Be Hallowed, Your Kingdom Come

The first and second petitions mark the clearest intersection between the Lord's Prayer and the great *Kaddish* prayer of the Jews:

> Exalted and hallowed be His great Name
> in the world which He created
> according to His will.
> May He establish His kingdom
> in your lifetime and in your days,
> and in the lifetime of the whole household of Israel,
> speedily and at a near time.
> And say: Amen.[22]

When praying the Lord's Prayer, it is critical for Christians to remember that their Lord was a devout Jew and that, when his followers pray as Jesus taught them, they sing an antiphon of praise with the synagogue. The Prayer perpetually reminds a predominantly Gentile church that Jesus is their one and only point of entrée to the gracious covenants, law, and promises of God to Israel (Rom 9:1-5; Eph 2:1-22).[23]

What is the "name" of God? What does it mean for God's name to be "hallowed"? Who hallows the name? In the Old Testament, one's name is no mere appellation but that one's peculiar essence (Gen 2:19; 32:28). Accordingly, when God causes his name to inhabit a place, it is a way of saying that God him-

---

22. Translated by Petuchowski in Petuchowski and Brocke, *The Lord's Prayer and Jewish Liturgy,* p. 37.

23. Invaluable in this regard is the essay by Asher Finkel, "The Prayer of Jesus in Matthew," in *Standing before God: Studies on Prayer in Scriptures and in Tradition,* ed. Asher Finkel and Lawrence Frizzell (New York: KTAV, 1981), pp. 131-69.

self dwells there (Deut 12:5-11). Similarly, in Ezekiel God promises to restore Israel from exile for his own sake, for the sake of God's name:

> Thus said the LORD GOD: Not for your sake will I act, O House of Israel, but for My holy name, which you have caused to be profaned among the nations to which you have come. I will sanctify My great name. . . . And the nations shall know that I am the LORD — declares the LORD GOD — when I manifest My holiness before their eyes through you. (Ezek 36:22-23, NJPS)

In the first instance, it is not Israel that hallows God's name; it is God who hallows — sets apart, consecrates, sanctifies — his own name. In other words, God demonstrates his singular, supreme divinity over all other gods and authorities by redeeming Israel. The ultimate purpose of that redemption is that all the nations may acknowledge God as God, the true Sovereign over all.

In Ezekiel, God's hallowing of the name purifies a profane Israel:

> I will sprinkle clean water upon you, and you shall be clean: I will cleanse you from all your uncleanness and fetishes. And I will give you a new heart and put a new spirit into you: I will remove the heart of stone from your body and give you a heart of flesh; and I will put My spirit into you. Thus I will cause you to follow My laws and faithfully to observe My rules. (Ezek 36:25-27, NJPS)

Leviticus also yokes God's election of Israel with its sanctification: "For I the LORD am He who brought you up from the land of Egypt to be your God: you shall be holy, for I am holy" (11:45).

Returning to the first petitions of the Prayer, we may reasonably surmise that it is God who, in the first instance, hallows his name, even as the Father is finally responsible for the establishment of God's kingdom and (in Matthew's form of the Prayer: 6:10bc) the universal execution of God's will (cf. Ps 135:6).[24] The three petitions in Matthew 6:9c-10 (hallow your name; let your kingdom come; may what you will, happen) resolve themselves into the two found in Luke 11:2b (hallow your name; let your kingdom come), which boil down to the first: May you, God, act in such a way that you may be truly acknowledged as God. As Paul puts it, with characteristic bite, "Though everyone is a liar, let God be proved true!" (Rom 3:4).

Here, plainly, is a point where our wants are stretched and disciplined. Like the Decalogue (Exod 20:2-17; Deut 5:6-21), the Prayer does not ignore hu-

---

24. These are examples of "divine passives": verbs conjugated in the passive voice as reverential surrogates for describing activities whose agent is God.

man need, but neither does it start there. It commences with God's holiness on God's own terms, God's sovereignty over every human desire or design. The Prayer, like the Law, begins with God.

It is not always so. Contemporary Christians who read the debates on prayer among classical and Hellenistic philosophers will find there many of the questions that arise in Sunday school.[25] If prayer is but a matter of asking and giving, how does God's relationship to us differ from that of a business transaction (Plato, *Euthyphro* 14de)? Assuming prayer's efficacy, what shall we ask for? What if we should unwittingly ask for something that would end up harming us (Aristotle, *Nicomachean Ethics* 5.14.1129b; Xenophon, *Memorabilia* 1.3.2; 4.2.36)? If we are governed by unchangeable Fate (or "a closed natural system," which amounts to the same thing), what difference could any prayer possibly make (Seneca, *Natural Questions* 2.35.1-2)? In essence, Epictetus's answer to that last question is "Go with the flow!" — rendered, to be sure, with genuine piety:

> Conduct me, Zeus, and thou, O Destiny,
> Wherever your decrees have fixed my lot.
> I follow cheerfully; and, did I not,
> Wicked and wretched, I must follow still.   (*Enchiridion* 51)[26]

The first petitions of the Lord's Prayer offer a different response that cuts the philosophers' knots, for the primary matter in Christian prayer is not what we may get out of it, nor how we may discover courage to live with "a theology that presents God as a great unblinking cosmic stare."[27] As we pray our Lord's Prayer, slowly, inevitably its words form us into people who realize that *our deepest need and most basic desire is for nothing but God himself and the grace to do God's will.* As aptly expressed in the Westminster Confession, humanity's chief end is to adore and enjoy God forever. Ultimately, our reason for being is to take our appointed place in the heavenly choir that encircles the throne and ceaselessly sings

> Holy, holy, holy is the Lord God Almighty
> Whose presence fills all the earth,
> Who was and is and is to come!

---

25. Some of those questions are considered by Oscar Cullmann in *Prayer in the New Testament*, trans. John Bowden, OBT (Minneapolis, Minn.: Fortress, 1995), pp. 119-42.

26. Epictetus, *The Enchiridion*, trans. Thomas W. Higginson, LLA (Indianapolis, Ind.: Bobbs-Merrill, 1948), p. 39.

27. Dallas Willard, *The Divine Conspiracy: Rediscovering Our Hidden Life in God* (San Francisco: HarperSanFrancisco, 1998), pp. 244-45.

That *sanctus,* a deliberate conflation of Isaiah 6:3 and Revelation 4:8, underlines the *eschatological* dimension in praise of God's holiness and prayers for the kingdom's coming.[28] The prayer of Epictetus faces backwards, "wherever [Destiny's] decrees have fixed my lot"; in contrast, the Prayer of Jesus leans into God's future, still in anguished labor for its deliverance (Rom 8:18-25). Following the lead of our Lord at its vanguard (Mark 1:14-15), we pray that God's sovereignty may extend from creation through redemption, from Alpha to Omega. Because God is truly God, our Father has been and even now is restoring all things to himself. We trust God's holy power to bring that restoration to fulfillment and ask that we may have a part in it — on the strength not of our merits but rather of God's purging our own profaneness. Through us who have received a Holy Spirit, a heart of flesh, and luster to reflect sacred brightness (Matt 5:16), God continues to reclaim this world in alignment with his holy will.

Keep Giving Us Each Day Our Daily Bread

The initial petitions of the Prayer have concentrated our mind on God's authority: parental, royal, and holy. The petition for bread opens a complementary series of requests for divine providence of nourishment, release, and protection. What has been to this point latent in the Prayer becomes patent: our intrinsic neediness. As creatures, we are wanting; we lack within ourselves the resources necessary for our sustenance. The Prayer of our Lord evokes those needs, draws to the surface our desires, and trains our gaze upon the Blessed One, the only One, who is capable of fulfilling them.

"Bread" bundled many connotations for the earliest Christians. In addition to simple food (Matt 7:9; Mark 6:8; Acts 20:11), it would have summoned up memories of manna, which the LORD rained from heaven upon Israel in the wilderness, every day for forty years (Exod 16:4-25). As Christians looked forward, bread would also be served at the heavenly table for the Messiah's end-time banquet (Luke 14:15; cf. Matt 8:11; Luke 22:29-30; Rev 7:13-17). In remembrance of Jesus' Last Supper with the Twelve, bread was a primary element in Christians' observance of the Lord's Supper (Mark 14:22-25; 1 Cor 11:23-26), whose celebration molded the ways they retold stories of Jesus' feeding of multitudes (Mark 6:30-44; 8:1-10). Manna, messianic feast, and eucharist all converge in John 6:

---

28. See Raymond E. Brown, "The Pater Noster as an Eschatological Prayer," in *New Testament Essays* (New York and Ramsey: Paulist, 1965), pp. 217-53.

My Father gives you the true bread from heaven. . . . I am the bread of life: the one who comes to me will by no means go hungry, and the one who believes in me will by no means ever thirst. . . . I am the living bread that came down from heaven. If anyone eats of this bread, he will live forever; and the bread that I shall give for the life of the world is my flesh. (John 6:32b, 35, 51)

For modern Christians whose imaginations have been blessedly stocked by Scripture and liturgy, it is practically impossible to screen out all but one of these connotations in praying the Prayer. Not only impossible, it is undesirable and theologically suspect. From Israel's ancient days in the Sinai until now, the people of God have experienced manifold hunger. Manna from heaven filled famished stomachs; loaves from the oven have been taken, broken, and thankfully offered as Christ's body to sustain the body of Christ. When we pray for bread, we are petitioning for nourishment in all forms, at kitchen table and communion table; we ask every day and all the time for "the sacrament of the present moment";[29] we beseech *God*, who is the Giver and, in Christ, the Gift (John 6:53-58).

To believe that, and to pray on that basis, may have been easier for the earliest Christians than for us. A culture that assumed one's next breath to be directly dependent on divine infusion (Job 34:14-15; Ps 104:29-30) was not timid to acknowledge its vulnerability.[30] With its nearly relentless confidence in self-reliance, its comparative wealth, and its almost pathological refusal to face death, North American culture does not well prepare its members to acknowledge insufficiency. The fact is, we are no less impoverished than Jesus' first followers, nor any less needy than the rest of our own world's population. Much of the time we manage to disguise that need from ourselves. That is why we chuckle, ruefully recognizing ourselves in television's Bart Simpson: asked by his parents to offer grace, the cartoon brat said, "God, we worked hard putting all this food on the table by ourselves. So thanks for nothing." Yet all our arrogance and possessions collapse when our reasons for getting up in the morning are stripped from us, when our families fall apart, when the lab tests come back positive.

If our Lord's Prayer did nothing but confront us with how desperate our need really is, in itself that would fill a gaping void in all of us. Worth pondering is George MacDonald's stark observation: "The one principle of hell is — I am my own!"[31] The way out of hell is to entrust ourselves, our loved ones, and

---

29. Jean Pierre de Caussade, *Abandonment: or, Absolute Surrender to Divine Providence,* trans. Ella McMahon (New York: Benziger Brothers, 1952 [1887]), pp. 92-94 passim.

30. Consult Hans Walter Wolff, *Anthropology of the Old Testament* (Philadelphia: Fortress, 1974), pp. 33-35.

31. C. S. Lewis, ed., *George MacDonald: An Anthology,* Touchstone Book (New York: Simon & Schuster, 1996), p. 88.

neighbors and enemies to God's safekeeping. Our wanting, and our want, cannot resist being disciplined by prayer, day in and out, that God will provide — and keep providing us — bread for the morrow (cf. Exod 16:12).[32]

And Forgive Us Our Sins,
for We Ourselves Forgive Everyone Indebted to Us

The ancients conventionally assumed that *paideia,* the shaping of character, required stringent discipline (Prov 3:11-12; Heb 12:5-11).[33] Forgiveness, its petition and pledge, is for many the Prayer at its toughest. Did ever a passage better exemplify Mark Twain's estimate, somewhere, that the passages in Scripture that troubled him most were not those he could not understand, but rather those that he did?

The incurring of debt and its forgiveness is as old as culture itself; its association with sin and salvation runs deep in Israelite soil (Isa 40:2; 55:6-7; Jer 31:34). Yet we shall stumble by confusing forgiveness with other things not implied by the metaphor. Forgetting, for instance, is no necessary consequence of forgiving; some malice or meanness we have suffered — or inflicted — in this life may be unforgettable and, in extreme cases, perhaps ought to be. Forgiveness is neither denying injury nor pretending no harm has been done. Injury denied is injury magnified; the efficacy of forgiveness depends on no-nonsense recognition of debt. Concocting excuses, clever or lame, for sin is no substitute for forgiveness: we may cut an offender slack by the yard without covering the offending inch that remains. Another mistake is to twist forgiveness into placing someone "on probation": the postponement of indignation until a later offense, or until our undissolved fury over the first can no longer be contained.

---

32. Praying today for "our bread *for the morrow*" *(ton arton hymōn ton epiousion)* is one of many ways that the phrase in Luke 11:3 may be interpreted. Other possibilities include "today's" bread, "essential" bread, "appropriate" bread, even "supernatural" bread. The exact translation is unattainable since we have not yet discovered the word *epiousios* in any ancient text not influenced by this passage. Much easier to spot is the verse's "iterative imperative": "Give, and keep giving [*didou*] to us."

33. Even at seventy-two, St. Augustine shuddered to remember his discipline as a child: "[T]he process of learning with its attendant punishment is so painful that children not infrequently prefer to endure punishments designed to compel them to learn, rather than to submit to the process of learning. In fact is there anyone who, faced with a choice between death and a second childhood, would not shrink in dread from the latter prospect and elect to die?" (*Concerning the City of God against the Pagans* [21.14], trans. Henry Bettenson [London: Penguin Books, 1972], p. 991). See also H. I. Marrou, *A History of Education in Antiquity* (London: Sheed and Ward, 1956), pp. 158-59, 272-73.

All these strategies fail the standard of forgiveness, which — in spirituality as in economics — is a deliberate decision to release someone indebted to us from compensation, however just that restitution may be. Forgiveness is finally a matter of mercy.[34]

Because our capacity for delusion seems infinite, we thank God for the forgiveness petition in the Prayer. So many are the lies in which we wrap ourselves — a guilt so thick that it feels impenetrable; egotism so woolly that we'd settle for the puny indifference of "getting a break" — that, apart from the Prayer's reminder, we might go frightening stretches of our lives oblivious that we are forgiven sinners — not one or the other but *both* sinners *and* forgiven. We learn that about ourselves, thus learning how critical it is that we repent, under the Prayer's direction. We cry to our *Father*, "whose property is always to have mercy";[35] we appeal to *our* Father, in the company of fellow Christians who, by the same Prayer, are learning to forgive *us* the abuse that we have heaped on *them*. There's the nub. In asking God for forgiveness, do we assume, following Pudd'nhead Wilson's Calendar, "Nothing so needs reforming as other people's habits"?[36] Or are we able to perceive what C. S. Lewis discerned: "To be a Christian means to forgive the inexcusable, because God has forgiven the inexcusable in you"[37] (thus, Matt 18:21-35; Luke 17:3-4)?

From the saints, the virtuosi of prayer, we learn most about forgiveness. Hear this, written by a Jewish prisoner in a German concentration camp:

> Peace to all men of evil will! Let there be an end to all vengeance, to all demands for punishment and retribution. . . . Crimes have surpassed all measure, they can no longer be grasped by human understanding. There are too many martyrs. . . . And so, weigh not their sufferings on the scales of thy justice, Lord, and lay not these sufferings to the torturors' charge to exact a terrible reckoning from them. Pay them back in a different way! Put down

---

34. In formulating this paragraph's thoughts, I have richly benefited from Marjorie J. Thompson's essay, "Moving toward Forgiveness," in *Weavings* 7/2 (1992): 16-26.

35. *The Book of Common Prayer, According to the Use of The Episcopal Church* (n.p.: Seabury, 1979), p. 337 (from the liturgy for "The Holy Eucharist: Rite I"). Thus, too, the modern Jewish prayerbook: "Forgive us, our Creator, when we have sinned; pardon us, our King, when we transgress; for You are a forgiving God" (*Gates of Prayer. The New Union Prayerbook: Weekdays, Sabbaths, and Festivals* [New York: Central Conference of American Rabbis, 1975], pp. 39, 63).

36. Mark Twain, *Mississippi Writings: The Adventure of Tom Sawyer, Life on the Mississippi, Adventures of Huckleberry Finn, Pudd'nhead Wilson* (New York: Library of America, 1982), p. 1005.

37. C. S. Lewis, "On Forgiveness," in his *The Weight of Glory and Other Essays*, Touchstone Book (New York: Simon & Schuster, 1996), p. 135.

in favour of the executioners, the informers, the traitors and all men of evil will, the courage, the spiritual strength of others, their humility, their lofty dignity, their constant inner striving and invincible hope, the smile that staunched their tears, their love, their ravaged broken hearts that remained steadfast and confident in the face of death itself, yes, even at moments of the utmost weakness. . . . Let all this, O Lord, be laid before thee for the forgiveness of sins, as a ransom for the triumph of righteousness; let the good and not the evil be taken into account! And may we remain in our enemies' memory not as their victims, not as a nightmare, not as haunting spectres, but as helpers in their striving to destroy the fury of their criminal passions. There is nothing more that we want of them. And when it is all over, grant us to live among men as men, and may peace come again to our poor earth — peace for men of goodwill and for all the others. . . .[38]

And Let Us Not Fall Victim to Temptation

"And when it is all over, . . . may peace come again." The one who offered that prayer intuited what many early Christians believed: that before this world is reclaimed by God's benevolent wholeness *(shalom)*, an intense, retaliatory outburst — "the messianic woes" or "great tribulation" — is predictable, overlapping with the present age (Matt 10:34-36 = Luke 12:49-53; Mark 13:5-13; 2 Thess 2:7; Rev 3:10; 7:9-17). Therefore, the last petition of the Prayer completes the eschatological arc described by earlier appeals for God's hallowing of his name, the kingdom's coming, and heavenly bread.[39] Severe attacks upon the faithful are neither punishments from God nor senseless, dumb luck. The Prayer trains us to locate such trials within the Vista–Visionary horizon of Christ's own death-and-life battle with "powers and principalities," before God's righteous peace can reassemble us among all things in everything (1 Cor 15:20-28; Eph 6:10-20).

Luke 11:4c can be translated in the way the Prayer is usually prayed: "And lead us not into temptation." Did Jesus assume that *God* is the agent of temptation? Not likely. None of the Evangelists regards temptation as "character-building": Jesus counsels his disciples to pray that they may not enter it (Matt 26:41; Mark 14:38; Luke 22:40, 46). Temptation is not divine but diabolical (Matt

---

38. Quoted by Metropolitan Anthony of Sourozh (Anthony Bloom), in *Living Prayer* (Springfield, Ill.: Templegate, 1966), pp. 17-18.

39. That end-time coloring is deepened by Matthew's addition of the prayer for deliverance from the Evil One (6:13b; also *Did.* 8.2) and by the doxology that scribes added to Matt 6:13 ("for yours is the kingdom, and the power, and the glory, forever; amen").

4:1 = Mark 1:13 = Luke 4:2; Luke 4:13; 1 Cor 7:5; 1 Thess 3:5). James (1:13) flatly denies that God tempts anyone. All this is in line with ancient Jewish prayers offered at morning and evening, some form of which Jesus himself probably prayed:

> Bring me not into the power of sin,
> And not into the power of guilt,
> And not into the power of temptation,
> And not into the power of anything shameful.   (*b. Ber.* 60b, twice)

For disciples no less than for Jesus, trials come in advance of the Ultimate Trial. We are not spared. We pray, though, that we may not be *victimized*, so overwhelmed by temptation that we lose faith and fall away (Luke 8:13). In that season, Paul was convinced, God understands and stands ready to succor: "God can be depended on not to let you be tried beyond your strength but, when temptation comes, to give you a way out of it so that you can withstand it" (1 Cor 10:13b, Goodspeed). To pray for strength to stand fast amid onslaught is a tacit vote of "no confidence" in our native heroism. Such prayer is offered by those who have learned to admit their human frailty, to wait for the One who alone is rock, deliverance, and haven (Ps 62:2, 7, 8), to trust that "behind the weird mask of pain is the face of Love."[40]

Authentically Christian prayer is answered in its asking (Mark 11:22-25; 1 John 5:13-15) and Trinitarian in its operation. If what we want is God, God is what we receive — because the Spirit of Holiness, moving among us, quickens our spirits to ask for God (Rom 8:14-17). That same Spirit dwelt in Christ the Son of God, who loved us and gave himself for us (Gal 2:20). Therein lies the extraordinary power of the Prayer for the formation of Christian character: inherently fertile, the Prayer accomplishes that which God purposes (cf. Isa 55:11). It is impossible for us to pray Jesus' Prayer and remain unreconstructed by the mind of Christ (cf. 1 Cor 2:16). By its praying, measure by measure, grace softens our self-centeredness, love enlarges our noblest capacities: trust in the Father, desire that God's name and all creation be sanctified, regarding our fellow creatures with merciful eyes. The Lord's Prayer is nothing other than Christ's own curriculum in the education of human wanting.

---

40. Ward, *The Use of Praying*, p. 105.

Character Formation or Character Transformation?
The Challenge of Cruciform Exegesis
for Character Ethics in Paul

Alexandra R. Brown

For reasons that are many and complicated, readings of Paul, and particularly of 1 Corinthians, have in the last decades tended to concentrate on his "worldly" side: his political identity within the Roman order, his use and, some argue, *abuse* of power, his kinship with other moral philosophers of his day, his pragmatism as a community organizer, his apostolic self-defense, and so on. Some of these studies, to be sure, work self-consciously from theological premises (the author's own or Paul's or both) that are nonetheless muted or blurred by other concerns; others offer avowedly nontheological readings that shed new and welcome light on matters that have been long shrouded in theological presupposition (our own or Paul's or both) and that, of course, carry their own ideological premises. Altogether, these recent studies of Paul reveal a remarkable spectrum of viewpoints and methods and a refreshing opening for debate about exactly what we are recovering and what we can or should do with the recovered material that comes of our exegetical efforts. Do we find in the Bible ethics whose recovery will help us form meaningful human community, or do we find there the very source of a Western hierarchical hegemony whose recovery is more threatening than helpful? I agree with Francis Watson that the introduction of new methodologies in exegesis, even anti-theological ones, cannot be fundamentally at odds with a biblical theology that values what he calls "the open text," for thus understood, the Bible remains, as he says, "the site of the proliferation of meanings that accords with its character as sacred text, constantly read and re-read without ever being exhausted."[1] Readings that are open both to the theological premises of the biblical texts and to a broader cultural

1. Francis Watson, ed., *The Open Text: New Directions for Biblical Study?* (London: SCM, 1993), pp. 3-4.

critique of those premises serve together to keep the text "open," free from any one controlling viewpoint.

Yet, when the inquiry into a text is inherently theological, as I assume the quest for a biblical character ethics to be, care must be taken to be clear (even if skeptically so) not only about one's own theological stance but also about the *text's* theological or ideological premises, and to take these seriously into account when discussing theories of character appropriate to that text. The tendency otherwise is to allow whatever conceptual frame is nearest to the culture of the reader or interpreter to become the overlay for understanding a given type of discourse, for example, the ethical discourse that is so central to 1 Corinthians. Because his pastoral advice has much in common with other ancient models of moral parenesis, and because the recovery of ancient moral philosophy is a principal theme in contemporary ethics, interpretations of the ethical sections of 1 Corinthians sometimes tend to emphasize formal aspects of its content in ways that mute or even subvert its theological foundations in the opening discourse on the cross. Such interpretations may inadvertently violate the integrity of Paul's ethical teachings by separating them from the theological perspective on which they are founded.

In this essay, I will argue that the opening theological argument of 1 Corinthians, Paul's discourse on the cross in chapters 1–2, is not incidental or merely introductory but fundamental to the argument on Christian practice and life in community that follows it. Moreover, I will argue that it is fundamental in a way that challenges what Paul takes to be the conventional morality in the ancient world by insisting upon a way of seeing and knowing that is powerfully at odds with that morality and with the conventional epistemology that lies behind it. Toward this end, for example, he draws provocatively upon the Isaiah text, "I will destroy the wisdom of the wise and the cleverness of the clever I will thwart" (1 Cor 1:19-20; Isa 29:14 [LXX]). To miss this connection is to fundamentally misapprehend Paul's thought on Christian character and moral formation for his own generation and, I will try to show, for succeeding generations. It is to fail, first of all, to recognize the rhetorical power of the first two chapters of the letter, where Paul presents the cross of Christ as nothing less than the apocalyptic turning point between worlds, including the worlds that define human character. Hence, it is to miss the signals given in those chapters for the ways in which, for Paul, the "Word of the Cross" actively seizes and reorients human *perception,* drawing believers out of what he calls "the wisdom of the world" (1:20) and into the transformed way of knowing and being that he defines as "having the mind of Christ" (2:16). The rest of the letter, including its overtly ethical sections, is grounded in the theological conviction that it is only by being cross-oriented, both in the sense of being transformed by the initial encounter with it and in the sense of being shaped by continual reflection upon it within the community (i.e., the task of Christian preaching and worship and, indeed, of all instances of discerning the Spirit), that one is drawn into genuinely Christian character.[2]

To be sure, the intervening history of the Christian church from Paul's day to ours has dramatically altered the circumstances under which we read this text so that, for example, its dichotomy of strength versus weakness (1:25) must now be read in light of later uses of the cross as a symbol of worldly, institutional power, uses that Paul could not have anticipated and would not have sanctioned. Nevertheless, the dichotomy between wisdom and *apocalypsis*, and especially the deep challenge to traditional epistemology embedded in the text, is in some ways timeless. Exegesis, especially when it is concerned with matters of character formation in contemporary Christianity, then, must take into account the changing cultural milieu in which the text is read without abandoning the context in which it was written. In what follows, I will first seek to show how Paul's apocalyptic theology of the cross addresses matters of character formation in his own context. In the second part of the essay, I will suggest through a reading of contemporary fiction one way Paul's theology of character might translate into modern idiom.

Paul's Apocalyptic Vision and Character Ethics

Key to the interpretation I will pursue here is that Paul is possessed of a distinctive and thorough-going apocalyptic worldview by which he sees in the advent of Christ and his faith, definitively revealed in his cross, the apocalyptic turning point between the ages. It is relatively easy to demonstrate that Paul draws heavily on the Jewish apocalyptic tradition to articulate his understanding of the Christ event and that he shapes the ideas and images of this tradition to fit the new circumstances revealed to him in Christ. The effects on human perception that follow this cosmic event are summarized in 2 Cor 5:16-17:

> From now on, therefore, we regard no one from a human point of view; even though we once knew Christ from a human point of view, we know

---

2. Victor Paul Furnish has recently called into question the view of some that Paul should be approached primarily as an apostle of "practical teachings," "first and foremost a man of practical religion." While Furnish does not suppose that Paul's letters yield anything approaching a systematic theology, he does find in the letters a "portrait of Paul as a *theologian* in that they disclose him engaged in serious reflection on Christian understandings of God and of human existence . . ." (*The Theology of the First Letter to the Corinthians* [Cambridge: Cambridge University Press, 1999], pp. xiv-xv).

him no longer in that way. So if anyone is in Christ, there is a new creation: everything old has passed away; see, everything has become new! (2 Cor 5:16-17)

That the event that marks the shift between "once" and "from now on" is the crucifixion itself is evidenced repeatedly in Paul's letters. In Galatians 2:19-20, Paul's crucifixion *with* Christ marks the turn from solitary "life in flesh" *(zō en sarki)* before the indwelling of Christ to life that is simultaneously "life in faith" *(en pistei zō tē tou huiou tou theou)*. In 3:1, he reminds the Galatians that his initial, liberating preaching among them was a "public portrayal of Christ crucified." In 6:14, the triple crucifixion of Christ, the world, and Paul is decisive evidence for the proclamation that *now* "neither circumcision nor uncircumcision is anything, but a new creation is everything" (6:15). Clearly, in Galatians, the cross is the turning point between the old world and the new creation.

In the Corinthian correspondence, as we see immediately in 1 Corinthians 1–2, the apocalyptic "once . . . but now" pattern continues to pivot on the cross, only now with more stress than in Galatians on the specifically *perceptual* shifts that accompany the transformation. In 1:17-18, it is the cross, rather than baptism by any apostle, that is the operative "power" in the simultaneous creation of comprehension and obduracy and, consequently, of salvation or destruction.[3] In 2:3, the Word of the Cross afflicts its utterer, like an apocalyptic visionary, with "fear and trembling." Throughout the discourse in 1:18–2:16, moreover, the cross is linked repeatedly and directly to shifts in human perception. Indeed, for Paul, the identification of the Son of God as the *crucified* one is the epistemological challenge that calls the foundations of all seeing and knowing into question. In this identification, too, we find the foundation of Paul's advice later in the letter to live in the world *as if* not in it, "for the form of this world is passing away" (7:31). Since the cross event, foundational structures of thought that once supported the universe, certainties that ordered social and moral life, are shattered by the image and reality of the power-filled scandal of the cross. When Paul insists a little later in this context that after the apocalypse of the cross "we no longer speak in words of human wisdom, but taught by the Spirit" (2:13), he calls upon, while at the same time calling into question, certain premises of the wisdom tradition in which human wisdom and divine Spirit

---

3. See Ulrich Wilckens, who combines the subjective and objective renderings of the dative nouns *sōzomenois* and *apollymenois* in 1:18: "The measure of their [the hearers'] distinction is therefore, on the one hand, *their* judgment about the *logos tou staurou*, but, on the other hand, the eschatological judgment of *God*, through which *God* will separate them as saved and lost" (*Weisheit und Torheit: Eine exegetische-religionsgeschictliche Untersuchung zu 1 Kor 1 und 2*, Beiträge zur historichen Theologie 26 [Tübingen: J. C. B. Mohr, 1959], p. 22 [emphasis mine]).

are closely identified in the figure of the sage who strives morally and intellectually toward the good as it is manifested in the cosmos. The ways in which Paul sees this wisdom epistemology in conflict with his own apocalyptic way of knowing bear directly, it seems to me, on how we understand his ethics.

The Word of the Cross in 1 Corinthians 1–2

A brief look at the flow of the argument in 1 Corinthians 1–2 reveals the striking association of the cross with perceptual transformation and the kinship of Paul's formulation with the thought world of apocalyptic. After he describes the context of community dissension that stimulates his writing, Paul begins his discourse on the Word of the Cross:

> For Christ did not send me to baptize but to proclaim the gospel, and not with eloquent wisdom, lest the cross of Christ be emptied. For the Word of the Cross is folly to those who are perishing, but to us who are being saved, it is the power of God. (1 Cor 1:17-18; author's translation)

The identification of the cross with divine power is the first step in a radical rearrangement of opposites in the discourse. At a later moment, as Paul reflects on divine election, new and surprising attributes define the constitution of the community itself:

> But God chose what is foolish in the world to shame the wise, God chose what is weak in the world to shame the strong, God chose what is low and despised in the world, even things that are not, to bring to nothing the things that are, so that no human being might boast in the presence of God. (1:28-29, RSV)

The capstone of the discourse on the cross comes at 2:16 as Paul brings the argument full circle to the opening call for unity in "the same mind":

> But who has known the mind of the Lord so as to instruct him? But we have the mind of Christ. (2:16, RSV)

The central themes of the discourse converge in this single image of transformed perception; the new creation revealed in the cross now comes to consciousness.

In the first step of the argument, the *logos tou staurou* (Word of the Cross) provokes scandal. For neither Greek nor Jew does death by crucifixion of God's

Son conform to the cosmic order that Logos, with its first-century synonyms (e.g., "reason," "wisdom," even "Law"), has come to signify. Surely for Paul, his own utterance of the term "logos" recalls the power-filled Word uttered by the prophets and apocalyptic visionaries of Israel: the Word of the Lord in Isaiah that goes out to accomplish God's purpose and will not return empty (Isa 55:1-11); Jeremiah's Word that "like a fire" breaks rocks in pieces (Jer 5:14; 23:29); the Word in 2 Esdras that created the world in the beginning and now prophesies its end (2 Esd 6:15, 43-44). Paul, however, has added a new apocalyptic dimension to the litany of the Word, defining this Word as a word with the power to break the cosmic order of opposites. It is obvious that Paul shatters conventional notions of wisdom and folly, weakness and power, in this discourse. What is not as obvious is the effect of this convention-shattering power of the cross on the moral order in Corinth or in successive Christian congregations who are informed by the Corinthian letter as Scripture.

The emphasis Paul places on the perceptual effects of the cross in 1 Corinthians reflects not only the apocalyptic character of his own vision (2 Cor 5:16-17; cf. Gal 1:11-12) but also the special vulnerability of the gospel in the Corinthian communal context to perceptual error. Indeed, Paul seems to locate the cause of the Corinthian fractiousness in an insufficient comprehension of the cross. In contrast, over against *their* divisive *gnosis* and cosmic spiritualism he reiterates his determination in 1 Corinthians 2:2 "to *know nothing* among [them] except Christ and him *crucified*." Moreover, in this section of the discourse (2:1-5), Paul turns to the language of paradigm and demonstration to make the point. To know Christ crucified is to *show* (demonstrate; 2:4) the power of the cross by one's own transformed "weakness, fear, and trembling," conditions that typically describe apocalyptic visionaries awed by their visions. In such paradoxical demonstration *(apodeixis)* of spirit *(pneuma)* and power *(dynamis)*, and not in persuasive words *(peithois sophias logois;* 2:4), the true *logos,* the true *kerygma,* is manifested. For Paul, the demonstration of weakness is no ordinary human weakness but rather the apocalyptic authentication of divine revelation.[4] The theme of power being manifested in his own weakness is a pervasive theme in Paul and comes into special prominence in 2 Corinthians, where his vocation to be a paradigm pointing to Christ is to "have this treasure in earthen vessels," showing "that transcendent power belongs to God not to us . . . always carrying in the body the death of Jesus so that the life of Jesus might also be manifested *(phanerōthē)* in our bodies" (2 Cor 4:7-10).

---

4. See also the resurrection narratives in the Synoptic Gospels where the Christ-event evokes the reaction of fear and trembling (Matt 28:4, 8; Mark 16:8; Luke 24:5, 37).

The Cross as the Apocalypse of Love

Somehow, then, the revelation of the cross alone that Paul knows and preaches among the Corinthians is meant also to transform them into manifestations of the same body of Christ, ending their fractious and competitive behavior. But what is it that is being revealed in the cross that can not only break down old ways of knowing but found the new community with its profound paradigm shifts? For Paul, to be sure, the cross has this power because it reveals something about God, namely, that God is love. Strangely, perhaps, Paul does not make this equation as explicit in 1 Corinthians as he does in Romans, where the power of the cross to reveal love is declared forthrightly: "But God shows his love toward us in that while we were yet sinners Christ died for us" (Rom 5:8, RSV). Yet the variations on this idea in 1 Corinthians are telling. In 2:9-10, for example, the priority of love to knowledge in the revelation of divine mystery is in view:

> But, as it is written, "What no eye has seen, nor ear heard, nor the human heart conceived, what God has prepared for those who love him," these things God has revealed to us through the Spirit. (1 Cor 2:9-10)

Elsewhere I have argued that the relative pronoun *ha* ("what" in 2:9a) is none other than that which is revealed in the preceding discourse, namely, the mystery of the cross of Christ.[5] Here the fuller dimensions of that revelation are given; the mystery of God revealed in the Word of the Cross is not, as the Corinthians might have it, what human faculties of knowing perceive. Not *gnosis* but *agapē* qualifies one for participation in God's mystery. With this qualification comes a jolting dislocation for those whose *gnosis,* or desire for it, has overshadowed or displaced the gift of love. The theme emerges again in the parenesis of 8:1-2, where Paul poses love as the alternative to the elitist boasting in knowledge that ravages this community:

> Now concerning food sacrificed to idols. . . . Knowledge puffs up but love builds up. Anyone who claims to know something does not yet have the necessary knowledge. But anyone who loves God is known by him. (8:1-2)

Again, the reference point for the play on *gnosis* and love is the perception-altering event of the cross. Here Paul goes a bit further than his apocalyptic

---

5. The perceptual terminology used in 1 Corinthians 1–2 is remarkably extensive. Elsewhere I have catalogued twenty-six terms relating to perception that occur between 1:5 and 2:16 (Alexandra R. Brown, *The Cross and Human Transformation: Paul's Apocalyptic Word in 1 Corinthians 1–2* [Minneapolis, Minn.: Fortress, 1995], pp. 119-22).

forebears when he intimates that in his vision something more than what he already knows to be true about God is revealed. It is not simply that what he knows is confirmed amid disconfirming events in history, as is often the case in apocalyptic literature. Rather, for him, the revelation given in the cross redefines both who God is and in what reality one participates by means of God's revelation. Loving God is the sign that one has correctly perceived what is revealed. He sees that, in light of the cross, the Corinthians, with all human beings, may cease to be oriented to God primarily in intellectual or merely moral ways. They are freed by participation in the love that is revealed, as Meister Eckhart put it, to "love with God's own love," and thus to be agents of love in the world. Most significantly, perhaps, for our purposes, is that the teaching Paul offers on participatory love is not left in speculative mists. The end of chapter 8 shows Paul once again turning to personal demonstration to make his point: "Therefore, if food is the cause of my brother's falling, I will never eat meat, lest I cause my brother to fall" (1 Cor 8:13).

1 Corinthians 13: Apostolic Paradigm for Reconciliation

The fullest development of revealed love in our letter, of course, is in the *agapē* discourse in chapter 13. Carl Holladay's argument that this chapter is best understood as a form of parenesis in which Paul presents himself as "a concrete paradigm" for the self-indulgent Corinthians is persuasive.[6] Although I would describe Paul's self-presentation not as a "paradigm of voluntary, responsible self-restraint" in the model of the Greco-Roman moralists, as Holladay does, but as an "apocalyptic paradigm of the irrepressible power of divine freedom to love," I am persuaded that chapter 13 *is* in the mode of apostolic paradigm. Functioning "not (as) a didactic explanation, but (as) a paradigmatic exhibition,"[7] it draws explicitly, as Holladay shows, on many elements of Paul's self-description elsewhere in the letter, and especially on the theme — so important across the entire Corinthian correspondence — of his apostolic afflictions. Holladay helps us further by pointing out Paul's declaration in 13:8 of the "absolute finality" of love: "Love never fails." The Corinthian values that have been percolating throughout the letter — knowledge, prophecy, charisms of all sorts

6. Carl R. Holladay, "1 Corinthians 13: Paul as Apostolic Paradigm," in *Greeks, Romans and Christians: Essays in Honor of Abraham J. Malherbe*, ed. David L. Balch, Everett Ferguson, and Wayne A. Meeks (Minneapolis, Minn.: Augsburg/Fortress, 1990), pp. 80-98.

7. See *hodon deiknymi* in 1 Cor 12:31. Holladay demonstrates that *deiknymi* ("show") is used here as in other parenetic contexts where a particular way of living is being promulgated (Holladay, "Apostolic Paradigm," p. 87).

— are at best penultimate and at worst distortions of divine reality; but love is ultimate. Moreover, Paul has this insight and lives this reality in a way he once did not. He, like the Corinthians, was once *nēpios,* an uninformed child, incapable of seeing what has now been revealed to him; but now he has entered into the realm of the coming perfection *(teleios),* already partially, "through a glass darkly," yet unmistakably revealed. To put away "childish things" is at the heart of the parenesis he offers, and so he enjoins the Corinthians themselves to live what Holladay calls (succumbing at last to apocalyptic vocabulary) "the essential eschatological reality . . . which reveals the interior of the Christ event that turned the ages . . . the only such reality to have invaded the now in any absolute sense."[8]

If love is for Paul the eschatological reality that turns the ages, its recognition in the cross is for him the key to perceptual, and thereby moral, transformation. But how do we move from the exegetical observation of this apocalyptic, love-generated worldview in Paul to its application in contemporary models of Christian character ethics?

Visionary Ethics and Pauline Apocalyptic

To see Christian existence as resulting from a divine invasion of conventional ways of knowing requires the revision of models of character ethics, ancient or modern, that rely heavily on individual free will, choice, reason, and the private and public cultivation of "virtues." Time and again in Paul's letters, where one expects the human being to be given a saving choice, some odd circumlocution occurs in the text to assure that it is God and not the human being who is in charge. In our text, for example, it is the Word of the Cross that divides the ones being saved from the perishing, not because the two groups freely choose their fate but because *God* has said, "I will destroy the wisdom of the wise and the cleverness of the clever I will thwart" (1 Cor 1:18-19). Moreover, in a typically Pauline move, the understanding comes first as gift, for as he says, "we have received the Spirit which is from God so that we might understand the gifts bestowed on us by God" (1 Cor 2:12). It is not that for Paul the will is uninvolved in living the cross-transformed life, but rather that it is of itself (that is to say, "autonomously") impotent apart from the gift revealed through the cross, which provides both the orientation and the impetus to act according to "what God has prepared for those who love him." Divine love, we might say, draws human love to itself. By analogy then, apostolic love, insofar as it makes present the love

---

8. Holladay, "Apostolic Paradigm," pp. 97-98.

of God, draws community love into practice and so love from member to member in the same manner.

Because Paul focuses on the revelation and perception of the cross as the basis for his ethical discourse in 1 Corinthians, ethical theories that rely more on vision than choice get closer to Paul's way of seeing the matter. When Stanley Hauerwas writes in an essay exploring Iris Murdoch's philosophical ethics that "what we can see and thus desire compels us. . . . [W]e are not free to change our moral self through choices,"[9] or that "the moral life is more than thinking clearly and making rational choices. . . . [I]t is a way of seeing the world," he is closer to the Pauline idiom than many ethical theorists of our time.[10] This is especially clear in 1 Corinthians, where the perception of the cross as divine power and love co-mingled for the liberation of the cosmos is the driving force behind the letter's several chapters of ethical discourse. Again, Hauerwas on Murdoch: "In the last analysis it is not so much by our effort that we are able to love as it is by the fact that reality itself lures us from our self-centeredness . . . the other forces us to attend to him as other."[11] For Paul, of course, the "reality itself" is none other than the divine love that creates the new world. Divine love, as we see in the line of argument extending from chapter 1 through chapter 13 of 1 Corinthians, both creates and elicits the (willing, yet not autonomous) response of human love.[12]

Although Hauerwas does not explicitly use apocalyptic language, his references in his "ethics of vision" to the clashing of worlds, the destruction of the old self and its illusions, and the creation of the new world now "under the mode of the divine" bear many resemblances to Paul's apocalyptic perspective. Setting himself in opposition to Murdoch's stark argument for the "virtue of humility" (i.e., that "one can stand the process of the destruction of illusion

9. Stanley Hauerwas, "The Significance of Vision: Toward an Aesthetic Ethic," in his *Vision and Virtue: Essays in Christian Reflection* (Notre Dame, Ind.: Fides Publishers, 1974), p. 33.

10. Hauerwas, "Significance of Vision," p. 36.

11. Hauerwas, "Significance of Vision," p. 44.

12. For Hans Urs von Balthasar, likewise, the beginning of theological reflection lies in the primordial human experience of the Thou, "the moment when the child first becomes aware of the smile of its mother and so becomes Geist. In that moment the child becomes an I. And with the experience of I is given also the experience of the world and the experience of the Thou. Thus the primary word is love and in this initial experience of love the child is given the glimpse that an infinite love is possible. In spite of subsequent disappointments and even the realization that the mother's love is finite [and *can* become contingent], the original intuition abides. And in that intuition lies the origin of the person's religious pilgrimage" (John O'Donnell, S.J., "Hans Urs von Balthasar: The Form of His Theology," in *Hans Urs von Balthasar: His Life and Work,* ed. David Schindler [San Francisco: Communio Books/Ignatius, 1991], p. 207 [with editorial insertion]).

without being oneself destroyed and that, moreover, there is a saving content in recognizing the meaninglessness of life"), Hauerwas insists that what makes the gospel "good news" is that we are told the truth about ourselves in such a way that the destruction brings healing and the assurance of a sustaining reality beyond us rather than merely the stark humility of nothingness.[13] Similarly, Paul in 1 Corinthians apparently intends for the Word of the Cross to have healing effect on the fractious congregation. The reconciling force of the Word he brings is apparent in the internal workings of the text itself. As the Word of the Cross enters into the discourse at 1:17, it causes a disruption of the conventions of language that both shape and reflect the old world of ordinary perception. In this capacity to disrupt perceptual structures, the Word has destructive force, but this is not its only force. The discourse, which reveals above all the liberating love of God, ends with the announcement in 2:16 of a newly created and communally shared perceptual organ, the "mind of Christ."

The capacity of the Word of the Cross to create anew in the rubble of destruction — a destruction and creation that are both reflected in and elicited by the vision of the cross itself — is also its character-transforming power. Not only does this Word point to a new world, but it draws human beings into that world where they now communally possess the "mind of Christ" (2:16). But is the action described here, like other instances of moral formation known to both the ancient and the modern world, taking place as those who hear it learn to imitate it, consciously choose it, and actively will to be formed by it? Or is it an action that takes place despite the human capacity to choose a program of moral formation, thus contradicting any general conception of ethics? It is of course an old question, as old at least as the rise of apocalyptic epistemology in ancient Israel.

The Word of the Cross and Character Ethics in Contemporary Fiction

Careful listening at this juncture will tell us that a great deal is at stake here for those who wish to derive an ethics of character from Paul. The language of mystery, vision, and apocalyptic perception seems to leave scant room for systematic reflection on moral formation, and this certainly has been one complaint leveled against apocalyptic hermeneutics from antiquity to the present:[14]

---

13. Hauerwas, "Significance of Vision," p. 47.

14. See the Midrash *Bava Metziah* 59b. For the rabbis behind this midrash, interpretation of the text, not reliance on miraculous intervention from heaven, is what God approves. In the

it is deterministic, stifles human freedom, and is flatly anti-responsible.[15] Or is there yet "a still more excellent way"? Paul is not concerned first of all to illuminate character ethics for later readers, but he does address in our hearing (and the basic problems of the letter remain far too audible) a congregation in what we might call character *crisis,* and we are given here an outline at least of a character-formation story in Corinth that finds analogues in more contemporary discourse. Our ethical and theological distance from this text may be not so much a cultural and temporal span — the sort that can be traversed by sound historical and philological study — as the result of our resistance — shared apparently by some among the Corinthians — to the good news that demands first the destruction of our conventional moral systems.[16]

To connect across that distance, there is help from the literary imagination. Often in my attempts to show how Pauline theology might inform contemporary life, especially as contemporary life is more and more estranged from the biblical idiom, I have turned for help to literary texts that are ordinarily classified as secular but that have remarkable capacity to bring to light theological themes and patterns that lie embedded in the texts of sacred tradition. I wish to claim slightly more here than the mere possibility of finding in some literature illuminating analogies for bringing Paul's distinctive perspective into view. That project, too, is one that I value as a teacher of biblical texts in, as it were, a foreign land (the modern secular university). What I see in certain literature is some-

---

midrash, Rabbi Joshua quotes Deuteronomy in a telling way (Burton Visotzky, trans., *Reading the Book: Making the Bible a Timeless Text* [New York: Doubleday, 1991], p. 55):

> The commandment I command you today is not hidden from you, nor is it too far from you. It's not in heaven that you might say, "Who can go up to heaven and bring it down and explain it so that we might do it?" . . . The word is very close to you, in your mouth and in your hearts. Do it.

15. This position is vigorously propounded by Johan Stohl, who argues that Paul's apocalyptic understanding, which he believes fuels what he calls "evangelical/Pentecostal threats to a free, creative, democratic society . . . undercuts humanistic freedom and responsibility" in ways that are not only "morally and psychologically inadequate for our age, but even dangerous." The moral consequences of the worldview in which one "surrenders" to the possession of Christ in order to be free are, according to Stohl, devastating. "If our acts are not our own," we "cannot be held morally responsible for them." We are "robbed of our self-respect as human beings" ("St. Paul and Moral Responsibility," *Free Inquiry* [Spring 1990]: 30-31).

16. "The most important discontinuities are not historical but moral and theological. That is, the most important discontinuities between Scripture and our contemporary settings are more likely found within us, specifically in our inability and unwillingness to provide and embody wise readings of the texts, than in gaps of historical time" (Stephen E. Fowl and L. Gregory Jones, *Reading in Communion: Scripture and Ethics in Christian Life* [Grand Rapids: Eerdmans, 1991], p. 63).

thing like what Nicholas Lash calls a "performance of Scripture," but in this case the performance occurs not directly in the community of Scripture's readers but indirectly, though no less paradigmatically, in the fictional narrative.[17] By such scriptural "performance" in literature we are enabled to see the impression Scripture makes when it is pressed into the story world. Scripture's capacity to mark character, like a seal in wax, is realized not directly in the paradigmatic lives of exemplars to be imitated in Christian practice but indirectly through the imagination of a whole narrative world that renders, not states, the mystery of its source and destiny. In the performance of some fiction, we are drawn into the rendering act in such a way that we are marked by it, not unlike the way in which hearers may be drawn into the transforming act of the Word of the Cross as it is rendered, and not merely said, in 1 Corinthians.

Flannery O'Connor and Christian Apocalyptic

I was introduced to the connection between Paul and the Southern Catholic writer Flannery O'Connor a number of years ago by J. Louis Martyn whose use of her story "Revelation" made Paul's apocalyptic come to life in extraordinary ways.[18] So I continued to read O'Connor and Paul side by side and to cast about for other ways of letting latter-day visionaries like O'Connor inform my theological work.[19] No writer yet has seemed so nearly on target for Paul. The more

17. Nicholas Lash, "Performing the Scriptures," in *Theology on the Way to Emmaus* (London: SCM, 1986), p. 42, as cited in Fowl and Jones, *Reading in Communion*, p. 62:

> Christian practice, as interpretive action, consists in the performance of texts which are construed as "rendering," bearing witness to, one whose words and deeds, discourse and suffering, "rendered" the truth of God in human history. The performance of the New Testament enacts the conviction that these texts are most appropriately read as the story of Jesus, the story of everyone else, and the story of God.

18. J. Louis Martyn, "From Paul to Flannery O'Connor with the Power of Grace," *Katallagete* 7/4 (Winter 1981): 10-17. Reprinted in revised form in J. Louis Martyn, *Theological Issues in the Letters of Paul* (Nashville: Abingdon, 1997), pp. 279-97. See Flannery O'Connor, "Revelation," in *The Complete Stories* (New York: Farrar, Straus and Giroux, 1946; reprinted 1980), pp. 488-509.

19. O'Connor herself noted explicitly the contribution of the novelist to theology ("Novelist and Believer," in *Mystery and Manners* [New York: Farrar, Straus and Giroux, 1957], p. 158):

> If the novelist is doing what as an artist he is bound to do, he will inevitably suggest that image of reality as it can be glimpsed in some aspect of the human situation. In this sense, art reveals, and the theologian has learned he can't ignore it. In many universities, you will find departments of theology vigorously courting departments of

deeply I read in his letters, and particularly in the Corinthian correspondence, the more I appreciate O'Connor's peculiar angle on the connection between the transforming moment — often initiated by some bizarre, grotesque, or invasive action — and the more mundane elements of character formation that surround the revelatory event. More precisely, the characteristic movement in her stories from prideful illusion to displacement and estrangement and finally to redemptive insight offers illuminating analogy to the workings of Paul's cross-based apocalyptic theology. Both apostle and writer also see the fullest implications of their respective theologies in communal contexts; neither has time or place for the solitary individual.

Perhaps it is the nearness of O'Connor's social context and its moral problems to our own that allows us to see so clearly by analogy in her stories the implications of Paul's apocalyptic theology for Christian moral life as a corporate reality. O'Connor lived in what can certainly be called "apocalyptic" times in the segregated South in the 1950s and 1960s. Her vision was inextricable from the experience of division, hatred, and violence that comes from individual and corporate pride: pride of place, pride of race, and pride of position, both social and moral, just as Paul's message arises time and again from the conflicts he encounters in the church about privilege and identity. That O'Connor continually sets her characters in view of their creation in the image of God and yet so often in grotesque perversion of or alienation from that identity also brings her into natural conversation, though probably not total agreement, with the Apostle who holds Christ to be the "second Adam" in whom "all shall be made alive" (1 Cor 15:22, KJV).

Authentic character ethics must, we are reminded by L. Gregory Jones and Stephen Fowl, take account of "socially-embodied traditions" that, for good or for ill, shape us.[20] O'Connor wrote to racially segregated audiences who were, to be sure, in earshot of the Bible, and who took their cues for morality from what they understood to be biblical cadences. She also understood the dictum of character ethicists from Aristotle on that "friendship is the very heart of the moral life," that "in and through friendship we become certain kinds of people rather than other kinds," and that imitation shapes character.[21] Yet she did not treat these ethical topics conventionally. In fact, we see everywhere in her stories caricatures of the standard *topoi* of moral education — the memora-

---

English. The theologian is interested specifically in the modern novel because there he sees reflected the man of our time, the unbeliever, who is nevertheless grappling in a desperate and usually honest way with intense problems of the spirit.

20. Fowl and Jones, *Reading in Communion*, p. 9.
21. Fowl and Jones, *Reading in Communion*, p. 68.

ble and self-righteous Mrs. Turpin in "Revelation" is a product of the sort of moral development that follows certain conventional patterns of vices and virtues.[22] The irony that she receives her revelatory and literal blow at the hand of Mary Grace, a mentally unstable Wellesley coed who hurls a book entitled "Human Development" directly at Mrs. Turpin, should not be missed. Mrs. Turpin's true character, the closest she will get to the *imago Dei* on this side of eternity, is most fully present at the end of the story in her vision in the purple streaked evening sky of "the whole vast hoard of souls rumbling toward heaven," the band of saints and sinners ascending, whites, blacks, freaks, and lunatics, all the people she had looked down on all her life, "going on ahead (of herself and her husband Claude) leaping and jumping like frogs." Then she sees dignified people like herself and Claude bringing up the rear, the only ones singing in tune, but now whose "shocked and altered faces show that *even their virtues are being burned away*."[23]

O'Connor understood that imitation is basic to character development and often in ways that are not to the good of her subjects in fiction. Her use of the grotesque is geared to reveal to her readers through radically nonimitable characters and events what she calls "our essential displacement," meaning, I think, our displacement from our true character in the *imago Dei*. In an essay entitled "The Grotesque in Southern Fiction," she defends her often misunderstood use of the freakish image or event to shake her reader into a redeeming recognition of the likeness in which he or she is really formed when the pretense of merely human imitation is stripped away.

> Whenever I am asked why Southern writers particularly have a penchant for writing about freaks, I say it is because we are still able to recognize one. To be able to recognize a freak you have to have some conception of the whole man, and in the South, the general conception of man is still, in the main, theological . . . I think it is safe to say that while the South is hardly Christ-centered, it is certainly Christ haunted. The Southerner who isn't convinced of it is very much afraid that he may have been formed in the image and likeness of God. Ghosts can be fierce and instructive. They cast strange shadows, particularly in our literature. In any case, it is when the freak can be sensed as a figure for our essential displacement that he attains some depth in literature.[24]

22. O'Connor, "Revelation," pp. 488-509.
23. O'Connor, "Revelation," p. 508 (italics added).
24. Flannery O'Connor, "The Grotesque in Southern Fiction," in *Mystery and Manners* (New York: Farrar, Straus and Giroux, 1957), pp. 44-45.

The necessity of such violent means to connect us to reality, one of the hallmarks of her fiction, is for her a natural extension of the cultural tradition in which she lives and writes. In an interview with another Southern Catholic writer, Walker Percy, reported by O'Connor, Percy is asked why there are so many good writers in the South, to which Percy replies, "Because we lost the War," meaning of course the Civil War. Losing the war, he intimated, meant among other things coming face to face with our fallenness, military and moral, but at the same time, through defeat, gaining a new and redeeming perspective of reality. O'Connor picks up this theme as she writes:

> We have gone into the modern world with an inburnt sense of human limitations and with a sense of mystery which could not have developed in our first state of innocence. . . . In the South we have, in however attenuated a form, a vision of Moses' face as he pulverized our idols.[25]

When we listen to what O'Connor is actually saying with her carefully selected vocabulary, we see that the human limitations of which she speaks are magnified in her story "The Artificial Nigger."[26] Here we are shown the powerful effects of Mr. Head's racism on his orphaned grandson, Nelson, as they journey on a "moral mission" to Atlanta where Mr. Head, described as a man whose "strong character . . . could be seen plainly in his features," intends to teach Nelson, a child with an "ancient" look, who the boy really is by his own (Head's) moral example.[27] Like other protagonists in O'Connor's stories, Head believes himself to be "in the know" on those matters about which his grandson needs educating and especially on worldly things pertaining to the city among which race is primary. On this last subject, Head claims special expertise that he constantly holds over the grandson who, to Head's irritation, knows and boasts of the fact that he was actually born in Atlanta and therefore has deep experience of all the city offers, even though he only lived there for a short time in infancy.[28] For various reasons, what Head thinks of as his "moral mission" goes awry and becomes in an unexpected and apocalyptic turn a chapter in his own, as well as the boy's, moral formation. Yet Head is at first successful in the character forming project *he*

---

25. Flannery O'Connor, "The Regional Writer," in *Mystery and Manners* (New York: Farrar, Straus and Giroux, 1957), p. 59.

26. Flannery O'Connor, "The Artificial Nigger," in *A Good Man Is Hard to Find and Other Stories* (New York: Harcourt, Brace & World, 1953), pp. 102-29.

27. O'Connor, "The Artificial Nigger," pp. 103, 105.

28. Compare the boasting in their Christian origins by the Corinthians depicted in 1 Cor 1:10-16.

has in mind. Moments after he and the boy Nelson board the train to Atlanta, a finely dressed dark-skinned man — obviously of a social class higher than Head's — walks the aisle toward and passes grandfather and his charge. Head grabs the boy's arm to get his attention and tightens his grip as the man passes. The educative moment has arrived. When the man has passed he loosens his grip and commences the lesson:

> "What was that?" [Head] asked.
>
> "A man," the boy said and gave him an indignant look as if he were tired of having his intelligence insulted.
>
> "What kind of man?" Mr. Head persisted, his voice expressionless.
>
> "A fat man," Nelson said. He was beginning to feel that he had better be cautious.
>
> "You don't know what kind?" Mr. Head said in a final tone.
>
> "An old man," the boy said and had a sudden foreboding that he was not going to enjoy the day.
>
> "That was a nigger," Mr. Head said and sat back. . . .
>
> "I'd of thought you'd know a nigger since you seen so many when you was in the city on your first visit," Mr. Head continued. "That's his first nigger," he said to the man across the aisle.
>
> The boy slid down into the seat. "You said they were black," he said in an angry voice. "You never said they were tan. How do you expect me to know anything when you don't tell me right?"
>
> "You're just ignorant is all," Mr. Head said and he got up and moved over in the vacant seat by the man across the aisle.[29]

A clearer account of a lesson in moral formation would be hard to find. Right down to the conscription of the larger community in the moral certainty he proclaims, Mr. Head is the model of one who passes on "socially embodied values" toward the end of character forming, and initially it works. O'Connor's insight into *how* it works is the sort of moment that marks her own moral genius. These are her words:

> Nelson turned backward again and looked where the Negro had disappeared. He felt that the Negro had walked down the aisle just to make a fool of him and he hated him with a raw fresh hate; and also, he understood now why his grandfather disliked them.[30]

29. O'Connor, "The Artificial Nigger," p. 110.
30. O'Connor, "The Artificial Nigger," pp. 110-11.

In these few words, which so aptly reveal the pathology of a newly formed racism, O'Connor gets us right to her point. Robert Coles has commented on the scene and its picture of a certain kind of character development:

> Now a youngster who has been fighting for a modicum of self-respect from the over-bearing Head is ready to surrender. Now, as today's psychology would put it, abstractly, an "identification with the aggressor" has taken place — at a high cost though: a boy's felt inadequacy and vulnerability had prompted him to find a scapegoat, one readily available in the "coffee-colored man" whom he originally had the innocent decency to describe as "a man," then as "a fat man," then as "an old man." Now, hustled and humiliated and cajoled and seduced by Head, the boy is ready to join the adult world; he is, as the contemporary language of psychology would have it, "socialized." Pain and self-doubt have become transmuted into hate — a grim kind of "education."[31]

Head and Nelson, now by Head's example, are headed way to the East of Eden, far from the *imago Dei*. Later when the train reaches Atlanta, the two walk through the streets, getting more and more lost in the city maze. At one point the boy, wishing to show himself wise, chides Mr. Head in words more true than he knows: "I don't believe you know where you're at." When they are both too tired to walk any further, Nelson sits down, back against a wall, and falls asleep. Mr. Head stays awake, and presently he sees another opportunity to educate this impudent child. He will hide in the alley and then make a loud racket, so that Nelson will awaken and find himself alone and disoriented. That should teach him to be grateful for the mentorship of his grandfather. The plan works all too well. At the crashing sound of boot against garbage can, Nelson leaps into the air and takes off running, block after block, helter-skelter until he plunges headlong into a woman carrying groceries and both sprawl to the pavement. When Head, by now himself in panic, comes upon the scene, Nelson runs to him, grabs him around the legs and holds on for dear life. The toppled woman and her friends meanwhile are calling for the police and shouting at Head that his boy is a "juve-nile delinquent."[32] Sensing the approach of policemen behind him, and working to disengage the terrified boy's fingernails from the backs of his legs, he lowers his head and utters distinctly, "This is not my boy. I never seen him before." O'Connor adds, "he felt Nelson's fingers fall out of his flesh." She continues,

31. Robert Coles, *The Secular Mind* (Princeton, N.J.: Princeton University Press, 1999), p. 138.

32. O'Connor, "The Artificial Nigger," p. 123.

The women dropped back, staring at him with horror, as if they were so repulsed by a man who would deny *his own image and likeness* that they could not bear to lay hands on him. Mr. Head walked on, through a space they silently cleared, and left Nelson behind. Ahead of him he saw nothing but a hollow tunnel that had once been the street.[33]

This is the signature O'Connor turning point, the revelatory blow that turns her characters toward redemption, but only through the sort of crisis that tears away all pretension. Nelson walks mechanically forward, making no effort to catch up, several yards behind Head. The two walk on, the elder feeling the full weight of his denial, his "disgrace," the younger neither feeling nor offering forgiveness. Head's feeble attempts to break the spell they have entered fail. To his "Let's us go get a Co' Cola somewheres," Nelson turns his back. A water spigot spotted by Head provides, he thinks, a last hope for forgiveness and reconciliation.

He had not had a drink of water since early morning but he felt he did not deserve it now. Then he thought that Nelson would be thirsty and they would both drink and be brought together. He squatted down and put his mouth to the nozzle and turned a cold stream of water into his throat. Then he called out in the high desperate voice, "Come on and getcher some water!"[34]

When Nelson rejects this final plea, Mr. Head feels that he himself has "drunk poison." He loses all hope. (Paul's familiar eucharistic words echo, "If anyone eats and drinks without discerning the body, he eats and drinks judgment upon himself" [1 Cor 11:29].) Meanwhile, the two have become hopelessly lost in the maze of unfamiliar streets. Head feels that if he sees a sewer entrance he will drop into it and be carried away. When at last he sees another human being he waves both hands above his head "like someone shipwrecked on a desert island."

"I'm lost!" he called, "I'm lost and can't find my way and me and this boy have got to catch this train and I can't find the station. Oh Gawd I'm lost! O hep me Gawd I'm lost!"[35]

The confession brings only temporary relief. The man knows how to direct them to the train. Head calls to Nelson, "We're going to get home!" But Nelson remains silent. "Home was nothing to him." The alienation overwhelms Head now.

33. O'Connor, "The Artificial Nigger," p. 123 (emphasis mine).
34. O'Connor, "The Artificial Nigger," p. 125.
35. O'Connor, "The Artificial Nigger," p. 126.

He felt he knew what time would be like without seasons and what heat would be like without light and what man would be like without salvation.[36]

But here, at the point of his deepest despair, something catches his attention. Just ahead he sees, "within reach of him, the plastic figure of a Negro sitting bent over on a low yellow brick fence that curved around a wide lawn."[37] By now Nelson is only a short distance behind, and he sees it too. Mr. Head, astonished, his voice in a whisper, breathes, "An artificial nigger!" Together they gaze, their first mutual act since before the awful betrayal. The figure they see was meant to look happy, "but the chipped eye and the angle he was cocked at gave him a wild look of misery instead." Now Nelson, too, in almost exactly the same voice, whispers the disorienting phrase, "An artificial nigger!" In an instant their identities undergo a strange merger. Head is like an "ancient child" and Nelson like a "miniature old man."[38] In the presence of this figure, their opposition to one another dissolves. O'Connor continues:

> They stood gazing at the artificial Negro as if they were faced with some great mystery . . . that brought them together in their common defeat. They could both feel it dissolving their differences like an action of mercy. Mr. Head had never known before what mercy felt like because he had been too good to deserve any, but he felt he knew now.[39]

What follows now bears some of the same features as Mrs. Turpin's revelation. The redemption is real, the transformation certain, but the human subjects remain. Head wants the boy to know that he is still wise; Nelson's eyes seem to implore him to explain "once and for all the mystery of existence." The cocksure moralizer has not simply evaporated from Head's character. He searches for something lofty to say, but what comes out is anything but lofty: "They ain't got enough real ones here. They got to have an artificial one."[40] No sooner does the action of mercy have its effect on Mr. Head than he is struggling again in what O'Connor calls elsewhere "territory held largely by the devil."[41] Yet something has changed fundamentally. As they arrive home, our attention is drawn to the

---

36. O'Connor, "The Artificial Nigger," p. 127.

37. O'Connor, "The Artificial Nigger," p. 127.

38. O'Connor, "The Artificial Nigger," p. 127.

39. O'Connor, "The Artificial Nigger," pp. 127-28.

40. O'Connor, "The Artificial Nigger," p. 128.

41. O'Connor writes, "I have found, from reading my own writing, that my subject in fiction is the action of grace in territory held largely by the devil" (Flannery O'Connor, "On Her Own Work," in *Mystery and Manners* [New York: Farrar, Straus and Giroux, 1957], p. 118).

light. The heavens are telling the glory of God. The moon is "restored to its full splendor"; it floods the scene with light. Even the sage grass points to the new-found truth; it "glitter[s] with a fresh *black* light."[42] Head is touched a second time by the action of mercy:

> [T]his time he knew there were no words in the world that could name it. He understood that it grew out of agony, which is not denied to any man and which is given in strange ways to children. He understood it was all a man could carry into death to give his maker and he suddenly burned with shame that he had so little of it to take with him. He stood appalled, judging himself with the thoroughness of God, while the action of mercy covered his pride like a flame and consumed it. . . . He realized that he was forgiven for sins from the beginning of time, when he had conceived in his own heart the sin of Adam, until the present, when he had denied poor Nelson. He saw that no sin was too monstrous for him to claim as his own, and since God loved in proportion as He forgave, he felt ready at that instant to enter Paradise.[43]

As the serpentine train slithers away from this new Eden, Nelson, too, brightens, and though he watches his grandfather with suspicion, he makes his own confession, "I'm glad I've went once, but I'll never go back again!"[44]

Conclusion

In O'Connor's stories, it nearly always takes an apocalyptic event to shake her characters out of their false identities, often characterized by varying kinds and degrees of moralism, so that they may be re-created in the image of God that is their true identity. Because the process is often destructive before it is redemptive, many readers prefer a gentler sort of story than O'Connor offers. Like the effects of Paul's Word of the Cross on the conventionally ordered mind, her stories often assault to heal. Here is an apocalyptic literature of engagement and seizing. It incarnates in its characters the reality O'Connor sees by her mystical eye, the reality of the real presence breaking in to ordinary life and the recovery of the image of God it initiates. In her oft-repeated expression "as if" — a phrase which for her signifies the distance between the concrete visible world and the mysterious invisible one — we sense the collaboration of our apocalyp-

---

42. O'Connor, "The Artificial Nigger," p. 128 (emphasis mine).
43. O'Connor, "The Artificial Nigger," pp. 128-29.
44. O'Connor, "The Artificial Nigger," p. 129.

tic Apostle. For he has said, "[L]et those who have dealings with the world live as if they had no dealings with it" (1 Cor 7:15).

These common elements of Paul's letters and O'Connor's work are the effects, I have argued, of a shared apocalyptic vision of the cross. For both writers, the encounter with the cross is at once a tearing down and a re-creating. This, for both, is a function not of the suffering alone but of the action of mercy "for us" that extends the liberating eschatological reality of *agapē* into the sin-encumbered world. Only by an encounter with the cross, revealed at the intersection of his own disgrace and despair with the startling plastic figure, does Head see at last that "God loves in proportion as God forgives." The sort of suffering that Head finally both sees in the figure and endures himself is what O'Connor identifies as true "compassion," which she defines in Pauline terms as "the sense of suffering with and for the creation in its subjection to vanity" (Rom 8:20-23). It "is a sense that implies the recognition of sin; this is suffering-with, but one which blunts no edges and makes no excuses."[45] While Paul is less focused on sins and forgiveness than upon bondage and liberation, he too finds divine love "suffering with and for" the creation, and he knows the power of this love to heal by cutting through pretense, vanity, and illusion. When he addresses the Corinthian congregation's division and strife, then, he makes haste to reiterate the Word of the Cross to draw them, by rendering the crucified, into loving, self-giving relations with one another. The clear message of 1 Corinthians, and of O'Connor's story too, is that this orientation toward the cross is the key to life together. In this cruciform existence,[46] the only norm is love, as the remainder of 1 Corinthians, and not least its paradigmatic 13th chapter, so richly demonstrates.

What can it mean, finally, for ethics to be situated in an apocalyptic worldview that radically distrusts human reason and imitative ethics as a means of passing on life-giving truth? Both Paul and his equally apocalyptically minded commentator O'Connor demand instead a powerful and transforming encounter with divine love that "blunts no edges and makes no excuses." This is a visionary tradition whose power now, as in antiquity, is to open a liberating space beyond "traditional boundaries of normative character"[47] so that the

---

45. O'Connor, "Novelist and Believer," pp. 165-66. I am grateful to Bill Oliver for pointing out this passage to me. See Bill Oliver, "Flannery O'Connor's Compassion," *The Flannery O'Connor Bulletin* 15 (Georgia College, 1986): 1.

46. A related point is made by Richard Hays when he discusses cruciform ethics: "the ethical norm is not a predetermined rule or set of rules for conduct; right conduct must be discerned on the basis of a christological paradigm with a view to the need of the community" (*The Moral Vision of the New Testament* [San Francisco: HarperSanFrancisco, 1996], p. 46).

47. William P. Brown (*Character in Crisis: A Fresh Approach to the Literature of the Old*

magnitude of divine love revealed in the cross might continually free human beings from the blinding egoism that so readily infects what is thought to be human moral progress. The vision of the freak, the misfit, the radically other will be first, as O'Connor put it, the measure of "our essential displacement,"[48] but then, as we enter into the mystery of the crucified, it will also be our transforming "action of grace."[49] For Paul and for O'Connor, what determines a distinctively Christian character is the impress of the crucified on one's own being. For Paul, this means not only living the paradigm of *agapē* (1 Corinthians 13), but "bearing the marks of the crucified" (2 Cor 4:10-12). He has, so to speak, the character of the crucified engraved on his body, "so that," as he says, "the life of Jesus may also be manifested" and "put to work" in the community of faith (2 Cor 4:11-12). Christian character is cruciform in both individual and communal life.[50]

With Paul and O'Connor, we have a come a long way from some of the definitions of character that mark modernity and postmodernity. This impress of the crucified is not, for example, the sort of character mark in view in John Stuart Mill's definition:

> A person whose desires and impulses are his *own* nature, as it has been developed and modified by his *own* culture, is said to have character. One

---

Testament [Grand Rapids: Eerdmans, 1996], p. 153) arrives at a similar conclusion to the one I draw here, although without the explicit reference to apocalyptic, when he finds that Job's character at the climax of the book

> exceeds the traditional boundaries of normative character . . . [when] Yahweh offers Job a new vision of cosmic community that explodes his restrictive world-view . . . [so that] now the wild creatures that Yahweh presents to Job become his new relatives and peers. Compelled to step back and look beyond his provincial world, Job discovers humility and awe before the grand sweep of creation as well as solidarity with it and thus finds a new responsibility toward all of existence.

48. O'Connor, "The Grotesque in Southern Fiction," p. 45.

49. O'Connor, "On Her Own Work," p. 118.

50. Also on "cruciform ethics," see Richard Hays, *Echoes of Scripture in the Letters of Paul* (New Haven, Conn.: Yale University Press, 1989), p. 191 (cited in Fowl and Jones, *Reading in Communion*, p. 64):

> No reading of Scripture can be legitimate, then, if it fails to shape the readers into a community that embodies the love of God as shown forth in Christ. . . . True interpretation of Scripture leads us into unqualified giving of our lives in service within the community whose vocation is to reenact the obedience of the Son of God who loved us and gave himself for us. Community in the likeness of Christ is cruciform; therefore, right interpretation must be cruciform.

whose desires and impulses are not his *own*, has no character, no more than a steam engine has character.[51]

Or still less is it what is envisioned in the definition given by R. S. Peters (in an entry in the *Oxford English Dictionary*, 2nd ed.): "Character traits are shown in the sorts of things a man can *decide* to do."[52]

For Paul as for O'Connor, character is manifested not in "the sorts of things one can decide to do" but in the mark left by the "action of mercy" on one who sees and now must live the vision of unconditional love. One last image from O'Connor makes the point vivid. In the story "Parker's Back," Obadiah Elihue Parker is prompted by an explosive, revelatory encounter between the tractor he was driving and a tree to have tattooed on his back the profile of a Byzantine Christ with "all-demanding" eyes, "eyes to be obeyed."[53] The revelation brings him to a crisis from which there is no return: "He knew that there had been a great change in his life, a leap forward into a worse unknown and that there was nothing he could do about it,"[54] nothing but to bear the image by which one is chosen and marked. As the story ends, Parker, who has been beaten with a broom by his pious but gnostic wife until welts form on his tattooed back, takes refuge, weeping as his wife looks on with "hardening eyes," beside a tree.[55] Now this tree, like the tree of his initial revelation, becomes a powerful cross-shaped symbol of death and life. With Parker's story, we are not far from Paul's image of gospel embodiment for the sake of the other in 2 Corinthians:

> We have this treasure in earthen vessels to show that the transcendent power belongs to God and not to us. We are afflicted in every way, but not crushed; perplexed, but not driven to despair; persecuted but not forsaken; struck down, but not destroyed; always carrying in the body the death of Jesus, so that the life of Jesus may also be manifested in our bodies. For while we live we are always being given up to death for Jesus' sake, so that the life of Jesus may be manifested in our mortal flesh. So death is at work in us, but life in you. (2 Cor 4:7-12)

51. John Stuart Mill, *On Liberty* (New York: Penguin Books, 1974), p. 124 (first published in London: John Parker and Son, West Strand, 1859) (emphasis mine).

52. R. S. Peters, "Moral Education and the Psychology of Character," *Philosophy* 37 (1962): 37 (emphasis mine), cited in the "character" entry in the *Oxford English Dictionary*, 2nd ed.

53. Flannery O'Connor, "Parker's Back," in *The Complete Stories* (New York: Farrar, Straus and Giroux, 1946; reprinted 1980), pp. 526, 527.

54. O'Connor, "Parker's Back," p. 521.

55. In her letters, O'Connor identifies Parker's wife as a heretic of what we might call the "gnostic" variety. "Sara Ruth," she writes, "was the heretic — the notion that you can worship in pure spirit" (Flannery O'Connor, *Collected Works* [New York: Library of America, 1988], p. 1218).

There is risk, of course, in leaving moral formation to revelation, and for this reason, as Paul knew well, the revelation that forms character and community must be mediated by and held accountable to the cross as the manifestation of God's liberating love. There is also risk in the handing down of moral precepts, especially Christian moral precepts, when they become detached from the revelation that first left its cruciform mark on the human being. Then the danger is that of reifying particular forms instead of allowing the dynamic process that Paul calls "hearing of faith," *akoēs pisteōs* (Gal 3:2). Ethics in this latter sense is controlled not by precept but by vision. Every ethical act hinges on who one perceives God to be and, especially, on the way in which one is both freed and claimed by the love revealed in the cross. There is room in this view, to be sure, for human effort. For Paul, the effort elicited by the hearing of faith is evident in his preaching and repreaching the gospel of the cross. For O'Connor, the effort called forth by Christian vision is the performance of the "action of grace," an action that for her is manifestly scriptural. For both apostle and writer, these efforts, like the action presented by the cross itself, are *for* the world and *for* the community with whom each groans for deliverance from bondage into the "glorious liberty of the children of God" (Rom 8:21). So each continues to do the hard work of proclaiming the gospel to audiences that are liable to be scandalized by it, scandalized even, as we see in both Galatians and the Corinthian correspondence, to the point of amnesia.

For Paul, finally, only when one knows God through the cross is one freed to hear and thus to obey God *in one's body,* that is, to act in love for the world. In 1 Corinthians, Paul shows himself again and again willing to abandon particular rules for the sake of building up the community in love, even Christ's rule against divorce if the unbelieving partner requests it, for the sake of peace. Because the theology of the cross determines his ethical stance at every juncture, he is driven to discern and align himself with dynamic and divine love in every historical relationship. Yet the impression made by the vision seems in this life vulnerable to miscomprehension or at least to fading comprehension. Christ crucified had been preached to the Galatians before they turned to circumcision; it had been preached to the Corinthians before their call to cruciform life evaporated into bodiless spiritual enthusiasm. For this reason, Paul continues, as he must, to preach Christ and him crucified. For this reason, too, O'Connor resorts again and again to the grotesque image or vision by which her characters are drawn to saving revelation. Both Paul and O'Connor see that love is, to use Carl Holladay's expression, the "essential eschatological reality . . . the only such reality to have invaded in any absolute sense."[56] But each in his or her own

---

56. Holladay, "Apostolic Paradigm," p. 97.

way sees too that as our vision from this earthly plane is incomplete — we see "through a glass darkly" — so too is Christian character in need of the renewed impression of the cross by which it is already formed. This renewal, we learn from Paul and from O'Connor, takes place in human communion, in life together where the impression of the cross is continually manifested in Word, sacrament, and deed. And so, says Paul, will all who look upon the Christ with unveiled faces be themselves, like Parker, transformed into icons of Christ, not all at once, but "from one degree of glory to another" (2 Cor 3:18).

Accepting Affliction:
Paul's Preaching on Suffering

L. Ann Jervis

Paul speaks often of suffering. He speaks about the suffering he caused the church prior to Christ's revelation to him,[1] as well as the suffering he himself experienced[2] and embraced.[3] Paul also speaks of the suffering of Christ[4] and of those who believe in Christ. This essay addresses the latter type of suffering, the suffering of believers. Its thesis is that Paul's initial preaching specified that acceptance of the gospel entails the acceptance of suffering; that is, Paul talked about suffering not only because it was happening either to himself or to his congregations but also, and perhaps primarily, because it was integral to the gospel message.[5]

The topic of Christian suffering in Paul's writings has been studied externally and internally, as it were. Some have investigated his references to Christian suffering historically by asking what made the new faith so offensive to Jews and pagans. Others have inquired about Paul's *Leidenstheologie*, his theol-

---

1. Gal 1:13; Phil 3:6.

2. 1 Cor 4:10-13; 2 Cor 11:23-28; 1 Thess 2:2. Not unrelatedly, Paul speaks openly about being imprisoned (Phil 1:7; Phlm 1).

3. Phil 3:10; Col 1:24.

4. Col 1:24; 2 Cor 1:5; Phil 2:6-8; 3:10, 18.

5. When Paul talks about suffering in his gospel message, he is *not* giving advice on how to handle the suffering that accompanies the human condition or encouraging an unhealthy embrace of suffering. Rather, Paul proclaims that beyond the difficulties and tragedies of life belief in the gospel entails a distinctive form of suffering. From indirect evidence, it should be noted that Paul appears to address *typical* human troubles in his preaching and that his gospel demonstrated, as did that of Jesus, God's desire and power to heal and restore. Paul's reference to signs and wonders (Rom 15:19), the power of the Spirit (1 Cor 2:4-5), and miracles (Gal 3:5) accompanying his preaching suggests that God worked through him to relieve human suffering (cf. Acts 14:8-10; 16:16-18, 25-26).

ogy of suffering. The method of this study is to combine these approaches by asking both about the circumstances in which Paul's talk of Christian suffering originated and about the meaning he attached to it. It will be argued that the primary *Sitz im Leben* for Paul's talk about the suffering of believers is his proclamation of the good news.

Many scholars recognize that Paul regarded suffering as necessary for believers in Christ[6] and that the certainty of affliction was fundamental to his gospel.[7] Yet because scholars have rarely entertained the possibility that Paul actually *preached* suffering,[8] his words on the matter have been typically regarded as part of his pastoral and theological *response* to the experience of suffering, as if to imply that Paul was merely reflecting on what had happened to himself and to his converts as a consequence of believing in Jesus Christ. To the contrary, Paul's words on suffering, I hope to demonstrate, were from the beginning integral to his gospel message. Paul spoke of Christian suffering not only after his hearers became believers but also before. Talk of Christian suffering belongs not only to Paul's catechizing[9] but primarily to his evangelizing activity.

Survey of Previous Discussions

The Historical Circumstances of Paul's References to Suffering

Since there is no evidence until Nero's rage in 64 c.e. for any persecution from the authorities, the tribulations to which Paul refers are understood to be unofficial forms of harassment,[10] largely instigated by Judean Jews against their kin-

---

6. E.g., E. Kamlah, "Wie beurteilt Paulus sein Leiden?" *ZNW* 54 (1963): 217-32, esp. p. 224; and C. H. Cosgrove, *The Cross and the Spirit: A Study in the Argument and Theology of Galatians* (Macon, Ga.: Mercer University Press, 1988), p. 186.

7. K. Plank, *Paul and the Irony of Affliction*, Semeia Studies (Atlanta: Scholars Press, 1987).

8. While several mention suffering as part of Paul's preaching, they do so without pausing to consider the significance of this. H. Ridderbos, for instance, says simply that Paul's preaching included "suffering, dying, and rising again with Christ" (*Paul and Jesus: Origin and General Character of Paul's Preaching of Christ*, trans. D. H. Freeman [Philadelphia: Presbyterian and Reformed Publishing Co., 1958], pp. 64-65). See also J. C. Hurd, "Concerning the Structure of 1 Thessalonians," in *The Earlier Letters of Paul — and Other Studies* (Frankfurt am Main: Peter Lang, 1998), p. 73; and R. F. Collins, *The Birth of the New Testament: The Origin and Development of the First Christian Generation* (New York: Crossroad, 1993), pp. 70-71.

9. See Cosgrove, *The Cross and the Spirit*, p. 185.

10. The earliest extant evidence for official involvement in persecution of Christians comes from the accounts of Pliny, Tacitus, and Suetonius (110-125 c.e.). E. Gibbon's perspective was that the earliest Christians were protected from persecution by virtue of appearing as Jews,

folk who had become believers in Jesus Christ.[11] Various reasons are proposed for why Jews may have persecuted Jewish Christians. Paul's gospel is understood to have caused offense to Jews because it disputed the validity of the law,[12] particularly in regards to the necessity for Gentiles to be circumcised.[13] Another aspect of disregard for the law would have been the affirmation that the Messiah was a crucified criminal.[14] There was also Jewish-Christian opposition to Paul and his converts.[15] The basis for information about this early period comes almost entirely from the NT, although some give credence to later records such as the account from John Malalas (ca. 490–ca. 575 C.E.) of Jewish agitation in Antioch in 48 C.E.[16] and information in Eusebius.

Paul's letters give evidence also of pagan harassment of Gentile believers (1 Thess 2:2, 14).[17] The conflict between pagan believers and their neighbors is understood to have arisen because the believers turned away from socially significant cultic practices.[18] C. S. de Vos argues that there would have been a dif-

---

whose religious practices were by and large tolerated by the Romans (*The Decline and Fall of the Roman Empire*, vol. 2 [London: Methuen & Co, 1896], p. 82). It was this seeming similarity that shortly became problematic for Christians in their pagan society: Christians became the targets of the same suspicion and resentment as the Jews (see P. Schäfer, *Judeophobia: Attitudes toward the Jews in the Ancient World* [Cambridge, Mass.: Harvard University Press, 1997], p. 55).

11. So G. E. M. de Ste. Croix, who relies heavily on Acts ("Why were the Early Christians Persecuted?" in *Studies in Ancient Society: Past and Present Series,* ed. M. I. Finley [London: Routledge and Kegan Paul, 1974], p. 212). See also E. P. Sanders, *Paul, the Law and the Jewish People* (Philadelphia: Fortress, 1983), p. 191; J. M. G. Barclay, *Jews in the Mediterranean Diaspora: From Alexander to Trajan (323 B.C.E.–117 C.E.)* (Edinburgh: T. & T. Clark, 1996), p. 395.

12. So W. Schmithals, *Paul and James* (London: SCM Press, 1965), p. 37.

13. So Sanders, *Paul, the Law and the Jewish People,* p. 191.

14. J. C. Beker, *Paul the Apostle: The Triumph of God in Life and Thought* (Philadelphia: Fortress, 1980), pp. 182-84.

15. On this, see G. Lüdemann, *Opposition to Paul in Jewish Christianity,* trans. M. E. Boring (Minneapolis, Minn.: Fortress, 1989). See also R. Jewett, who suggests that the escalation of Zealot activity in 48/49 C.E. extended to the diaspora where Jews who were not fully obeying the law (in which category those Jewish Christians who had communion with Gentile Christians fell) were punished by Jewish Christians who were "stimulated by Zealot pressure" ("The Agitators and the Galatian Congregation," *NTS* 17 [1970-71]: 205).

16. So R. Riesner, who interprets the account to indicate Jewish persecution of other Jewish believers in Jesus (*Paul's Early Period: Chronology, Mission Strategy, Theology,* trans. D. Stott [Grand Rapids: Eerdmans, 1998], p. 196).

17. See T. Still, who argues convincingly that other Gentiles are the source of the tribulation experienced by Gentile Thessalonians (*Conflict at Thessalonica: A Pauline Church and Its Neighbours,* JSNTSup 183 [Sheffield: JSOT Press, 1999], pp. 218-27); also A. J. Malherbe, *The Letters to the Thessalonians,* AB 32B (New York: Doubleday, 2000), p. 172.

18. So J. M. G. Barclay, "Conflict in Thessalonica," *CBQ* 55 (1993): 512-30; see also R. L. Fox, *Pagans and Christians* (New York: Knopf, 1989), p. 425.

ferent degree of conflict depending on whether a community's ethos was Greek or Roman, for Romans were generally more tolerant toward foreign ideas.[19]

What has not been entertained historically is the idea that the topic of suffering arose *in* Paul's introduction of the gospel;[20] that even prior to their having firsthand experience of the affliction connected with the gospel Paul told his potential converts that they would suffer. Such an idea does not presume that the initial gospel message was a call to be provocative, or that it was an invitation to martyrdom. Rather, this suggestion opens the possibility that, while Paul both responds pastorally to the suffering that comes to his converts as a result of their faith in Christ and reflects theologically on the significance of such suffering, his talk about Christian suffering came before his converts' afflictions. It *originated* not in response to his converts' experience of rejection and persecution,[21] but rather in Paul's initial preaching. Paul's kerygma not only included, then, the story of Jesus' preexistence, incarnation, cross, and resurrection,[22] but also gave notice that those who believed in Jesus would suffer.

The contention of this study is that Paul includes, for whatever reason, tribulation in his gospel message.[23] Those who heard his gospel were told that suffering came with belief. The historical circumstances that caused Paul to talk about suffering are, then, more complex than simply the afflictions visited on him or his converts by angry nonbelievers: Paul spoke of suffering at the point at which he talked about the gospel.

The Meaning of Suffering in Paul

Among those who study Paul's words on Christian suffering to understand what he meant by them, rather than the historical circumstances that occa-

---

19. C. S. de Vos, *Church and Community Conflicts: The Relationships of the Thessalonian, Corinthian and Philippian Churches with Their Wider Civic Communities*, SBLDS 168 (Atlanta: Scholars Press, 1999).

20. While some recognize that Paul understood and proclaimed that suffering and persecution were the norm (e.g., Barclay, *Jews in the Mediterranean Diaspora*, p. 393; Malherbe, *Thessalonians*, p. 194), they do not explicitly locate this in Paul's evangelistic message.

21. For example, de Vos suggests reading 1 Thessalonians as a letter of consolation, seeking to comfort and reassure his readers in the midst of their tribulations (*Church and Community Conflicts*, pp. 170-73).

22. So R. B. Hays, *The Faith of Jesus Christ: An Investigation of the Narrative Substructure of Gal 3:1–4:11*, SBLDS 56 (Chico, Calif.: Scholars Press, 1983), p. 256.

23. It may be that Paul's own experience of persecuting the church and being persecuted contributed in large measure to his understanding of the gospel.

sioned them, there lacks any serious pondering of whether Paul might have preached suffering at the point at which he introduced his gospel. Paul's words on suffering are regarded as *ad hoc,* arising out of a concern to find meaning or significance in the suffering he and his converts experience as a result of their faith in Christ.

There are three main ways or explanations by which Paul is understood to have given meaning to the suffering he and his converts experienced: an eschatological framework, unity with Christ, and the suffering of others for their faith.

Eschatological Framework

Those who claim that Paul approached the gospel with an eschatological framework suggest that he regarded the suffering of the church as a necessity[24] and accounted for the suffering of believers on the basis of his conviction that Jesus is the Messiah who has brought the promised salvation. Suffering is an essential part of the apocalyptic agenda. The end of this age necessitates the suffering of the righteous so that the new age can be born.[25]

Most helpful is the recognition that Paul changed traditional Jewish apocalyptic ideas about the significance of the suffering of the righteous in light of his belief that the new age was already present since Christ's crucifixion and resurrection.[26] Thus, while the suffering of believers relates to the messianic woes,[27] sufferers can do more than simply wait; because of Jesus' resurrection they can rejoice in their sufferings.[28] The suffering of believers results from the fact that the powers of sin and death are still at work, even though Christ

24. E.g., N. T. Wright, *The Epistles of Paul to the Colossians and to Philemon,* TNTC (Grand Rapids: Eerdmans, 1986), pp. 88-89; E. Güttgemanns, although focusing almost exclusively on Paul's suffering, states that Paul thought that the church shared in his apostolic suffering (*Der leidende Apostel und sein Herr. Studien zur paulinischen Christologie* [Göttingen: Vandenhoeck & Ruprecht, 1966], p. 327).

25. So J. Gundry Volf, *Paul and Perseverance: Staying In and Falling Away,* WUNT 2/37 (Tübingen: J. C. B. Mohr [Paul Siebeck], 1990), pp. 54, 61; C. Wolff, "Humility and Self-Denial in Jesus' Life and Message and in the Apostolic Existence of Paul," in *Paul and Jesus: Collected Essays,* ed. A. H. M. Wedderburn, JSNTSup 37 (Sheffield: JSOT Press, 1989), p. 157.

26. R. Tannehill, for instance, understands that the cross is an eschatological event for Paul; a new world has been created with the death and resurrection of Christ (p. 71). Nevertheless, "fullness of salvation is *not yet*" (*Dying and Rising with Christ: A Study in Pauline Theology* [Berlin: Töpelmann, 1967], pp. 71, 74).

27. So W. Schrage, "Leide, Kreuz und Eschaton: Die Peristasen Kataloge als Merkmale paulinischer Theologia Crucis und Eschatologie," *Evangelishe Theologie* 34 (1974): 165.

28. Wright, *Colossians and Philemon,* p. 88.

has ultimately defeated them.[29] Because of the cross, Christian suffering is a sign of God's power to redeem the world,[30] a sign of final salvation.[31] In fact, Paul may have thought suffering necessary to complete the end-time afflictions and hasten the coming of the End.[32]

United with Christ

Others claim that Paul considered suffering to be essential because of his conviction about having been united with Christ. A. Deissmann spoke of Paul's "mysticism of suffering." Believers are members of the Body of Christ and so share "mystically in all that that Body experienced and now experiences."[33] A. Schweitzer contended that Paul's "mystical doctrine" of union with Christ, combined with Paul's recognition that this time was not the time of the premessianic tribulations but the time of fulfillment (the messianic time), resulted in his focusing on believers' dying with Christ.[34] The suffering of believers is sharing in Christ's death. Others regard Paul's conviction that believers are united with Christ to mean that believers' afflictions are an extension both of Christ's suffering and of his death.[35] A version of the mystical view understands Paul's frame of reference as imitation. Believers actualize their union with Christ by imitating in this time the crucifixion. This means that, while they will know resurrection at the parousia, they must in the present endure suffering for the sake of the church.[36]

Another development of the mystical view understands Paul's frame of reference to be participation in Christ.[37] Paul thought that suffering was neces-

---

29. Tannehill, *Dying and Rising*, pp. 75-77, 127.

30. Beker, *Paul the Apostle*, p. 146.

31. Gundry Volf, *Paul and Perseverance*, p. 62; Tannehill, *Dying and Rising*, p. 129.

32. W. H. C. Frend, *Martyrdom and Persecution in the Early Church: A Study of a Conflict from the Maccabees to Donatus* (New York: New York University Press, 1967), p. 65.

33. A. Deissmann, *Paul: A Study in Social and Religious History*, trans. W. E. Wilson (New York: Harper & Row, 1957), p. 159. This view is shared by J. Lambrecht, "Paul and Suffering," in *God and Human Suffering*, ed. J. Lambrecht and R. F. Collins (Louvain: Peeters, 1990), pp. 47-68, esp. p. 55.

34. A. Schweitzer, *The Mysticism of Paul the Apostle*, trans. W. Montgomery (Baltimore: The Johns Hopkins University Press, 1998), p. 147.

35. E.g., G. W. H. Lampe, *Reconciliation in Christ* (London: Longmans, Green and Co., 1956), p. 61.

36. E. E. Ellis, "Christ Crucified," in *Prophecy and Hermeneutic in Early Christianity* (Tübingen: J. C. B. Mohr [Paul Siebeck], 1978), p. 78.

37. Although Hays does not discuss Paul's view of suffering, he makes a fine distinction between participation and standard understandings of the imitation of Christ. The latter refer

sary because he understood God's work in Christ to entail believers' participation in Christ.[38] It is not that Christian suffering comes from following Christ's example; rather, Christians suffer because they are *in* Christ.[39] It is as believers are in Christ that God's work is accomplished in them. A version of this view is that of J. H. Schütz, who claims that Paul thinks of himself and other Christians as standing "'in' the gospel."[40] Consequently, the whole of the believers' lives reflects the forces of the gospel, including "God's weakness which is God's power."[41]

Others take a crossover view. A. T. Hanson thinks that the root of Paul's theology is eschatology[42] and that Paul believed that Christians suffer in the Messiah, manifesting "the same pattern of life, and because Christ lives in them, [they] continue God's saving activity based on the once-for-all events of Jesus Christ's career."[43]

The Suffering of Others

The third approach to studying Paul's *Leidenstheologie* conceives of him making meaning of the suffering he and his converts were experiencing by seeing it in concert with his religious tradition. Paul makes sense of suffering by using images and understandings of other sufferers for God. For instance, K. T. Kleinknechts regards Paul as coming to understand Christian suffering in light of righteous sufferers in the OT.[44] J. Pobee thinks that Paul understood his and

---

to repetition of Christ's actions, whereas participation enables "those who are redeemed to complete [God's story in Jesus] by carrying out their own mandate, by becoming active subjects who fulfill God's original purpose by loving one another" (*The Faith of Jesus Christ*, p. 261). However, see on imitation, W. P. de Boer, who argues that it means "bringing to expression in one's life something he has witnessed in another" (*The Imitation of Paul: An Exegetical Study* [Kampen: Kok, 1962], p. 14).

38. B. M. Ahern, "The Fellowship of His Sufferings (Phil 3,1)," *CBQ* 22 (1960): 1-23, esp. p. 30; Cosgrove, *The Cross and the Spirit*, p. 189.

39. M. Hooker, "Interchange in Christ," *JTS* 22 (1971): 349-61.

40. J. H. Schütz, *Paul and the Anatomy of Apostolic Authority*, SNTSMS 6 (Cambridge: Cambridge University Press, 1975), p. 248.

41. Schütz, *Anatomy of Apostolic Authority*, p. 248.

42. A. T. Hanson, *The Paradox of the Cross in the Thought of St. Paul*, JSNTSup 17 (Sheffield: JSOT Press, 1987), p. 12.

43. Hanson, *The Paradox of the Cross*, p. 37. See also L. G. Bloomquist, *The Function of Suffering in Philippians*, JSNTSup 78 (Sheffield: JSOT Press, 1993).

44. K. T. Kleinknechts, *Der leidende Gerechtfertigte: Die alttestamentlich-jüdische Tradition vom 'leidenden Gerechten' und ihre Rezeption bei Paulus*, WUNT 2/13 (Tübingen: J. C. B. Mohr [Paul Siebeck], 1988).

his converts' sufferings in light of the Jewish-martyr theology that was prevalent in the Intertestamental period.[45]

What distinguishes my perspective on Paul's *Leidenstheologie* from those mentioned above is that I take into consideration the initial setting in which Paul spoke of suffering.

Suffering in Paul's Initial Preaching

The occasion for Paul's talk about suffering is not only found in his pastoral response to his converts and in his theological reflections, but first and foremost in his initial presentation of the gospel. In order to argue this, it must be demonstrated that Paul did not talk about suffering only *after* he or his congregations encountered suffering. Consequently, we will focus on Paul's first preaching, that is, on determining within the limitations imposed by the nature of the evidence whether Paul talked about suffering when he first preached the gospel to an audience. Before taking this step, we must first address certain preliminary matters: the meaning of preaching the gospel for Paul, the kind of suffering entailed by the gospel, and the identity of Paul's first gospel.

Preaching the Gospel

Paul's preaching of the gospel was not divorced from an enactment of the good news. The gospel was not simply presented orally; it was also demonstrated through the accompanying power of the Spirit (Gal 3:1-4; 1 Cor 2:1-5). Moreover, the good news was made visible through Paul's person when he was with his converts; Paul reminds the Philippians of what they saw in him when he was with them (1:30) and asks his converts to imitate him (1 Cor 4:16; Gal 4:12; Phil 3:17; 2 Thess 3:7). The preaching of the good news involved nurture and teaching (1 Cor 3:1-2; 1 Thess 2:7). Paul's first gospel is not, then, a speech with a certain content. Rather, it is Paul's presentation of the good news in "word and deed" (Rom 15:18). Paul understands himself as the servant of the gospel (Rom 15:16) and knows that when he has spoken or demonstrated the good news he has been used by Christ (15:18). Proclamation of the gospel is, then, accomplished in the power of the Holy Spirit (15:19) and demonstrated in Paul's behavior, which includes his teaching and nurture of believers.

45. J. Pobee, *Persecution and Martyrdom in the Theology of Paul*, JSNTSup 6 (Sheffield: JSOT Press, 1985).

We must also think not only of the preaching of the gospel but about the gospel itself. For Paul, the gospel is not a set of doctrines but God's power (Rom 1:16).[46] The gospel is God's (Rom 1:1; 2 Cor 11:7; 1 Thess 2:2, 8) and Christ's (Rom 1:9; 1 Cor 9:12; 2 Cor 9:13; 10:14; Gal 1:7; 1 Thess 3:2; 2 Thess 1:8),[47] and so obedience to God now involves serving the gospel, as epitomized by Paul (Rom 1:9; 15:16) and his co-workers (Phil 2:22). God calls through the gospel (2 Thess 2:14). Consequently, the gospel is to be obeyed (Rom 10:16; 2 Cor 9:13; 2 Thess 1:8).[48] The gospel is an entity in which one participates (1 Cor 9:23; Phil 1:5), stands (1 Cor 15:1),[49] labors (Phil 4:3), and serves (Phil 2:22; 1 Thess 3:2; Phlm 13). The gospel is a dynamic entity that enters the world (Col 1:5-6), coming in both word and spiritual power (1 Thess 1:5). Those who speak the gospel are called apart (Rom 1:1), for they are entrusted with an entity from God (1 Thess 2:4).

The gospel is a standard of action. Paul criticizes Cephas and Barnabas for not walking straight toward *(orthopodeō pros)* the truth of the gospel through their actions at Antioch (Gal 2:14). The goal of the gospel is to create one spirit and one mind (Phil 1:27). The gospel has the power to make a new community. Indeed, it has enabled Paul to become the Corinthians' father in Christ (1 Cor 4:15). The gospel provides a spirit for those who accept it (2 Cor 11:4). The gospel is a way of seeing (Gal 1:12) and provides a vision of God's likeness, the glory of Christ (2 Cor 4:3-4).[50] The gospel is not abstract but directed toward particular contexts (Gal 1:7), suggesting that its content is more dynamic than fixed.

Rather than a set of doctrines, the gospel is a transforming power; it is God's and Christ's way of entering and changing the human story. The gospel creates a new people with a new set of standards and hopes. If Paul talked about suffering when he preached the gospel, it would have been not as one in a series of theses to be believed, but rather as a way of life that came with obeying the gospel, as demonstrated by Paul himself.

---

46. Schütz notes that Paul does not use *pisteuein* in the sense of "believe" with *euangelion* as its object. Concerning 1 Cor 15:1-11, "the focus is less on the gospel as *what* they *believed* than on the gospel as *where* they *are*" (*Anatomy of Apostolic Authority,* pp. 41-42).

47. When Paul talks about "my gospel," he understands that his gospel is God's and Christ's (e.g., Rom 2:16) and that it is synonymous with preaching Christ (Rom 16:25).

48. Cf. Rom 1:5, where the obedience of faith is the proper response to the gospel.

49. Schütz notes something similar: "the gospel is an on-going entity 'in' which one can 'be' or 'stand'" (*Anatomy of Apostolic Authority,* p. 43).

50. I understand the three clauses as conveying parallel ideas.

What Kind of Suffering?

Another preliminary matter must be discussed before we may proceed: the kind of suffering entailed by the gospel. Our subsequent discussion will bring out the shades and nuances of the type of suffering Paul's gospel guaranteed converts, and so at this point it will suffice to determine what kind of suffering is *not* included in the gospel.

Christian suffering is not the result of being slaves of sin (Rom 6:12). The negative, life-destroying dispositions and actions that are the result of being in bondage to the power of sin are outlined at various places in Paul's letters (e.g., Rom 1:29-31; Gal 5:19-21). Such destructive attitudes and conduct create suffering for both individual and community. While believers still live in an age in which the power of sin is at work, they are not enslaved to it.[51] The affliction that is part of Paul's gospel is the affliction of being part of the solution to the problem of sin rather than the affliction that comes from being in bondage to it. This is not to say that believers do not still struggle with sin and its accompanying suffering, but that this is not the suffering that believers take on when they accept Paul's message.

Furthermore, Paul does not tie Christian suffering to disease or demons. While he himself knows physical suffering,[52] Paul seems to think that God's healing of such suffering is not inconsistent with the gospel, even though in his case God has chosen that he live with "a thorn in the flesh" (2 Cor 12:7). The believer may know spiritual and physical pain, but it is not this suffering that he speaks of as the affliction that comes with belief.

Paul's First Gospel

A final preliminary matter presents itself: the question of how to identify Paul's first gospel. What we have from Paul is, in most cases, not his original preaching but only epistolary responses to subsequent developments to his preaching. Nevertheless, we do have two forms of access to what Paul initially preached.

One kind of access is Paul's reference to what he said when he was first with his converts. Phrases such as that found in 1 Thessalonians 3:4 — "and when I was with you, I told you in advance" — introduce information about

---

51. Cf. J. C. Beker, "Suffering and Triumph in Paul's Letter to the Romans," *HBT* 7 (1985): 113.

52. See G. B. Caird's discussion on Paul's physical suffering in his *Principalities and Powers: A Study of Pauline Theology* (Oxford: Clarendon, 1956), pp. 75-76.

Paul's earliest preaching. A thorough treatment of our topic would demand that we use every reference to what Paul might have said in his evangelistic visits, but space allows investigation of only one letter. We will begin with Paul's earliest letter, 1 Thessalonians.[53]

The other form of access is found in the letter to the Romans. While the purpose of Romans is a controversial scholarly topic, the consensus is that Paul has not been to Rome, has not converted the audience he addresses in the letter, and, for whatever reasons, is seeking credibility with the Roman Christians through an epistolary performance of his convictions about the faith. Along with others, I argue that in Romans Paul is preaching his gospel for the first time to the church at Rome.[54] This is not to say that Romans is simply the essence of Paul's gospel. Like all of Paul's letters, Romans is situation specific,[55] as was Paul's first preaching to other groups of people.[56] One of the most obvious specifics about the situation to which Paul preaches in Rome is that his audience already knows the gospel. Paul's preaching in Romans was tailored so as to present his gospel as the same as, yet different from, the one the Roman believers accepted. While recognizing the particularity of the gospel Paul preaches in Romans, we must nonetheless take advantage of what this letter offers — an example of Paul's first address.

Now to the task at hand — investigating whether Paul's initial gospel included the promise of suffering, and, if it did, what he said about it.

1 Thessalonians

In 1 Thessalonians, Paul turns quickly to the matter of *thlipsis* (affliction). In the course of expressing gratitude to his converts for their faith, love, and hope, as well as reminiscing about their conversion (1:2-10), Paul reminds them that they received the word in much affliction, with joy from the Holy Spirit (1:6).

53. That 1 Thessalonians is Paul's first extant letter is standard scholarly opinion. See, e.g, G. Lüdemann, *Paul, Apostle to the Gentiles: Studies in Chronology,* trans. F. S. Jones (Philadelphia: Fortress, 1984).

54. L. A. Jervis, *The Purpose of Romans: A Comparative Letter Structure Investigation,* JSNTSup 55 (Sheffield: JSOT Press, 1991). See also, e.g., D. E. Aune, who designates Romans a speech of exhortation in which Paul attempts to convince the Roman Christians of the truth of his gospel ("Romans as a *Logos Protreptikos,*" in *The Romans Debate,* ed. K. P. Donfried [Peabody: Hendrickson, 1991], pp. 278-96).

55. See K. P. Donfried, "False Presuppositions in the Study of Romans," in *The Romans Debate,* ed. K. P. Donfried [Peabody: Hendrickson, 1991], pp. 102-25, esp. p. 103.

56. There is no reason to assume that Paul preached and enacted the gospel in the same way in every location he visited.

This is typically understood as a reference to some sort of social or even physical suffering inflicted on the Thessalonians as a result of believing Paul's gospel,[57] perhaps including the killing of some believers.[58] The line of scholarly inquiry extends to investigating the probable character of and reasons for such persecution,[59] sometimes using evidence also from Acts.[60] Paul's words are regarded as words of consolation.[61] The assumption in such interpretations is that Paul's talk about suffering is a pastoral response, that Paul here "interprets the persecutions which came on the Thessalonian church."[62] Consequently, attention is turned to Paul's "doctrine on suffering,"[63] so that, as mentioned above, Paul's talk about suffering is located in his catechesis. The suggestion of this study is that we entertain the idea that the letter's words on suffering are not merely reactive but reiterative. Paul's response to his converts' afflictions is not only to teach them how to handle suffering but to remind them that when they accepted the gospel they accepted also suffering.

There are two types of evidence in the letter indicating knowledge that Paul and the Thessalonians have shared since he first spoke the word of the gospel to them. The first kind of evidence is where Paul reminds his converts of what they know *(oidate)* and the second is where Paul expresses thanks-

---

57. E.g., Barclay, "Conflict in Thessalonica"; R. Jewett, *The Thessalonian Correspondence: Pauline Rhetoric and Millenarian Piety* (Philadelphia: Fortress, 1986), pp. 93-94. However, see A. Malherbe, who thinks *thlipsis* refers primarily to the psychological distress of the newly converted (*Paul and the Thessalonians* [Philadelphia: Fortress, 1987], pp. 46, 65), an opinion broadened somewhat in his commentary, where he understands it to refer to "social, intellectual, and religious dislocation with attendant confusion, bewilderment, dejection, and even despair" (*Thessalonians*, p. 128). Elsewhere, Malherbe argues that *thlipsis* refers to the "emotionally destabilizing experience" of conversion ("Conversion in Paul's Gospel," in *The Early Church in Its Context: Essays in Honor of Everett Ferguson*, ed. A. J. Malherbe et al. [Leiden: Brill, 1998], pp. 230-44, esp. pp. 233-36).

58. K. P. Donfried argues that the "dead in Christ" (4:16) were killed during the persecutions in Thessalonica ("The Cults of Thessalonica and the Thessalonian Correspondence," *NTS* 31 [1985]: 349-50).

59. E.g., J. M. G. Barclay, "Thessalonica and Corinth: Social Contrasts in Pauline Christianity," *JSNT* 47 (1992): 49-74; idem, "Conflict in Thessalonica"; Still, *Conflict at Thessalonica*, p. 217; de Vos, *Church and Community Conflicts*.

60. So F. F. Bruce, *1 and 2 Thessalonians*, WBC 45 (Waco, Tex.: Word Books, 1982), pp. xxii-xxvi.

61. de Vos, *Church and Community Conflicts*, p. 178; K. P. Donfried, "The Theology of 1 Thessalonians as Reflection of Its Purpose," in *To Touch the Text: Biblical Studies in Honor of Joseph A. Fitzmyer, S.J.*, ed. M. P. Horgan and P. J. Kobelski (New York: Crossroad, 1989), pp. 243-44.

62. Pobee, *Persecution and Martyrdom*, p. 109.

63. Ahern, "Fellowship of His Sufferings," p. 2.

giving *(eucharistoumen)*.[64] Throughout 1 Thessalonians, Paul states that his converts know something because of what he knows they heard or experienced when he was with them (1:5; 2:1, 2, 5, 11; 3:3; 4:2; 5:2).[65] When he tells them that they know *(oidate)*, he is not interpreting for them what they *should* know but rather affirming what they *have* known since accepting the gospel.[66] When Paul gives thanks for the Thessalonians, he makes reference not only to their continued growth but also to the circumstances of their reception of the gospel (1:5-6; 2:13-14).[67] We can take his expressions of gratitude regarding what happened on his evangelistic visit as evidence for what he knows that they know. While it is true that the letter "speaks incidentally of the founding and shaping of the community," yet is "devoted to its nurturing,"[68] the incidental references should be treated as significant in any investigation of Paul's initial preaching.

Paul says that the Thessalonians know what kind of people he and his co-workers were when they were with them, and how the Thessalonians became imitators of them and of the Lord (1:5-6). E. Castelli rightly notes that here (and at 2:14) Paul uses *mimētēs* with the indicative (in comparison to his use of the same word with the imperative in Phil 3:17; 1 Cor 4:16; 11:1); thus, Paul's words in

64. As J. Lambrecht says, "[T]hanksgiving essentially means remembering the past" ("Thanksgivings in 1 Thessalonians 1–3," in *The Thessalonian Correspondence*, ed. R. F. Collins [Leuven: Leuven University Press, 1990], p. 192).

65. Paul also uses *oidate* in 3:4b, where it refers to what they know now. Nevertheless, what they know now accords with what he had told them when he was with them.

66. So Hurd, "Concerning the Structure of 1 Thessalonians," p. 73; Bruce, *1 and 2 Thessalonians*, ad loc.; D. Juel, "1 Thessalonians," in *Galatians, Philippians, Philemon, 1 Thessalonians*, ACNT (Minneapolis, Minn.: Augsburg, 1985), p. 213. Jewett's opinion that the Thessalonians did not expect the persecutions they experienced and found them "inconsistent with their faith" (p. 94) is not consonant with his determination that, in a letter using demonstrative/epideictic rhetoric, Paul is *reminding* his readers of praiseworthy and blameworthy behavior (*The Thessalonian Correspondence*, p. 72).

67. Though many include only 1:2-5 in the first thanksgiving period (e.g., P. T. O'Brien, *Introductory Thanksgivings in the Letters of Paul*, NovTSup 49 [Leiden: Brill, 1977], pp. 146-53), I understand the first thanksgiving section to be 1:2-10 (see my *The Purpose of Romans*, pp. 91-94). I regard 2:13-16 also as a thanksgiving (cf. Hurd, "Concerning the Structure of 1 Thessalonians," p. 82) and accept the authenticity of 2:14-16. See particularly the arguments against B. A. Pearson, "1 Thessalonians 2:13-16: A Deutero-Pauline Interpolation," *HTR* 64 (1971): 79-94, in C. J. Schlueter, *Filling up the Measure: Polemical Hyperbole in 1 Thessalonians 2.14-16*, JSNTSup 98 (Sheffield: JSOT Press, 1994); and in K. P. Donfried, "Paul and Judaism: 1 Thessalonians 2:13-16 as a Test Case," *Int* 38 (1984): 242-53. For review of scholarship that argues for the letter's unity, see Riesner, *Paul's Early Period*, pp. 409-11.

68. E. Richard, *First and Second Thessalonians*, SP 11 (Collegeville, Minn.: Liturgical, 1995), p. 10.

1 Thessalonians 1:6 and 2:14 are historically descriptive.[69] When the Thessalonians received the word in much affliction with the Holy Spirit's joy (1:6), they did so in imitation of Paul, his co-workers, and the Lord. The imitation in which they engaged consisted not only in the fact of their reception of the word[70] but also in the circumstances of their receiving the word: in much affliction with joy of the Holy Spirit.[71]

Later in the letter, Paul reminds the Thessalonians that they know *(oidate)* the circumstances of his speaking the gospel to them: Paul and his co-workers came to them as sufferers who courageously spoke the word to the Thessalonians in the face of hostility (2:2).[72] Given the references to tribulation (1:6) and the fact that the Thessalonians appear actually to be suffering (3:3),[73] it is best to understand the hostility as some form of social harassment[74] rather than as the typical resistance to new and challenging ideas one might encounter in public debate.[75]

The Thessalonians, then, knew from the outset that suffering accompanied belief in the gospel. They knew this because the ones who spoke the good news to them had suffered as a consequence of the gospel; because they witnessed the circumstances of opposition that surrounded Paul and his co-workers speaking the gospel; because Paul told them when he was with them that suffering would come (3:3);[76] and because of what they themselves experi-

69. E. Castelli, *Imitating Paul: A Discourse of Power*, LCBI (Louisville, Ky.: Westminster/ John Knox, 1991), p. 92.

70. So W. Michaelis, *"mimeomai," TDNT* 4:670.

71. I see no reason to make a syntactical distinction between the first prepositional phrase *(en thlipsei pollē)* and the second *(meta charas pneumatos hagiou)*, as does Richard, who makes the first an expression of attendant circumstances ("despite all the attendant difficulty") and the second an adverbial complement to the participle (the community "accepted the word . . . with joy inspired by the Holy Spirit") (*Thessalonians*, p. 67).

72. I accept V. C. Pfitzner's understanding that Paul's reference to *pollō agōni* in 2:2 is to "the opposition which accompanied the preaching of Paul and his companions" (*Paul and the Agon Motif: Traditional Athletic Imagery in the Pauline Literature* [Leiden: Brill, 1967], p. 113).

73. Taking *tautais* to refer to the Thessalonians' tribulations, as well as Paul's (so E. Best, *The First and Second Epistles to the Thessalonians*, HNTC [New York: Harper & Row, 1972], p. 135).

74. So Barclay, "Social Contrasts in Pauline Christianity," p. 53.

75. R. F. Collins reduces the nature of the hostility to that which occurs in the course of a public debating contest, such as among moral philosophers (*The Birth of the New Testament*, p. 39). See also Richard, *Thessalonians*, p. 79.

76. Paul's choice of *keimai* in 3:3, a word that literally means to recline or lie down and metaphorically means set apart or destined, suggests that Paul thinks (and communicated to his potential converts) that believers in the gospel are set apart to be in affliction. John Calvin captures part of this nuance: "Paul teaches that there is no reason why believers should feel dis-

enced by becoming imitators of Paul and the Lord in receiving the word with suffering accompanied by the Holy Spirit's joy.[77]

Paul's expressions of gratitude also indicate what his converts know that they know. In the context of the first thanksgiving (1:2-10), Paul, as noted above, affirms that the Thessalonians knew what kind of people he and his co-workers were when they were with them, and that the Thessalonians' reception of the word made them imitators of Paul, his co-workers, and the Lord. Later Paul gives thanks again, this time filling out what he had said the first time he expressed gratitude.[78] When the Thessalonians received the word, they did so truly, recognizing it as the word of God, with the result that they became imitators of the churches of God in Judea and so suffered from their compatriots (2:13-14).[79]

Taking these passages as Paul's affirmations of what the Thessalonians know, Paul's talk about the Thessalonians' afflictions is not only a pastoral response designed to put a meaningful face on the unfortunate result of believing his gospel, or Paul's theological reflection on the significance of suffering, but mainly a reminder of what he had said and been in person. Paul's response to the Thessalonians' tribulations is to remind them of what they know from their first introduction to the gospel: acceptance of the gospel entails the acceptance of suffering.[80]

We then see in Paul's talk about suffering in 1 Thessalonians a representation of what he demonstrated and declared when he was with them: to believe the good news is also to accept affliction; those who believe truly become sufferers. Those who receive the word spoken by Paul as the word of God become like other true believers, like the "churches of God in Judea in Christ Jesus,"

---

mayed on occasion of persecutions, as though it were a thing that was new and unusual, inasmuch as this is our condition, which the Lord has assigned to us . . . we are appointed to it" (*Commentaries on the Epistles to the Philippians, Colossians and Thessalonians,* trans. J. Pringle [Grand Rapids: Eerdmans, 1948], p. 266).

77. Note the important observation of de Boer, cited earlier, that the character of imitation is "a bringing to expression in their own lives of what they had seen and detected outside themselves" (*The Imitation of Paul,* p. 124).

78. Tannehill also regards 2:13-16 as a second epistolary thanksgiving and argues that the first thanksgiving (in which he includes 1:2-5) and the second "are parallel in thought and must be interpreted together" (*Dying and Rising,* p. 100). See also Donfried, who argues that 1:6-9a and 2:13-16 must be interpreted together ("The Theology of 1 Thessalonians," p. 250).

79. See Still's argument that *sumphuletoi* is best understood as the converts' fellow Gentiles (*Conflict at Thessalonica,* pp. 218-26).

80. Cf. de Boer, who thinks that Paul made "a plain and open declaration in his preaching to non-Christians that Christianity brings one into affliction. It had been a part of his message repeatedly (cf. the imperfect tense)" (*The Imitation of Paul,* p. 115, n. 71).

who suffered from their compatriots (2:14). The Thessalonians' current suffering is confirmation that the word of God is at work among them. Their suffering is also confirmation that they are modeling themselves after Jesus, consequently setting an example for other Christians (1:7).

What is the nature of this affliction? With 2:14-16 as part of the letter, we can say that affliction involves being rejected by compatriots, and that it is akin to what Jesus experienced. While some downplay[81] or dismiss[82] the idea, the most straightforward reading of 1:6 is that being afflicted is part and parcel of the *imitatio Christi*.[83] Although Paul does not flesh out the nature of Jesus' afflictions as they relate to the believers', one can conjecture with some warrant.

The word *thlipsis* can mean a woman's birth pangs.[84] That Paul refers later in the letter to his converts as children (*tekna;* 2:7) suggests that Paul evokes the image of birth in connection with receiving the word in 1:6. While it is something of a mangled metaphor — those who are born are at the same time those who experience the tribulation of giving birth[85] — it does convey the significance of what they have received (given birth to) and who they have become (like children). By recognizing the eschatological fervor of Paul's initial gospel (e.g., 1:9-10) and the use of birthing imagery in apocalyptic texts that refer to the coming of the new age,[86] we might understand Paul's reference to Jesus' tribulation (1:6) as resonating with the idea of birthing the new age. Those who now are chosen (1:4; 5:9) imitate him in these afflictions, for while the gospel holds out promises of eternal life (4:14-17; 5:10) and escape from the wrath to come (1:10; 5:9), it also assures believers that they must wait (1:10). In the period of waiting for the new age, believers know the tribulations of birthing.

81. Michaelis, *"mimeomai,"* p. 670.

82. Richard, *Thessalonians,* pp. 67-68.

83. Cf. Bruce, *Thessalonians,* p. 16. Note also that this interpretation is corroborated by other passages in Paul (e.g., Phil 3:10).

84. E.g., John 16:21, where here too tribulation is accompanied by joy.

85. B. R. Gaventa notes something similar in regards to 1 Thess 2:7, where she reads Paul comparing himself and his co-workers both to babes *(nēpioi)* and the nurse who cares for them. She suggests that Paul's use of a mixed metaphor at 2:7 is caused by his struggle to talk about two aspects of being an apostle: childlikeness and responsible caregiving ("Apostles as Babes and Nurses in 1 Thessalonians 2:7," in *Faith and History: Essays in Honor of Paul W. Meyer,* ed. J. T. Carroll, C. H. Cosgrove, and E. E. Johnson [Atlanta: Scholars Press, 1990], pp. 204, 206).

86. We see this in 1 Thess 5:3. Cf. *1 Enoch* 62:4 and *4 Ezra* 4:42. We also see in the prophets the birthing metaphor used to speak of the day of the LORD (Mic 4:10; Isa 13:6, 8; Jer 6:24). See B. R. Gaventa, "The Maternity of Paul: An Exegetical Study of Galatians 4:19," in *The Conversation Continues: Studies in Paul and John,* ed. R. T. Forna and B. R. Gaventa (Nashville: Abingdon, 1990), p. 193.

When Paul preached about tribulation to potential converts, it was not merely the practical advice of a wise father — if you take this road you may get hurt.[87] Nor is it simply what we find in Jewish apocalyptic literature's pastoral response to people who currently are experiencing, or who have in the past experienced, suffering,[88] assuring them of God's ultimate control (*1 Enoch* 108; *4 Ezra* 6:1-6; *2 Bar* 73-76). Paul told his hearers that the salvation offered in the gospel *required* those who accepted it to be afflicted.

Though Paul's words do not allow us to know exactly how he might have explained the reason for or nature of the tribulation that accompanied belief, the fact that he says his converts' tribulation imitates the Lord's is suggestive. He may have described the reason for tribulation in the context of the birthing of a new age. Just as Jesus suffered in order to be raised and, thereby, open the way for the resurrection of believers (1 Thess 4:14-17) and protect them from the coming wrath, so believers in Jesus suffer as they wait for the day of the Lord. If this is how Paul thought, then clearly he regarded the suffering of believers as constructive and distinctive. The suffering of believers comes because they are participants in the process of God's bringing about the completion of this age, even though their role is different from that of Jesus. It should be noted, then, that the suffering received by those who receive the gospel is suffering specific to believers.[89]

87. Donfried writes regarding 3:4 that "[Paul] and his co-workers *warned*" the Thessalonians about persecution ("The Theology of 1 Thessalonians," p. 251 [italics mine]).

88. J. J. Collins wisely notes that the social setting of apocalyptic does not always indicate a situation in which suffering is actually present; it may also reflect, as in the case of *4 Ezra* and *2* and *3 Baruch*, the aftermath of a crisis (*The Apocalyptic Imagination: An Introduction to the Jewish Matrix of Christianity* [New York: Crossroad, 1984], p. 29).

89. C. B. Cousar puts it well: "The sufferings mentioned by Paul are the result of deliberate, voluntary discipleship and are not just 'bad things' that happen" (*A Theology of the Cross: The Death of Jesus in the Pauline Letters*, OBT 24 [Minneapolis, Minn.: Fortress, 1990], pp. 170-71). Richard misses this point in his argument against those who recognize that Paul saw suffering as essential to faith in Christ when he writes: "suffering and pain are certainly constituents of the human condition, but it is ludicrous to maintain, on the basis of a text such as 1 Thess 3:3, that persecution is either normal for or the destiny of Christians. Also it is clear that Paul often exhorts his audience to see its sufferings and misfortunes in light of Jesus' death, but this is more central to his paraenesis and soteriology than to his anthropology" (*Thessalonians*, p. 148). The tribulation to which Paul refers is not normal "suffering and pain"; he is not discussing anthropology. Rather, Paul is talking about the tribulation that is part of the good news.

Romans

There are several references to Christian suffering in Romans. It is difficult to know whether the references to suffering are Paul's effort to teach the Romans something essential to his gospel, or whether they confirm an understanding the Romans already have. If Paul were wishing to teach as something new that Christian suffering was part of belief, he would almost certainly have placed more emphasis on it and given more extended teaching than he does. At the same time, if he were merely confirming what the Romans believed, we might expect to see reference to it in those places where he affirms a shared faith (e.g., in 1:1-4).[90] As will be seen, the evidence suggests that the gospel the Romans believed included the expectation of tribulation and that Paul both affirms this understanding and focuses it in a particular way.

Paul speaks first of *thlipsis* in chapter 5. This is a pivotal point in the letter. Since 1:16, Paul has been in conversation with interlocutors, but at 4:23 he again turns to his audience, directly including them as he explains and explores the nature of the gospel.[91] The reference to tribulation in chapter 5 is at once casual and formal. Paul does not strain over introducing suffering as if it were a foreign idea, but neither does he treat it nonchalantly. He speaks of suffering both as if his audience were aware of its relevance to the gospel and as if he has something important to which he wishes to call their attention.

In 5:3, Paul writes, *kauchōmetha en tais thlipsesin* ("let us boast in the af-

90. Most accept that these verses contain material that Paul inherited. See commentaries and H. Schlier, "Zu Röm 1,3f," in *Neues Testament und Geschichte*, ed. H. Baltensweiler and B. Reicke (Zürich: Theologischer Verlag, 1972), pp. 207-18. Yet see J. M. Scott, who argues against the theory that this is a pre-Pauline creed (*Adoption as Sons of God: An Exegetical Investigation into the Background of YIOTHESIA in the Pauline Corpus*, WUNT 2/48 [Tübingen: J. C. B. Mohr (Paul Siebeck), 1992], pp. 223-44). When the passage's pre-Pauline character is accepted, its function is generally understood to be that of resonating with what the Roman audience believes (Jervis, *The Purpose of Romans*, pp. 75, 85; S. Brown, *The Origins of Christianity: A Historical Introduction to the New Testament* [Oxford: Oxford University Press, 1984], p. 127).

91. S. K. Stowers argues convincingly that 4:23–5:11 is significant as a section that "draws conclusions from the preceding argument and provides hortatory application for the letter's audience" and observes that for the first time since the letter opening Paul directly addresses his audience (*A Rereading of Romans: Justice, Jews, and Gentiles* [New Haven, Conn.: Yale University Press, 1994], pp. 247, 249). Others determine different parameters and provide other reasons for regarding this as a pivotal section. For example, R. N. Elliott thinks the pivotal section is 5:1-21, noting the connections between what precedes ch. 5 and 5:1-11 and the connections between what follows 5:12-21 and the content of that passage (*The Rhetoric of Romans: Argumentative Constraint and Strategy and Paul's "Dialogue with Judaism"* [Ann Arbor, Mich.: U.M.I., 1990], pp. 233-34).

flictions").[92] This exhortation follows the previous one in 5:2 ("let us boast in the hope of the glory of God"). Whereas earlier in the letter boasting was disparaged because it concerned a false confidence about the divine-human relationship (2:17, 23; 3:27; 4:2), now Paul encourages boasting that is focused on the hope of God's glory and present tribulations. The experience of tribulations as part of faith is not at issue. He is addressing suffering not as a "problem" for his audience but rather as an accepted part of Christian existence.[93] Paul's contribution to the Romans' faith is to encourage a particular approach to Christian suffering.

Again in 8:18 (where he uses not *thlipsis* but the word *pathēma*), Paul talks about the fact of suffering without awkwardness and the need to defend the fact of suffering in believers' lives (cf. 1 Pet 3:14-17). This present time involves sufferings, at once for the creation and for believers (Rom 8:23). There is a similarity between 8:23 and 5:3 both of thought and of linguistic expression *(ou monon de, alla kai)*. In both verses, Paul affirms that believers are those who suffer.

Christian suffering is not merely "the troubles of this world"[94] that all know but a particular affliction that comes from being in Christ.[95] Paul underscores for his Roman audience that suffering is an intrinsic feature of being justified (5:1-3), and it is best to understand him talking about a kind of suffering that is peculiar to believers.

In Paul's view, believers must face *thlipsis, stenochōria* (distress), and *diōgmos* (persecution), along with famine, nakedness, peril, or sword (8:35). We should think of these various distresses as different manifestations of Christian suffering.[96] Whereas evildoers will experience *thlipsis* and *stenochōria* at the end

92. *Kauchōmetha* should probably be translated in the subjunctive in vv. 2-3, but this depends on whether an indicative or subjunctive is chosen for *exō* in v. 1. Given the weight of textual evidence favoring the latter choice for *exō* and the occurrence of *kauchaomai* in v. 11 as a participle having imperatival force (so Stowers, *Rereading of Romans*, p. 249), the best option is to translate the phrase with the hortatory subjunctive.

93. Contrast Pelagius, who sees Paul addressing suffering as a problem and seeking to assure his readers that suffering is the price to be paid for gaining the reward of eternal life and saving one from everlasting suffering (*Pelagius's Commentary on St. Paul's Epistle to the Romans*, trans. T. de Bruyn [Oxford: Clarendon, 1993], on 5:3).

94. J. A. Fitzmyer, *Romans*, AB 33 (New York: Doubleday, 1992), p. 397.

95. J. D. G. Dunn writes regarding 8:18 that since Paul "nowhere else thinks of his Christian suffering without seeing it also as a sharing in the sufferings of Christ . . . the thought is probably implied here" (*Romans 1–8*, WBC 38a [Dallas, Tex.: Word Books, 1988], p. 468). Cf. E. Käsemann who writes in regard to 5:3 that "*thlipsis* is the end-time affliction which comes on the Christian as a follower of the messiah Jesus" (*Commentary on Romans*, trans. G. W. Bromiley [Grand Rapids: Eerdmans, 1980], p. 134).

96. The list of troubles in 8:35 should be understood in context with 8:38 and, thus, seen

(2:9), believers experience such things now. Paul does not seek to explain present suffering or counsel merely to endure it. He rather exhorts boasting of it, as if a full embrace of Christian suffering were a positive and necessary aspect of faith (cf. 2 Cor 12:9-10). As elsewhere, Paul places suffering in the context of hope (8:23) and certainty about a relationship with God (5:1; 8:35).

While many interpret the type of suffering mentioned in 8:35 as part of the messianic woes,[97] Paul does not make this explicit. He may well here, as in 1 Thessalonians, think of the suffering of believers as part of birthing the new age. It is important to note, however, that his use of the apocalyptic narrative outline is not the same as that of his Jewish kinfolk. In the service of encouraging hope and endurance (see *4 Ezra* 6:25-28), apocalyptic literature has a strong focus on the vindication of the righteous, typically speaking of current suffering as a problematic but necessary part of the conclusion of this age and the bringing in of the new one (e.g., *4 Ezra* 5:1-13). Paul, however, expresses no awkwardness about suffering, no need to justify God to his audience in the face of suffering. He speaks of Christian suffering not as a predicament but as a cause for boasting. Unlike his fellow Jews, Paul does not use the apocalyptic framework in service of theodicy (cf. Dan 7:17-27; *1 Enoch* 102-5). His reference to suffering is not, as Byrne suggests, occasioned by the question "how to reckon with suffering within the framework of religious belief."[98] Paul states that suffering is part of this time for believers, and that, more than enduring it, believers are to boast in it. Christian suffering is not simply to be endured until it can be vindicated.

In 8:36, Paul quotes almost verbatim from the LXX of Psalm 44:22 (43:22 [LXX]) in order to describe the situation of believers. Commentators typically claim that Paul incorporates this psalm to assure his audience that God's people have always known tribulation,[99] that tribulations are a sign of God's care,[100] or that God foresaw the present suffering of believers.[101] Yet we should not miss the graphic descriptive quality of the text Paul has chosen — he describes him-

---

as the "manifestation of the hostility of super-human forces" (B. Byrne, *Romans*, SP 6 [Collegeville, Minn.: Liturgical, 1996], p. 277) that attack those in Christ.

97. So Dunn, *Romans 1–8*, p. 469; see B. Byrne, *"Sons of God" — "Seed of Abraham": A Study of the Idea of the Sonship of God of All Christians in Paul against the Jewish Background,* AnBib 83 (Rome: Biblical Institute, 1979), p. 108, n. 115, for references to other scholars taking this view. However, see E. P. Sanders, who observes that it is difficult to find before 135 C.E. the view that suffering must precede the end of the age (*Jesus and Judaism* [Philadelphia: Fortress, 1985], p. 124).

98. Byrne, *Romans*, p. 275.

99. C. E. B. Cranfield, *Romans*, ICC 45 (Edinburgh: T. & T. Clark, 1985), 1:440.

100. So Fitzmyer, *Romans*, p. 534.

101. Byrne, *Romans*, p. 277; L. Tisdale, "Romans 8:31-39," *Int* 42 (1988): 70.

self and other believers as living while being killed and destined for slaughter. Nor should we miss the fact that such suffering has purpose — "for your sake."[102] When Paul's talk of suffering is assumed to be a pastoral response or theological reflection, the psalm is understood as a further justification of present suffering; but when we locate Paul's talk about suffering in his gospel preaching, the psalm becomes an illustration of the tribulation-ridden way of the life of believers and an affirmation that Christian suffering has a focus beyond simply enduring until the end.

Near the end of the letter, Paul includes advice on *thlipsis* (12:12) and *diōgmos* (12:14). The context of 12:12, in which Paul advises on the best approach to various Christian activities, such as hope and prayer, suggests that tribulation is to be seen also as a Christian activity.[103] This particular activity is best engaged in through standing one's ground *(hupomenō)*. Positive response to tribulation as a Christian activity is here enjoined.[104] In 12:14, Paul describes an even more proactive response to Christian suffering — believers are to bless those pursuing them. Clearly, enemies are on the landscape (12:20). In fact, Paul informs the Roman believers of the persecution he fears he might soon face in Jerusalem (15:31). Tribulation and persecution are, then, a fact of life for believers. Paul thinks such suffering is not an accident but rather a necessary mode of life for those in Christ.

What is the nature of the suffering that believers must expect? It is akin to the suffering of Christ, for believers suffer not on their own but with Christ (*sumpaschomen*, 8:17). The nature of their suffering is as Christ's is in the face of hostility, loss, rejection, and death. Since Paul understands believers to suffer together with Christ, we should not understand Christ's suffering as an *example* of how to suffer. Rather, the suffering of believers is also Christ's suffering, and vice versa. The character of such suffering is that it attunes believers to current circumstances in the whole of creation. Through the spirit (8:23), believers groan, as does the creation (8:22),[105] because of the sufferings of the present time (8:18). Both await redemption and, because of this, there is a reaching forward, a positive thrust, to this groaning.[106] There is a groaning peculiar to those who have

102. The *sou* is normally taken to refer to God rather than Christ.

103. A. Hultgren notes that Paul's use of the verb "persecute" here and elsewhere (e.g., 1 Cor 4:12) indicates that he thought of it as an ongoing condition ("Paul's Pre-Christian Persecutions of the Church: Their Purpose, Locale and Nature," *JBL* 95 [1976]: 108). I am suggesting that Paul understood it as more an activity than a condition.

104. Cf. Dunn, *Romans*, p. 743, who also reads *hupomenō* as implying a positive response.

105. I take *ktisis* as nonhuman creation, while recognizing that both human and nonhuman creation are intimately connected. Cf. Byrne, "Sons of God," p. 105.

106. So Byrne, "Sons of God," p. 108.

the first fruits of the Spirit.[107] It is a groaning that knows (*oidamen;* 8:22) for what it hopes and the significance of that hope for all creation. As W. Sanday and A. C. Headlam put it, Paul understood the movement to be "truly cosmic. The 'sons of God' are not selected for their own sakes alone, but their redemption means the redemption of a world of being besides themselves."[108]

Believers hope for adoption and the redemption of their bodies (8:23). Paul uses the metaphor of adoption here in a manner somewhat different from how he uses it either in Galatians or earlier in the Romans passage. It served his purpose in Galatians to stress that believers were already adopted and so already heirs (Gal 3:25-26; 4:3-7). In Romans 8:15, Paul says that believers have received a spirit of adoption. In 8:23, however, Paul reserves the concept of adoption for the end,[109] when believers' bodies will be redeemed and they will know the freedom of glory as the children of God (8:21).[110]

Believers have received a part of what is promised them, and so now they live in hope. The hope Paul expresses in Romans 8:19-23 is that the bondage to decay intrinsic to the current creation and human bodies will be broken.[111] This hope resonates with the conviction expressed in Romans 1:4 about Jesus' resurrection.[112] For Paul, the hope for resurrection is not for the reassumption of a body that is subject to decay but rather for a new spiritual body (1 Cor 15:44). Just as Jesus is declared God's Son at his resurrection, that is, when his body is redeemed,[113] so believers trust that they will be adopted and their bodies redeemed because of Jesus' resurrection. In this time, however, they groan.

We might also hear resonances from Romans 6:4. While this verse refers not to Christ's suffering but to his death, and does so for the purpose of ex-

---

107. Cf. Scott, *Adoption as Sons of God*, p. 257.

108. W. Sanday and A. C. Headlam, *The Epistle to the Romans*, ICC 45 (New York: Charles Scribner's Sons, 1896), p. 212.

109. J. D. G. Dunn catches the dynamic of the passage well: "(the Spirit's) coming at conversion makes us sons (8.15), and his life-long work brings our sonship to maturity and makes us perfect sons (8.23) . . . with the very image of God himself and manifested in glory (8.29)" (*Baptism in the Holy Spirit* [Naperville, Ill.: Allenson, 1970], p. 150).

110. In 8:21, Paul promises that when the children of God are liberated to be in their glory as God's children, then the creation, too, will know liberty.

111. Paul shares this hope, of course, with his Jewish kinfolk. See, for example, 2 *Bar.* 51:3; *1 Enoch* 104:2; Wis 3:1-4.

112. For references to some of the important discussions of the connection between Rom 1:4 and 8:23, see Scott, *Adoption as Sons of God*, pp. 220-23.

113. Note Scott's wise comment that speaking of Jesus' adoption as Son at the resurrection does not preclude his predestination to sonship (*Adoption as Sons of God*, p. 222, n. 6), and J. D. G. Dunn's point that the idea of the preexistence of Jesus is not at issue in this passage ("Jesus-Flesh and Spirit: An Exposition of Rom 1:3-4," *JTS* 24 [1973]: 59).

plaining the significance of Christ's death for sin, the idea of waiting for resurrection is similar to 8:23. This similarity suggests that Paul thinks that the groaning of believers (8:23) is connected to having been baptized into the death of Christ (6:4). The nature of the suffering that believers agree to in accepting the good news is the suffering of Christ. Believers suffer with Christ and are in the death he died.

Such suffering has a purpose. In believers, it produces patience or endurance (5:3). Such perseverance is the basis of character *(dokimē)* and hope (5:4). Suffering's purpose is ultimately, then, hope. As we have seen, the hope of believers is for resurrection (6:4; 8:23) and sharing in the glory of Christ (8:17).[114] This hope is dependent on suffering. As Paul writes: "we suffer with (Christ) in order that we will also be glorified with him" (8:17). Suffering comes with accepting the gospel.[115]

While the purpose of suffering is for believers to receive the glory for which they hope, it is also for the sake of God, who acts on behalf of the world (8:32). Quoting Psalm 44:22, Paul writes that it is for the sake of God that he and other believers suffer (8:36). In these sufferings *(en toutois pasin; 8:37)*, believers triumph gloriously, not *over* these things, but *in* or *through* them, according to the Greek. Suffering has, then, a positive benefit in this time. In the midst of suffering there is victory, victory akin to that achieved by Christ in his death. Just as God handed over God's son to death for the sake of humanity (8:32) and then gave him all things, so believers are victors in their suffering, knowing that they too will receive all things (8:32), since they suffer with Christ for humanity. Christian suffering has a purpose, and that purpose is both for Christians themselves — to receive glory with Christ — and for the world. As J. C. Beker puts it in regard to 8:17, "the phrase 'provided we suffer with him' points to our redemptive suffering in — for — the world . . . for the 'sufferings of Christ' have a redemptive power that furthers the coming glory of God."[116]

---

114. Christ's glory is also God's (5:2), and as Christ now possesses God's glory, so will believers. Cf. R. Scroggs, *The Last Adam: A Study in Pauline Anthropology* (Philadelphia: Fortress, 1966), p. 64.

115. Byrne rightly rejects interpreting *eiper* (8:17) as indicating an option not to suffer, but sees it rather either as a statement of fact ("seeing that," cf. 8:9; so also Cranfield, *Romans*, p. 407) or as an obvious condition ("provided that") (Byrne, *Romans*, pp. 253-54).

116. Beker, *Paul the Apostle*, pp. 364-65. Cf. G. B. Caird: "because the life of the church is Christ's own life, it is of necessity a life of suffering. . . . The powers of evil have been defeated by the obedience of Christ; they are constantly being defeated whenever Christians face them in the panoply of God; but the final triumph comes only when divine love has absorbed the whole momentum of evil . . . this final triumph is to be the revelation of God's glory reproduced in the sons of God . . . the summing up of all things in Christ" (*Principalities and Powers*, p. 101).

Given the nature and purpose of Christian suffering, Paul encourages believers to take a positive and proactive position in the midst of their affliction (12:12, 14) and even to boast of it (5:3). Since their suffering is the suffering of Christ, they are to behave as Christ would in situations of persecution, blessing their persecutors (12:14), not avenging themselves (12:19), and recognizing that acts of goodness defeat evil (12:20-21).

The evidence of Romans strongly suggests that Paul and his audience, who had been converted through people other than himself, accepted suffering as part of the gospel.[117] It appears that Paul sought to provide a richer understanding of suffering as part of the Christian call with the following claims. One of the activities of believers is to suffer, along with, for instance, praying and hoping (12:12). Believers are sufferers because they are the ones with the first fruits of the Spirit (8:23; 5:5), which produces *(katergazomai)* hope, especially for the redemption of their bodies (8:23), for the glory promised to be revealed to believers (8:18; 5:2), and for the completion of God's purposes for all creation (8:19-21). Finally, the nature of Christian suffering is that it is in partnership with Christ (8:17).

Summary of Evidence

Evidence from both 1 Thessalonians and Romans indicates that talk about suffering took place in Paul's initial gospel preaching. Part of the first message Paul's hearers heard was that those who accepted his gospel accepted also tribulation. The two letters we have examined suggest that Paul could shed different shades of meaning on Christian suffering. In 1 Thessalonians, Christian tribulation is imitation of Jesus Christ; in Romans, Christian suffering is suffering with Christ. In 1 Thessalonians, Paul speaks of Christians suffering only social harassment and, consequently, of suffering believers as marginalized people waiting for the end. In Romans, however, Paul relates Christian suffering to the desire for bodily redemption and the defeat of decay; consequently, suffering believers are seen as central to the whole hope of creation. In both letters, the suffering about which Paul speaks is peculiar to believers and is understood as part of God's work in bringing this age to completion.

Both the evidence of his preaching the gospel when he was with his con-

---

117. This confirms, although on a different basis, Schweitzer's insight that the idea of suffering with Christ did not originate with Paul. Schweitzer argues this on the grounds that Paul inherited the earliest church's understanding of its sufferings as being part of the premessianic tribulation (*Mysticism*, pp. 144, 147).

verts (1 Thessalonians) and the evidence of his first address to an audience (Romans) indicate that Paul regarded suffering as an organic part of preaching the gospel. Moreover, the fact that he brings out a variety of its aspects further indicates that, like the other key features of his gospel message, Christian suffering was a basic element of his preaching.[118]

Christian Suffering and Christian Character

While the classic creeds do not mention the suffering of believers,[119] our investigation has indicated that the first gospel, at least in Paul's time and place, did regard suffering as part of the gospel message. Paul's epistolary words on suffering are not only pastorally responsive and theologically reflective but integral to his proclamation. For those for whom Paul's gospel has a degree of authority there are certain implications regarding how his words shape our understanding of the Christian life.

While Christians suffer like everyone else from disease, loss, and death, Paul's words on Christian suffering (at least those we have examined) do not offer answers or consolation. They do not address the same challenge Abraham put to God in Genesis 18:25: "Far be it from you to do such a thing, and bring death upon the innocent as well as the guilty; so that the innocent and guilty fare alike. Far be it from you! Shall not the Judge of all the earth deal justly?" Paul's concern is not to present a theodicy in the face of human suffering.[120] The troubles that accompany every human life are not the issue when Paul talks about the affliction that comes with receiving the gospel.

Paul expects Christians to know that they have accepted a message that promises them suffering; that there is for the Christian a peculiar and distinctive type of suffering that comes with belief in God's work in Jesus Christ. For all his misguided approach to Christian suffering, Ignatius understood Paul's

118. Cf. the variety of uses and meanings Paul gives to matters as fundamental to gospel preaching as Christ's crucifixion, resurrection, and Lordship.

119. Cousar suggests that the authors of the creeds did not mention suffering because suffering will end at the last day (*Theology of the Cross,* p. 175). Perhaps the reason for the omission of suffering from the creeds is related rather to the fact that martyrdom had become a problem for the church.

120. Contrast the rabbinic concern to find an explanation, such as vicarious atonement: "R. Gurion, or, some say, R. Joseph son of R. Shemaiah, said: When there are righteous men in a generation, they are taken for the sin of the generation. When there are no righteous in a generation, school-children are taken for the generation" (*b. Šabb.* 33b; cited from Y. Elman, "The Suffering of the Righteous in Palestinian and Babylonian Sources," *JQR* 80 [1990]: 321).

basic point that acceptance of the gospel was acceptance of a particular form of suffering: "I glorify Jesus Christ, the God who made you so wise, for I observed that you are established in an unshakable faith, having been nailed, as it were, to the cross of the Lord Jesus Christ."[121]

The suffering that comes with acceptance of the gospel is akin to the suffering of Jesus: it is suffering that is productive (Rom 5:3-4), that brings to expression who Jesus is (1 Thess 1:6), and that suffers with (Rom 8:22-23) and for (Rom 8:36) him. Suffering is a necessary part of God's work in this time. In the material we have investigated, there is one specific example of an instance of such suffering — social harassment by compatriots (1 Thess 2:14). Paul also describes general sufferings in Romans 8:35. By and large, however, the exact features of Christian suffering are left unspecified. Nevertheless, what is not to be missed is that to be a believer is to be in tribulation of a particular sort.

What is also not to be missed is that, since Christian suffering comes with belief in the gospel, it need not be sought. Paul's gospel is not an encouragement to martyrdom.[122] Rather Paul's gospel, as God's transforming power through which God changes the human story, entails suffering for those who, like Christ, receive God's word (1 Thess 1:6). There is no benefit in seeking out martyr-type suffering. The suffering appropriate and intrinsic to believers simply is a fact of our lives. It is one of the Christian activities. Obeying the gospel means accepting a suffering way of life.

Beyond recognizing that Paul preached suffering, we have noted on the basis of two of his letters ways in which he interpreted suffering. Paul's understanding in this regard also has implications for Christian character.

Christians are those who imitate Christ, bringing to expression who Jesus

---

121. "To the Smyrnaeans" 1 (quoted from *The Apostolic Fathers: Greek Texts and English Translations of Their Writings,* ed. and trans. J. B. Lightfoot and J. R. Harmer [Grand Rapids: Baker, 1992], p. 185).

122. Contrast St. Cyprian's use of Rom 8:17 (Ep. 6.2.1) and his words in Letter 31 (Ep. 31.3, cited from *The Letters of St. Cyprian of Carthage,* trans. G. W. Clarke, ACW 44 [New York: Newman, 1984], 2:34-35 [italics mine]):

> What could befall any man which might bring him greater glory or greater bliss than this: in the midst of his executioners, undaunted to confess the Lord God; in the midst of the varied and refined instruments of torture, employed, in their savagery, by the powers of this world, even with body racked, mangled and butchered, to confess Christ the Son of God with breath, though failing, yet free; . . . *to have become . . . a partner with Christ in his passion;* . . . to have gained through death itself undying life; butchered and racked by every instrument of savagery, to have overcome the tortures through those very same tortures; . . . to have looked without horror upon his own blood streaming forth.

is. An aspect of this imitation is suffering (1 Thess 1:6). As sufferers, Christians know themselves to suffer not alone but together with Christ (Rom 8:17); not for nothing but for God (Rom 8:36); not in despair but for hope (Rom 5:3-4). Christian suffering is productive. It produces in believers that which is positive (Rom 5:3-4). Its purpose is to bring believers into glory (Rom 8:17), to redeem bodies subject to decay (Rom 8:23). Christian suffering, moreover, works toward the fulfillment of God's project of liberating the world.

When Christians suffer that type of suffering that is unique to them, it will manifest itself not in martyr-like actions, grim perseverance, or a negative and self-focused disposition. Christian suffering is, rather, a dynamic, forward-moving activity. It will be recognized for its capacity to be as Christ is, to proclaim hope, to reach towards God's promise of liberty. Christians suffering in this way will not complain but celebrate (boast), knowing that they are part of God's work in this time by sharing in Christ's work of suffering.

The character of the Christian is the character of the voluntary sufferer. In regards to Christian (as opposed to general human) suffering, there is for the believer no sense of suffering unfairly, no sense of being beleaguered, no angry questions to God. Christians are those who have accepted suffering because they have believed in Christ, the suffering one, knowing that as Christ's suffering changed the story for humanity from one of bondage to the promise of freedom, their suffering also contributes to making that promise a reality.

Believing Forms Seeing: Formation for Martyrdom in Philippians

Stephen E. Fowl

In his 1930 commentary on Philippians, Ernst Lohmeyer interpreted the entire epistle in terms of the theme of martyrdom.[1] In writing Philippians, Paul was writing a manual of martyrdom. There are numerous reasons for modern scholarship's strong aversion to Lohmeyer's account. The most obvious are found in Lohmeyer's rather heavy-handed attempts to find references to martyrdom under every exegetical stone. In an apparent reaction to this, very few contemporary commentators are willing to find any consideration of martyrdom in Philippians. This position is further solidified when one compares Philippians with second- and third-century martyrological texts.[2] Philippians is very different from these. Nevertheless, in Philippians Paul pays rather persistent attention to his own disposition towards his imprisonment, trial, and possible death (1:12-26; 2:17). He is concerned that the Philippians manifest a common life worthy of the gospel of Christ in the face of opposition. He goes so far as to say that he and the Philippians have been granted the opportunity not only to believe in Christ but to suffer for his sake (1:29-30). Paul presents the story of Christ in terms that are very similar to the suffering servant of Isaiah (2:6-11).[3] In addition, he informs the Philippians of his desire to know "the power of [Christ's] resurrection, the fellowship of his sufferings and to be conformed to his death" (3:10).

---

1. See E. Lohmeyer, *Die Briefe an die Philipper, an die Kolosser, und an Philemon* (Göttingen: Vandenhoeck and Ruprecht, 1930).

2. See H. Musurillo, *The Acts of the Christian Martyrs* (Oxford: Clarendon, 1977).

3. For a recent strong defense of the connections between Phil 2:5-11 and Isaiah 40–55, see Richard Bauckham, *God Crucified* (Grand Rapids: Eerdmans, 1998), pp. 47-53. It would seem that the question for NT scholars today is not whether there are allusions in Phil 2:5-11 to Isaiah 40–55 but how strong these allusions arc and what one makes of them.

If it is the case that Philippians is not explicitly a manual of martyrdom, I think one can, nevertheless, claim that one of the aims of the epistle is to display and to help form habits of perception, attention, and action necessary for life as a faithful Christian in a world often hostile to Christianity. If this is right, then it is also fair to claim that such habits are those necessary for forming people to be martyrs. This is because being a martyr is not an end in itself; steadfast obedience and fidelity are appropriate ends of Christian living. Whether or not faithful Christians become martyrs is in large part out of their hands. It depends to some degree on the acts and responses of a hostile world. Hence, while Lohmeyer might be wrong in thinking Philippians is directly about martyrdom, he was on the right track to the extent that Philippians is about the habits and dispositions that would enable people to offer their lives back to God in the face of intense hostility with martyrdom as a possible consequence.

To make this case as strongly as I would like would require a thorough accounting of the entire epistle. Such a task would, obviously, require more than my allotted space. Instead, I will have to be satisfied with working through an important chunk of Philippians 1, particularly verses 12-26. While these verses present a number of interesting exegetical conundra, they are not the verses one would normally first turn to in order to make a case that Philippians is centrally concerned about forming people capable of offering their lives back to God. Instead, passages such as 1:27-30 (with its concern about how the Philippians comport themselves in the face of opposition), 2:6-11 (with its emphasis on Christ's self-emptying and obedience unto death), 2:15-18 (where Paul applies sacrificial language to himself), 2:19-30 (which features the exemplary lives of Timothy and Epaphroditus), and 3:9-21 (which conveys Paul's own commitment to living in conformity with Christ's sufferings and his repudiation of the enemies of the cross) — all seem like more obvious places to start.

Nevertheless, offering one's life back to God in the face of hostile powers requires both theologically formed and christologically acute perceptual skills and habits. These habits allow one to give an account of one's circumstances — no matter how dire — that fit the narrative of one's own situation into the larger story of the divine economy of salvation. Only when one can do this can the refusal to abandon one's faith and hope become intelligible as an act of steadfast fidelity rather than an act that is stubborn, criminal, or insane. That is, this habit of seeing oneself and one's circumstances in a certain way makes it possible to distinguish between the empire's execution of recalcitrant, stubborn, or insane subjects and offering one's life back to God in martyrdom. In Philippians, Paul both displays these perceptual habits and skills and seeks to contribute to the formation of these skills in the Philippians. While Paul rhetorically works to form these skills and habits in the Philippians in many and various ways throughout the epistle, it is in 1:12-26 that Paul begins this task in earnest. Hence, it is here that I wish to focus my attention.

In 1:12-26, Paul offers a reading of his own situation. That is, he provides the Philippians with news about himself and how he is faring in prison. Following that, Paul expresses his hope that he will soon hear from the Philippians how they, too, are faring (1:27-30). This is not particularly remarkable. Within the genre of the so-called "letter of friendship," such sharing of news, commenting on received news, and requesting further news from the recipients are to be expected.[4] What is distinctive about Philippians in this regard is that in the course of sharing news about himself Paul is also involved in a particularly theological endeavor. That is, Paul does not simply relate news to the Philippians. Rather, he narrates an account of his circumstances in prison in the light of his larger reading of God's economy of salvation. Paul's account is not simply about episodes in his life, but also about his life as an episode in the larger drama of God's saving purposes. By fitting his account within the larger story of God's activity, Paul is able, by means of inference and analogy, to see how he should comport himself in his particular situation. Moreover, because Paul knows something of the Philippians' situation, he is able to offer an account of that situation that shows the similarities between his circumstances and theirs. Hence, Paul can make the crucial claim that the Philippians are engaged in the same struggle he is (1:30). Further, because they are in the same struggle he is in, they, too, should see their story in the light of the divine economy. Thus, they should comport themselves in a manner similar to Paul.

Those familiar with the epistle will recognize that this pattern of argument becomes much more explicit in 3:15-21 and especially in 3:17 with the command to become *summimētai mou*. I want to argue here that the strength of Paul's argument in chapter 3 depends upon two interrelated moves that are first made in chapter 1. The first thing is Paul's ability to see his circumstances in the light of the divine economy. The second is Paul's ability to see the Philippians' circumstances as similar to his own, both in their material conditions and in their relationship to God's economy. To make this case, an examination of 1:12-26 is required.

"I want you to know, brothers and sisters, that my circumstances have actually led to the advancement of the gospel." This is the way Paul begins a sec-

---

4. This point has been convincingly made by Stanley Stowers in *Letter Writing in Greco-Roman Antiquity* (Philadelphia: Westminster, 1986), pp. 50-70; idem, "Friends and Enemies in the Politics of Heaven," in *Pauline Theology*, vol. 1, ed. J. Bassler (Philadelphia: Fortress, 1991), pp. 107-10; L. Alexander, "Hellenistic Letter Forms and the Structure of Philippians," *JSNT* 37 (1989): 87-101.

tion that, at least on its surface, is a friendly account of how things are with him. Instead, what Paul presents is both an account of his own circumstances in prison and an account of the advance of the gospel. Paul's use of the term *mallon* here makes it clear that advancement of the gospel is not what one would have expected to be the result of Paul's imprisonment. In fact, it is easy to imagine the various ways in which the gospel might be hindered or brought into disrepute by Paul's imprisonment. The sociological contours of dishonor, shame, and loss of status associated with imprisonment in the Greco-Roman world have recently been laid out in Craig Wansink's monograph.[5] Moreover, the manifestly gruesome conditions of imperial prisons induced despair in virtually all those subjected to them.

The term *prokopē*, usually translated as "advancement" or "progress," has a rich heritage in Stoicism, and some have found Stoic overtones here. Paul's usage, however, seems to conform to the more straightforward usage found in 2 Maccabees 8:8 and Josephus's *Antiquities* 4.59, where the word is used in a nonphilosophical sense to refer to progressive movement toward an objective. Thus, despite, indeed in the light of, Paul's imprisonment, the gospel has moved on toward its goal.

In terms of the next two verses, it would seem that the progress of the gospel is manifested in the fact that many have learned that Paul's imprisonment is the result of his life in Christ[6] rather than the result of a straightforwardly criminal act. Moreover, many who might have otherwise been silent have been emboldened to proclaim the gospel in Rome. As Paul offers his account, two things become clear. First, it is Paul's life in Christ that has landed him in chains. Second, and more importantly, there is the clear implication that being in chains is not inconsistent with being "in Christ." Paul's current circumstances are not only consistent with his convictions about Christ but are the sorts of circumstances one who shared those convictions might also expect to share.

The text is silent here about the identity of the agent advancing the gospel. Presumably, the implied agent is God. In a situation that by all appearances should have threatened the gospel, God has, instead, insured the gospel's advancement. Paul's own abilities to control his circumstances are quite circumscribed. God is the agent who advances the gospel and forms Paul in such a way

---

5. See C. Wansink, *Chained in Christ: The Experience and Rhetoric of Paul's Imprisonments*, JSNTSup 130 (Sheffield: Sheffield Academic Press, 1996), pp. 27-95.

6. The terse phrase *en Christō* in 1:13 must imply a great deal. The context does little to determine which of several possible lines of implication to pursue. In 3:3, 14; 4:19, 21, Paul also uses *en Christō*. In these cases, the context works to determine the way one ought to take the phrase.

as to see progress in circumstances that might lead others to see God's purposes as frustrated.

Having made the bold assertion that God has used his bonds, contrary to expectation, to advance the gospel, Paul does recognize some problems in the newfound boldness that some have to proclaim the word. We learn that some proclaim the word out of "envy" and "strife" (1:15a). Paul offers his interpretation of their rationale for preaching in this way in 1:17. They preach Christ from *eritheia*. This is a rather unusual word. Prior to the NT, it occurs only in Aristotle, where it denotes self-serving pursuit of political office by unfair means.[7] Within the NT, *eritheia* occurs here in 1:17 and in Romans 2:8; 2 Corinthians 12:20; Galatians 5:20; as well as James 3:14, 16. In addition, the word also appears in Philippians 2:3, where it is paired with *kenodoxia*. This word pair is contrasted with the habit of seeking the benefit of others in humility. In the light of these uses, it is probably best to take the term in 1:17 to describe selfish ambition, a sort of self-absorption that is ultimately destructive of a common life. As Paul sees it, the aim of those preaching from such motives is to deepen the pain of his imprisonment. In this particular context, it is unlikely that those who preach Christ from selfish motives have fomented a deliberate plot to exacerbate Paul's physical sufferings or to cause actual bodily harm. Instead, the aim would be to create "inward annoyance," or, in Lightfoot's words, "to make my chains gall me."[8] In this light, the aims of those who preach Christ from selfish ambition stand directly opposed to God's ends in using Paul's imprisonment to advance the gospel.

While those who preach Christ from selfish motives hope to increase Paul's tribulations, Paul's claims indicate that they have failed. As verse 18 makes clear, despite the efforts of those who aim to trouble him, Paul rejoices because Christ is preached. The motives of the preachers, while notable, seem secondary to the act of proclamation. This seems to be an odd notion. Why might Paul think this way?

Paul seems able to take this stance because throughout verses 12-18 he displaces himself as the subject of what is ostensibly a discussion of his own circumstances. Let me elaborate on this by looking at the way Paul phrases several key claims in 1:12-18. In 1:12, Paul notes that the gospel progresses through God's agency rather than his. In verse 16, when he mentions those who preach Christ out of *agapē*, Paul notes that they do so because they have seen that Paul is im-

---

7. See BAGD, p. 309.

8. "Inward annoyance" comes from P. T. O'Brien, *The Epistle to the Philippians* (Grand Rapids: Eerdmans, 1991), p. 102. See J. B. Lightfoot, *St. Paul's Epistle to the Philippians* (Lynn: Hendrickson, 1981 [1896]), p. 90.

prisoned for the defense of the gospel. The phrase *keimai eis* here indicates being established, appointed, or destined for something (cf. 1 Thess 3:3; Luke
2:34). In this case, it is the defense of the gospel for which Paul is appointed. The
emboldened preaching of these Christians stems from having perceived that
Paul's circumstances are both the result and the manifestation of his defense of
the gospel. Hence, there is a sense in which the gospel is on trial rather than, or
in addition to, Paul. Attending to these turns of phrase should indicate that we
are not dealing with a letter of friendship in any straightforward sense.

According to the standard conventions of a letter of friendship, Paul begins in 1:12 to reveal "the things concerning me." As Paul narrates them, however, "the things concerning me" turn out to be only indirectly about Paul.
What is clear here, as elsewhere in the epistle, is that Paul and Paul's own story
are integrated so thoroughly into the story of God's economy of salvation that
it becomes difficult to separate the two. Paul has learned to see his circumstances as part of this larger, ongoing story. Hence, in telling his story he, quite
naturally, ends up talking about the progress of that story. Ultimately, then, because Paul is convinced that God is directing both his personal circumstances
and the more general spread of the gospel, he need not be overly concerned
about the motives of any particular set of preachers. This discussion allows Paul
to display a pattern of being able to perceive oneself in the light of the larger
movement of God's economy and then responding in the appropriate ways. It
allows Paul a certain ironic distance from his own circumstances. He is able to
see that, despite appearances and contrary to expectations, God is advancing
the gospel. To use the language Paul applies to the Philippians in 1:6, God is
bringing to completion the good work God initiated in Paul.

As verse 19 picks up the discussion of Paul's own circumstances, we see
him displaying this same point of view. As with verses 12-18, however, we will
also see that Paul's discussion about his imprisonment illustrates a more general
pattern of self-perception and action that Paul displays for the Philippians. As
the rest of the epistle makes clear, it is precisely this pattern of self-perception
and action that Paul wants the Philippians to display in regard to their circumstances.

In verse 18, Paul ends his discussion of various types of preachers with an
expression of joy. The last clause of verse 18 serves to introduce verse 19 and reiterates Paul's commitment to rejoicing. As verse 19 makes clear, this commitment is based on a certain knowledge Paul has *(oida)*. The two subsequent *hoti*
clauses explicate the nature of this knowledge.

The first clause is a direct quotation of the LXX of Job 13:16: "This will result in my salvation." Paul does not introduce the quote with any of his standard phrases. Moreover, the claim is intelligible to anyone who does not know

the text of Job. However, as Richard B. Hays has noted, for someone who does pick up and identify the quote, there are some "intriguing resonances."[9]

In Job 13:16, Job is in the midst of defending his integrity in the light of his friends' accusations that Job's circumstances are the result of some hidden sin in his life. He claims in 13:16 both that he will ultimately be vindicated before God, and that those who have spoken falsely will not be welcomed into God's presence. While there may be more to say about these resonances, for my purposes it is enough to note that Paul appears to take on Job's voice "to affirm confidence in the favorable outcome of his affliction."[10] In the midst of seemingly hopeless circumstances, Paul shares Job's hopeful confidence of salvation. Paul then goes on to note that his salvation or vindication will come through the prayers of the Philippians and the subsequent supplying of the Spirit.

In this verse, there seems to be an inherent ambiguity in Paul's use of the term "salvation" *(sōtēria)*. On the one hand, this term clearly reflects Paul's expectation that he will be vindicated before God.[11] On the other hand, some scholars have argued that the term has more immediately material connotations, referring to Paul's hoped-for release from prison.[12] It is unclear to me why both of these possibilities cannot be heard.[13] If Jeffrey Reed is correct, Paul may be playing on the standard epistolary meaning of *sōtēria* as physical well-being and safety in order to undermine any excessive desire on the part of the Philippian Christians for deliverance from physical suffering taken on in Christ.[14]

In verse 20, we learn of the second reason for Paul's rejoicing. It is Paul's eager expectation and hope that he will in no way be disgraced. The language here about being put to shame *(aischunēsomai)* is quite common in the LXX. In context, the term does not reflect an inner feeling of shame so much as a failure of faith (in word or deed) that brings disgrace with it.[15] Given the way this no-

9. See R. B. Hays, *The Echoes of Scripture in the Letters of Paul* (New Haven, Conn.: Yale University Press, 1989), pp. 21-24. For much of the following, I am indebted to Hays's work.

10. Hays, *The Echoes of Scripture*, p. 22.

11. So, among others, O'Brien, *The Epistle to the Philippians*, p. 110.

12. So, among others, G. F. Hawthorne, *Philippians*, Word Biblical Themes (Waco, Tex.: Word Books, 1987), p. 40.

13. See the arguments for this view in Jeffrey Reed's *Discourse Analysis of Philippians: Method and Rhetoric in the Debate over Literary Integrity*, JSNTSup 136 (Sheffield: Sheffield Academic Press, 1997), pp. 212-15. G. Fee (*Paul's Letter to the Philippians*, NIBCNT [Grand Rapids: Eerdmans, 1995], pp. 131-33) moves in a similar direction.

14. See Reed, *Discourse Analysis of Philippians*, p. 215. This view would get some support from 2:14, where Paul urges the Philippians to avoid "grumbling and dissention," using language that evokes Israel's response to physical hardships.

15. See especially LXX Pss 24:3; 68:7; 118:80; Jer 12:13.

tion is developed in Philippians, it would appear that Paul is using the term in much the same way here. In this light, Paul's usage conforms more to his use of *aischunēsomai* in 2 Corinthians 10:8 than in Romans 1:16.

Rather than being disgraced, Paul plans, with all boldness and as he has always done heretofore, that Christ will be magnified in his body. The notion of "magnifying the Lord" has strong links to the Psalms.[16] Luke uses the same word in the Magnificat, where the term ascribes glory to God. What is striking in Philippians is that the passive voice of the verb allows Paul to make a significant distinction. While it is Paul who might be disgraced, it is Christ who will be magnified by Paul's body whether the apostle lives or dies. Because the quotation from Job in 1:19 speaks of a heavenly vindication, there is a tendency among commentators to think that Paul here is also talking about a confidence directed toward the eschaton. Such an eschatological view, however, seems to miss some important points. First, Paul's discussion of Christ being magnified in his body notes not only that such magnification will happen in the future but that Christ is regularly magnified in Paul's body. This is the force of *hōs pantote kai nun*.[17] Paul's confidence is not primarily about the eschaton but about his ability to continue, with the Spirit's help, in circumstances of extreme adversity, a practice he has carried on for some time.

A second interpretive issue here concerns Paul's use of the term *sōma*. Under Rudolf Bultmann's influence, it became common to weigh down Paul's use of *sōma* with quite a bit of anthropological baggage.[18] In explicit reaction to Bultmann, Robert Gundry has argued that Paul's use of *sōma* simply cannot bear such a load.[19] In general, Gundry would seem to have the weight of exegetical evidence on his side. He misses something, however, when he limits Paul's use of *sōma* to Paul's physical body.[20] Although Gundry correctly warns against investing Paul's use of *sōma* with a great deal of anthropological weight, we have to recognize that Paul's claims imply that whether he dies or lives there is, in each instance, an opportunity for magnifying Christ or disgracing him-

---

16. See LXX Pss 33:3; 34:27; 39:16; 56:10.

17. Fee (*Paul's Letter to the Philippians*, p. 137) is correct to pick this up. However, he incorrectly limits the practice of "magnifying Christ in my body" to the practice of the "praise of Christ."

18. See R. Bultmann, *New Testament Theology*, 2 vols., trans. K. Grobel (London: SCM, 1952), 1:194-95; see also E. Schweizer, *TDNT* 7:1065-66.

19. See R. H. Gundry, *"Sōma" in Biblical Theology with an Emphasis on Pauline Anthropology* (Cambridge: Cambridge University Press, 1976).

20. "*Soma* therefore does not signify the whole 'I' of Paul, but only that part of him more immediately affected by the outcome of his trial and through which he bears witness to the visible world around him" (Gundry, *"Sōma" in Biblical Theology*, p. 37).

self. In dying, Paul could either be disgraced or magnify Christ; in living, he faces the same option. Magnifying Christ in life, however, will require a different set of practices than magnifying Christ in death. Aquinas recognizes this in his commentary when he observes: "Christ is honored in our body in two ways: in one way, inasmuch as we dedicate our body to his service by employing our bodies in his ministry . . . ; in another way by risking our body for Christ. . . . The first is accomplished by life, the second by death."[21]

What Paul understands, and what Bultmann and Gundry in their own ways both miss, is that in this particular matter Paul's body will display the disposition of his character whether he lives or dies. For example, in dying in a way that disgraces himself (by recanting under torture, for example), Paul's body would display something crucial about his character.[22] Paul understands what virtually all ancient moral philosophers would have recognized: bodily actions and bodily responses to specific situations display elements of a person's character. It is not simply Paul's death that is discussed here, but the manner of his death and Paul's abilities to describe that death as something that might either give glory to God or bring shame on himself. In this respect, Paul's claims are not particularly surprising.

Yet a Roman prison would be the last place in which one would be expected to have any control over one's own body. In the context of imperial imprisonment, the prisoner's body becomes the text on which the empire's power is inscribed.[23] In a situation where the Roman empire would be expected to have complete control over Paul's body, Paul asserts that Christ will be magnified by the way in which he comports himself. Whether he lives or dies, Paul (especially his body) will be, as he has always been, Christ's text rather than the empire's.

Having confidently asserted that he intends to continue to glorify Christ

21. Thomas Aquinas, *Commentary on Saint Paul's First Letter to the Thessalonians and the Letter to the Philippians*, trans. F. Larcher (Albany, N.Y.: Magi Books, 1969), p. 69.

22. As Chrysostom comments on this passage, "For if fear of death had cut short my boldness, death would have been worthy of shame, but if death at its approach cast no terror on me, no shame is here; but whether it be through life I shall not be put to shame, for I still preach the Preaching, or whether it be through death I shall not be put to shame; fear does not hold me back, since I exhibit the same boldness" (Homily 3).

23. This general point in regard to imprisonment and punishment was first made by M. Foucault in *Discipline and Punish*, trans. A. Sheridan (New York: Vintage, 1979). One further issue that has generated some scholarly interest in regard to Phil 1:19-26 concerns whether or not Paul was here contemplating suicide. Due to space considerations I will not address this issue. Some of the initial positions in this debate were staked out by A. Droge. His views were revised and summarized in his book with J. Tabor, *A Noble Death* (San Francisco: Harper Collins, 1992); see also Wansink's comments on this in *Chained in Christ*, pp. 96-125.

in his body whether he lives or dies, Paul now turns in verses 21-26 to reflect at greater length on what is at stake in living and dying. I think it is best to let verses 22-23 add more precision to the laconic comment in verse 21: "For me to live is Christ, to die is gain."[24] That is, to live entails that Paul will continue to magnify Christ, engaging in fruitful labor for Christ, such as founding and building up various congregations. To die is to enter into a deeper union with Christ than is possible in the flesh.[25]

Of particular interesting is Paul's claim in verse 22 that he does not know which of these two options for magnifying Christ in his body he will choose. The Greek here is somewhat obscure because of the verb *gnōrizō*. The most straightforward way to take the clause *kai ti hairēsomai ou gnōrizō* would be something like "I don't know which [of these two options] I will choose."[26] The complication comes from the fact that this is not the normal way Paul uses this verb. He normally uses *gnōrizō* to speak of disclosure, of making known — often in regard to God's mysteries (cf. Rom 16:26; 1 Cor 15:1; 2 Cor 8:1; Gal 1:11). There are various ways commentators have tried to bring this sense of *gnōrizō* to bear on this verse. The results of these attempts range from the unsatisfying[27] to the downright confusing.[28] Moreover, although Paul does not tend to use *ou gnōrizō* in the sense of "I don't know," there are a host of extrabiblical references to support such usage.[29] Given that this makes the best sense of the passage, we should read the verb in this way.

Paul here seems to be deeply torn between his desire to die, his personal preference, and the needfulness of living. He speaks as one faced with two incompatible possibilities, each with a certain appeal. By verse 25, however, Paul has both made up his mind and given the reasons for his resolve. While his personal preference is to die and be with Christ, it is more beneficial to the

24. See O'Brien, *The Epistle to the Philippians*, p. 120.

25. See A. Lincoln, *Paradise Now and Not Yet* (Cambridge: Cambridge University Press, 1981), p. 106, who says, "The state into which Paul will enter at death is far better, bringing with it a greater closeness of communion with Christ, and yet . . . it is still a state of expectation, less than the fullness of redemption described in 3.20f." Presumably, if Paul was radically unsure of what lay beyond the grave for him, then death would have held little appeal.

26. I take Paul's use of *hairēsomai* in the conventional sense of indicating a choice not a preference. For the best arguments in favor of this see Wansink, *Chained in Christ*, pp. 96-102.

27. For an example of this, see Fee, *Paul's Letter to the Philippians*, p. 164, who denies that Paul had any real choice to make.

28. See Lohmeyer, *Die Briefe an die Philipper*, pp. 60-61; and O'Brien, *The Epistle to the Philippians*, pp. 127-28, who thinks that Paul cannot make his decision known because God's mind had not yet been revealed to Paul. This is confusing because by v. 25, Paul has both made up his mind and does not attribute his decision to a direct message from God.

29. See Philo *Jos.* 165; *Conf.* 183; Josephus *Ant.* 2.97; *Life* 420; see also *TDNT*.

Philippians for him to remain in the flesh, engaging in fruitful labor for Christ. Contrary to his own desire, Paul has decided to live. Paul's reasoning displays the habit of seeking the benefit of others, a habit that plays a crucial role in the argument of the epistle.

As I think will become clear to those who read to the end of chapter 2, it is precisely this activity of seeking the benefit of others that God has decisively displayed to the world in the life, death, and resurrection of Jesus. When faced with the choice of life or death, Paul opts for life. This is not because life is obviously superior to death. For Paul, this is far from the case. Rather, Paul's choice analogously replicates the climactic movement in the divine economy of salvation. By seeing his situation as part of that larger story, Paul is provided with a compelling exemplar of how he should comport himself in his imprisonment.

Paul claims that he has decided to live and remain with the Philippians, engaging in fruitful labor for Christ, because it is more beneficial to the Philippians and will advance their "progress and joy in the faith." Here in verses 25-26, Paul is making a transition from speaking (at least ostensibly) about his own affairs to a discussion of the Philippians' affairs, a discussion he will take up directly in verses 27-30. He does this by bringing his affairs and their affairs into the same story.

This conclusion is supported by several verbal links in verses 25-26 to themes Paul has already introduced. For example, the phrase *touto pepoithōs oida* introduces a bold statement about how Paul's situation will work itself out for the Philippians' advantage — they will advance and have joy. It also recalls the equally bold statement in 1:6 *(pepoithōs auto touto)* about God's continued work in the life of the Philippian congregation.

Further, Paul had already introduced in 1:12 the discussion of his circumstances in prison by asserting that, contrary to expectation, his circumstances have worked to advance the gospel *(eis prokopēn tou euangeliou)*. In 1:18, Paul notes that, despite the motives of some, he rejoices in the advance of the gospel. In verse 25, he asserts that his remaining with the Philippians will lead to their advancement *(eis tēn humōn prokopēn)* in joy and faith. These verbal connections remind us that from the very first part of the epistle, when Paul asserts his conviction that God has worked and will continue to work in the lives of the Philippians, he has already been reading the Philippians into the narrative of God's economy of salvation in much the same way he has read himself into that story. His claims in verse 25 simply resume that activity. In reading the Philippians into his account of the divine economy from the beginning of the epistle, Paul is already laying the groundwork for the claim he is going to make in 1:30 that he and the Philippians are engaged in the same struggle. This claim is essential for the larger aims of Paul's argument. If he can establish that he and the Philippians are in similar circumstances, then he can argue that the Philippians ought to act in a similar manner. Moreover, offering an account of their situation in a way that both ties their situation to his and accounts for their circumstances in the light of the larger movements of the divine economy, Paul is implicitly encouraging them to learn how to see their situation in a similar way. By the time the argument reaches the explicit claim in 3:17 that the Philippians should "join together in imitating" *(summimētai)* Paul, he has already laid so much conceptual and rhetorical groundwork that the claim comes as no surprise.

According to verse 26, the end result of Paul's decision to remain in the flesh, engaging in fruitful labor for and with the Philippians so that their joy and faith may advance, is the "boasting" that will happen when Paul and the Philippians are reunited and can see each other face to face. In the Greco-Roman world, boasting is quite compatible with a cultural system based on honor and shame. It is a way of rightly locating honor.[30] Of course, boasting in Christ, one who suffered a slave's death, would have struck many in Paul's world as foolishness. Paul makes this quite clear in 1 Corinthians 1:18-31, a passage that concludes with a citation from Jeremiah 9:23-24, "Let the one who boasts, boast in the Lord." As the passage from Jeremiah indicates, this practice of boasting or giving glory is a practice that, if done in the right way and for the right reasons, is the paradigmatic activity of the believer. If done in the wrong way or for the wrong reasons, it is fundamentally destructive of a believer's relationship with God. In Philippians 1:26, the grounds for boasting are in Christ Jesus and, more precisely, what Christ Jesus has done through Paul.[31] This displacement of the self as the ground and focus of boasting is consistent with the pattern I have noted above. Paul is not the object of his own or the Philippians' boasting. Rather, Christ is the object, and Paul's circumstances simply provide the occasion.

More synthetic comments about Paul's account of his circumstances can now be offered. I will begin by relating 1:12-16 to the overall argument of the epistle. In this passage, Paul has consistently displaced himself as the primary actor in a story that is ostensibly about himself. Thus Paul's account here makes clear that his story is part of a larger story, the story of God's economy of salvation. In the light of his persistent emphasis on the *koinonia* that he shares with the Philippians, Paul starts to draw them into this larger story as well. Paul

30. See B. Witherington's discussion of this issue in *Friendship and Finances in Philippi: The Letter of Paul to the Philippians* (Valley Forge, Pa.: Trinity Press International, 1994), pp. 47-49.

31. As Witherington rightly suggests, "Paul is trying in part of this discourse to de-enculturate his audience from such values by indicating that they are part of a different commonwealth, holding a different sort of citizenship" (*Friendship and Finances*, p. 47).

makes this explicit in 1:5, where he claims that he and the Philippians are fellow sharers in the gospel. It is also explicit in 1:30, where Paul claims that he and the Philippians are part of the same struggle. It is also evident in Paul's expression of thanks in 4:10-20. Hence, on both sides of the argument in 1:12-26, Paul explicitly notes that he and the Philippians share a common situation. Within 1:12-26, Paul's reflections about his own life and death and how his views and plans are shaped not only by his commitment to continue magnifying Christ in his body but also by what is most beneficial to the Philippians indicate that he and the Philippians share a common situation. Further, he has indicated that his future joy and boasting in the Lord are intimately connected to the destiny of the Philippian community, a point he makes explicit in 2:12-18.

In short, Paul sees that he and the Philippians are engaged in a project greater than themselves. This project is nothing less than participation in the economy of God's saving purposes. Because they are fellow participants in the divine economy, Paul's sufferings and the Philippians' sufferings can be narrated within the scope of that common project. As a result, it will be neither Paul's beliefs that might require the Philippians to suffer nor the Philippians' beliefs that might require Paul to suffer. Rather, it is their common convictions about God's work in the world, most particularly as that work is revealed in and through the story of Christ narrated in 2:6-11, that lead Paul to claim that the Philippians have been granted the opportunity not only to believe in Christ but to suffer for his sake (1:29).

In the light of present or immanent suffering, it is crucial for Paul to help the Philippians develop the skills of being able to interpret the movement of God's economy and so to situate themselves both within the movements of that story and in the light of that story's ultimate end, that they, as a community, can remain as a faithful witness to the gospel in a hostile world. This point is explicitly brought home in 1:27-28. Of course, the divine economy is not a self-interpreting text; its movements can at times be hard to decipher — particularly in the midst of material realities such as suffering and imprisonment. As already noted, Paul tends to adopt an ironic point of view in these matters, about which more can be said.

When I speak of Paul's ironic point of view in regard both to his own circumstances and to the movements of the divine economy, it is important that I qualify that judgment in several important respects. Paul's point of view is ironic in that he is able to see that, despite their present appearance and contrary to expectation, his circumstances are working and will work to advance the gospel. Despite the fact that he is in prison and utterly powerless, he will magnify Christ in his body. In spite of the obvious benefits of death, he will pursue a course that is more beneficial to the Philippians. The stable point that can sustain this ironic perspective is Paul's unwavering confidence that God will ultimately bring all things to their proper end. This is very different, then, from a perpetual irony that infinitely defers judgment and commitment, an irony that cannot but lapse into cynicism.

Instead, Paul's ironic perspective is christologically dense. It is a perspective that is shaped by a narrative of God's economy of salvation that reaches its climax in the life, death, and resurrection of Jesus, especially as that story is told in 2:6-11. In these verses, we read about a Christ who, contrary to expectation, does not use equality with God for his own advantage.[32] Instead, seeking the benefit of others, Christ willingly empties himself, takes on the form of a slave, and obediently submits to crucifixion. As verses 9-11 indicate, surprisingly, this is precisely the pattern of seeing and acting that God vindicates by exalting the crucified one. Having been shaped by this narrative, Paul can see the temporal contingency of present circumstances and current configurations of power. As a result, he can comport himself in the midst of adverse circumstances in the knowledge that these circumstances are ultimately ordered by God's providential will. Moreover, this ordering ultimately ensures that all things will be subject to Christ.

In Philippians, these perceptual skills and habits are not explicitly tied to martyrdom. Nevertheless, by displaying these skills for the Philippians and by urging them to manifest these same skills and habits in their own context (e.g., 2:1-4), Paul is contributing to their formation as Christians who, when called upon, have the resources to narrate their own deaths as willed offerings of themselves to God. To those with the requisite perceptual habits and skills, such deaths can be made intelligible under the term "martyr."[33]

---

32. In this respect, the term *alla* in 2:7 plays a role similar to that of *mallon* in 1:12. I owe this observation to Mike Gorman.

33. I am grateful to my colleagues Mike Gorman and Jim Buckley for reading an earlier version of this paper and offering helpful comments, criticisms, and corrections.

The Function of Moral
Typology in 2 Peter

J. Daryl Charles

On a textbook level, there is a curious absence of 2 Peter in discussions of NT ethics. To illustrate, in Richard B. Hays's magisterial work, *The Moral Vision of the New Testament*,[1] believed by many to be the best and most comprehensive work available in the discipline of NT ethics, not a single page is devoted to the General Epistles, much less Jude or 2 Peter. Indeed, this is typical in varying degrees of most comparable treatments.[2]

The conspicuous absence of 2 Peter in NT ethics confronts us with the obvious question: Why do primers on NT ethics almost uniformly fail to include this epistle in their discussions? Surely the reason is not a lack of moral vocabulary. Moral grammar, as it turns out, is highly dense in this epistle, as throughout the General Epistles. (Only in the Johannine Epistles does this feature recede.) Ethics and virtue, exhortation and moral typology abound in

1. R. B. Hays, *The Moral Vision of the New Testament — Community, Cross, New Creation: A Contemporary Introduction to New Testament Ethics* (San Francisco: HarperSanFrancisco, 1996). In this important volume, Hays argues for a unified ethical vision in the NT. The scriptural loci in Hays's study are Paul, Mark, Matthew, Luke-Acts, Johannine literature, and Revelation.

2. Little or no discussion of 2 Peter is found in the following works: W. Marxsen, *New Testament Foundations for Christian Ethics,* trans. O. C. Dean, Jr. (Minneapolis, Minn.: Fortress, 1993); H. Merklein, ed., *Neues Testament und Ethik* (Stuttgart: KBW, 1989); S. Schulz, ed., *Neutestamentliche Ethik* (Zürich: Theologischer Verlag, 1987); W. Schrage, *The Ethics of the New Testament,* trans. D. E. Green (Philadelphia: Fortress, 1988); J. T. Sanders, *Ethics in the New Testament* (Philadelphia: Fortress, 1975); C. Spicq, *Théologie Morale du Nouveau Testament,* 2 vols. (Paris: Gabalda, 1970); R. Schnackenburg, *The Moral Teaching of the New Testament,* 2 vols., trans. J. Holland-Smith and W. J. O'Hara (Freiburg: Herder, 1965); R. H. Marshall, *The Challenge of New Testament Ethics* (London: SPCK, 1947); W. A. Meeks, *The Moral World of the First Christians* (Philadelphia: Westminster, 1986).

2 Peter, which exhibits similarities to James, 1 Peter, and Jude in its paraenetic-rhetorical character. As a form of prescriptive and proscriptive exhortation,[3] paraenesis serves to promote practical rules for behavior and adopts styles that range from censure to consolation.[4] Moral categories are assumed and thus are not explicated in paraenesis. Because the exhorter proceeds on the basis of what is already plainly known, he disavows the need for further instruction, merely reminding his audience of knowledge they already possess. It is helpful to compare two samples of paraenesis: one from 2 Peter and one from literature roughly contemporaneous to the NT, the markings of which are quite similar:

> I know you need no telling, but my love for you prompts me to remind you to keep in mind and put into practice what you know already, or else it would be better for you to remain ignorant. Remember . . . (Pliny, *Letter to Maximus* 8.24)[5]

> Therefore I intend to keep on reminding you of these things, though you already know them and are established in the truth that has come to you. . . . I think it right . . . to refresh your memory . . . so that . . . you may be able at any time to recall these things. . . . I am trying to arouse your sincere intention by reminding you: remember . . . (2 Pet 1:12-15; 3:1a-2a)[6]

Where concreteness is necessary for the reader's instruction, moral paradigms and types are a common feature in the paraenetic tradition and serve the purposes of illustration.[7] In addition to its characteristic use of paradigms, paraenesis (the *logos parainētikos*) typically incorporates the elements of regulatory rules of conduct, ethical proscriptions, ethical justifications, warnings, and catalogs of vice and virtue.[8] The social situation of paraenesis, moreover,

3. The role of *exhortatio* or *logos parainētikos* in Hellenistic rhetoric is delineated by Quintilian, for example, in *Inst.* 3.6.47; 9.2.103.

4. A. Malherbe, *Moral Exhortation: A Greco-Roman Sourcebook* (Philadelphia: Westminster, 1986), pp. 124-25.

5. The English translation appears in *Letters and Panegyricus*, trans. B. Radice, LCL (Cambridge, Mass.: Harvard University Press, 1969), pp. 72-73.

6. Author's translation.

7. Malherbe, *Moral Exhortation*, pp. 124-29.

8. On the paraenetic tradition in general, see K. Berger, "Hellenistische Gattungen im Neuen Testament," in *Aufstieg und Niedergang der römischen Welt: Geschichte und Kultur Roms im Spiegel der neueren Forschung*, ed. W. Haase (Berlin and New York: Walter de Gruyter, 1984), 2:25.2, pp. 1075-77. For examples of the use of paraenesis in the General Epistles, see L. G. Perdue, "Paraenesis in the Epistle of James," *ZNW* 72 (1981): 241-56; P. H. Davids, "Tradition and Citation in the Epistle of James," in *Scripture, Tradition, and Interpretation*, ed. W. W. Gasque

dictates a relationship of the author to his readers, namely, that of a father figure to a son, or a mentor to his disciple, the purpose of which is to exercise moral authority through exhortation.[9]

Consonant with the reminder terminology that characterizes paraenetic literature, the readers of 2 Peter are exhorted to recall, and validate, what they already know (1:8-15; 3:1-2, 11, 17). Incomparable divine resources have been placed at their disposal for "life and godliness" (1:3). To concretize the matter, moral examples are served up from the past (2:4-10a). The angels who rebelled were disenfranchised and have been reserved for the day of judgment. Noah's generation was condemned because of hardened moral skepticism, while faithful Noah, with his family, was saved. Lot, as well, was rescued by the Lord from the judgment that beset the cities of the plain, thus serving as an example of one who faced the daunting challenges of living in a pagan society where moral standards were continually subject to assault and compromise.

The burden of 2 Peter (i.e., ethical lapse)[10] is communicated not only by

---

and W. S. LaSor (Grand Rapids: Eerdmans, 1978), pp. 113-26; and T. Martin, *Metaphor and Composition in 1 Peter*, SBLDS 131 (Atlanta: Scholars Press, 1994), pp. 103-21.

9. Berger, "Hellenistische Gattungen," p. 1076; S. K. Stowers, *Letter Writing in Greco-Roman Antiquity* (Philadelphia: Westminster, 1986), p. 95.

10. Traditional commentary on 2 Peter proceeds on the assumption that the letter is pseudepigraphal and "early Catholic," reflecting second-century developments in the church. Thus Willi Marxsen, in his influential work, states,

> This document gives us a glimpse of the situation of the Church at a relatively late period. The eschatology which looks to an imminent End has fallen into the background, and one has to adjust oneself to living in the world (cf. esp. the Pastorals). The Church is in process [sic] of becoming an institution. The Spirit is linked with tradition and with the ministry — and is passed on by the laying on of hands. The point has now been reached where one has to make clear where one differs from those among whom the Spirit is still "freely" active. In the post-Pauline period — long after Paul, in fact, for he has already become a "literary entity" belonging to the past — the futurist eschatology of the Church is attacked by the Gnostics. "Where is the promise of his coming? For from the day that the fathers fell asleep, all things continue as they were from the beginning of the creation" (iii.4). Though far removed from the beginnings of the Church, the author is seeking to remain in continuity with these beginnings and sets out an "apologia for the primitive Christian eschatology" in its apocalyptic form (*Der 'Frühkatholizismus' im Neuen Testament*, BibS(N) 21 [Neukirchen: Neukirchener Verlag, 1958], p. 244).

Here Marxsen is referring to an essay by another influential proponent of the early Catholic thesis, Ernst Käsemann. See the latter's "An Apologia for Primitive Christian Eschatology," in *Essays on New Testament Themes* (London: SCM, 1964), pp. 135-57. While an "early Catholic" reading of the NT is by no means confined to 2 Peter — or the "catholic epistles" for that matter — it is here applied in its most concentrated form. For a recent evaluation of the early Catholic

the language of paraenesis but also by the descriptions of the underlying pastoral problem. Consider the writer's vocabulary: "pleasure" *(hēdonē)*, "licentiousness" *(aselgeia)*, "depravity" *(phthora)*, "lusts of the flesh" *(epithymiai sarkos)*, "covetousness" *(pleonexia)*, "defilement" *(miasma)*, "lawless" *(anomos)*, "vanity" *(mataiotēs)*, "irrational beasts" *(aloga zōa)*, "morally corrupt" *(athesmos)*, "adulterous" *(moichalidos)*, "returning to one's own vomit" *(epistrepsas epi to idion exerama)*, and "wallowing in mud" *(kylismon)*. Those being described are individuals who have lost their moral sense.

The Moral Life in 2 Peter

2 Peter 1: Setting the Context

Probing the letter's paraenetic character and the author's marshaling of sources is useful in illuminating the role that moral typology plays in 2 Peter. The author's purpose for writing, sealed in the solemn testimony that his "death will come soon" (1:14), is expressed in 1:12-15: "I am making every effort so that following my [earthly] departure you might be able at any time to recall these things." Precisely what is it that should be so urgently "recalled" by the readers? The writer challenges his readers to cultivate an ethos that "offers proof" *(poieisthai bebaian,* 1:10) of their calling. That proof lies in a virtuous lifestyle, which furnishes proof both to the one who has provided abundant resources for life and godliness (1:3-4, 11) and to the moral skeptic (3:3-7). "What sort of persons should you be in holy conduct and piety?" (3:11) is the ringing question that readers are left to ponder at the conclusion of the letter.

Following the epistolary greeting, which accents received righteousness and grace (1:1), a catalog of virtues (1:5-7) is given.[11] The catalog itself, intended

---

thesis, see J. D. Charles, *Virtue amidst Vice: The Catalog of Virtues in 2 Peter 1,* JSNTSup 150 (Sheffield: Sheffield Academic Press, 1997), pp. 11-42.

11. As A. Vögtle (*Die Tugend- und Lasterkataloge im Neuen Testament,* NTAbh 16.4, 5 [Muenster: Aschendorff, 1936], pp. 58-62) has demonstrated, the emergence of ethical catalogs in the Hellenistic period can be seen as the result of philosophical reflection, initially within an "academic" but later a more popular context. In time, however, the focus of philosophical ethics moves from the theoretical basis of *aretē* (virtue or moral excellence) in the direction of its concrete and practical expression. Rhetorically speaking, the ethical catalog has an epideictic function: it is intended to instill praise or shame within the listener. Vice and virtue lists perform this practical rhetorical function equally in Stoic and Christian usage. Because the ethical contours of both were shaped against the backdrop of Greco-Roman culture, connections between Stoic discourse and the New Testament are numerous, as would be expected. Second Peter 1:5-7 is a

to outline the contours of Christian "life and godliness" (1:3), includes several commonly cited features that appear in standard Stoic virtue lists and are adapted to the Christian paraenetic tradition. Although Stoic categories are utilized, they serve a distinctly Christian purpose. The letter's greeting clarifies and highlights grace, a significant departure from the Stoic understanding of ultimate things. Both Stoic and Christian moral traditions compel moral progress or *prokopē* (cf. Phil 1:25; 1 Tim 4:15). The latter tradition, however, can be said to be less rigorous and absolute, based on the fact that it is predicated on divine grace and not human achievement per se.

In the mind of the writer, to possess these things (i.e., the virtues) is to prevent an ineffective and unfruitful life; to lack them is analogous to blindness resulting from a neglect of truth (1:8-9). At issue is moral responsibility.

The language of paraenesis presses to the fore in 2 Peter 1: "for this reason" (v. 5); "if these things are yours" (v. 8); "anyone lacking these things" (v. 9); "if you do these things" (v. 10); "for this reason I intend to remind you, even though you know them already and are established[12] in the truth that has come to you" (v. 12); "I think it right to stir you up" (v. 13); and "recall these things" (v. 15). Reflected in 2 Peter 1 is a markedly Gentile social environment in which the Christian community finds itself.[13] The rhetorical effect of this ethical terminology, though easily lost on the modern reader, would have been unmistakable to its intended audience. Theirs is not a faith that is void of the moral life; rather, the distinctly Christian ethic is to shine forth in bold contrast to surrounding culture. Tragically, in the view of the author, some have disregarded the divine "promises" (1:4; implied in 1:9, 12, 15) and as a result of their intercourse with the surrounding culture have "forgotten" their "cleansing from past sins" (1:9). These are to confirm their election through a robust Christian ethic (1:10). Worse yet, some are even aggressively propagating that there is *no* moral authority before which they must make account (2:1; 3:3-5).

---

prime example (see J. D. Charles, "The Language and Logic of Virtue in 2 Pet. 1:5-7," *BBR* 8 [1998]: 1-14; and idem, *Virtue amidst Vice*, pp. 99-111).

12. An interesting ethical observation is offered by N. Hillyer (*1 and 2 Peter, Jude*, NIBCNT 16 [Peabody: Hendrickson, 1992], p. 170), who suggests that if the epistle is genuinely Petrine, the use of the verb "firmly establish" *(stērizō)* is a conscious and poignant echo of the word Jesus spoke to the Apostle years prior at a time when he would be tempted toward denial.

13. This is the guiding assumption of T. Fornberg's thorough study, *An Early Church in a Pluralistic Society: A Study of 2 Peter*, ConBNT 9 (Lund: Gleerup, 1977). See also Charles, *Virtue amidst Vice*, pp. 44-83.

2 Peter 2: The Power of the Moral Paradigm

Notable examples of moral typology, as well as a detailed sketch of the opponents, are featured in 2 Peter 2. The verb tenses in 2:1-2 indicate a *future* time in which the *pseudodidaskaloi* ("false teachers") will manifest their destructive pattern. That the word "destruction," *apōleia,* occurs three times in 2:1-3 is indicative of an intense struggle that is foremost moral. Characteristic of that struggle are licentiousness *(aselgeia),* reviling truth *(hē hodos tēs alētheias blasphēmēthēsetai),* greed *(pleonexia),* and deception *(plastois logois).* Before false doctrine can proceed, it is typically introduced by moral departure, that is, a denial of moral authority *(despotēn arneomai).* The present struggle in the community involves the flight of those who had been purchased by — and thus, were the property of — the Master *(ton agorasanta autous despotēn arnoumenoi,* 2:1; cf. Jude 4). Significantly, slave-market imagery appears twice in 2 Peter.[14]

In addition, the link between 2:1-3 and 2:4-10a — and the material that follows — is decidedly ethical. The defining features of the pastoral dilemma, delineated in 2:10b-18 following the examples from the past, are "licentiousness" (twice), "defiling passion," "squalor," "moral depravity," "corruption," "seduction," and "lawlessness." The paradigms of 2:4-10a are relevant to the present, given the description of the reprobate who appear to be reveling in a like condition (2:13).

Complementing the allusions to the fallen angels and to Sodom and Gomorrah that resemble Jude[15] is flood typology — notably absent in Jude — which is intended to be prototypical of eschatological judgment.[16] In 2 Peter, Noah and Lot become types of faithful Christians who are to expect deliverance from God *(phylassein,* 2:5; *rhyomai,* 2:7, 9) despite enormous social obsta-

---

14. 2 Pet 2:1, 19. Cf. also 1 Cor 6:20; 7:21-23; Gal 3:28-29; 1 Pet 1:18-19; Rev 5:9.

15. While M. Desjardins ("The Portrayal of the Dissidents in 2 Peter and Jude: Does It Tell Us More about the 'Ungodly' than the 'Godly'?" *JSNT* 30 [1987]: 89-95), speaking for most NT scholars, is right to conclude that it is only natural that Jude and 2 Peter be viewed together, owing to their considerable literary correspondence, this very tendency has prevented fresh inquiry into both epistles. It may very well be useful to look beyond the correspondences to the *uniquenesses* (without becoming overspeculative) and, thereby, gain new insight into the meaning and message of both.

16. In 3 Macc 2:3-7, the flood, Sodom, and Pharaoh together serve as a *paradeigma* of judgment, similar to the angels, flood, and Sodom in 2 Peter 2, where they function as a *hypodeigma* of the ungodly (2:6). Leonard Goppelt (*TYPOS: The Typological Interpretation of the Old Testament in the New,* trans. D. H. Madvig [Grand Rapids: Eerdmans, 1982], p. 159) makes the distinction between type and symbol or analogy, identifying the fallen angels and Sodom with the latter.

cles.[17] The catchword "savior," occurring five times in the epistle (1:1, 11; 2:20; 3:2, 18), is intended to have more than a christological thrust. God saves a righteous remnant:

> For in this way, entry into the eternal kingdom of our Lord and *Savior* Jesus Christ has been abundantly provided for you. (1:11)

> For if, after having escaped the defilements of the world through the knowledge of our Lord and *Savior* Jesus Christ, they are again entangled. . . . (2:20)

> Remember the past words spoken by the holy prophets and the commandment of the Lord and *Savior* spoken through your apostles. (3:2)

> But grow in grace and knowledge of our Lord and *Savior* Jesus Christ. (3:18)

The message of 2 Peter, unlike Jude, is not mere condemnation; rather, it is the assurance of rescue from the midst of the cultural "furnace." While 2 Peter shares the same eschatological outlook as Jude, the paradigms in 2 Peter have a different function. This use of moral typology, however, requires a qualification. While Noah is a herald of righteousness[18] both in the OT and in Intertestamental literature,[19] Lot is by no means a righteous model in the OT. According to the Genesis 19 narrative, Lot appears to be fully inculturated in Sodom. In the end, he must be removed from the city by physical force (v. 16). Lot's "righteousness" — thrice he is depicted as *dikaios*[20] in 2 Pet 2:4-10 — is developed more fully in Jewish Intertestamental literature,[21] although it can be

17. Noah's generation is prototypical of a faithless generation in Jesus' teaching as well (Matt 24:37-39; Luke 17:26-28). In Luke's Gospel, Noah's and Lot's generations appear side by side, where both are united by a common thread: life proceeding as normal in spite of pending judgment. For a thorough examination of the use of flood typology in both Jewish and Christian literature, see J. P. Lewis, *A Study of the Interpretation of Noah and the Flood in Jewish and Christian Literature* (Leiden: Brill, 1968). On Noah and Lot as types in the synoptic tradition, see J. Schlosser, "Les jours de Noé et de Lot. A propos de Luc xvii,26-30," *RB* 80 (1973): 13-36.

18. See J. C. VanderKam, "The Righteousness of Noah," in *Ideal Figures in Ancient Judaism*, ed. J. J. Collins and G. W. E. Nickelsburg, SBLSCS 12 (Chico, Calif.: Scholars Press, 1980), pp. 13-22.

19. E.g., Sir 44:17-18; Wis 10:4; *1 Enoch* 106-7; *Jub.* 5:19; Josephus *Ant.* 1.3.1; *Gen. Rab.* 30:7; cf. Heb 11:7.

20. The frequent occurrence of *dikaios/dikaiosynē* in 2 Peter (seven times: 1:1, 13; 2:5, 7, 8, 21; 3:13) has a distinctively ethical quality. Moreover, *dikaiosynē* occurs often in Hellenistic catalogs of virtue, even when its sense is wholly anthropocentric ("justice") as opposed to theocentric with social implications ("righteousness").

21. Wis 10:6; 19:17; also Philo *Mos.* 2.58.

indirectly attributed to Abraham's pleading with God recorded in Genesis 18:16-33. Contrast, not essential nature, is the point of the Lot typology,[22] as clarified by the structural pattern of the text itself: *ouk epheisato . . . ouk epheisato . . . errysato.*[23] Important connections exist between the social environment of the readers and the "days of Noah"[24] and Lot. One commentator captures the sense of these verses in considering the significance of the flood typology:

> Peter thus maintains his pastoral purpose of encouraging his readers to keep faith with God in their own situation. Such a loyal stand will neither go unnoticed nor fail to attract a similar divine protection from the consequences of sin of the godless. . . . Yet, as God kept Noah and his family from perishing in the Flood which carried off the wicked of those times, so the same God will protect believers who remain faithful to him in later generations.[25]

In the typology of 2 Peter, the flood performs two functions: it both saves and judges.

Lot, by contrast, is not Noah. In 2 Peter, he is described as "tormented" *(kataponeō)* in his soul by unrestrained, lawless men day after day. Yet, in spite of this, in spite of his comfort in Sodom (cf. the portrait in Genesis 19), he too is rescued by God, which only serves to underline *the unmerited graciousness* of God's action.[26] The catastrophe that befell the cities of the plain is intentionally didactic. The visitation of divine judgment made Sodom and Gomorrah "an example" or "pattern" *(hypodeigma)*[27] for succeeding generations.[28] And what

22. Therefore, some modification is needed in T. D. Alexander's statement that "for the author of 2 Peter there could have been little doubt that Lot . . . clearly deserved the epithet 'righteous'" ("Lot's Hospitality: A Clue to His Righteousness," *JBL* 104 [1985]: 289). This premise is based on rabbinic understanding, according to which Lot was willing to offer shelter and food to strangers in Sodom (cf. Ezek 16:49; 22:29).

23. 2 Pet 2:4-9 contains language, moral paradigms, and a structural pattern that are very much akin to Sir 16:7-11.

24. The "days of Noah" and the flood also appear in 1 Peter in a similar context — suffering for doing right in an evil age (1 Pet 3:20). Moreover, "imprisoned spirits" surface in both epistles (1 Pet 3:19; 2 Pet 2:4).

25. Hillyer, *1 and 2 Peter, Jude,* pp. 188-89.

26. Hillyer, *1 and 2 Peter, Jude,* p. 190.

27. Cf. Jude 7. On Sodom and Gomorrah as a paradigm in Jude, see J. D. Charles, *Literary Strategy in the Epistle of Jude* (Scranton, Toronto, and London: University of Scranton, Associated University Presses, 1993), pp. 116-18.

28. Also *Jub.* 16:5, 6, 9; 20:5; 22:22; 36:10; Wis 10:6-7; Sir 16:8; *Tg. Ash.* 7:1; *Tg. Naph.* 3:4; 3 Macc 2:5; *Gen. Rab.* 27:3; *m. Sanh.* 10:3; *m. 'Abot* 5:10; Philo *QG* 4.51; Josephus *J.W.* 5.566.

is the pattern? Sin (i.e., moral lapse), when it is allowed to take root, leads to a moral departure and darkening of one's heart, which invariably incurs judgment. While the moral paradigms in 2 Peter address both the apostate and the faithful, their thrust — consistent with moral exhortation — is to encourage the latter. God continues to be "savior" amid the community's overwhelming cultural struggles.

The description accorded the adversaries in 2:10b-21 both contains significant parallels to Jude and is differentiated by a notable expansion of the Balaam typology (2:15-16). The moral corrosion that characterizes these individuals in 2 Peter is striking. They act as irrational beasts, slander, and revel in their corruption. They are boastful, irreverent, disobedient, and scornful. They are adulterous, insatiable in their appetite for sin, and actively seduce others.

Moreover, whereas only a brief standardization of type appears in Jude ("the error of Balaam," v. 11), in 2 Peter these individuals are more fully typologized; they are depicted as "having abandoned the upright way and gone astray" *(kataleipontes eutheian hodon eplanēthēsan)*, following the road of Balaam son of Bosor, who "loved the wages of wrongdoing" (2:15). The language strongly suggests apostasy. A paradigm of self-seeking and greed in Jewish tradition,[29] Balaam more importantly (for the immediate context) was seduced by pagans, the fruit of which meant apostasy for Israel. Balaam is prototypical of some in the community, who are depicted with Balaam as actively pursuing wickedness.[30] The downfall of a prophet of God is a singular phenomenon — and one that is highly instructive. Balaam over time became ethically divorced from the message that he bore. The psychology and character of apostasy are such that a moral cynicism causes one to loathe what was formerly embraced; in the end, one "loves the rewards of wrongdoing." Such a tragic case is not only a possibility that can befall the individual; from the standpoint of 2 Peter, it is also a cancer that threatens everything around it.

The Noah and Balaam typology indicates that not doctrinal strife but ethical lapse is the focus of the writer's polemic. In addition, two further clues — in 2:19 and 2:20-22 — magnify the pastoral dilemma. The opponents are antinomian in character and boast of their freedom from moral constraints. In

29. See G. Vermes, *Scripture and Tradition in Judaism: Haggadic Studies*, 2nd ed., StPB 4 (Leiden: Brill, 1973), pp. 127-77; also, Charles, *Literary Strategy*, pp. 120-24.

30. Note a similar link to Balaam in the message to the church at Pergamum (Rev 2:12-17). Significantly, idolatry and fornication are the two identifying characteristics in Pergamum (2:14), as in Thyatira, which is said to be under the influence of "Jezebel" (Rev 2:20-22). Balaam and Jezebel, given the trajectory of the related OT narratives, are symbols for apostasy in the early church. See G. Forkman, *The Limits of the Religious Community*, ConBNT 5 (Lund: Gleerup, 1972), pp. 157-58.

casting off divine moral authority, these individuals end up as slaves (2:19) to their own lusts (*epithymia*, v. 18) and pleasure (*hēdonē*, v. 13). In the Pastoral Epistles, this very linkage of *epithymia* and *hēdonē* by means of the slave metaphor is also employed to illustrate the Christian's servitude to the former life.[31] This combination, well-known in Hellenistic ethics, would have had even greater meaning for the Christian looking back on his or her preconversion state than for the Greek moralist. Second Peter 2:19, as well as verses 20-22, describes the moral degeneration that characterizes the pagan lifestyle, a decidedly pre-Christian condition. The implication for the readers, rhetorically speaking, is that even moral pagans are better off than some in the community.[32]

The language found in verses 20-22 adds to the picture in a way that should give the readers pause. The adversaries, tragically, had previously escaped worldly defilement but have become entangled and overpowered therein once more — a horrendous state of affairs in which the latter condition eclipses the original. The picture that follows, though conventional, is meant to shock. A double proverb (v. 22) consisting of one part OT (Prov 26:11) — the dog returning to its vomit — and one part extrabiblical (Arabic, Syriac, and Armenian versions of *The Story of Ahiqar*)[33] — the pig returning to the mud — is employed. The readers are struck by the graphic simplicity of proverbial wisdom and will appreciate its appropriateness to the situation. The use of common proverbial stereotyping resonates with the audience, especially in a pagan social environment.

2 Peter 3: Dealing with the Moral Skeptic

Traditional commentary has read 2 Peter 3 through the lens of eschatology, typically interpreting this material as evidence of *doctrinal* deformation in need of adjustment.[34] Viewed structurally, 3:1-13 consists of the following components: an exhortation to remembrance, a caricature of the hardened moral skeptic, a declaration of incontrovertible moral accountability, pastoral remarks concerning theodicy, and concluding admonitions. Theologically, it is not the *timing* of the parousia but its inescapable *fact* that is vigorously asserted. The day of moral reckoning and death, as aptly stated by J. B. Mayor,[35] removes the skeptic

31. Cf. Jas 4:1-2 and Titus 3:3, where both elements are associated.
32. Cf. Titus 3:3-5, which has a similar rhetorical function.
33. *APOT* 2:772.
34. See, e.g., Käsemann, "An Apologia for Primitive Christian Eschatology," pp. 135-57.
35. J. B. Mayor, *The Epistle of St. Jude and the Second Epistle of St. Peter* (New York: Macmillan, 1907), p. 211.

from the realm of illusion and into the sphere of reality. On this basis, paraenetic language is employed once more for the purpose of warning the saints. The author of 2 Peter concludes: "I am arousing you by way of reminder" (v. 1); "what sort of people should you be?" (v. 11); "therefore . . . , make every effort . . ." (v. 14).

Destruction of the cosmos by fire, alluded to in 3:10-13, mirrors the Stoic belief that the universe underwent periodic renewal by means of burning *(ekpyrōsis)*. This restoration was understood to take place over and over again, without terminus. While the author of 2 Peter does not endorse this view of the universe and advances an apocalyptic eschatological perspective, he would seem to be borrowing Stoic ideas and imagery for the sake of argument.[36] These are marshaled not with a view toward emphasizing chronological timing but in order that the *certainty* of divine judgment be firmly established.[37] Moreover, the opponents not only question the reality of the parousia; they challenge the very stability and preservation of the cosmos.

Our encounter in chapter 3 with the writer's moral apologetic leads us to a conclusion contrary to that proposed by traditional biblical scholarship. The literary units of the epistle are not in fact disconnected or haphazardly assembled, nor do they "betray embarrassment rather than force."[38] The epistle does not close "with the admission that the doctrine of the Last Things is already landing the Church in difficulties, and her apologetic is in fact the demonstration of a logical absurdity."[39] Rather, the material in chapter 3 is a calculated response to the current moral state of affairs brought about by those who have forgotten the binding power of Christian truth-claims, resulting in various levels of embracing the old (i.e., heathen) way of life. An alternative reconstruction of 2 Peter 3 is to be preferred, to the extent that it preserves the literary arguments and integrity of the letter. .

---

36. Cf. J. H. Neyrey, "The Form and Background of the Polemic in 2 Peter," *JBL* 99 (1980): 407-31; R. Riesner, "Der zweite Petrus-Brief und die Eschatologie," in *Zukünftserwartung in biblischer Sicht: Beiträge zur Eschatologie,* ed. G. Maier (Wuppertal: Brockhaus Verlag, 1984), pp. 124-43; C. P. Thiede, "A Pagan Reader of 2 Peter: Cosmic Conflagration in 2 Peter 3 and the OCTAVIUS of Minucius Felix," *JSNT* 26 (1986): 79-96; and M. E. Boring et al., eds., *Hellenistic Commentary to the New Testament* (Nashville: Abingdon, 1995), pp. 537-38. A most useful discussion of the nature and origins of Stoic cosmology is found in D. E. Hahm, *The Origins of Stoic Cosmology* (Columbus: Ohio State University Press, 1977), pp. 200-215.

37. J. Chaine ("Cosmogonie aquatique et conflagration finale d'après la Secunda Petri," *RB* 46 [1937]: 207-16) captures the proper sense of the use of eschatology in 2 Peter 3 and, not unlike Neyrey, adduces several texts from antiquity concerned with cosmic conflagration.

38. Käsemann, "An Apologia for Primitive Christian Eschatology," p. 194.

39. Käsemann, "An Apologia for Primitive Christian Eschatology," p. 194.

The affirmation of cosmic renewal in 3:13 mirrors interplay of pagan and Judeo-Christian cosmology, behind which stands a fundamental question: What is the relationship of human beings to matter? Yet behind this question stands an even more fundamental question, namely: What is the relationship of *moral* human beings to matter? Cosmology and eschatology in the strictest sense, however, are not showcased. Rather, the author's purpose is to develop a response to a caricature of the moral skeptic (v. 4). Because the opponents are championing moral self-determination (2:1, 2, [implicit in 4-10a], 13, 15, 18, 19), they must justify their ethical departure — hence, the function of the caricature in 3:3-5, which presents the moral question from the standpoint of someone on the outside.[40] Furthermore, they "deliberately ignore" *(lanthanei gar autous touto thelontas)* past examples of divine retribution (3:5-6), which typologically point to the ultimate day of moral reckoning: "and the earth and all deeds done on it will be revealed" (3:10). The point of the teaching is not to adjust theology; rather, it is to stress that judgment will be the expression of a *judicial* process and a *moral* reckoning.[41]

From the standpoint of the faithful (i.e., the "beloved" of 3:8), this divine "delay" is disconcerting and requires a proper perspective.[42] The faithful, like Noah and Lot (2:5-8), will be rescued at the appointed time. Until then, however, they must resist the social forces at work within culture that would undermine faith and morality. Theodicy and divine long-suffering, not a fading parousia hope, constitute the pastoral burden of the writer (3:8-13). His is a response not to a warped eschatological framework or theology per se but to a militantly resistant skepticism that denies any moral claims over one's life. For the faithful, patiently enduring (vv. 12, 15) in a hostile social environment is part of God's call to "holiness and godliness" (v. 11). The final exhortation in the epistle is instructive, for it clarifies the writer's priority: "You, then, beloved, since you have been forewarned, be on guard, so that you are not carried away by the error of the morally depraved" *(athesmoi;* v. 17).[43]

---

40. S. S. Smalley ("The Delay of the Parousia," *JBL* 83 [1964]: 54) correctly sees in these verses a concern not to adjust eschatology but to address the moral skeptic, i.e., the "outsider."

41. This important exegetical and contextual point is made by H. Lenhard, "Ein Beitrag zur Übersetzung von II Ptr 3.10d," *ZNW* 52 (1961): 128-29; and F. W. Danker, "II Peter 3:10 and Psalm of Solomon 17:10," *ZNW* 53 (1962): 84.

42. Contrary to the regnant assumptions of "early Catholicism," there is no disappearance or "fading" of the eschatological hope in 2 Peter 3; rather, it is the matter of *timing* that invites clarification.

43. The opponents are characterized as "morally depraved" or "lawless" three times in the epistle (2:7, 8; 3:17). Twice they are depicted as creatures or slaves of moral "corruption" (2:12, 19).

Conclusion

A unitary reading of 2 Peter brings us to an important determination. Ethical lapse and apostasy lie at the heart of that which plagues the community to whom the epistle is addressed. The combined ingredients of literary style and paraenetic language, Stoic and mystic categories, the catalog of virtues, moral typology, and caricatures of the adversaries all add up to a cultural setting permeated by pagan Hellenistic influence. Moral corruption, licentiousness, antinomianism, and irreverence vex the church set within a pluralistic society. For this reason, moral skepticism, not dissatisfaction with orthodoxy,[44] is the object of the author's highly stylized polemic. It is for this reason that piety and immorality, virtue and wickedness, are juxtaposed throughout the epistle.[45]

Strongly suggested throughout the epistle is a fundamental denial of moral self-responsibility. In its advanced stages, this denial has resulted in the apostasy of certain members of the community. While it is true that "theological" justification (i.e., "heresy") necessarily accompanies any departure from the faith, apostasy (i.e., an ethical departure from the moral truth of Christian revelation) is the scourge of the community. The present situation calls for a roundly prophetic and eminently pastoral word of exhortation — a word aimed foremost at enunciating the ethical foundations of the Christian faith.[46]

Moral types, hence, figure prominently in the author's paraenetic scheme. Examples from the past — some notorious, all instructive — illustrate in graphic terms the author's burden. In 2 Peter, types perform two functions: they simultaneously reiterate judgment and salvation. To the apostate, they underscore a day of moral reckoning for which the unrighteous are being reserved; to the faithful, they offer encouragement, insofar as God continues to be "savior" amid the community's overwhelming cultural struggles. Second Peter constitutes a prophetic, and eminently pastoral, word of exhortation *(logos parainētikos)* aimed at enunciating the ethical foundations of the Christian faith.

---

44. Contra J. N. D. Kelly (*A Commentary on the Epistles of Peter and Jude*, BNTC [London: A. & C. Black, 1969], p. 305) and others. Orthopraxy, not orthodoxy, is underscored.

45. So P. Perkins, *First and Second Peter, James, and Jude*, IBC (Louisville, Ky.: John Knox, 1995), p. 163.

46. The situation being addressed in the epistle may be reasonably compared with that encountered by Paul in Corinth in 55 c.e. Moral lapse, credibility of confession, and cultural idolatry, matters thoroughly discussed in 1 Corinthians 1–11, all have a theological bearing (cf. 1 Corinthians 15). Nevertheless, the burden of Paul's letter is foremost ethical.

"A Sharp Two-Edged Sword":
Pastoral Implications of Apocalyptic

Ellen T. Charry

Where there is perceived to be a cosmic struggle between goodness and evil, in which it appears that the forces of darkness are about to swallow up the followers of light, the faithful remnant, the pious, the virtuous, the holy ones, or the elect, in a violent and devastating change of eons, there crouches apocalypticism. Wherever there is a longing for a future era of peace and righteousness in which God will wipe away every tear, there peeps the eschaton, the fullness of time. In the nineteenth century, these concepts helped scholars distinguish literary genres in New Testament and other texts. Yet these two notions joined together — the decay of the present age in which the righteous are alone and persecuted, and the transformation of the future into God's reign, where evil will be vanquished — speak a truth that enables the literature to reach across time and space.

A God who is good, powerful, and faithful must be willing and able to rescue the persecuted faithful from rebels against God's will who threaten them. The parousia, the final judgment, the defeat of the Antichrist, and chiliasm all bespeak hope in the vindication of the righteous against their enemies. Even so, the vivid scenes painted by apocalyptic prophecy also catch one up in the fear of being caught on the wrong side of the divide. Apocalyptic not only gives hope of God's power to rescue, it also "interpret[s] how things were, are, and ought to be. [Its] purposes are to inform and influence human life by means of the values and insights expressed in the symbolic and narrative form."[1] It is, or can be, an instrument of spiritual nurture.

1. A. Yarbro Collins, "Reading the Book of Revelation in the Twentieth Century," *Int* 40 (1986): 231.

Reprinted with permission from *Int* 53 (1999): 158-72.

Although the church's appropriation of apocalyptic has changed over time, one attribute seems to remain constant: clarity. It is always clear to those who are, or sense that they are, wronged that goodness is readily distinguishable from evil, and that they are on the right side of the cosmic divide. Even if it looks like the forces of evil have the upper hand in the struggle, there is no real acceptance of evil's eventual triumph. Apocalypticism is born of hope and fear, not despair and cynicism. Goodness will prevail in the long run, even if not in one's own lifetime; evil will be vanquished by the universal reign of God. This latter instinct — that evil simply cannot finally (be allowed to) win — allays despair, anger, and fear and encourages trust in the power of God's reign, even in troubled times. While a source of courage, apocalyptic is also a source of anxiety. The power of God — whether poised to take down Israel, Rome, the medieval papacy, or Adolf Hitler — keeps the faithful alert. Punishment of God-resisters as well as rescue of God-worshippers are expressions of divine power that aim to instill awe and reverence in both groups. Yet, they can switch places far too easily.

A deeper source of anxiety reflected in apocalyptic is the expectation of conflict and suffering built into the gospel itself. Paul anticipates conflict between those who embrace and those who reject the gospel of the crucified Lord when he warns Christians that their message is countercultural in both pagan and Jewish worlds (1 Cor 1:18-31). Yet he also proclaims that the lordship of Christ is universal, that every knee shall bow and every tongue confess that Jesus Christ is Lord (Phil 2:10-11). If, toward the end of the century, Christians did not know what they were getting into, they had no excuse. Later texts press the point even more clearly. Matthew's community already knows, probably firsthand, how divisive the Christian gospel really is. Matthew 5:10 and 10:34-36, as well as the Gospel as a whole, are like boot-camp for Christians: they teach the strenuous standards they are to live by. John 15:18-25, perhaps most directly, warns of future persecution. In sum, whether referring to the initial hostility from Jews or enduring hostility from the Roman Empire, the New Testament shows that Christianity is not for the fainthearted.

This dramatic eschatology is central to an important interpretation of Christ's victorious work, which guided the early church through its struggle with Rome. Christ triumphed over the devil who had brought down creation and humankind. His victory is not personal but cosmic; it consecrates a new age. Sin, death, and bodily corruption at death are conquered in his rising from the dead. The power and goodness of God overpower human weakness and the forces that seem impervious to the voices of reason and honor. It is this victory of God that Christians read about in their Scriptures, confess in their creeds, proclaim in their preaching, and recall and celebrate in their feasts and in the sacraments. So they upbuild one another in a hostile environment.

The two biblical texts that modern scholars have identified as apocalyptic in a technical literary sense are Daniel and Revelation. They both meet the scholarly definition of apocalyptic as prophetic revelatory visions of a supernatural world delivered to an individual.[2] We will turn to Daniel along with other Old Testament themes shortly. The strongest New Testament call to stouthearted Christians comes in Revelation. This prophecy seeks to arouse intense commitment to Christ in keeping with the fearsome circumstance of Christians in Asia Minor. The prophecy is delivered by a two-edged sword in Christ's mouth (1:16). It calls for the establishment of Christ's kingdom and counters both pagan culture and the church. Emotional intensity is volatile. When everything is at stake and danger looms, emotions may lurch out of control. In condemning the forces of evil, one may find oneself condemned or trapped in the dizzying eddy of anger, fear, anxiety, and embarrassment as one longs for a new day. Here we will sample how Christian writers have appropriated and reoriented the emotionally destabilizing aspects of apocalyptic in various circumstances.

Ambiguity in the Struggle of Good and Evil: Revelation 2–3

Apocalyptic varies with historical circumstances. New Testament writers anticipated, or perhaps even provoked, Christian clashes with the Roman Empire. Christians, like Jews, were unpatriotic "atheists" because they would not, or could not, participate in sacrifices to the emperor (although some permitted a pinch of incense to appease the powers).[3] When fire, famine, or plague unsettled Rome or the provinces, Christians were ready scapegoats for the emperor or a provincial governor. Christians were indeed a religious and political threat to the unity of the empire. In light of Philippians 2:10-11, we can see that confessing the name of Jesus intended to provoke the state. Jesus Christ was the proper threat to all counterclaims to divine authority.

Deemed legal by the state, Jews were nevertheless seriously harassed and penalized. The first uprising of Jews against Rome in 66 C.E. created hostility against Christians as well.[4] When Christians separated from Judaism, their situation became more precarious. They became a hated, exposed minority "asso-

---

2. This definition of apocalyptic literature was developed by a group of scholars and published in John J. Collins, "Introduction: Towards the Morphology of a Genre," in *Apocalypse: The Morphology of a Genre*, ed. J. J. Collins, *Semeia* 14 (1979), p. 9. It is cited in A. Yarbro Collins, "Reading the Book of Revelation," p. 236.

3. Robin L. Fox, *Pagans and Christians* (New York: Knopf, 1987), p. 426.

4. Fox, *Pagans and Christians*, p. 432.

ciated with 'evil religion.'"[5] Individuals were captured, tried, and on occasion exiled or martyred for refusing to comply with civil standards, although classwide persecution came later. By the second century, simply being a Christian was enough to arouse persecution.[6] The vicious pursuit of adoration by Domitian extended to the provinces as well.[7] The gods clashed.

The revelation of Christ through one named John to the seven churches — lampstands or shining lights of western Asia Minor and their patron spirits or perhaps angels — interprets the situation of these Christians. It suggests that they were being called out for a special role in the divine plan: to proclaim the triumph of God over the gods. The Apocalypse was written to hold their feet to the fire.

Yet John's Apocalypse sounds another note at the outset, a note that disturbs the clarity of readers' understandable identification with the Lamb against the Beast. Although apocalyptic clarity pits the pure church against the evil empire, this relationship of adversity is set in a complex frame. To begin, it is striking that the prophecy against Rome is delivered to Christians. The church is the target of the vision because it carries Christ's mission to the world. In John's vision, the ascended Christ is surrounded by seven lampstands, indicating the symbolic significance of the seven churches being addressed. As successors to the household of God, symbolized by the candelabra in the destroyed temple in Jerusalem, the churches have a high profile. Because the mission is to bring down the false gods of Rome, Christian conduct must be scrupulous. Christians are, as Paul put it, "ambassadors for Christ" (2 Cor 5:20). The credibility of the gospel now relies on them.[8] Christ holds seven stars in his right hand (symbolizing the angels of these churches) and speaks (presumably to them) with a double-edged sword.

The power of the two-edged sword is evident in five of the individualized cover letters delivered by the appointed angels that accompany the dissemination of the prophecy to the churches in the midst of the enemy. All but two of the letters (to the Smyrneans and the Philadelphians) are double-edged. The other five are patterned after Pauline parenesis, which first praises the congregation's faithfulness to the gospel but then chastises it for failing to live up to the gospel it confesses. With this rhetoric the writer allies himself with the audience's best intentions, thus gaining their initial trust. The purpose is to con-

---

5. W. H. C. Frend, *The Rise of Christianity* (Philadelphia: Fortress, 1984), p. 110.

6. Fox, *Pagans and Christians*, p. 434.

7. Fox, *Pagans and Christians*, p. 426.

8. Christopher Rowland, *Revelation*, Epworth Commentaries (London: Epworth, 1993), p. 62.

front them with their complicity in the evil they fear. Some Christians, surrounded by pagans like those Paul chastises in Romans 2:1-11, lose their grip on the gospel's demand to separate radically from the dominant culture. As Richard Bauckham points out, "Worshipping the beast was something many of John's Christian readers were tempted to do or were actually doing or even . . . justified."[9] Admonition of the faithful is never popular, especially in such delicate situations. The double-edged sword, of course, cuts both ways; it strengthens the troops for battle yet calls them to ever more strenuous standards as God's witnesses.

While attending to this dialectical dimension of most of the letters to the seven churches of the Apocalypse, it is important to note that this pattern, while prevalent, is not universal. The letters to the churches at Smyrna and Philadelphia lack the criticism found in the other five. Nevertheless, the criticism in five of the seven letters is sufficient to suggest that this theme is not incidental. For readers struggling to make sense of the delicate situation, it is a reminder of their own frailty in the face of the call to proclaim the universal rule of God in a hostile environment. Encouragement and critical self-examination go hand in hand, proclaimed by Christ himself through the angels who deliver his revelation. Even the despised are scrutinized for the quality of their worship of the one true God.

The cover letter to the church at Ephesus reveals a variegated picture of the Christians there (2:1-7). Ephesus was the main seaport of Asia Minor and was dominated by a huge temple to Artemis (Romanized as the goddess Roma) and the divine Julius.[10] Christians there are vigilant for the faith; they will not tolerate wickedness. They do not take members' self-testimony at face value but test it. They are willing to suffer for God's sake (vv. 2-3). They seem to pass the test of a faithful congregation. Yet, despite this strong record, they cannot fulfill the mission to which Christ calls them (vv. 4-5). Although Christians of great integrity, their faith has lost the dew of its first flowering; they are "complacent"[11] and have compromised their "lampstand" status (v. 5b). Their ministry is on shaky ground. Those with acute hearing who can regain their Christian integrity will eat of the tree of life when they are put to the test (v. 7).

The sharp double-edged sword is next unsheathed against the church in Pergamum (2:12-17). Pergamum was the seat of Roman power in western Asia.

---

9. Richard Bauckham, *The Theology of the Book of Revelation,* New Testament Theology (New York: Cambridge University Press, 1993), pp. 15-16.

10. G. B. Caird, *The Revelation of St. John the Divine,* BNTC (London: A. & C. Black, 1984), p. 29.

11. Rowland, *Revelation,* p. 67.

The populace worshipped Asclepius, the god of healing. The Romans erected a temple to Rome and Augustus to whom absolute allegiance was due. Christian confession runs upstream against imperial power. Yet, here too, God is not pleased (v. 14a). There are still sexual immorality and signs of idolatry among the Christians in Pergamum (v. 14b). Their ministry, too, is compromised. The burden of being a Christian is not only to be intellectually faithful to Christ but to use one's body, including the gastro-intestinal tract and the genitals, in a manner that serves and honors him. There is no separation of mind and body here. Repent, the angel says, or Christ will fight — and already is fighting, by means of this very revelation — the "soft" Christians with his two-edged sword. Here we see that the Lord upholds the faithful in the face of their impending destruction by the state. Yet in the midst of this external pressure he ups the ante of Christian faithfulness. God threatens Christian sinners even while they are persecuted. Lax Christians are in double jeopardy, from God's enemies and from God himself.

Next, Christ speaks directly to the Christians in Thyatira (2:18-29), a commercial center that worshipped the god Tyrimnos, identified with Apollo.[12] On the surface, these Christians seem to be strong: eager in faith, love, and good works (v. 19). Yet some of them, too, have a deeper hidden life in which they protect, perhaps even participate in, the idolatry and adultery that they claim to have left behind, symbolized by consorting with Jezebel (v. 20). Christ divides the truly postpagan Christians from those who never really detached themselves from a pagan lifestyle. The latter will be struck dead that God may be glorified among the churches, but the truly postpagans who endure with Christ to the end will inherit secular authority when the enemy is defeated (vv. 26-27).

Sardis was a prosperous industrial and commercial city whose local worship of Cybele had merged with Greek goddesses. The deified empress Livia was impressed on their coins.[13] Like most congregations the church at Sardis is a "mixed bag" of Christians (3:1-6). Although they have a good reputation, the reality is more complicated. A few members of the church have not "soiled their clothes," but most have need of a laundromat. They do not obey the gospel that they received when they were converted. They too must repent, lest the anger of God visit them, stealthily, like a thief (v. 3b).

The final dialectical letter is to the church in Laodicea (3:14-22), another cosmopolitan, wealthy, and educated city with a fine medical school.[14] Here we find tepid Christians. They are wealthy and self-satisfied, indifferent to their

12. Caird, *The Revelation of St. John the Divine*, p. 43.
13. Caird, *The Revelation of St. John the Divine*, p. 47.
14. Caird, *The Revelation of St. John the Divine*, p. 56.

spiritual wretchedness, poverty, blindness, and nakedness (v. 17). God is especially angry with this sort of Christian, who should be strong enough to withstand the temptations of wealth and luxury. In this letter, the prophet alludes to the source of the dialectical apocalyptic: "My child, do not despise the LORD's discipline or be weary of his reproof, for the LORD reproves the one he loves, as a father the son in whom he delights" (Prov 3:11-12).

From the Roman side, the problem was that Christians, like Jews, simply refused to assimilate and so aroused hostility — a sensibility Christians themselves would readily lose when Jews refused to assimilate into the "Christian" world after Christians assumed power. From the Christian side, the issue was that this weak and motley band was called to proclaim God's defeat of the Roman order.

In sum, even from its opening chapters, John's apocalyptic suggests that struggle between forces of good and evil is more complex than meets the eye. First, the tone set by these letters suggests that not all Christians are the same (a word to the wise seminarian). Local congregations cannot be generally categorized. Some Christians are stouthearted and read the gospel militantly. Others are of softer mien and seek a low profile. According to the Apocalypse, Christ desires a militant church that will absorb suffering rather than accommodate the powers that be. Indeed, to preach Christ by employing the same tactics as the Beast would give Rome the victory.

Next, the pastoral function of apocalyptic is twofold. It is both to bolster the faithful in their precarious situation and to hold their feet to the fire. Christ's demand for self-searching prevents self-righteousness from setting in. Fighting the Beast can become a path to self-esteem rather than a means of testifying to Christ. Third, clearly these five letters offer a radical Christian teaching. Instinctively, if one is dealt with unkindly by those in authority, one responds with anger and perhaps a desire for revenge. That is not Christ's teaching here. None of the seven letters ever suggests revenge or violence as an appropriate response to the situation in which Christians find themselves. Christianity is an alternative way of life. Christians' own spiritual well-being is God's primary concern. Christians who endure suffering for their confession fight for Christ by maintaining their integrity, not by becoming what they hate.

Finally, this Christian understanding of the struggle between goodness and evil is multivalent. Evil cannot simply be projected or introjected. As the author of 1 Peter put it, "Be sober, be watchful. Your adversary the devil prowls around like a roaring lion, seeking someone to devour. Resist him, firm in your faith" (5:8-9a). True vigilance is not only against the disobedience of others, but also against temptation. God's revelation points out just how thin the line between sin and righteousness really is. The enemy is both within and without. In short, the cover letters undercut the clarity often associated with the cosmic struggle between God and Satan.

Apocalyptic Suffering and Self-Examination

The ambiguity of apocalyptic prophecy is not unique to Revelation but is embedded deep in biblical thinking as, for example, in the Old Testament pattern of prophecy and punishment. In Genesis 1–11 and Isaiah 24, divine wrath smites or threatens the whole earth. Both the nations and Israel are threatened with destruction in Isaiah 3–23 and in Amos 1–2.

While the corruption of the world prior to the call of Abraham sets up a distinction between Israel and the nations, later history proves that the elect of God are as sinful as the nations who do not know God. The ambiguity articulated in the cover letters of the Apocalypse is evident as early as Sinai in institutional memory. God plagues, plunders, and destroys the Egyptians in order to rescue Israel, only to rage against the paganized Israelites. Moses, like Abraham with the Sodomites, has to intercede to prevent God from destroying them too, even though Moses himself is so furious with the dancing calf-worshippers that he smashes the newly carved law at the sight of them (Exod 32:19). These memories, however, seem to have had little far-reaching effect in Israel. The temptation of paganism continues unabated. Like the Apocalypse, classic Israelite prophecy is a tool to call Israel to repent and all the world to worship God.

Israel is elected as the infantry in God's battle against the gods. The Egyptian enslavement bespeaks Israel's suffering in the midst of ancient Near Eastern power politics in pursuit of God's goal: God's power, justice, and mercy arrayed before the nations. In the Exodus story, Israel's suffering is the necessary prelude to God's deliverance. Finally, in the midst of the slaying of the firstborn, Pharaoh pleaded for blessing from this God who is more powerful than the gods of Egypt (Exod 12:32b). Samson's triumph over the Philistines (Judges 16), the conversion of the widow of Zarephath (1 Kgs 17:24), the triumph of Elijah's God over the priests of Baal (1 Kings 18), the conversion of Naaman the Syrian (2 Kings 5), and of course Jonah are other examples of this theme.

Another dramatic match of God against the gods is Daniel's survival of the lions, in which God's power so sobered King Darius that he decreed that God was to be feared and reverenced throughout his kingdom, which included Babylon, Media, and Persia (Dan 6:26). Indeed, Israel's captors are called to worship God. Most of these conversion or near-conversion stories occur among Israel's enemies. Imagine Hitler converting to Judaism in the midst of the war! Now, the Old Testament stories enumerated here are not of apocalyptic urgency. The circumstances are difficult, however: slavery, famine, military danger, captivity, and exile. Understandably, the characters in these narratives see and react only at the level of their own interest and need in the immediate events that confront them. Ironically, Israel, perhaps without assent and apparently without even realizing it, is the instrument of God's redemption of her enemies all along, and the conversion they undergo is not to affection for Israel herself. It is to God who has co-opted Israel into this grand mission.

In most of these stories, Israel is an unsuspecting instrument of the divine plan, but Daniel's representation of the exiled Israelites at the Babylonian court displays this role directly. His terrifying apocalyptic visions and dreams explain God's struggle to be known amid contemporary politics. Israel, it appears, will long be instrumental in spreading God's reign.

Although Daniel is called as a missionary to the Gentiles and a comforter to Israel, he, like John of the Apocalypse, is also concerned for the spiritual health of Israel. Astonishingly, in the midst of his prophecy portending the fall of the neo-Babylonian empire, Daniel's prayer in chapter 9 is a lengthy confession of Israel's sins that concludes with a plea for the restoration of God's temple: "We do not present our supplication before you on the ground of our righteousness, but on the ground of your great mercies" (Dan 9:18c). Daniel parades Israel's sins before its captors!

The vision of both Daniel and John is wide enough to relate the current troubles of God's people to their spiritual well-being. Daniel's prayer reflects the Deuteronomic and later rabbinic view that suffering is brought on by sin, and calls all Israel to repent in his prayer for divine mercy. The five cover letters to the "shining lights" of the church in the Apocalypse do not argue strongly that the suffering of the church was brought on by Christian laxity. Only the allusion to the divine discipline of the psalmist in the letter to the Laodiceans suggests this. Yet, for both Daniel and John, the dread created by the threat of impending suffering should spur introspection leading to conversion. Learning self-criticism is a gift — painfully learned, but a gift nonetheless.

Self-criticism, as an appropriate response to humiliation, is not limited to the Bible. It seems to have been Socrates' point to his fellow citizens after the Athenian debacle in the Peloponnesian War. If it would not be too distorting to paraphrase Socrates in prophetic biblical terms, we might say that he was criticizing the Athenians (though without the God of Abraham) for putting their trust in the power of the sword rather than in the power of goodness in order to turn them around. For this, Socrates was put to death.

Daniel and John integrate two elements that display the ambiguity of apocalyptic and bring them to bear on the interpretation of the suffering of God's people. First, self-examination is required, even on the part of those being persecuted. Second, God's rescue of the faithful is cause for self-examination among those who have persecuted. Thus, victim and oppressor are joined together in a common search for the truth about themselves and about God who is in the midst of their struggle.

Augustine and the Spiritual Transformation of Apocalyptic

By the fourth century, Christians grew weary under the persecution of Diocletian. When it ended, the struggle between good and evil turned inward. Accommodationists battled rigorists in the Donatist controversy. The struggle threatened to divide the church. Internally fragmented and externally threatened, the church was vulnerable. People became caught up in anticipating a date for the parousia. Suddenly, the conversion of Constantine and the legalization of Christianity in 313 changed everything. Rome was transformed from the enemy into an instrument for the spread of the faith. Predicting a date for the end of the world no longer fit the need of the rapidly growing church.

Augustine of Hippo stepped into the breach by converting the violent apocalyptic framework of Revelation for peacetime use. He recognized that the legalization and rapid spread of Christianity meant that a new eon was indeed at hand, and that the old pagan world would collapse by gradual conversion to the Catholic faith, not by cataclysm. The day of the church was at hand. A gentler reading of scriptural eschatology was needed.

Personally, Augustine had already made the spiritual shift from the old to the new world of the Catholic faith, and he determined that the age of the church should supersede the pagan age. Rather than a sudden violent apocalypse, Augustine watched Roman civilization decay from within and in response created structures to nurture the growth of Christian civilization. To this end, he domesticated apocalyptic by redirecting it from the violent overthrow of the state to the final judgment each individual would have to face.[15] This had the effect of both moralizing and spiritualizing eschatology and of setting the day of judgment in the distant future. Rather than focusing on tyrannical state regimes outside the church, he turned attention to the day Christians would have to take account of themselves. The chapters on the final judgment offer spiritual guidance for new converts. In this regard, whether intentionally or not, Augustine was forwarding the self-critical spiritual admonition of Daniel and Revelation. Augustine's ecclesiology offers one example of his refocusing apocalyptic on the church itself, more in line with the Old Testament and

15. Augustine *City of God,* book 20.

Jesus' eschatology that focused on the people of God. To counter Donatist rigorism, Augustine, looking at the clergy, defined the church as a mixed body of saints and sinners.[16] Although this may be read as an anti-apocalyptic move, it actually follows the precedent of unclarity or ambiguity in apocalyptic texts. He introjected the apocalyptic divide between goodness and evil into the church itself. This strategy sustained the church for centuries and was only fully dispensed with in the sixteenth century when Protestants were willing to sacrifice the unity of the church for the sake of purity.

Another point at which Augustine outfitted the church for the long haul was his teaching on celibacy and marriage. He equated spiritual readiness for the Catholic faith with his own readiness for celibacy, and he never explicitly relinquished the idea that celibacy is superior to marriage. By early in the fifth century, however, he recognized that married life was appropriate for most Christians. It was not only a concession to human weakness, as Paul had suggested, but a positive good in itself. In his treatise "On the Good of Marriage," he elevated marriage to sacramental status and argued for its three goods. First, stable marriages assure the health and stability of society through the rearing of children in families. Next, the friendship and companionship of marriage and the fidelity that it requires are an honorable way of life that promotes friendliness in society. Finally, and here his defense of marriage moves in a radically new direction, the marital bond is a sacramental relationship that constitutes a holy way of life before God or perhaps (he is not clear on this) mediates God's holiness to the couple.[17]

With Augustine, marriage came out of the closet into the light of God in the church. Without criticizing celibacy directly, he implied that it no longer suited the church's situation. Celibacy is possible for a select group, or if the world really is about to end. He also realized that disorderly sex is unable to sustain a cohesive social fabric. Extramarital sex had to be ruled out in order for Christians to steward civilization. Marriage is the only institution able to deal with both problems.

As suggested above, the baptism of Europe required a change in the direction of eschatology because there was no longer an external regime that delegitimated the church. With its minority status ended, Christians had to learn to rule themselves. Could the church learn from its own experience of persecution? Augustine used the allegorical method to symbolize and spiritualize the characters and events of Scripture (including the Apocalypse) in order to render it a pastoral rather than a political instrument.

---

16. See, e.g., Augustine *City of God* 20.9.

17. Augustine, "The Good of Marriage," in *Marriage in the Early Church*, ed. David G. Hunter (Minneapolis, Minn.: Fortress, 1992), pp. 120-21.

Nonapocalyptic eschatology charted a new path for the long-term future by becoming an instrument of moral self-scrutiny for those who live in peaceful times. Together with his teaching on the moral ambiguity of the church, Augustine crafted an eschatology that acknowledged the weaknesses of Christians and assumed a long future for the church. The struggle between God and Satan would continue, but now within the story of the church itself.[18]

Joachim and Apocalyptic's Return to History

Beginning with the eleventh century, the church's appropriation of apocalyptic took another turn.[19] With the consolidation of papal power from the late eleventh through the thirteenth centuries, the Western church became a bureaucratic institution like any other secular power. The papacy became the center of authority in the West. Eschatological longing returned, now targeted against the secularized church itself. This took the form of calls for the reform of monasticism, church governance, and the papacy.

The Gregorian Reform of the late eleventh century, named for its chief exponent, Gregory VII, rallied around the slogan "the freedom of the church." This meant freedom from lay control, as the feudal system was being constructed. It also called for moral renewal and a monastic spirit against the proprietary church system and the king's church.[20] This reform movement sparked the Investiture Controversy (1075-1122) between the pope and King Henry IV over ecclesiastical power. The church was combating simony that occurred when the laity invested bishops and priests with authority over lands and churches. The king was protecting his power over his subjects. The result of the reform movement was the Petrine apostolic principle, the doctrine of papal primacy. It gave the pope administrative authority far beyond the church's spiritual mandate.[21] The Gregorian Reform thus secularized the church. This in turn led to another pivotal turning point in the church's appropriation of apocalyptic.

The struggle between vice and virtue occurs within both individuals and institutions.[22] In the high Middle Ages, apocalyptic writing and art revived and were reshaped by the struggle for the spiritual integrity of the church. Apoca-

18. Bernard McGinn, ed., *Apocalypticism in the Western Tradition*, Collected Studies Series 430 (Brookfield, Vt.: Variorum, 1994), 3:269-70.

19. McGinn, *Apocalypticism in the Western Tradition*, 3:277.

20. I. W. Frank, *A Concise History of the Medieval Church* (New York: Continuum, 1995), pp. 57-58.

21. Frank, *A Concise History of the Medieval Church*, p. 61.

22. McGinn, *Apocalypticism in the Western Tradition*, 3:227.

lyptic moved away from Augustine's ecclesiological-spiritual interpretation of John's Apocalypse. This shift was accompanied by the loss of the two-edged sword built into the biblical apocalyptic vision. Instead of being spiritualized, in keeping with patristic allegorical exegesis, the bizarre images were rehistoricized, as they had been in the mind of the original author. The symbolic images and scenes were again interpreted in terms of contemporary events and figures. This left little room for the tonic of unclarity. The enemy was named.

The greatest exponent of this renewed historical appropriation of apocalyptic was Joachim, the Abbot of Fiore (d. 1202). His apocalyptic categories helped make sense of, and gave direction to, historical events and possibilities. He offered a Trinitarian interpretation of history, in order to look beyond the Petrine principle that currently reigned. He identified the rule of the Father with the age of the Old Testament and the age of the Son with the age of the church, and he anticipated a turn to the age of the Spirit as a millennial age of peace and love, to occur dramatically in 1260. His approach threatened papal authority.

Joachim's vision of the age of the Spirit did not, however, envision overthrow but renewal of the papacy. Joachim based his salvation history on Revelation 14:6: "Then I saw another angel flying in midair, and he had the eternal gospel to proclaim to those who live on the earth — to every nation, tribe, language, and people." This new vision of the pope as an Angelic Pastor proclaiming the eternal gospel, a suffering servant who would turn the church from worldly to spiritual matters, was patterned on the monastic life Joachim himself had adopted.[23] Joachim was a transitional figure; he advocated a strong but a spiritually pure papacy that could be a spiritual model for the people.

Nevertheless, the subordination of the spiritual life to the financial and imperial interests of the church bureaucracy continued through the thirteenth century, disheartening more radical Christians. Francis of Assisi made his own protest against the worldliness of the church, sharpening Joachim's position. Viewing the church's wealth, ostentation, and power as signs of corruption, Francis and later the Franciscans countered that poverty was the plumbline not only of the monastic life but also of the Christian life in general. Militant Franciscan spiritualists, appealing to Joachim, longed for a future Angel Pope. They considered themselves the vanguard of the future, purified church that would usher in Joachim's age of the Spirit.[24] For them, the threat of evil was no longer from external regimes but from within: the Antichrist now headed the church!

---

23. McGinn, *Apocalypticism in the Western Tradition*, 5:158.
24. McGinn, *Apocalypticism in the Western Tradition*, 5:162.

Augustine's distant, spiritualized eschatology seemed too weak in the direct confrontation between Christian rigorists and papal bureaucrats and flatterers. Visionaries and bureaucrats rarely see eye to eye. The debate between worldly and spiritual orientations lost the grace of ambiguity. The struggle between Franciscan rigorists and accommodationists divided the order and unsettled matters more broadly.[25] The laity sought means of devotion and piety outside regular channels.

The decline of the church spurred widespread, often highly politicized, debate on two visions of the church. Should the church be out and about, like a multinational corporation, or should it be a spiritual leader modeling the life of prayer, modesty, and simplicity? Yearning for an Angel Pope, a monastic who would defeat the Antichrist and lead the church back to the norm of evangelical poverty, brought class conflicts to the fore, as positions hardened on both sides. Clarity and conflict walked hand in hand. The classic call for the vindication of the righteous and the destruction of the wicked rang out.

In response to the frenzy created by followers of Joachim who predicted the imminent change of eons, Thomas Aquinas turned to the issue, taking Augustine as his guide.[26] Like the master, he identified the basic point of apocalyptic to be "the ability to predict the end of the world with security."[27] Skittish about violent certainty, Thomas voted for Christian life in the trenches over the long haul. As the storm of theological and social upheaval gathered, Thomas amassed several arguments against Joachim, among them that the abbot had an erroneous understanding of theological history (there are two, not three, decisive ages of salvation history — before and after Christ) and a wrong scriptural (i.e., typological) hermeneutic.[28] Thomas, like Augustine before him, argued that Christ's rule on earth would never be smooth. Nonapocalyptic eschatology was prepared to live with that reality, but it stretched the limits of what rigorous Christians could tolerate.

Apocalyptic's Two-Edged Sword: Self-Critical Indignation

We have touched on only a sample of the apocalyptic texts and movements in Christian history. We have seen apocalyptic turn outward to bolster the church against external threat and inward to purify it in times of ease. We have seen es-

---

25. McGinn, *Apocalypticism in the Western Tradition*, 5:168-69.
26. McGinn, *Apocalypticism in the Western Tradition*, 9:38.
27. McGinn, *Apocalypticism in the Western Tradition*, 9:37.
28. McGinn, *Apocalypticism in the Western Tradition*, 9:40.

chatology adapted for times of crisis and in anticipation of peace. We have seen that crisis promotes a religious rigorism that precipitates more crisis, and that prosperous times encourage accommodation to the larger culture. These impressions leave us without a systematic presentation of apocalyptic but provide some insights to ponder at the new millennium.

Apocalypticism is a powerfully emotional force. It is birthed by rigorists and activists. Yet cooler heads perceive its dangers and seek to sand its rough edges to prevent violence and debilitating wars of attrition. Apocalyptic encourages endurance in times of crisis and concedes to panic when the End seems near. It is a cry for succor and rescue when human resources seem unable to stem the coming tide of evil and destruction, yet it thrives on moral outrage that burns out when the crisis passes.

Beneath the emotional urgency experienced by a weaker party to the disputes resides a deep longing, a longing for help in the form of holy leadership. In our own day, it is implicit, for example, in contemporary feminism, which craves a rigorous standard of "holiness" throughout the church. Apocalyptic feminism is, however, an anomaly in today's world. Ours is more nearly an age of apathy, or perhaps paralysis, in the face of the massive impersonal forces involving all of us: for example, the debasement and violence of modern secular culture, materialism, and overpopulation. Perhaps the amorality that we embrace comforts us not only because we find morality tedious in times of peace and general prosperity but also because we feel helpless against the contemporary evils we deplore. The disclosure of corrupt leaders and the debasement of public and personal life have not stimulated rigorist moral fervor for holy leadership. Instead of longing for virtuous leaders, modernists have become cynical about virtue and leadership altogether. Classic apocalyptic may be difficult to fathom through this sensibility.

Biblically and theologically speaking, the visible reign of God has always been somewhat elusive. In the Old Testament, the people betray God almost immediately after their liberation from Egypt. In the New Testament, the lordship of Christ has already arrived and yet is clearly incomplete both because it embraces so few and because these few so often waffle in their adherence to Christ's lordship and the way of life it authorizes. It is present already because believers taste it and are transformed by the new identity and mission Christ has given them. Yet it is still far off because it is partial and ephemeral. Christians struggle to remain uncomfortable in a comfortable culture, which compels them to conform. Perhaps this tension, built into Paul's eschatology, is the reason why realized and future eschatologies have so readily interacted. Or, perhaps it contributes to apocalyptic's fading more broadly. Christians no longer experience themselves as a minority in a larger host culture.

The agent of conversion and sanctification — who gives believers the ability to be Christians, builds up the church, and Christianizes the general culture — is the Holy Spirit, the agent of faith and holiness. The church's mission, under the guidance of the Holy Spirit, is two-sided, as is the eschatological vision itself. The Christian is charged to await the coming of the Lord with patience but also to participate actively in preaching Christ throughout the world. The challenge is to remain aloof enough from one's surroundings to maintain a distinctively Christian voice, yet to become involved enough so that Christ's call can be grasped in an alien setting. The faith required to live Christianly under duress, the hope that Christ will vindicate his followers, and the love that enables one to minister to one's enemies are possible only by the grace and comfort of the Holy Spirit.

A final theological observation has to do with the relation between eschatology and ecclesiology. Apocalyptic eschatology generally presumes a corporate nature of the church whose members identify with it as a corporate reality, whether under external intimidation or internal corruption. Nonapocalyptic eschatology introduces the notion of individuals facing the final judgment after this life. This is usually linked with a focus on an individual's fate rather than the fate of the church. Apocalyptic eschatology works with a corporate ecclesiology, while a nonapocalyptic eschatology fits well with an individualized ecclesiology.

There is tension, then, between eschatology and ecclesiology, depending on which models are employed. Classically speaking, the church is normally one, holy, catholic, and apostolic. Sadly, normalcy is not usual for the church. Apocalyptic eschatology lends itself more readily to corporate ecclesiology than to individualized ecclesiology, where believers constitute the church.

Let us now return to the starting point of our reflection. The two apocalyptic Scripture texts we examined, Daniel and the Apocalypse of John, both bring the crises they address under the judgment of Christ's two-edged sword. From the perspective of scriptural apocalyptic, it is not enough to be filled with righteous indignation when persecuted. Even where outrage is warranted, it must be tempered by self-criticism. The tenor of Daniel's prayer and the five cover letters we examined suggest that the experience of persecution, evil as it is, does not imply the righteousness of the oppressed. In short, according to the Scriptures, victims are sinners, too, even if not in the same manner that oppressors are. Daniel and John call both the tyrant and the persecuted to repentance: an odd, but perhaps fitting place for them to meet. Ironically, this strange companionship may itself suggest a way forward in the face of frustration.

Apocalypticism, it turns out, is itself a two-edged sword. It can be dangerous when it breeds self-righteous indignation. Yet, without it and the hope that it nourishes, the Christian project would collapse. Fortunately, Christian texts themselves offer an antidote in what we might call self-critical indignation. It is, admittedly, a difficult teaching by which to live. The texts themselves, however, warn the reader that faithfulness to God under pressure has never demanded less.

Although we have focused on apocalyptic eschatology, it is noteworthy that a gentler, though perhaps not kinder, eschatology has prevailed in the church. Augustine taught that the body of Christ is not a club for saints but a school for sinners, all of whom must account for themselves in God's good time.[29] Combining a corporate ecclesiology that embraces both accommodationists and rigorists with a nonapocalyptic eschatology for the long term may be the highest road for the church to travel, for it places the militant and the laid-back all under the standards of holiness, unity, catholicity, and apostolicity. Perhaps the struggles of the past two millennia will yet bring us strength for the third.

29. Thanks to Rowan Greer for this phrasing.

PRACTICE

Embodied Remembering:
Wisdom, Character, and Worship

Jill Y. Crainshaw

She remembers. It was summer, 1931. Across the street from the front porch where she is sitting, people rush in and out of the Wal-Mart parking lot. In another era, she spent her girlhood days where that parking lot is now, baking in the hot summer sun, in what were then her grandfather's farming fields. But it is the evenings of those days whose seeds have found the deepest roots in her memory, because each day at sunset that thirteen-year-old girl, an old man, and a bluegrass band of crickets created a daily summer benediction.

Each evening, during those misty moments that teeter on the edge of nightfall, she and two of her friends made a pilgrimage down the winding dirt road to where "old man Fauber" could always be found, sitting on the front porch of an old farmhouse, moving back and forth to the rhythms of a weathered rocking chair. Smiling, the glow of summer fireflies twinkling in his eyes, Mr. Fauber taught them.

Sixty-eight years later, the young girl is a woman, but she still remembers. She remembers the daily pilgrimage, and she remembers the words of the mountain ballad that she learned on that front porch. She laughs. Those old mountain ballads take fifteen verses to tell their stories, and Mr. Fauber taught them that ballad's story one verse, sometimes only one line, each evening.

The lyrics themselves exhibited no explicit philosophical or existential meaning, and the song was not the creation of a Bach or a Beethoven. Even so, a particular kind of wisdom was discovered in that daily ritual, a wisdom beyond the words of the song. They laughed together, talked about farming and baseball, discussed techniques for growing the sweetest tomatoes, and then she and her friends headed home, the song and an unexpected wisdom growing in their hearts and in their minds as the summer slipped away.

During those summer evenings in 1931, a ritual was created, a ritual whose meaning was about more than the words of a playful mountain ballad. Three adolescents and a grandfatherly neighbor created a communal space where wisdom of a deeper kind could be shared, a wisdom that cannot be adequately articulated in human language. A ritual was created that provided a structure of meaning in a world that soon would be plunged into the uncertain complexities of the Great Depression. In the midst of the rhythms of daily living, they created a particular rhythm of being together that shaped hearts and minds for a lifetime.

The ritual structure of worship connects our daily lived experience to our experiences of God's presence. As worship juxtaposes the everyday objects and actions of bread and water, eating and washing, to God's Word, a rhythm is created that over time shapes hearts and minds so that people are enabled to glimpse God's presence in the daily-ness of their lives.[1] Through the ongoing rhythms of the Lord's Day worship and the liturgical year, the gospel story is told, verse by verse, week after week; the community's story is also told as people bring with them to the worship event the joys and despairs of living in the complex world of the twenty-first century. In worship, as the human story is woven together with the peculiar idiom of the divine story, space is created where the community can encounter the mystery of God's presence in Christ.[2]

A major challenge to the formative power of Christian worship is the pluralism of the contemporary world. People's thoughts and actions today are shaped by a multiplicity of societal images and influences ranging from the media to the sports industry to the internet. For the Christian community, however, the paschal mystery, God's presence in Christ's death and resurrection, is the generative source of character formation.[3] Worship creates a pathway into this mystery as those gathered remember Christ through the proclamation of the Word and in celebrations of the eucharist.

Worship's weekly rhythm of liturgical remembering has the power to

---

1. Don Saliers, *Worship as Theology: A Foretaste of Glory Divine* (Nashville: Abingdon, 1994), pp. 194-96.

2. Gordon Lathrop (*Holy Things: A Liturgical Theology* [Minneapolis, Minn.: Fortress, 1993], pp. 33-34) argues that meaning occurs in worship as symbols, actions, and words are set next to one another in the actions of the *ordo*. This patterning of the liturgy "evokes and replicates the deep structure of biblical language, the use of the old to say the new by means of juxtaposition."

3. In my *Wise and Discerning Hearts: An Introduction to a Wisdom Liturgical Theology* (Collegeville, Minn.: Liturgical, 2000), I argue that the shaping of cognitive and affective dispositions toward God is never merely a matter of adopting certain behaviors. Character formation is a dialectical and ongoing process of critical reflection and action; it involves continual practicing of the "good" within the patterns of liturgy.

paint on the landscape of every lived experience a vision of a world in which the hungry are fed and the bitterness of injustice is replaced by the taste of God's goodness and grace. It is a vision the church embodies when in its liturgies the gathered community wrestles with the realities of evil and ritually images an alternative.[4]

L. Gregory Jones suggests that many faith communities today have "lost a sense of the Bible as a (or the) central text in the formation of Christian character and identity."[5] Important to rediscovering Scripture as "the Word that journeys with us" in our work and in relationships on Monday through Saturday is the ritual act of "remembering." In worship, we "remember" God's Word. This remembering happens as the church, in its proclamations of God's Word, retrieves from within the Judeo-Christian tradition the liberating truths embedded in Scripture and creatively imagines the "world that Scripture imagines."[6]

Retrieving the power of Scripture for today does not involve merely an analysis of ancient texts and languages. In worship, rather, contemporary communities weave their language together with the ancient language of the texts in an intentional and poetic seeking after the truth.[7] This essay will examine the relationship between liturgical remembering, character formation, and the emerging role of the Christian church in the contemporary world marketplace.

This exploration involves two interrelated tasks: (1) to establish a correlation between the ritual framework of worship and feminist efforts to reinterpret Christian tradition by retrieving from within tradition liberating alternatives to patriarchal structures; and (2) to suggest concrete ways in which such a correlation contributes to recovering the formative power of Scripture for the

4. Mary Catherine Hilkert, *Naming Grace: Preaching and the Sacramental Imagination* (New York: Continuum, 1997), p. 97. Edward Farley ("Toward a New Paradigm for Preaching," in *Preaching as a Theological Task: World, Gospel, Scripture*, ed. Thomas G. Long and Edward Farley [Louisville, Ky.: Westminster/John Knox, 1996], pp. 165-75) argues that in the context of worship it is possible for redemptive discourse to disrupt evil and give hope to the concrete situations of people's lives.

5. L. Gregory Jones, "The Word That Journeys with Us: Bible, Character Formation, and Christian Community," *ThT* 55 (1998): 70.

6. Jones, "The Word That Journeys with Us," p. 71.

7. Walter Brueggemann (*Theology of the Old Testament: Testimony, Dispute, Advocacy* [Minneapolis, Minn.: Augsburg/Fortress, 1997], p. 743) suggests that the discovery of "true speech both evokes and requires a certain kind of community — a community with an intentional speech practice of its own." He makes a distinction between the work of interpretation in the academic community and that in the ecclesial community. He considers the work of both to be necessary for a full understanding of Scripture.

church today.[8] Biblical wisdom literature, particularly as it has been interpreted by William P. Brown, provides a hermeneutical frame for this exploration.[9]

*   *   *

> A poem can momentarily heal not only the alienation of thought and feeling . . . but can fuse the different kinds of knowing and at least in some instants weld mind back into body seamlessly.[10]

People long for frameworks that can help them make sense out of the chaos and ambiguities of human living. Rituals, says Tom Driver, provide frameworks for meaning making because of their ability to "link our most 'advanced' ideas and aspirations with some of our most 'primitive' tendencies. They are profoundly integrative." Rituals link the stories we tell about ourselves to certain actions and to a reality beyond the limits of human knowing. At their best, rituals are embodied poetry that "seamlessly" integrate mind, body, and spirit.

For example, the stories of our birth and of our belonging both to the human family and to God's family are ritually immersed in the water of baptism, water that symbolizes both a basic human need and the human desire for life beyond the pain of this world. In a similar way, a funeral ritual becomes a tapestry onto which we weave the stories of our living and our dying, the ritual's language and actions providing the ambiguity and uncertainty of human death with an eternal framework.

From birth, a human being's prereflective intuitions about God, humanity, and the world are mediated into conscious reality and action through ritual

---

8. Shannon Schrein (*Quilting and Braiding: The Feminist Theologies of Sallie McFague and Elizabeth A. Johnson in Conversation* [Collegeville, Minn.: Liturgical, 1998], pp. 1-4) suggests two categories of feminist theological response to the ideological dominance of patriarchal structures in the Christian tradition. "Revolutionary" feminism has in large measure determined that the patriarchal structures of the tradition are not redeemable. "Reformist" feminism seeks to discover liberating alternatives within the tradition that have been suppressed by patriarchal hegemony.

9. See William P. Brown, *Character in Crisis: A Fresh Approach to the Wisdom Literature of the Old Testament* (Grand Rapids: Eerdmans, 1996). In an earlier publication, I outlined the parameters of a "wisdom liturgical theology" that contributes to liturgical renewal by developing a "theological method grounded in the dialogical movement between the horizons of everyday reality and tradition in Old Testament wisdom as it is developed in the structural forms of Proverbs 1–9 and Job" (*Wise and Discerning Hearts*, p. 6).

10. Marge Piercy, *Circles on the Water: Selected Poems* (New York: Knopf, 1982), p. xii, quoted in Elisabeth Schussler Fiorenza, *But She Said: Feminist Practices of Biblical Interpretation* (Boston: Beacon, 1992), p. 9.

and symbolic structures such as gestures and language. As Driver explains, our humanity is in large part learned, a learning that happens as we "enact, rehearse, work, and play our way into the human condition."[11] The threads of this learning are woven throughout history as human communities of every era both learn and teach. In this learning/teaching dialectic, ritualization provides rhythms for passing one generation's wisdom on to the next one.[12]

To ritualize, says Driver, is to seek pathways for those almost daily journeys we make into landscapes that we have not experienced before. He offers the example of a child learning to walk or to dance. Her learning is imagination, invention, and experiment, but it is also more than that. Much of what the child learns is formed as she patterns her actions, with some risk and creative nuance, after the examples she sees in her culture. These patterned examples shape and are shaped by each succeeding generation and make up a society's ritual pathways.

Many of society's ritual pathways, or patterns for action and decision making, were cut through the wooded forests of earlier eras as our predecessors learned how to weather storms, survive droughts, plow barren fields, make friends, and heal disease. Much of the wisdom gained in this learning has endured through the years, some of it even gaining the status of treasured tradition. Driver explains that

> as a particular act of ritualizing becomes more and more familiar . . . it comes to seem less like a pathway and more like a shelter. These two images — pathway and shelter — reflect the tension in ritualization between the

11. Tom Driver (*The Magic of Ritual: Our Need for Liberating Rites That Transform Our Lives and Our Communities* [San Francisco: Harper Collins, 1991], pp. 15-16) argues that ritualizing activity is basic to the human condition. Anthropologists and archeologists have discovered the prevalence of ritual in all cultures throughout human history. Rituals in religious life are thus created and perdure in a broader historical and socio-cultural context of ritual.

12. Driver, *The Magic of Ritual*, pp. 15-16. Driver makes a distinction between ritual and ritualization. Ritualization is more implicit to everyday life; common behavioral actions such as shaking hands or saying "hello" or "good-bye" are examples of ritual pathways that are a more or less unnoticed part of daily life. These acts of ritualizing, says Driver, are a vital part of human and animal living: "Human beings share with other animals a communicative world that depends upon gestural routines. Ethologists, who study animal behavior, have learned that animals of many different species engage in behaviors so highly patterned and so necessary for the animals' communication with each other that the scientists view them as akin to the rituals that humans perform. . . . Ritualized activities became, countless generations ago, necessary for our survival, and have remained necessary to a far greater extent than is commonly recognized" (p. 14). Ritualized activities are the "stuff" of which the more clearly delineated parameters of rituals, such as the great liturgies of various historical epochs or the elaborate rites of passage in many cultures, are made.

verb and the noun. Some ritualizations have become in the course of time such elaborate shelters that they are like architecture. . . . What were once newly blazed pathways are now old forms invested with rich symbolic content and carefully guarded by explicit traditions and rules. These are the great liturgies and ceremonies of stable institutions. . . . They both guide and shelter the passing of generations.[13]

The ritual process of meaning making described by Driver is an important part of religious structures throughout the world. Ritual and story, moving together in a poetic dance, are the ways people interpret their world; this is also the way we connect God's story to our human stories.

Images parallel to "pathway" and "shelter" appear in the recorded wisdom of the early Hebrew sages. The implied movement between "pathway" and "shelter" in the canonical book of Proverbs reflects a pattern for critically remembering tradition that can benefit contemporary struggles to appropriate inherited wisdom.

William Brown argues that the book of Proverbs is "essentially about the journey from home to community and back again, a *rite de passage*."[14] An image that reflects this, not unlike Driver's ritual "pathway," appears in Proverbs 1–9 in the symbolism of the "way":

Hear, my child, and accept my words,
    that the years of your life may be many.
I have taught you the way of wisdom;
    I have led you in the paths of uprightness.
When you walk, your step will not be hampered;
    and if you run, you will not stumble.
Keep hold of instruction; do not let go;
    guard her, for she is your life.
Do not enter the path of the wicked,
    and do not walk in the way of evildoers.
Avoid it; do not go on it;
    turn away from it and pass on.   (Prov 4:10-15)

This metaphor of the "way," or pathway, is a primary symbolic expression in Proverbs 1–9.

A goal of early Hebrew wisdom, Brown argues, was to shape the character of persons in the community such that they would have "eyes to see and ears to

13. Driver, *The Magic of Ritual*, p. 17.
14. Brown, *Character in Crisis*, p. 49.

hear" God's presence in their everyday lives and could develop the wisdom for making ethical and moral choices that would lead to communal and personal well-being. In biblical understanding, he continues, *derek*, or way, is marked by the footprints of many generations of travelers. In other words, the tested wisdom of past generations has the power to guide new generations in particular directions. Norman Habel notes that the symbol of the way in Proverbs is elaborated and clarified in terms of its opposite. To travel the way of wisdom is to choose life; the "path of the wicked" leads to chaos and death (4:16-19).[15]

Another primary symbol in Proverbs, expressed in the image of the "two houses," parallels the ritual "shelter" described by Driver:

> For at the window of my house
> I looked out through my lattice,
> and I saw among the simple ones,
> I observed among the youths,
> a young man without sense,
> passing along the street near her corner,
> taking the road to her house
> in the twilight, in the evening,
> at the time of night and darkness.   (Prov 7:6-9)

The symbolism of the "house" dots the landscape of the journey of the wise person in Proverbs.

For example, the book of Proverbs begins in a communal setting where a father instructs his son in the way of wisdom. From this communal "shelter" that has provided him with religious understandings and with particular patterns for decision making, the son journeys into the world where the traditional wisdom of his community is challenged. As his community's traditional symbols and images run headlong into the dissonant images of the marketplace, and as he struggles to appropriate the wisdom of his tradition in landscapes beyond his community, the possibility arises for reformulation of moral principles and consequent reshaping of character.

In Proverbs 9, another house appears along the journey, the house of Woman Wisdom:

> Wisdom has built her house;
> she has hewn her seven pillars.
> She has slaughtered her animals, she has mixed her wine,
> she has also set her table.

---

15. Norman Habel, "The Symbolism of Wisdom in Proverbs 1–9," *Int* 26 (1972): 131-57.

> She has sent out her servant-girls,
>> she calls from the highest places in town,
>> "You that are simple, turn in here!"
> To those without sense she says,
>> "Come, eat my bread
>> and drink the wine I have mixed.
> Lay aside immaturity and live,
>> and walk in the way of insight."   (Prov 9:1-6)

In this image, Woman Wisdom (Greek, *sophia*) stands in the doorway inviting all who hear her words to enter her house. People from all walks of life are welcomed at her table, and her house becomes a metaphorical "shelter" of meaning in which the diverse aspects of life can be integrated.[16]

In feminist interpretations of the wisdom tradition, the presence of Sophia challenges patriarchy and embraces pluralism. In Proverbs, Wisdom is characterized as a female who is at God's side in the act of creation, who pervades nature and the world with her presence, and in whom God delights. In fact, as Elizabeth Johnson explains, throughout the Hebrew wisdom literature, God's presence is personified in the figure of Sophia, who is cast as "sister, mother, female beloved, chef and hostess, preacher, judge, liberator, establisher of justice, and a myriad of other female roles wherein she symbolizes transcendent power ordering and delighting in the world."[17] To enter her house is to enter Wisdom's house and to have one's image of God and of the world expanded and enriched by metaphors vastly different from metaphors common within the dominant patriarchal system.

The image at the end of Proverbs again implies that of a "shelter" (31:10-31). The son has journeyed beyond the parameters of tradition and returned to establish his own home in partnership with a woman of wisdom who is both wife and entrepreneur in the marketplace (vv. 16-24). Integrating the wisdom of tradition with the wisdom gained along the journey, the pilgrim now begins to create a "ritual shelter" that reflects parts of the tradition of his formative community but at the same time engages the issues and concerns of the wider mar-

---

16. Mircea Eliade (*The Sacred and the Profane: The Nature of Religion — the Significance of Religious Myth, Symbolism and Ritual within Life and Culture* [New York: Harper and Row, 1957]) explores how the door into the church represents a threshold between the sacred and the profane. While the categories of "sacred" and "profane" are less clearly delineated in a desecularized world, Eliade's understanding of the church as that space where time intersects eternity is valuable for current discussions of ritual integrity and vitality.

17. Elizabeth Johnson, *She Who Is: The Mystery of God in Feminist Theological Discourse* (New York: Crossroad, 1992), 87.

ketplace. The shelter he creates, Brown argues, is a sanctuary of meaning whose frameworks mediate a new vision for relating to God, others, and the world.[18]

The ongoing movement between pathway and shelter exemplified in Proverbs is vital to worship if its ritual structure is "to point beyond itself to deeper realities or beliefs held, often unconsciously, by the individuals who perform it." No shelter should become permanent; there are always new paths to blaze, new theological truths to uncover. The dialectical movement between pathway and shelter is what gives ritual its poetic quality. When ritual maintains this quality, the theological knowledge and interpretations mediated by it are not allowed to become static. Instead, biblical truths and their proclamation in worship are understood in a constantly moving and shifting dynamic into which insights never before encountered can be always be woven.[19]

Such a dynamic relationship between pathway and shelter is necessary for a critical retrieval of Scripture for current contexts. If the poetic quality of ritual, and thus of worship, is diminished, ritual "shelters" become concretized as houses of ideological authority, outmoded and complicit in perpetuating oppression. Within such ideological structures, patriarchal and dogmatic principles for Scripture interpretation are often substituted for the more metaphorical and liberating content of Scripture, content characterized by a plurality of voices and contexts. When this happens, worship becomes mere ceremony that fails to tell the stories of all of God's creation and to connect the divine story to the realities of people's lives.

Mark Searle uses the metaphor of "journey" to name the dialectical or tensive quality of ritual and explores it in relationship to worship and conversion.[20] It is part of human living that people almost daily make journeys through unfamiliar landscapes. Sometimes these journeys take us into wildernesses that appear unexpectedly on the horizon in the form of various crises. Sometimes wildernesses are discovered as people make conscious choices to step off the pathways they are on and explore new frontiers.

The journey away from the familiar, away from traditional shelters, initiates what Arnold van Gennep termed a rite of passage.[21] In rites of passage, the journeyer moves outside the parameters of normative social structures into the unfamiliar, into a stage of destabilization or what is called "liminality." Growth occurs as the wilderness wanderer recognizes that her long-held beliefs about

---

18. Brown, *Character in Crisis*, pp. 154-55.

19. Fiorenza, *But She Said*, p. 52.

20. Mark Searle, "Journey of Conversion," *Worship* 54 (January 1980): 41-42.

21. Arnold van Gennep, *The Rites of Passage*, trans. Monika B. Vizedom and Gabrielle L. Caffee (Chicago: University of Chicago Press, 1908), pp. 12-13.

the world are not adequate for dealing with the realities she now faces. Having wrestled with this unexpected and disorienting juxtaposition of traditional values with conflicting views of reality, she can return to society with a nuanced or revised understanding of tradition and with a transformed vision of the world.

Van Gennep focused his work on those momentous life events in which people move from one social situation to another. Rites of passage, from his standpoint, are rituals through which "individuals are detached from their established and normal role in society by being placed outside the social nexus in an in-between state."[22] In folk cultures, rites of passage mark transitional phases of life such as baptism, marriage, or Bar/Bat Mitzvah.

Ritual anthropologist Victor Turner expanded upon van Gennep's work to suggest that all ritual reflects a movement from separation (from an established societal role), to liminality (a stage of antistructure or disengagement from familiar established norms), to reaggregation (reintegration into societal structure with a new role or identity).[23] Turner argues that common to this process are transforming religious experiences during which new truths about God are discovered and the identities of individuals and communities are formed.

Human living is characterized by a constant movement between times of clarity and certainty about beliefs, on the one hand, and crisis times of uncertainty and ambiguity, on the other. When this movement is suppressed or masked, the poetic and imaginative quality of ritual is lost. So, too, is its ability to initiate change and growth.

How is the dynamic relationship between ritual pathways and ritual shelters to be nurtured in the church's worship? Or, to express it as Elisabeth Schüssler Fiorenza does, how can people today whose lives are still influenced by the Bible "read 'against the grain' of its patriarchal rhetoric" and breathe new life into its language and content, allowing its ancient words to speak the truth anew in a constantly changing world?[24]

As the faith community has encountered societal change at other times in its history, certain patterns of response and action have emerged. Many of these patterns of action, some liberating and some oppressive, have endured over time even through the most difficult historical situations the church has faced.[25]

---

22. Alan J. Roxburgh, *The Missionary Congregation, Leadership, and Liminality* (Harrisburg, Pa.: Trinity Press International, 1997), p. 24.

23. Driver, *The Magic of Ritual*, pp. 157-59. See also Victor Turner, *The Ritual Process: Structure and Anti-Structure* (Baltimore: Penguin, 1969).

24. Fiorenza, *But She Said*, p. 7.

25. Edward Farley, *Ecclesial Reflection: An Anatomy of Theological Method* (Philadelphia: Fortress, 1982), pp. 190-96.

Edward Farley links these enduring patterns of response and action to the development of tradition. For archaic people, tradition provided an accumulation of wisdom that guided them in making decisions in difficult situations. It was a collective wisdom that grew out of each faith community's lived experience of God's presence in its particular historical context and that was passed from generation to generation:

> Having a distinctive "tradition" meant that they did not have to re-invent or rediscover "truth" in its entirety each time they faced a new situation; they could turn to the wisdom of their history to find the enduring elements of truth and construct on this foundation a solution to problems appropriate for current circumstances.[26]

The church faced enormous societal change early in its history and created "vehicles of duration" for protecting the distinctiveness of its tradition within the religious plurality of the surrounding Mediterranean culture.

These protective structures or shelters became increasingly rigid over time, and a hierarchical house of authority was created. Farley and other scholars have suggested recently that many of the interpretations and norms growing out of the house of authority are incompatible with the liberating and imaginative nature of the gospel because they are too tied to the power elite who developed them.[27] Such critiques of the house of authority point to a challenge the faith community faces today as it seeks to provide meaningful structures for mediating God's presence in our own pluralistic age.

The community of faith is a historical entity connected to particular historical events. Because of this, acts of faith in past generations cannot be isolated from acts of faith in subsequent generations. At the same time, there is an aspect of God's presence that overflows the edges of historical parameters and remains veiled in mystery. There is a wisdom about God that cannot be articulated in any human language or thought pattern.

That is one reason why the poetic quality of ritual is so vital to worship. Authentic worship is both pathway and shelter; it taps into the cadences of tradition's enduring rhythms, but it also explores and envisions realities beyond those inherited rhythms. When the poetic quality of its worship is lost, the faith community risks substituting temporal frameworks for the deeper realities of God's presence encountered in the paschal mystery.[28]

---

26. Crainshaw, *Wise and Discerning Hearts*, p. 129.

27. Crainshaw, *Wise and Discerning Hearts*, p. 129.

28. Edward Farley, *Ecclesial Man: A Social Phenomenology of Faith and Reality* (Philadelphia: Fortress, 1975), p. 177.

One of the greatest threats to worship's transformative potential arises, then, when oppressive patterns are institutionalized as liturgical forms and passed on uncritically from generation to generation. Much liturgical discussion related to this has focused on what is called *anamnesis* or liturgical remembering.

These discussions suggest that those theologies that are too tied to a methodological house of authority perpetuate structures of oppression and injustice. Liturgical remembering is more than a mere reenactment of past events.

Remembering Christ's self-gift in the eucharistic narrative allows past events to become a matrix of meaning in the present. In fact, liturgical remembering in the eucharist can itself create a rite of passage or ritual pathway through which people enter more deeply into the mysteries of God's grace. As communities of faith gather around a common table and remember Christ, they discover their own stories in the gospel story; they are cut loose from the restrictive moorings of normative societal frameworks and understandings; and it becomes possible for them to discover a new vision for life, relationships, and action in the midst of personal crisis and societal change:

> The source of the liturgy's power to challenge consists at least partially in its memory. We make memory (re-actualize) of God's past promises in such a way that we recall our future hope. Here liturgy not only makes memory of the little and lost ones as well as the injustices propagated, but it also recalls the promise of future justice when the poor will be fed, the imprisoned freed, the lame walk, and the narratives of the forgotten proclaimed.[29]

As such, in its remembering, liturgy has enormous potential to shape the praxis of faith communities.

However, as feminist liturgical scholar Marjorie Proctor-Smith suggests, the "past" contains more than what has been given authoritative and even narrative status. Traditionally, liturgy has had an androcentric basis and has grown out of patriarchal structures.[30] It has thus often failed to remember the victims of the world's evils and injustice, reducing its power for transformation.

As Driver argues in relation to ritual, "we have not given birth to ourselves." In our acts of participatory remembering around the Lord's table, we do

---

29. Mark Whalen, "In the Company of Women? The Politics of Memory in the Liturgical Commemoration of Saints — Male and Female," *Worship* 73 (November 1999): 485.

30. Marjorie Proctor-Smith, *In Her Own Rite: Constructing Feminist Liturgical Tradition* (Nashville: Abingdon, 1990). See also David Power, *Eucharistic Mystery: Revitalizing the Tradition* (New York: Crossroad, 1995).

more than "bring the past to mind." Instead, our remembering becomes an invocation, a drawing of the wisdom of earlier communities and the pathways they forged into the present. For transformation to occur in our remembering, this invocation must involve a retrieval of those stories that were suppressed or devalued within the dominance of patriarchy. Such a retrieval is essential to the ongoing development of the church's identity.

A central question for faith communities today focuses on their identity in the culture of postmodernity. What is the role of the Christian church, its worship, and its sacred texts, in shaping the hearts, minds, and actions of persons and communities in this era of fragmentation and religious pluralism? How are North American Christians "faithfully to indwell the gospel in a culture that has disembedded itself from that tradition"? For many churches, wrestling with this question has sparked a double crisis, namely, of internal identity and identity in relation to the larger culture, as the church is increasingly being pushed to the margins of that culture.[31]

Jones argues that in order to nurture the kind of scriptural awareness that shapes the church's identity in this era when many people's childhoods have not been seasoned by the stories of the Bible, "we need to rediscover Scripture as the 'word that journeys with us' in Christian living."[32] This rediscovery involves reading the Bible with eyes that see the stories its interpreters have not told and that our world's children have never heard.

Liturgical remembering is vital to this process of rediscovery, because it is in the church's liturgical celebrations that Scripture, read and interpreted, engages contemporary realities and concerns. The remainder of this essay will briefly explore how critical remembering happens in the church's ritual celebrations of Word and table, and how Wisdom can provide a hermeneutical structure for that remembering. By "critical remembering," I mean both the community's remembering of Christ's death and resurrection in the eucharist and the critical retrieval and embodiment of God's Word such that it shapes the identity and character of the faith community in ways that enable it redemptively to engage the current socio-cultural context.

---

31. Roxburgh, *The Missionary Congregation*, p. 1. See also Douglas John Hall, *The End of Christendom and the Future of Christianity* (Valley Forge, Pa.: Trinity Press International, 1997). Hall argues that Christianity potentially has a significant cultural future if faith communities will "stop trying to have the kind of future that nearly sixteen centuries of official Christianity in the Western world have conditioned us to covet." The "coveted future" he terms "Christendom," or the imperialism of the Christian religion. He views the marginalized status of Christianity in contemporary culture as a positive return to its earliest radical and revolutionary New Testament beginnings.

32. Jones, "The Word That Journeys with Us," p. 71.

Its voice was silent. At least, that's how it seemed at first. One summer evening I journeyed with a friend down a winding country road past cows and fences and farmlands. We came to a narrow dirt path that took us to a place in the woods camouflaged by oaks and pines. There in a clearing stood the skeletal remains of a building that was once a church. Abandoned. Silent. Only the trees and squirrels were gathered around to hear its message. The steps leading to its doorway were broken; even its eyes were hollow, the glass long since broken out. In the eave where an oval window used to be, two buzzards stared out at us. The church belongs to the forest now. Its voice is silent; or is it?[33]

A table. Breaking bread. Eating. Drinking. They are ordinary objects and actions of daily living, but, when they are "held together with the word and spirit of God's holiness," they become the shapes and rituals of Christian worship.[34] The early church, reflecting its Jewish heritage, discovered its identity around a table. Gathering to hear the gospel story and to share a simple meal, people from diverse religious traditions who faced many different daily struggles encountered the mystery of God's presence in objects and actions common to their daily lives. In the worship of the early church, as they broke bread together, those who gathered became more than they were as individuals. They became a community of new life in Christ, the church.

Because of its rootedness in the ancient Judeo-Christian tradition and perhaps because of its connectedness with the common objects and actions of human living, table fellowship is a ritual whose importance continues as the twenty-first-century church struggles to rediscover its identity. To their gatherings around the Lord's table, people bring the wonderment stirred within them by the dazzling colors of springtime's annual symphony; they also bring with them horrific images of a world where rage and tragedy destroy the lives of innocent victims and where political ideology silences the voices of the powerless.[35]

The promise of authentic worship is that the spectrum of human experience and history is drawn into a transforming encounter with God's redemptive presence as God continues to be made known in the breaking of the bread. One way to explore the meaning of the eucharistic ritual for worship and character formation today is to juxtapose it to the metaphor of "voice."[36]

What language about God does the faith community of this era articulate

33. Crainshaw, *Wise and Discerning Hearts*, p. 125.
34. Lathrop, *Holy Things*, p. 11.
35. Saliers, *Worship as Theology*, p. 28.
36. Karen Baker-Fletcher, "Soprano-Obligato," in *A Troubling in My Soul: Womanist Perspectives on Evil and Suffering*, ed. Emilie M. Townes (Maryknoll, N.Y.: Orbis, 1993), p. 184.

in its gatherings around the table? How do those articulations mediate the voice of God's wisdom in the cacophony of a contemporary world marketplace? To what extent do the actions of the church in its table fellowship give voice to the silenced victims of the world's evils and injustices?

Thomas Troeger writes that the church is under "reconstruction."[37] Historically dominant images of God are fading or have crumbled, leaving in the church's institutional edifice what Troeger calls a "God-shaped" hole where once there were clarity and doctrinal certainty. During this time of reconstruction, the church has, in a sense, been drawn to the threshold of the liminal, a time of marginalization and restabilization. As it decides whether to embrace liminality with all of its potential for transformation, questions of identity rise to the surface.

Wisdom theology, as articulated in the Hebrew Scriptures, offers responses to these questions on two levels. First, growing in the soil of the Judeo-Christian heritage, the metaphorical language of wisdom speaks about God from within the tradition using the female symbol of Wisdom. Second, the literary structure of wisdom, particularly as expressed in Proverbs and Job, reflects a ritual framework for critical remembering.

There are several reasons why the wisdom literature is a dynamic dialogue partner for the church's contemporary struggle with its identity. Brueggemann argues that the period of the United Monarchy (1000-921 B.C.E.) brought to Israel an unprecedented visibility and affluence. The response to this societal change, reflected in the early wisdom of Proverbs, was "a radical reformulation of the old tradition with reference to the new situation" of cultural pluralism for which the Mosaic tradition had no adequate answers.[38] One way the sages accomplished this reformulation of tradition was by avoiding dogmatic claims of tradition and instead focusing on the potential human beings have for discovering within the created order the necessary wisdom for virtuous living.[39]

Similarly, early wisdom refused to separate the sacred and profane into neat categories, an emphasis Alexander Schmemann brought to his work on li-

---

37. Thomas Troeger, *Preaching While the Church Is under Reconstruction: The Visionary Role of Preachers in a Fragmented World* (Nashville: Abingdon, 1999), pp. 1-5.

38. Walter Brueggemann (*In Man We Trust: The Neglected Side of Biblical Faith* [Atlanta: John Knox, 1972], p. 48) dates the earliest proverbs to the Solomonic period (1000-921 B.C.E.). Within this historical context, Proverbs is viewed as an attempt at reformulating the faith in a time when existing understandings and traditions were found inadequate. The same could be said of the book of Proverbs as a whole, finalized in the Persian period, a time of historical transition and restoration for Israel.

39. Crainshaw, *Wise and Discerning Hearts*, pp. 161-92.

turgical renewal. He argues, similar to the theological perspective of the early sages, that the whole created world "is an epiphany of God."[40] That is why a sacramental understanding of both the world and liturgy are so vital; in the objects and actions of daily life, as they are symbolically juxtaposed to God's Word in liturgical celebrations, the community encounters God's presence as it permeates all of the created universe. Wisdom, too, reflects an understanding that the whole world is God's creation; life in its daily-ness mediates "connections with the mystery of the Holy One, hidden and present."[41] For example, individual wisdom sayings in Proverbs 10–31 metaphorically use common objects in creation such as ants or grasshoppers to speak the truth about God, self, and the world. This emphasis on God's presence in everyday life blurs ethnic, cultural, and gender boundaries to make wisdom accessible to the whole world. God is no longer located solely or even primarily in the temple or in the Israelite community but can be discovered throughout the created universe. The breadth and depth of God's presence in wisdom nurture the potential for those parts of creation that exist outside the power structures of society to be heard as "voices" that contain theological wisdom. It thus becomes profoundly significant that wisdom is characteristically personified as female.

Two early wisdom texts, Proverbs 1:20-21 and 8:1-9, provide an intriguing framework for addressing the church's contemporary questions of identity. In these texts, the female voice of wisdom, Sophia, can be seen as a metaphor for the relationship of the church to today's world marketplace:

> Wisdom cries out in the street;
>> in the squares she raises her voice.
> At the busiest corner she cries out;
>> at the entrance of the city gates she speaks.   (Prov 1:20-21)

> Does not wisdom call,
>> and does not understanding raise her voice?
> On the heights, beside the way,
>> at the crossroads she takes her stand;

---

40. Alexander Schmemann (*For the Life of the World: Sacraments and Orthodoxy* [New York: St. Vladimir's Seminary, 1973], p. 26) explores how the purpose of liturgy is to embody Christ's vision of the world redeemed. In this sacramental understanding of all life, it is not possible to see the church as a sacred enclave in a profane world. Rather, in liturgy, the categorical lines between sacred and profane are blurred as the whole world is viewed as being permeated by God's presence.

41. Elizabeth Johnson, "Redeeming the Name of Christ: Christology," in *Freeing Theology: The Essentials of Theology in Feminist Perspective*, ed. Catherine Mowry LaCugna (San Francisco: Harper Collins, 1993), pp. 115-17.

beside the gates in front of the town,
    at the entrance to the portals she cries out:
"To you, O People, I call,
    and my cry is to all that live.
O simple ones, learn prudence;
    acquire intelligence, you who lack it.
Hear, for I will speak noble things,
    and from my lips will come what is right;
for my mouth will utter truth;
    wickedness is an abomination to my lips.
All the words of my mouth are righteous;
    there is nothing twisted or crooked in them.
They are right to the one who understands,
    and right to those who find knowledge.   (Prov 8:1-9)

Standing as Wisdom does at the world's busy intersections in the midst of a public discourse characterized by multiculturalism and religious pluralism, to what vision does the church give voice? Can the contemporary church continue to provide a horizon where humanity's gnawing affective and cognitive hungers for meaning and truth intersect with the mysteries of God's presence? How does the mediation of God's presence in the ritual of table fellowship shape the character of those who have gathered such that a new vision of reality and a new way of interpreting life are made possible?

As suggested earlier, this time of reconstruction is for the church a liminal time. A liminal phase or stage is one in which individuals become disengaged from normative social roles and, in a sense, lose their identity:

> Liminality is paradoxical. It places a group in great tension. Even in complex societies the impulses of groups in the liminal state move in two directions at the same time: turning backward to recover the lost identity and risking moving forward.[42]

The importance of the tensive relationship between "shelter" and "pathway" emerges again in relation to this.

Caught in the shifting tides of cultural change, many of the principles by which the relationship between the church and culture was defined historically have been swept away. The "shelters" of authority have been dismantled. As a result, the church finds itself in that ambiguous place where old rules no longer apply and where it is uncertain what pathway to forge into the future.

---

42. Roxburgh, *The Missionary Congregation,* p. 34.

Because of this, at least from the standpoint of ritual process, the church has entered a liminal phase and thus stands at the threshold of unprecedented transformation.[43]

Ritual can create a framework of meaning making, a shelter, in the midst of cultural chaos and change. In fact, in their gatherings around the Lord's table, people are drawn out of normative societal structures to the threshold of the liminal where traditional symbols and forms can be reconsidered, recreated, or even changed. This transformation occurs, similar to the process in early wisdom, as objects and actions of daily living are juxtaposed to God's Word.

In its celebrations of the eucharist, the faith community engages liminality through narrative remembering of the paschal mystery. In this remembering, the community establishes a framework within which participants engage ancient texts and tradition in ways that infuse tradition with alternative meanings that are more liberating and more appropriate to current realities.

One obstacle to engaging texts in this way is that historically the church's tradition, dominated by patriarchy and hierarchy, has diminished the tensive quality of its worship by making the humanity of the dominant group normative. Because it temporarily suspends normative social structure, ritual liminality makes possible the creation of a different kind of space, something that Turner calls "communitas." In this space, hierarchies of relationship lose their power to determine the character of the group, and people can meet one another at deeper, less socially stratified levels.[44]

Elizabeth Johnson, a Roman Catholic feminist theologian, offers some insight into how transformative critical remembering can happen. She engages the church's current situation of liminality by asking what she considers to be a crucial question for a contemporary church seeking to rediscover its identity: "What is the right way to speak about God?"[45] This question is of tremendous liturgical importance as contemporary churches seek in their Sunday gatherings to "name grace" in their hymns, their prayers, and their proclamations.[46]

Johnson's response to this question represents a significant effort to reappropriate classical theology by recovering suppressed or neglected elements within traditional structures of the faith. Her revisionist approach, in

43. Roxburgh, *The Missionary Congregation*, p. 34.

44. Roxburgh, *The Missionary Congregation*, p. 50. See also Driver, *The Magic of Ritual*, pp. 160-61.

45. Johnson, *She Who Is*, p. 19.

46. See Mary Catherine Hilkert, *Naming Grace: Preaching and the Sacramental Imagination* (New York: Continuum, 1997).

particular its retrieval of the Hebrew wisdom tradition, exemplifies one way of critically remembering Scripture and tradition; it is an approach that explores the metaphorical language and alternative wisdom of the ancient texts in an effort to "speak a good word about the mystery of God recognizable within the contours of Christian faith that will serve the emancipatory praxis of women and men, to the benefit of all creation, both human beings and the earth."[47]

In her critical retrieval of Scripture and of classical theology, Johnson seeks to "unmask the hidden dynamic of domination in the Christian tradition's language, custom, memory, history, sacred texts, ethics, symbolism, theology, and ritual."[48] Developing a wisdom hermeneutic, she accomplishes this through a three-step process that has some interesting parallels with the stages of ritual process discussed above and with worship's journey of conversion.[49]

First, Johnson analyzes tradition to see what societal norms or agendas are being implicitly and/or explicitly supported by its language, interpretive principles, customs, symbolisms, and rituals. Drawing on liberation theology, feminist theology, and ecological concerns, she addresses questions that are vital for the faith community to ask in its ritual process of remembering: Who is being remembered here? What is being remembered or not remembered about particular persons, places, or events? How are these remembered?[50]

Liturgical memory is always interpreted memory and thus ideological activity. Particular articulations of reality often have encoded within them agendas that support the interests of existing power structures, structures that can be ideological and marginalizing. That is why critical remembering is so important to the reconstruction of the church.

The second step in Johnson's methodological process is also important to reconstruction. This second step involves searching tradition and Scripture for those "lost" fragments of wisdom, those untold stories that have embedded within them the foundations for a different construal of reality. Johnson's hope is that as the stories of historically silenced voices are heard, the contemporary church will be challenged to become more faithful to the liberating essence of its tradition.[51]

This second step correlates Turner's concept of liminality in ritual processes. For Turner, social structure is "the patterned arrangement of role-sets, status-sets, and status-sequences consciously recognized and regularly opera-

---

47. Johnson, *She Who Is*, p. 8.

48. Johnson, *She Who Is*, p. 29.

49. Johnson, *She Who Is*, pp. 29-30.

50. Schrein (*Quilting and Braiding*, p. 19) notes also the influences of Wolfhart Pannenberg, Karl Rahner, David Tracy, and Edward Schillebeeckx on Johnson's work.

51. Johnson, *She Who Is*, p. 30.

tive in a society."[52] Liminality is a stage of "anti-structure" in which groups or individuals become aware that the assumptions and/or role-sets of societal structures are no longer viable or are not relevant to current circumstances. During this stage, symbol systems that have become static or limiting are destabilized, and the discovery of less ideological images for God, church, and the world is made possible.

The third step in Johnson's process is the reconstruction of Christian theology and symbol to promote the equality of all humanity. As Johnson describes it, this is a creative moment when "life and faith are thought in new ways that promote the equality of women and all the oppressed in a genuine community of mutuality with those who formerly dominated."[53]

Central to Johnson's method is her critical retrieval of the wisdom tradition, a tradition that she argues offers a way of speaking about God that challenges Christianity's historically androcentric bias. In *She Who Is*, Johnson presents an analysis of the appearances of Sophia in both the Hebrew and Christian Scriptures. In Proverbs 1:20-33, noted above, Sophia is a "street preacher, a prophet who cries aloud in the market and at the city gates a message of reproach, punishment, and promise." Elsewhere in Proverbs, Sophia is with God in the act of creation (8:22-31). Johnson also traces Sophia's appearances in the book of Sirach, the Wisdom of Solomon, and the book of Baruch.[54]

In each of these wisdom texts, Johnson uncovers "potent female images of the living God present and active throughout the world."[55] Exploring these images within the framework of feminist principles, she argues that these are ancient symbols that point to ways the church today can shape emancipatory discourse about the mystery of God. Such emancipatory discourse ultimately shapes emancipatory praxis.

52. Victor Turner, *Dramas, Fields, and Metaphors* (Ithaca, N.Y.: Cornell University Press, 1974), p. 237.

53. Johnson, *She Who Is*, p. 30.

54. David Power ("Liturgical Praxis: New Consciousness at the Eye of Worship," *Worship* 61 [July 1987]: 292-305) argues that a recovery of the name Sophia as an image for God and Jesus is important for the renewal of liturgy. A retrieval of the wisdom tradition, and in particular of the metaphor Sophia in liturgical praxis, Power argues, draws attention to the ways that the faith community's worship and belief shape praxis. In particular, he suggests that Christ "and his transformation in the Spirit are testimony to that wisdom whereby the God who dwells in the cosmos, dwells in a people who through the *pathos* of suffering and compassion become a community in which there is neither Jew nor Greek, neither slave nor free, no male and female. This persuasion shapes the world in which, in the name of Christ, Christians are invited to live, and to which they can, in the same name, invite all humanity to enter." Such a worldview is not shaped apart from the faith community's worship of God.

55. Johnson, *She Who Is*, p. 103.

Worship is an ongoing dialectical process. The symbols and metaphors of worship over time shape the community and guide people in thinking critically about who God is and who they are in relation to God and to the world. They also shape the actions of people. Much worship today, however, has become merely a reflection of the dominant consumer-driven culture and its values; liturgy that engages the liminal pulls people out of these normative values to reveal different metaphors and images for God.[56]

This revelation is ultimately determinative of communal identity and action. That is one reason why Johnson's work is significant for liturgical renewal and for reclaiming Scripture as the "Word that journeys with us through the diverse contexts of our lives."[57] Using a feminist and liberation hermeneutic, Johnson destabilizes the normative structures of classical theology, thereby revealing metaphors for Holy Spirit ("Spirit-Sophia"), Christ ("Jesus-Sophia"), and God ("Mother-Sophia") that establish a Trinitarian relationship of radical equality. This radical equality, reflected in theological language and images that have been shaken loose from the dominance of patriarchy, can then be reflected in faith communities of radical equality or *communitas*.

Metaphorical language and symbols, such as that of Sophia, are vital to liturgical rites. Equally vital is that the tension be maintained between a descriptive remembering of history that attempts to order events into a cohesive whole and a constructive remembering of history that leaves room for the elusiveness of God's presence in the Christ event.

Johnson echoes a similar concern when she asks: "If God is essentially incomprehensible, above all names and thought, beyond every ideal and value, a living God! — how is it possible to say anything at all about the divine?"[58] Appropriating Thomas Aquinas's use of analogy, Johnson concludes that religious language is analogical by nature.

Recognizing the analogical nature of language prevents the faith community, particularly in its articulations of God's presence in worship, from diminishing the ultimate mystery of God:

A word whose meaning is known and prized from human experience is first affirmed of God. The same word is then critically negated to remove any association with creaturely modes of being. Finally, the word is predicated of God in a supereminent way that transcends all cognitive capabilities. . . . Every concept and symbol must go through this purifying double

---

56. Saliers, *Worship as Theology*, pp. 161-70.
57. Jones, "The Word That Journeys with Us," p. 75.
58. Johnson, *She Who Is*, p. 112.

negation, negating the positive and then negating the negation to assure its own legitimacy. In the process an unspeakably rich and vivifying reality is intuited while God remains incomprehensible.[59]

Because God is ultimately mystery, Johnson concludes along with Aquinas the necessity of following Scripture's example of giving many names to God, each of which open up a different perspective of the divine.

At this point, some conclusions can be drawn. To absolutize structures or images for God is to limit the faith community's ability to grow in its understanding of God and God's vision for the world; it also limits the ability of the church, in its worship and its theology, to remember or retrieve the gospel in its fullest expression. Liturgy can guard against the tendency of the community to substitute temporal or provincial frameworks for the realities of God's presence that exist beyond those frameworks. One way it can accomplish this is by maintaining the dynamic tension between "pathway" and "shelter" in its ritual expressions.

This involves creating and utilizing worship forms that intentionally embrace the liminal. In this, the everyday world and its normative structures are, in a sense, temporarily suspended. Turner writes:

> Just as the subjunctive mood of a verb is used to express supposition, desire, hypothesis, or possibility rather than stating actual facts, so do liminality and the phenomena of liminality dissolve all factual and common sense systems into their components and "play" with them in ways never found in nature or in custom, at least at the level of direct perception.[60]

Again, wisdom literature provides a framework within tradition for tapping into the transformative power of the liminal.

While Proverbs establishes a particular moral worldview, that worldview is challenged in Job. The character of Job encounters a crisis of suffering for which the theological constructs of his tradition do not provide answers. As Brown argues, by entering into a process of critical reflection about his tradi-

---

59. Johnson, *She Who Is*, p. 113. Johnson notes that the "negating power of analogy was forgotten in the face of the onset of nominalism and of ecclesiastical desire to make simple positive and authoritative statements about the divine." David Tracy has used the analogical imagination to point to the inability of human language to grasp or adequately "name" the mystery of God. See *Analogical Imagination: Christian Theology and the Culture of Pluralism* (New York: Crossroad, 1981).

60. Victor Turner, quoted in Driver, *The Magic of Ritual*, p. 159. See also Victor Turner, *The Anthropology of Performance* (New York: Performing Arts Journal Publications, 1986).

tion and facing circumstances of inexplicable tragedy and alienation, Job is drawn into a place of liminality. On the ash heap, Job's worldview is reoriented:

> Then the LORD answered Job out of the whirlwind:
>   "Who is this that darkens counsel by words without knowledge?
> Gird up your loins like a man,
>   I will question you and you shall declare to me."   (Job 38:1-3)

> "Have you entered into the springs of the sea
>   or walked in the recesses of the deep? . . .
> Have you comprehended the expanse of the earth?
>   Declare, if you know all this?"   (38:16, 18)

> "Look at Behemoth, which I made just as I made you;
>   it eats grass like an ox. . . .
> It is the first of the great acts of God —
>   only its Maker can approach it with the sword.
> For the mountains yield food for it
>   where all the wild animals play."   (40:15, 19-20)

In these speeches from the whirlwind, God challenges Job's worldview and theological understandings with a radically inclusive view of the cosmos. God questions Job with queries that touch on the whole of creation: earth (38:4-7), Sheol (38:16-18), heavenly beings, (38:7), and primeval mythic monsters (Behemoth in 40:15-24 and Leviathan in 41:1-34). Drawn into a vision far from the familiarity of his own dominant social status as a sage, Job is urged toward a deeper contemplation of the world around him.

Emerging from this experience, Job reenters the world of his tradition with a different understanding of himself, God, and others. This is reflected in part by the fact that contrary to the common practice of his tradition, Job's daughters are named and "given an inheritance along with their brothers."[61] He returns to his community "as a more fully human character because he has a more mature, a more authentic, sense of gratitude. He has learned that 'virtue' exists only in recognition of human interconnectedness with all of creation."[62]

The challenge facing the contemporary church and its worship is not unlike that faced by Job — namely, to push beyond tradition's absolutized shelters

---

61. Job 42:15. See also Brown, *Character in Crisis*, pp. 116-19, for further discussion of the shaping of character as it is reflected in Job.

62. Crainshaw, *Wise and Discerning Hearts*, p. 244. See also Carol Newsom, "The Moral Sense of Nature: Ethics in Light of God's Speech to Job," *PSB* 15 (1994): 9-27.

of authority to catch sight of God's wisdom that is still at the center of tradition. Johnson, as a revisionist feminist theologian, believes this can happen by unmasking those aspects of tradition that conceal faith's essence and by remembering the stories of those in our history and in our contemporary communities whose voices have been silenced by oppression and injustice. Proverbs and Job, along with feminist theology and ritual criticism, suggest a process of ongoing critical reflection and a framework for liturgical remembering that can challenge the church as it seeks to reclaim its place as a voice of redemption in this era's pluralistic marketplace.

*   *   *

The worship of the faith community in its thousands of different expressions throughout the world, when it is its most authentic, is a mystery, a mystery of creation and transformation. Even in the simple act of gathering, the creative mystery is present. The age-old story of God's presence with God's people is retold in doxological conversations of laughter and tears, praise and lament; and in the actions of the gathered community, in its worship and in its praxis, the gospel story is created brand-new again. New rhythms are learned. New meanings are discovered. The community taps into a cadence of creation that has never been heard quite that way before and that will never be heard in quite that way again. A wisdom is mediated in those unrepeatable moments of communal worship that cannot be articulated within the limits of human language.

Worship is the power of the faith community to shape the dispositions of persons — their hearts, their minds, and their actions — toward the things of God. What the church sings and prays determines how prereflective intuitions of God are articulated in language, symbols, and action in the world. Because the contemporary church is in a time of tremendous change, of liminality, when historically dominant images and language have been drawn into question, it is possible that new unexplored meanings about God await us on the horizon.

In this era of fragmentation and destabilization, it is important the church's celebrations of Word and table draw people into the different kind of reality mediated in times of liminality. A primary goal of the ritual journey of conversion is to enable the faith community to engage the realities of the world with a redeemed vision of what is ultimate. In other words, a goal of worship is to transform the faith community's worldview and thus its action.

If worship is to accomplish this, if the church is to embrace the liminal and be transformed, what changes must happen in its liturgical structures?

First, worship cannot merely mirror the structures that are dominant in this consumer-driven culture. In the contemporary era, Alan J. Roxburgh argues, the church's social role has "shifted into the realm of personal, private piety."[63] In many cases, to accommodate this shift, the church has either adopted worship structures that appeal to the perceived needs and desires of its "consumers" or maintained traditional structures without adequately considering how they intersect contemporary issues and concerns.

To embrace the liminal in liturgical practice is to invite people to enact an alternative mode of being through face-to-face encounters with one another. In this, the church can reclaim *communitas* as its primary symbolic foundation without abandoning the traditional structures of worship reflected in the worship practices of the early church. In its liturgical remembering, the church must work to restore the metaphorical nature of those traditional structures by engaging the forgotten stories of its history more fully and by restoring the tensive quality of celebration and lament, singing and silence, confession and forgiveness, and law and gospel.

Second, part of restoring the dynamic interplay between "shelter" and "pathway" in our worship involves retrieving metaphors and language for God that urge us beyond the dominance of monarchical and male-centered symbols to see the broad spectrum of symbols that are available to us in Scripture. To sing and pray to, of, and for God's presence using the many names of God found in Scripture is to hear God called mother, father, companion, friend, dairymaid, shepherd, farmer, potter, midwife, physician, bakerwoman, teacher, artist, warrior, king, physician, and nurse.[64] Expanding the metaphorical spectrum in this way draws the lived experience of a wider diversity of the world's peoples into our remembering of God's story with God's people around the eucharistic table. Such remembering of the tradition's many names for God is necessary if the church's discourse about God is to acknowledge the ultimate inaccessibility of God's mystery in any human language.

Finally, ritual is a "'transformance' — a performance designed to change

---

63. Roxburgh, *The Missionary Congregation*, p. 37.

64. Johnson (*She Who Is*, pp. 118-19) explores images for God within the Christian tradition, within the postbiblical Jewish heritage, and within other religious expressions of humankind beyond Judeo-Christian parameters. As she suggests, "Western language of recent centuries appears thin and paltry when brought into contact with this polyphony resulting from the human search for appropriate names for God. Western language has focused on male symbols to the virtual exclusion of female and cosmic ones. . . . Remembering the Christian and indeed the world tradition of the many names for God opens up space for the renewal of God-language, showing that pluriform speech is not only legitimate but religiously necessary for a proper discourse about the mystery of God."

a situation."[65] This means that liturgical remembering is embodied remembering; the actions of the community around the table are a rehearsal for the community's actions in the world. Encountering God and one another in the hearing of the Word, praying, breaking bread, passing the peace, singing, and preaching, the worshipping community emerges from the liminal to return to the world. The gospel, remembered in its fullest sense around the table, empowers the community to challenge "all powers in the world that enforce inequality and destroy peace."[66] Too often, as the church struggles to dialogue meaningfully with a world that has relegated it to the margins, its worship becomes tied to personal, ecclesiastical, or societal agendas, and this dimension is lost.

Leitourgia, or liturgy, is grounded in the belief that in Christ the whole world is redeemed. In its most dynamic sense, worship is both the "performance of freedom" within the ritual itself and the "working for freedom" in the world. To embody our remembering of the paschal mystery is to allow the narrative of Christ's death and resurrection to become the foundation and the life breath of all the actions — moral, political, personal, communal, and social — of our daily lives.

Restoring Scripture as the "Word that journeys with us" in our contemporary lives is closely connected to the church's liturgical remembering and its power to form a community of liberation and hope. As the church searches for its contemporary identity, the journey is about meeting personal needs of people who may enter our doors, but it is ultimately about much more. The journey is about more than engaging in a fond remembrance of the past; it is also about more than creating new methods of worship. Rather, the task of the church's worship today is that of the artist, poetically weaving together the plurality of contemporary voices, the diversity of voices in Scripture, and the voices of the world's silenced ones so that the gospel story is heard in its rich and boundless fullness, ancient but new every day.

---

65. Driver, *The Magic of Ritual,* p. 212. Here Driver uses Richard Schechner's term "transformance" by which he means that performances are embodied means of transforming persons and communities from one status or identity to another. See Richard Schechner, *Essays on Performance Theory, 1970-1976* (New York: Drama Book Specialists, 1977), p. 76.

66. Driver, *The Magic of Ritual,* p. 222.

Sightings of Primal Visions: Community and Ecology

Larry L. Rasmussen

A cluster of concerns determines my approach to character ethics and the reading of Scripture. The primary concern is community spiritual-moral formation in a double sense: the spiritual-moral formation of the community itself and the community's ongoing formation of its members by way of its practices. Formation and practices are inextricably related. They are often but different ways of describing the same reality. The moral character of the community and its members, how it came to be and continues, is, in any event, the overriding interest here.

The character of God in shaping such communities is real but secondary in this particular inquiry. It is not my point of departure. Nonetheless, it moves to the fore as soon as I turn to communities of Jewish and Christian faith or assume them, as I do below. This interest in forming and sustaining moral community has its own stimulus. However, I have yet to find an apt description that is mercifully brief. In what follows, I shall try in several different, related ways.

My preoccupation with community spiritual-moral formation, and the role of Scripture in generating and sustaining it, is provoked in part by an analysis of modernity. It goes like this. The ascendancy of individualism and other workings of capitalist markets mean a concomitant erosion and displacement of community values that have staying power. Social processes in the grip of maximally deregulated corporate capitalism yield less and less community participation in character formation and grant more and more spiritual-moral influence to media and markets. The erosion of settled and intact community (which is not, I hasten to add, a synonym of just or good community) means the progressive removal of moral formation from face-to-face relationships and its reinstatement in other, less direct and less accountable arenas of human interaction. Since I find media- and market-driven mythmaking and values spiritually and morally deceptive and shallow, if not corrupting, I am concerned ("Under that false tinsel is real tinsel," to recall H. L. Mencken). Rampant global materialism intent on creating human beings as individual consumers is, in any case, hardly a force for community character with a sense for the numinous and the transcendentally moral!

The present malformation of character would be reason enough, but there is more. The same forces that created what Troeltsch, Marx, Weber, and others identified as "the social question" or "the modern social problem" — the collective agonies that accompany the dissolution of settled, intact human communities in industrializing orders — are forces that also banish any lingering sense of a moral community inclusive of more-than-human reality. These forces not only radically secularize, or desacralize (cf. Weber's "disenchantment of the world"); they also reduce membership in the moral world to one species only and then argue its capacity to legislate its own moral laws as it fashions a whole world "after its own kind" (with apologies to Genesis 1). Most importantly, these forces have worked, and continue to work, in ways that now generate "the ecological question" or "the modern ecological problem" — that is, grave and unprecedented threats to life systems themselves — on a global scale. Any effort to form communities as just and sustainable must now address "the social question" and "the ecological question" *as causally joined questions.*

In other words, the spiritual-moral formation of communities must by necessity happen by way of practices that assume the interrelatedness of the socio-communal, biophysical, and geo-planetary spheres, since the cumulative impact of human activity is felt on all levels. The moral cosmologies of such communities need routinely to locate each individual community and its members within an inclusive "Community of Life" and foster a sense of moral responsibility and accountability that populates the moral universe with otherkind as well as humankind. Indeed, the preservation and enhancement of this comprehensive community must be the primary concern of human communities, for their own survival. Yet that cannot happen if the utilitarian and "commoditized" treatment of Earth overrides aesthetic, emotional, and mystical orientations. "Earth as a biospiritual planet,"[1] and not the dumb stage and stockpile of resources for human community and character, ought to be the guiding notion for moral formation now.

To anticipate our interrogation of Scripture: Are there ways of properly reading Scripture that assume the whole community of Life as the subject of the moral universe? If there are, what might they yield for community formation and its practices? Are there ways of legitimately reading Scripture that as-

---

1. Thomas Berry, *The Great Work* (New York: Bell Tower, 1999), p. 59.

sume human activities are integral with the larger Earth community and that play this out in the details of a people's way of leaning into the world? Do bath and table, for example, splashing water and poured wine, render a way of life with obligations inclusive of all water and soils? Are justice across the human community and treatment of the land so bound up together as to be a "tight fit," morally speaking? Is the world contiguous so that "social" and "natural" are always causally intertwined? If so, is the world also morally bonded in such a way that "righteousness" is uppermost for the well-being of the whole? Furthermore, what is God's character in such approaches to the text, not as an afterthought but as the formative force, "the power behind the masks," as one Yupik Alaskan told me?

Yet let me offer yet another way to say what provokes this effort. It mimics Thomas Berry's notion of "the great work" and subscribes to his contention about "macrophase ethics." Each epoch, Berry contends, has in retrospect its "great work." The great work of Israel was to convey a new and dramatically influential experience of the divine in human affairs; the great work of the classical Greek world was to forge a profound understanding of the human mind and create a strong Western humanist tradition; the great work of Rome was to gather Mediterranean peoples and those of Europe into a civilizational *oikoumenē*; the great work of India was to lead human thought into subtle and unsurpassed experiences of time and eternity; and the work of the Native peoples of the Americas was to establish a rapport with the natural powers of these continents in ways that established integral relationships with them.[2] Berry's thesis is that we now stand between the great work of the modern epoch — manifest in the dramatic achievements of science, technology, industry, commerce, and finance — and another path, one demanding a different "great work." The reason is a crisis of sufficient magnitude to require that the work of the present epoch be abandoned; this includes its dominant ethos, systems, and practices. The crisis is that "commercial-industrial obsessions" have disrupted indispensable biosystems to such a degree that life as we have come to live it is unsustainable on modernity's terms. The great work ahead, then, is to effect the transition from a period of "the human devastation of Earth to a period when humans [are] present to the planet in a mutually beneficial manner."[3]

If we grant Berry's conclusion, it goes without saying that any such great work means changed cosmologies and moral universes, together with altered institutions and different habits. It means different inner disciplines as well as outward arrangements, different languages of understanding as well as differ-

2. Berry, *The Great Work*, pp. 2-3.
3. Berry, *The Great Work*, p. 3.

ent religious, cultural, and moral imagination. Like past "great works," these will be decades long, perhaps centuries long, in the making. Whatever the duration, community spiritual-moral formation of a kind appropriate to humans as "present to the planet in a mutually beneficial manner" will be somewhere near the heart of such work.

Berry's analysis has direct implications for moral theory. He contends that the next great work requires "macrophase ethics," something beyond "our ordinary ethical judgments, involving individual actions, the actions of communities, or even of nations."[4] Humans collectively exercise "macrophase power" on the planetary life systems of which we are an integral part, but we have a microphase sense of responsibility, and we "do" spiritual-moral formation on a microphase scale. Our human identity and our religio-cultural traditions do not act (and actions are finally what count, morally) in ways that assume Earth as the comprehensive community. Humans are considered to have inherent rights, but other-than-human life does not. Individuals and (human) communities claim our loyalties while a bioregion and the planet as a whole do not. Commercial transactions are to be fair and honest — and subject to legal recourse when they are not — yet these are not requisites of their impact beyond the human transactors. And spiritual values routinely address our dissatisfactions by reference to transearthly experience and its consolation.[5] Berry's point is not simply the unrelenting anthropocentrism of reigning moral notions and practices, including the anthropocentrism of most Christian character ethics and its catechesis. It is that our necessarily "microphase" formation of character and conscience, including community character and conscience, may have some idea about where to begin in matters of suicide, homicide, and genocide, for example, but it does not carry notions that can even contemplate, much less respond to, biocide or geocide. The necessarily small-scale and day-to-day ways of "growing people up" and arranging the systems within which and through which we live out our lives simply do not "take in" the comprehensive Earth community we increasingly dominate, are inextricably part of, and totally depend upon. Differently and normatively said: the ecological imperative necessary to the "great work" before us does not derive from human ethics; human ethics derive from the ecological imperative.[6] Human beings are integral to the comprehensive Earth community; we are not some transcendent and ecologically segregated species. Our microphase ethics — which includes the details of character formation — must derive from the macrophase ethics befitting this reality.

4. Berry, *The Great Work*, p. 101.
5. This discussion is from Berry, *The Great Work*, pp. 100-102.
6. Berry, *The Great Work*, p. 105.

To summarize: with a billion other folks, my concern is to help foster moral community that counters the negative spiritual-moral formation of much of modernity, nurtures a moral universe comprehensive of the Community of Life as a whole, and habituates community members to the great work of an era Berry hopes will be "ecozoic" rather than "technozoic," and that will see "microphase ethics" reflective of "macrophase power."

Yet such communities do not simply appear — poof! — on command. Like the "great work" itself, they are created over time in the unpredictable evolution of circumstance and intention. Part of their creation and transformation includes the rereading of formative texts — the Bible in Jewish or Christian renditions for our time, the Qur'an in Islam, and so forth. So the question becomes: What might point us to rereading Scripture and another look at the character of God and of our communities, in order to help direct community spiritual-moral formation appropriate to the macrophase ethics of an "eco"-age?

On the basis of site visits to selected Christian communities in the United States, Asia, Africa, and Europe, I have a hunch that there are glimpses of a "primal vision" or "primal visions" in Jewish and Christian biblical texts that can be teased out by approaching these texts through the practices and cosmologies of the above-mentioned and similar communities. These communities, chosen because their practices and moral universes address social justice and environmental well-being together, show a double-stranded commonality. I had anticipated one strand and in fact selected these communities because of it. Stated in the negative: the moral universes of these communities did not routinely engage in apartheid thinking at the species level — that is, they did not assume that humans are an ecologically separated species with a mandate to dominate. Nor was theirs an utterly utilitarian "take" on material reality. However, the second strand I did not anticipate: namely, that all these communities drew upon the cosmologies and cultures of indigenous peoples. The communities to which I refer are "Orthodox Alaska" (the Orthodox Church in the hands of Native Alaskans), the Maryknoll Ecological Sanctuary in the Philippines, the African Association of Earthkeeping Churches in Zimbabwe, the Khanya Programme of the Methodist Church in the Eastern Cape, South Africa, the Coptic monasteries of the Wadi al-Natrun in the Desert of Scetis, Egypt, and the Iona Community of Scotland. Because these are wildly diverse communities that have little contact with one another, my curiosity about the double thread of Earth-inclusive and indigenous cosmologies with a "cosmic" bent was piqued. It led me to a different set of questions from those modern scholars have asked of biblical texts.

(That indigenous peoples routinely ask them may be the case, but they have not won the day in biblical scholarship. Despite its explosion of methods and proliferation of entry points, biblical scholarship remains largely captive to intellectual traditions that distinguish history from nature in species-apartheid fashion.)

Let me say this differently. The interrogation of Scripture, like the writing of history itself, is always done backwards — from the present to the past (and "the present" includes our sense of feared or hoped-for futures). We "crawl back through"[7] history, including the history of interpretation, from a location landscaped with the years of our own lives. On this terrain, we confront texts whose previous meanings and uses are then encountered, adapted, reconfirmed, reconfigured, or newly discovered. In this case, it is community formation to address planetary socio-ecological degradation that drives me to crawl back through history. And it is the spiritual-moral tracings of indigenous people in Christian communities that sends me anew to the Scriptures as sources of community moral formation.

Cautions are in order, and I promised my interviewees I would utter them. The very notion of "indigenous peoples" is a construct of modernity, as is their shared consciousness. That is, these peoples, native to their lands from time immemorial, were not a collectivity in the premodern era. They no more thought of themselves as "indigenous peoples" than peoples enslaved from diverse communities of the African continent thought themselves Negroes or African-Americans once they disembarked slave ships on this end of Middle Passage terrors. Indigenous peoples' sense of any common identity is the outcome of contact with globalizing European tribes. That so-called common identity issues from contact in the form of colonization, commerce, and Christianity in a complex those European tribes considered their mandated *mission civilisatrice*. Before this shared indigenous identity was forged on the anvil of oppression, a Zapotec villager growing maize on one side of the world was as different from an Australian aboriginal spearing fish on the other side, or an Aleut tanning hides in the polar sun, or an Iboloy terracing hillsides, as any human beings could be. They spoke different languages, prayed to different divinities, furnished their worlds with different symbols, practiced different crafts, crossed different borders into each others' lives, knew different flora and fauna and waters and soils, and fought one another from fears, hopes, and claims rooted in different ways of life.[8] I do not assume, then, some genetically derived "indigenous perspective" and some single primal vision common to these dis-

7. Charles Long, *Significations: Signs, Symbols, and Images in the Interpretation of Religion* (Philadelphia: Fortress, 1986), p. 9, as cited by Dale Irvin, *Christian Histories, Christian Traditioning: Rendering Accounts* (Maryknoll: Orbis Books, 1998), p. 102.

8. The idea about difference expressed here is taken from Richard J. Perry, *From Time Immemorial: Indigenous Peoples and State Systems* (Austin: University of Texas Press, 1996), p. 3.

parate peoples. In fact, I worry about the continuing propensity of Euro-American scholarship to homogenize the diverse beliefs of native peoples. Not least, such scholarship violates the very sense of place and kinship each native people stipulates as critical. The authority of elders to interpret, to find meaning, and to change community ways, all in a manner tied to the intimacies of a particular land, is then subtly transferred to interpreters who do not live as part of this land (or even "on" it, as they might say) and whose own sense of livable worlds is modern, that is, much more artifactual and portable.

All this said, the experience of native peoples in the neo-Europeanizing of their lands and its cultures has been deeply formative of their collective consciousness and lays down the contours of their present causes.[9] This shared ex-

---

9. Common denominators shared by previously autonomous indigenous worlds, inexplicable apart from the neo-Europeanizing of the globe, are succinctly gathered in the United Nations work of rapporteur José R. Martinez Cobo. *Study of the Problem of Discrimination Against Indigenous Populations* is a report in five volumes assembled by indigenous peoples themselves. A major task was agreement on "the definition of indigenous populations from the international point of view." Paragraphs 378-80 are the summary.

378. Indigenous populations may, therefore, be defined as follows for the purposes of international action that may be taken affecting their future existence:

379. Indigenous communities, peoples and nations are those which, having a historical continuity with pre-invasion and pre-colonial societies that developed on their territories, consider themselves distinct from other sectors of the societies now prevailing in those territories, or parts of them. They form at present non-dominant sectors of society and are determined to preserve, develop and transmit to future generations their ancestral territories, and their ethnic identity, as the basis of their continued existence as peoples, in accord with their own cultural patterns, social institutions, and legal systems.

380. This historical continuity may consist of the continuation, for an extended period reaching into the present, of one or more of the following factors:

(a) Occupation of ancestral lands, or at least of part of them;
(b) Common ancestry with the original occupants of these lands;
(c) Culture in general, or in specific manifestations (such as religion, living under a tribal system, membership of an indigenous community, dress, means of livelihood, life-style, etc.);
(d) Language (whether used as the only language, as mother-tongue, as the habitual means of communication at home or in the family, or as the main, preferred, habitual, general or normal language);
(e) Residence in certain parts of the country, or in certain regions of the world;
(f) Other relevant factors. (Cited from J. R. Martinez Cobo, *Study of the Problem of Discrimination Against Indigenous Populations*, vol. 5: *Conclusions, Proposals and Recommendations* [New York: United Nations Publications, 1986], p. 29)

perience formulates the questions brought by indigenous peoples to biblical texts, or brought by communities that still have the impress of their ways. (In my site visits, an example of this was dramatic. Virtually every inquiry I made about native cosmologies showed the face and place of such cosmologies in *community resistance,* community resistance to "globalization," globalization that began with European contact and continues as an economy treating all things, land included, as commodities in a "free trade" system. Or, in another articulation of the same campaign of resistance, every community sought control of lands and their uses in keeping with their own identification as a people of the land. Differently said, what many scholars, including biblical scholars, blandly name "worldviews" were more accurately political-moral topographies tied to peoples' communal survival in the face of forces long disruptive of "the land" as placed and rooted community.

All this said, we finally come to the topic in recognizable form. The question has become this one: Do the biblical accounts betray an ecology of community in which the most fruitful way to understand the stories told of a people's creation, together with the land, is to see them as stories of community formation and fortification? Moreover, does "community" include the more-than-human as integral to the human, in ways as concrete as the flora and fauna, rocks and soils and waters of a place deemed essential, if not actually sacred? If so, do such biblical accounts extend an earlier experience, essentially the "indigenous" experience of the creation of a people and the land together, as their experience of the cosmos and its story?

If the answer is "yes" to any of these questions, what might we venture as the historical-geographical influence? The reply here, too, is only a hunch. At the same time, it is a question put to biblical scholars and a premise to be tested.

My hunch is that we should revisit the impact of Canaanite religion and its seasonal cycles upon early Israel. Yet not exclusively Canaanite, at least not if Thorkild Jacobsen's scholarship holds true in his classic work *The Treasures of Darkness: A History of Mesopotamian Religion.* Jacobsen's conclusion about the fourth millennium B.C.E. is that the "basic character" of ancient Mesopotamian religion as a whole is "the worship of forces in nature," forces he describes as "the life principle [intuited] in observed phenomena."[10] He goes on to say that worship seems to turn on selective attention to the powers important for human survival and that the next millennia will witness a "progressive humanization" of these powers. By this, he means a growing preference for human forms and human patterns over nonhuman ones in religious discourse. Briefly put,

---

10. Thorkild Jacobsen, *The Treasures of Darkness: A History of Mesopotamian Religion* (New Haven: Yale University Press, 1976), p. 73.

anthropomorphizing and historicizing, even personalizing, take place. None-theless, the earlier shared cosmology of one integral, numinous world is not lost even when it is displaced by the new reigning cosmology.[11]

So, for example, the same Psalms that beautifully address a personal God in the most intimate ways also attend to the presence of this God of Life in the details of the surrounding world, moving with utter ease between the humanly transformed world and the rest of nature. It is one seamless world. Or, to cite an-other possibility of retention, the direct address of the majestic creator and ruler of the universe in the book of Job is as intense and personal as any human play-ers in any epic psychodrama. At the same time, the author cannot, as a modern author well might, omit terrifying and awesome cosmic powers of creation from the hands of an awesome God. Furthermore, where does the impulse arise in apocalyptic literature, from Isaiah to John of Patmos, always to portray the new or restored world as fecund and harmonious, with landscapes painted in the de-tail of regional flora and fauna, mountains and waters, valleys and by-ways? Or, to go straight to the heart of Israel's formation as a people of the covenant, why the prominence of forces of nature as media of God's power and presence, as hierophanies and theophanies, from the Exodus out of Egypt to the giving of the Law on Sinai? One reads of earthquake, wind, and fire as voices of judgment and signs of God's majesty; mountains as places of dramatic meeting with God (in both Testaments); and thunder, lightning, and a thick cloud (even Sinai "wrapped in smoke" and the LORD descending upon it "in fire" [Exod 19:18]). There simply is none of the later parsing of history from nature here, or Creator God from Redeemer, or culture from land and landscape. The God who spins out the galaxies and assigns the cells of all life their unending tasks is the God of pathos who commands human transformation of the world in accord with the canons of righteousness. The Creator redeems, and the Redeemer creates, in a reach spanning inner spirit and moral character, social and even cosmic realms.

Yet let us return to the perspectives of indigenous peoples and offer com-mentary in some detail. The belated discovery across these diverse communi-ties is that premodern cosmologies share much in common and apparently did so prior to invasion and colonization. It is motifs of these shared primal visions that I bring to biblical texts, in conjunction with their appearance in my recent site visits. In broad consideration, I will attend to shared cosmologies inclusive of all life and centered in the land. To make this manageable, I will focus on no-tions of restoration (or healing), reciprocity, and responsibility as common moral dimensions of these cosmologies and ask whether or not we see a coun-terpart in biblical texts.

---

11. Jacobsen, *The Treasures of Darkness*, p. 73.

"Healing" community is "healing" creation in these cosmologies, and vice versa. Community and creation are, of course, inextricable for peoples of primal visions, visions of all life as an interrelated, interdependent community possessing a diffused sacrality.

For indigenous peoples, healing (or restoration) normally works with assumptions of restraint, reciprocity, and balance throughout "creation" (a word for cosmically extended community).[12] Everything we do has an effect in (not "on") the world around us. Some kind of reciprocity must therefore exist among "the relatives" (human and other-than-human co-siblings of creation). The need for reciprocity itself rests in a notion that harmony and balance characterize healthy or whole creation (again, including human community) and that such harmony and balance were invested in the natural-social order by the One who brought it forth and continues to sustain it through powers present in the cosmos itself and pervasive of it.

Acts of reciprocity are most apparently needed where violence occurs, even when it is the necessary violence of harvesting and hunting. (Such acts, I add, are invariably ritualized in these communities.) It is apparent to all, of course, that the taking of life is necessary for ongoing life, but without spiritual acts of reciprocation — a prayer or song of gratitude, a blessing of seeds or waters, a festival of firstfruits, rites of preparation (e.g., fasting before the hunt) or rites of purification afterward (a cleansing bath) — harmony and balance suffer with deleterious consequences for the land and its peoples.[13] Often the land itself cries out, weeps, and mourns. (*'Ădāmâ* is an actor in this universe, to recall the Genesis narrative.) In short, restorative actions must be taken at human initiative if any and all are to survive and be "redeemed."

In Orthodox Alaska, the Aleut synthesis of indigenous and Orthodox spiritualities carries these "cosmic" elements into common practices. It may be in the stipulations about the construction of both house and church as microcosms of macrocosm, or in the way to dress, wash, eat, hunt, fish, and observe seasons of the year. There is even an assumption that the whales or seals killed for the life of the village somehow allowed their sacrifice and "gave themselves"

12. See George E. Tinker, "An American Indian Theological Response to Ecojustice," in *Defending Mother Earth: Native American Perspectives on Environmental Justice*, ed. Jace Weaver (Maryknoll: Orbis Books, 1996), pp. 160-62.

13. To give but one example among some Native Alaskans, the men hunted and observed certain preparatory rites for the taking of a life — e.g., the deer's, the seal's, the whale's. Women did not hunt because they were the givers of life, the mothers of all living, and the violation of life on their part would have been even more serious if they were the hunters. Yet the men, too, had violated a life in the necessary taking of it and thus needed to undergo rites of purification before hunting again.

for the life of the village. They did so, it is believed, in the knowledge that their kind will be treated with respect, even in death, and that future generations of their kind will be allowed to be born and thrive in that fecund conjoinery of land, sea, and sky. The proper human relationship with the rest of creation, then, is a collective, ritualized responsibility arranged so as to ensure the survival — and respect — of all. This responsibility assumes relationships that are reciprocal at the core, though the partners are not thereby necessarily equal.

In the so-called Priestly tradition of the Hebrew Bible, the Israelites, and before them Noah and his family (see Gen 9:4), are not "to eat the blood of any creature, for the life of every creature is its blood" (Lev 17:14). When hunters kill a wild animal for food, they must "pour out its blood and cover it with dust" (Lev 17:13), thereby returning it to the ground (*'ădāmâ*) from which it, and indeed the hunters themselves, came. Apparently the efficacy of "atonement" itself (17:11) in animal sacrifice to YHWH rests in the value of the life contained in the blood, now returned to YHWH. Richard Hiers's conclusion is that "the life of animals that are killed for food must be respected, either by sacrificing them on YHWH's altar, thereby returning their life to Him, or in the case of wild animals . . . by pouring their blood out on the ground."[14] These stipulations were to be carried out not only by Israelites but also by any aliens sojourning among them (see 17:10, 12, and 13). This, together with the fact that the instructions are given to Noah and his descendants, suggests these provisions derive from a sense of reverence for animals — or at least respect and regard — that is assumed to hold universally.

In a backhanded sort of way, this sense of reverence, even identification — life in the blood — is also seen in the substitution of animal sacrifice for sinful Israelites. What was holy — the animal's lifeblood — could cleanse or cure what was not — the unclean Israelite. That is, the life of an animal could substitute for a human life. This even raises the question of whether, before God the giver of all life, these lives and this blood — and perhaps the ground as well — are not somehow *equivalent*, or if that is too strong a word, then at least of comparable significance in the community's ethic of harmony and responsibility.

An even older source, the Deuteronomic, also prohibits eating the flesh with the blood, "for the blood is the life" (Deut 12:23), and stipulates that the animal's blood be poured "out upon the earth like water" (v. 24; cf. v. 27). This seems to carry overtones of the ancient creation narrative in which life returns to that ground from which all creatures had been formed (Gen 2:18-19). In another direction, it seems to fit P's creation account and its "second round." Cre-

14. Richard H. Hiers, "Reverence for Life and Environmental Ethics in Biblical Law and Covenant," *Journal of Law and Religion* 13/1 (1996-98): 153.

ation's second round leads to the first and most inclusive of all biblical covenants, namely, God's covenant with Noah *and every living creature* (a point made almost *ad nauseum* in each of the covenant's five formulations [see Gen 9:8-17]). This, in turn, is apparently the covenant Isaiah refers to as "the everlasting covenant" in Isaiah 24:5. Here is a covenant in which all creatures are "partnered" to God and pronounced "good" and "very good." Furthermore, it is a universal covenant intended to remain valid and in play throughout history. To any indigenous person, all this sounds utterly aboriginal!

I return to Orthodox Alaska. Here community responsibility extends to nonbiotic sources of life. Again, this is commonly ritualized. The Orthodox Feast of Theophany, for example, is heavily observed in rural and coastal Alaska, where the river or sea is the source of community livelihood and represents it. The feast includes an annual sanctification of water. Cross-shaped holes are cut in the ice in late January, and water is carried by villagers to their homes, which is also their "mini-church," complete with icons. There the village priest offers prayers for the blessing of the dwelling and its inhabitants. Here, if I may speculate, talk of "heaven" is really talk of creation and community together purified, sanctified, and renewed or made "new" (i.e., full harmony realized).[15] Ontologically the world is one; "heaven" is earth in all its aboriginal glory, its peoples and their land redeemed.

And the character of God in Orthodox Alaska? The cosmos is alive with God; everything is potentially an icon. As one priest, complaining of the secularism of modernity, put it: "'Show us God,' say many of our contemporaries, 'and we will believe.' But how? Do not these people who despise miracles and do not believe in them demand a greater miracle? We must say to them: Show us what is *not* God!"[16] Differently said, for Orthodox Alaskans the life force of the Creator (the *inualyua* of the Eskimo) is a sacred reality present as diverse *logoi* of the Divine Logos. (The Orthodox theologian would say it this way: "Whatever is true and beautiful and good is of Christ.") The life force is present as manifestations of the Spirit alive in all things alive, the very Breath of Life itself, the "Holy" Spirit.

Another example from Orthodox Alaska comes from the visit of Bishop Innocent. In his sermon during the 1999 pilgrimage to Spruce Island to remember St. Herman of Alaska, the Bishop declared: "This land is holy, and was so long before St. Herman worked wonders here. As God's creation, it was holy even before the ancient peoples of this place traversed Beringia [the grassy land

---

15. Michael Oleska, *Orthodox Alaska: A Theology of Mission* (Crestwood, N.Y.: St. Vladimir's Seminary Press, 1998), pp. 200-201.

16. Cited in Oleska, *Orthodox Alaska*, p. 39.

bridge from Asia]. But St. Herman and all who tend this land, these pilgrims included, sanctify it further with their good works."[17]

This is, of course, classic Eastern Orthodox creation theology and a statement of Orthodoxy's pan-en-theism. It happens to also fold nicely into the Aleut pre-Christian cosmology of land, sea, and sky. So a Russian Christian saying that "Earth is the icon that hangs around God's neck" finds a ready embrace by Native Christians and is genuinely their own conviction as well.

But I digress. The salient point is that spiritual-moral formation in this community cosmology is a term for learning stipulated ways of restraint, reciprocity, and harmony for the sake of a community that survives and thrives as part of a greater creation that survives and thrives. That creation is God's; that creation is where God is.

Issues of land are always central. Given the lifeways and cosmogonies of indigenous peoples, this is inevitable. The people emerge from the land itself and share its identity. They, with all else alive, are *of* the land (*'ādām,* and all else, is from *'ădāmâ,* to cite the biblical counterpart). Yet the centrality of land is also an outcome of the collective consciousness that emerged from shared oppression. The loss of the land — the center of the cosmos, the *axis mundi,* for an indigenous people — to conquest, colonization, and commerce means that land and sovereignty issues are the burning political agenda. "Self-determination" may be the rallying call and demand, but it is a word borrowed from modernity and here actually means community resistance to cultural and economic imperialism to the extent that is tied to severed relationships with land sacred to the ancestors and crucial to present identity.

For the Association of African Earthkeeping Churches, it means reclaiming "the lost lands." Initially, the ancestral lands were lost to British settlers in the first wave of the globalizing economy. The lands remain lost, however, because land reform expected with independence (Southern Rhodesia to Zimbabwe, Ian Smith to Robert Mugabe) did not materialize (and a neo-colonial economy geared to world markets, with abundant national corruption, did). For the Shona peoples, the overriding concern in the struggle for independence was precisely the recovery of these lands as "rooted in a religiously inspired sense of place." The land, Inus Daneel explains, "is the people, the animals, the plants, the entire earth-community — unborn, living, dead . . . the totality of known and unknown existence." Thus losing the land to foreigners is both an "inner" and "outer" trauma that leaves the indigenous inhabitants "rootless serfs and aliens."[18]

---

17. From my notes of the bishop's homily, Spruce Island, Alaska, August 8, 1999.

18. Inus Daneel, *African Earthkeepers: Interfaith Mission in Earth-Care,* vol. 1 (Pretoria: Unisa Press, 1998), p. 242.

The lands are "lost" in still another sense, namely, through extensive deg-radation resulting from overuse. This includes the overpopulated communal lands in southern Zimbabwe. To counter the further loss of these lands, and as a part of a continuing "war of independence" that aims at redistribution and re-generation of the lands lost to settlers, the Earthkeeping Churches of Masvingo Province presently carry on their "war of the trees" to "reclothe the Earth." When eucharist or "passover" is celebrated in the African Initiated Churches, to cite one example, trees are planted. There is a "pascha" of "booths" at the time of harvest, as there is a "pascha" of seeds at the time of planting, land-oriented ritual events that can linger several days and that take their inspiration from these African Zionists' reading of the Hebrew Bible. Or, to cite another case of belonging to the land, this one from practitioners of traditionalist Shona ances-tor veneration: beer and snuff are employed ritually when reafforestation work is undertaken. Seedlings are placed next to beer pots, and the ritual officiant pours ancestral beer from a calabash down the sides of the pots into the soil around the seedlings. Communion with the spirit world is invoked in the cause of reclamation and in responsibility before the ancestors and to posterity. To quote vaZarira, the woman spirit medium presiding at one of the earth-"reclothing" efforts:

> Today we want to place our own spirits with those of our ancestors, to-gether with our activities in their land. We cannot simply act on our own without informing them. If we do so, we would be transgressing. Then all the trees we plant will die. We will have been working to no purpose, with-out directing our action in truth. . . . To the ancestors [while she is perform-ing the beer libation ritual]: Oh, you people, you who have received the staff [authority for the land] from Negovano [regional chief], the staff which has existed since ancient times, we did not initiate this [responsibil-ity for the land]. You did that long ago. You venerable ones, go and tell Negovano. You, Negovano, lift to your forefathers this action. . . . Let your fathers in turn notify their forefathers so that they can inform Musikvanhu [God or, literally, "creator of people"] of the work of the children . . . here in the land of Negovano.[19]

A cosmic order is present here, kept in balance through mystical union and sanction appropriately ritualized. That it also serves socio-ecological well-being in a liberationist struggle of peasants mobilized around traditional values may be striking to many of us, but it comes as no surprise to other indigenous peoples, including those of Christian faith.

19. Daneel, *African Earthkeepers*, p. 131.

Yet my point is less the struggle itself than the primordial ties with Earth in an identification with the land and the sense of responsibility to the generations *of* the land who have gone before but whose spirits still live *in* the land. These ties with Earth are aboriginal and binding and manifest themselves with both nonlingual and lingual members of the land *as* cosmic community in this place.

Take the trees, for example. A favorite passage of the Earthkeeping Churches is Isaiah 41:17-20, along with many other passages drawn from "Second" Isaiah. One reason is surely the text's correspondence to events that precipitated the tree plantings. Subsistence farmers were restricted to communal lands that suffered terrible drought in the 1980s. So a poor people living in a hilly, parched land was the prophet's audience, whether in ancient Zion or among these African Zionists. This people, repenting of their sins of land abuse, clung in faith to the promise of "open rivers on the bare [now deforested] heights, and fountains in the midst of the valleys" (v. 18).

Yet the attraction of the text also rests with the trees themselves. In Isaiah 41:19-20, the trees "put in the wilderness" are named, species by species. Together with the watered and again fertile land, the trees reflect a people and their land restored.[20]

There is something both whimsical and profound when this text is read vis-à-vis a practice among African Earthkeeping tree planters. If individual trees are not sacred, groves are. Sacred groves are the dwelling places of traditional deities, or the burial places of prominent elders, or sites associated with wonders. Even when these deities or wonders are rejected as pagan by Christian Africans, the groves are retained as designated sites of festivals, burials, life passages, community deliberation, and a place of Christian worship itself. In some ways, reafforestation work is but an extension of traditional ecological practices associated with these sacred groves.

The whimsical side is this: many planters take on tree nicknames, given most often by others. The spirit and "character," including the "moral" virtues, of a certain species of tree is associated with the character and spirit of one of the planters. So Solomon Zvanaka, who doggedly keeps in touch with everyone and knits the organization together, is "grapevine." Old Chief Murinye, patron of the ZIRRCON cause from the side of the traditionalists, is "baobab," the ancient, imperturbable, and unmistakable hulk on the horizon who observes all and is as old and sturdy as a rock. Leonard Gono, a leader who gave himself totally for the cause, only to die much too young, is remembered posthumously as *mabvamaropa*, the tree "which produces blood."

---

20. See the detailed analysis given by William P. Brown in *The Ethos of the Cosmos: The Genesis of Moral Imagination in the Bible* (Grand Rapids: Eerdmans, 1999), pp. 241-48.

Still, personal identification with trees is not the main point; identification with the land as inclusive community is. From topsoil we and all else — trees included — come, and to topsoil we return. The humus is "our bodies, ourselves" and the place of our responsibility in a community that includes ancestors and posterity.

This intimacy with the land and its generations is sometimes startling, at least to a child formed by Western modernity with its erasure of "place." The same speech of vaZarira, cited above, includes this: "Now that we come to address our ancestors, we do so in the knowledge that the ancestors are the land, the ancestors are the water, the ancestors are the *sadza* [porridge] we eat, and the ancestors are the clothes we wear. Without our ancestors, we will be without water, without food, without clothes. All our well-being [*upenyu hwakanaka*, literally "good life"] will be lost. So at this point we arrive at a moment of truth, one of great importance."[21]

Here I simply raise the question of whether the land ethic implicit, sometimes explicit, in the Hebrew Bible does not offer far more than we have made of it for community spiritual-moral formation. Christian African, or vaZarira's, identification with the land may send us back anew to those numerous texts about restoring the land (e.g., sabbath legislation) and about keeping it undefiled or unpolluted. It may also give insight into the tenuous nature of possessing the land, dependent as it is on being righteous and doing justice. Furthermore, it may reassert that which is biblically basic, namely, that the land is YHWH's, as is "all the earth" (Exod 19:5).[22]

To summarize: my questions for scholarly deliberation are the consequences of a hunch, served up for discussion with biblical scholars. The hunch was put this way by Ewert Cousins. We should face the ecological imperative and what it asks of us for community spiritual-moral formation with "the earth as our prophet and the indigenous people as our teachers."[23] This leads to the hints outlined above and questions such as the following. Is not the Yahwist trajectory in the Hebrew Bible especially striking in its strong affinities with indigenous perspectives, so striking that it should be fully interrogated from this angle? Or, if the materials sometimes identified as the Yahwist's are not a trajectory, should they not, in their separate elements, be interrogated from this

---

21. Daneel, *African Earthkeepers*, p. 131.

22. In this respect YHWH's instruction to Moses is quite fascinating: "Consecrate to me all the first-born: whatever is the first to open the womb among the people of Israel, both of man and beast, is mine" (Exod 13:1-2).

23. Cousins is quoted by Tu Wei-ming, "Beyond the Global Mentality," in *Worldviews and Ecology*, ed. Mary Evelyn Tucker and John Grimm, Bucknell Review 37/2 (Lewisburg, Pa.: Bucknell University Press, 1994), p. 28.

point of view? Not least noteworthy is the fact that some of these materials may be among the oldest of the formative biblical strands. They may reach back to the era that Jacobsen argues bore the marks of widespread nature religion. They may in fact incorporate influences from a time when there was no abstraction of the human whatsoever, even to speak, as we have, of "humanity" or "earth" or "religion." There are the Spirit or God and the land, a particular land of specific flora and fauna and a people who belong to it as bone of their bone. The tiller is a "plain citizen and member" of the land (Leopold) and, yes, its servant among many servants, in a community built upon reciprocal relationships that, when disordered, bring disaster to all, but when rightly ordered bring abundance. Even the (Yahwist) altar is prescribed of rock and soil only, unadorned by human artifice (see Exod 20:24). Moreover, the cosmology itself is "moral," both in the sense that a moral purposiveness is inscribed in creation itself by Yahweh and in the sense that righteousness on the part of the people is the requisite for creation's surviving and thriving. The social order, which is part and parcel of the greater natural and cosmic order, must be just if vines are not to languish and fish die (see, e.g., Hos 4:1-3). Bonds with the earth, the universe, and its Creator are rent when injustice reigns.

Or, we might interrogate not only major biblical trajectories and the connections there of cosmology to ethos and spiritual-moral formation but also specific texts, additional to those cited above. Are the two "wombs" of Psalm 139 remnants of a primal vision? "For it was you who formed my inward parts; you knit me together in my mother's womb" (v. 13). "My frame was not hidden from you, when I was being made in secret, intricately woven in the depths of the earth" (v. 15).[24] Are we all born of two wombs, our mother's and Earth Mother's, and does this intuition of a primordial bond with Earth still echo in the traditions behind the received texts?

Another instance of such text interrogation might take up the famous third chapter of Ecclesiastes. It begins, "For everything there is a season," and continues, in speaking of workers, this way: "I know that there is nothing better for them than to be happy and enjoy themselves as long as they live; moreover, it is God's gift that all should eat and drink and take pleasure in all their toil" (3:12-13). A despairing tone sets in here and in the next chapter, in view of "all the oppressions that are practiced under the sun," with no one to comfort the oppressed and wipe their tears (4:1). The dead are in fact envied over the living and the not yet born, fortunate not to have been witnesses of

---

24. See, most recently, William P. Brown, "*Creatio Corporis* and the Rhetoric of Defense in Job 10 and Psalm 139," in *God Who Creates*, ed. William P. Brown and S. Dean McBride, Jr. (Grand Rapids: Eerdmans, 2000), pp. 112-13.

any evil (4:2-3). Yet in chapter 3 the conviction reigns that God will judge both the righteous and the wicked, and the effort is made to understand why justice is seemingly a perpetual "no-show." In this connection, the chapter ends with a passage that may echo the strong identification with Earth characteristic of earlier eras:

> I said in my heart with regard to human beings that God is testing them to show that they are but animals. For the fate of humans and the fate of animals is the same; as one dies, so dies the other. They all have the same breath, and humans have no advantage over the animals; for all is vanity. All go to one place; all are from the dust, and all turn to dust again. Who knows whether the human spirit goes upward and the spirit of animals goes downward to the earth? So I saw that there is nothing better than that all should enjoy their work, for that is their lot; who can bring them to see what will be after them? (3:18-22)

Joel offers a similar possibility. There is, in this case, lament over the ruin, including the vast ecological ruin, of the community. Amid the ruin, the prophetic word of comfort is declared, but to whom?

> Do not fear, O soil: be glad and rejoice, for the LORD has done great things! Do not fear, you animals of the field, for the pastures of the wilderness are green; the tree bears its fruit, the fig tree and vine give their full yield. O children of Zion, be glad and rejoice in the LORD your God; for he has given the early rain for your vindication, he has poured down for you abundant rain, the early and the later rain, as before. The threshing floors shall be full of grain, the vats shall overflow with wine and oil. (2:21-24).

We also might ask, What sits in the background or even foreground of that oft-cited verse from Micah, "He has told you, O mortal, what is good; and what does the LORD require of you but to do justice, and to love kindness, and to walk humbly with your God" (6:8)? This chapter begins with a command by God to the people to make their case "before the mountains, and let the hills hear [their] voice" (6:1). Furthermore, the mountains, as well as "the everlasting foundations of the earth" (6:2), are told to listen to this controversy God now conducts with Israel. It is a jury-like setting, with the people making their case before the mountains and hills, as the latter in turn listen to the accusations against the people by the God of the mountains and hills and of Israel. Incidentally, the failure to have done justice, loved kindness, walked humbly with God has a distinctly ecological outcome: "You shall sow, but not reap; you shall tread olives, but not anoint yourselves with oil; you shall tread grapes, but not drink wine" (6:15). The people's unrighteousness breaks sustaining life links with the land, and those breaks redound to the people's own suffering.

We might revisit the Deuteronomic reforms and ask what in them may go deeper than the interests named in the received texts: in the reforms of Hezekiah and Josiah, for example, and the efforts to destroy the complex of altar, tree, hill, and megalith — efforts that met, it seems, with only limited success. Or the complaints of Hosea and Jeremiah that these backsliding people are worshipping on every lofty hill and under every green tree, even blowing kisses to calves (Hos 13:2).

Indeed, the prejudice that generations of Christians were raised on and that shaped much of the moral "cosmos" of many Christians and Jews alike, that the battle between YHWH and Baal is the battle against nature religion, must be revisited. The rich display of, say, trees and mountains in Israelite art, and its later absence in the wake of monotheistic reforms, may not be a case at all of ridding Israelite faith of that which is genuinely alien to it (i.e., Canaanite religion) but a case of rejecting that which is genuinely embedded in it from its earliest days. More careful study needs to be given to the precise reasons why the reforms of Hezekiah and Josiah are waged, or the complaints of Hosea and Jeremiah are registered. More study needs to be given to the imagery employed by Israel's poets and prophets and the worlds denoted by them in the texts. It is not enough to say, for example, that Micah's mountain-and-hills jury and Joel's consolation of soils, animals, and Zion betoken "only" the artistry of metaphor. Such a claim only begs the question of both origins and ongoing meaning of such artistry. If I might suggest one criterion for proceeding, it would be this. We should not assume, as so much biblical scholarship has, that the strong Jewish and Christian refusal to identify the Creator with the creation[25] brings with it a parallel break of the human with (the rest of) creation. Instead, we should proceed with the strong motif present in the Hebrew Bible that the world is one and contiguous.

To conclude: this exercise has been driven by a need to revisit our own formative sources, Scripture among them, in the interests of the spiritual-moral formation of communities whose basic point of moral reference and responsibility is the comprehensive Community of Life. One potentially fruitful way to

---

25. For the record, most indigenous peoples do not make this identification either. Most, in fact, are quite close to the wisdom literature of the Hebrew Bible and its sense of God's power and presence throughout the created order. This is not pantheism. For recent analyses of the wisdom literature with respect to creation and character, see Leo G. Perdue, *Wisdom and Creation: The Theology of Wisdom Literature* (Nashville: Abingdon, 1994); William P. Brown, *Character in Crisis: A Fresh Approach to the Wisdom Literature of the Old Testament* (Grand Rapids: Eerdmans, 1996); idem, *The Ethos of the Cosmos*, esp. pp. 271-380.

do that is to take cues and clues from peoples who have resisted the intrusive and corrosive effects of modernity on their communities and whose resistance resides in cosmologies and lifeways that graciously spare us the dysfunctional approaches to life of species-apartheid thinking. I have sought to bring that kind of stance from communities trying to live Christianity as an "Earth faith." At best, it can be an opening and can have genuine legitimacy only if peoples from such communities, whether these are indigenous peoples or not, are part of the scholarly conversation itself. They and the rest of us could then investigate the broader contours of character and community that seem to recur among those most intimate with Earth. Those contours are, specifically, a sense of place, a sense of community, rites and responsibilities appropriate to integral human-earth relations, an insistence that the spiritual and material are inextricable dimensions of the same reality, and awareness of the divine presence as a presence experienced in all the powers that bear upon us.[26] Far too little has been done in the way of constructive spiritual-moral formation, drawing from "the earth as the prophet and indigenous peoples the teachers" (Cousins). The suggestion is to ask what place biblical materials might play in this formation when refracted through these prisms.

A poem of praise encountered on yet another visit to Iona, with its Celtic heritage, is a fitting finale. Celtic Christianity was, in contrast to many other versions, markedly local, with an interpenetration of faith and landscape that surpasses not only modern experience but even the Christian "classical" world of its own time. In this Christian cosmology, God speaks to the human community precisely within its encompassing environment, and nature belongs part and parcel to the dialogue with God. Nature comprehensively is in fact the medium of the Trinity's revelation itself. Moreover, Celtic language is direct and inclusive. It is utterly without the Western classical world's tendency to abstract and universalize the human community and assign religious dialogue to the realm of the spirit. It is a language of the land and "the everlasting covenant" and a language of uncanny psalmic quality.

This particular poem is Welsh, probably from the tenth or eleventh century, and kept alive, as many Celtic (and indigenous) works, in the oral traditions of a people identified with a place.[27]

Hail to you, glorious Lord!
May church and chancel praise you,

---

26. This is Daneel's arrangement for discussing the contributions of African earthkeepers to the broader, even global, community (see above).

27. For a comparable litany of praise from Scripture, see Psalm 148.

May chancel and church praise you,
May plain and hillside praise you,
May the three springs praise you,[28]
Two higher than the wind and one above the earth,
May darkness and light praise you,
May the cedar and sweet fruit-tree praise you,
Abraham praised you, the founder of faith,
May life everlasting praise you,
May the birds and the bees praise you,
May the stubble and the grass praise you.
Aaron and Moses praised you,
May male and female praise you,
May the seven days and the stars praise you,
May the lower and upper air praise you,
May the books and letter praise you,
May the fish in the river praise you,
May thought and action praise you,
May the sand and the earth praise you,
May all the good things created praise you,
And I too shall praise you, Lord of glory,
Hail to you, glorious Lord![29]

28. In native Celtic cosmology, the "three springs" are sun, moon, and sea.

29. Cited with permission from Oliver Davies and Fiona Bowie, eds., *Celtic Christian Spirituality: An Anthology of Medieval and Modern Sources* (New York: Continuum, 1995), p. 28. I also draw from this source for the introduction to this poem (pp. 6-7). My gratitude to colleagues in Biblical Studies at Union, Professors Alan Cooper and David Carr, for their helpful responses to an earlier draft of this paper.

Character Ethics and Moral
Education for Liberation

Marcia Y. Riggs

Introduction

As interest in character formation blossomed in the discipline of Christian ethics, I found myself hesitant, if not resistant, to engage in the new (renewed?)
emphasis upon the moral formation of persons rather than upon the ethics of
decision making. There were two reasons for this hesitation. First, I thought
that we all knew that credible decision making is not forthcoming from persons
of "deficient" character and that the social context of the United States made it
difficult for moral formation in our communities to occur without attention to
the ways those communities (even Christian communities) are complicit in the
historical and ongoing social processes of race, class, and gender oppression.
Second, those of us who are members of oppressed social groups (e.g., African-
American, female, lower class) are most often characterized as either lacking
character, incapable of moral maturation, or morally depraved. Therefore, I
conjectured, persons in social groups such as I embody will be either further
vilified or ignored by those who set the terms of the discussion.

As discussions of character ethics proceeded, it seemed that neither of
my concerns was going to be an explicit part of the conversation. Then Gloria
Albrecht published *The Character of Our Communities*,[1] and sustained attention was given to differences of social location and experiences (deriving
from race, gender, class, ethnicity, sexual orientation) and their impact upon
Christian communities and their interpretation of the Christian narrative.
Albrecht speaks out of her "white, middle-class, heterosexual, Christian femi-

---

1. Gloria Albrecht, *The Character of Our Communities: Toward an Ethic of Liberation for
the Church* (Nashville: Abingdon, 1995).

nist"[2] social location and experience to answer two questions, "What should be the character of the Christian communities composed of people like myself, people privileged by race and class, to be part of the dominant culture of the U.S.? And how can our communities shape characters of resistance to violence, both the violence of war and the violence inherent in all relationships of domination?"[3]

Like Albrecht, I speak out of my particularity seeking to make relevant the emphases of character ethics for my African-American community.[4] This paper has two sources. First, it derives from my work as an educational consultant to the African Methodist Episcopal Zion Church's summer camp program for children and youth. Specifically, it represents a critical reflection upon my praxis in the writing and implementation of a moral education curriculum for that program several summers ago. Second, it represents an attempt to develop further ideas in my first book, *Awake, Arise, & Act: A Womanist Call for Black Liberation.*[5] In this paper, I will outline those ideas that pertain to moral education for liberation. I will then present the methodologies and assumptions that informed the moral education curriculum I developed and offer as conclusion and illustration the litany I designed for the summer camp.

Moral Education for Liberation

As a social group, African-Americans experience oppression in this country through structures of social inequality and ethnic stratification or, in Iris Marion Young's words, through "faces of oppression."[6] However, such an understanding of our oppression points to only one dimension of black oppres-

2. Albrecht, *The Character of Our Communities*, p. 12.

3. Albrecht, *The Character of Our Communities*, p. 15.

4. For discussions that set forth the emphases of character ethics (e.g., narrative and communal identity, moral evaluation, assessing values and commitments, moral psychology, theory of human fulfillment, and its opposition to central elements of neo-Kantianism), see William C. Spohn, "Current Theology: Notes on Moral Theology, 1991 (The Return of Virtue Ethics)," *TS* 53 (1992): 60-75; Gregory Trianosky, "What is Virtue Ethics All About?" *APQ* 27/4 (1990): 335-44; Stanley Hauerwas, *Character and the Christian Life* (Notre Dame, Ind.: University of Notre Dame Press, 1975); and idem, *A Community of Character: Toward a Constructive Christian Social Ethic* (Notre Dame, Ind.: University of Notre Dame Press, 1981).

5. Marcia Y. Riggs, *Awake, Arise, & Act: A Womanist Call for Black Liberation* (Cleveland, Ohio: Pilgrim, 1994).

6. Iris Marion Young, *Justice and the Politics of Difference* (Princeton, N.J.: Princeton University Press, 1990), pp. 44-62. The faces of oppression are (1) exploitation, (2) marginalization, (3) powerlessness, (4) cultural imperialism, and (5) violence.

sion, an external dimension. It is my contention that there is a complexity to black oppression (external and internal dimensions; constitutive and derivative factors) that must be exposed and addressed. This is important because a crucial task for African-Americans at this present time is to examine the internal dimension of black oppression, our responses to life under the conditions of racist-capitalist-patriarchal oppression, as prerequisite to black liberation.

I perceive at the heart of the internal dimension of black oppression this socio-ethical dilemma: competitive individualism versus intragroup social responsibility.[7] This dilemma betrays the African-American response as accommodation to liberal individualism rather than to a sense of communalism more consistent with an African-Christian religious worldview.[8] Accommodation to liberal individualism and the society's competitive class consciousness (its emphasis upon individual effort and competition over and against others) has led to a diminished corporate race-class consciousness that would undergird black liberative struggle.

Two manifestations of this dilemma are false black consciousness and "sympathy without empathy." First, false black consciousness means that black people lack an awareness of one another as interrelated; in other words, we lack an understanding of what the relationship between individual autonomy and communal autonomy should and might be for black people. All African-Americans are caught in this false black consciousness, but leaders in particular do not promote the liberation of blacks as a *group* from oppression in the United

7. See Riggs, *Awake, Arise, & Act*, chs. 2-3, for a full explication of this dilemma. A summary of that explication is as follows: the race versus class debate is the point of departure for my explication of the internal dimension of black oppression. The contending positions in this debate are: (1) class is a more determinative factor than race in the oppression of African-Americans today, and (2) race and class constitute a complex interrelated systematic reality wherein African-Americans are oppressed. In actuality, both positions are needed to understand the current plight of African-Americans, because to argue whether race or class is more determinative of black life today is to engage in a misleading debate.

If we, instead, maintain that there is a race-class dialectic of black oppression, then it is clear that there are both policy dimensions (e.g., civil rights legislation) and intracommunal issues that need to be discerned when assessing the current African-American situation. Because it is my contention that the intracommunal issues must be addressed first, I suggest that we consider the socio-ethical dilemma that derives from the impact of the race-class dialectic. This dilemma is competitive individualism versus intragroup social responsibility and has its basis in the social stratification of the African-American community.

8. For illumination of this notion of an African-Christian worldview that takes community seriously, see, e.g., Peter J. Paris, *The Spirituality of African Peoples* (Minneapolis, Minn.: Fortress, 1995); Albert J. Raboteau, *Slave Religion* (New York: Oxford University Press, 1978); and Gayraud S. Wilmore, *Black Religion and Black Radicalism* (Maryknoll: Orbis Books, 1983).

States.[9] Second, there is "sympathy without empathy." Upper-class and middle-class blacks may be willing emotionally and/or intellectually to advocate the plight of the lower classes but do not participate in movements on behalf of or with lower classes of blacks to effect mutual liberation. In fact, upper-class and middle-class blacks entrapped by competitive class consciousness often do not believe that they are in need of liberation. This disbelief leads to isolation of the upper and middle classes from the lower classes and alienation of the lower classes from the upper and middle classes, creating disunity where *functional* unity is essential. In order to address the overarching dilemma of competitive individualism versus intragroup social responsibility and the described manifestations of that dilemma, I suggest that we need moral education for liberation.

The task of moral education may be generally defined as "the development of persons who are capable of responsible moral action."[10] When I use the term moral education, I am referring to a process whereby we nurture in African-Americans the ability to mediate between the tensions intrinsic in oppressive socio-historic contexts and the creative vision and praxis required for and generated by living in those tensions. With specific reference to the dilemma outlined above, the overall aim of such moral education is that all classes of African-Americans will be enabled to discern authentic responsibilities of interrelationship and mutuality as members of a social group within the context of the United States as a site of oppression. From my perspective as a religious ethicist, moral education into a socio-religious mediating ethical stance is imperative.

This focus upon moral education should be distinguished (1) from those African-American neo-conservatives who place an overwhelming emphasis upon the need for individuals to clarify their values rather than acknowledge systemic realities that circumscribe African-Americans as a social group, and (2) from black separatists who espouse the need to maintain a value system that

---

9. Although this tendency is most often ascribed to black neo-conservatives, there is a sense in which more liberal black leadership also is captive to the tenets of liberal individualism. Cf. Joseph G. Conti and Brad Stetson, *Challenging the Civil Rights Establishment: Profiles of a New Black Vanguard* (Westport, Conn.: Praeger, 1993); and Cornel West, *Race Matters* (Boston: Beacon, 1993).

10. See James Gustafson, "Educating for Moral Responsibility," in *Moral Education,* ed. Nancy and Theodore Sizer (Boston: Harvard University Press, 1970), as cited in John L. Elias, *Moral Education: Secular and Religious* (Malabar, Fla.: Robert E. Krieger Publishing Company, 1989), pp. 136-42. Cf. Daniel Vokey, "Objectivity and Moral Judgment: Towards Agreement on a Moral Education Theory," *JME* 19/1 (1990): 14-23. Vokey states, "Moral education must help participants to learn (a) to choose the values that will inform their moral judgments, (b) to deal with moral conflicts, and (c) to appropriate critically the assumptions underlying their value-choices" (p. 23).

not only distinguishes itself from that of the dominant culture, but also makes total separation from or obliteration of that culture central to rejecting its values. Instead, I submit we need a socio-religious ethical stance for African-Americans that enables us to name the negative values that we have assimilated (values that do not engender liberative consciousness or conscience) and, at the same time, does not require that we relinquish our separate black cultural ethos and the values embraced therein in light of our socio-political goal of integration into the larger society. I insist that we African-Americans face some hard facts about ourselves and our condition: our present value systems are not strong enough to sustain us amid our anger and hatred, which derive from the reality that we will never be integrated into U.S. society and that we are dying either at the hands of one another or from the despair we feel. Facing this, we can become authentically creative again — nurturing values for liberative moral agency and vision that do not deny our past attempts at integration or separatism but cultivate a present hope for inclusion on terms that require neither assimilation of a single normative "white" standard for humanity nor separation out of bitter resentment.

The socio-religious ethical stance into which we must be nurtured is one that contains at least the elements of a moral vision of God's justice and the core values of renunciation, inclusivity, and responsibility.[11] The moral vision of God's justice establishes a theocentric frame of reference for critiquing moral life within both the internal and external dimensions of black life. This vision reminds the African-American community that God liberates and that we are called to be co-participants with God in God's liberating activity within society; thus, we are to make nonoppressive relationships both the means and end to liberation. Black persons as individuals-in-community are called to be responsible moral agents who work for just relations within, and justice for, the African-American community as a command of God, a command that must be determined empirically in socio-historic context.

11. See Bruce C. Birch and Larry L. Rasmussen, *Bible and Ethics in the Christian Life*, rev. ed. (Minneapolis, Minn.: Augsburg/Fortress, 1989), pp. 59-60. I am adopting their understanding of moral vision as "the vision of the good we hold, a part of which is how we perceive and regard ourselves and others. It is our integrated grasp of the moral realm." This vision is internalized and derived from the community from which we receive our moral identity. Although most moral education literature would differentiate between values and virtues, I use the terms interchangeably, presupposing that certain values practiced over time become virtues (i.e., enduring traits, attitudes, or dispositions) that constitute the earmarks of matured moral character. I am adopting Thomas Lickona's definition of moral values: "Moral values tell us what we *ought* to do. We must abide by them even when we'd rather not" (*Educating for Character* [New York: Bantam Books, 1989], pp. 38-39).

The values of renunciation, inclusivity, and responsibility are consonant with this moral vision of God's justice. Renunciation means both acknowledging that we are created by God and, thus, have worth, and renouncing any privileges deriving from achieved worth and status that produce divisiveness and exclusion. In short, we are to remember whose we are. Inclusivity signifies the ability to respect and embrace differences across permeable boundaries of distinctive groups who maintain their distinct identities, while nurturing functional interrelationships for specific aims. In other words, inclusivity means reconciliation and does not require loss of the particularity God created us to be. Responsibility requires that we discern our moral responses in context; moral agency is an act of interpreting the context and moral dilemmas therein, evaluating past and present responses applicable to such dilemmas, and acting in a manner that breaks complicity with oppression and manifests accountability for the present and a liberated future.

Importantly, moral education premised upon a vision of God's justice and the values of renunciation, inclusivity, and responsibility will enable African-Americans to mediate between an "ethics of survival" and an "ethics of freedom."[12] Out of such education will emerge a community enabled to grapple with tensions and conflicts as moments of creative moral living. Yet this can only happen if we are able to muster the courage to acknowledge (1) those values that have sustained us in the past (deriving from our historical communal African consciousness and spirituality in synthesis with our appropriation of Christianity) and (2) that God's Spirit may do a "new thing" in and for us (Rev 21:1-5). My thematic conceptual framework for this moral education is entitled "From Generation to Generation." This framework suggests that the collective wisdom of generations is critical to the survival and vitality of African-American people, for it is finally the dialogical engagement between generations that will serve as the basis of a mediating ethical process of communal character reclamation and formation to ensure life for present and future generations.

In sum, moral education for liberation will prepare African-Americans anew to provide moral leadership within their own community and for the larger society. We will be able to transmit what we have learned about mediating ethical process, that is, about living within the tensions endemic to the quest for a common good mediated with individual rights, for integration mediated with separatism, and so forth. We will be able to embody the values of renunciation (overcoming the destruction caused by socially constructed meanings of human worth), inclusivity (realizing interrelationships that re-

---

12. These terms are borrowed from Enoch Oglesby, *Ethics and Theology from the Other Side: Sounds of Moral Struggle* (Washington, D.C.: University Press of America, 1979).

spect difference), and responsibility (maintaining an alternative vision of reality and moral agency for liberation in the face of the normative one premised upon ideologies of domination). As moral education for liberation takes place, we will learn to thrive as a community within the constraints of oppression while seeking to abolish those constraints.

From Generation to Generation: Moral Education for African Children and Youth

The undergirding assumption of the moral education curriculum, "From Generation to Generation," is that the nurture of a community's character derives from reclamation of past moral wisdom and the moral formation of present generations of children and youth. This reclamation and formation must be determined by a moral vision that will guide our collective destiny into the twenty-first century.[13]

As stated in the previous section, a moral vision premised upon God's justice with the core values of renunciation, inclusivity, and responsibility is critical. This moral vision and its core values represent a maturation of the historical communal values of self-reliance and self-respect, which are foundational to institutions and practices of self-determination established by the African-American community in order to resist the dehumanization of black persons and to empower the collective will to fight racism. Such vision and values also call for a radical break from dominant cultural values such as defensive individualism, classism, and personal freedom to the detriment of a common good.

An assessment of the moral education curriculum that I developed with reference to the moral vision and values I propose yields the following insights about character ethics in the formation of liberated consciousness and conscience in African-American children and youth:

1. Assumptions about a normative narrative and its values must be qualified by the particularity of the group's history, social reality, and projected hopes for the future. Although the curriculum assumes the biblical narrative of creation/new creation and that some commonly held values (i.e., respect, honesty, friendship, responsibility, justice/fairness, self-discipline, compassion or empathy, gratitude, generosity, and moral courage) are

13. See Birch and Rasmussen, *Bible and Ethics in the Christian Life*, for a discussion of moral vision as a comprehensive framework that delimits our understanding of what is included and excluded from our moral sphere and anchors the interrelationship between the ethics of being (character formation) and the ethics of doing (decision making and action).

normative, both the narrative and the values are interpreted through the real-lived experiences of the community and stories from a cultural memory that must be kept alive.

2. Character formation is an act of faith; the outcomes we await. Character formation for liberated consciousness and conscience is a testament to faith in God as one whose justice endures. At a time when the language of conservative religious and political public discourse decries the loss of "traditional values," it may be difficult for those of us who assert a progressive or liberationist agenda to promote moral education. However, if we do not believe that the conservative interpretation of values should be normative, then we must be intentional about asserting the interpretations of values within and by communities in light of moral visions that will foster liberation for all.

Methodologies

The two primary methodologies undergirding this curriculum are literature-based moral education and moral discipline. Literature-based moral education[14] is particularly suited to this first-year program, which focuses on reclaiming symbols and stories. The rationale for the use of literature is that it provides the following significant aspects of moral education: a view of the world outside the self, experiences of values and decisions, and child models of moral behavior.[15] Also, an understanding of the importance of story to the church's tasks of moral identity formation and the transmission of moral tradition can be found in Christian education and Christian ethics literature, providing an important connection between this general methodology and moral education within the Christian tradition.[16] The process of story linking devel-

14. See Linda Leonard Lamme, Suzanne Lowell Krogh, and Kathy A Yachmetz, *Literature-Based Moral Education* (Westport, Conn.: Oryx, 1992).

15. For a full discussion of each of these aspects, see Lamme, Krogh, and Yachmetz, *Literature-Based Moral Education*, pp. 12-16.

16. See, e.g., Anne Streaty Wimberly, *Soul Stories: African American Christian Education* (Nashville: Abingdon, 1994); Thomas H. Groome, *Christian Religious Education* (San Francisco: Harper & Row Publishers, 1980); Gustafson, "Educating for Moral Responsibility"; Stanley Hauerwas, "Character, Narrative, and Growth in the Christian Life," in *Toward Moral and Religious Maturity: The First International Conference on Moral and Religious Development*, ed. Christiane Brusslemans et al. (Morristown, N.J.: Silver Burdett, 1980), pp. 441-84; Craig Dykstra, *Vision and Character: A Christian Educator's Alternative to Kohlberg* (New York: Paulist, 1981); and Birch and Rasmussen, *Bible and Ethics in the Christian Life*.

oped by Anne Streaty Wimberly is our particular point of contact with this general methodology. Wimberly defines "story-linking [as] a process whereby we connect parts of our everyday stories with the Christian faith story in the Bible and the lives of exemplars of the Christian faith outside the Bible."[17] She also proposes the following "four primary phases [of story linking]: (1) engaging the everyday story, (2) engaging the Christian faith story in the Bible, (3) engaging Christian faith stories from the African American heritage, and (4) engaging in Christian ethical decision making."[18]

The second methodology is moral discipline. I am considering this a methodology because it presupposes that it is necessary for those teaching and participating in this curriculum to be guided by an understanding that discipline is a tool of moral growth.[19]

> A moral education approach to discipline (or "moral discipline" . . .) uses discipline as a tool for teaching the values of respect and responsibility. This approach holds that the ultimate goal of discipline is self-discipline — the kind of self-control that underlies voluntary compliance with just rules and laws, that is a mark of mature character. . . . Discipline without moral education is merely crowd control — managing behavior without teaching morality.[20]

Basic Assumptions

1. Moral education is a process of inculcating values (virtues)[21] and developing critical moral reasoning. In order for the process to be effective, it must be appropriate with reference to the age and faith development of the children and youth, as well as consistent with the ultimate aim of a matured character. The portrayal of moral character as interlocking circles of moral knowing, moral feeling, and moral action is at the heart of this view of moral education. This portrayal assumes a holistic process that is consistent with Africentric value assumptions and the African-American religious tradition's quest for holism.
2. Christian tradition (scripturally based) and African-American religious tradition and cultural history are an appropriate, distinctive basis for the moral education of African-American children and youth. The need for

17. Wimberly, *Soul Stories*, p. 39.
18. Wimberly, *Soul Stories*, p. 39.
19. This discussion is adapted from Lickona, *Educating for Character*, ch. 7.
20. Lickona, *Educating for Character*, p. 110.
21. See n. 11.

an appropriate, distinctive basis derives from insights of black religious ethical thought:

A. Black religious ethical thought is seeking to mediate between an "ethics of survival" and an "ethics of freedom."[22]

B. At the heart of this mediation is the quest to nurture values for liberative moral agency that have sustained us in the past, deriving from our historical communal African consciousness and our synthesis of Christianity and African spirituality.

By way of illustration and conclusion, the litany I designed to provide a liturgical framework for liberative moral education is given below.

FROM GENERATION TO GENERATION
(A Litany for Bearers of Moral Tradition)

All: From generation to generation,

Leader: In the beginning was the Word and the Word created the world because the Word was with God and is God.

All: We must understand that we are God's helpers and keepers of human and earthly resources; we cannot make any claims for ourselves because we are here but for a season. "A generation goes, and a generation comes, but the earth remains forever" (Ecclesiastes 1:4).

Leader: The Word lives within the world through the church; therefore we the church must be the bearers of moral tradition in our community and to our future children.

All: From generation to generation.

Leader: Some of us have listened and heeded the call of God "to do justice, love mercy, and walk humbly with our God" (Micah 6:8).

         Some of us have sought justice in the society:

Female: Harriet Tubman was called "Moses" because she helped lead black people from slavery to freedom despite the $50,000 reward for her

---

22. These terms are borrowed from Oglesby, *Ethics and Theology from the Other Side.* Cf. Delores S. Williams, *Sisters in the Wilderness: The Challenge of Womanist God-Talk* (Maryknoll: Orbis Books, 1993). Williams speaks of a liberation tradition and a survival/quality of life tradition.

capture. This means that each following generation may continue the same love of liberty and independence, which drove our ancestors to unity and equality. We claim our freedom!

Male: Martin Luther King, Jr. advocated civil rights in the 1960s — "One may ask, 'How can you advocate breaking some laws and obeying others?'. . . I advocate obeying just laws. Conversely, one has a moral responsibility to disobey unjust laws. . . . I had hoped that the white moderate would understand that law and order exist for the purpose of establishing justice and that when they fail to do this they become dangerously structured dams that block the flow of societal progress."

Leader: Others of us have reminded the church of the responsibility to be a house of justice and a movement for change:

Female: Julia Foote, first woman ordained an elder in the A.M.E. Zion Church, reported in the 1890s — ". . . there was no justice meted out to women in those days. Even ministers of Christ did not feel that women had rights which they were bound to respect."

Male: To paraphrase Bishop Walls's thoughts: The A.M.E. Zion Church is moving upward and ongoing. It is not as much upward moving as ongoing. The church appears to be conforming to the world gradually. It is our duty to see that as time continues we transform the church and that we continue to renew our minds in the process.

Male: Bishop Ruben Lee Speaks, the senior bishop of the A.M.E. Zion connection, advocates breaking ground with new visions. For example, at Camp Dorothy Walls, he has envisioned a gymnatorium that seats over 1,000 people in order to help further the mission of the church.

Leader: We now name aloud or remember silently the faithful witnesses who have touched our lives and communities:

        (Persons participating call out names or remember silently witnesses in their present or past)

All: From generation to generation,

Leader: The cloud of witnesses call us to our responsibility and duty.

All: From generation to generation,

Leader: We must remember who is almighty; "But you, O Lᴏʀᴅ, reign forever; your throne endures to all generations" (Lamentations 5:19).

All: Let us pray: O God, we confess that we are not always mindful that you are almighty and that we can do nothing without you. We sometimes belittle the gift of your grace by being an ungrateful and ungracious people — not loving one another, not feeding the hungry, not opening our doors to the homeless and others rejected by the world. We ask now for your forgiveness. Amen.

All: From generation to generation,

Leader: In the countryside, in the suburbs, in cities and small towns, in plain wooden buildings, in stone and brick structures,   .

All: In (name aloud the name of your church),
We weep, remember Zion, and sing our song in a strange land:[23]
Lift every voice and sing,
Till earth and heaven ring,
Ring with the harmonies of Liberty;
Let our rejoicing rise
High as the listening skies;
Let it resound loud as the rolling sea.
Sing a song full of the faith that the dark past has taught us,
Sing a song full of the hope that the present has brought us.
Facing the rising sun of our new day begun,
Let us march on till victory is won.

Stony the road we trod,
Bitter the chastening rod,
Felt in the days when hope unborn had died;
Yet with a steady beat,
Have not our weary feet
Come to the place for which our parents sighed?
We have come over a way that with tears has been watered,
We have come, treading our path through the blood
of the slaughtered
Out from the gloomy past,
Till now we stand at last,
Where the white gleam of our bright star is cast.

23. The following part of the litany features James Weldon Johnson's famous poem (1900), popularly known as the African-American national anthem (James Weldon Johnson, *Lift Every Voice and Sing: Selected Poems* [New York: Penguin Books, 2000], pp. 101-2). It is reprinted with permission.

God of our weary years,
God of our silent tears,
Thou who hast brought us thus far on the way;
Thou who hast by Thy might
Led us into the light
Keep us forever in the path, we pray.
Lest our feet stray from the places, our God, where we met Thee,
Lest, our hearts drunk with the wine of the world, we forget Thee;
Shadowed beneath Thy hand,
May we forever stand,
True to our God,
True to our native land.

All: From generation to generation

Leader: "His mercy is for those who fear him from generation to generation" (Luke 1:50).

Leader: His mercy is for those who are in awe from generation to generation.

His mercy is for those who worship in spirit and truth from generation to generation.

His mercy is for those who love God with all their heart and mind and soul from generation to generation.

All: From generation to generation,
We worship you God, our Creator, Redeemer, Sustainer.
From generation to generation *(softly)*.
From generation to generation *(a little louder)*.
From generation to generation *(as loud as possible)*.
AMEN. AMEN. AMEN. *(May be spoken or sung as the threefold Amen.)*

Acknowledgments

Excerpts from "The Word That Journeys with Us: Bible, Character Formation, and Christian Community" by L. Gregory Jones, reprinted by permission of *Theology Today*.

"Ecumenism as the Shared Practice of a Peculiar Identity" by Walter Brueggemann, reprinted by permission of *Word and World*.

Excerpts from "The Artificial Nigger," in *A Good Man Is Hard to Find and Other Stories*, copyright © 1955 by Flannery O'Connor and renewed 1983 by Regina O'Connor, reprinted by permission of Harcourt, Inc.

"'A Sharp Two-Edged Sword': Pastoral Implications of Apocalyptic" by Ellen T. Charry, reprinted by permission of *Interpretation: A Journal of Bible and Theology*.

"Lift Every Voice and Sing," from *Saint Peter Relates an Incident* by James Weldon Johnson, copyright 1917, 1921, 1935 by James Weldon Johnson, copyright renewed © 1963 by Grace Nail Johnson. Used by permission of Viking Penguin, a division of Penguin Putnam Inc.

Excerpts from *Celtic Christian Spirituality: An Anthology of Medieval and Modern Sources*, edited by Oliver Davies and Fiona Bowie. Copyright © Oliver Davies and Fiona Bowie 1995. Reprinted by permission of The Continuum International Publishing Company, Inc.

Index of Subjects and Names

Albrecht, Gloria, xv, 410-11
Alderman, Harold, 209
Apocalyptic, 266-74, 344-60
Appadurai, Arjun, 34
Aquinas, Thomas, xii, 189, 191, 357
Aristotle, xii, 41, 122, 257, 325
Augustine, xii, 21, 22-23, 24-26, 28-29, 33, 41, 353-55, 356-57

Bakhtin, Mikhail, 131, 134
von Balthasar, Hans Urs, 21
Barth, Karl, 6, 43-44
Bauckham, Richard, 348
Beker, J. Christiaan, 312
Benhabib, Seyla, 38-39
Berry, Thomas, 390-92
Berry, Wendell, 196-97
Betz, Hans Dieter, 15-16
Birch, Bruce, xv, 98
Bondi, Richard, xv, 99, 107, 113, 117-18
Bonhoeffer, Dietrich, xv
Booth, Wayne, 122-24, 126, 130
Brown, William P., xv, 207, 208-9, 366, 368-69, 384-85
Brueggemann, Walter, 145-46, 214-15, 218, 219, 377
Bultmann, Rudolph, 324-25
Byrne, B., 309

Capitalism, 146

Carder, Kenneth, 20
Carroll, Robert, 219
Castelli, Elizabeth, 11, 13, 302
Catechesis, 22-23
Celtic Christianity, 408-9
Character: definition of, 3; ethics, 4-6; formation of, 150
Coles, Robert, 280-81
Collins, John, 11
Colonialism, 11
Community, 7, 57-72, 107-10, 231-45, 383, 389-409
Conscience, 44-45, 49-50
Crainshaw, Jill Y., 376
Creation, 187, 310-11, 389-409
Crenshaw, James L., 150-52
Cyprian, 248, 253

Daneel, Inus, 401-2
David, 73-97, 100-102, 108, 119
Davis, Ellen F., 32-33
Decalogue, 55-72, 256
Deissmann, A., 295
DeMent, Iris, 139
Descartes, 38
Desire, 65, 122
Donahue, John, 13
Driver, Tom, 366-68, 369, 374-75

Earth, 390-409

Ecology, 186, 390-409
Economy, 196-97
Education (moral), 151, 249, 410-22
Encounter ethics, 43-44
Epictetus, 257, 258
Esarhaddon, 64
Eschatology, 294-95
Ethos, xii

Farley, Edward, 373
Fichte, Johann Gottlicb, 39, 42
Fiorenza, Elisabeth Schüssler, 372
Foote, Julia, 420
Forgiveness, 260-62
Fowl, Stephen, xv, 277
Fox, Michael V., 205
Francis of Assisi, 356
Freedom, 66-67, 412-13
Friedman, Thomas, 146
Friendship, 158-59
Freud, Sigmund, 38

Giotto, Ambrogio Bondone, 188-89, 193
Globalization, 396
God: xi, 29, 211-30, 344-54; agency of, 221-
    23; as "Father," 250-55; freedom of, 217-
    19; language for, 229; relatedness of,
    217; sovereignty of, 215-17
Gula, Richard, 5
Gundry, Robert, 324-25
Gustafson, James, 16, 36

Hanson, J. T., 296
Happiness, 139-40, 142
Harmless, William, 22-23
Hauerwas, Stanley, xii, xv, 5, 41, 42, 98,
    110, 204, 273-74
Hays, Richard B., xv, 9, 31, 323, 331
Headlam, A. C., 311
Henley, William Ernest, 252
Heschel, Abraham, 43
Hillyer, N., 335
Hitler, Adolf, 11
Holiness, 33
Holladay, Carl R., 271-72
Holladay, William L., 147, 214
Hospitality, 33

Hütter, Reinhard, 65

Identity, 203-6, 231-47
Ignatius, 314-15
Imagination, 45, 49

Jacobsen, Thorkild, 396-97
Janzen, Waldemar, xvi
Jeanrond, Werner, 11
Jennings, Willie J., 22
Jesus (historical), 13-14
Joachim, 356-57
Johnson, Elizabeth, 380-84
Johnson, James Weldon, 421-22
Johnson, Mark, 39
Jonah, 20
Jones, L. Gregory, xv, xvi, 31, 277, 365, 375
Justice, 140, 198

Kant, Immanuel, 5-6, 17, 39, 41
Keenan, James, 203, 206
Kempis, Thomas à, 209
Kierkegaard, 17
King, Martin Luther, Jr., 18-19, 21, 23-26,
    30, 33, 420
Kinship, 61, 158-59
Kleinknechts, K. T., 296

Lamott, Anne, 139
Land, 67, 404-5
Lapsley, Jacqueline E., xvi, 62
Lash, Nicholas, 276
von Laue, Theodore, 234
Lessing, Doris, 206-7
Levinas, Emmanuel, 43-44, 67-68, 130
Lewis, C. S., 261
Liberation, 410-22
Lightfoot, J. B., 321
Liminality, 371-72, 379, 381-82, 384, 386-87
Liturgy, 388
Lochman, Jan M., 56
Lohmeyer, Ernst, 317
Lord's Prayer, 248-63
Love, 13-14, 270-72, 273
Luther, Martin, 65

McClendon, 41

MacDonald, George, 259
MacIntyre, Alasdair, xii, xvi, 6
Mack, Burton, 8, 35
Martyn, Louis J., 276
Martyrdom, 317-30
Matties, Gordon, xvi
Mayor, J. B., 340
Mays, James L., 137, 141
Media, 34-35, 37, 44-47, 48
Meeks, Wayne A., xvi, 7
Memory, 71-72
Mill, Stuart, 286-87
Murdoch, Iris, 40, 273-74

Narrative (story), 5, 17, 36, 40-42, 74, 110-
    11, 416-18; ethics, 121-34
Neighbor, 69
Newsom, Carol A., 10, 13
Newton, Adam Zachary, 122, 129-31
Niebuhr, H. Richard, 6
Nietzsche, Friedrich, 38, 126, 209
Nussbaum, Martha, 122-23, 126, 129

Obedience, 63-64
O'Connor, Flannery, 276-89
O'Connor, Kathleen, 214, 216
Order, 66-67
Otto, Echart, 63-64

Paideia, 260
Percy, Walker, 279
Perdue, Leo, 8, 11, 218
Peters, R. S., 287
Peterson, Eugene, 141
Pinches, Charles, xv
Pipher, Mary, 136, 138-40, 143, 148
Plato, 41, 257
Pobee, J., 296-97
Postmodern, 49
Poverty, 162, 194
Power, 232-34
Prayer, 248-63
Proctor-Smith, Marjorie, 374
Prudence, 185, 188, 189, 190, 193
Putnam, Robert, 139

Rafferty, Terrence, 75

Reed, Jeffrey, 323
Reich, Charles, 234
Repentance, 186
Ricoeur, Paul, 46
Riggs, Marcia Y., 411
Ritual, 366-71, 379-80
Roth, Philip, 96
Rushdie, Salman, 74-75, 96

Sabbath, 63, 66, 70, 71, 404
Sanday, W., 311
Sartre, 39
Schmemann, Alexander, 377-78
Schütz, J. H., 296
Schweiker, William, 56
Schweitzer, Albert, 295
Scripture (or Bible), xi, xii, xiv, 8, 9-10,
    19, 21, 27-32, 35, 38, 45-47, 51-52, 264,
    389-91, 394
Searle, Mark, 371
Self-control, 185, 198
Seneca, 257
Sermon on the Mount, 15-16
Shema, 64
Singer, Isaac Bashevis, 141
Society of Biblical Literature, xiii
Space, 61, 66-67
Speaks, Ruben Lee, 420
Speech, 160-62
Spohn, William, 17
Stone, Elizabeth, 203
Story. *See* narrative
Stulman, Louis, 215-16
Suffering, 290-316, 351-53

Taylor, Charles, xvi, 56
Temperance, 193-94
Ten Commandments. *See* Decalogue
Tertullian, 248
Thoreau, 209
Time, 61, 66-67
Torah (or *tôrâ*), 59, 137-38, 140, 172, 194-
    95
Tracy, David, 36
Trinity, 383
Troeger, Thomas, 377
Tubman, Harriet, 420

Turner, Victor, 372, 381-82, 384
Twain, Mark, 261

Van Gennep, Arnold, 371-72
Van Seters, John, 236-37
Vices, 188-98
Violence, 220, 224-30
Virtue(s), 32, 41, 183, 184-89, 191, 197, 200-201, 203, 272, 335; cardinal, 185, 188; theological, 188
Vision (moral), 12-14

Wansink, Craig, 320
Ward, Neville, 249
Watson, Francis, 264
Weber, Max, 390

Weil, Simone, 248
Wealth, 162, 194
Westminster Confession, 257
Whalen, Mark, 374
Williamson, H. G. M., 108
Wimberly, Anne Streaty, 417-18
Wisdom, 153-55, 375
Wisdom literature, 150-51, 187, 377-78, 382
Worship, 365-88

Xenophon, 257

Yamada, Frank, 68
Yoder, John Howard, 41
Young, Iris Marion, 411-12

Index of Scripture References

OLD TESTAMENT

Genesis

1–11	351
1	390
2:18	252
2:18-19	399
2:19	255
3:19	126
9:4	399
9:8-17	400
18:25	314
19	338
32:28	255

Exodus

1–15	235
3:1	57
3:8-10	221
4:27	57
8:23	239
9:6	239
9:26	239
10:1-2	235
11:7	239
12–13	235, 236
12:16	235
12:19	60
12:32b	351
12:49	60
16:4-25	258
16:12	260
18:5	57
18:8	235
18:14	235
19	62
19:3	57
19:3-8	61
19:5	404
19:8	62
19:18	397
20:2-17	256
20:10	60
20:24	405
22:7	133
23:10	71
23:12	60, 71
24:13	57
32–33	62
32:19	351
36:2-7	116

Leviticus

9:6	32
9:14	60
11:29	58
15:15-16	60
15:29-30	60
16:29	60
17:8	60

17:10	60, 399
17:11	399
17:12	60, 399
17:13	60, 399
17:14	399
17:15	60
18:26	60
19:18	12
19:33-34	60
24:22	60
25:3-4	71
35:15	60

Deuteronomy

5:3	72
5:6-21	256
5:14	60
5:15	67
6:5	12
8:11-20	195
9:5	30
10:16	62
10:17-19	242
10:18-19	216
11:1-7	72
12:5-11	256
12:23	399
12:24	399
12:27	399
13:2-12	64

14:18-29	242	17:28	80	7:18	88
15	7, 71	17:29	81	7:18	88
15:1-18	239	17:32	81	7:18-21	88-89
15:15	240	17:33	81	7:19	88
16:1-8	236	17:37	81	7:21	88
16:9-17	236	17:39	81	7:22	88
16:11	236, 242	17:40	82	7:25	89
16:12	236, 242	17:42	82	7:29	89
16:14	242	17:43	82	8	89
17:14-20	172	17:44	82	8:1	89
17:18-20	64-65	17:45	82	8:1-14	95
24:17	242	17:46	82	8:2	89
24:18	242	18:3	83	8:3	89
24:19-21	242	18:7	83	8:5	89
24:22	242	18:8	83	8:6	89
26:12-13	242	18:12	83	8:9	89
30:6	63	18:14	83	8:10	89
30:8	63	18:16	83	8:13	89
30:11-14	63	18:20	83	8:15	73, 89
		18:28-29	83	11:25	90
				11:27	90
Joshua				12:1	90
2	30	**2 Samuel**		12:7	90
		1:12	58	12:9	91
Judges		2:1	84	12:10	92
5:11	58	2:6	84	12:11	225
5:13	58	2:7	84	12:13	90
16	351	2:8	84	12:22	91
		3:1	85	12:24	91
1 Samuel		5:1-2	85	12:25	91
2:24	58	5:10	85	15:6	92
13:14	77	5:12	85	15:13	92
15:1	77	5:19	86	15:14	92
15:3	77	5:20	86	15:25-26	92
15:8-9	77	5:23	86	15:27	93
15:10	77	5:24	86	15:30	93
15:18	77	6:2	86	15:31	93
15:28	77	6:7	86	15:32	93
16:6	76	6:8	86	15:33	93
16:7	76	6:9	86	17:14	94
16:12	76, 82	7	84, 87	23:4	163
16:13	78	7:1	87, 89		
16:16	78	7:9	87	**1 Kings**	
16:18	78, 79, 82	7:10	87-88	2:3	94
16:21	83	7:12	88	2:22-24	94
17:8	79	7:14	88	2:33	94
17:10	79	7:15	88	2:44	94
17:26	80	7:16	88		

4:33	192
15:5	73
17:24	351
18	351

2 Kings

5	351
6:28-29	225
16:2	73
23:21-23	236

1-2 Chronicles   110-11, 119

1 Chronicles

1–9	100
10–36	100
12:38-39	118
16:8-36	101
17–29	101
21–29	100
22	100
22:7	118
22:19	118
28–29	101, 116, 117
28	99
28:1	101, 109
28:2	118
28:2-7	116
28:2-10	101
28:8	116
28:9	118
28:9-10	116
28:11-19	101, 102
28:20-21	101
29	100, 116
29:1	117
29:1-5	101, 102, 112
29:1-9	116
29:1-25	99, 119
29:5b	114
29:6-9	101, 103
29:8	118
29:9	114
29:10	104
29:10-19	100, 101, 104, 114
29:14	104, 113
29:15	104

29:15-16	113
29:17	108, 114, 118
29:17a	118
29:17b	118
29:17-18	104
29:18	112, 118
29:18-19	104
29:19	113, 117, 118
29:20-25	101, 104
29:20-30	100
29:21-25	105
29:22a	114
29:22b	102
29:22-23	109
32:31	118

2 Chronicles

1–9	100
1:11	118
6–7	117
7:10	118
10	115
11:16	118
12:14	118
13:7	118
15:12	118
15:15	118
15:17	118
16:9	118
17:6	118
19:3	118
20:33	118
22:9	118
24	111
24:2	112
24:4	118
24:20-22	108
25:2	118
26:13	118
26:16	118
29:2	111
29:10	118
29:31	118
29:34	118
30	115
30:12	109, 118
30:19	118

30:26	108
31:21	118
32:25	118
32:26	118

Nehemiah

2:5-8	237
5	243
5:8-11	244
8:1-12	237
8:13-18	237
9	240
9:36-37	240
9:38–10:39	241

Job

1–42	151, 397
1	124
1:1	124-25
1:1-3	126
1:1-5	124
1:5	128, 133
1:6-12	124
1:6–2:10	124
1:8	131
1:9-10	126
1:13-19	125
1:13-21	124
1:21	126-27
2:1-7	124
2:3	133
2:3b	127
2:5b	127
2:7	125
2:7-10	124
2:9	127
2:10	124
12:11	155
13:16	322-23
34:14-15	259
38:1-3	385
38:2-30	176
38:4-7	385
38:16	385
38:18	385
40:15	385
40:15-24	385

40:19-20	385	41:9	142	137:9	226
41:1-34	385	42–49	135	139:13	405
42:10	124	44:22	309, 312	139:15	405
42:11	128	46:1	254	145:1	250
42:11-17	124, 125	50	135	145:8	254
		51	142	148	145
Psalms		55:20-21	142	150:6	145
1–150	150	62:2	263		
1–2	138, 140, 142, 145,	62:7	263	**Proverbs**	
	147	62:9	263	1–9	152-53, 154
1:1	136, 137	68:6	250	1:2-3	200
1:2	137	69:7-12	142	1:3	186, 187, 195
1:3	137	69:9	149	1:4	190
1:3-5	136	69:21	149	1:7	184, 190
1:5	136-37	72	135	1:8	166
1:6	135, 136, 137	73–83	135	1:8-19	153, 166
2:11	138	73:22	175	1:19	164
2:12	137	80:1	250	1:20-21	378
3	141-42	84–85	135	1:20-33	382
3:1-2	141	86:15	254	2:1-3	205
3:2	138	87	135	2:1-22	166
3:3-4	141	88	135	3:1-18	166
3:5-6	141	88:8	142	3:5-8	191
6:1	142	88:18	142	3:11-12	260, 350
8:1	250	89	135	3:13-26	186
8:10	250	89:27	250	3:19	186, 192
10:2-4	142	90	135	3:21	186
10:10-11	142	93	138, 145	3:21-35	166
13	141	93:1	250	4:1-9	166
13:1	142	95–99	138, 145	4:10-27	166
18:1	250	96:13	140	5:1-23	166
18:2	250	98:9	140	6:1-15	166
22	147, 149	99:1	250	6:6-11	191-92
22:1	149	100	144-46	6:20	166
22:26	147	100:1	145	6:20-35	166
22:29	147	100:2	138	7	196
23	146-48	100:3	145	7:1-9	166
23:1	250	103:13	250	7:6-27	154
23:4	146	104:29-30	259	7:7	196
23:5-6	147	109:6-19	145	7:16	154
31:5	149	109:9-10	226	8:1-9	378-79
32:1	142	111:4	144, 254	8:22-31	382
34:12	184	112:4	144, 254	8:22-36	186
35:13-14	142, 144	117:1	145	8:27, 29-34	197-98
38:1	142	119:44-46	241	9	154
38:11	142	127	135	9:1-6	369-70
41:1	140	135:6	256	9:5	154-55, 181

9:6	155	12:23	161	15:30	159
9:7-18	166	12:24	162	15:31	159
9:17	155	12:28	159	15:32	190
10:1	156, 158	13:1	158	15:33	164
10:1–15:32	152, 158	13:2a	155	15:33–22:16	156, 157
10:1–22:16	154, 155-65	13:3	161	16–22	152
10:1b	179	13:4	155	16:1	158, 164
10:2	156, 159, 160	13:9	159	16:1-2	156
10:3	156, 162, 163-64	13:11	162	16:2	158, 163
10:4	156, 159	13:18	162	16:4	164
10:6	156, 161	13:23	160, 162	16:8	193, 160
10:8	156, 161	13:24	158	16:9	158, 164
10:11	160-61	13:25	155	16:10	160, 163, 172
10:12	156, 159	14:1	158	16:11	160
10:15	156	14:2	163	16:12	157, 163
10:19	156, 161	14:7	156, 165, 173	16:13	163
10:21	155, 161	14:8	190, 200	16:14	163
10:22	162	14:21	162	16:15	172
10:26	156	14:22	163	16:15a	163
10:27	163	14:23	162	16:15b	163
10:30	159	14:25	161	16:19	162, 173, 193
10:32	161	14:26	164	16:21	161
11:1	157	14:26-27	163	16:23	161
11:3	156	14:28	163	16:24	155, 161
11:4	159	14:31	162	16:28	159
11:4-6	159	14:33a	159	16:32	193
11:9	161	14:35	163	16:33	160, 164
11:10-11	159	15:1	161	17:1	155, 159, 193
11:12	161	15:2	161	17:3	158
11:14	159, 164	15:3	164	17:5	162
11:16b	162	15:4a	161	17:7	161
11:18-19	159	15:5	158, 190	17:9	159
11:20	163	15:6	156, 158-59	17:13	159
11:22	156	15:7	161	17:14	159
11:26	156	15:8	160, 163	17:15	160
11:29a	159	15:9	163	17:17	159, 174
12:2	163	15:16	156, 163, 193	17:19	159
12:3	160	15:17	156	17:21	158, 159
12:5	160	15:20	158	17:23	160
12:6	161	15:21	190, 196	17:24	199
12:7b	159	15:22	164, 168	17:25	158, 159
12:9	16	15:23	161, 170	17:26	160
12:14a	155	15:25	158, 164	17:28	161
12:17	157, 161	15:26	163	18:5	160
12:18	156, 161	15:27	158	18:6	159
12:19	161	15:28	161	18:11	162
12:22	156	15:29	163, 164	18:18	159

18:19	159	22:4	164	24:12a	166
18:21	161	22:6	158	24:12b	166
18:22	159	22:7a	162	24:13	166, 181
18:24	159	22:9	162	24:13-14	155
19:1	162, 173	22:10	165	24:14	167, 168
19:5	157, 161	22:11	159, 180	24:14b	166
19:6	159	22:15	158	24:15	168
19:7	159	22:16	162	24:16	168
19:9	157-58, 191	22:17–24:22	154, 165-69	24:17	169
19:10a	162	22:19	166	24:18	166
19:12	172	22:20	165	24:19	168
19:12a	163	22:21a	166	24:20	168
19:12b	163	22:21b	175	24:21	165, 166, 180
19:13	158, 159	22:23	166, 167	24:21-22	166, 172
19:18	158, 159	22:27a	166	24:23-34	154, 164-69
19:19b	165	22:27b	166	24:24-25	168
19:21	164	22:28	167	24:26	167
19:22	162	22:29	166, 168, 169, 180	24:27	167
19:26	158, 159	23:1-2	180	24:28	167
19:27	158, 159, 165	23:1-3	168, 169	24:30-31	167
19:28	158, 160, 161	23:4	167	24:30-34	165, 196
20:2	163, 172	23:4-8	168	24:33-34	167, 174
20:3	159	23:6	167	25:1–29:27	154, 169-75
20:8	163	23:9	168	25:2	171, 180, 182
20:10	157	23:10	167	25:6	169
20:11	158, 159	23:10b	167	25:7	169
20:20	159, 165	23:11	166, 167	25:7b-10	174
20:21	162	23:13b	166	25:8	169
20:23	157	23:14	166	25:11	170, 198
20:24	158	23:15	166	25:15	170, 171
20:26	163	23:15-16	165	25:16	169, 181
20:27	158	23:16	167	25:17	169, 174
20:28	163	23:17	165, 166	25:18	170
21:1	163, 172, 180	23:18	167, 168	25:18-19	175
21:3	160	23:21	167	25:20	171
21:6	162	23:22	166	25:21	169
21:7	160	23:22-25	167	25:21-22	173
21:9	159	23:23	165	25:24	169
21:12	159	23:26	165	25:25	175
21:13	162	23:29	166	25:26	172
21:15	160	24:1-2	168	26:1	173
21:19	159	24:2	167	26:3	173
21:20	162	24:3-7	165	26:4-5	169, 181
21:28	158, 161	24:5-6	168, 169	26:5	173
21:30	164	24:7	168	26:7	173
21:31	158, 164	24:9	165	26:8	173
22:2	162	24:10-11	166	26:9	173

26:10	173	29:9	169	31:7-9	179
26:11	170, 173, 340	29:10	172	31:9	171, 179, 181
26:12	173, 177	29:12	169, 171, 172	31:10-31	153, 154, 195, 370
26:12a	169	29:13	171	31:13	154
26:13-16	174	29:14	169, 171, 174	31:14	195
26:18-19	170, 174, 175	29:16	172	31:15	181
26:20	173	29:18	172	31:16-24	370
26:24	173, 175	29:18b	169	31:17a	181
26:24-26	173	29:20	169, 173	31:19	154, 195
26:26	173	29:25	174	31:20	195
26:28	173	29:26	171, 174, 181	31:22	154
27:1	169	29:27	172, 175	31:23	181
27:2	169	30:1-3	175	31:26	195
27:4	169	30:1-6	175	31:27	195
27:5	169	30:1-33	154, 175-78	31:28	196
27:6	174	30:2	175, 177	31:31	196
27:9	171	30:2-3a	177		
27:10	169, 174	30:3b	176	**Ecclesiastes**	
27:11	169	30:4	175, 176, 177	1–12	151, 202-10
27:12	181	30:6	177	1:1-2	205
27:13	169	30:7-8	175	1:4	419
27:17	170	30:7-9	194	1:13	205
27:22	173	30:8-9	177	1:13a	203
27:23	169	30:10	177	1:13-14	204
27:23-27	170	30:11-14	176	1:16-17	205
28:1	172, 181	30:13	177	1:17-18	204
28:3	170, 171, 172	30:14b	178	2	207
28:4	172	30:15-16	176, 192	2:1-3	205
28:5	174	30:17	176	2:3	205
28:6	174	30:18	176	2:14-16	204
28:7	172	30:18-19	176, 177, 192	2:15	206
28:9	172	30:20	176	2:17	202, 204
28:11	174	30:20-23	177	2:19	206
28:12	172	30:21-23	176	2:21-23	204
28:14a	169	30:22a	178	2:24	204
28:15	170, 171, 172, 174	30:24-28	176, 177	3:10	204
28:15-16	171	30:24-31	192	3:12-13	405
28:16a	171	30:27	178, 181	3:15	204
28:20	174	30:28	178	3:18-22	406
28:25	173, 174	30:29-31	176, 177	3:19b	202
28:25-26	173	30:31	178	4:1	405
28:26	199	30:32	177, 178	4:1-3	204
28:27	174	31:1-9	154, 178-79, 181	4:2-3	405-6
29:2	172	31:2	179	5:1-5	208
29:4	171	31:3	181	5:1-7	209
29:5	171, 174, 175	31:3-9	179	5:13-17	204
29:7	174	31:5b	179	5:18-19	210

6:1-5	204	**Jeremiah**		11:23	224	
7:16b	208	1–25	215	12:3	223, 224	
7:21	208	2:35	211	12:5-6	211	
7:23	206	3:4	211	12:12	221	
8:3-5	208	4:4	224	12:22	224	
8:10-13	204	4:6	224	13:4	220	
8:12-13	209	4:7	221	13:9	219, 220	
8:16-17	204	5:6	221	13:14	222	
9:9	208	5:9	224	13:17	212	
9:10	208	5:14	269	13:24	220	
9:11-12	204	5:29	224	14:7-9	211	
10:4	208	6:7	224	14:7-11	224	
10:5-7	204	6:11	223, 224	14:12	221, 224	
10:20	208	6:11a	227	14:16	224, 226	
11	207	6:11-12	225	14:17	212	
11:5	208, 210	6:11b-12	224	14:19-22	211	
11:9	208	6:14	218	14:21	218	
		6:15	224	15:2	224	
Isaiah		6:19	224, 226	15:6	224	
3–23	351	6:21	224, 225	15:7-9	224	
6:3	258	6:22	220	15:8	224	
23:1-18	233	7:7	218	15:9	221, 224	
24	351	7:32	224	15:15	223, 224	
24:5	400	8:3	214	15:17	222, 224	
29:14	265	8:9	224	15:18-19	212, 224	
36:18-20	233	8:11	218	16:18	224	
40:2	260	8:12	224	17:18	223, 224	
41:17-20	403	8:18–9:1	212	18:13	224	
41:18	403	8:19c	214	18:17	220, 224	
42:1-4	243	9:9	224	18:19-23	226	
42:6	243	9:10	212, 214	18:21	224, 225	
45:1-7	221	9:10-11	213	18:21-23	222	
47:6-7	222	9:11	214	18:22	224	
47:7-10	233	9:16	220	18:23	224	
49:6	243	9:17-19	214	19:6	224	
49:8	243	9:21	225	19:9	225	
49:26	225	9:22	214	19:11	220, 224	
51:1-2	236	9:23-24	218, 328	20:4	221	
54:7-8	240	10:12	217	20:8	224	
55:1-2	237, 240	10:15	224	20:9	224	
55:1-11	269	10:21	224	20:11	224	
55:6-7	260	10:25	223, 224	20:12	223, 224	
55:8	240	11:5	218	21:2	211, 220	
55:11	263	11:11-12	224	21:5	220	
55:12	240	11:12-14	224	21:6	220	
56:2-8	243	11:20	223, 224	21:7	220, 222	
58:6-7	243	11:22	224	21:12-14	226	

21:14	220	43:10	220, 221	**Joel**	
23:1-2	220	43:13	220	2:21-23	406
23:1-4	214	47:6	221		
23:2	220	48:12	220	**Amos**	
23:2-3	214	49:19	221	1–2	351
23:8	214	49:20	220		
23:9-22	218	49:30	220	**Micah**	
23:16-17	211	49:38	220	6:1-2	406
23:29	269	50–51	222	6:8	406, 419
24:9	214, 220	50:9	220	6:15	406-7
25:8	221	50:17	214, 220		
25:9	221	50:41	220	**Zechariah**	
25:12-14	222	51:1	220	1:14	220
25:15-17	226	51:4	221	1:15	222
25:32	220	51:15	217		
25:33	221	52	222		
25:34	224	52:8	220, 221	**NEW TESTAMENT**	
27–29	222				
27:5	217	**Lamentations**		**Matthew**	
27:6	221	1:5	225	3:17	251
27:8	221	1:16	225	4:1	263
27:10	220	2:19-21	225	4:4	149
28:1-17	218	4:4	225	4:17	149
29:1	221	4:10	225	5–7	14
29:1-14	218	5:11	225	5:1-11	149
29:4	221			5:10	345
29:7	221	**Ezekiel**		5:12	149
29:14	221	1–48	62	5:16	258
30:3	218, 221	5:10	225	5:17	149
30:9	218	11:45	256	5:38-48	14
30:11	220	26–28	233-34	5:42	149
31:1-3	218	28:2	234	5:44	149
31:1-6	218	29:3	233	6:9	250
31:18	218	36:22-23	256	6:9b	253, 254
31:20	221	36:25-27	256	6:10	256
31:34	260			6:11-13	253
31:35-37	218	**Daniel**		6:14	254
32:17	217	1–12	237, 346, 359	6:33	149
32:29	220	6:26	351	7:9	258
33:14-26	218	7:17-27	309	7:9-12	254
36:29	220	9	352	7:21	254
38:17-18	222	9:18c	352	7:21-23	251
39	222			8:11	258
39:5	221	**Hosea**		8:21-22	254
42:10	222	4:1-3	405	9:6	251
42:12a	221	13:2	407	9:8	251
42:12b	221			10:34-36	345

11:27	252	6:36	216-17	**Romans**	
12:18	251	8:13	263	1—16	313-14
13:31-32	35	10:22	252	1:1	298
15:21-28	30	10:27	12	1:1-4	307
16:24	149	11:1	248	1:4	311
17:5	251	11:1-13	249	1:6	324
18:1-4	251	11:2	250	1:9	298
18:10	251	11:2b	256	1:16	298, 307
18:23-35	251	11:2b-4	248	1:29-31	290
19:13-15	251	11:3-4	253	2:1-11	238
21:15-16	251	11:11-13	254	2:8	321
22:37-39	12	11:13	254	2:9	308-9
23:9	254	14:15	258	2:17	308
25:31-46	253	15:11-32	253	2:23	308
27:29	216	20:13	251	3:4	256
27:46	149	22:29-30	258	3:27	308
27:48	149	22:39-46	253	4:2	308
28:18	251	23:24	228	4:23	307
28:19	149	23:46	149	5:1-3	308
				5:2	308, 313
Mark		**John**		5:3	307-8, 312, 313
1:13	263	2:17	149	5:3-4	316
1:14-15	258	4:27	251	5:4	312
1:22	251	5:19	252	5:5	313
2:10	251	5:26-27	251	5:8	270
6:8	258	5:30	251	6:4	311, 312
6:30-44	258	6:32b	259	6:12	299
8:1-10	258	6:35	259	8:4-5	254
8:33	255	6:51	259	8:12-13	254
9:7	251	6:53-58	259	8:12-39	253
10:1-12	251	9:18-23	252	8:14-17	251, 263
10:28	252	10:14-18	253	8:15	311
10:29-31	252	11:41-42	252	8:17	310, 312, 313, 316
11:22-25	263	13:16	254	8:18	308, 310, 313
12:6	251	14:8-9	251	8:18-25	258
12:29-31	12	15:18-25	345	8:19-21	313
13:9-13	252	20:17	253	8:19-23	311
14:22-25	258			8:20-23	285
14:32-42	253	**Acts**		8:21	288, 311
14:36	253	1:7	251	8:22	310, 311
15:34	149	3:15	251	8:22-23	315
		17:26-28	251	8:23	308, 310, 311, 312,
Luke		20:11	258		313, 316
1:50	422	24:22	183	8:32	254, 312
2:34	322	24:26	183	8:35	308, 309
4:2	263			8:36	309, 312, 315, 316
4:13	263			8:37	312

9–11	61
9:1-5	255
10:16	298
12:12	310, 313
12:14	310, 313
12:19	313
12:20	310
12:20-21	313
15:16	297, 298
15:18	297
15:19	297
15:31	310
16:26	326

1 Corinthians

1–2	265, 267, 268-70
1:12	272
1:17-18	267, 268
1:18-19	272
1:18-31	328, 345
1:18–2:16	267
1:19-20	265
1:20	265
1:25	266
1:26	255
1:26-31	268
2:1-5	269, 297
2:2	269
2:3	267
2:4	269
2:9	270
2:13	267
2:16	250, 265, 268, 274
3:1-2	297
4:15	298
4:16	297, 303
7:5	263
7:15	285
7:31	267
8:1-2	270
8:13	271
9:12	298
9:23	298
10:13b	263
11:1	303
13	285
15:1	298, 326

15:44	311

2 Corinthians

2:16	263
3:18	289
4:7-10	269
4:10-12	286
4:11-12	286
4:34	298
5:16	255
5:16-17	266-67, 269
5:20	347
8:1	326
9:13	298
10:2	255
10:8	324
11:4	298
11:7	298
11:18	255
11:23-26	258
12:7	290
12:9-10	309
12:20	321

Galatians

1:7	298
1:11	326
1:11-12	269
1:12	298
2:14	298
2:19-20	267
2:20	263
3:1	267
3:1-4	297
3:2	288
3:25-26	311
3:28	35
4:1-20	253
4:3-7	251, 311
4:12	297
5	30
5:17	255
5:19-21	299
5:20	321
6:10	253
6:14	267
6:15	267

Ephesians

2:1-22	255
6:1-4	255
6:18	255

Philippians

1–4	317-30
1:5	298, 329
1:6	322
1:12	321, 327
1:12-18	321, 322
1:12-26	317, 318-19, 329
1:15a	321
1:16	321
1:17	321
1:18	322, 327
1:19	322, 324
1:21	326
1:21-26	326
1:22	326
1:22-23	326
1:25	326, 327, 335
1:25-26	327
1:26	328
1:27	298
1:27-28	329
1:27-30	318, 319, 327
1:29	329
1:29-30	317
1:30	319, 329
2:1-4	330
2:3	321
2:6-11	317, 318, 330
2:9-11	330
2:10-11	345, 346
2:12-18	329
2:15-18	318
2:17	317
2:19-30	318
2:22	298
3:9-21	318
3:10	317
3:15-21	319
3:17	297, 303, 319, 328
4:3	298
4:10-20	329

Colossians

1:5-6	298

1 Thessalonians

1	300-306, 313
	314
1:2-10	301, 304
1:4	305
1:5	298, 302
1:5-6	302
1:6	301, 303, 305,
	315, 316
1:7	305
1:8	298
1:9-10	305
1:10	305, 305-6
2:1	302
2:2	292, 298, 302,
	303
2:4	298
2:5	302
2:7	297, 305
2:8	298
2:11	302
2:13-14	302, 304
2:14	292, 302, 305,
	315
2:14-16	305
3:2	298
3:3	302, 303, 322
3:4	299
3:5	263
4:14-17	305, 306
5:2	302
5:9	305
5:10	305

2 Thessalonians

1:8	298
2:14	298
3:7	297

1 Timothy

4:15	335

Philemon

13	298

Hebrews

1:2-3	254
5:7-10	253
5:8-9	254
12:3-11	254
12:5-11	260

James

1:13	263
3:14	321
3:16	321
5:11	254

1 Peter

1:17	251
3:14-17	308
5:8-9a	350

2 Peter

1–3	331-43
1	334-35
1:1	334, 337
1:3	333, 335
1:3-4	334
1:4	335
1:5	335
1:5-7	334
1:8	335
1:8-15	333
1:9	335
1:10	335
1:11	334, 337
1:12	335
1:12-15	332, 333
1:13	335
1:14	334
1:15	335
2	336-40
2:1	335, 336, 342
2:1-3	336
2:2	342
2:4-10	333, 336, 337, 342
2:5	336
2:5-8	342
2:7	336
2:10b-18	336
2:13	340, 342

2:15	342
2:15-16	339
2:18	340, 342
2:19	339, 340, 342
2:20	337
2:20-22	339, 340
3	340-42
3:1-2	333
3:1a-2a	332
3:1-13	340
3:2	337
3:3-5	335, 342
3:3-7	334
3:4	342
3:5-6	342
3:7	342
3:8	342
3:8-13	342
3:10-13	341
3:11	333, 341, 342
3:12	342
3:13	342
3:14	341
3:15	342
3:17	333, 342
3:18	337

1 John

4:20	48
5:13-15	263

Jude

4	336
11	339

Revelation

1–22	346, 359
1:16	346
2–3	346-51
2:1-7	348
2:2-3	348
2:4-5	348
2:5b	348
2:7	348
2:12-17	348
2:14	349
2:18-29	349

2:19	349	**DEUTERO-**		2 Esdras	
2:20	349	**CANONICAL**		6:15	269
2:26-27	349			6:43-44	269
3:1-6	349	**Wisdom of Solomon**			
3:3b	349	14:3	250	1 Maccabees	
3:14-22	349			1:11-14	245
3:17	350	**Sirach**			
4:8	258	23:1	250	2 Maccabees	
7:13-17	258	23:4	250	8:8	320